Animal Skulls

Animal Skulls

A Guide to
North American Species

Mark Elbroch

STACKPOLE
BOOKS

Published by
STACKPOLE BOOKS
5067 Ritter Road
Mechanicsburg, PA 17055
www.stackpolebooks.com

Printed in the United States

First edition

Cover design by Caroline Stover
Cover photo by Mark Elbroch

Illustrations and photographs by Mark Elbroch unless otherwise noted.

Endorsed by the American Society of Mammalogists.
Published with advice and support from the Santa Barbara Museum of Natural History.

Library of Congress Cataloging-in-Publication Data

Elbroch, Mark.
    Animal skulls : a guide to North American species / Mark Elbroch.
       p.   cm.
    Includes bibliographical references.
    ISBN-13: 978-0-8117-3309-0
    ISBN-10: 0-8117-3309-2
    1. Skull. 2. Mammals—Anatomy. 3. Zoological specimens—Catalogs and collections—North America. I. Title.
QL822.E43   2006
573.7'616097—dc22

                                                 2006000818

For my great-uncle and great-aunt,
Robert and Mary Cross

Editor's Notes:

The following abbreviations are used when providing specimen numbers, indicating in which collection each specimen is held:

SBMNH: Santa Barbara Museum of Natural History
MVZ: Museum of Vertebrate Zoology at the University of California, Berkeley
MCZ: Museum of Comparative Zoology at Harvard University
LACM: Natural History Museum of Los Angeles County, often called the L.A.
  County Museum

Color tabs are used throughout this book to provide aid in species identification. The colors represent the overall species groups. Mammal skulls and mammal jaws are found in the red tab color sections. Birds are located in the blue tab color sections. Amphibians and Reptiles are represented in the green tab color sections.

MAMMALS

Virginia opossum, *Didelphis virginiana*

BIRDS

Canada goose, *Branta canadensis*

AMPHIBIANS AND REPTILES

Western toad, *Bufo boreas*

CONTENTS

ACKNOWLEDGMENTS

This work would have been impossible without the incredible support provided by collections, institutions, and most important, the people who cared for and monitored the vast number of specimens I have been lucky enough to handle. First and foremost among them are the three people who constitute the Department of Vertebrate Zoology at the Santa Barbara Museum of Natural History: Paul W. Collins, curator; Krista A. Fahy, associate curator; and Michelle L. Berman, assistant curator. For nearly an entire year, the Santa Barbara Museum acted as a second home, and these three people welcomed me and supported this work in every way, exceeding all my expectations. My heartfelt thanks to all three for their incredible patience, generosity, and enthusiasm.

Paul, Krista, and Michelle each contributed expertise to the project in his or her own way. Paul's vast experience with mammals and encyclopedic knowledge of useful publications and osteology have left an everlasting imprint in the shape and content of this book; for instance, it was he who encouraged me to widen my search for existing cranial measurements and compile them for the benefit of others. Krista's continuous warmth, lightning-fast resource acquisitions, and expertise in ornithology have shaped the bird accounts. And Michelle's knowledge of marine mammals helped fill that complete void in my own experience.

By the end of several trips to the Museum of Vertebrate Zoology at the University of California–Berkeley, many people had aided and supported my time spent in the beautifully laid-out, upkept, and species-rich collections; after a visit to the MVZ, there is no question as to why its collections have such a wonderful reputation. Special thanks to Christopher Conroy, curator and researcher; Carla Cicero, curator and researcher; Jim Patton, emeritus professor, curator of mammals; and Eileen Lacey, associate professor, curator of mammals.

Staff members at the Museum of Comparative Zoology at Harvard University were warm, welcoming, and incredibly helpful; the collections are diverse and beautiful, and the old building is a wonderful environment in which to work. Tremendous thanks to the following people, who fully supported my time amid the stacks: Judy Chupasko, curatorial associate (collection manager), and Mark Omura, curatorial assistant, both with the Department of Mammalogy; and Jeremiah Trimble, curatorial assistant, with the Department of Ornithology.

The beautiful space and large and diverse collections at the Natural History Museum of Los Angeles County were also of great help; the shelves extend so high you need a ladder to access all the specimens. A special thanks to Jim Dines, collections manager, Section of Mammalogy, and Kimball Garrett, collections manager, Section of Ornithology, for their generosity and support. Thank you also to Kate Doyle, collections manager at the University of Massachusetts in Amherst for allowing access to the ornithology osteology collection.

Neal Wight on the West Coast and Max Allen on the East both contributed uncountable measurements to the birds accounts, saving me weeks of time and helping expand this project immensely. Thanks to them both for their contributions and maintaining the focus one needs to measure skulls in back rooms with accuracy.

Thanks also to Prescott College for allowing Neal Wight to join me as an intern in the project, and to Linda Butterworth in the library at Prescott, who tracked down numerous articles at my request. Thanks to Jim Anderson for introducing me to the world of professional skull collecting, which he did with zeal and generosity, and for the interview he contributed to this publication. Thanks to Craig Holdrege of the Nature Institute in New York for reminding me to keep a broader perspective when interpreting the forms that are animal skulls and for sharing his enthusiasm for the subject matter. And thanks to Tiffany Morgan, who contributed a day as numbers transcriber in the Museum of Comparative Zoology.

Several individuals shared artwork and research. Thanks to Donald Hoffmeister for sharing figures from *Mammals of Arizona,* a comprehensive volume that sets an incredible standard for state mammals publications. Thanks to Jim Heffelfinger for incredible generosity in sharing much from his own publication on aging Arizona game species. Thanks to Shai Meiri for sharing unpublished cranial measurements. Thanks also to Randy Babb, Patricia Hansen, and Matt Alderson for sharing drawings. And thank you to Eric York for sharing the remains of a raccoon killed by a cougar he'd gathered during kill site analysis.

Special thanks to those who reviewed all or a portion of the finished manuscript: B. Miles Gilbert (archaeologist, author *Mammalian Osteology,* coauthor, *Avian Osteology*), Paul Collins (curator, Vertebrate Zoology, Santa Barbara Museum of Natural History), Richard Zusi (Division of Birds, Smithsonian Institution), Krista Fahy (associate curator, Santa Barbara Museum of Natural History), and three anonymous reviewers with the American Society of Mammalogists.

While sharing a house in expensive Santa Barbara, several people suffered my rather obsessive work habits and skull collection. Thanks to both Chris Duncan, who tolerated the stink of active dermestids without fuss, and Mike Kresky for their patience and understanding. Mike, also a skull collector, shared enthusiasm for everything dead, artwork, and energy to keep me going through much of the writing and research. Thanks to Kristin Magnussen for hours and hours of scanning artwork and typing corrections as I neared the deadline for the project and found myself juggling too many pieces; her calm work ethic helped make the last weeks more peaceful. Thanks also to

Donna Ryczek at Goleta Typing, who also spent many an hour typing in corrections to save me time.

Looking farther back in time, a tremendous thanks to my great-uncle Robert and great-aunt Mary, for while I was a small boy, Robert worked with the Natural History Museum in London. When my family visited, he gave us tours of the many stuffed creatures on display, with their vacant stares and dusty coats, as well as the back rooms filled with stacks and stacks of uncountable specimens, where scientists moved like ants in an aquarium. My explorations of these back rooms and taxidermied wildlife are among my fondest memories and have fueled the work that produced this publication. Thanks to all my family: Daddidar, the great naturalist and poet; Lizzie, the great supporter and party thrower; Mary, my grandmother, one of the most generous people I've ever met; and Larry, my grandfather, who lived life just the way he liked. For my amazing parents, who—while I lived with them and still after I've been gone for so many years—have tolerated frozen specimens clogging the freezers and skulls buried in the yard or placed under protection to stink and invite the flies and beetles to come and do their work. Not many parents would welcome their son into their home, after so many months away, carrying some roadkilled beast procured en route.

Thanks to Mark Allison and Stackpole Books for this opportunity and continuing to support and encourage so many of my writing projects. Warm thanks to Ken Krawchuk with Stackpole, who welcomed me into the book design process, and suffered my meddling with calm patience and a keen attention to detail. Thanks also to Anne Hawkins, who deftly negotiated this contract and continues to aid and promote new projects with a critical eye, sharp mind, and warm enthusiasm.

And last, my thanks to the many animals whose lives have now touched mine; your diverse forms will haunt me for years to come. For in collections, animals live on and continue to inspire, teach, and share something of what it means to be a truly wild creature.

Introduction

People have always been fascinated with skulls and bones. Browse through any natural history museum, environmental education center, or university collection and you will find them: big, small, reptile, amphibian, bird, mammal, predator, and prey. Perhaps skulls are a reminder of our own mortality—that we, too, will eventually be just skull and bones. Or perhaps it's our fascination with living organisms. The diversity and complexity of life is ever apparent in the equally varied and beautiful forms that are animal skulls. For skulls are sculptures in a vast array of shapes and textures that excite and inspire our imagination.

Reaching far back to the Neanderthal people who inhabited what are now Switzerland and Germany, much evidence supports that these ancient ancestors of modern man created cults around skulls and bones. Deep in cave dwellings high in the mountains are the remains of stone cabinets and shelves, lined with numerous cave bear skulls arranged with symbolic intentions and protected from deterioration and prying eyes. We can only guess at their significance (Campbell 1988).

Along the Atlantic and Gulf Coasts of North America, the Mi'kmaq and Wuastukwiuk used skulls in varied rituals, many of which were married to hunting and sustenance. Hunters often carried charms to help them while they hunted: claws, beaks, or weasel skulls. Skulls were woven into their culture in other ways: "Before killing a bear the hunter would talk or sing to the animal. A further demonstration of this respect involved cleaning the skulls of hunted bears and beavers, and then placing them high on a pole or in a tree where dogs could not defile them" (University of Calgary 2000).

For some, skulls represent all that is evil, and for others, all that is good. Skulls are part of ceremonies and religions the world over, appearing in stories and art of many cultures. They symbolize life, death, good luck, bad luck, power, and rebellion. They are used to inspire awe or fear, represent secret societies, and voice outrage over modern wars. Skulls hold power. They've also become the stuff of imagination, of science fiction and horror movies. I've encountered several *Star Wars* figures, aliens, and other characters while perusing museum collections.

In 1142, a monastery was founded in the town of Sedlec, in what is now the Czech Republic, where it was said an abbot sprinkled earth from Jerusalem. People flocked

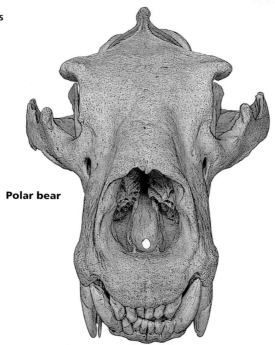

Polar bear

to be buried or bury others on this small parcel of land. In 1870, an effort was made to increase the space necessary to allow others to continue to be buried on the property. The skulls and bones of forty thousand people were used to decorate a small chapel built on site in the fourteenth century, a window into history and culture you may still visit today (California Academy of Sciences 2002).

Skulls have been painted in cultures past and present and have appeared in the work of ancient and modern artists. Painted skulls of mammoths and bison have been exca-

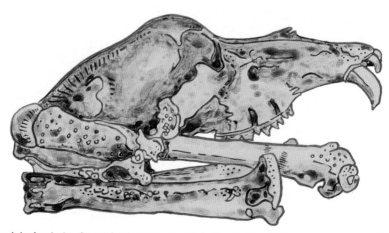

An original painting by Michael Kresky depicting the skull and femur arrangements of cave bears discovered in mountain caves of central Europe, which were photographed and included in Campbell (1988). Used with permission of the artist.

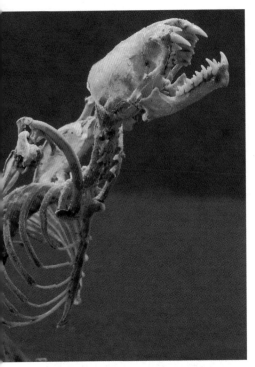

The fantastic skeleton of a hoary bat *(Lasiurus cinereus)* may have inspired popular movie characters. SANTA BARBARA MUSEUM OF NATURAL HISTORY 2716.

vated from the earth and speak of cultures long past. Georgia O'Keeffe's famous paintings of horse and cow skulls are stark and bold, like animal bones themselves, like the desert landscape and sky above. Her words on the subject: "So I brought home the bleached bones as my symbols of the desert. To me they are as beautiful as anything I know. . . . The bones seem to cut sharply to the center of something that is keenly alive on the desert even tho' it is vast and empty and untouchable—and knows no kindness with all its beauty" (Robinson 1998, 365).

Today the Andamanese still live much as they always have, as was evident on televisions the world over when they seemed to have survived the 2005 tsunami off Thailand completely unscathed. They are a hunting and fishing people, spearing fish with long arrows projected from bows as tall as or taller than the one who wields it. The Andamanese fear a power called *otkimil,* which they believe can influence or

An original painting by Michael Kresky created from a photograph of the Andamanese people in Campbell (1988). Note the central figure, a recent widow, who still wears her dead husband's skull to ward off evil powers. Used with permission of the artist.

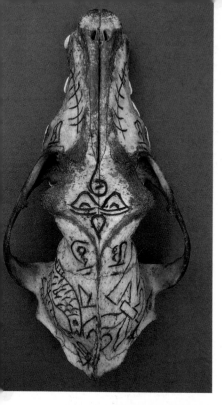

This skull is reported to be an antique wolf skull decorated in Tibet. What do the symbols mean? PRIVATE COLLECTION.

hurt them during times of stress or life crisis. Joseph Campbell's *Historical Atlas of World Mythology* (1988) includes several photographs that depict charms worn in defense. In one, a woman wears her sister's skull trailing down her back to ward off *ot-kimil*. In another, a widow wears her husband's skull strapped to her shoulder, which she will wear until she finds a new husband and the threat of *ot-kimil* has passed.

Regardless of reason, belief, or understanding, the allure of animal skulls is very real. It's exciting to hold the skull of the last grizzly killed in California. He lived, he died, and yet one can still hold his remains, a tangible line to the living, breathing creature that so stirred the imagination near a century ago. Words cannot describe the feelings.

The Importance of Collections

Referring to the Museum of Comparative Zoology of Harvard University, Edward O. Wilson said, "Biology could not have advanced without collections of museums like this one. Absent their priceless resources, there would be no coherent system of classification, no way to identify the vast majority of organisms, no theory of evolution, no foundation for ecology" (Pick 2004).

This book likely would have taken a lifetime to compile and complete were it not for the amazing natural history collections sprinkled across our country and the world. These massive collections are rich reservoirs of accumulated knowledge and understanding about the earth's natural systems and their components, including living organisms. In 2004, some 20.4 million visitors walked amid the displays at the National Museum of Natural History at the Smithsonian. Today the Smithsonian collection boasts about 121.6 million specimens, of which some 580,000 are mammals and more than 600,000 are birds. Each specimen in the collections is tagged with the collector's name and where and when the animal was taken. Curators point proudly to specimens they have contributed, aware that the skin and bones will long outlive them and be handled by unknown numbers of people far into the future.

Collections are the bedrock foundations for our understanding of evolution, taxonomy, and phylogeny. These sciences have advanced immeasurably through the simple exercise of comparing specimens over hundreds of years. They are accumulated experience, the tangible culmination of generations of scientists and naturalists working and

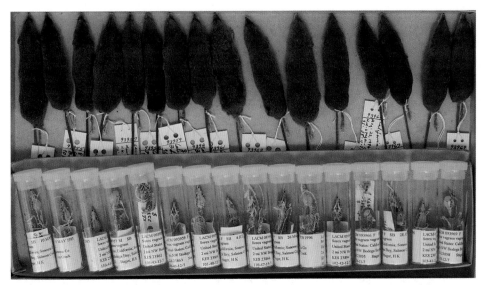

A tiny fraction of a drawer of skins, skulls, and bones of vagrant shrews *(Sorex vagrans)* from California. NATURAL HISTORY MUSEUM OF LOS ANGELES COUNTY.

interacting with our world. Collections are pooled community knowledge, touchable, smellable, visible materials for comparison and experimentation. They consist of the actual specimens, not renditions, pictures, or illustrations. You can hold the skulls of creatures that died hundreds of years ago.

Collections also hold histories of people. In addition to the artifacts of people who lived before us human history is found among the animal skins and skulls. Collections show cultural trends: the great exploration years into unknown terrain; the species documenting races when researchers traveled far and wide to discover as many new species as possible; wars against predators such as wolves, bears, and others; the conservation days; the era of traveling zoos and exotic fur farms; the increased incidence of roadkill

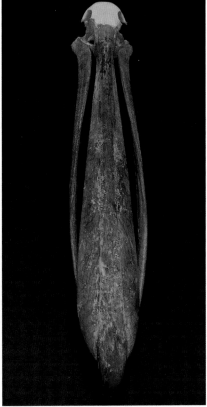

The complete skull of a female brown pelican *(Pelecanus occidentalis).* SANTA BARBARA MUSEUM OF NATURAL HISTORY 868.

in new specimen acquisition. In collections, histories of people lie side by side with other natural phenomena.

There was a time when natural history collections were at the center of academic learning and research, but this is not the case today. The first natural history museum in the United States, Peale's Museum, opened in 1786 in Philadelphia. The second, the Museum of Comparative Zoology at Harvard University, opened in 1859, the same year Darwin's theories of evolution were released to the world.

During the second half of the nineteenth century and the first half of the twentieth, natural history collections thrived. Collecting became an avenue for adventurous scientists to explore unknown, rugged terrain in hopes of discovering undocumented species and achieving renown as a contributor to science. Buildings and warehouses across America quickly filled with countless specimens from around the globe, and whole animal studies supported and strengthened our understanding of evolution and phylogeny.

The discovery of DNA in 1953 provided an amazing new tool to increase this understanding. Yet with this advancement, interest in collections waned, more compartmentalized approaches to studying wildlife were favored, and funding, support, and care for collections quickly diminished. Some were dismantled, sold off, or given away. Curators were laid off, and staffing in most museums was greatly reduced.

But the 1980s saw a resurgence of interest in collections, as scientists realized the specimens held a grand reservoir of DNA samples dating back hundreds and even thousands of years. In addition, specimens can provide knowledge of what the animals were eating during their lifetime, the chemical pollution that surrounded them while they foraged, and possibly a great deal of other information we do not yet have the tech-

A single drawer of common vampire bats *(Desmodus rotundus)* from southern Mexico. NATURAL HISTORY MUSEUM OF LOS ANGELES COUNTY.

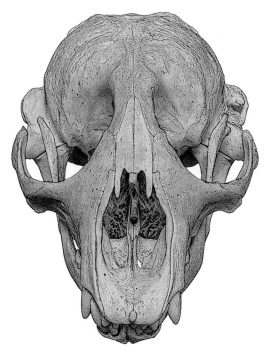

The complete skull of a female harbor seal *(Phoca vitulina)*. SANTA BARBARA MUSEUM OF NATURAL HISTORY 1683.

nology to reveal. Collections may also hold unknown specimens, undiscovered beasts awaiting someone with the perseverance and curiosity to find them hidden in dark rooms in boxes, on shelves, or even incorrectly labeled.

Consider this thought: The depth of a collection lies not only in the diversity of specimens held, but also in the length of a series, meaning the number of a given species held. If a museum held an agile kangaroo rat captured in the Los Angeles basin every year from 1850 until now, the skins would embody a gripping story of changes in air quality, soil contaminants, plant pollution, evolution, and so much more. Thus active collecting is still a necessary component to modern science.

Collections have never fully recovered from the blow dealt half a century ago, with the discovery of DNA and the move away from whole animal studies in traditional academia. Nowadays, not only are collections often understaffed, poorly funded, and underappreciated, but also the curators who might best care for, understand, and contribute to them are nearing extinction. Unfortunately, today's academic programs often provide less-than-ideal training for curatorship. Where is our next generation of curators? Who will care for our collections?

The Bones of the Skull   **1**

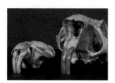

The tough, flexible portion of bones that grows, bends, and heals in living animals is called collagen. The macromolecules of collagen pack together tightly, providing flexibility and strength. Yet in weight, approximately 50 percent of bone is further reinforcement in the form of tiny crystals of the mineral hydroxyapatite, a form of calcium. It is this mineral material that make bones incredibly strong, durable, and rigid. There is also a tiny portion of additional organic material that is responsible for maintaining the blood supply and nourishment to living bones.

The skull, as addressed in this book, is the collection of bones that house and protect the brain, which acts as the control network for the entire nervous system, as well as protects the sensory organs: eyes, inner ears, taste organs, and nasal receptors. The skull also protects the trachea and inner mouth, the initial portions of the breathing apparatus and digestive tract. The skull is both receptacle and protector of what are vital to survival.

The skull is composed of two obvious pieces: the cranium and mandible, or jaw. They work in unison to acquire and prepare food for the body, to communicate, and so much more. This book is primarily about mammal skulls, but it also includes many bird species and several reptiles and amphibians; yet most of the discussion in this chapter refers to mammal skulls. The mammal skull can be further divided into five general areas, the last three of which are subdivisions of the cranium: *teeth,* or dentition; the *mandibles,* or jaws, of which every species has two; the *rostrum,* that part of the cranium anterior to the zygomatic arches, generally holding all the teeth, the palate, and the entire nasal cavity; the *braincase,* that part of the cranium posterior to the rostrum with the exception of the zygomatic arches; and the *zygomatic arches,* the bones arching outward from the braincase and rostrum to form the orbits.

The bones of skulls are each members of one of two large groups: paired or unpaired bones. There is an obvious symmetry to all skulls, though detailed analysis will reveal that it's very rare to find an animal in which the right side is identical to the left. Any bone that appears on both the right and left sides of the skull is considered a "paired bone." Any bone that appears only once in a given animal is an "unpaired bone," and these are generally associated with the midline of the skull. For example, mammals

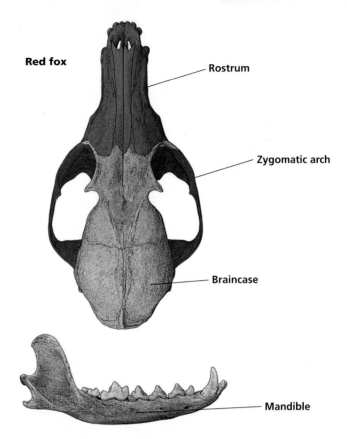

Red fox

Rostrum

Zygomatic arch

Braincase

Mandible

The four regions of the skull discussed next are presented here on this red fox *(Vulpes vulpes)* skull.

and some reptiles have two occipital condyles, bones that protrude from the posterior of the skull and articulate with the atlas, the first bone in the vertebral column. In these animals, they are paired bones. Birds, however, have but one occipital condyle on the midline of the skull, and thus in birds it is an unpaired bone.

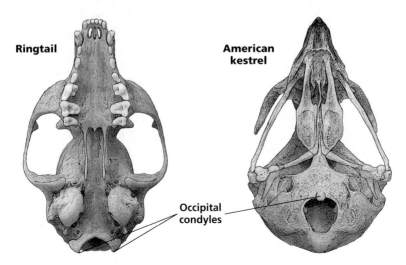

Ringtail

American kestrel

Occipital condyles

Skull Vocabulary

Common names do not exist for bones of the skull, and there is no way around the unfamiliar and technical language associated with bones. For those invested in learning to identify skulls and discuss them with others, my advice is to learn the bones that are quickly and easily observed and most often used in identification, and then keep labeled diagrams close at hand for those odd bones mentioned under certain species accounts. Learning new vocabulary requires a certain enthusiasm and even stamina. The pages of this book holding detailed diagrams are marked for easy referencing. Like every biologist and naturalist before you, you'll refer to diagrams frequently as you get started.

Following are some terms you should become familiar with for the study of skulls:

Anterior: Toward the front of the skull or specific region.

Cingulum: A structure that encircles another structure or body, girdlelike.

Commissure: The ventral line of a bird's bill; the line created by the bill and mandible when they are joined and closed.

Concave: Curving downward, forming a depression.

Condyle: A rounded projection of bone that articulates and moves to form a joint with another bone.

Convex: Curving outward, creating a swollen region, or bump.

Culmen: The dorsal surface of a bird's bill.

Cusp: A peak on an individual tooth.

Deciduous: Describes the milk teeth, which fall out and are replaced before the animal reaches full adult status.

Dorsal: On or near the top of the skull or specific region.

Emarginated: Notched, or with a series of notches.

Foramen: A hole through which blood vessels and nerves may pass.

Fossa: A depression, pit, or troughlike vacuity in bone surface, or an empty space, as in the temporalis fossa.

Infraorbital: Lying below the eye.

Interorbital: The space between the orbits, or eyes.

Labial: The outside edge, toward the lips and cheeks. In reference to teeth.

Lateral: A side perspective of the skull or specific region.

Lingual: The inside edge, toward the tongue. In reference to teeth.

Posterior: Toward the back of the skull or specific region.

Orbit: The vacuity in which the eye sits and is supported by bony structures.

Process: A projection of bone sticking outward on the skull or a specific bone.

Procumbent: Jutting forward.

Septum: A partition, or something that separates.

Suture: The meeting point between two bones in the skull, often visible as a crack or line.

Ventral: On or near the bottom of the skull or specific region.

Studying Skulls

Any modern mammalogy or zoology text includes a detailed discussion of each bone in the skull. This section describes bones and regions of the skull that are especially important in identification. This is followed by diagrams illustrating all of the bones in the cranium.

Overall Shape

The first thing you should notice about a skull is its overall shape, whether it is, for example, boxy, round, squat, or slender. The overall skull outline provides much information to the observant. Consider the following examples:

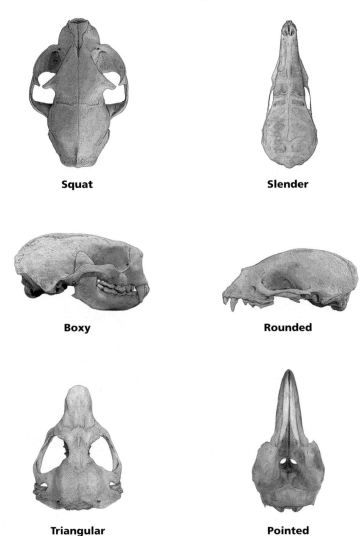

Squat

Slender

Boxy

Rounded

Triangular

Pointed

Tall

Flat

The Teeth

At the center of each tooth is a living and growing material termed *pulp*. A tough, bonelike material called *dentin* provides the bulk of protection for the pulp, and the shiny, hard outer layer that is visible above the gum line is *enamel*. In most species, a rougher layer of *cementum* covers the roots of the teeth.

Most mammals are *diphyodont,* meaning they have two sets of teeth over the course of their lives. The first set is *deciduous* and is often called the *milk teeth;* these are the teeth children place under their pillows in hopes of the tooth fairy's visit. Molars and occasionally other teeth do not have deciduous precursors, so they and those that replace the milk teeth are all referred to as *permanent dentition.*

The exposed portion of the tooth that we see and analyze is referred to as the *crown* of the tooth, and that which sits hidden in the socket is the *root.* The points of the crown of the tooth are referred to as *cusps.* Teeth may be unicuspid, or single-pointed, such as canine teeth; bicuspid, or double-pointed; tricuspid; and so on. If a mammal has two or more kinds of teeth—for example, canines and incisors—it is classified as a *heterodont.* Most mammals are heterodonts, though there are a few species in which every tooth is identical, such as armadillos. Mammals with only a single kind of tooth are called *homodonts.*

Typical carnivores and omnivores have four kinds of teeth: incisors, canines, premolars, molars. Rodents and some ungulates lack canines completely. Among the great diversity of mammals of North America, there is tremendous variation in the presence and number of incisors, canines, premolars, and molars. Each of these tooth groups is further discussed and explained in chapter 2. Studying the teeth begins to

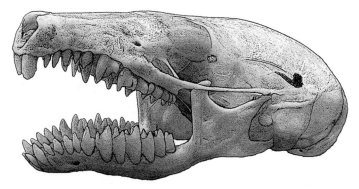

The dentition of insectivores, such as this broad-footed mole (*Scapanus latimanus*), is jagged and impressive. SANTA BARBARA MUSEUM OF NATURAL HISTORY 4708.

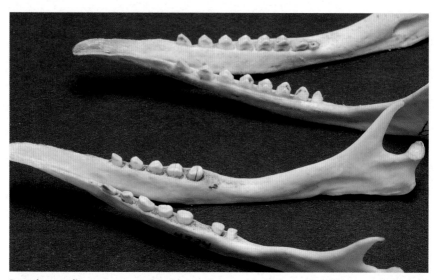

Dental anomalies are common in wide-ranging species. Here are mandibles and their corresponding dentition of two nine-banded armadillos (Dasypus novemcinctus), to illustrate variation. SANTA BARBARA MUSEUM OF NATURAL HISTORY, 4234, 1379.

open doors to visualizing the entire animal and understanding its ecology from just the skull in hand.

The dental formula was developed by mammalogists to efficiently summarize the dentition and dental patterns of a particular animal. *Capital* letters refer to teeth in the cranium, and *lowercase* letters to those in the mandible. An "i" is short for incisors, "c" for canines, "p" for premolars, and "m" for molars. The dental formula is always given in the same order, which represents teeth from front to back, even if none are present at all. Also, teeth in the cranium always precede the same teeth in the mandible. The formula represents only one side of the mouth; therefore, to determine the total number of teeth for a given animal, you must take the sum of all the teeth in a given dental formula and multiply by two. Consider the large rodent mountain beaver *(Aplodontia rufa)* and the coyote *(Canis latrans)*.

The mountain beaver's dental formula is written as such: i 1/1 c 0/0 p 2/1 m 3/3, total 22.

(upper teeth)	1		0		2		3
incisors	—	+ canines	—	+ premolars	—	+ molars	—
(lower teeth)	1		0		1		3

The sum of all the numbers present is 11; 11 × 2 = total teeth, 22.

The coyote's dental formula is written as such: i 3/3 c 1/1 p 4/4 m 2/3, total 42.

(upper teeth)	3		1		4		2
incisors	—	+ canines	—	+ premolars	—	+ molars	—
(lower teeth)	3		1		4		3

The sum of all the numbers present is 21; 21 × 2 = total teeth, 42.

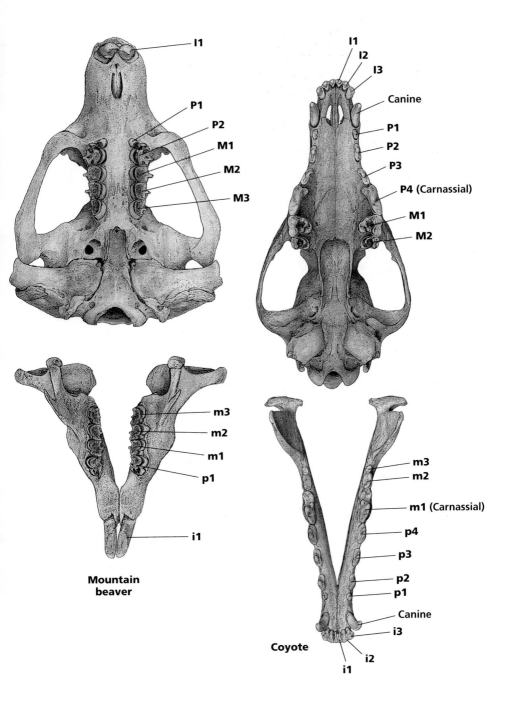

Compare the relative number and sorts of teeth present in this mountain beaver, representing the rodents, and this coyote, representing the carnivores. Note that the upper teeth in the cranium are differentiated by capital letters, and the teeth in the mandibles are designated with small letters: I, i = incisor; P, p = premolar; M, m = molar.

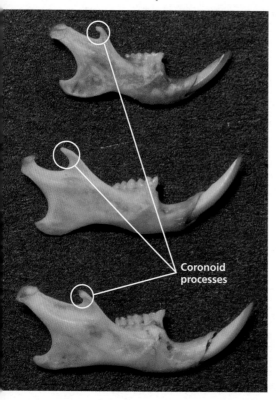

Coronoid processes

The Mandible

The mandible is a much simpler form than the cranium, with which it joins. Yet there is subtle variation in the sizes and shapes of the three processes, which form the posterior of the mandible and provide the surfaces to which muscles may attach, and the bone structures that articulate with the cranium. These are the *angular, condyloid,* and *coronoid processes,* and variation exists across diverse species as well as within a given family. The *condyle* is the actual bone that makes contact and articulates with the cranium. In this book, the *ramus* refers to the central area in between the three processes at the posterior of the

Note the variation in the three posterior processes in three mice species, especially the dramatic variation in the coronoid process. From top to bottom, western harvest mouse *(Reithrodontomys megalotis)*, northern grasshopper mouse *(Onychomys leucogaster)*, and deer mouse *(Peromyscus maniculatus)*. SANTA BARBARA MUSEUM OF NATURAL HISTORY.

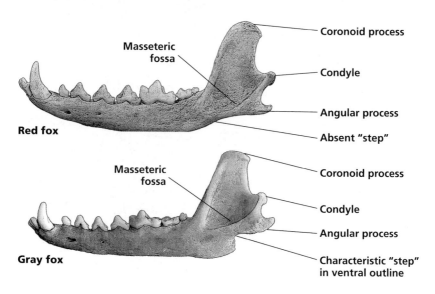

Masseteric fossa

Coronoid process

Condyle

Angular process

Absent "step"

Red fox

Masseteric fossa

Coronoid process

Condyle

Angular process

Gray fox

Characteristic "step" in ventral outline

In the closely related red and gray foxes, compare the subtle differences in the forms and sizes of the three processes that form the posterior of the mandible in mammals. Also note the relative size of the masseteric fossa, which is much smaller in the gray fox.

mandible, and the *body* to that part of the jaw anterior to the ramus, in which the teeth are rooted.

Consider the gray and red fox mandibles illustrated here; look carefully at the "step" in the ventral surface of the angular process. Also scrutinize the photograph of the three mandibles of mouse species; look for the evident variations in the coronoid and the other processes.

The Rostrum

The overall shape of the rostrum varies across animals considerably, from long and slender in the long-tongued bat to short, broad, and notched in the hoary bat. The length and shape of the *nasals* on the dorsal surface are often key in identification; *nasal sutures* may also be fused and obliterated, meaning that you'll no longer be able to determine where nasal bones begin or end. Compare the shapes and sizes of the nasal bones in the closely related moose and caribou with the fused nasals of the striped skunk.

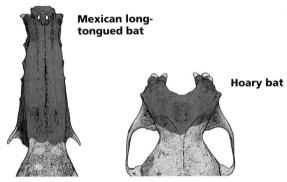

Mexican long-tongued bat

Hoary bat

Note the extreme variation in the shapes of the rostrums of these two bat species. On the left the Mexican long-tongued bat *(Choeronycteris mexicana)*, and on the right the hoary bat *(Lasiurus cinereus)*.

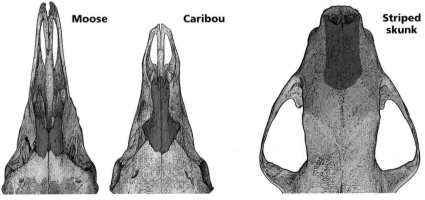

Moose   **Caribou**   **Striped skunk**

Even among cervids there is tremendous variation in the size and shape of the nasal bones; compare the short and stubby nasals in the moose *(Alces alces)* on the left with the long and flaring nasals of the caribou *(Rangifer tarandus)* on the right. In many mammals, including this striped skunk *(Mephitis mephitis)*, the nasal sutures fuse and become difficult to see in adult animals.

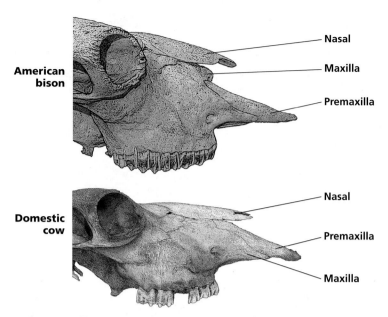

American
bison
— Nasal
— Maxilla
— Premaxilla

Domestic
cow
— Nasal
— Premaxilla
— Maxilla

The premaxillaries, maxillaries, and nasals are especially important when comparing ungulate skulls. For example, the premaxillaries often touch the nasals in domestic cows *(Bos taurus)*, yet are separated by a wide space in our native American bison *(Bos bison)*.

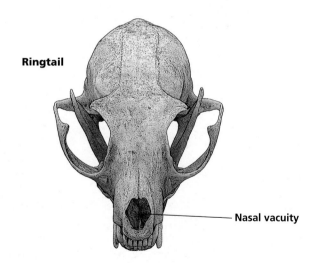

Ringtail

— Nasal vacuity

The posterior edge of the nasals is often important as well, especially as it compares in length and shape with the *premaxillary* and *maxillary bones,* which form the lateral and ventral surfaces of the rostrum. In many ungulates, it is important to note whether the nasals are in contact with the premaxillaries.

The *nasal vacuity* is the hole created by the nasals, premaxillaries, and maxillaries, within which are the olfactory nerves and receptors. The nasal vacuity may be large or small, and steeply angled or vertical. It is useful in differentiating among species.

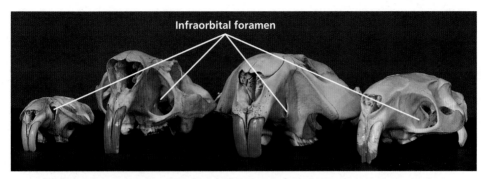

Infraorbital foramen

From left to right, compare the size and shape of the infraorbital foramen in Common muskrat *(Ondatra zibethicus)*, North American porcupine *(Erethizon dorsatum)*, American beaver *(Castor canadensis)*, and Nutria *(Myocastor coypus)*. MUSEUM OF VERTEBRATE ZOOLOGY, UC BERKELEY 37415, 68707, 90732, 97349.

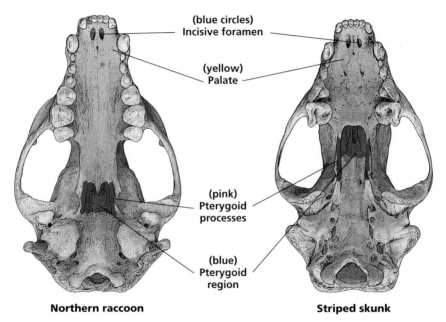

(blue circles)
Incisive foramen

(yellow)
Palate

(pink)
Pterygoid processes

(blue)
Pterygoid region

Northern raccoon   **Striped skunk**

The *infraorbital canal* is located most often on the lateral side of the rostrum. It is a passageway for nerves and arteries, and sometimes muscles as well. The size and shape of the *infraorbital foramina* vary tremendously across species. In rodents, they are quick characters to help differentiate among large species. Beavers are sciuromorphs, meaning that no part of the *masseter muscles* passes through the infraorbital foramina. At the other end of the spectrum are the hystricomorphs, such as porcupines and nutrias, in which much of the masseters pass through this very large opening. The masseter muscles are discussed in detail in chapter two.

On the ventral surface of the rostrum are the ever-important *palate* and *incisive foramina*. The length and shape of the palate are critical in analysis, and often the exact point where the palate terminates is as well. The incisive foramina are holes in the palate, and they range in size from small in carnivores to very large in cottontails and hares. Their size, shape, and the alignment of their anterior and posterior edges are all critical in identification.

The Braincase

The interorbital region of mammal skulls is primarily formed by the *frontal bones.* The *interorbital breadth* is an important variable in identification, especially in how it compares with the *postorbital breadth* (page 37). *Postorbital processes* are bone extensions that protrude from the frontal bones to support and define the orbit; the narrowest breadth anterior to the postorbital processes is the interorbital breadth, and posterior to the processes is the postorbital breadth.

The overall shape and proportionate size of the braincase varies from tiny and slender in the opossum to very large and oval in weasels. Running along the dorsal surface of the braincase are the *temporal ridges,* which also vary in size and form. Compare the distinctive and well-developed U-shaped temporal ridges on gray fox skulls with the less-developed V-shaped ones in red foxes.

At the posterior of the braincase, the temporal ridges may join to form a *sagittal crest,* which may or may not be present in various mammal species. It may be small or large, extending to the posterior or growing vertically above the braincase. *Occipital crests* also may be formed at the posterior of the skull or may be absent altogether. Large occipital crests often contribute to a *supraoccipital shield,* which extends to the posterior over the occiput and the foramen magnum.

The ventral surface is a complex formation of numerous bones and foramina. The *pterygoid region* is a vacuity created just posterior to the edge of the palate and lead-

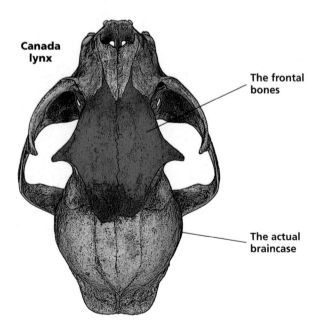

Canada lynx

The frontal bones

The actual braincase

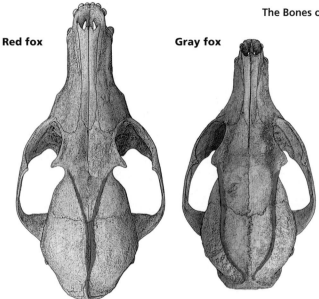

Red fox   **Gray fox**

Compare the temporal ridges in red and gray foxes. In the red fox *(Vulpes vulpes)*, ridges are less developed and converge to the posterior in a V-shape, while in gray foxes *(Urocyon cinereoargenteus)*, the temporal ridges are large, distinctive, and converge to the posterior in a U-shape.

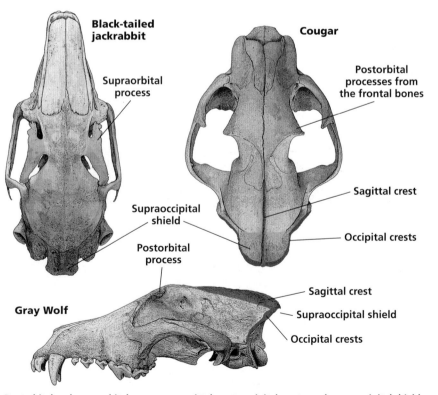

Black-tailed jackrabbit

Supraorbital process

Cougar

Postorbital processes from the frontal bones

Sagittal crest

Supraoccipital shield

Occipital crests

Postorbital process

Sagittal crest

Supraoccipital shield

Occipital crests

Gray Wolf

Postorbital and supraorbital processes, sagittal crest, occipital crests, and supraoccipital shield.

Desert cottontail   **Ermine**   **Cinereus shrew**

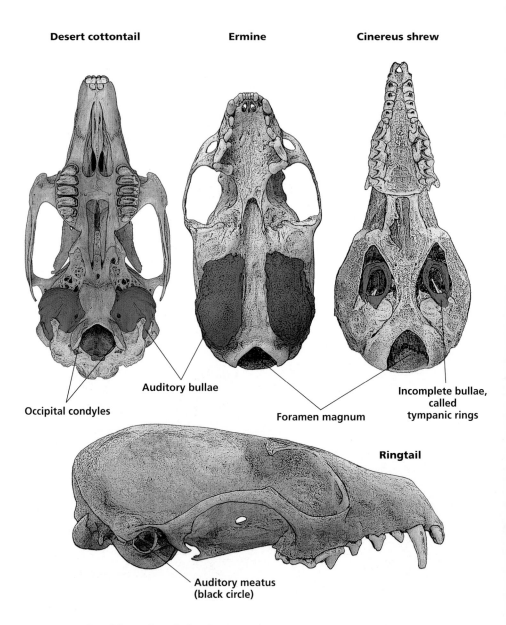

Occipital condyles

Auditory bullae

Foramen magnum

Incomplete bullae, called tympanic rings

Ringtail

Auditory meatus (black circle)

Occipital condyles, auditory bullae, foramen magnum, tympanic rings, and the auditory meatus.

ing to the anterior through the nares, the foramina connecting the nose to the back of the mouth; *pterygoid processes* extend to the posterior and form the lateral boundaries of the pterygoid region. These are illustrated on page 19.

Toward the posterior are the *auditory bullae,* which may be swollen and large or tiny and deformed, and may or may not have neck extensions. They are critical in cross-species comparisons. The lateral, tubular entrance to the auditory bullae is called the *auditory meatus*. The height, size, and shape of the auditory meatus are also key characteristics in identifying certain mammals.

The *occipital condyles* are two large protrusions on either side of the *foramen magnum,* a large hole at the posterior of the cranium that is the entrance to the braincase through which passes the spinal cord. The occipital condyles are the articulation points for the vertebrae and the start of all the bones posterior to the skull.

Zygomatic Arches

The zygomatic arches, or cheekbones, may be wide or narrow, slender or robust, parallel or converging to either the anterior or posterior of the skull. The *maxillary arm* of the zygomatic arch connects the anterior of the arch to the skull, and the *squamosal arm* connects it at the posterior. Often the ventral surface of the maxillary arm includes a *zygomatic plate,* whose pitch when viewed from the lateral is a useful clue when differentiating among rodents and other animals.

The zygomatic arches are composed of various other bones. The middle piece, called the *jugal bone,* is often important in identification. In some mammals, *postorbital processes* protrude from the jugal bones, providing structural support and boundaries for the orbit. *Postorbital processes* may extend from the frontals as well.

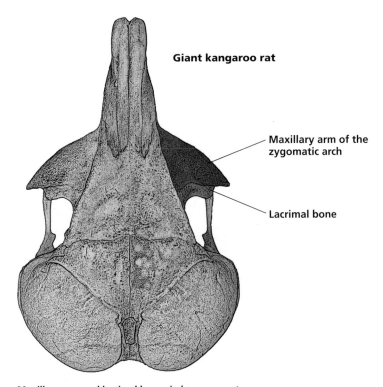

Giant kangaroo rat

Maxillary arm of the zygomatic arch

Lacrimal bone

Maxillary arm and lacrimal bones in kangaroo rats.

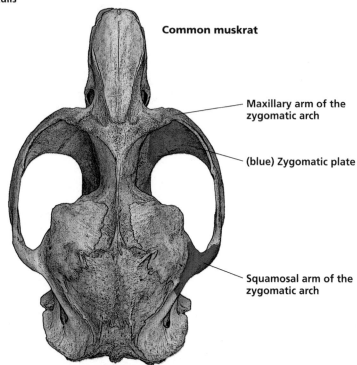

Common muskrat

Maxillary arm of the zygomatic arch

(blue) Zygomatic plate

Squamosal arm of the zygomatic arch

Maxillary arm of the zygomatic arch, zygomatic plate, and squamosal arm of the zygomatic arch.

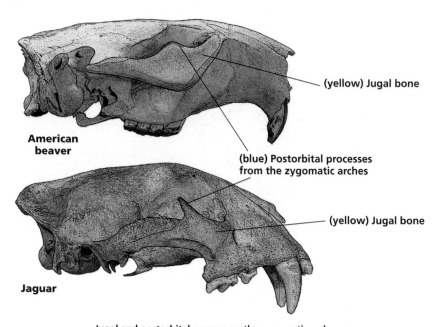

(yellow) Jugal bone

American beaver

(blue) Postorbital processes from the zygomatic arches

(yellow) Jugal bone

Jaguar

Jugal and postorbital process on the zygomatic arch.

Reference Diagrams

Following are detailed reference diagrams for your use while exploring the species accounts. Terms are listed below in alphabetical order.

Mammals

1. alisphenoid bone D3, D7
2. alisphenoid canal D3
3. angular process of the mandible D4, D8
4. auditory bulla (tympanic bulla) D2, D3, D5, D6, D7
5. basioccipital D2, D6
6. basisphenoid D2, D6
7. body of the mandible D4, D8
8. carotid foramen D2
9. condylar foramen D9
10. coronoid process of the mandible D4, D8
11. external auditory meatus D3, D7
12. foramen magnum D2, D6
13. foramen ovale D2, D6
14. frontal D1, D5
15. hypoglossal foramen D2
16. incisive foramen (palatal foramen) D2, D6
17. infraorbital foramen or canal D3, D7
18. interparietal bone D5, D12
19. jugal D3, D5, D7, D10
20. jugular foramen D2
21. lacrimal D3, D12
22. lambdoidal crest (occipital crest) D1, D5
23. mandibular condyle D4, D8
24. mandibular fossa D2
25. masseteric fossa on the mandible D4, D8
26. maxilla (maxillary) D1, D3, D5, D7, D12
27. maxillary arm of the zygomatic arch D5, D12
28. mental foramina on the mandible D4
29. nasal D1, D3, D5, D7
30. nasal vacuity D1, D3, D7
31. occipital bone (occiput) D2, D3, D6, D7
32. occipital condyle D2, D3, D7
33. orbit D1, D5
34. orbitosphenoid D3
35. palatal foramen (see incisive foramen)
36. palatine D2, D3, D6
37. paraoccipital process D2, D3, D6, D7
38. parietal D1, D5, D7
39. posterior lacerate foramen D2, D9
40. postorbital processes on the frontal bones D1, D3, D10
41. postorbital processes on the jugals D10
42. premaxilla (premaxillary) D1, D2, D3, D5, D7
43. presphenoid D2
44. pterygoid D2, D3, D6, D7
45. ramus of the mandible D4, D8
46. sagittal crest D1, D3, D11
47. spheno-pterygoid canal D6
48. squamosal D1, D3, D5, D7
49. squamosal arm of the zygomatic arch D1, D5
50. temporal fossa D1, D5
51. temporal ridge D1
52. vomer D2
53. zygomatic plate D5

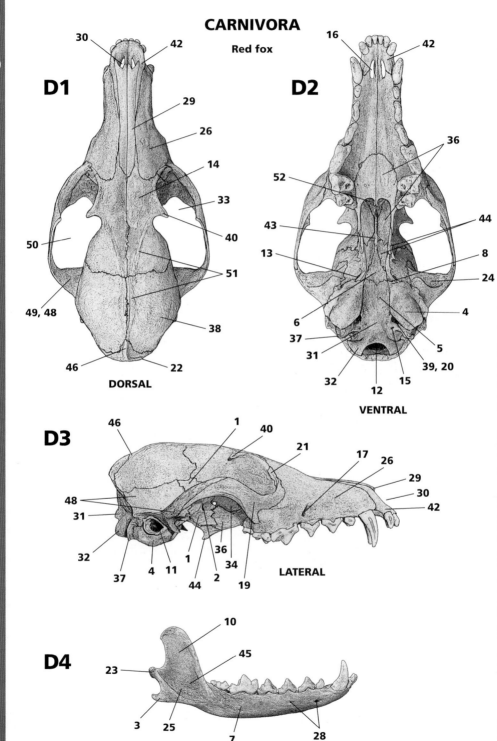

CARNIVORA

Red fox

D1

30
42
29
26
14
33
40
50
51
49, 48
38
46
22

DORSAL

D2

16
42
36
52
43
44
13
8
24
4
6
37
5
31
39, 20
32
15
12

VENTRAL

D3

46
1
40
21
17
26
29
30
42
48
31
32
4 11
37
1
36
44 2 19
34

LATERAL

D4

10
45
23
3 25
7
28

RODENTIA

Common muskrat

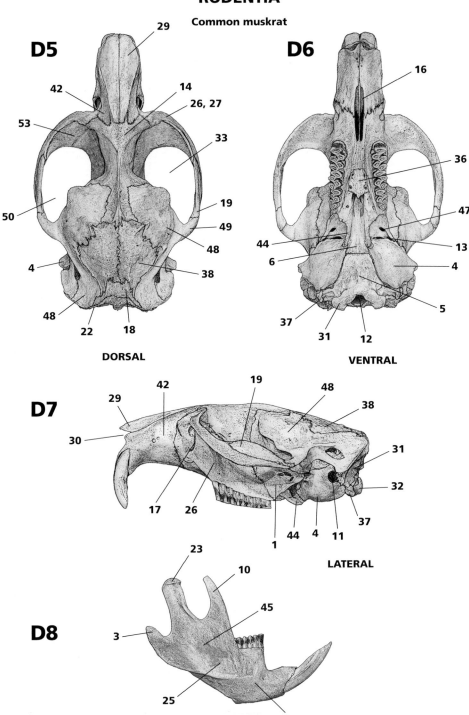

D5 — 29, 42, 14, 26, 27, 53, 33, 50, 19, 49, 48, 4, 38, 48, 22, 18

DORSAL

D6 — 16, 36, 47, 13, 44, 6, 4, 5, 37, 31, 12

VENTRAL

D7 — 29, 42, 19, 48, 38, 30, 31, 32, 17, 26, 37, 44, 4, 11, 1

LATERAL

D8 — 23, 10, 45, 3, 25, 7

California sea lion

D9

D10 Bobcat

40

41

19

39

9

Fisher

46

Chisel-toothed
kangaroo rat

D12

27, 26

21

D11

18

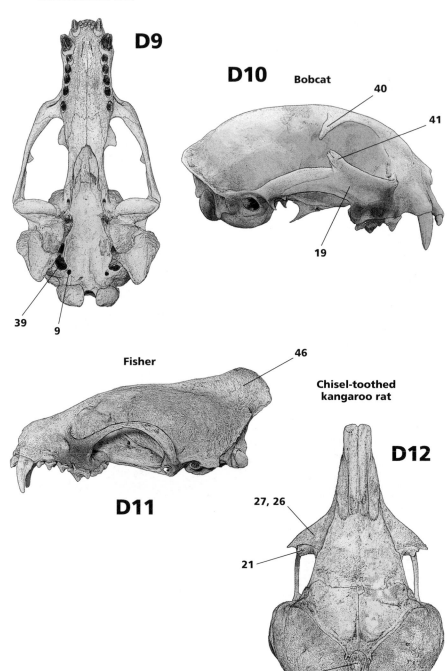

Birds

1. basitemporal plate B2
2. cranio-facial hinge B1, B3, B5
3. culmen (dorsal surface of the bill) B3
4. ectethmoid B3
5. exoccipital
6. external acoustic meatus B4
7. foramen, external occipital vein B2
8. foramen magnum B2
9. frontal B1, B3
10. frontal process of the premaxillary B1, B3, B6
11. interorbital fenestra B3
12. interorbital septum B3
13. jugal arch B1, B2
14. lacrimal B1, B3, B5
15. maxillary B2, B3, B6
16. maxillary process of the premaxillary B6
17. nasal B1
18. nasal aperture B3, B5, B6
19. occipital B3
20. occipital condyle B2
21. occipital crest B5
22. palantine B2
23. parasphenoid rostrum B2
24. parietal B1
25. paroccipital process B3
26. postorbital process B3, B5
27. premaxillary B3
28. pterygoid B2
29. quadrate B2, B3
30. quadratojugal B2, B3
31. sclerotic ring B7
32. squamosal B1, B3
33. supraocular bone B1, B3
34. tomium (cutting edge) B3
35. vomer B2

Cooper's hawk

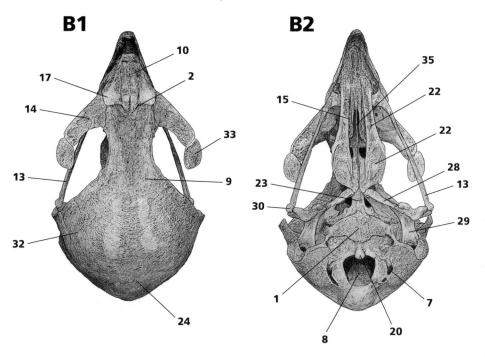

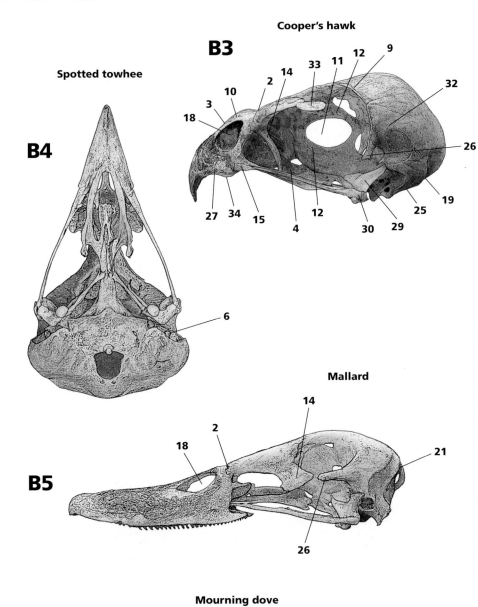

Cooper's hawk

B3

Spotted towhee

B4

Mallard

B5

Mourning dove

B6

California thrasher

31

B7

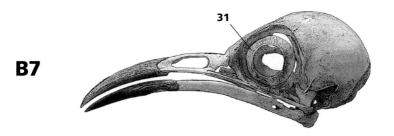

Toad and Salamander

Labeling for diagrams of all reptiles and amphibians adapted from Hildebrand and Goslow (2001).

1. chondrocranium
2. exoccipital
3. foramen magnum
4. frontal
5. frontoparietal
6. maxillary
7. nasal
8. occipital condyle
9. parietal
10. prefrontal
11. premaxillary
12. prootic
13. pterygoid
14. quadrate
15. quadratojugal
16. squamosal
17. vomer

Western toad   **Pacific giant salamander**

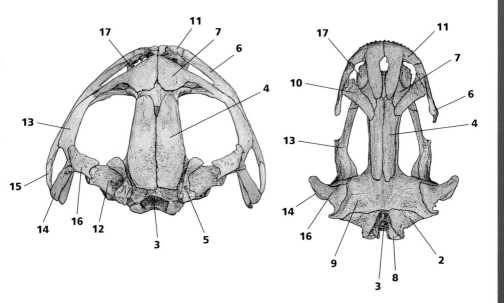

Turtle, Lizard, Alligator

1. anterior palatine foramen
2. basisphenoid
3. ectopterygoid
4. external nares
5. frontal
6. internal nares
7. jugal
8. lacrimal
9. maxilla (maxillary)
10. nasal
11. palatine
12. parietal
13. posterior palatine foramen
14. postorbital
15. prefrontal
16. premaxilla (premaxillary)
17. pterygoid
18. quadrate
19. quadratojugal
20. sclerotic ring
21. squamosal
22. superciliary
23. supra-angular
24. supraoccipital
25. temporal openings

American alligator

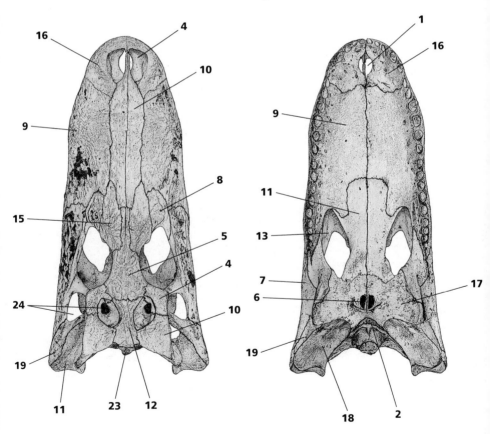

Leatherback sea turtle

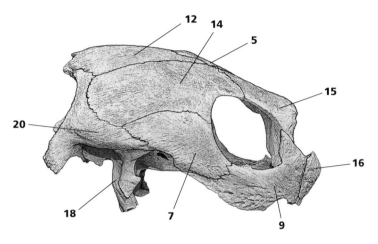

Common chuckwalla

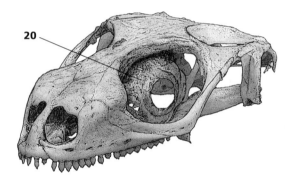

Measuring Mammal Skulls

Numerous potential measurements have been recorded for mammal skulls in the many scientific resources. Those employed for a particular species are often different for those of a mammal in a different family, given that certain measurements are more useful for identification than others depending on the shape of the skull. For example, to measure the length of the entire skull, you can measure the greatest length of skull or the condylobasal, basilar, basal, or occipitonasal length. Some measurements are more useful when you hope to answer a specific question, such as the sex of a given species. In this case, the interorbital breadth would be less useful than the zygomatic breadth.

Following are brief descriptions and visual presentations of the many measurements included in the book. When using tables that include measurements of specific bones, it would be more useful to refer to the diagrams of the bones of the cranium to best understand the bone in question. Also note that skulls are nearly always measured in millimeters.

Reference Diagrams

Measuring Mammal Skulls

Basal length: M2, from the tip of the premaxillae anterior to the lower edge of the foramen magnum.

Basilar length: M2, from the posterior edge of the upper incisors to the lower edge of the foramen magnum.

Breadth across the maxillary arms: M4, the greatest distance across the maxillary arms of the zygomatic arches, often useful in animals with arches that are fragile and break easily.

Breadth of braincase: M3, the greatest width of the braincase posterior to the zygomatic arches.

Breadth of rostrum: M3, the narrowest breadth across the rostrum just anterior to the zygomatic arches and posterior to the canines.

Condylobasal length: M2, from the tip of the premaxillae anterior to the incisors to the posterior of the occipital condyles.

Depth of skull : M1, the greatest height of the skull while it sits on a flat surface.

Greatest length of skull: M1, from the tip of the rostrum to the posteriormost part of the skull.

Interorbital breadth: M5, the narrowest breadth between the orbits, and anterior to the postorbital processes when present. In ungulates, often measured at the orbital notches.

Length of incisive foramen: M9, the longest length of an incisive foramen.

Length of mandible: M6, M7, a linear line from the anterior edge of the mandible *below* the incisors to the posterior edge of the condyloid process.

Length of mandibular toothrow: M8, the length of the lower toothrow *excluding* the incisors.

Length of maxillary toothrow: M9, M1, the length of the upper toothrow *excluding* the incisors.

Length of nasals: M5, the longest linear length of a nasal bone.

Length of palatal bridge: M10, the shortest length of the palatal bridge.

Length of rostrum: M5, from the tip of the rostrum to the anterior edge of the zygomatic arch.

Mastoidal breadth: M3, M5, the greatest width across the mastoid processes and braincase.

Occipitonasal length: M11, from the tip of the nasals to the posterior of the occipital condyles.

Palatal length: M2, from the tip of the premaxillae anterior of the upper incisors to the posterior edge of the palatines.

Palatilar length: M2, from the posterior edge of the upper insicors to the posterior edge of the palatines.

Postorbital breadth: M5, the narrowest distance just posterior to the postorbital processes.

Postpalatal length: M2, from the posterior edge of the palatines to the lowest edge of the foramen magnum.

Zygomatic breadth: M3, M4, the greatest width across the zygomatic arches.

Measuring bird, reptile, and amphibian skulls is discussed and illustrated at the start of their respective species accounts.

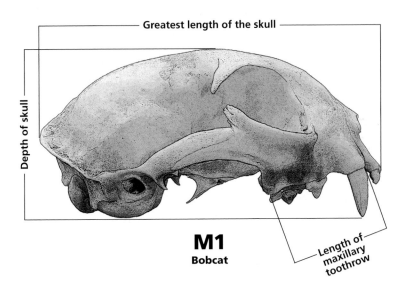

M1
Bobcat

Greatest length of the skull

Depth of skull

Length of maxillary toothrow

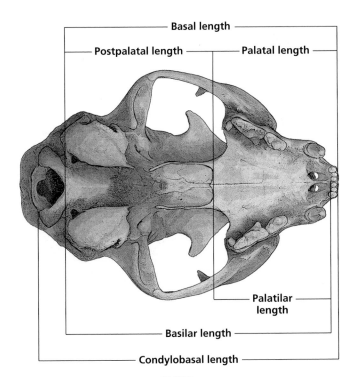

Basal length

Postpalatal length

Palatal length

Palatilar length

Basilar length

Condylobasal length

M2
Bobcat

Measuring Mammal Skulls

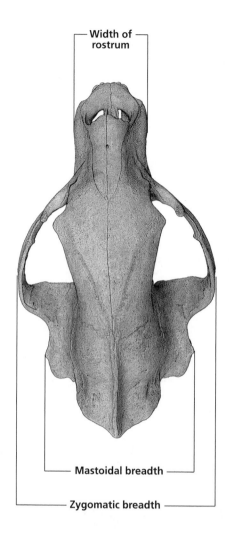

Width of rostrum

Mastoidal breadth

Zygomatic breadth

M3
American black bear

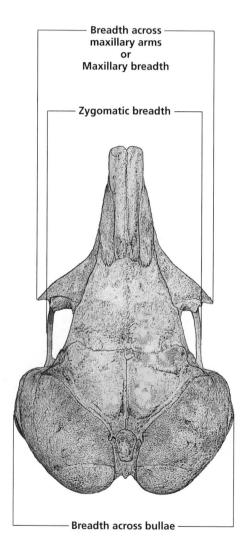

Breadth across maxillary arms or Maxillary breadth

Zygomatic breadth

Breadth across bullae

M4
Chisel-toothed kangaroo rat

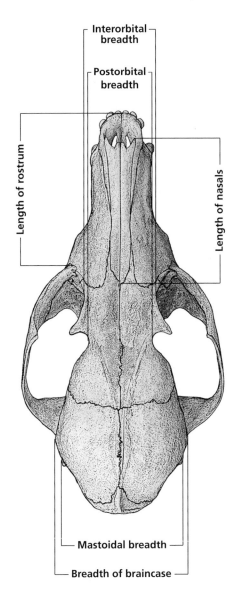

Interorbital breadth

Postorbital breadth

Length of rostrum

Length of nasals

Mastoidal breadth

Breadth of braincase

M5
Red fox

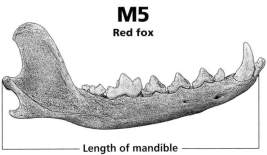

Length of mandible

*The jaw is angled.

M6
Red fox

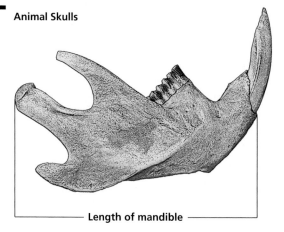

Length of mandible

M7
Common muskrat

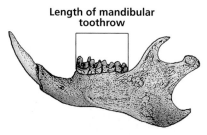

Length of mandibular toothrow

M8
Thirteen-lined ground squirrel

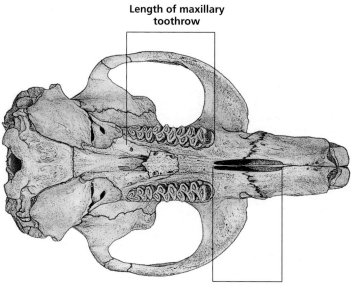

Length of maxillary toothrow

Length of incisive foramen

M9
Common muskrat

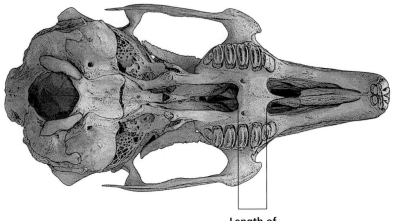

Length of
palatal bridge

M10
Brush rabbit

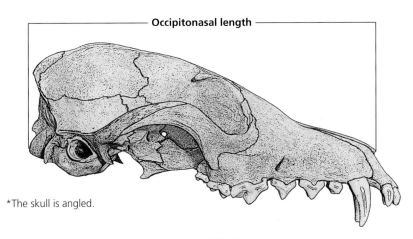

Occipitonasal length

*The skull is angled.

M11
Red fox

Understanding and Interpreting Form

2

The Natural History of Animal Skulls

Should you visit the La Brea tar pits in Los Angeles, California, pay the price to enter the Page Museum, where you can stand before several hundred dire wolf skulls displayed on a single wall, all excavated from the surrounding black pools. The stained skulls of saber-toothed cats and dire wolves are all about killing, relics of an ancient past when muscle, tooth, and claw seemed on a much larger scale than today. You can also study the bulk and musculature of these animals and their prey, as realistic life-size models are displayed amid the bones of diverse fauna. From remains of animals and ecosystems, archaeologists and paleontologists have re-created the entire bodies of ancient creatures and tell their stories of hunting and foraging thousands of years ago. They do this by interpreting the shapes of the remaining skulls and bones.

Every animal is a streamlined expression of evolution and ecology, its very form a set of variables in a unique equation balancing energy requirements with energy expenditure and the equipment necessary to meet those demands. You too can begin to re-create the life of some animal from a skull you hold, just a piece of the whole. It takes curiosity, imagination, perseverance, and some good questions to get you started. The skull, like all parts of a whole, reveals patterns that likely reappear in other aspects of the animal's morphology and ecology. For example, the slender skulls of deer are connected to long, slender bodies supported by long, slender legs on long, slender toes, and deer leave long, slender tracks. The squat skulls of cats are supported by squat, muscular bodies and squat, muscular legs, and their tracks are squat and flat.

What do the teeth tell you about what your animal ate and how it foraged? And even more, what do the teeth tell you about the whole animal? What do the shapes of the cranium and jaws relay about the development of the masseter and temporalis muscles, which determine whether power is emphasized in biting or crushing or grinding? What do the shape of the nasal cavity, the size of the brain, and the direction of the orbits reveal? Your goal is to visualize the entire animal, an active animal engaged

The imposing image of an agitated female cougar *(Puma concolor)*. From just bone and teeth, we attempt to visualize the whole living animal, and to see patterns that occur in the skull recurring throughout the remaining anatomy, physiology, and ecology of a given species. Always remind yourself the skull you hold was once part of something larger.

in its environment, and avoid the pitfalls of becoming lost in analyzing the pieces and never understanding the whole.

Holdrege (2003) talks about the importance of stepping back after each new analysis, each revelation, and asking yourself how the entire animal is expressed in the small piece you are studying, be it the teeth, mandible, or sagittal crests. Function is often a very descriptive way to share insights into skull morphology, but Holdrege reminds us of its limitations. I use my hands to type, yet perhaps it would be going a bit too far to say that my hands have evolved to type. Remain open to questions, and remember that every bone form has multiple functions, many of which we may yet have to witness or comprehend.

The natural history surrounding an animal's life is revealed further as you develop more detailed interpretations of the forms that are animal skulls, and begin to see those same patterns throughout the entire animal. Each skull tells the story of how that animal survived in the world—what it ate, what were its predators, and which senses it relied on the most to successfully stalk, hunt, feed, and hide. The skull also provides evidence on which to base further interpretations: the relative age of the animal at its death, whether it was a male or female, hardships endured while it was alive, and even on occasion how it met its demise. Following are some distinguishing characteristics to look for, along with a few interpretations to get you started. Other clues as to how an animal lived can be found all over the surface of the skull. Be creative, and ask more questions than those raised here—you are limited only by your imagination. The more you know about wildlife, the easier it is to formulate questions and to realize potential answers and larger patterns. Thus you are encouraged to cross-reference as much and as often as possible—with other skull guides; tracking guides; mammal, bird, and reptile and amphibian identification guides; and any other source that might teach you something about the natural history of wildlife. Any knowledge you acquire will aid your imagination in re-creating some beast from the skull and jaw you discovered while exploring the countryside.

The Teeth

Studying the myriad shapes and function of teeth is instrumental in interpreting the life of an animal. The analysis of teeth has been a cornerstone in understanding evolution, developing taxonomy, and classifying mammals and other animals. Whether animals are predators or prey is unveiled by the presence or absence of canines and carnassials, incisors, or flattened molariform teeth. Incisors, canines, premolars, and molars provide our first window into the lives of the creatures that have left us with only skulls and bones.

In rodents and ungulates, the great variety of cusps, prisms, and shapes formed along the crowns of the teeth are essential in identifying to the species level, especially when trying to distinguish between two very closely related animals, such as the various woodrat *(Neotoma)* species. A high-quality microscope or powerful loupe magnifier is required when studying microfeatures of the teeth of many small mammals, and for this reason I have not included detailed tooth descriptions. Rather, I've prioritized characteristics that are more easily visible with the naked eye or a magnifying glass when the skull is in hand. For a detailed description of rodent teeth, please refer to Chomko's essay in *Mammalian Osteology* (Gilbert 1980).

Incisors

Incisors are small, chisel-shaped teeth located at the front of the mouth and rooted in the premaxillary bones of the cranium, and the corresponding teeth in the mandibles. They are used for nipping, scraping, and tearing. Ungulates, the hoofed animals, use their incisors to nip buds from trees and herbaceous vegetation; carnivores and omnivores use the sharp edges to cut into fruits, vegetables, and soft meats, as well as to aid in gripping when tearing or dragging food or other items. Morse (2001) writes that a cougar uses its incisors much like a razor to shave away fur on large prey before opening the body cavity to feed on internal organs.

Shrews have large, procumbent incisors that are used to capture and hold insect prey. The enlarged, razor-sharp incisors of vampire bats are used to shave away layers of skin to reach blood sources, and the saliva acts as an anticoagulant.

The dentition of rodents and lagomorphs (rabbits, hares, and pikas) is distinctive, with four very large, sharp incisors at the anterior of the mouth. The upper and lower pairs of incisors close together in such a way as to slice and chisel both green and woody vegetation or gnaw at wood, bones, or anything short of metal the animal encounters. Colorful enamels are most evident on the anterior surfaces; the softer posterior is more easily worn away when the animal clicks its teeth together to maintain a sharp and ready edge.

The complete skull of a mountain goat *(Oreamnos americanus)*. Note the complete lack of upper incisors in the cranium. MUSEUM OF VERTEBRATE ZOOLOGY, UC BERKELEY, male, 43450.

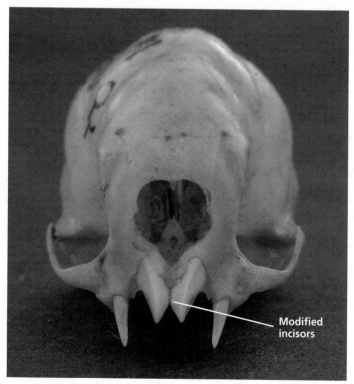

Study the modified incisors of this hairy-legged vampire bat *(Diphylla ecaudata)*, which have become the tools that allow it to shave skin and lap up flowing blood. NATURAL HISTORY MUSEUM OF LOS ANGELES COUNTY, female, 6070.

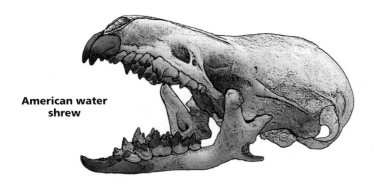

American water shrew

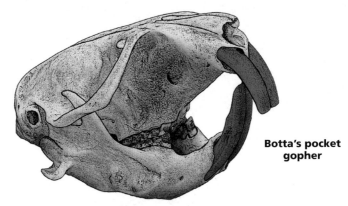

Botta's pocket gopher

In both rodents and shrews, the first incisors are well developed and distinctive. The infamous and distinctive incisors of rodents, as in this Botta's pocket gopher *(Thomomys bottae)*, are used as chisels and shears. In shrews like this American water shrew *(Sorex palustris)*, the procumbent, pointed incisors may function like forceps to capture, hold, and maneuver wiggly prey.

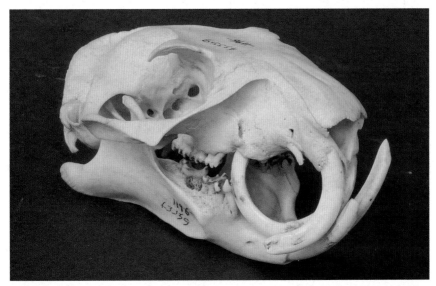

Carefully follow the line of each upper and lower incisor in this incredible woodchuck *(Marmota monax)* skull from Massachusetts. Dental anomalies are not uncommon in rodents and other mammal species. MUSEUM OF COMPARATIVE ZOOLOGY, HARVARD U., 43359.

Canines

Canines are the teeth of nightmares and horror movies, and are largely responsible for our fear of big carnivores. The canines are the most forward teeth in the maxillae bones of the cranium, and the corresponding teeth in the mandibles. Omnivores and carnivores have four unicuspid canines, whereas other animals have just two or none at all. In carnivores and omnivores, the canines are large, conspicuous conical teeth used to puncture, capture, hold, and kill other animals. They are the teeth with which a wolf attaches to the flank of a fleeing elk and a fisher kills a snowshoe hare while holding

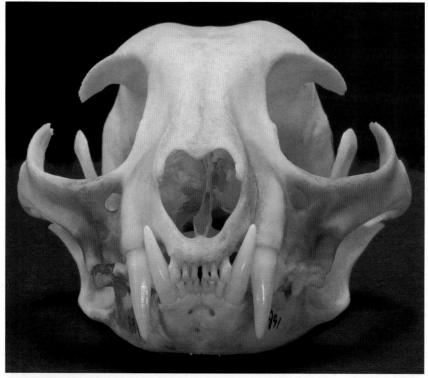

Note the four very long, sharp canines at the anterior corners of the mouth in this male bobcat *(Lynx rufus)*. SANTA BARBARA MUSEUM OF NATURAL HISTORY 891.

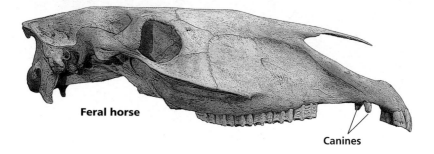

Feral horse

Canines

it close with all four paws. Canines are also instrumental in fighting for breeding rights, over territory, and in self-defense.

In rodents and rabbits, canines have disappeared altogether. In many ungulates, they remain as rudimentary small teeth in the maxillae bones, thought to be associated with displays during breeding season. In the mandibles of most ungulates, the canines mimic the incisors in shape and function and thus are easily overlooked by the casual observer. Yet in peccaries and wild hogs, the canines are large and distinctive, thought to be used as weapons in battles over breeding and in defense against predators, including humans.

Premolars and Molars

Premolars and molars are the posterior teeth responsible for chewing, shearing larger and tougher foods, and milling fibrous materials. The amazing diversity of foods that North American mammals chew is reflected in the great diversity of shapes and forms exhibited by premolars and molars. Thus they are a wonderful source of insight into the lives of animals.

Premolars differ from molars in that they are deciduous, being replaced as an animal reaches maturity. Premolars sit central on the mandible, whereas molars are farther to the posterior. Experts still disagree as to whether molars are more technically milk teeth that are never replaced or permanent teeth that had no predecessors. They tend to erupt latest among the teeth, and when fully erupted, they are often used as evidence that an animal is an adult.

In carnivores and omnivores, premolars and molars are most often jagged and serrated and used for gripping and tearing. Among the premolars and molars are the carnassials, specialized teeth that serve as shears to cut large meals into bite-size pieces. Give any dog a large slab of meat and watch it maneuver the food to the back of the mouth and off to one side. It is using its carnassials to shear off a smaller piece. When milk teeth are still present, the carnassials are formed by the fourth upper and lower premolars; in permanent dentition, the shearing carnassials are formed by the first premolar above and the first molar in the lower mandible. Note that the impressive

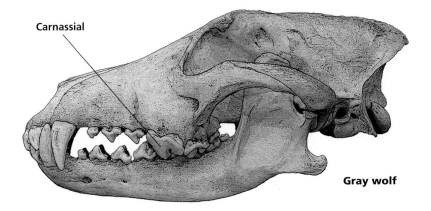

Carnassial

Gray wolf

skulls of bears, with their daunting canines and massive zygomatic arches, lack carnassials, the characteristic shearing teeth of true predators.

Depending on a carnivore's diet, the last molar in the toothrow may be flattened or serrated. In wolves and wolverines, flattened molars provide ideal surfaces for trapping and crushing large bones, and in black and brown bears, the equipment for crushing and grinding plant materials. Carnivorous sea otters use their very flat molars to crack and crush tough mollusks. Felines, on the other hand, have jagged premolars and molars, which they use to tear and slice flesh meals.

In many sea mammals, the premolars and molars have evolved into sharp, conical teeth, ideal for holding slippery prey. This is especially true in animals that gulp their food whole, such as dolphins. This strategy of first grasping, then holding, repositioning, and finally gulping prey whole is an ancient and a time-proven model; many identical teeth line the mouths of reptiles and amphibians, including the gulping alligators, salamanders, and frogs of today. In insectivores like shrews and moles, pointed premolars and molars crush and cut into tough insect exoskeletons.

Functionally, the role of premolars and molars seems very similar in rodents, rabbits, and ungulates, and they are often referred to as a single group, called either the cheek teeth or molariform teeth. These teeth are the crushing and grinding equipment responsible for pulping tough plant and mast fibers. The sharply cusped molari-

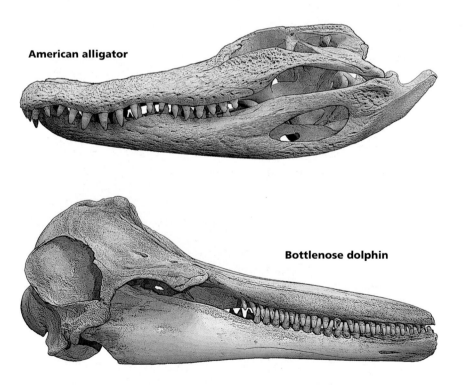

American alligator

Bottlenose dolphin

Both American alligators *(Alligator mississippiensis)* and Bottlenose dolphins *(Tursiops truncatus)* exhibit the simple conical teeth of animals which tend to gulp meals whole.

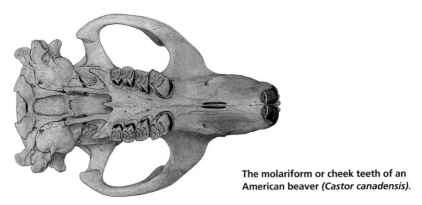

The molariform or cheek teeth of an American beaver *(Castor canadensis).*

form teeth in deer have evolved for grinding woody browse, buds, and limbs, and the taller, flatter ones in bison for grinding herbaceous plants and graze and withstanding years and years of inevitable tooth wear.

The Jaws

Two large groups of muscles are primarily associated with the closing of the jaws, the temporalis and masseter muscles. The shapes of the mandibles, braincase, and zygomatic arches tell us much about the size and purpose of the temporalis and masseter muscles in an animal, which in turn reveal much about their natural history. Another group of muscles, the digastric muscles, is responsible for opening the jaws. These muscles attach at the mastoid processes and extend to the lower posterior portion of the jaws, though they are less useful in identification and interpretation.

The temporalis muscles originate on the lateral side of the braincase (and temporal ridges or crests if present), as well as the posterior ligaments of the eye, and they run down through the temporalis fossa to attach to the anterior surface and upper portion of the coronoid process. These muscles determine the power driving the closing of the jaw at the front of the mouth and the teeth associated there, such as the canines. Mammals that kill with their canines often have well-developed temporalis muscles, whereas they tend to be poorly developed in animals that grind vegetation.

The masseter muscles attach along the ventral side of the zygomatic arches and extend down to attach to the angle of the mandible and the masseteric fossa. The masseter muscles provide power to the posterior portion of the mandible and the premolars and molars located there. Masseter muscles are well developed in herbivores, for it is the molars that are responsible for processing the foods on which they depend.

The development of these two large muscles groups varies tremendously across species, and understanding their relative sizes in an animal is critical in interpreting the creature's natural history. There are many modifications to the cranium and mandible that aid these muscle groups in providing further power in biting, shearing, or crushing, including the shape of the cranium, the presence of crests, pitted surfaces, the overall shape of the lower jaw, and the presence of depressions at attachment sites.

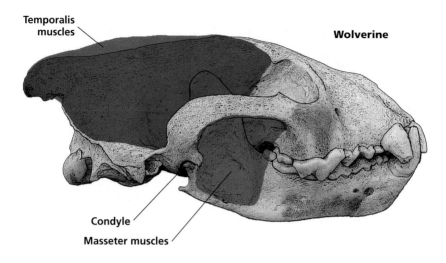

Temporalis muscles

Wolverine

Condyle

Masseter muscles

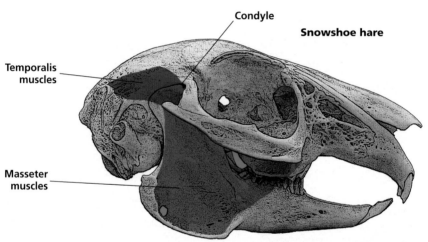

Condyle

Snowshoe hare

Temporalis muscles

Masseter muscles

Compare the relative sizes and proportions of masseter and temporalis muscles in this wolverine *(Gulo gulo)* and snowshoe hare *(Lepus americanus)*. The masseter muscles are relatively well developed in the wolverine, an animal capable of crushing and eating large bones of ungulates, which other predators cannot crack. In the hare, note the extreme development of the masseter muscles. Also compare the position of the mandibular condyle in relation with the toothrows of each species.

The Temporalis Muscles

Perhaps the most apparent character to aid in envisioning the relative size of the temporalis muscles is the width of the temporalis fossa, the vacant space behind the orbit (and postorbital processes if present), defined by the cranium on one side and the zygomatic arches on the other. More widely spreading zygomatic arches indicate an animal with strong temporalis muscles, as the wider the arches spread, the more muscles that could fit in the space between them and the cranium. Carnivores and many omnivores show wide-spreading zygomatic arches. Some rodents do as well—those

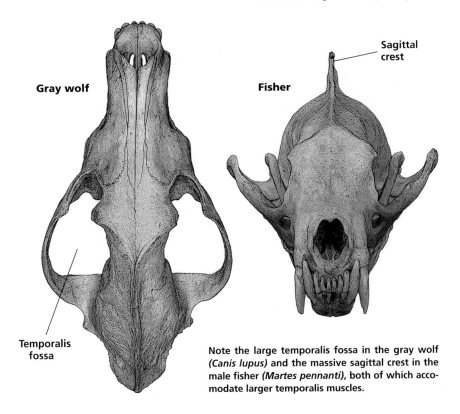

Note the large temporalis fossa in the gray wolf *(Canis lupus)* and the massive sagittal crest in the male fisher *(Martes pennanti),* both of which accomodate larger temporalis muscles.

that require suitable force behind their incisors to chisel mast, wood, or even bone. Ungulates, on the other hand, require little upward force of the mandible with regard to incisors and canines, and this is reflected in the narrow spread of their zygomatic arches and the reduced size of their temporalis muscles.

Temporalis muscles can be even more enlarged, increasing power still further, with a greater surface area at attachment points, as reflected in the development of sagittal crests. Male fishers, wolverines, and California sea lions develop exceptional sagittal crests to accommodate incredible temporalis muscles. Yet nearly all carnivores and omnivores, and some rodents too, exhibit development of sagittal crests. Pitted craniums also allow more surface area and deeper attachments for muscles, and thus can increase the power exerted by the jaw. On the other hand, a smooth, rounded skull provides the least surface area for temporalis muscles to attach readily, and therefore indicates a lifestyle that is less dependent on power at the anterior of the mandibles.

A portion of the temporalis muscles is also connected to the posterior of the orbit, and thus there is a relationship between the size of the orbit and modifications necessary to accommodate larger temporalis muscles. A large orbit and large temporalis, as in bobcats, require tough bone supports in the form of large postorbital processes extending from either the frontal or zygomata bones, or both and in some cases a complete postorbital bar. If the orbit is small and the temporalis muscles large, as in wolverines, smaller postorbital processes are adequate to support musculature. And

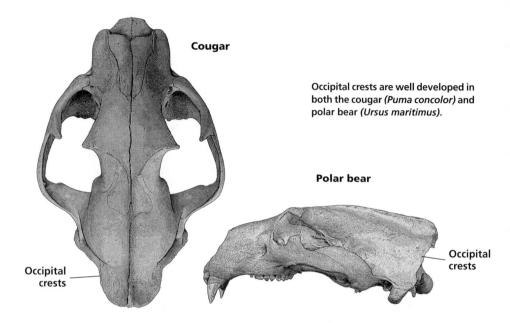

Cougar

Occipital crests are well developed in both the cougar *(Puma concolor)* and polar bear *(Ursus maritimus).*

Polar bear

Occipital crests

Occipital crests

where eyes are large but the temporalis muscles are weak, as in seals, postorbital processes too can be weak or absent altogether.

Muscles in the neck are often strengthened with an increase in temporalis muscles, and this is evidenced by the development of occipital or lambdoidal crests at the posterior of the skull. Consider the polar bear, which sometimes hunts by patiently waiting next to a hole in the ice where 250-pound seals briefly appear to breathe. In that moment, the bear clamps down on its prey with canines and mouth and yanks the seal from its watery sanctuary—often breaking a foot of ice to do so—with mind-boggling strength of jaw, neck, and body. The occipital crests of polar bears are exceptionally well developed, as are the sagittal crests. They are also well developed in the cougar, which will leap onto the back of an elk, up to seven times its size, clamp its canines into the back of the neck, and then ride the panicked beast as it charges forward with a burst of adrenaline. The cougar's neck muscles are all-important in such endeavors. Or consider the badger, which moves earth with its head and neck, and even fights creatures much larger than itself with the strength of a bear. The badger is able to do all this thanks to its well-developed occipital crests and strong neck muscles.

Temporalis muscles also can be increased by modifications of the mandible. A scooped-out surface called the masseteric fossa may run down the coronoid process, allowing for larger temporalis muscles to secure to the mandible. This is especially apparent in the mandibles of cats. Larger masseter muscles also attach to the lower portion of the masseteric fossa.

Considering the power and size of the temporalis muscles and the physics of increasing pressure at the anterior of the mandibles allows a glimpse at patterns in the lifestyle of the animal. In the cougar, large canines are evident, teeth designed to puncture and hold prey, as well as to tear chunks from large meals. Carnassials are

Cougar

knifelike, shearing teeth extraordinaire. The well-developed sagittal crests, wide-spreading zygomata, long postorbital processes, and scooped coronoid process all allow for increased development of the temporalis muscles. The slightly curved mandible increases the power exerted upward at the front of the jaw, and the shortened muzzle increases the power of the bite still further. The lambdoidal crests indicate powerful neck muscles. In analyzing a cougar skull, you thus find numerous features that indicate a natural history dependent upon killing living animals quickly.

Now consider this pattern in the context of the whole animal. The skull and dentition of the cougar contribute to killing quickly and efficiently. The musculature of the body and legs is ideal for quick, short chases and pouncing, again for killing quickly. The heart and lungs are small and inadequate for long chases, much better for killing quickly. The broad feet and sheathed claws aid in pouncing and holding prey—helpful equipment when killing quickly. Thus the pattern that you observed in the skull reappears in other aspects of the animal's morphology and ecology.

Take the mule deer, common prey for wild cougars, as another example. Deer have long, slender skulls; smooth, rounded braincases; narrowly spreading zygomatic arches; and countless other adaptations to shift the power of the jaws from the anterior to the posterior of the mouth. Yet their occipital crests are developed, indicating strong neck muscles as used in grazing and sparring.

Think about what each revelation contributes to your understanding of the whole animal as expressed in each bone form. Use your imagination—it may be your greatest tool in assessing animal skulls.

The Masseter Muscles

Thick, heavy zygomata are excellent indicators of large masseter muscles, whose power is delivered at the posterior portion of the mandibles. This is the location of the grinding molars in omnivores and herbivores and the shearing carnassials in carnivores. Ungulates have narrow zygomatic breadths, which means the passage for temporalis muscles is small, indicating that power at the anterior of the mandibles is unnecessary. Yet their zygomatic arches are often thick and heavy, providing solid anchorage for masseter muscles that are larger than their temporalis muscles. Grinding and chewing are essential to these animals' lifestyle. The same model is perhaps more dramatically exhibited in the armadillo, where a smooth, rounded braincase and narrowly spreading

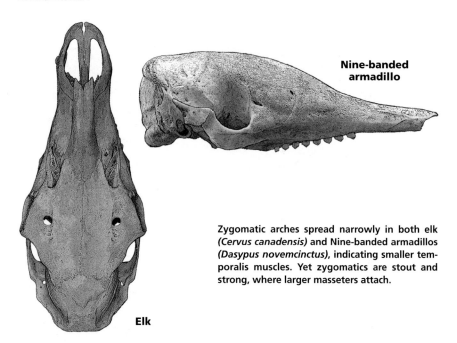

Nine-banded armadillo

Zygomatic arches spread narrowly in both elk *(Cervus canadensis)* and Nine-banded armadillos *(Dasypus novemcinctus)*, indicating smaller temporalis muscles. Yet zygomatics are stout and strong, where larger masseters attach.

Elk

zygomata allow for poor development of the temporalis muscles. These animals have no teeth at the anterior of the mouth at all. Their short zygomatic arches are stout, though, and a bony ridge extends forward onto the maxillaries, allowing well-developed masseter muscles, with the power of the jaws focused on the premolars and molars.

The opposite is true in many carnivores, whose masseter muscles are much smaller than the temporalis muscles. These animals need more power to capture and hold prey than to shear off chunks to swallow. And as is often the case, the omnivores provide a middle ground between true carnivores and herbivores, balancing power at the anterior of the jaws with power at the posterior for grinding varied meals. Omnivorous bears have both wide-spreading and thick zygomatic arches, allowing the development of both muscle groups.

The Shape and Articulation of the Mandibles

The overall shapes of the mandibles also influence the physics of upward pressure exerted by the lower mandible. Herbivores and carnivores exhibit different jaw shapes. In herbivores, jaws are either long and thin (as in armadillos and deer) or thickest at the posterior and tapering toward the anterior (as in horses and rabbits). Both of these shapes concentrate the real strength of the jaws on the middle and posterior teeth, those responsible for grinding and chewing. Shortened and curved jaws, as are especially apparent in gnawing rodents and carnivores, increase the power exerted at the anterior of the jaw.

Loose articulation between the cranium and mandibles allows a greater range of movement from side to side and back to front, which is especially useful when grind-

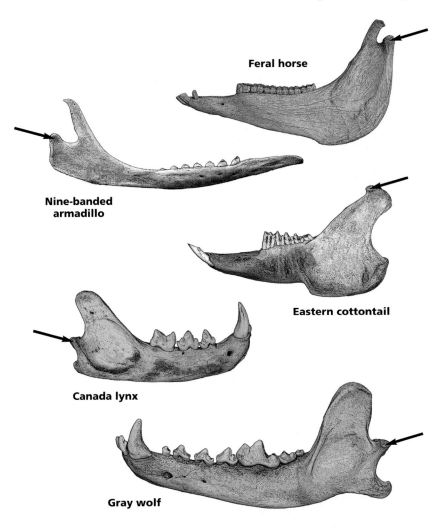

Compare the relative shapes of these various mandibles, as well as the relationship between the condyles (marked by arrows) and the level of the tooth rows.

ing plants and masts; visualize a cow grazing in a field. Tight articulation created by a barrel-shaped condyle and snug mandibular fossa is more useful when teeth need to meet in a particular way, as when shearing chunks of meat from a carcass. Tighter articulation also focuses the power of closing jaws on a vertical axis, rather than allowing some spreading of force to either side as well. In wolverines, the mandibular fossa allows no wiggle room for the condyle, and often the jaws cannot be removed from the cranium in mature specimens without damaging the bones securing the articulation point. At the opposite extreme are rabbit skulls, in which the articulation point is so vague that it may be difficult to guess exactly where to position the lower jaw when reassembling a specimen.

According to Hildebrand and Goslow (2001), when the mandibular condyle, which forms the "hinge," is on the same plane as the toothrows, as in carnivores, the arc of approaching teeth as the jaw closes is opposite, and therefore ideal for slicing, shearing, or working the teeth like a mortar and pestle. When the condyle sits well above the toothrows, as in herbivores, the teeth approach each other at a more oblique angle, wedging and rolling food as the teeth come together, like a mill for vegetation illustrated on page 50.

The Senses

Other bone forms are associated with the senses of smell, sight, and hearing. The overall size of the brain cavity is also relevant to interpreting an animal's sensory capabilities. Analyzing these structures and characteristics will help you determine how the animal interpreted and interacted with its environment so that you can better understand its natural history. Did your animal rely strongly on vision, like humans, or more on scents or sounds to move about and survive in its environment?

Smell

The importance and strength of an animal's sense of smell can be roughly gauged from the length, width, and height of the rostrum; the dimensions of the nasal vacuity; and the development of turbinate bones, which support olfactory nerves. Canines are renowned for their keen sense of smell and for scent-tracking potential prey. Their ros-

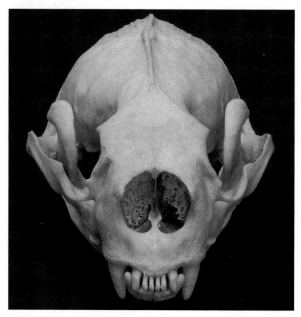

Note the large nasal vacuity and complex turbinate bones within of this male California sea otter *(Enhydra lutris)*. SANTA BARBARA MUSEUM OF NATURAL HISTORY 3377.

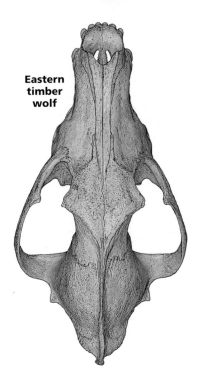

Eastern timber wolf

A large, well developed rostrum aids wolves in scent trailing.

trums are long and stout, compared with the much shorter rostrums of visual hunters such as cats. In the hoary bat, little of the skull is devoted to rostral development; perhaps scent-trailing is less important in the aerial hunting strategies of this insect predator.

Sight

Consider the size of the orbital vacuities in proportion to the overall size of the skull. The very large orbits of felines reveal the visual hunting strategies on which they depend for survival. The large orbits of seals and sea lions house eyes that need to see in the diminished light of deeper waters. Nocturnal creatures such as the great horned owls, night monkeys, and flying squirrels also have large orbits. Compare the southern flying squirrel's shorter skull and larger orbits with those of its sympatric cousin, the diurnal eastern chipmunk.

The angle of the orbits, which directs the animal's gaze, also tells you much about its natural history. Orbits that point at near right angles to the midline of the skull, as in many ungulates, enable the animal to view the world in monocular vision, which means that it watches any movement in its environment with each eye individually. The advantages of monocular vision include an almost 180-degree field of view with each eye, so nearly 360 degrees can be watched simultaneously. This is ideal equipment for animals in danger of being preyed upon, such as deer and rabbits, which need to constantly monitor as much of their environment as possible. Monocular vision is also very sensitive to movement, allowing prey species to detect any small motion that might reveal a sneaking predator. The greatest disadvantage to monocular vision is in

Great horned owl

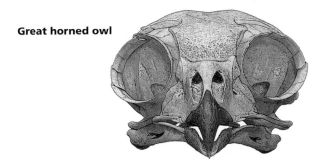

The large orbits and sclerotic rings of a great horned owl *(Bubo virginianus)*.

American buffalo

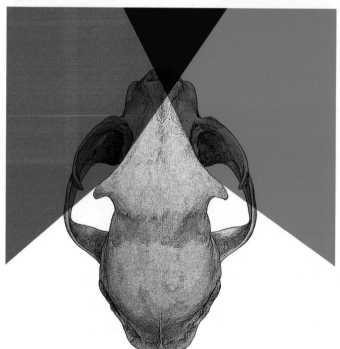

Bobcat

Compare the monocular field of view awarded each eye in the American buffalo *(Bos bison)*, with the binocular vision of the bobcat *(Lynx rufus)*. As stated in the text, each system of sight provides both benefits and detriments.

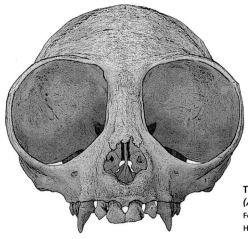

The amazing orbits of the night monkey (*Aotus trivirgatus*) dominate its skull. Female, SANTA BARBARA MUSEUM OF NATURAL HISTORY 2259.

the decreased ability to assess depth of field; motion is easily observed, but at what distance and on what path that movement might approach is obscured. It would seem that detection skills are prioritized, for at the first signs of danger, it is fleeing that saves these animals' lives.

As the orbits are angled more forward, there is a greater degree of overlap between the field of view covered by each eye. This overlap allows for binocular vision, which boosts interpretation and awareness of depth perception, but has a smaller field of overall coverage than that provided by monocular vision. Animals that pounce on animals, leap from branch to branch, or hunt moving targets tend to have the greatest need for depth perception and thus the greatest degree of binocular vision. Cats, owls, and primates are the most compelling examples, yet to a varying degree, all the carnivores and omnivores have binocular vision.

The position of the orbits is also a useful clue to the animal's lifestyle. Water-loving creatures, such as alligators and beavers, have orbits high on the head to let them see while swimming with the head partially submerged. Grazing creatures have eyes at the far posterior of the skull, allowing them to see while their heads are down cropping herbaceous greens and clover, a great advantage, especially when grasses are longer.

Hearing

The size and shape of auditory bullae can give some indication of the strength of hearing in an animal, though it is possible to have excellent hearing even with small or flattened bullae. In general, however, larger and more swollen, or inflated, auditory bullae indicate an increased ability to hear. Rabbits, which are exceptional in their hearing and dependent on this sense to reveal potential threats in areas where vision might be obscured, have inflated auditory bullae. In 1962, D. B. Webster studied the enlarged auditory bullae and swollen mastoid regions in kangaroo rats (Ewer 1973). The enlargement increased the air space behind the tympanic membranes, creating a chamber that resonates perfectly with the sound frequencies created by an owl swoop-

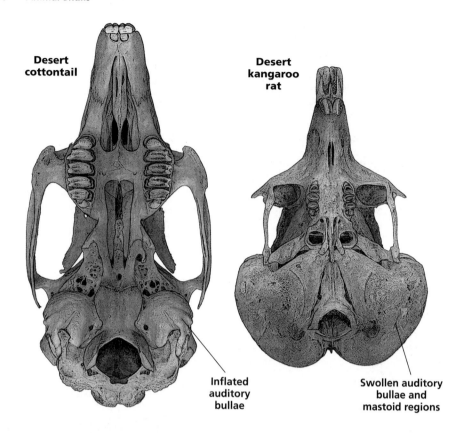

Desert cottontail

Desert kangaroo rat

Inflated auditory bullae

Swollen auditory bullae and mastoid regions

ing in for a kill and a rattlesnake making a strike. Thus the auditory system of kangaroo rats is thought to allow them to avoid threats on their lives at the last moment, if they leap and veer with lightning speed.

Canines have well-inflated auditory bullae too. River otters, which rely less on hearing while underwater and in such environments, have flattened and smaller auditory bullae. In opossums, the bullae are barely perceptible at all; certainly opossums can hear, but they always seem startled when they see you approach in the field.

Braincase

The size of the braincase in proportion to the overall skull and body can give you some clues as to the relative intelligence of an animal, though this is a very inexact interpretation. The brain is involved in interpreting sensory information, decision making, and memory. Larger brains are often associated with greater creativity and curiosity, which allow for greater plasticity and adaptation to circumstances, and sometimes even tool use. For example, the polar bear has a very large braincase; the polar bears in Manitoba stalk and hunt the tourists on the tundra buggies. People are thrilled that the bears come right up to the vehicles and explore about their undersides, many unaware that this intent curiosity is a hunting strategy that gives the polar bear an edge in environments where food can be scarce.

A Review of the Main Interpretive Features

Let's quickly review the tools we've discussed to help you recognize patterns in the life of an animal from its skull:

1. Consider the dentition, the kinds of teeth and their shapes.
2. Envision the development of the temporalis and masseter muscles, which are revealed in the spread of the zygomata and the development of sagittal crests and such.
3. Examine the shape and articulation of the mandibles.
4. Study the shape and size of the rostrum and nasal vacuity.
5. Contemplate the size and angles of the orbits.
6. Scrutinize the size and shape of the auditory bullae.
7. Ponder the size of the braincase and what you might guess about the animal's thinking and interpretive capabilities.

If possible, practice identifying the above characteristics on skulls you are familiar with so that you get a feel for skull features and how natural history is reflected in bone form. Let's examine the gray fox *(Urocyon cinereoargenteus)* skull as a specific example:

1. Foxes are canids, and all members of this family have forty-two teeth, including incisors, canines, premolars, and molars. Compared with those of other members of this family, the gray fox's teeth are smaller and less aggressive, used for hunting smaller, more manageable prey. Carnassials are developed, though proportionately smaller than in other canids; shearing is possible, but gray foxes lack the equipment necessary for very large, tough prey. The hindmost molars are proportionately wider and flatter, supporting a more omnivorous diet, and the canines are slightly blunter, still excellent for

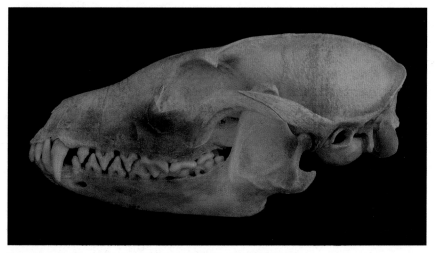

Common gray fox *(Urocyon cinereoargenteus)*. PRIVATE COLLECTION.

gripping and holding, but not as efficient for puncturing. Also note the slimmer and shorter rostrum; the teeth are not rooted in the same way as in the larger canids, which hunt prey larger than themselves. All in all, the gray fox has a dainty dentition. Some members of the canid family are social hunters, allowing them to tackle prey much larger than themselves. In such hunting forays and battles to the death, large, strong teeth well rooted in substantial bone are essential to success and survival.

Lessons at a Gray Fox Den

I recently monitored a gray fox den to learn more about these fascinating creatures, paying particular attention to the food that both the male and female parents contributed to their litter of five pups. In the several weeks I devoted to the foxes, I witnessed the following food items brought into the den: five brush rabbits, seven black rats, one garter snake, five dusky-footed woodrats, three California voles, one Trowbridge's shrew, three Botta's pocket gophers, and one mule deer fawn of the black-tailed subspecies. I also witnessed one of the pups eat a banana slug. It was the fawn that most fascinated me.

When I approached the den entrance one morning and saw the fawn carcass lying there, I was dubious about whether a gray fox could kill such a large animal. I checked my trusty digital Camtrakker camera, which kept up the watch while I slept. The male had dragged the fawn to the den entrance at 3:30 A.M. Perhaps it was a roadkill, though this was unlikely because of the remoteness of the site and low road density in the immediate area. So I decided further forensic study was needed and analyzed the exterior of the carcass, then skinned it out to look further for signs of trauma at the time of death. The hooves of the animal were used, which meant the tiny deer had lived and moved about. But it was a very young fawn, perhaps only a week old. It was certainly the age when its greatest defense was lying motionless in cover to avoid the notice of potential predators.

As much as I worked to deny the obvious hypothesis that the fox had killed the fawn, I could not do so. Everything pointed to strangulation. The canines had not punctured the neck, but while the fawn twitched and fought, they had removed fine lines of fur. If the fox had stolen a bobcat's kill, there would be punctures and signs of feline canines. But signs of trauma were present only on the neck. I could not find any evidence that the tiny creature had been struck in any way.

I can only guess that the fox had stumbled upon the fawn lying in some nearby field, grasped it by the neck, and strangled its life away before the fawn could escape. The most compelling signs that I relied on to re-create this story, which is only my best guess as to what happened, were the strength and power of the jaws that strangled the fawn.

2. Among the most striking features of the gray fox skull are the well-developed U-shaped temporal ridges, which act as anchors and boundaries for the temporalis muscles, those that provide power to the anterior teeth. This U-shaped system greatly limits the development of this muscle group, and strength is considerably hampered in comparison with other members of the canid family. The pitted surface along the sides of the braincase do add further anchorage points, but not enough to compensate for and balance the loss of power from such reduction in the temporalis muscles. The orbits are proportionately larger than in other canids, and the temporal fossa smaller. The masseteric fossa, the anchoring points for muscles on the coronoid process, is also smaller and shallower than in other canids. The masseter muscles are not exceptional, interpreted from the zygomata of medium weight and size. Both the dentition and the development of these two large muscle groups indicate a lifestyle that involves hunting small prey and eating mast and fruit crops.

The lambdoidal crests are also proportionately smaller in the gray fox than in the larger canids. This is another indicator that hunting large game, which will fight and flee forward while the attacker clings on, is not the lifestyle pursued by the gray fox.

3. The snug articulation of the mandibles and the location of the condyle in relation to the toothrows are both characteristic of all the canids though the condyle is slightly more elevated above the toothrows; the more elevated the condyle the less effective teeth will be in shearing and crushing. There may be greater side-to-side mobility in the jaw of the gray fox, but this may or may not be significant. The body of the mandible is straighter than in other canids, sharing power among all the teeth in the mouth, rather than focusing strength at the anterior. The mandible as a whole is daintier than in other canids, further evidence of a life hunting small game and eating soft fruits and plant materials.

4. The rostrum is doglike, being long and well developed, so the sense of smell is excellent. Oddly, the gray fox has a distinctively shorter and narrower rostrum than other canids, and one wonders what this indicates about the relative importance of smell in locating foods.

5. Gray fox orbits are large and point forward, providing the binocular vision of carnivores and omnivores. It is not the binocular vision of a bobcat, but enough that hunting moving targets is successful.

6. The auditory bullae in the gray fox are small but well inflated, indicating that the sense of hearing is excellent. Gray foxes may be hunters, but they are also prey for coyotes, bobcats, domestic dogs, and others. Hearing potential dangers approach is essential.

7. The gray fox has a large braincase in proportion to the overall size of the skull. Foxes are certainly adaptable and curious, and they work to avoid numerous predators. Michael Fox compared gray foxes with red and arctic foxes, noting that they are more social because they engage in allogrooming with partners (Fritzell and Haroldson 1982). He also reports that gray foxes had the least obvious facial expressions of the three.

Individual and Geographic Variation

When you are among friends and coworkers, it's obvious that everyone's head is not the same shape. Yet we are all humans, *Homo sapiens*. It is the same with every creature: Although certain shared cranial features identify animals as members of a given family, genus, and species, there is remarkable variation in the size and shape of their bodies and skulls across their geographic ranges, as well as among individuals within a given population.

Gould and Kreeger (1948) studied 2,092 muskrats from various locations along a 250-mile stretch connecting the far eastern edge of Louisiana with its far western marshes. They discovered that muskrats increased in body and skull size from east to west across the state; thus the largest muskrats were on the westward boundary of the state. How would muskrats differ from east to west and south to north across our entire continent?

In another study, Goheen et al. (2003) observed that a red squirrel population that had only recently migrated south into the hardwoods of Indiana had already developed larger craniums and longer jaws than their northern counterparts. These variations were related to a change in diet rather than latitude. Southern red squirrels are feeding on harder mast, such as acorns and walnuts, while their northern ancestors still feed on the smaller seeds of conifers. The researchers were able to prove that the cranial evolution resulted in greater mandibular force, which gives the southern population an adaptive edge when feeding on harder mast.

Maine   **California**

Bergman's rule, a classic in wildlife biology, says that in many species with a large geographic distribution, the northern populations are larger than their southern counterparts. Raccoons, for example, are largest in the Northwest and smallest in the Southeast (Gehrt, 2003). But this is not always the case, as there are numerous variables at play, and animals and their skulls only hint at the complexity of natural ecosystems. Consider the male long-tailed weasel skulls pictured here.

Determining the Age of Mammal Skulls

Several methods can be employed to determine the relative, and sometimes specific, age of a mammal when it died, given only the skull in hand. Certain laboratory methods involve counting or measuring cementum layers in teeth. In some mammals, rings of cementum occur like growth rings of a tree, each representing a year of life; in others, a greater width of cementum accumulates at the tooth roots with predictability and can be measured to estimate age. Other lab methods require chemical testing and color tests. The discussion below focuses on methods that do not require a lab. They are visual in nature and can be done by anyone with a skull in hand.

There are ample resources to help you determine the age of animals from their skulls and mandibles, but much of it is sprinkled among numerous scientific journals and papers. Three valuable resources include considerable information on aging animals from skull specimens. The first is a very user-friendly, inexpensive, visual publication compiled by Jim Heffelfinger (1997) for the Arizona Game and Fish Department, called *Age Criteria for Arizona Game Species*. The second is a large and expensive book called *Wild Mammals of North America: Biology, Management, and Conservation*, edited by G. Feldhamer et al. (2003). The third is Miles Gilbert's *Mammalian Osteology* (1980) which invites contemplation on how historical context might be inferred from bone remains and reveal an animal's age. All are worth having on hand.

Keep in mind, however, that there is too much variation even within a given species, too much diversity of form, to make aging an exact science that can be applied to every skull.

Milk Teeth and Tooth Eruption

Teeth are excellent indicators of age. In all mammals, teeth will at least separate out adults from immature animals, and in some cases, they will give you a much more specific range for the potential age. Incomplete dentition is an obvious sign of immaturity. For example, opossums will not have fifty teeth until they reach adulthood. The presence of the smaller milk teeth, the deciduous dentition, also indicates an immature animal. Often immature specimens will be in the process of tooth replacement or the permanent molars may be erupting from the bone. Depending on the species, the sequence in which some teeth erupt before others is used to age specimens with great accuracy. When relevant, such information is given in the notes under the species accounts.

In American bison, the presence of milk teeth and permanent teeth among the incisors and canines in the mandibles can be used to age animals up to five years old. Refer to the illustrations on page 66 to help you visualize the sequence of replacement, which occurs from the midline outward to either side (Heffelfinger 1997). The milk teeth are much smaller than the permanent dentition, and as a general rule, this is true in most mammals.

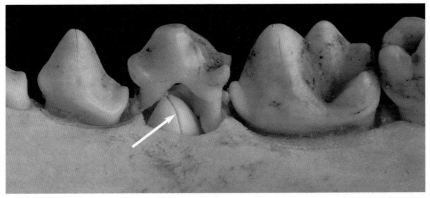

Tooth eruption and replacement in a subadult female white-nosed coati *(Nasua narica)*. NATURAL HISTORY MUSEUM OF LOS ANGELES COUNTY 59442.

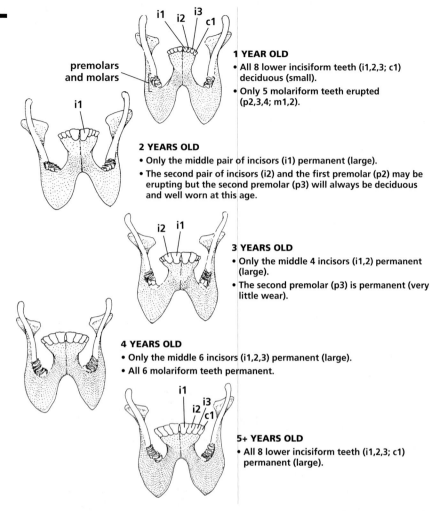

1 YEAR OLD
- All 8 lower incisiform teeth (i1,2,3; c1) deciduous (small).
- Only 5 molariform teeth erupted (p2,3,4; m1,2).

2 YEARS OLD
- Only the middle pair of incisors (i1) permanent (large).
- The second pair of incisors (i2) and the first premolar (p2) may be erupting but the second premolar (p3) will always be deciduous and well worn at this age.

3 YEARS OLD
- Only the middle 4 incisors (i1,2) permanent (large).
- The second premolar (p3) is permanent (very little wear).

4 YEARS OLD
- Only the middle 6 incisors (i1,2,3) permanent (large).
- All 6 molariform teeth permanent.

5+ YEARS OLD
- All 8 lower incisiform teeth (i1,2,3; c1) permanent (large).

Each of the two lower mandibles in American bison *(Bos bison)* have 3 incisors and 1 incisor-form canine at the anterior of the mouth, and in the posterior, 3 premolars and 3 molars. The eruption pattern of these teeth can be used to age bison up to 5 years old. Found in Heffelfinger (1997). Drawings by Randy Babb, and used with permission of Jim Heffelfinger.

Tooth Wear, Gum Line Recession, and Missing or Broken Teeth

Tooth wear is a wonderful tool for quickly assessing the relative age of an animal. As an animal lives and feeds, its teeth wear down. In some species, researchers have a reasonably good understanding of how much tooth wear to expect in a given age class and thus use this method for quite accurate aging of individuals. In other species, tooth wear still can be used to differentiate juvenile from adult, and early, middle, or late adulthood.

In omnivores and carnivores, gum line recession on the canines is another good relative guide to an animal's age. With a bit of experience, you'll be able to identify a skull as young, early adult, middle-aged, or very old. As you gain more experience handling

Female

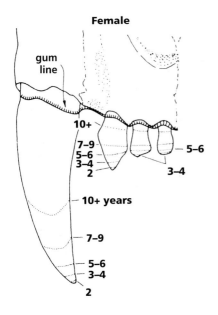

Male

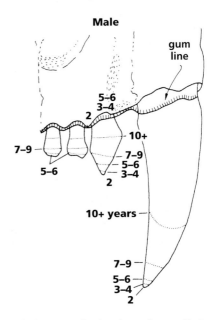

Tooth wear with relative age in cougars *(Puma concolor)*. You are viewing the canines and incisors from the front of the skull. Drawing by and with permission of Matt Alderson, Arizona Game and Fish Department.

skulls of a given species, you will be able to age by gum line recession with greater accuracy within a population.

Older animals often have teeth missing, which can be differentiated from teeth lost after the animal died by the healing of the socket where the tooth would have been held. Or teeth may have broken and then worn smooth with continued living; broken and smoothed canines in carnivores or omnivores usually are characteristic of the oldest age classes. LeCount (1986) uses broken canines in his criteria for aging black bears either in the field or from skulls alone. Two or more broken, yellowed, and smoothed canines are descriptive of bears sixteen years old or more.

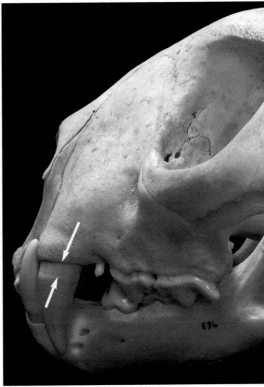

Gum line recession is clearly evident in this mature male cougar, the measurable height of which is delineated between the two arrows.
SANTA BARBARA MUSEUM OF NATURAL HISTORY 886.

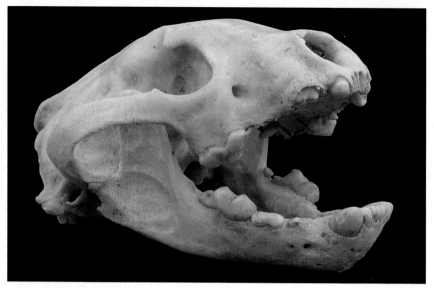

Note the incredible tooth wear in this very old female wolverine *(Gulo gulo)* trapped near Nome, Alaska. She may have further broken her upper canines when struggling with the trap, which is quite common in wolverines. PRIVATE COLLECTION.

Bones with a Pitted Appearance

Certain bones or regions of the skull may be smoother than others. The surface of immature bone has a certain roughness or sponginess; these areas have not yet completely ossified and remain porous. Mature bone is shiny and hard. Refer to the photo of the immature coyote skull, in which different types of bone are present. Roughness on the bone surface usually indicates an immature animal, but it also appears in

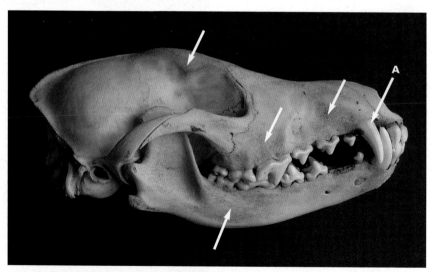

Look carefully for the rough porous bone that is still rapidly growing in this subadult coyote *(Canis latrans)*, several portions of which are delineated with arrows. The more mature bone surfaces are shiny. Also note the very small gum line recession (A). PRIVATE COLLECTION.

mature animals at areas where a wound was in the process of healing. Ossification of the bones seems to occur last at their growing edges, though the patterns of development vary with bone forms. Note that in the coyote, the postorbital processes remain porous, yet much of the frontal bones has already ossified.

Oddly enough, skulls of very old animals may also be quite pitted, though in such cases the pits are less uniform and deeper, and the bone is mature and shiny. Also in very old animals, all the sutures have fused, and the teeth show considerable wear.

Sutures

A suture is the meeting place between two bones on the skull, often visible as a line or crack between two obviously separate plates or bone forms. Nearly all the sutures on a skull are very visible at birth and into immaturity, but as most mammals age into adulthood, certain sutures fuse and become difficult to discern with the naked eye. In some mammals, however, such as the opossum, sutures remain visible through adulthood and are therefore far less useful as guides in aging. Yet in others, specific sutures are very useful in separating juveniles from adult ani-

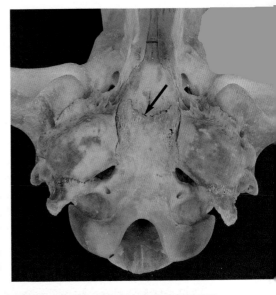

This large male gray wolf (Canis lupus) skull can be identified as a subadult by the open basioccipital suture. PRIVATE COLLECTION.

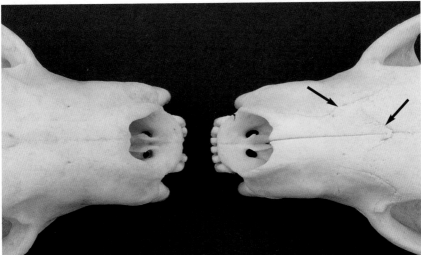

Compare the nasal sutures of the mature fisher (Martes pennanti) on the left with the subadult animal on the right. PRIVATE COLLECTION.

mals. The rates with which sutures fuse is variable, and is much slower in animals in poor nutritional health as well as in domestic species which are castrated (Amorosi 1989).

Perhaps the most universal in applications across diverse species are the sutures associated with the basioccipital region on the ventral surface of the skull between the auditory bullae. In mustelids and skunks, the sutures associated with the nasals are also useful.

Temporal Muscle Coalescence

Temporal muscle coalescence is described in Poole et al. (1994) as one method to separate American martens *(Martes americana)* into age classes. As an immature marten moves from juvenile to adult status, the temporalis muscles grow rapidly, and the corresponding temporal ridges on the cranium, which indicate their boundaries, move closer and closer together, eventually forming a larger and larger sagittal crest in adult animals. This is also true in bears and some other species as well. With some experimentation, it may be that temporal muscle coalescence might have broader applications than just in American martens.

Martens reach adult size by their first fall and are classified as juveniles if less than one year old, and adults if one year or more. Poole et al. measured two distances to determine relative age: the length of temporal muscle coalescence (LTMC), which is the measure of contact between the temporalis muscles (the sagittal crest or ridge) from just below the occipital crests forward; and the width between temporal muscles (WBTM), which is the distance between muscles that are not in contact at all, also taken just below the occipital crests. Refer to the photograph for a visual aid. In Alaska, males with an LTMC of less than 10 millimeters identified 97 percent of the juveniles, and in the Northwest Territories, a measure of less than 20 millimeters identified 97 percent of the juveniles. In Alaskan females, a WBTM of greater than 3 millimeters described 93 percent of juveniles, and less than 3 percent of juveniles had any measurable LTMC at all, whereas in the Northwest Territories, 11 percent of juvenile females exhibited some measurable LTMC. This is also a wonderful example of variation between geographic populations.

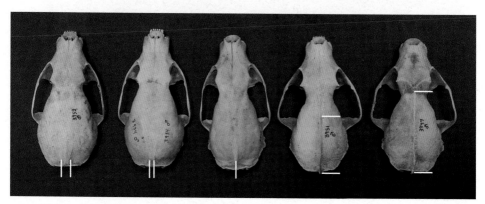

Male martens *(Martes americana)* from Alaska, which from left to right exhibit temporal muscle coalescence with age. SANTA BARBARA MUSEUM OF NATURAL HISTORY 3952, 3934, 3940, 3951, 3949.

Development of Sagittal and Lambdoidal Crests; Widening of the Zygomata; Lengthening of the Postorbital Processes

The development of sagittal and lambdoidal crests is related to the further growth and development of the temporalis and neck muscles, which continues from juvenile to early adulthood and on into late adulthood. The fisher and California sea lion are both dramatic examples of this development, yet many mammals exhibit similar changes with time to a lesser degree.

As an animal continues to age and the jaw and neck muscles continue to grow and develop, the temporal fossa is also enlarged to accommodate the passage of larger muscles. This is evident in the widening of the zygomata, which occurs quite rapidly when moving into adulthood and continues while the animal is an adult. Captive animals that eat softer foods and live an easier life may not develop crests to the same degree as their wild counterparts or at all (Ewer 1973).

The length of the postorbital processes also increases with greater age, and they may even form a postorbital bar in very old animals of some species. This characteristic is particularly evident in felines, especially house cats, though this may be because these animals are nurtured and protected, and therefore live much longer than their native counterparts.

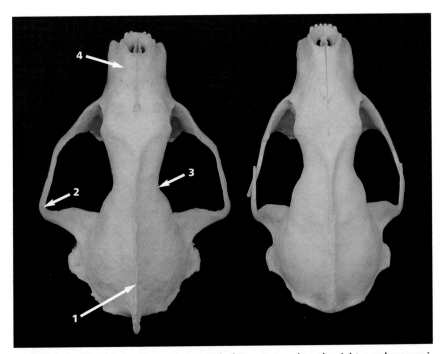

On the left is a male fisher *(Martes pennanti)* of 5+ years, and on the right a male approximately 10–11 months old. Note the many changes with age, including: 1. the development of the sagittal crest, 2. the widening and lowering of the zygomatic arches, 3. the narrowing of the postorbital constriction, and 4. the fusing of the nasal sutures. PRIVATE COLLECTION.

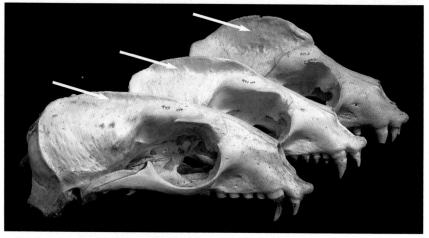

Sagittal crest development in male California sea lions *(Zalophus californianus)*; subadult males look very similar to females. SANTA BARBARA MUSEUM OF NATURAL HISTORY 239, 941, 945.

Horns

Bovid skulls are characterized by their ever-growing and permanent horn sheaths and cores. Researchers often use the size and shape of horns to determine relative age. On page 503 is a further discussion of how horn size and shape in buffalo, mountain goats, and mountain sheep are clues to determining age.

Relative Size of the Skull

As an animal ages and grows, the overall skull grows larger as well. Numerous factors influence the degree of bone growth during the life of an individual, including the health of the animal, its genetics, the geographic population of which it is a member,

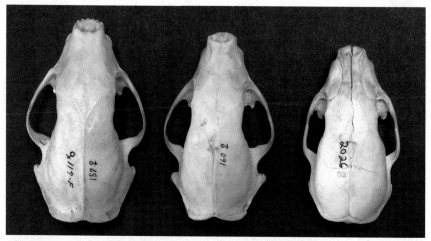

Three female striped skunks *(Mephitis mephitis)* from southern California, which from right to left exhibit numerous characteristics associated with aging and maturity. Note the increase in overall size, the development of occipital and sagittal crests, the widening of the zygomata, and the fusing of sutures associated with the braincase and nasals. SANTA BARBARA MUSEUM OF NATURAL HISTORY 2026, 157, 160.

Two brown bear *(Ursus arctos)* skulls: one adult male and a cub of unknown gender. Note the dramatic increase in size with maturation, as well as the fusing of numerous sutures, the coalescence of temporal muscles, and the development of postorbital processes and the occipital and sagittal crests. PRIVATE COLLECTION.

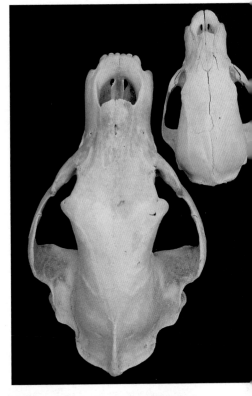

and a host of environmental conditions, such as the nutritional value and availability of meals and the temperatures the animal endures. Thus size must be weighed along with other characteristics and used simply as a guide; there are no hard and fast rules.

Sometimes dramatic size variation occurs within a species across its geographic range. An old adult male marten's skull from Maine may have a shorter overall length than an animal less than a year old from Alaska. In such cases, other methods of aging are more useful, unless you know well the size parameters for the population you study.

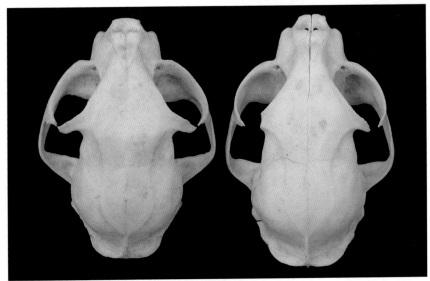

The skulls of two male bobcats *(Lynx rufus)* killed on the very same road near Santa Cruz, California. Individual variation is evident within each distinctive geographic population as well. In this case, the shorter, squatter skull also had a shorter mandible, yet was the older animal of the two. PRIVATE COLLECTION.

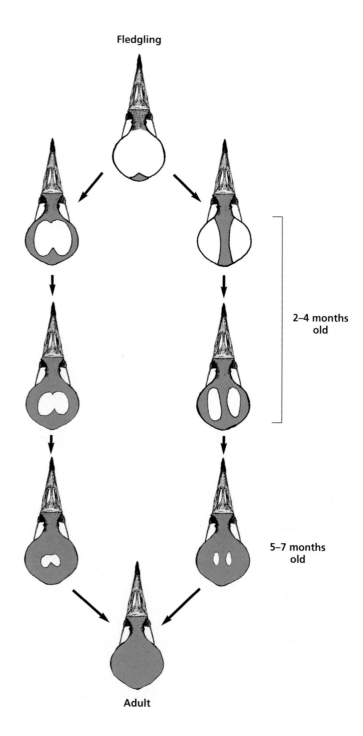

A visual representation of two variations on the pneumatization process in bird skulls, which can be used to differentiate young from adult birds either alive and in hand, or from remains. Drawn after Evans and Heiser (2004).

Determining the Age of Passerine Skulls

"Skulling" is a technique used with living passerines, or perching birds, in the field by researchers banding birds during the fall migration. Without any injury to the birds, they part the feathers of the cranium and wet the thin translucent layer of skin. This allows them to view the ossification of the cranial bones, estimate the relative age of birds less than a year old, and therefore separate young from adult birds. By one year, a bird's skull has completely ossified. Age classes as described for living birds also have applications for skulls in hand.

Birds are born with a single layer of cartilage and bone forming the cranium. Within their first year of life, they develop a second layer, which further supports and strengthens the first; this process of growing the second layer is called skull pneumatization. Podulka et al. (2004) illustrate two common patterns of skull pneumatization, adapted and re-created here.

Sexing Skulls

Determining the sex of an animal from its skull is often a tricky business. In some species, males or females may have some growth or feature that is absent in the other sex. For example, male moose and deer grow antlers, but females do not.

From there, sexing becomes a bit more challenging. Many animals exhibit some degree of sexual dimorphism, with one sex being significantly larger than the other.

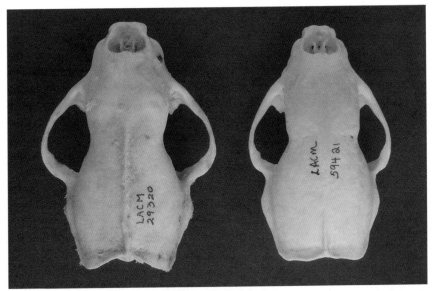

A large male white-backed hog-nosed skunk *(Conepatus leuconotus)* on the left, and female on the right exhibit classic male-female features. Male carnivores are often more robust and with wider spreading zygomatics and more developed crests and ridges. NATURAL HISTORY MUSEUM OF LOS ANGELES COUNTY 29320, 59421.

This may be due to a number of variables, including the greater energy expenditure invested in reproduction by females, the fighting in mating rituals by males, or males and females feeding on slightly different diets and better sharing a given niche. In the case of cougars, the males become much larger than the females; in the case of red-tailed hawks, the opposite is true. This discrepancy is obvious in the tables of measurements provided in the species accounts, most of which are divided into males and females for a given species. Sometimes a good pair of calipers will reveal the sex of a specimen. In pronghorn, a comparison of the interorbital and zygomatic breadths will provide the means to determine sex; in polar bears, the length of the toothrows; in caribou, the length of the mandible; and in raccoons and opossums, the length of the upper canines.

Yet determining the sex of a skull is not an easy business. Morphological and even measurement parameters are often subtle or have considerable overlap—enough that many skulls you attempt to classify will fall right in the middle. Variation due to geographic range will also confound inquiries. In these cases, try several measurements, for some are more revealing of sexual variation than others. In most carnivores, the mastoidal and zygomatic widths are especially useful, as is the greatest length of the skull.

Little research has been done to discover whether the degree of sexual dimorphism varies across populations. One such undertaking was done for raccoons by Ritke and Kennedy (1993). They compared a great many cranial features of raccoons taken from across North America and found that the width of canines was the only measurement to exhibit any variation across geographic populations with any statistical significance. Thus they concluded that the sexual pressures on male and female raccoons are likely consistent across populations.

Morphologic variation between the sexes of a given species are often obscured or absent when dealing with immature animals. Thus determining the relative age of the skull you are studying is the first order of business. If sutures and tooth wear indicate a younger animal, the methods presented in individual species accounts might not be adequate to determine the sex of the skull in question.

Tracking across the Surfaces of Animal Skulls

3

Some skulls reveal further stories about other, unrelated animals that have somehow marked the bone while the skull's owner still lived, at its death, or long after soft tissues faded away. In these cases, the stories of more than one animal are told simultaneously.

Marks Made before Death

Disease, fighting, and parasites all will leave visible signs on animal skulls and bones. Parasites and disease may re-form bones, causing swollen portions, or bubbles, much like the galls created on leaves and woody material by growing fly and wasp larvae. Great vacant holes or permeated surfaces where roots of teeth should be or bone should grow may reveal some disease or parasite that the animal endured while alive.

Healed wounds may also be apparent. Fighting for territory or breeding rights within a species is common, just as are fights between species, the sagas of predators and prey. Wounds to the head are very serious and often result in death, but if the animal lives beyond the encounter, healing will take place. I've held polar bear skulls with creased, spongy bone that had grown in where another breeding male had gouged the skull while asserting dominance to hold his position in the breeding ranks and ensure that his strong genes were passed onto the next generation. Bullet holes and holes where teeth were lost sometimes heal in the same manner, starting with a spongy, softer bone and eventually filling in or being covered from encroaching sides, much like the healing of wood on a living tree.

Broken canines are often evidence of biting leg-hold or cage traps or attempting to open something that should not have been tried. Wolverines are infamous for breaking their canines in an attempt to free themselves from leg-hold traps. In the case of traps, the broken teeth show no smoothing, for the animal often dies shortly after—unable to break free. Yet if the animal survives, broken canines will smooth and color

Sinus infections by nematode parasites in three female hooded skunks *(Mephitis macroura)* from Mexico. NATURAL HISTORY MUSEUM OF LOS ANGELES COUNTY 59413, 59416, 34934.

Note the hole low on one mandible of this woodchuck *(Marmota monax)* where a bullet passed through the bone and then healed.

Healed
bullet
wound

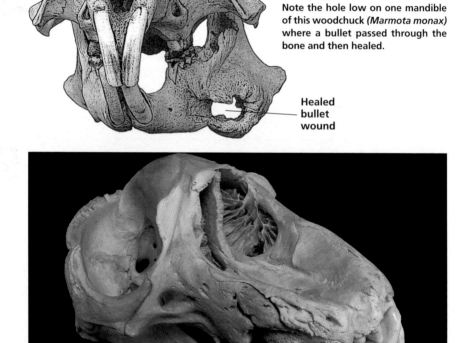

Paul Collins, curator, thought the bone deterioration in this male elephant seal *(Mirounga angustirostris)* might have started with broken canines and even torn gums and splintered mandibles resulting from a battle with another male during breeding. He suspected infection moved into the wounds and literally ate away tissue and bone alike, potentially leading to the demise of the animal over time. SANTA BARBARA MUSEUM OF NATURAL HISTORY 2331.

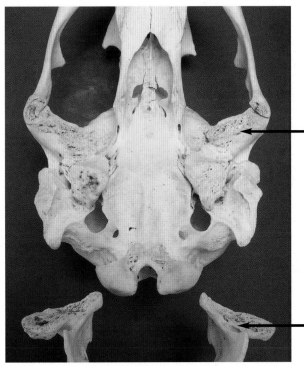

Arthritis is evident in this male California sea lion *(Zalophus californianus)* where the jaws connect with the cranium. Characteristic signs of arthritis include bone swelling and "bubbling" at joints and where bone surfaces make contact with one another. SANTA BARBARA MUSEUM OF NATURAL HISTORY, 243.

with time. It is quite common to find old carnivores and omnivores with broken, yet smoothed and rounded canines—signs of some earlier encounter with traps, fighting, or a meal too tough for old teeth. The ways in which it is possible to break a canine are numerous.

Marks Made at the Time of Death or Shortly Thereafter

Predators often strike the head when making a kill, especially to the posterior. Look for marks made by canines piercing the braincase, and if you have the vertebrae as well, look for signs on the uppermost bones. According to Childs (1998), damage to the rostrum is one clue to help differentiate between jaguar and cougar kills; jaguars often attack and pull down large prey by the nose and face, whereas cougars either bite the back of the neck, killing by piercing the braincase or severing the spinal column, or bite the jugular, killing by suffocation.

Carnivores may also eat the brains of their prey, which are high in nutrition and often a select food for many animals. Raptors leave a characteristic triangular cut in

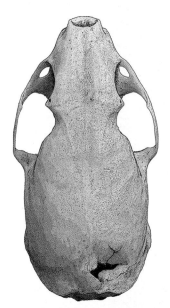

A raccoon killed by a cougar. The canines have created gaping holes.

A weasel killed by a domestic cat—note the canine puncture in the braincase.

A red fox killed by a trapper's bludgeon.

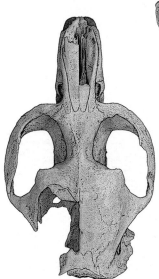

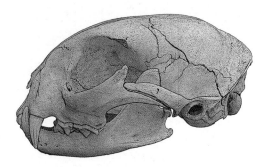

A muskrat killed by a snowy owl, which also opened the brain cavity, leaving the characteristic triangular sign of feeding raptors.

A bobcat killed by a vehicle moving approximately 30 mph. Note the broken postorbital process and several other cracked bone surfaces.

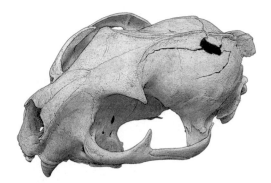

A cougar shot at close range with a rifle.

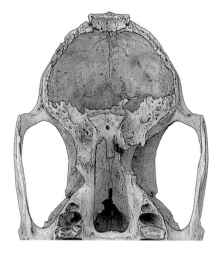

An Eastern cottontail skull, showing the characteristic signs of feeding rodents, which opened the braincase of the rabbit shortly after it died.

skulls they have opened to feed on the brain, whereas mammal predators often crush much of the cavity.

Trappers' signs are sometimes evident in damage done to the skull. Depending on how a trapper kills animals, the skull may be cracked, dented, or broken, or hold a small, concise hole from a small-caliber bullet shot at close range. This is a sure sign of a trapped and confined animal, whether by trapper, poacher, or someone operating on a depredation permit. The close range and perfect aim are very telling. Look also for scoring or piercing by knives made when an animal was skinned.

When an animal is struck by a car, the skull is usually crushed, flattened, or falls apart as soon as the soft tissues decompose or are removed. There are too many variables to describe the skull of the typical roadkill victim. The speed of the vehicle, the size of the animal, and where the animal is struck are the three largest variables. Suffice it to say, many roadkilled animals do not leave intact skulls to study.

Very soon after an animal dies, rodents will feed on the prized brain if another creature hasn't beaten them to it. They leave a characteristic round opening, and the entrance to the brain cavity will be large and ragged.

Intercanine Widths as a Tool in Depredation Studies

The distance between the wounds inflicted by paired canines has for many years been instrumental in identifying the predator from its prey's carcass remains (Shaw 1979, LeCount 1986, and others); this has most often been employed to determine large predators of large prey, including cattle and sheep. More recently, this method has been used by researchers with success to determine the predators of chicks at seabird nests (Lyver 2000 and others), and with mixed results to identify the predators of bird eggs (Lariviere and Messier 1997 and others).

Forensic dentistry is the field that studies bite wounds on people in contribution to or substantiation of evidence; this field primarily has focused publications and research on human bite marks, which are often inflicted during sexual crimes and other acts of violence and can be matched to individuals to identify the culprit. Recently, Murmann (in press) has contributed new work that begins to analyze the bite structure of cats, canines, and other wildlife.

For all these reasons and many more, it seems evident that intercanine measurements are a useful tool in field research and detection. Yet little published reference material exists for such endeavors. With this in mind, Neal Wight joined me from Prescott College to undertake a project to begin building such a resource. Yet there are legitimate concerns as to whether "dry" measurements taken from skulls can be applied in the field. I've had success applying this data set in depredation cases where the predator was identified by other means, and feel at the very least these numbers offer field technicians a place to start. Skulls and antlers you find may wear the signs of some predator, and an analysis of intercanine distances may help reveal the culprit. Others parameters are recorded in additional publications, including but not limited to Elbroch (2003), Murmann et. al. (in press), LeCount (1986), and Shaw (1979).

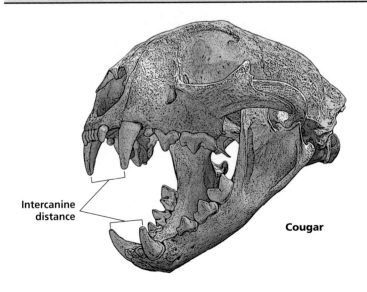

Intercanine distance

Cougar

Intercanine Widths

Mammals	Sex	Distance between upper canines (mm) median (parameters)	Distance between lower canines (mm) median (parameters)
Order Didelphimorphia: American marsupials			
Family Didelphidae: Opossums			
Virginia opossum, *Didelphis virginiana*	♀	19.04 (15.90–22.12) N=6	15.96 (13.20–17.73) N=6
	♂	22.15 (16.81–25.00) N=9	17.96 (13.08–22.16) N=8
Mexican mouse opossum, *Marmosa mexicana*	♀♂	5.00 (4.36–5.46) N=4	3.92 (3.54–4.30) N=4
Order Chiroptera: Bats			
Family Phyllostomidae: New World leaf-nosed bats			
California leaf-nosed bat, *Macrotus californicus*	♀	2.84 N=1	1.92 N=1
	♂	2.64 N=1	1.88 N=1
Mexican long-tongued bat, *Choeronycteris mexicana*	♀♂	4.39 (3.80–4.80) N=4	3.82 (3.51–4.06) N=4
Family Vespertilionidae: Vesper bats			
Hoary bat, *Lasiurus cinereus*	♀♂	5.56 (5.14–6.18) N=6	4.73 (4.46–5.26) N=7
Big brown bat, *Eptesicus fuscus*	♀♂	4.40 (3.94–4.66) N=7	3.29 (3.00–3.56) N=6
Pallid bat, *Antrozous pallidus*	♀♂	4.58 (4.20–5.14) N=11	3.85 (3.48–4.30) N=9
Family Molossidae: Free-tailed bats			
Western bonneted bat, *Eumops perotis*	Unknown sex	6.67 N=1	3.56 N=1
	♂	6.84 N=1	4.02 N=1
Order Carnivora: Carnivores			
Family Canidae: Dogs, foxes, and wolves			
Coyote (northeastern), *Canis latrans*	♀	30.42 (27.10–32.22) N=4	28.22 (25.52–29.54) N=5

Intercanine Widths continued

Mammals	Sex	Distance between upper canines (mm) median (parameters)	Distance between lower canines (mm) median (parameters)
Coyote (northeastern), *Canis latrans*	♂	33.20 (30.95–35.90) N=6	30.28 (27.00–35.10) N=6
Coyote (western), *Canis latrans*	♀	27.47 (25.68–30.24) N=10	25.55 (23.40–28.05) N=10
	♂	29.48 (25.90–32.97) N=9	27.06 (25.21–28.79) N=10
Gray wolf, *Canis lupus*	♀	43.50 (35.87–50.01) N=10	39.94 (34.40–46.86) N=10
	♂	45.51 (40.45–54.46) N=10	40.70 (32.06–47.13) N=10
Arctic fox, *Vulpes lagopus*	♀	21.19 (19.40–24.20) N=10	18.65 (16.42–20.77) N=10
	♂	22.12 (19.97–23.85) N=10	19.51 (17.32–20.62) N=10
Kit fox, *Vulpes macrotis*	♀	15.26 (14.08–16.26) N=11	13.30 (11.58–15.03) N=11
	♂	15.79 (13.78–17.51) N=13	13.86 (11.29–15.45) N=13
Swift fox, *Vulpes velox*	♀	17.00, 17.01 N=2	13.56, 15.09 N=2
	♂	16.07 (15.04–16.64) N=3	14.77 (14.47–15.22) N=3
Red fox, *Vulpes vulpes*	♀	21.25 (19.06–23.18) N=10	19.73 (16.96–23.13) N=9
	♂	22.05 (19.96–25.03) N=10	19.11 (16.15–21.85) N=9
Common gray fox, *Urocyon cinereoargenteus*	♀	16.76 (15.41–19.31) N=10	14.89 (13.76–17.10) N=10
	♂	16.46 (14.50–19.50) N=10	15.68 (13.81–17.10) N=10

Mammals	Sex	Distance between upper canines (mm) median (parameters)	Distance between lower canines (mm) median (parameters)
Family Ursidae: Bears			
American black bear, *Ursus americanus*	♀	48.59 (45.95–55.24) N=10	45.39 (37.52–53.89) N=10
	♂	52.59 (44.04–60.37) N=10	49.11 (38.44–57.03) N=10
Brown or grizzly bear, *Ursus arctos*	♀	60.06 (51.73–70.55) N=10	56.95 (50.86–64.52) N=10
	♂	65.28 (51.52–76.42) N=10	61.58 (47.74–73.47) N=10
Family Phocidae: Earless or hair seals			
Harbor seal, *Phoca vitulina*	♀	32.05 (27.49–36.34) N=10	28.49 (23.00–36.06) N=10
	♂	32.79 (29.90–35.33) N=10	28.51 (24.44–32.82) N=10
Family Procyonidae: Ringtails, raccoons, and coatis			
Ringtail, *Bassariscus astutus*	♀	10.56 (9.46–11.78) N=10	10.01 (8.92–10.91) N=10
	♂	11.36 (10.18–12.29) N=10	10.65 (8.57–11.83) N=10
Northern raccoon, *Procyon lotor*	♀	22.67 (20.15–28.23) N=10	20.77 (16.07–25.56) N=10
	♂	23.47 (19.38–26.83) N=10	22.95 (19.26–27.10) N=10
White-nosed coati, *Nasua narica*	♀	20.74 (19.07–24.71) N=12	18.85 (16.42–22.12) N=9
	♂	25.24 (19.99–29.31) N=9	22.16 (17.97–27.11) N=11
Family Mustelidae: Weasels, otters, and badgers			
American marten, *Martes americanus*	♀	10.36 (8.60–12.54) N=15	9.47 (8.24–11.19) N=15

Intercanine Widths continued

Mammals	Sex	Distance between upper canines (mm) median (parameters)	Distance between lower canines (mm) median (parameters)
American marten, *Martes americanus*	♂	11.99 (9.80–14.61) N=15	10.57 (8.62–12.48) N=15
Fisher, *Martes pennanti*	♀	14.97 (13.11–17.12) N=14	13.16 (11.88–16.15) N=13
	♂	17.96 (14.96–21.95) N=18	15.75 (13.60–17.60) N=17
Ermine or short-tailed weasel, *Mustela erminea*	♀	4.53 (3.47–6.04) N=10	3.66 (2.44–4.57) N=10
	♂	5.34 (4.07–7.08) N=10	3.93 (2.62–5.12) N=10
Long-tailed weasel, *Mustela frenata*	♀	6.69 (5.79–7.58) N=11	5.45 (4.56–6.46) N=11
	♂	7.91 (7.33–9.03) N=10	6.72 (6.13–7.96) N=10
Least weasel, *Mustela nivalis*	♀	4.32 (3.24–4.99) N=11	3.27 (2.70–4.00) N=11
	♂	4.71 (3.89–5.30) N=9	3.79 (3.56–4.40) N=10
American mink, *Mustela vison*	♀	9.45 (8.33–10.44) N=10	7.47 (6.20–8.27) N=10
	♂	10.43 (9.33–12.37) N=10	8.20 (6.26–10.13) N=10
Wolverine, *Gulo gulo*	♀	29.01 (25.39–32.24) N=10	25.46 (23.80–27.06) N=8
	♂	32.78 (30.40–35.61) N=6	29.42 (26.10–31.30) N=6
American badger, *Taxidea taxus*	♀	27.15 (24.83–30.01) N=10	26.40 (24.33–28.82) N=10

Mammals	Sex	Distance between upper canines (mm) median (parameters)	Distance between lower canines (mm) median (parameters)
American badger, *Taxidea taxus*	♂	29.81 (25.69–33.89) N=10	28.51 (23.81–32.34) N=10
Northern river otter, *Lontra canadensis*	♀	19.80 (17.80–22.72) N=13	16.87 (14.55–18.75) N=13
	♂	19.83 (16.66–22.58) N=12	18.23 (16.50–21.43) N=12
Family Mephitidae: Skunks			
Western spotted skunk, *Spilogale gracilis*	♀	9.50 (8.65–11.16) N=10	8.53 (7.53–9.81) N=10
	♂	10.69 (8.54–12.29) N=11	9.63 (8.03–10.53) N=10
Striped skunk, *Mephitis mephitis*	♀	13.59 (11.95–15.27) N=10	12.30 (10.31–14.21) N=10
	♂	14.52 (12.25–16.36) N=9	13.47 (11.30–14.80) N=9
White-backed hog-nosed skunk, *Conepatus leuconotus*	♀	13.06 (11.47–15.65) N=10	10.41 (8.59–12.35) N=10
	♂	14.63 (12.38–16.30) N=10	12.40 (9.60–14.86) N=9
Family Felidae: Cats			
Cougar or mountain lion, *Puma concolor*	♀	36.26 (31.89–41.40) N=10	32.43 (28.93–35.56) N=10
	♂	41.25 (37.55–45.96) N=11	36.38 (33.18–37.77) N=11
House cat, *Felis catus*	♀	15.77 (14.73–17.84) N=7	13.93 (11.53–16.77) N=7
	♂	17.75 (15.82–19.27) N=11	15.48 (13.79–17.07) N=12
Ocelot, *Leopardus pardalis*	♀	23.81 (22.10–25.68) N=4	20.73 (18.60–24.25) N=4

Intercanine Widths continued

Mammals	Sex	Distance between upper canines (mm) median (parameters)	Distance between lower canines (mm) median (parameters)
Ocelot, *Leopardus pardalis*	♂	25.26 (20.29–33.10) N=7	20.84 (15.29–23.90) N=7
Margay, *Leopardus wiedii*	♀	14.81 (14.26–15.20) N=5	13.70 (13.10–13.98) N=5
	♂	16.58 (15.40–17.67) N=4	14.38 (12.61–15.49) N=4
Jaguarundi, *Herpailurus yaguarondi*	♀	16.47 (14.44–18.25) N=4	14.33 (12.54–15.07) N=4
	♂	17.95 (16.68–20.30) N=4	15.63 (13.25–18.29) N=4
Canada lynx, *Lynx canadensis*	♀	24.48 (22.66–25.68) N=10	23.40 (22.25–24.42) N=10
	♂	25.38 (23.73–27.62) N=10	23.60 (21.91–27.82) N=10
Bobcat, *Lynx rufus*	♀	21.47 (19.47–23.49) N=10	19.98 (17.66–21.95) N=10
	♂	22.75 (19.47–25.01) N=10	21.01 (18.66–23.08) N=10
Jaguar, *Panthera onca*	♀	45.36, 45.50 N=2	42.13 (39.42–45.98) N=3
	♂	50.37, 55.84 N=2	43.16, 43.89 N=2

N=number of specimens measured

Marks Made after the Soft Tissues Have Decomposed

Skulls and antlers remain long after soft tissues such as muscles, fat, and tendons decompose or are eaten by insects. Yet there is still a resource here, a reservoir of calcium on a landscape where calcium-rich foods are scarce. Rodents of every size, as well as numerous other species, will chew bones, skulls, and antlers, sometimes eating them in their entirety. To some extent, the size of the incisor widths can help you differentiate between these species. O'Connor (2000) describes the gnawing on bones by several mammal families: Canines gnaw on bones, leaving an overlapping, large number of blunter, shallower, and wider depressions. Felines tend to gnaw less and bite down harder, leaving a smaller number of narrower, deeper marks in bones. Sheep and members of the deer family will also gnaw bones, leaving characteristic prismatic tooth markings, much like those made by deer chewing acorns, which can be found in *Mammal Tracks & Sign* (Elbroch 2003), along with other useful text regarding signs surrounding kill sites.

Elk and caribou have been observed chewing each other's antlers just after the rut, when hormones have calmed and males begin to spend time together; look for tines with ragged, rough nubs. Coyotes and wolves also eat moose and caribou antlers, and their canine impressions are common on the antlers of both species. Feeding is concentrated in the softer central portion of the dish, to which the tines attach. You may find moose antlers with just the tines remaining and the entire central portion of the antler eaten away.

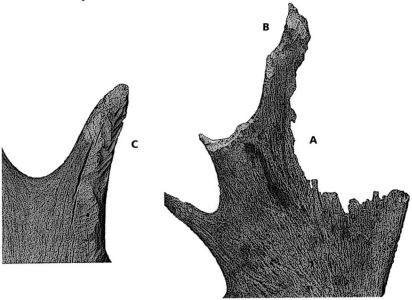

On the left is a close-up of marks made by porcupine incisors (C) on a moose antler. On the right is a moose antler partially eaten by a coyote (A) as well as shared with other rodents (B).

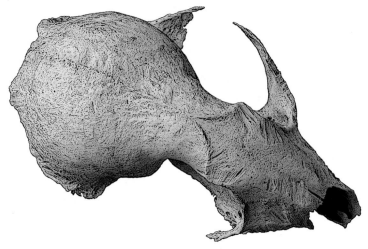

A raccoon skull gnawed by small rodents. White-footed mice and Southern red-backed voles were common where it was found.

Incisor Widths as a Tool in Depredation Studies

As with intercanine widths, the width inflicted by individual or paired incisors of rodents and other animals on bones, skulls, and antlers allows us to significantly narrow down the list of potential culprits. Further, incisor widths can also be used in the analysis of wood or plant remains, as is often employed by those studying crop predation. Fruit trees are destroyed by numerous species, both aboveground and from subterranean tunnel systems. Knowing the relative sizes of the teeth can help in determining what animal is responsible for gnaw marks you observe.

Measuring the width of incisors from the sign itself is a skill that improves with experience. The deeper the gouge in that which is bitten, the wider the impression made. Natural surfaces swell and shrink as well, depending on many variables, including the surface itself, the water content of the material being bitten, whether the wood was alive or dead, outside temperatures, and the age of the bite marks. Certainly the freshest sign provides the best circumstances for correct identification of the culprit, for the measurements are likely less influenced by the many variables that accompany time. If you have found a fresh skull which has been gnawed, you may also find associated sign such as fur, tracks, and scats, evidence you should consider along with the measurements of the incisor widths (refer to Elbroch 2003).

The accompanying table gives measurements of many species known to eat crops, damage trees, and chew on bones, skulls, and antlers. These numbers reflect the parameters of a single incisor of a given species, and were created from "dry" specimens in collections; there will be limitations in their application. Measurements were recorded by Neal Wight from Prescott College, who joined me for this purpose.

Incisor Widths

Mammals	Sex	Upper incisor widths (mm) median (parameters)	Lower incisor widths (mm) median (parameters)
Order Lagomorpha: Pikas, hares, and rabbits			
Family Ochotonidae: Pikas			
American pika, *Ochotona princeps*	♀	1.82 (1.62–1.98) N=10	1.56 (1.43–1.79) N=10
	♂	1.90 (1.65–2.17) N=10	1.53 (1.32–1.67) N=10
Family Leporidae: Hares and rabbits			
Desert cottontail, *Sylvilagus audubonii*	♀	2.35 (1.98–2.65) N=10	2.51 (2.28–2.78) N=10
	♂	2.21 (1.94–2.43) N=10	2.35 (2.18–2.71) N=10
Eastern cottontail, *Sylvilagus floridanus*	♀	2.69 (2.45–2.87) N=10	2.79 (2.55–2.90) N=10
	♂	2.66 (2.42–2.89) N=10	2.81 (2.61–3.04) N=10
Snowshoe hare, *Lepus americanus*	♀	2.18 (1.73–2.46) N=10	2.11 (1.78–2.27) N=10
	♂	2.20 (1.92–2.45) N=10	2.10 (1.94–2.25) N=10
Black-tailed jackrabbit, *Lepus californicus*	♀	2.80 (2.54–3.06) N=10	2.95 (2.58–3.26) N=10
	♂	2.72 (2.29–3.46) N=10	2.82 (2.36–3.36) N=10
White-tailed jackrabbit, *Lepus townsendii*	♀	3.02 (2.30–3.44) N=10	2.93 (2.37–3.37) N=10
	♂	2.84 (2.11–3.26) N=10	2.72 (1.93–3.02) N=10
Order Rodentia: Rodents			
Family Aplodontiidae: Aplodontia			
Mountain beaver or aplodontia, *Aplodontia rufa*	♀	3.72 (3.28–4.23) N=10	3.41 (2.94–3.98) N=10

Incisor Widths continued

Mammals	Sex	Upper incisor widths (mm) median (parameters)	Lower incisor widths (mm) median (parameters)
Mountain beaver or aplodontia, *Aplodontia rufa*	♂	3.59 (3.17–4.34) N=10	3.19 (2.20–4.01) N=10
Family Sciuridae: Squirrels			
Least chipmunk, *Neotamias minimus*	♀	.85 (.77–.97) N=10	.76 (.66–.83) N=10
	♂	.86 (.76–.98) N=10	.74 (.68–.81) N=10
Eastern chipmunk, *Tamias striatus*	♀	1.14 (.94–1.32) N=10	1.13 (.95–1.30) N=10
	♂	1.08 (.98–1.18) N=11	1.06 (.91–1.19) N=11
Yellow-bellied marmot, *Marmota flaviventris*	♀	3.33 (2.74–4.35) N=10	3.14 (2.36–3.77) N=10
	♂	3.68 (2.72–4.93) N=10	3.38 (2.58–4.57) N=10
Woodchuck or groundhog, *Marmota monax*	♀	3.96 (3.14–4.70) N=10	3.59 (2.66–4.24) N=10
	♂	3.40 (2.68–3.83) N=10	3.11 (2.11–3.61) N=10
Eastern gray squirrel, *Sciurus carolinensis*	♀	1.53 (1.24–1.70) N=10	1.22 (1.17–1.55) N=10
	♂	1.64 (1.52–1.74) N=10	1.45 (1.22–1.54) N=10
Western gray squirrel, *Sciurus griseus*	♀	2.01 (1.71–2.25) N=10	1.60 (1.19–1.95) N=10
	♂	2.06 (1.79–2.20) N=10	1.54 (1.28–2.00) N=10
Eastern fox squirrel, *Sciurus niger*	♀	2.10 (1.90–2.30) N=10	1.77 (1.40–2.18) N=10

Mammals	Sex	Upper incisor widths (mm) median (parameters)	Lower incisor widths (mm) median (parameters)
Eastern fox squirrel, *Sciurus niger*	♂	2.02 (1.83–2.20) N=10	1.77 (1.50–2.09) N=10
Red squirrel, *Tamiasciurus hudsonicus*	♀	1.54 (1.31–1.68) N=10	1.27 (1.06–1.43) N=10
	♂	1.43 (1.09–1.69) N=10	1.23 (1.09–1.41) N=10
Family Geomyidae: Pocket gophers			
Botta's pocket gopher, *Thomomys bottae*	♀	2.10 (1.86–2.60) N=10	1.69 (1.67–2.07) N=10
	♂	2.36 (1.94–2.88) N=10	2.06 (1.78–2.57) N=10
Northern pocket gopher, *Thomomys talpoides*	♀	1.88 (1.63–2.10) N=10	1.64 (1.43–1.78) N=10
	♂	2.05 (1.70–2.45) N=10	1.79 (1.49–2.22) N=10
Plains pocket gopher, *Geomys bursarius*	♀	2.57 (2.29–2.95) N=10	2.34 (2.08–2.81) N=10
	♂	2.79 (2.47–3.33) N=10	2.61 (2.32–3.07) N=10
Family Castoridae: Beavers			
American beaver, *Castor canadensis*	♀	6.61 (4.95–7.71) N=10	6.73 (4.65–7.90) N=10
	♂	6.71 (4.89–7.98) N=10	6.65 (4.72–7.80) N=10
Family Muridae: Mice and rats			
Marsh rice rat, *Oryzomys palustris*	♀	.85 (.64–.95) N=10	.77 (.59–.92) N=10
	♂	.91 (.81–1.12) N=10	.83 (.73–1.06) N=10
Deer mouse, *Peromyscus maniculatus*	♀	.72 (.64–.78) N=10	.68 (.62–.78) N=10

Incisor Widths continued

Mammals	Sex	Upper incisor widths (mm) median (parameters)	Lower incisor widths (mm) median (parameters)
Deer mouse, *Peromyscus maniculatus*	♂	.74 (.67–.86) N=10	.64 (.59–.68) N=10
Hispid cotton rat, *Sigmodon hispidus*	♀	1.39 (1.12–1.66) N=10	1.30 (1.11–1.55) N=10
	♂	1.47 (1.10–1.78) N=10	1.40 (1.08–1.73) N=10
Bushy-tailed woodrat, *Neotoma cinerea*	♀	1.60 (1.37–1.88) N=10	1.45 (1.25–1.67) N=10
	♂	1.62 (1.47–2.02) N=10	1.48 (1.35–1.81) N=10
Desert woodrat, *Neotoma lepida*	♀	1.47 (1.40–1.65) N=10	1.40 (1.25–1.53) N=10
	♂	1.57 (1.37–1.70) N=10	1.53 (1.42–1.61) N=10
Norway rat, *Rattus norvegicus*	♀	1.36 (1.10–1.94) N=6	1.33 (1.01–1.72) N=6
	♂	1.48 (1.31–1.68) N=6	1.41 (1.31–1.56) N=6
Black rat, *Rattus rattus*	♀	1.21 (.96–1.43) N=8	1.06 (.89–1.17) N=8
	♂	1.25 (1.16–1.34) N=8	1.16 (1.07–1.22) N=8
House mouse, *Mus musculus*	♀	.54 (.47–.62) N=10	.52 (.38–.67) N=10
	♂	.52 (.45–.63) N=10	.52 (.41–.65) N=10
Southern red-backed vole, *Clethrionomys gapperi*	♀	.80 (.68–.93) N=10	.65 (.64–.72) N=9

Mammals	Sex	Upper incisor widths (mm) median (parameters)	Lower incisor widths (mm) median (parameters)
Southern red-backed vole, *Clethrionomys gapperi*	♂	.75 (.65–.85) N=10	.62 (.54–.70) N=10
Meadow vole or field mouse, *Microtus pennsylvanicus*	♀	1.20 (.93–1.30) N=10	1.04 (.86–1.19) N=10
	♂	1.25 (1.13–1.36) N=10	.98 (.90–1.11) N=10
Muskrat, *Ondatra zibethicus*	♀	3.26 (2.66–3.77) N=10	2.98 (2.55–3.32) N=10
	♂	3.39 (3.00–3.99) N=10	2.94 (2.49–3.52) N=10
Family Erethizontidae: New World porcupines			
North American porcupine, *Erethizon dorsatum*	♀	4.32 (3.81–4.89) N=10	4.33 (3.83–4.75) N=10
	♂	4.23 (3.63–4.72) N=10	4.16 (3.66–4.70) N=10

N=number of specimens measured

Collecting and Preparing Skulls

4

For some, the excitement and mysteries surrounding bones and skulls in the field is quite enough, and simple identification is sufficient for their purposes. Others might like to bring the skulls home, start collections, use them in education or research, or integrate them into sculpture. In this chapter are described the steps for finding and preparing specimens to keep or use in some fashion.

Obtaining Animal Skulls

Finding and acquiring animal skulls is perhaps as much fun as the actual holding and examining of the cleaned specimen. Nothing is more fascinating than contemplating the events that led up to the demise of a creature whose remains you've found while exploring woods near your home. Did the animal die from predation, a disease, or some other natural cause? *Mammal Tracks & Sign* (Elbroch 2003) and *Bird Tracks & Sign* (Elbroch and Marks 2001) are among the tracking guides that can help you interpret the clues surrounding kill sites.

Perhaps you've found the cleaned and scattered skull and bones of some mystery creature long since dead. Skulls and bones exist sprinkled across the landscape; the challenge is learning to find them. In the North, spring is an excellent time to search for skulls, as numerous diverse animals die from hardship or starvation during the harsh winter season. Start searching before new vegetation begins to cover what lies on the flattened debris from the previous year.

Seek out predator dens. Active fox and coyote dens are especially good for animal remains, though over time, every chewable object present will be damaged by playful, experimenting teeth.

Owl roosts and the nests of many raptors are hot spots for animal skulls of all sorts. In fact, they are the source of nearly all the small-mammal skulls in my own collection. Whenever I arrive in a new bioregion, I seek out great horned owl roosts, for this is a widespread species, and these owls regurgitate massive pellets, which keep many a skull intact. Michael Kresky, a friend, and I once visited a great horned owl roost he'd discovered in the Malibu area in Southern California. Without exaggeration, what we found was a deep, narrow drainage flowing with animal skulls and bones from years of owls roosting in the canyon walls above. We collected several hundred animal skulls, of which more than half were Botta's pocket gophers *(Thomomys bottae)*. The remainder mostly consisted of California voles *(Microtus californicus)*, along with a handful of partial California pocket mouse skulls and a single California towhee skull. White-footed mouse and woodrat species were absent, as were cottontails. Individual raptors often become specialists in their particular hunting styles and preferred species, a good reason to seek out as many roosts as possible. Yet this flood of gopher and vole skulls taught us much about the environment in which we stood—so many gophers, so many voles, and so few other small mammals.

A bit of advice when dissecting owl pellets. If you work in the field and the pellets are dry, fragile skulls often break. Harvest as many pellets as possible, and then soak them in a bucket of water before beginning to lightly tease them apart. The skulls of certain species, especially mice, are fragile and separate into the various bones with ease. If you have the patience, collect each piece and glue them back together to re-create the skull. Raptors of all kinds will also bring kills back to nests. A hawk will not likely swallow the head of an animal such as a ground squirrel whole, but will push its decapitated head and stripped remains from the nest. Look for sign and skulls accumulated below.

Riverbanks and floodplains where soil is constantly moving and being reshaped are reservoirs for skulls that were buried sometime in the past and then from time to time are revealed for sharp eyes to recognize. Recently, some friends were standing on a riverbank when a portion of it collapsed into the moving water, revealing a perfect California ground squirrel encased within. Several days later, we discovered a cow skull protruding from another stream bank, either revealed or deposited there by recent flooding. I've pulled bison, beaver, and bobcat skulls from other stream banks.

Perhaps you have hunted or trapped an animal yourself or picked up a whole animal that was struck by a vehicle or died by some other means. You may also acquire entire dead animals, or just their heads, from numerous sources. Local taxidermists often dispose of the "green" heads of wild animals, as they use a framework or form to hold the skin on a mount. Fish and game departments dispose of a number of animals through depredation permits and are also called in when wounded animals are found or certain animals have been killed by cars. Private zoos, pet stores, and wildlife rehabilitators also incur casualties and dispose of animals. Any of these are good leads to acquiring whole animals.

Skulls can also be bought very easily. In fact, skull collecting is a popular pastime both in our country and abroad. Jim Anderson, professional skull collector, provides the following advice: Start on EBAY and search for "Animal skulls," or for individual animal skulls, like "coyote skull." Once you've mastered searching and moving about on ebay, you'll find ample and varied specimens for sale. You might then want to graduate to Taxidermy.net, where you can buy skulls, "green heads," or entire animals. Go to http://www.taxidermy.net/forums/ and click FOR SALE. You can also score your own skulls to see whether they are world record worthy with either of one of two systems:

The Safari Club International standard (http://www.safariclub.org/SCIMeasurers/) or the Boone and Crockett Club (http://www.boone-crockett.org/, then click on Big Game Records). Jim himself owns several world record skulls, as well as such odd beasts as a Tion and Liger.

There are numerous federal and state laws pertaining to hunting, collecting, or keeping animals, whether living or just their remains, and the laws vary considerably from state to state. Across the country it is illegal to possess any bones of non-game birds (Migratory Bird Treaty Act, 1973). Take the time beforehand to research what is legal and illegal where you will be collecting. Permits are often required to collect specimens and even to pick up roadkills for study or collection purposes. Call your state fish and game office to inquire about obtaining the correct permits.

Cleaning and Preparing Specimens

For skulls from whole animals or ones that are only partially decomposed, follow the steps described below to prepare them for presentation. You begin by removing the soft tissues using one of several methods. This is followed by degreasing and whitening, if you want to lighten the skull further. Finally, if desired, you can add a protective coating.

If you've found a cleaned skull in the woods, you won't need to do as much to prepare it for your collection. If the skull has greened with algae or browned with earth, soak it in water and then use an old toothbrush to clean it up as much as possible. To whiten it further, follow the degreasing and whitening procedures described below. The peroxide or ammonia will also help prevent potential health risks from bacteria.

Removing the Soft Tissues

There are several alternative methods for removing the soft tissues, which include the muscles, fats, and ligaments, as well as the blood vessels. Four methods are described here: cold-water or hot-water maceration, chemicals, dermestid beetles, and other insects that feed on dead or decaying flesh.

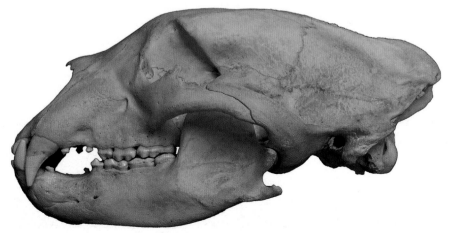

American black bear *(Ursus americanus)*. Adult male, SANTA BARBARA MUSEUM OF NATURAL HISTORY 2049.

Each of these methods should be begun with similar preparation, removing as much of the soft tissues as you can with a knife or other tool. At a minimum, you should remove the skin and fur, but the more of the meat, brain, and other soft materials you cut away at this point, the easier the rest of the removal process will be. If you are worried about damaging the skull, only skin the head. And if you don't want to touch the remains at all, just go ahead with the next stage of the process.

Cold-water maceration. Maceration is the process of wearing away or decomposing the soft tissues with water. Cold-water maceration is a very simple process and requires only a bucket for equipment.

Fill the bucket with water and place the animal head within, so that it is completely submerged. Some people prefer to cover the bucket with a lid; I only do so enough to prevent animals from stealing my macerating skulls, though in truth, the water seems to keep most animals at bay. Place your bucket as far away as is necessary to protect the sensitive noses of nearby humans, for it will smell bad quickly. Quite simply, the head is rotting in water, and as more bacteria join the process, which occurs best in warmer temperatures, the breakdown of the soft tissues increases in speed.

I've also macerated skulls in the shallows of still ponds within protective measures I've constructed to keep out marauding animals. It has worked in a pinch, such as when I'm in a remote location for an extended period. I avoid water currents, which might carry away loose teeth or bones when the maceration is well under way.

Cold-water maceration is a very effective method of cleaning skulls, but the process is extremely slow, taking several weeks to several months, depending on the size of the skull. It's also smelly. With larger skulls, I tend to replace a portion of the water when it becomes dark and murky, every few days or so. Always retain some of the existing water to maintain the bacteria population that is cleaning your skull.

Once the skull is completely macerated, place it in a bucket of clean water for three to four days, changing the water completely every twenty-four hours. This helps reduce the odor of the final specimen.

Hot-water maceration. Hot-water maceration completes in minutes what may take months with cold-water maceration. In simple terms, hot-water maceration is boiling the skull and is a quick, easy, and efficient method of cleaning it. A few warnings when considering this method: It's a smelly process, so it's best to work outside or in a well-ventilated area. It shrinks the skull slightly, so if you're hoping for a record breaker and don't want to lose a millimeter, consider another method. Boiling breaks down all tissues rapidly, often resulting in sutures further separating and teeth falling

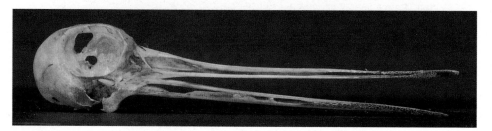

Wilson's snipe *(Gallinago delicata)*. MUSEUM OF VERTEBRATE ZOOLOGY, UC BERKELEY, male, 53893.

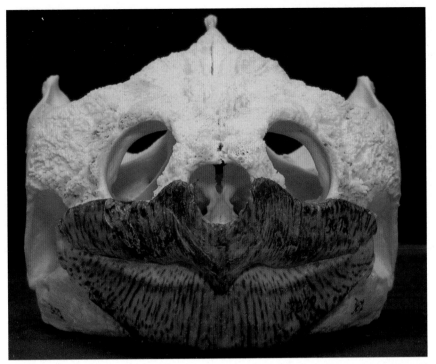

The complete skull of a male snapping turtle *(Chelydra serpentina)* with armorlike skin still attached to the cutting surfaces of the mouth. SANTA BARBARA MUSEUM OF NATURAL HISTORY 3672.

out. Be prepared to glue any wandering pieces. Remove the brain before you put the skull in hot water, for as the brain heats, it expands and may crack the braincase. The hot water may also crack the teeth, especially of larger animals.

To remove the brain, use something long and thin, such as an unbent paper clip for small animals or a coat hanger for larger ones. Stick your implement into the brain cavity and carefully stir, taking care not to break any of the interior supporting structure. Then hold the skull under running water and shake, allowing bits of the brain to fall out. Fill the brain cavity with water, and repeat the stirring, shaking, and refilling until the entire brain has been removed.

Cold-water and hot-water maceration are at opposite ends in a continuum of water temperatures you might use to help clean your skulls. Many people prefer to place skulls in water and then heat it slowly, stopping just before boiling. This is easier on the specimen than boiling, yet still greatly increases the speed of the process. I've boiled a number of skulls with very satisfactory results and have yet to experience any teeth cracking. Boiling is an ideal method when time is short, such as when traveling.

Chemicals. Gilbert (1980) describes the use of antiformin, papain, and sodium perborate in removing soft tissues. Lacking the personal experience with these chemicals, please consult his excellent reference *Mammalian Osteology* for suggested solutions.

Dermestid beetles. Dermestid beetles are exceptionally efficient cleaners of skulls and leave every small bone intact for the skull enthusiast. Nearly every large osteology collection across the country maintains an active colony for cleaning animal skulls and bones. There are also a number of private businesses to which you can send animal remains to have them cleaned by beetle colonies; the Internet is a good place to search for such obscure services.

Dermestes vulpinus, the carpet or hide beetle, is the common species of choice, but many dermestid beetles can be used to clean skulls of tissues, including the more colorful varieties found in the wild. Dermestids take several forms over their lifetime. The larval form is a short, bristled worm of sorts, which sheds its exoskeleton often as it enlarges until molting into the adult beetle. The adults are the breeding portion of the colony, but it's the larval stages that do the most feeding, the tiniest of which clean the smallest bones and cracks. The adults can fly, but only when it's warmer than 85 degrees.

Dermestid beetles require a bit more preparation and equipment, but the results are superb, especially for small and fragile specimens. If you want to keep your own beetle colony, you can find suppliers on the Internet. You'll need an aquarium in which to keep them, with a screen top to prevent them from escaping. Ideally, your dermestid colony should not be in your house, for they are notorious for escaping and will do very well living in your carpets. Dermestids need cover—something to burrow into to keep warm, lay eggs, and molt. I've had the best success with small pieces of tight 3/4-inch shag rug, which they definitely prefer over layered newsprint or cardboard, both of which would be adequate. They also seem to prefer protection within pieces of rug set vertically along the sides of their aquarium, rather than horizontal pieces, which quickly become covered in frass.

Dermestids eat only dried soft tissues, meaning you can't throw a freshly skinned head or wet material into their tank and expect any results. Moister environments also can draw other unwanted visitors, such as flies and mites, the latter of which may wipe out your beetle colony.

To prepare specimens for dermestids, it is best to skin the animal and remove the eyes and brain, which hold moisture the longest, and which the larvae just don't seem to like eating as much. Then you must dry the specimen to a jerkylike state; depending on humidity, it should be dry enough within several days. Hang the skull to dry, protected against animals and insects. After trying all sorts of crazy schemes to protect drying skulls from ants and flies, I now place them in brown paper bags and hang them on my clothesline. An outside screened-in closet would be ideal. Obviously, the climate in which you live will greatly influence how you decide to dry your skulls.

When the prepared head is dry, place it in a shallow cardboard box or wire mesh to catch loose teeth or any small bones the larvae might knock loose while feeding. Put it in the aquarium with the beetles and larvae.

Dermestids seem to better maintain feeding while under cover and in warmer temperatures. When you place a skull into their holding tank, cover it with some paper towels to speed up the process. If you are in a colder climate or want your dermestids to keep working through all seasons, add a lamp. The suggested temperature is around 80 degrees. Many people also suggest keeping them in the dark, either by placing the tank in a closet or shed or darkening the sides of the aquarium. I've never done this and can't speak to whether it increases productivity.

Even though it's necessary to dry out the soft tissue first, dermestids like some moisture, so spray the paper towels covering the skull once a day with just enough water to provide moisture for an hour. The mature beetles and larvae will flood out of every orifice to take advantage of the moisture, which can be fun to watch. Don't overdo the watering, though, for the tank environment should be dry to protect against mite invasions. I know many people who add no water to their beetle colonies at all, and they seem to do just fine.

At times when you have no skulls for the insatiable beetles to clean, they can easily live ten days without food. If necessary, you can give them dry cat or dog food to keep them going until you next need their help in cleaning a skull.

Other insects. Dermestid beetles are not the only insects that like to feed on dead and decaying flesh. Flies and maggots will efficiently clean a skull as well, especially if it is kept in moister conditions. Maggots are unable to eat flesh that has dried thoroughly. I've heard that maggots secrete a waste product as they feed, which will dye the skull a slightly yellow or light brown color. I've not found this to be a problem, if it is true, but for those of you who prefer a very white skull, it can always be whitened further as described below.

Ants are also a good alternative, especially if you are aware of an active colony. If you place a skull by a large ant mound, it will be stripped clean in short order, especially if kept moist.

Whether you're using flies or ants to do this job, make sure your skull is secure, so that it cannot be gnawed on by rodents, dragged away by a marauding raccoon, or picked up and carried off by a coyote. I only had to learn that lesson once—well, maybe twice—to remember to somehow protect the skull from large and small mammals. I use a self-created "rot trap," a simple wood framework covered in tight chicken wire fencing. The holes are about 1/2 inch square, and the entire enclosure is 4 by 4 feet and 18 inches tall. This is large enough to allow the remains of several animals to rot under protection simultaneously. I weigh down the enclosure to prevent bears from overturning it, for they'll feed on the rotting meat—and the maggots as well, if they are congregated in large numbers. I've also created enclosures for skulls with all sorts of other materials, such as stones or bricks, leaving enough space for flies and beetles to enter, but not enough for mice and other mammals. Be sensitive to prevailing winds and human noses when choosing a location.

Another alternative is to bury your animal skulls in nice loamy earth, where ample beetle and worm species will clean the skull for you. This is a slightly slower process than allowing insects to feed aboveground, taking up to several months. The earth will stain the skull a browner color, but you can whiten it following the procedure below. If you use this method, be careful not to lose any teeth or smaller bones when digging up the cleaned remains.

Degreasing

Fat in the bones of animals will leach outward over time and turn skulls shades of yellow and brown. For some collectors, this makes skulls more appealing; for others, it is far from preferable. The fat content in skulls and bones also varies tremendously across species. Certain animals will definitely require this extra step of degreasing,

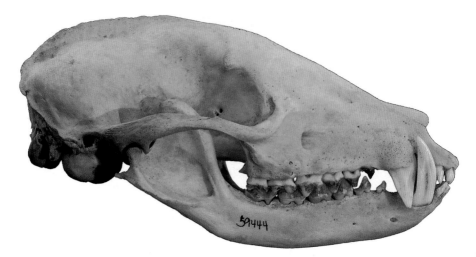

White-nosed coati *(Nasua narica)*. NATURAL HISTORY MUSEUM OF LOS ANGELES COUNTY, male, 59444.

but for many others it will be unnecessary. If a skull is greasy or sticky to the touch or continues to smell after the water treatment and drying completely, then degreasing is advisable.

The most easily obtained degreasing agent of choice is household ammonia. A solution of one part ammonia to two parts water makes a good overnight to 24-hour soak for specimens. This is also a wonderful way to clean skulls of beetle frass and germs. Ammonia will also lighten the color of the skull and may make further whitening unnecessary. Ammonia hydroxide is another product that works in much the same way.

Acetone is another popular degreasing agent, generally available where paint is sold. Acetone is highly toxic and should not be allowed to touch your skin or be breathed for extended periods, so wear rubber gloves and use a fume hood or outdoor workshop. It is also highly flammable. To degrease specimens, submerge them in acetone for up to three weeks, replacing the acetone when there is significant color change due to heavy leaching of fats. Note that acetone is considered a hazardous material and requires you to contact your local municipal disposal unit to find out where and when to drop off your discarded liquids.

Acetone is also useful in reclaiming compromised skulls, such as ones that have been painted or have their jaws glued in place. Elmer's glue can be softened and dissolved by soaking the skull in water, but acetone may be necessary to remove industrial glue or paint. Recently I used acetone and a bucket to free a very old bear skull that had been painted white, a popular method of prepping skull trophies in the past, and had its jaws glued in place. Within half an hour, the glue had begun to soften and release its grip, and the paint was coming off. Using old rags and a plastic brush, I was able to remove the paint and pry the industrial glue from around the condyle and the teeth. I would scrub and pry, then return the skull to the acetone. Within a little over an hour, the skull was fully restored. It had been perfectly preserved beneath.

Whitening

Only you can decide how white you'd like your skulls. Some people prefer skulls of a darker hue, but others opt for very white. Depending on your preference, you may choose to invest considerable time in whitening your skulls or skip this step altogether.

Never use Clorox or other bleach to whiten skulls. Hold to this rule with religious vigor, as even the mildest bleach solutions will greatly reduce the longevity of your skull. It may be two years or ten, but eventually skulls that were soaked in bleach solutions become chalky and break down. I know the horror of admiring cherished specimens only to have them slowly crumble with each handling, my hands removing a thin layer of bone, which appears like powder on my fingers. Save yourself this grief.

The whitening agent of choice is hydrogen peroxide, which can be bought at drugstores in varying strengths. Buy the lowest concentration you can, and this still can be further diluted with water before use. I've heard varying recommendations of what strength of peroxide to use; some suggest as low as 1 to 5 percent, others as high as 15 percent. Submerge your skulls completely for ten minutes to overnight, depending on the size of the specimen and how white you would like the finished specimen. After removing the skulls from a hydrogen peroxide solution, soak them overnight in a bucket of plain water so as to remove any remaining hydrogen peroxide and better end the bleaching process. Hydrogen peroxide is also a nice way to cleanse the skull of any unwanted refuse and germs, and it can be reused several times before disposed of. Spot whitening can also be achieved with hydrogen peroxide; paint a higher concentration on blotches or stains with a paintbrush.

Another method of whitening skulls is with solar power. Sun bleaching is free and very efficient. Place your specimen in a sunny window or outside in a spot where it is

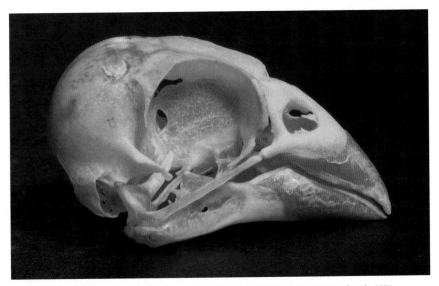

Cardinal *(Cardinalis cardinalis).* MUSEUM OF COMPARATIVE ZOOLOGY, HARVARD U., female, 7974.

well exposed to sun but won't be dragged off by some creature. Depending on how much sunlight your neck of the woods gets, whitening may occur in a week to a month.

Adding Protective Coatings

Skulls and bones are porous, meaning they soak up water, peroxide, ammonia, or acetone like sponges. This is why, regardless of the methods employed, a long soak in clean water afterward is imperative. After this, a skull needs to fully dry, which either eliminates or greatly reduces any lingering odors.

At this point, some folks choose to coat their skulls with a clear shellac of some sort. If this appeals to you, beware the sprays and varnishes that brown with age. I prefer a more natural skull, so I steer away from any coatings, unless I am attempting to salvage a bleached skull that is beginning to crumble.

Living bone is a very strong and flexible material, but dead and dry bones become more brittle and stiff. The teeth and bones of your skulls will easily chip, crack, and break if mishandled.

Recording Information

There was a time when my memory was enough to tell the stories of each of the skulls on my shelves. Perhaps my collection has grown considerably, or perhaps it is old age, but now I need to make notes so as not to forget all the details. Also, skulls with accompanying data become far more valuable down the line and allow for greater possibilities in education and research. Document as much information as you know: the genus and species, sex, approximate or definite age at death, place where you found or acquired the skull or entire animal, person who collected the material, and date of collection. You may want to take measurements and include them as well.

This information can be written on tags you attach to your skulls or on small slips of paper that are rolled and then inserted into the braincase through the foramen magnum. Another system is to use file cards or computer files to record the information, with matching reference numbers that you either attach or write directly on your skulls. Use whatever works best for you. More important than the data is that you enjoy the process.

Skull Illustrations and Measurements

The species accounts are arranged phylogenetically. Whole animal studies and comparative analysis are the foundation for our understanding of evolution and how animals are related to each other. But with the discovery of DNA, that understanding has been influenced by a microanalysis of animal matter on the genetic level. Thus taxonomy, the study of naming creatures, and phylogeny, which represents our understanding of how and in what order animals have evolved, continue to be revised and updated. For that reason, the order in which animals appear in this guide might not match that in older guides, and it likely will not match those written in the future; science is a dynamic and ever-expanding body of knowledge.

In theory, the first mammal to have finished evolving into the mammal it is today comes first in the book, the next second, and so on, until the very last. But the order reflects more than individual evolution, for evolution is not a linear event. Groups of animals, such as cats or moles, split off in their evolution and appear before other groups of animals; evolution occurs on numerous fronts simultaneously. Visualize the many branches of a tree, rather than a single time line. The Virginia opossum has long been considered the oldest mammal in North America, in evolutionary terms, and thus still appears first in this book. But thereafter begin some re-sorting and changes in both common and scientific names.

For the mammal portion of the species accounts, I have followed the *Revised Checklist of North American Mammals North. of Mexico, 2003,* by Baker et al. For birds, the checklist of the American Ornithologist's Union (http://www.aou.org/checklist/index.php3). For reptiles and amphibians, *Scientific and Standard English Names of Amphibians and Reptiles of North America North of Mexico, with Comments Regarding Confidence in Our Understanding,* by Crothier et al. (2000).

Several excellent keys to identifying mammal skulls are available, including *A Key to the Skulls of North American Mammals* (Glass and Thies 1997), *Illustrated Key to Skulls of Genera of North American Land Mammals* (Jones and Manning 1992), and *A Key-Guide to Mammal Skulls and Lower Jaws* (Roest 1991). In using a dichotomous key, you follow a series of questions, the answers to which refer you to further sets of questions, and eventually to a species identification. The species accounts provided here will complement such publications with visual presentations of animal skulls from across North America. In addition, there are invaluable essays on differentiating between similar species, aging specimens, and so much more in *Mammalian Osteology* (Gilbert 1980).

Dichotomous keys encourage a linear approach to identifying skulls, which is not how I interpret and identify skulls, nor do many other qualified naturalists, biologists, and taxonomists; though they still prove useful for determining between closely related species within a genus. For those who have handled enough skulls and carefully analyzed enough diagrams and illustrations, a more holistic way of identification emerges. This, I hope, is what this book will encourage, through undistracted engagement with real animal skulls alongside more artistic presentations of their diverse forms.

Organization

Supporting this approach to identifying skulls is first a visual quick-reference guide delineated with color tabs for easier referencing. Skulls are arranged from smallest to largest in three categories: mammals, birds, and reptiles. You may find that the skull in question resembles several illustrations in the quick-reference guide. If so, great! This is where real learning begins, for you'll be referred to species accounts where more views of the skull will support a more critical analysis to discover which tiny features might better aid in identification. It's this flipping of pages among species, further encouraged by lists of similar species, and rechecking your skull over and over again, that should create a more holistic appreciation of what you hold and increase learning over time.

Following the quick-reference illustrations are the species accounts. Each section begins with a brief general description of a family or group of animals, often accompanied by discussions of distinguishing characteristics of one or more species, as well as how to differentiate between similar members of the group. The individual species accounts each include four views of mammal skulls and three for birds, reptiles, and amphibians. Illustrations were made from actual specimens with painstaking accuracy, and the reference numbers for these particular skulls are included in case you're inspired to hold the real thing. Individual species accounts include more specific information on identification, as well as discussions on aging specimens, sexing animals, and relevant tidbits of natural history. Similar species are often listed to encourage you to cross-reference other potential candidates for identification. Mammals are the focus of this guide and so are placed first, followed by birds, and finally amphibians and reptiles.

Tables summarizing various cranial measurements have been compiled from various sources for many animals, allowing easy cross-species comparisons. Linear tables of numbers might arouse a certain anxiety in readers or perhaps outright panic, spurring a dash for the door or a burning of the book. Please breathe deeply and take whatever time you need to look at and study the tables, for they are an incredible resource compiled for your ease. Such questions as the sex, relative age, and size of an animal can often be answered by taking a few measurements and referencing the tables. They are also incredibly useful in species identification. To accurately measure skulls, use precision callipers with millimeter units.

Dividing species into geographic populations within the tables was beyond the scope of this book. For those who are interested in regional or subspecies variations, the references for original sources are included within the tables for follow-up research, and there are certainly a great many more resources on cranial morphometrics that were not included. Diagrams that will help you understand how measurements are taken are included earlier in this book, along with detailed diagrams of the bones of animal skulls. In order to streamline referencing for the reader, color tabs mark the detailed diagrams of both bones and measurements in one place in the book.

Mammal Skulls

Eastern pipistrelle
Pipistrellus subflavus
GL: 12.2–13.5 mm (5/10 in)

Little brown bat or myotis
Myotis lucifugus
GL: 13.7–15.6 mm (5/10–6/10 in)
page 232

Ghost-faced bat
Mormoops megalophylla
GL: 14.8–15.7 mm (5/10–6/10 in)
page 226

Least shrew
Cryptotis parva
GL: 14.2–18.0 mm (6/10–7/10 in)
page 208

Merriam's shrew
Sorex merriami
GL: 15.2–17.5 mm (6/10–7/10 in)
page 202

Crawford's desert shrew
Notiosorex crawfordi
GL: 15.0–17.6 mm (6/10–7/10 in)
page 210

Cave myotis
Myotis velifer
GL: 15.8–17.0 mm (6/10–7/10 in)

Cinereus or masked shrew
Sorex cinereus
GL: 14.6–17.2 mm (6/10–7/10 in)
page 201

Vagrant shrew
Sorex vagrans
GL: 14.9–19.5 mm (6/10–8/10 in)
page 205

Hoary bat
Lasiurus cinereus
GL: 13.1–19.0 mm (5/10–7/10 in)
page 233

Trowbridge's shrew
Sorex trowbridgii
GL: 16.5–18.0 mm (6/10–7/10 in)

Big brown bat
Eptesicus fuscus
GL: 15.1–23.0 mm (6/10–9/10 in)
page 235

Smoky shrew
Sorex fumeus
GL: 18.4–19.2 mm (7/10–8/10 in)

American water shrew
Sorex palustris
GL: 18.9–22.4 mm (7/10–9/10 in)
page 204

Silky pocket mouse
Perognathus flavus
GL: 19.5–22.0 mm (8/10–9/10 in)

Greatest length in millimeters and (inches)

Pallid bat
Antrozous pallidus
GL: 18.7–23.3 mm ($^7/_{10}$–$^9/_{10}$ in)
page 236

Western harvest mouse
Reithrodontomys megalotis
GL: 18.4–22.8 mm ($^7/_{10}$–$^9/_{10}$ in)
page 324

Little pocket mouse
Perognathus longimembris
GL: 20.2–22.6 mm ($^8/_{10}$–$^9/_{10}$ in)
page 304

House mouse
Mus musculus
GL: 19.5–23.5 mm ($^8/_{10}$–$^9/_{10}$ in)
page 342

Northern short-tailed shrew
Blarina brevicauda
GL: 16.9–25.2 mm ($^7/_{10}$–1 in)
page 207

American shrew mole
Neurotrichus gibbsii
GL: 20.7–24.2 mm ($^8/_{10}$–1 in)
page 213

Hairy-legged vampire bat
Diphylla ecaudata
GL: 21.6–23.3 mm ($^9/_{10}$–1 in)
page 230

California leaf-nosed bat
Macrotus californicus
GL: 22.4–23.9 mm ($^9/_{10}$–1 in)
page 227

Meadow jumping mouse
Zapus hudsonius
GL: 20.8–23.8 mm ($^8/_{10}$–$^9/_{10}$ in)
page 354

Marsh Shrew
Sorex bendirii
GL: 22.3–24.2 mm ($^9/_{10}$–1 in)

Woodland jumping mouse
Napaeozapus insignis
GL: 22.2–24.5 mm ($^9/_{10}$–1 in)
page 355

Southern red-backed vole
Clethrionomys gapperi
GL: 22.5–26.4 mm ($^9/_{10}$–1 in)
page 344

Pacific jumping mouse
Zapus trinotatus
GL: 24.0 mm ($^9/_{10}$ in)

Sonoran desert pocket mouse
Chaetodipus penicillatus
GL: 22.6–27.1 mm ($^9/_{10}$–1$^1/_{10}$ in)
page 308

Western jumping mouse
Zapus princeps
GL: 25.0 mm (1 in)

Great basin pocket mouse
Perognathus parvus
GL: 23.2–29.0 mm (⁹/₁₀–1¹/₁₀ in)
page 306

Deer mouse
Peromyscus maniculatus
GL: 23.3–28.0 mm (⁹/₁₀–1¹/₁₀ in)
page 328

Southern grasshopper mouse
Onychomys torridus
GL: 23.8–27.2 mm (⁹/₁₀–1¹/₁₀ in)

Southern long-nosed bat
Leptonycteris curasoae
GL: 25.7–27.3 mm (1–1¹/₁₀ in)

Northern grasshopper mouse
Onychomys leucogaster
GL: 25.0–29.9 mm (1–1²/₁₀ in)
page 330

Montane vole
Microtus montanus
GL: 25.4–30.2 mm (1–1²/₁₀ in)
page 346

White-footed mouse
Peromyscus leucopus
GL: 23.8–28.7 mm (⁹/₁₀–1¹/₁₀ in)
page 326

Long-tailed vole
Microtus longicaudus
GL: 25.9–28.9 mm (1–1¹/₁₀ in)

Dark kangaroo mouse
Microdipodops megacephalus
GL: 25.2–29.3 mm (1–1²/₁₀ in)
page 310

California vole
Microtus californicus
GL: 26.1–31.4 mm (1–1²/₁₀ in)

Bailey's pocket mouse
Perognathus baileyi
GL: 28.5–29.7 mm (1¹/₁₀–1²/₁₀ in)

Marsh rice rat
Oryzomys palustris
GL: 26.2–35.3 mm (1–1⁴/₁₀ in)
page 323

Meadow vole or field mouse
Microtus pennsylvanicus
GL: 23.8–31.0 mm (⁹/₁₀–1²/₁₀ in)
page 347

Mexican long-tongued bat
Choeronycteris mexicana
GL: 28.5–31.0 mm (1¹/₁₀–1²/₁₀ in)
page 229

Least chipmunk
Neotamias minimus
GL: 27.4–33.2 mm (1¹/₁₀–1³/₁₀ in)
page 268

Least weasel
Mustela nivalis
GL: 29.0–35.5 mm (1¹/₁₀–1⁴/₁₀ in)
page 430

Western bonneted bat
Eumops perotis
GL: 29.7–33.0 mm (1²/₁₀–1³/₁₀ in)
page 238

Brown lemming
Lemmus trimucronatus
GL: 27.6–35.1 mm (1¹/₁₀–1⁴/₁₀ in)
page 351

Hairy-tailed mole
Parascalops breweri
GL: 30.3–35.2 mm (1²/₁₀–1⁴/₁₀ in)
page 218

Water vole
Microtus richardsoni
GL: 30.1–37.7 mm (1²/₁₀–1⁵/₁₀ in)

Eastern Mole
Scalopus aquaticus
GL: 29.3–40.9 mm (1²/₁₀–1⁶/₁₀ in)
page 219

Yellow-pine chipmunk
Neotamias amoenus
GL: 31.4–34.8 mm (1²/₁₀–1⁴/₁₀ in)

Mexican spiny pocket mouse
Liomys irroratus
GL: 29.8–37.8 mm (1²/₁₀–1⁵/₁₀ in)
page 317

Mexican mouse opossum
Marmosa mexicana
GL: 29.9–40.8 mm (1²/₁₀–1⁶/₁₀ in)

Star-nosed mole
Condylura cristata
GL: 32.1–35.2 mm (1³/₁₀–1⁴/₁₀ in)
page 221

Southern flying squirrel
Glaucomys volans
GL: 32.0–37.2 mm (1³/₁₀–1⁵/₁₀ in)
page 293

Broad-footed mole
Scapanus latimanus
GL: 30.5–38.1 mm (1²/₁₀–1⁵/₁₀ in)
page 215

Cliff chipmunk
Neotamias dorsalis
GL: 33.7–38.3 mm (1³/₁₀–1⁵/₁₀ in)

Colorado chipmunk
Neotamias quadrivittatus
GL: 33.5–37.1 mm (1³/₁₀–1⁵/₁₀ in)

Uinta chipmunk
Neotamias umbrinus
GL: 33.7–36.6 mm (1³/₁₀–1⁵/₁₀ in)

Townsend's chipmunk
Neotamias townsendii
GL: 36.4–41.4 mm (1⁴/₁₀–1⁶/₁₀ in)

Chisel-toothed kangaroo rat
Dipodomys microps
GL: 32.6–38.5 mm (1³/₁₀–1⁵/₁₀ in)

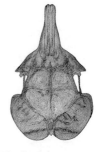

Merriam's kangaroo rat
Dipodomys merriami
GL: 33.5–37.9 mm (1³/₁₀–1⁵/₁₀ in)
page 313

Northern pocket gopher
Thomomys talpoides
GL: 33.7–40.8 mm (1³/₁₀–1⁶/₁₀ in)

Round-tailed ground squirrel
Spermophilus tereticaudus
GL: 34.7–39.8 mm (1⁴/₁₀–1⁶/₁₀ in)

Hispid cotton rat
Sigmodon hispidus
GL: 30.5–40.6 mm (1²/₁₀–1⁶/₁₀ in)
page 332

Thirteen-lined ground squirrel
Spermophilus tridecemlineatus
GL: 33.2–45.8 mm (1³/₁₀–1⁸/₁₀ in)
page 279

Botta's pocket gopher
Thomomys bottae
GL: 34.0–46.4 mm (1³/₁₀–1⁸/₁₀ in)
page 296

Ord's kangaroo rat
Dipodomys ordii
GL: 34.0–42.1 mm (1³/₁₀–1⁷/₁₀ in)
page 315

California kangaroo rat
Dipodomys californicus
GL: 34.0–42.1 mm (1³/₁₀–1⁷/₁₀ in)

Desert woodrat
Neotoma lepida
GL: 33.3–46.0 mm (1³/₁₀–1⁸/₁₀ in)
page 338

Ermine or short-tailed weasel
Mustela erminea
GL: 33.9–46.0 mm (1³/₁₀–1⁸/₁₀ in)

White-tailed antelope squirrel
Ammospermophilus leucurus
GL: 35.6–43.1 mm (1⁴/₁₀–1⁷/₁₀ in)
page 274

Agile kangaroo rat
Dipodomys agilis
GL: 39.9 mm (1⁶/₁₀ in)

Northern flying squirrel
Glaucomys sabrinus
GL: 36.0–44.2 mm (1⁴/₁₀–1⁷/₁₀ in)
page 291

Heermann's kangaroo rat
Dipodomys heermanni
GL: 40.9 mm (1⁶/₁₀ in)

Black rat
Rattus rattus
GL: 35.7–46.9 mm (1⁴/₁₀–1⁸/₁₀ in)

Townsend's mole
Scapanus townsendii
GL: 39.5–44.6 mm (1⁶/₁₀–1⁸/₁₀ in)
page 216

Eastern chipmunk
Tamias striatus
GL: 36.4–49.6 mm (1⁴/₁₀–2 in)
page 269

American pika
Ochotona princeps
GL: 38.8–47.3 mm (1⁵/₁₀–1⁹/₁₀ in)
page 248

Golden-mantled ground squirrel
Spermophilus lateralis
GL: 36.2–49.6 mm (1⁴/₁₀–2 in)
page 277

White-throated woodrat
Neotoma albigula
GL: 37.2–46.3 mm (1⁵/₁₀–1⁸/₁₀ in)
page 334

Plains pocket gopher
Geomys bursarius
GL: 40.5–60.0 mm (1⁶/₁₀–2⁴/₁₀ in)
page 298

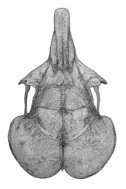

Desert kangaroo rat
Dipodomys deserti
GL: 41.5–46.7 mm (1⁶/₁₀–1⁸/₁₀ in)
page 312

Giant kangaroo rat
Dipodomys ingens
GL: 43.6–47.5 mm (1⁷/₁₀–1⁹/₁₀ in)

Red squirrel
Tamiasciurus hudsonicus
GL: 42.4–51.3 mm (1⁷/₁₀–2 in)
page 290

Norway rat
Rattus norvegicus
GL: 43.0–51.5 mm (1⁷/₁₀–2 in)
page 339

Yellow-faced pocket gopher
Cratogeomys castanops
GL: 41.5–58.3 mm (1⁶/₁₀–2³/₁₀ in)
page 300

Maine   California

Long-tailed weasel
Mustela frenata
GL: 38.4–53.6 mm (1⁵/₁₀–2¹/₁₀ in)
page 426

Pygmy rabbit
Brachylagus idahoensis
GL: 46.3–52.2 mm (1⁸/₁₀–2¹/₁₀ in)
page 249

Bushy-tailed woodrat
Neotoma cinerea
GL: 43.0–55.6 mm (1⁷/₁₀–2²/₁₀ in)
page 336

Big-eared woodrat
Neotoma macrotis
GL: 44.0–54.3 mm (1⁷/₁₀–2¹/₁₀ in)

Eastern woodrat
Neotoma floridana
GL: 43.9–55.6 mm (1⁷/₁₀–2²/₁₀ in)

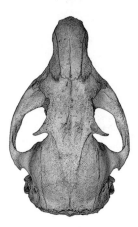 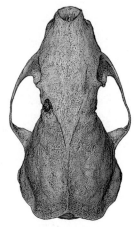 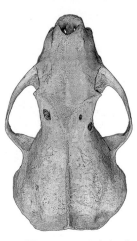

Columbian ground squirrel
Spermophilus columbianus
GL: 49.5–57.0 mm (1⁹/₁₀–2²/₁₀ in)

Eastern spotted skunk
Spilogale putorius
GL: 49.4–63.6 mm (1⁹/₁₀–2⁵/₁₀ in)

Western spotted skunk
Spilogale gracilis
GL: 49.4–63.6 mm (1⁹/₁₀–2⁵/₁₀ in)
page 446

California ground squirrel
Spermophilus beecheyi
GL: 51.6–65.4 mm (2–2⁶/₁₀ in)
page 276

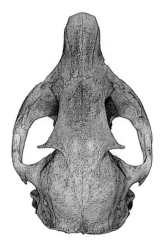

Arctic ground squirrel
Spermophilus parryii
GL: 50.7–65.8 mm (2–2⁶/₁₀ in)

Rock squirrel
Spermophilus variegatus
GL: 54.4–67.7 mm (2¹/₁₀–2⁷/₁₀ in)
page 281

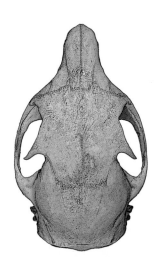

Abert's or tassel-eared squirrel
Sciurus aberti
GL: 58.1–62.9 mm (2³/₁₀–2⁵/₁₀ in)

Eastern gray squirrel
Sciurus carolinensis
GL: 53.8–66.5 mm (2¹/₁₀–2⁶/₁₀ in)
page 284

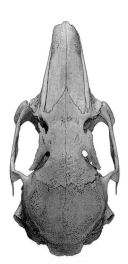

Brush rabbit
Sylvilagus bachmani
GL: 57.9–66.0 mm (2³/₁₀–2⁶/₁₀ in)
page 252

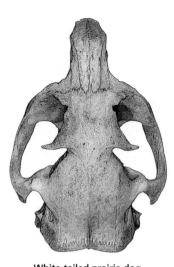

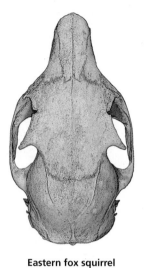

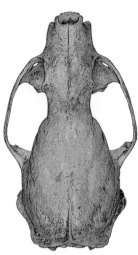

Eastern fox squirrel
Sciurus niger
GL: 47.1–71.8 mm (1^9/$_{10}$–2^8/$_{10}$ in)
page 288

White-tailed prairie dog
Cynomys leucurus
GL: 53.2–64.1 mm (2^1/$_{10}$–2^5/$_{10}$ in)

American mink
Mustela vison
GL: 53.3–70.6 mm (2^1/$_{10}$–2^8/$_{10}$ in)
page 432

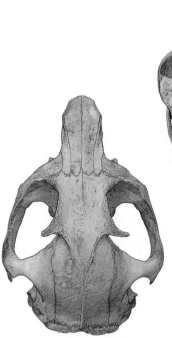

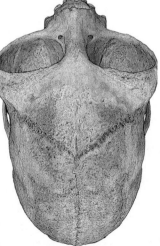

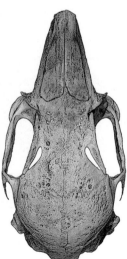

Night monkey
Aotus capucinus
GL: 66.2 mm (2^6/$_{10}$ in)

Black-tailed prairie dog
Cynomys ludovicianus
GL: 60.4–67.8 mm (2^4/$_{10}$–2^7/$_{10}$ in)
page 282

Mountain cottontail
Sylvilagus nuttallii
GL: 56.6–72.6 mm (2^2/$_{10}$–2^9/$_{10}$ in)

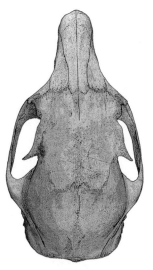

Western gray squirrel
Sciurus griseus
GL: 63.1–70.4 mm (2⁵/₁₀–2⁸/₁₀ in)
page 286

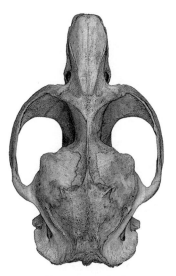

Common muskrat
Ondatra zibethicus
GL: 58.2–72.3 mm (2³/₁₀–2⁸/₁₀ in)
page 349

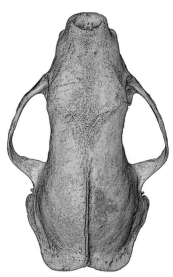

Hooded skunk
Mephitis macroura
GL: 51.8–72.4 mm (2–2⁹/₁₀ in)

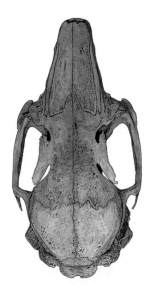

Desert cottontail
Sylvilagus audubonii
GL: 61.1–74.1 mm (2⁴/₁₀–2⁹/₁₀ in)
page 251

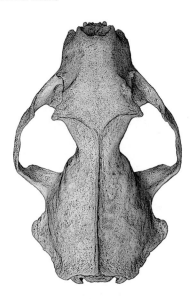

Black-footed ferret
Mustela nigripes
GL: 62.5–70.0 mm (2⁵/10–2⁸/10 in)
page 429

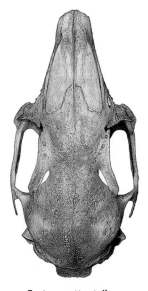

Eastern cottontail
Sylvilagus floridanus
GL: 62.3–82.0 mm (2⁵/10–3²/10 in)
page 254

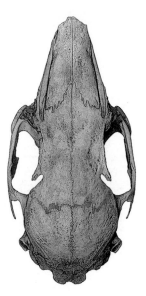

New England cottontail
Sylvilagus transitionalis
GL: 65.5–75.0 mm (2⁶/10–3 in)

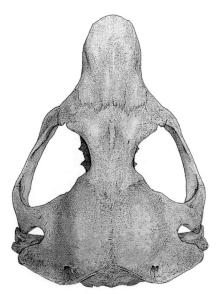

Mountain beaver or aplodontia
Aplodontia rufa
GL: 62.2–77.1 mm (2⁴/10–3 in)
page 263

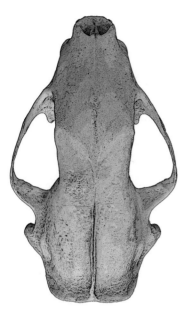

Striped skunk
Mephitis mephitis
GL: 67.9–88.0 mm (2⁷/₁₀–3⁵/₁₀ in)
page 449

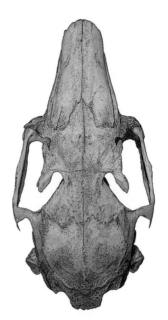

Snowshoe hare
Lepus americanus
GL: 72.9–85.5 mm (2⁹/₁₀–3⁴/₁₀ in)
page 256

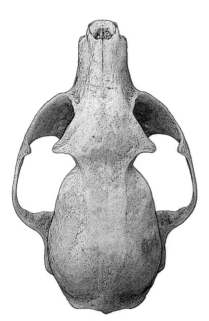

Ringtail
Bassariscus astutus
GL: 70.4–84.8 mm (2⁸/₁₀–3³/₁₀ in)
page 410

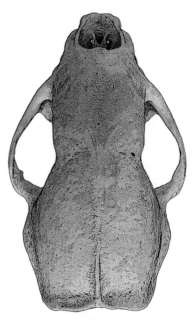

White-backed hog-nosed skunk
Conepatus leuconotus
GL: 65.0–84.5 mm (2⁶/₁₀–3³/₁₀ in)
page 451

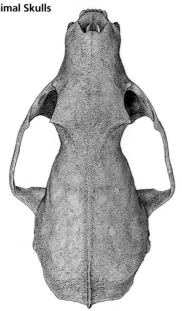

American marten
Martes americana
GL: 67.7–87.9 mm (2⁷/₁₀–3⁵/₁₀ in)
page 419

Yellow-bellied marmot
Marmota flaviventris
GL: 73.2–93.4 mm (2⁹/₁₀–3⁷/₁₀ in)
page 271

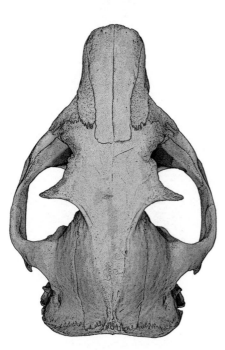

Woodchuck or groundhog
Marmota monax
GL: 73.6–102.0 mm (2⁹/₁₀–4 in)
page 272

Swamp rabbit
Sylvilagus aquaticus
GL: 83.7–99.6 mm (3³/₁₀–3⁹/₁₀ in)

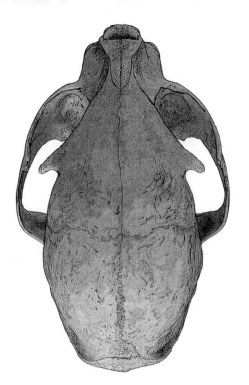

Margay
Leopardus wiedii
GL: 86.6–107.0 mm (3^4/$_{10}$–4^2/$_{10}$ in) page 463

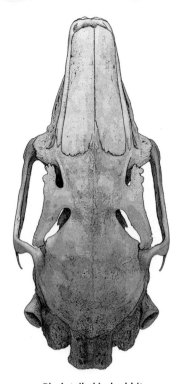

Black-tailed jackrabbit
Lepus californicus
GL: 85.4–101.9 mm (3^4/$_{10}$–4 in) page 258

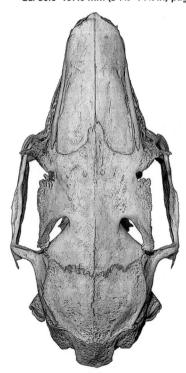

White-tailed jackrabbit
Lepus townsendii
GL: 76.8–102.5 mm (3–4 in) page 259

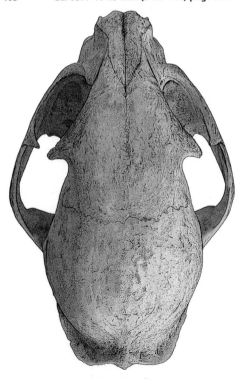

Jaguarundi
Herpailurus yaguarondi
GL: 86.7–116.1 mm (3^4/$_{10}$–4^6/$_{10}$ in) page 464

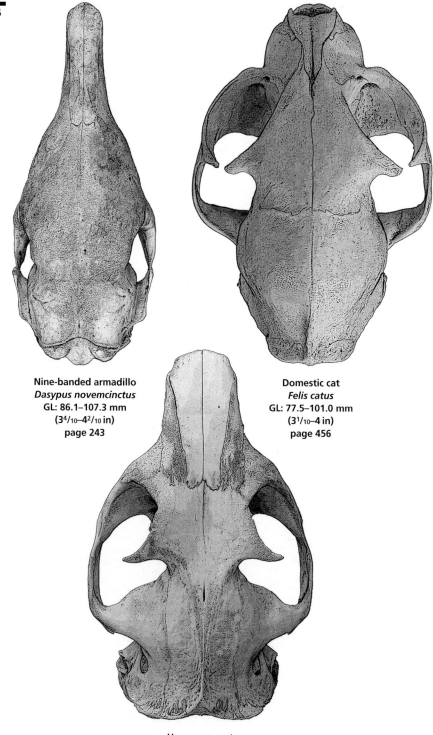

Nine-banded armadillo
Dasypus novemcinctus
GL: 86.1–107.3 mm
($3^4/_{10}$–$4^2/_{10}$ in)
page 243

Domestic cat
Felis catus
GL: 77.5–101.0 mm
($3^1/_{10}$–4 in)
page 456

Hoary marmot
Marmota caligata
GL: 82.8–108.8 mm
($3^3/_{10}$–$4^3/_{10}$ in)

Island fox
Urocyon littoralis
GL: 96.8–110.3 mm
(3^{8}/$_{10}$–4^{3}/$_{10}$ in)
page 390

Fisher (female)
Martes pennanti
GL: 98.7–105.3 mm
(3^{9}/$_{10}$–4^{1}/$_{10}$ in)
page 421

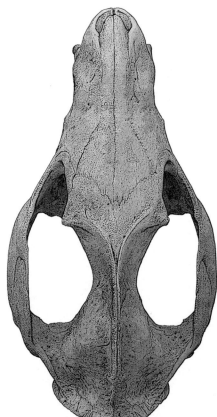

Virginia opossum
Didelphis virginiana
GL: 77.9–145.8 mm
(3^1/$_{10}$–5^7/$_{10}$ in)
page 195

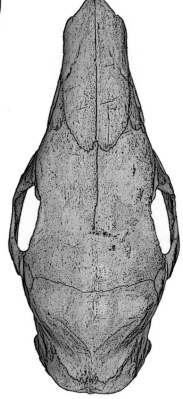

Mexican black agouti
Dasyprocta mexicana
GL: 106.7 mm
(4^2/$_{10}$ in)
page 363

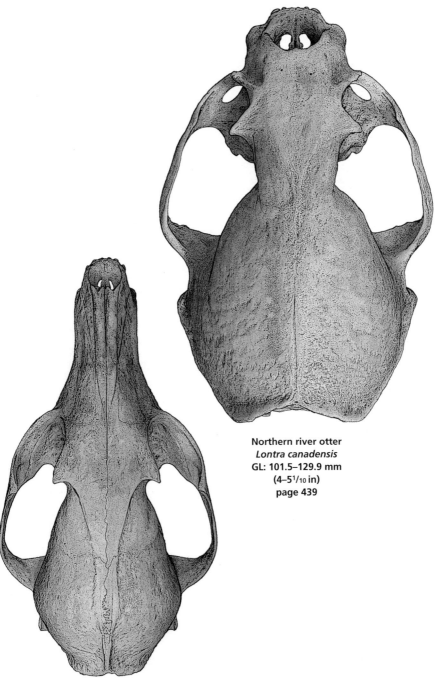

Northern river otter
Lontra canadensis
GL: 101.5–129.9 mm
(4–5^{1}/$_{10}$ in)
page 439

Kit fox
Vulpes macrotis
GL: 101.0–120.3 mm
(4–4^{7}/$_{10}$ in)
page 382

Life-size Mammal Skulls

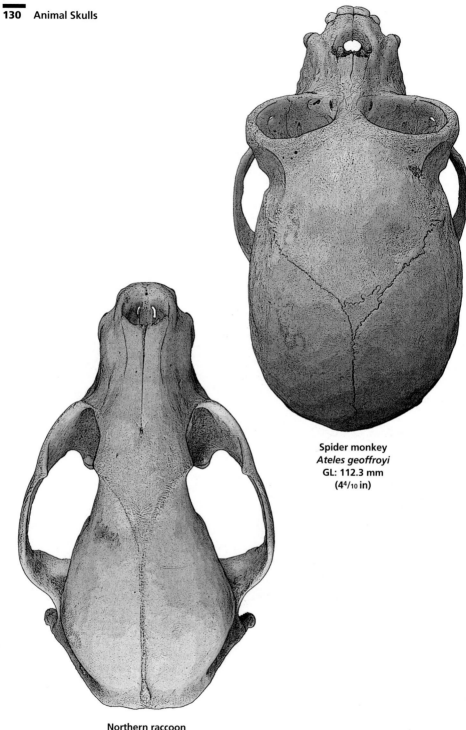

Spider monkey
Ateles geoffroyi
GL: 112.3 mm
(4⁴/₁₀ in)

Northern raccoon
Procyon lotor
GL: 93.6–135.5 mm
(3⁷/₁₀–5⁵/₁₀ in)
page 412

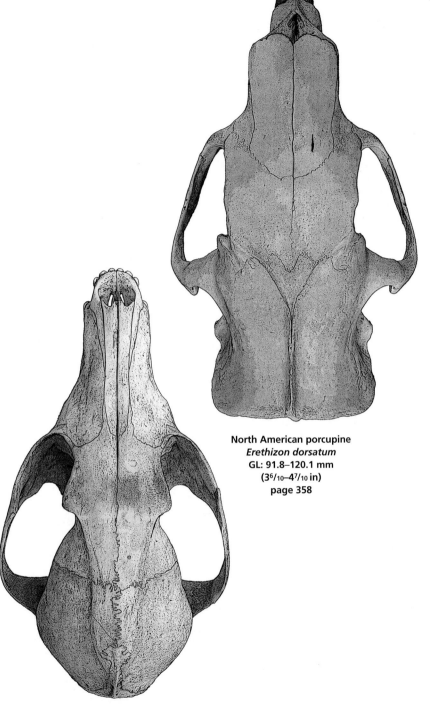

North American porcupine
Erethizon dorsatum
GL: 91.8–120.1 mm
(3⁶/₁₀–4⁷/₁₀ in)
page 358

Swift fox
Vulpes velox
GL: 111.4–116.8 mm
(4⁴/₁₀–4⁶/₁₀ in)
page 384

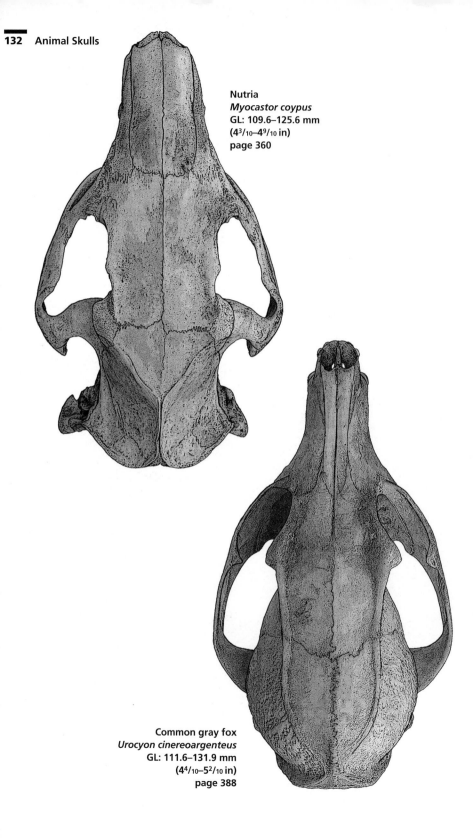

Nutria
Myocastor coypus
GL: 109.6–125.6 mm
(4^3/$_{10}$–4^9/$_{10}$ in)
page 360

Common gray fox
Urocyon cinereoargenteus
GL: 111.6–131.9 mm
(4^4/$_{10}$–5^2/$_{10}$ in)
page 388

Life-size Mammal Skulls

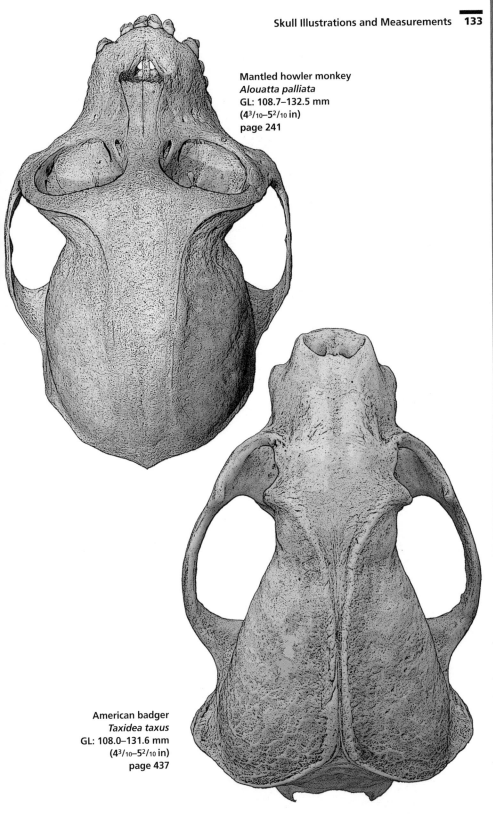

Mantled howler monkey
Alouatta palliata
GL: 108.7–132.5 mm
(4³/₁₀–5²/₁₀ in)
page 241

American badger
Taxidea taxus
GL: 108.0–131.6 mm
(4³/₁₀–5²/₁₀ in)
page 437

Life-size Mammal Skulls

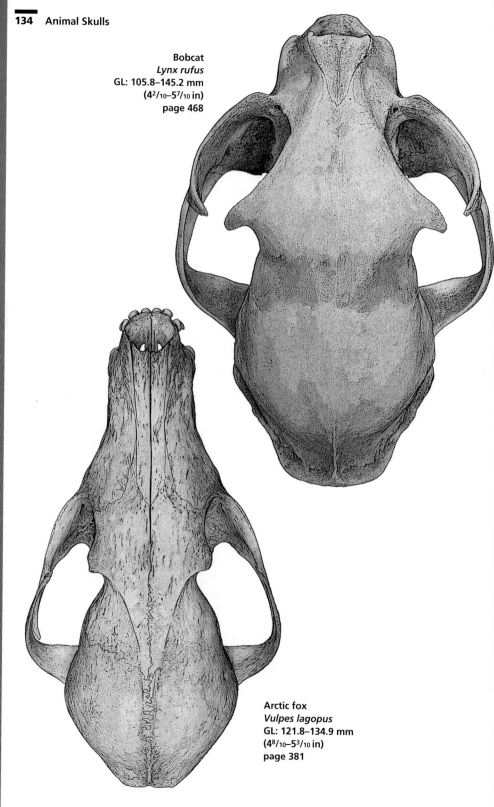

Bobcat
Lynx rufus
GL: 105.8–145.2 mm
($4^2/_{10}$–$5^7/_{10}$ in)
page 468

Arctic fox
Vulpes lagopus
GL: 121.8–134.9 mm
($4^8/_{10}$–$5^3/_{10}$ in)
page 381

Life-size Mammal Skulls

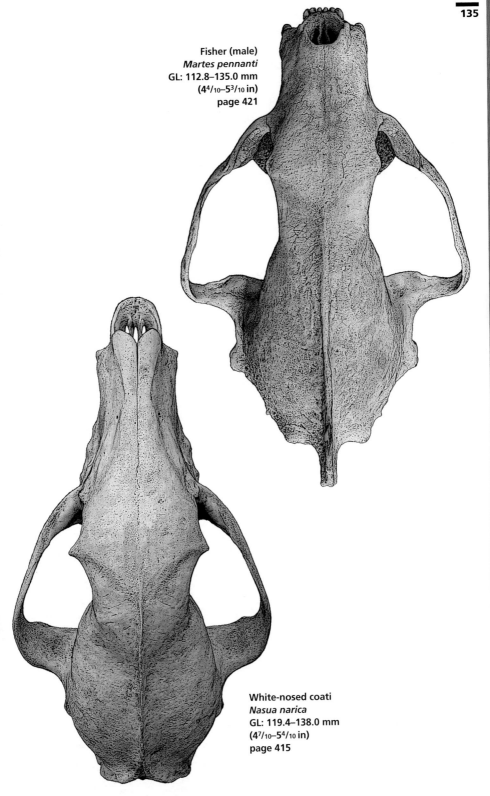

Fisher (male)
Martes pennanti
GL: 112.8–135.0 mm
(4^4/$_{10}$–5^3/$_{10}$ in)
page 421

White-nosed coati
Nasua narica
GL: 119.4–138.0 mm
(4^7/$_{10}$–5^4/$_{10}$ in)
page 415

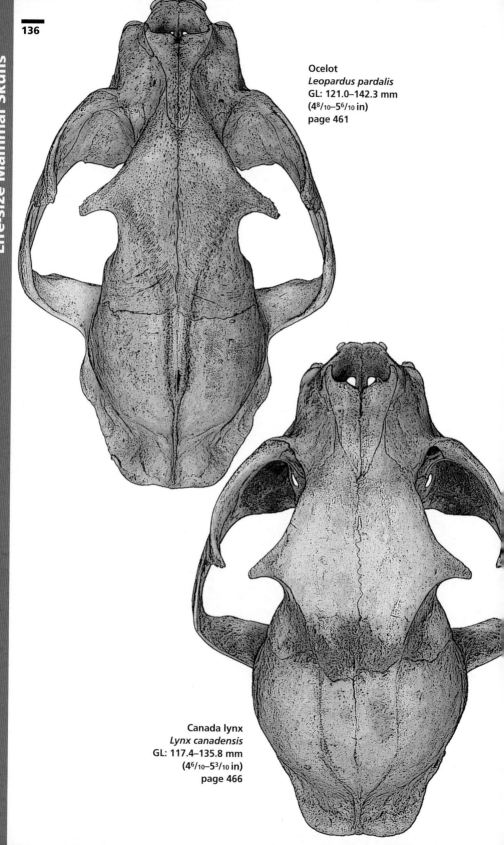

Ocelot
Leopardus pardalis
GL: 121.0–142.3 mm
(4^8/$_{10}$–5^6/$_{10}$ in)
page 461

Canada lynx
Lynx canadensis
GL: 117.4–135.8 mm
(4^6/$_{10}$–5^3/$_{10}$ in)
page 466

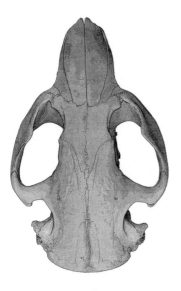

American beaver
Castor canadensis
GL: 100.8–158.6 mm
(4–6²/₁₀ in)
page 320

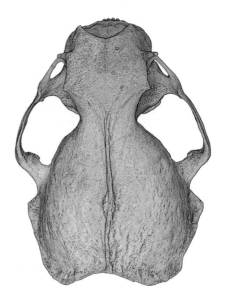

Sea otter
Enhydra lutris
GL: 125.1–148.6 mm
(4⁹/₁₀–5⁹/₁₀ in)
page 441

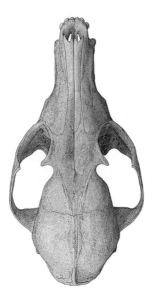

Red fox
Vulpes vulpes
GL: 124.5–157.2 mm
(4⁹/₁₀–6²/₁₀ in)
page 386

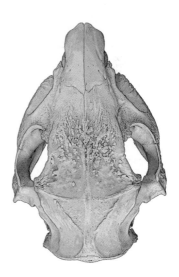

Paca
Agouti paca
GL: 141.0–160.2 mm
(5⁵/₁₀–6³/₁₀ in)
page 365

Greatest length of all craniums 50 percent of life-size

Greatest Length of Mammal Skulls at 50 Percent

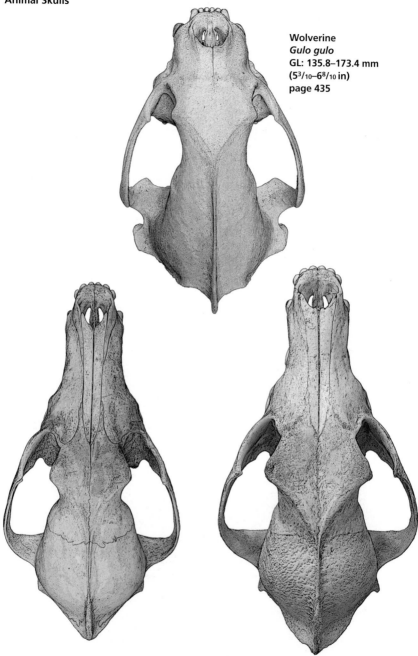

Wolverine
Gulo gulo
GL: 135.8–173.4 mm
($5^3/_{10}$–$6^8/_{10}$ in)
page 435

Coyote (west)
Canis latrans
GL: 170.0–213.0 mm
($6^7/_{10}$–$8^4/_{10}$ in)

Coyote (northeast)
Canis latrans
GL: 173.8–220.3 mm
($6^8/_{10}$–$8^7/_{10}$ in)
page 373

Greatest length of all craniums 50 percent of life-size

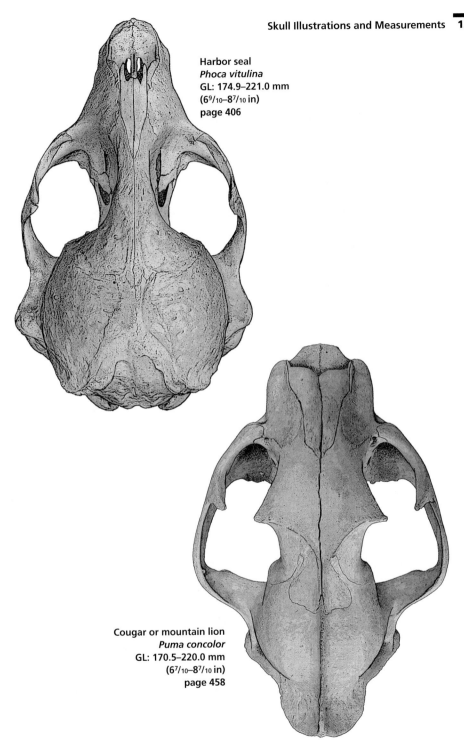

Harbor seal
Phoca vitulina
GL: 174.9–221.0 mm
(6⁹/₁₀–8⁷/₁₀ in)
page 406

Cougar or mountain lion
Puma concolor
GL: 170.5–220.0 mm
(6⁷/₁₀–8⁷/₁₀ in)
page 458

Greatest length of all craniums 50 percent of life-size

Greatest Length of Mammal Skulls at 50 Percent

Red wolf
Canis rufus
GL: 198.5–261.0 mm
(7^8/$_{10}$–10 ^{3}/$_{10}$ in)
page 379

California sea lion (female)
Zalophus californianus
GL: 232.9–253.3 mm
(9^2/$_{10}$–10 in)
page 401

Greatest length of all craniums 50 percent of life-size

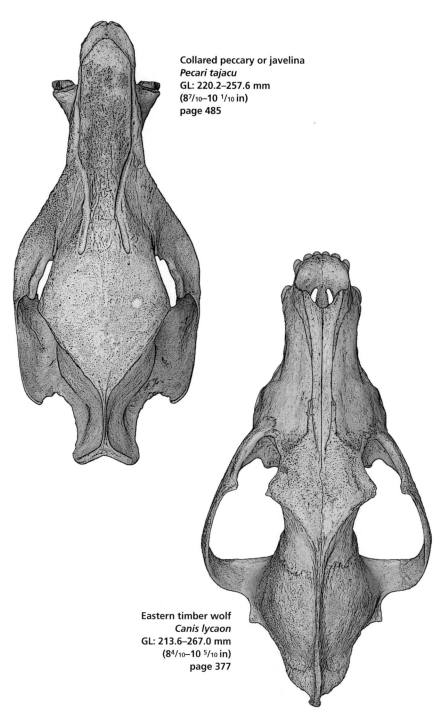

Collared peccary or javelina
Pecari tajacu
GL: 220.2–257.6 mm
(8⁷/₁₀–10 ¹/₁₀ in)
page 485

Eastern timber wolf
Canis lycaon
GL: 213.6–267.0 mm
(8⁴/₁₀–10 ⁵/₁₀ in)
page 377

Greatest length of all craniums 50 percent of life-size

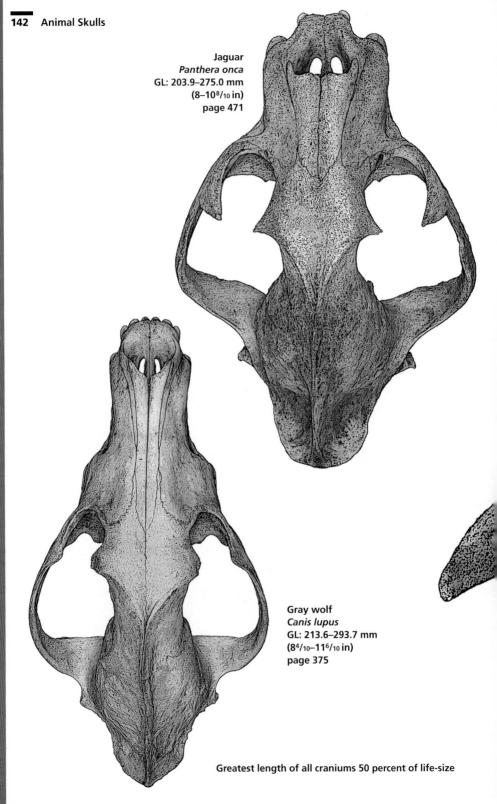

Greatest Length of Mammal Skulls at 50 Percent

Jaguar
Panthera onca
GL: 203.9–275.0 mm
(8–10^8/$_{10}$ in)
page 471

Gray wolf
Canis lupus
GL: 213.6–293.7 mm
(8^4/$_{10}$–11^6/$_{10}$ in)
page 375

Greatest length of all craniums 50 percent of life-size

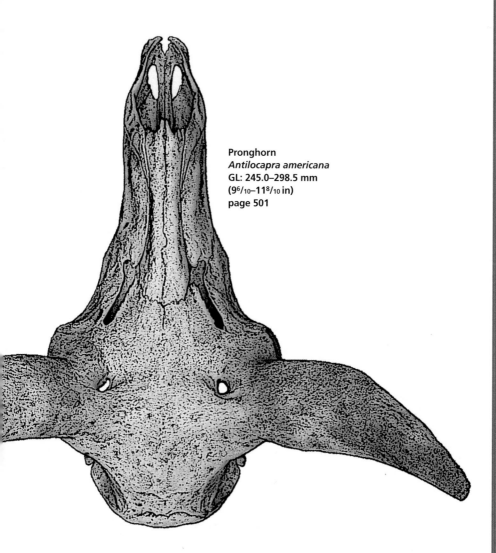

Pronghorn
Antilocapra americana
GL: 245.0–298.5 mm
(9⁶/₁₀–11⁸/₁₀ in)
page 501

Greatest Length of Mammal Skulls at 50 Percent

Greatest length of all craniums 50 percent of life-size

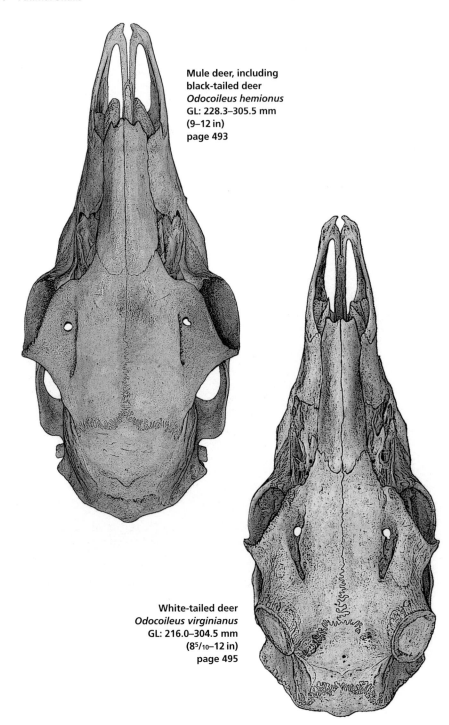

Mule deer, including
black-tailed deer
Odocoileus hemionus
GL: 228.3–305.5 mm
(9–12 in)
page 493

White-tailed deer
Odocoileus virginianus
GL: 216.0–304.5 mm
(8⁵/₁₀–12 in)
page 495

Greatest length of all craniums 50 percent of life-size

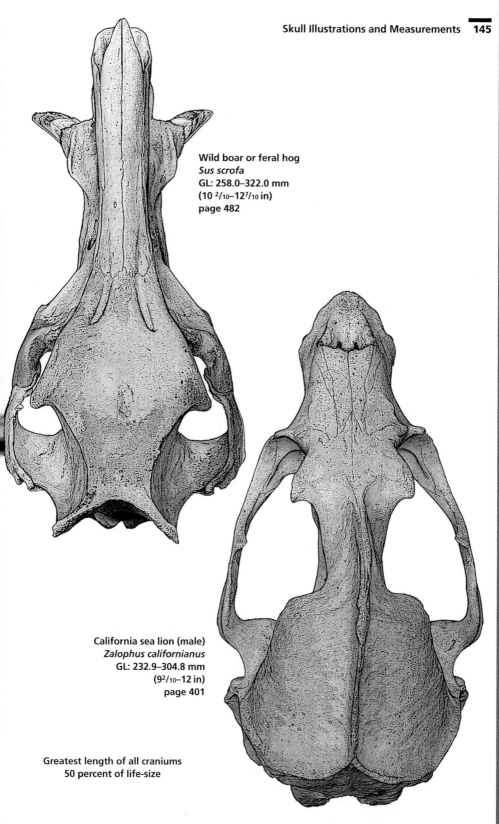

Wild boar or feral hog
Sus scrofa
GL: 258.0–322.0 mm
(10 $^2/_{10}$–12$^7/_{10}$ in)
page 482

California sea lion (male)
Zalophus californianus
GL: 232.9–304.8 mm
(9$^2/_{10}$–12 in)
page 401

Greatest length of all craniums
50 percent of life-size

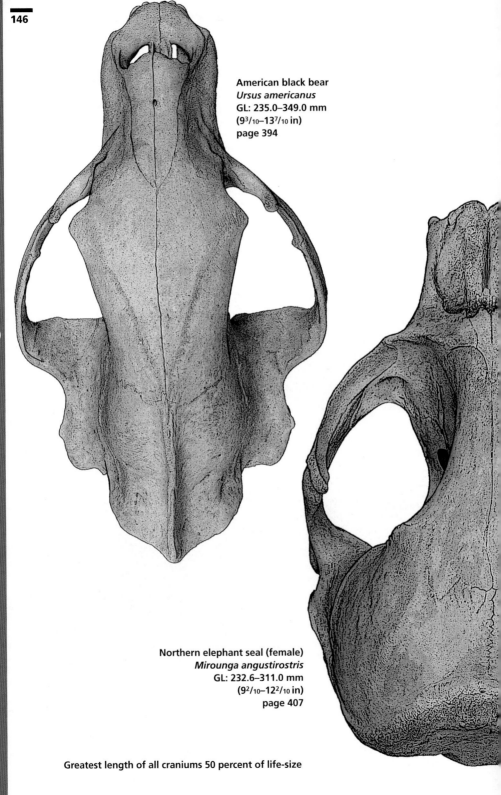

American black bear
Ursus americanus
GL: 235.0–349.0 mm
(9^3/$_{10}$–13^7/$_{10}$ in)
page 394

Northern elephant seal (female)
Mirounga angustirostris
GL: 232.6–311.0 mm
(9^2/$_{10}$–12^2/$_{10}$ in)
page 407

Greatest length of all craniums 50 percent of life-size

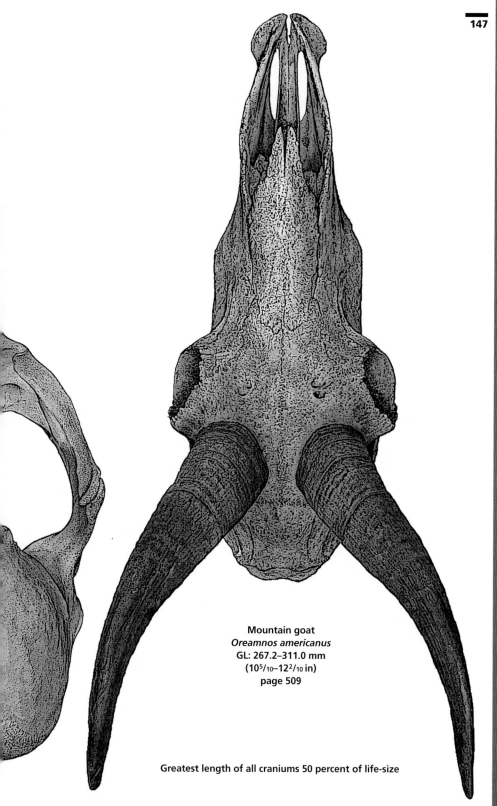

Mountain goat
Oreamnos americanus
GL: 267.2–311.0 mm
($10^5/_{10}$–$12^2/_{10}$ in)
page 509

Greatest length of all craniums 50 percent of life-size

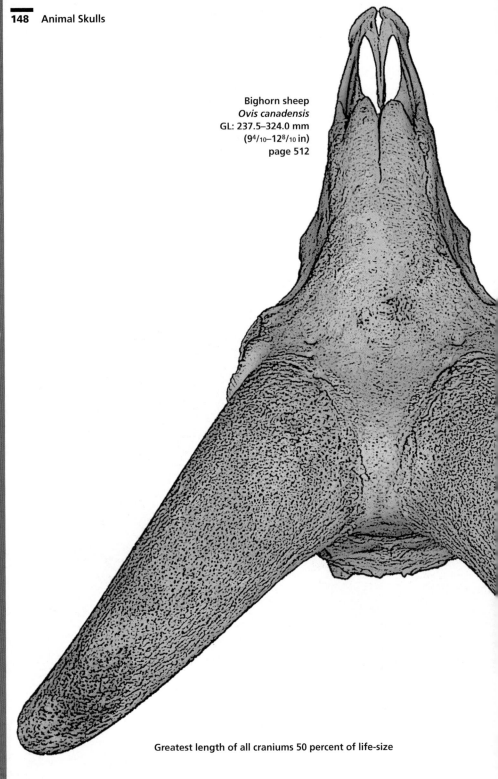

Bighorn sheep
Ovis canadensis
GL: 237.5–324.0 mm
($9^4/_{10}$–$12^8/_{10}$ in)
page 512

Greatest length of all craniums 50 percent of life-size

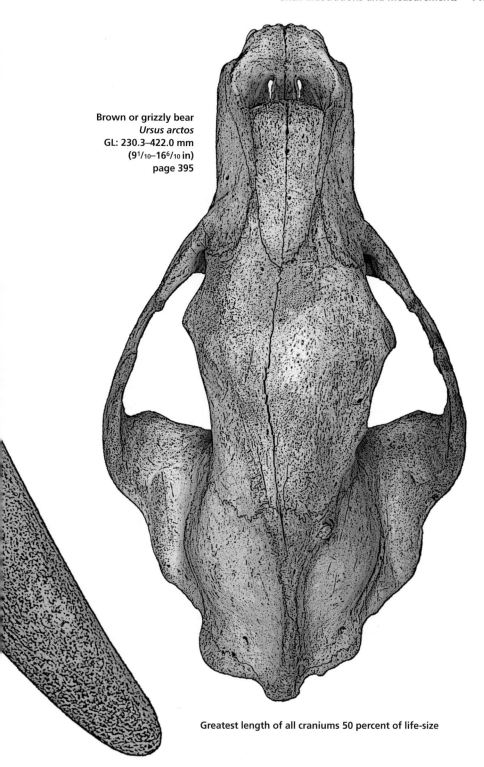

Brown or grizzly bear
Ursus arctos
GL: 230.3–422.0 mm
(9¹/₁₀–16⁶/₁₀ in)
page 395

Greatest length of all craniums 50 percent of life-size

Greatest Length of Mammal Skulls at 50 Percent

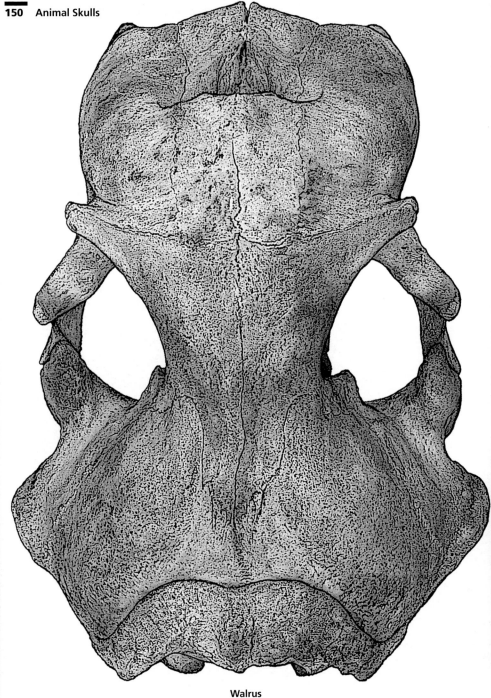

Walrus
Odobenus rosmarus
GL: 319.0–396.0 mm (12^5/$_{10}$–15^6/$_{10}$ in)
page 403

Greatest length of all craniums 50 percent of life-size

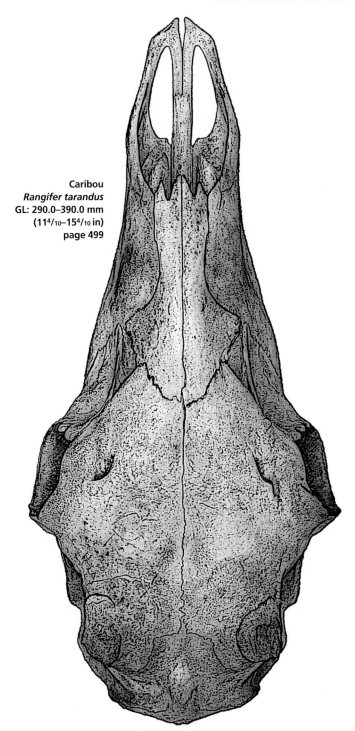

Caribou
Rangifer tarandus
GL: 290.0–390.0 mm
(11^4/$_{10}$–15^4/$_{10}$ in)
page 499

Greatest length of all craniums 50 percent of life-size

West Indian manatee
Trichechus manatus
GL: 325.0–418.0 mm
(12^{8}/$_{10}$–16^{5}/$_{10}$ in)
page 478

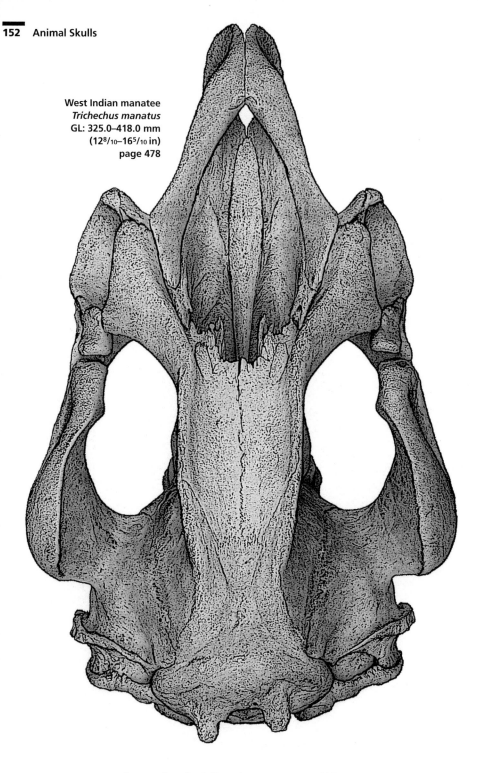

Greatest length of all craniums 50 percent of life-size

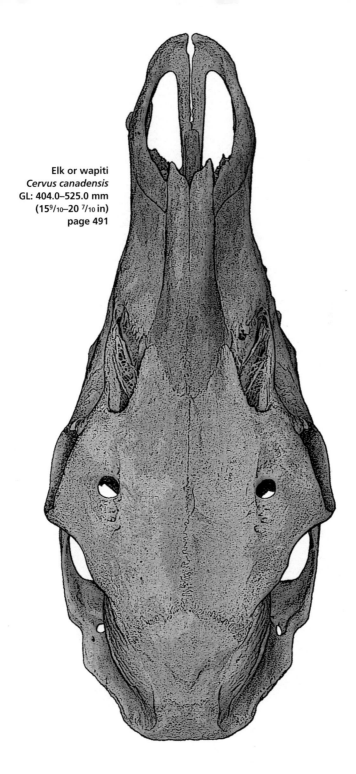

Elk or wapiti
Cervus canadensis
GL: 404.0–525.0 mm
(15^9/$_{10}$–20 ^{7}/$_{10}$ in)
page 491

Greatest length of all craniums 50 percent of life-size

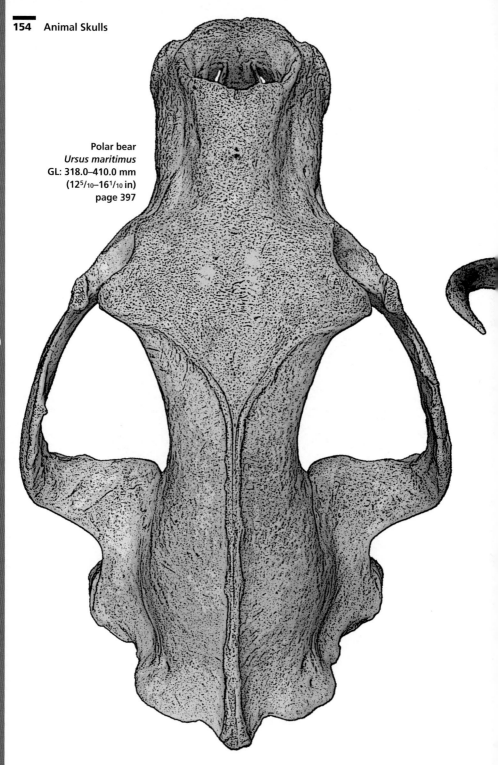

Polar bear
Ursus maritimus
GL: 318.0–410.0 mm
(12^{5}/$_{10}$–16^{1}/$_{10}$ in)
page 397

Greatest length of all craniums 50 percent of life-size

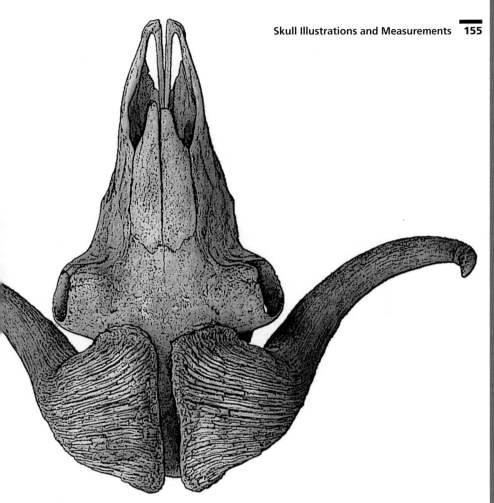

Muskox
Ovibos moschatus
GL: 428.5–528.0 mm
(16⁹/₁₀–20 ⁸/₁₀ in)
page 511

Greatest length of all craniums 25 percent of life-size

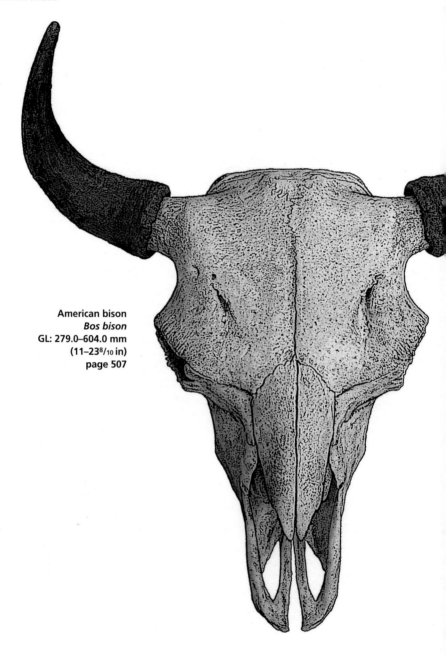

American bison
Bos bison
GL: 279.0–604.0 mm
(11–23^{8}/$_{10}$ in)
page 507

Greatest length of all craniums 25 percent of life-size

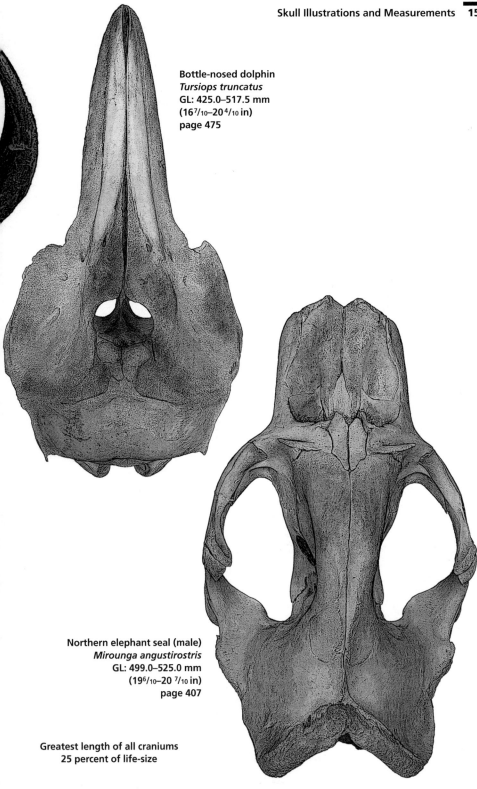

Bottle-nosed dolphin
Tursiops truncatus
GL: 425.0–517.5 mm
(16^{7}/$_{10}$–20^{4}/$_{10}$ in)
page 475

Northern elephant seal (male)
Mirounga angustirostris
GL: 499.0–525.0 mm
(19^{6}/$_{10}$–20 ^{7}/$_{10}$ in)
page 407

**Greatest length of all craniums
25 percent of life-size**

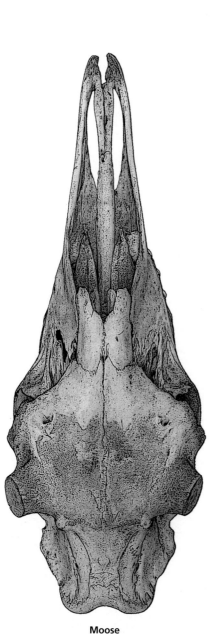

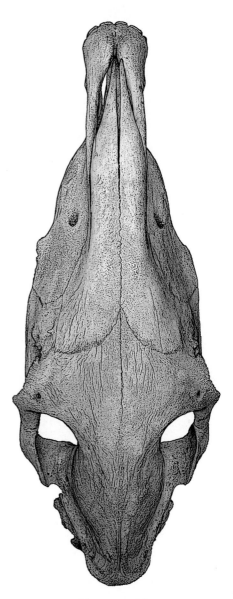

Feral horse or wild pony
Equus caballus
GL: 567.0–628.0 mm
(22³/₁₀–24⁷/₁₀ in)
page 480

Moose
Alces alces
GL: 540.0–633.0 mm
(21³/₁₀–24⁹/₁₀ in)
page 497

Greatest length of all craniums 25 percent of life-size

Mammal Jaws

Vagrant shrew
Sorex vagrans
L: 6.3–8.8 mm ($^2/_{10}$–$^4/_{10}$ in)
page 205

Merriam's shrew
Sorex merriami
L: 6.5–8.5 mm ($^2/_{10}$–$^4/_{10}$ in)
page 202

Least shrew
Cryptotis parva
L: 7.0–8.1 mm ($^3/_{10}$ in)
page 208

Cinereus or masked shrew
Sorex cinereus
L: 6.5–8.3 mm ($^2/_{10}$–$^3/_{10}$ in)
page 201

Crawford's desert shrew
Notiosorex crawfordi
L: 7.3–8.8 mm ($^3/_{10}$–$^4/_{10}$ in)
page 210

Little pocket mouse
Perognathus longimembris
L: 8.5–9.7 mm ($^3/_{10}$–$^4/_{10}$ in)
page 304

American water shrew
Sorex palustris
L: 8.5–9.7 mm ($^3/_{10}$–$^4/_{10}$ in)
page 204

Little brown bat or myotis
Myotis lucifugus
L: 8.9–10.5 mm ($^3/_{10}$–$^4/_{10}$ in)
page 232

Dark kangaroo mouse
Microdipodops megacephalus
L: 9.3–10.9 mm ($^3/_{10}$–$^4/_{10}$ in)
page 310

Western harvest mouse
Reithrodontomys megalotis
L: 9.4–11.5 mm ($^3/_{10}$–$^5/_{10}$ in)
page 324

Sonoran desert pocket mouse
Chaetodipus penicillatus
L: 10.2–11.5 mm ($^4/_{10}$–$^5/_{10}$ in)
page 308

Ghost-faced bat
Mormoops megalophylla
L: 12.0–13.1 mm ($^4/_{10}$–$^5/_{10}$ in)
page 226

Great basin pocket mouse
Perognathus parvus
L: 9.7–12.9 mm ($^4/_{10}$–$^5/_{10}$ in)
page 306

House mouse
Mus musculus
L: 10.4–12.0 mm ($^4/_{10}$–$^5/_{10}$ in)
page 342

Meadow jumping mouse
Zapus hudsonius
L: 10.6–12.0 mm ($^4/_{10}$–$^5/_{10}$ in)
page 354

Northern short-tailed shrew
Blarina brevicauda
L: 10.7–12.0 mm ($^4/_{10}$–$^5/_{10}$ in)
page 207

Woodland jumping mouse
Napaeozapus insignis
L: 11.6–12.7 mm ($^4/_{10}$–$^5/_{10}$ in)
page 355

Deer mouse
Peromyscus maniculatus
L: 12.0–13.8 mm ($^5/_{10}$–$^6/_{10}$ in)
page 328

Hoary bat
Lasiurus cinereus
L: 12.1–13.9 mm ($^5/_{10}$–$^6/_{10}$ in)
page 233

White-footed mouse
Peromyscus leucopus
L: 12.7–14.0 mm ($^5/_{10}$–$^6/_{10}$ in)
page 326

Hairy-legged vampire bat
Diphylla ecaudata
L: 13.1–14.4 mm ($^5/_{10}$–$^6/_{10}$ in)
page 230

Length (L) in millimeters and (inches)

Southern red-backed vole
Clethrionomys gapperi
L: 12.7–15.7 mm ($^5/_{10}$–$^6/_{10}$ in)
page 344

American shrew mole
Neurotrichus gibbsii
L: 12.6–16.0 mm ($^5/_{10}$–$^6/_{10}$ in)
page 213

Big brown bat
Eptesicus fuscus
L: 12.8–14.9 mm ($^5/_{10}$–$^6/_{10}$ in)
page 235

Northern grasshopper mouse
Onychomys leucogaster
L: 12.5–15.1 mm ($^5/_{10}$–$^6/_{10}$ in)
page 330

Merriam's kangaroo rat
Dipodomys merriami
L: 13.6–15.1 mm ($^5/_{10}$–$^6/_{10}$ in)
page 313

Pallid bat
Antrozous pallidus
L: 13.7–16.6 mm ($^5/_{10}$–$^7/_{10}$ in)
page 236

California leaf-nosed bat
Macrotus californicus
L: 14.4–15.1 mm ($^5/_{10}$–$^6/_{10}$ in)
page 227

Ord's kangaroo rat
Dipodomys ordii
L: 13.9–15.9 mm ($^5/_{10}$–$^6/_{10}$ in)
page 315

Least weasel
Mustela nivalis
L: 13.7–16.8 mm ($^5/_{10}$–$^7/_{10}$ in)
page 430

Mexican spiny pocket mouse
Liomys irroratus
L: 14.1–19.3 mm ($^5/_{10}$–$^8/_{10}$ in)
page 317

Least chipmunk
Neotamias minimus
L: 14.4–18.4 mm ($^5/_{10}$–$^7/_{10}$ in)
page 268

Marsh rice rat
Oryzomys palustris
L: 15.2–18.5 mm ($^6/_{10}$–$^7/_{10}$ in)
page 323

Montane vole
Microtus montanus
L: 15.1–18.5 mm ($^6/_{10}$–$^7/_{10}$ in)
page 346

Meadow vole (field mouse)
Microtus pennsylvanicus
L: 15.6–19.3 mm ($^6/_{10}$–$^8/_{10}$ in)
page 347

Southern flying squirrel
Glaucomys volans
L: 18.2–20.0 mm ($^7/_{10}$–$^8/_{10}$ in)
page 293

Ermine or short-tailed weasel
Mustela erminea
L: 15.2–24.9 mm ($^6/_{10}$–1 in)
page 424

Desert kangaroo rat
Dipodomys deserti
L: 17.8–20.5 mm ($^7/_{10}$–$^8/_{10}$ in)
page 312

Hispid cotton rat
Sigmodon hispidus
L: 17.9–22.6 mm ($^7/_{10}$–$^9/_{10}$ in)
page 332

Eastern mole
Scalopus aquaticus
L: 19.4–21.8 mm ($^8/_{10}$–$^9/_{10}$ in)
page 219

Hairy-tailed mole
Parascalops breweri
L: 19.2–21.6 mm ($^8/_{10}$–$^9/_{10}$ in)
page 218

Star-nosed mole
Condylura cristata
L: 19.5–21.9 mm ($^8/_{10}$–$^9/_{10}$ in)
page 221

Thirteen-lined ground squirrel
Spermophilus tridecemlineatus
L: 18.3–25.4 mm ($^7/_{10}$–1 in)
page 279

Mexican long-tongued bat
Choeronycteris mexicana
L: 20.9–22.5 mm ($^8/_{10}$–$^9/_{10}$ in)
page 229

Broad-footed mole
Scapanus latimanus
L: 19.7–23.5 mm ($^8/_{10}$–$^9/_{10}$ in)
page 215

White-tailed antelope squirrel
Ammospermophilus leucurus
L: 20.2–23.4 mm ($^8/_{10}$–$^9/_{10}$ in)
page 274

Brown lemming
Lemmus trimucronatus
L: 17.9–23.0 mm ($^7/_{10}$–$^9/_{10}$ in)
page 351

Eastern chipmunk
Tamias striatus
L: 20.7–23.7 mm ($^8/_{10}$–$^9/_{10}$ in)
page 269

Western bonneted bat
Eumops perotis
L: 21.9–24.0 mm ($^8/_{10}$–$^9/_{10}$ in)
page 238

Northern flying squirrel
Glaucomys sabrinus
L: 21.7–27.2 mm ($^8/_{10}$–1$^1/_{10}$ in)
page 291

Botta's pocket gopher
Thomomys bottae
L: 20.3–30.1 mm ($^8/_{10}$–1$^2/_{10}$ in)
page 296

Desert woodrat
Neotoma lepida
L: 22.0–26.2 mm ($^9/_{10}$–1 in)
page 338

White-throated woodrat
Neotoma albigula
L: 21.1–26.1 mm ($^8/_{10}$–1 in)
page 334

Golden-mantled ground squirrel
Spermophilus lateralis
L: 23.0–27.7 mm ($^9/_{10}$–1$^1/_{10}$ in)
page 277

Long-tailed weasel
Mustela frenata
L: 19.7–31.9 mm ($^8/_{10}$–1$^3/_{10}$ in)
page 426

Red squirrel
Tamiasciurus hudsonicus
L: 24.5–29.3 mm (1–1$^2/_{10}$ in)
page 290

Norway rat
Rattus norvegicus
L: 25.8–29.0 mm (1–1$^1/_{10}$ in)
page 339

Townsend's mole
Scapanus townsendii
L: 26.4–29.7 mm (1–1$^2/_{10}$ in)
page 216

Bushy-tailed woodrat
Neotoma cinerea
L: 26.0–30.2 mm (1–1$^2/_{10}$ in)
page 336

Plains pocket gopher
Geomys bursarius
L: 25.8–39.5 mm (1–1$^6/_{10}$ in)
page 298

Life-size Mammal Jaws

American pika
Ochotona princeps
L: 25.8–34.6 mm (1–1^4/$_{10}$ in)
page 248

Yellow-faced pocket gopher
Cratogeomys castanops
L: 27.0–38.2 mm (1^1/$_{10}$–1^5/$_{10}$ in)
page 300

Eastern gray squirrel
Sciurus carolinensis
L: 31.0–36.0 mm (1^2/$_{10}$–1^4/$_{10}$ in)
page 284

Eastern fox squirrel
Sciurus niger
L: 26.4–42.7 mm (1–1^7/$_{10}$ in)
page 288

Rock squirrel
Spermophilus variegatus
L: 32.5–40.3 mm (1^3/$_{10}$–1^6/$_{10}$ in)
page 281

Western spotted skunk
Spilogale gracilis
L: 29.7–40.5 mm (1^2/$_{10}$–1^6/$_{10}$ in)
page 446

California ground squirrel
Spermophilus beecheyi
L: 31.8–39.7 mm (1^3/$_{10}$–1^6/$_{10}$ in)
page 276

Pygmy rabbit
Brachylagus idahoensis
L: 31.5–40.4 mm (1^2/$_{10}$–1^6/$_{10}$ in)
page 249

American mink
Mustela vison
L: 30.6–47.3 mm (1^2/$_{10}$–1^9/$_{10}$ in)
page 432

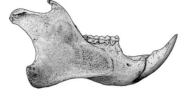

Western gray squirrel
Sciurus griseus
L: 37.8–42.3 mm (1^5/$_{10}$–1^7/$_{10}$ in)
page 286

Black-footed ferret
Mustela nigripes
L: 39.0–44.3 mm (1^5/$_{10}$–1^7/$_{10}$ in)
page 429

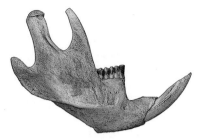

Common muskrat
Ondatra zibethicus
L: 38.8–47.3 mm (1⁵/₁₀–1⁹/₁₀ in)
page 349

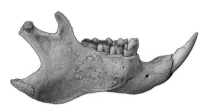

Black-tailed prairie dog
Cynomys ludovicianus
L: 39.2–45.1 mm (1⁵/₁₀–1⁸/₁₀ in)
page 282

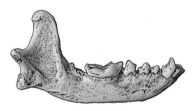

White-backed hog-nosed skunk
Conepatus leuconotus
L: 40.7–52.6 mm (1⁶/₁₀–2¹/₁₀ in)
page 451

Mountain beaver or aplodontia
Aplodontia rufa
L: 42.0–51.3 mm (1⁷/₁₀–2 in)
page 263

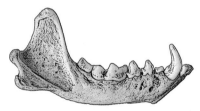

Striped skunk
Mephitis mephitis
L: 42.0–56.2 mm (1⁷/₁₀–2²/₁₀ in)
page 449

American marten
Martes americanus
L: 41.2–57.4 mm (1⁶/₁₀–2³/₁₀ in)
page 419

Desert cottontail
Sylvilagus audubonii
L: 43.2–52.5 mm (1⁷/₁₀–2¹/₁₀ in)
page 251

Brush rabbit
Sylvilagus bachmani
L: 48.1–54.6 mm (1⁹/₁₀–2¹/₁₀ in)
page 252

Ringtail
Bassariscus astutus
L: 46.5–58.7 mm (1⁸/₁₀–2³/₁₀ in)
page 410

Yellow-bellied marmot
Marmota flaviventris
L: 46.6–62.7 mm (1⁸/₁₀–2⁵/₁₀ in)
page 271

Snowshoe hare
Lepus americanus
L: 52.2–64.2 mm (2¹/₁₀–2⁵/₁₀ in)
page 256

Eastern cottontail
Sylvilagus floridanus
L: 53.2–60.1 mm (2¹/₁₀–2⁴/₁₀ in)
page 254

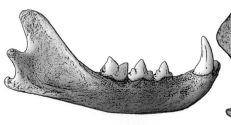

Margay
Leopardus wiedii
L: 52.5–61.7 mm (1⁶/₁₀–2⁴/₁₀ in)
page 463

Mexican black agouti
Dasyprocta mexicana
L: 60.8 mm (2⁴/₁₀ in)
page 363

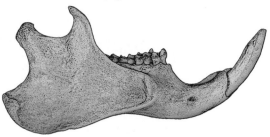

Woodchuck or groundhog
Marmota monax
L: 52.1–70.5 mm (2¹/₁₀–2⁸/₁₀ in)
page 272

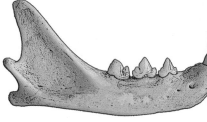

Domestic cat
Felis catus
L: 50.8–65.9 mm (2–2⁶/₁₀ in)
page 456

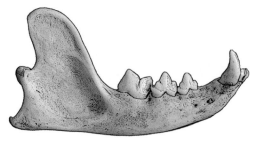

Jaguarundi
Herpailurus yaguarondi
L: 54.9–67.8 mm
(2²/₁₀–2⁷/₁₀ in)
page 464

Black-tailed jackrabbit
Lepus californicus
L: 60.4–73.7 mm
(2⁴/₁₀–2⁹/₁₀ in)
page 258

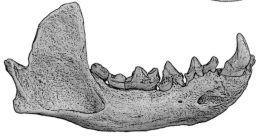

Northern river otter
Lontra canadensis
L: 59.8–72.6 mm
(2⁴/₁₀–2⁹/₁₀ in)
page 439

White-tailed jackrabbit
Lepus townsendii
L: 58.4–72.9 mm
(2³/₁₀–2⁹/₁₀ in)
page 259

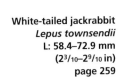

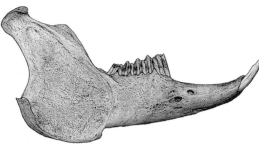

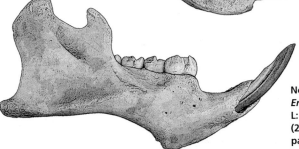

North American porcupine
Erethizon dorsatum
L: 62.8–82.7 mm
(2⁵/₁₀–3³/₁₀ in)
page 358

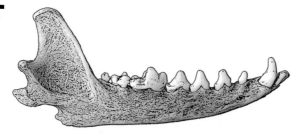

Island fox
Urocyon littoralis
L: 66.5–75.3 mm
($2^6/_{10}$–3 in)
page 390

Nine-banded armadillo
Dasypus novemcinctus
L: 71.6–79.2 mm
($2^8/_{10}$–$3^1/_{10}$ in)
page 243

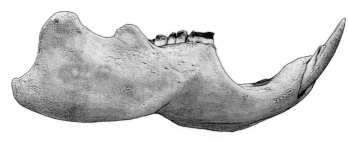

Paca
Agouti paca
L: 63.7–100.1 mm
($2^5/_{10}$–$3^9/_{10}$ in)
page 365

Bobcat
Lynx rufus
L: 72.2–94.9 mm
($2^8/_{10}$–$3^7/_{10}$ in)
page 468

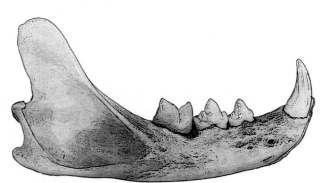

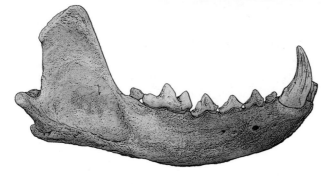

Fisher
Martes pennanti
L: 64.1–87.2 mm
($2^5/_{10}$–$3^4/_{10}$ in)
page 421

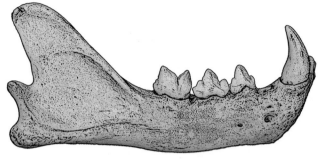

Ocelot
Leopardus pardalis
L: 74.7–96.4 mm
(2⁹/₁₀–3⁸/₁₀ in)
page 461

Canada lynx
Lynx canadensis
L: 76.6–88.2 mm
(3–3⁵/₁₀ in)
page 466

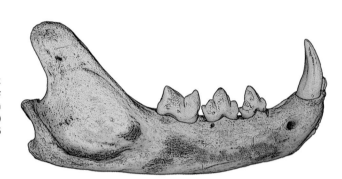

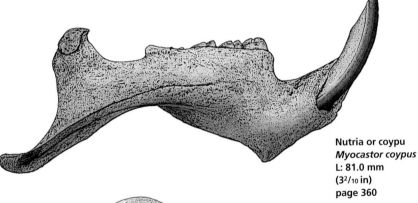

Nutria or coypu
Myocastor coypus
L: 81.0 mm
(3²/₁₀ in)
page 360

Northern raccoon
Procyon lotor
L: 72.5–91.3 mm
(2⁹/₁₀–3⁶/₁₀ in)
page 412

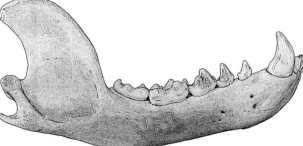

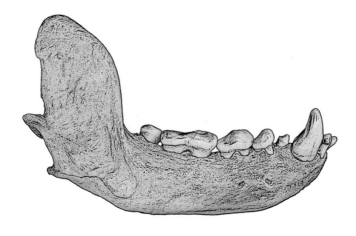

Sea otter
Enhydra lutris
L: 77.3–95.8 mm
(3–3⁸/₁₀ in)
page 441

Kit fox
Vulpes macrotis
L: 75.6–92.0 mm
(3–3⁶/₁₀ in)
page 382

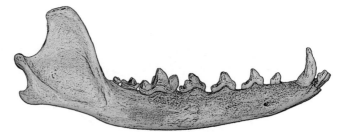

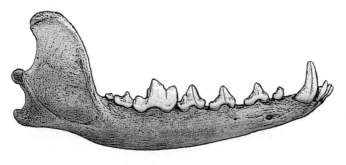

Swift fox
Vulpes velox
L: 80.1–95.6 mm
(3²/₁₀–3⁸/₁₀ in)
page 384

Virginia opossum
Didelphis virginiana
L: 62.4–116.9 mm
(2⁵/₁₀–4⁶/₁₀ in)
page 195

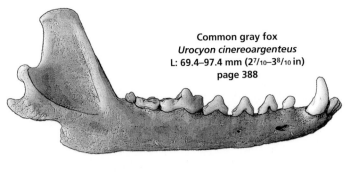

Common gray fox
Urocyon cinereoargenteus
L: 69.4–97.4 mm (2^{7}/$_{10}$–3^{8}/$_{10}$ in)
page 388

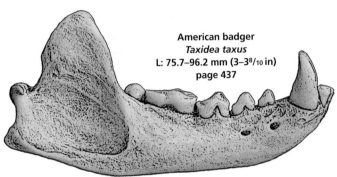

American badger
Taxidea taxus
L: 75.7–96.2 mm (3–3^{8}/$_{10}$ in)
page 437

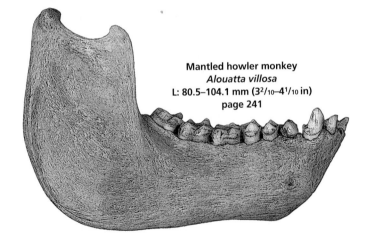

Mantled howler monkey
Alouatta villosa
L: 80.5–104.1 mm (3^{2}/$_{10}$–4^{1}/$_{10}$ in)
page 241

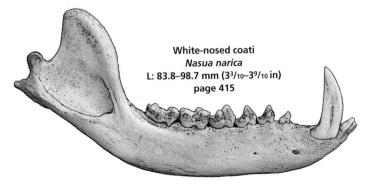

White-nosed coati
Nasua narica
L: 83.8–98.7 mm (3^{3}/$_{10}$–3^{9}/$_{10}$ in)
page 415

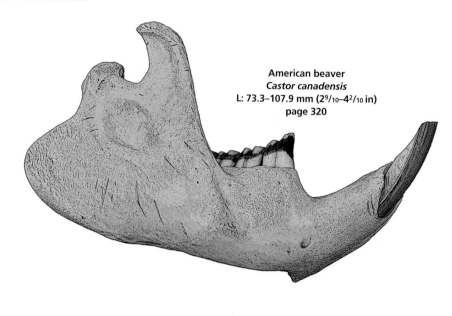

American beaver
Castor canadensis
L: 73.3–107.9 mm (2^9/$_{10}$–4^2/$_{10}$ in)
page 320

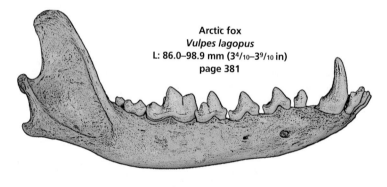

Arctic fox
Vulpes lagopus
L: 86.0–98.9 mm (3^4/$_{10}$–3^9/$_{10}$ in)
page 381

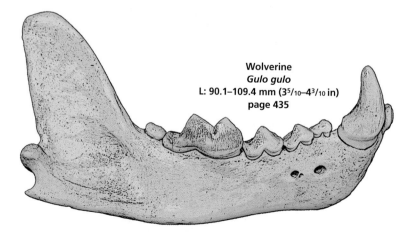

Wolverine
Gulo gulo
L: 90.1–109.4 mm (3^5/$_{10}$–4^3/$_{10}$ in)
page 435

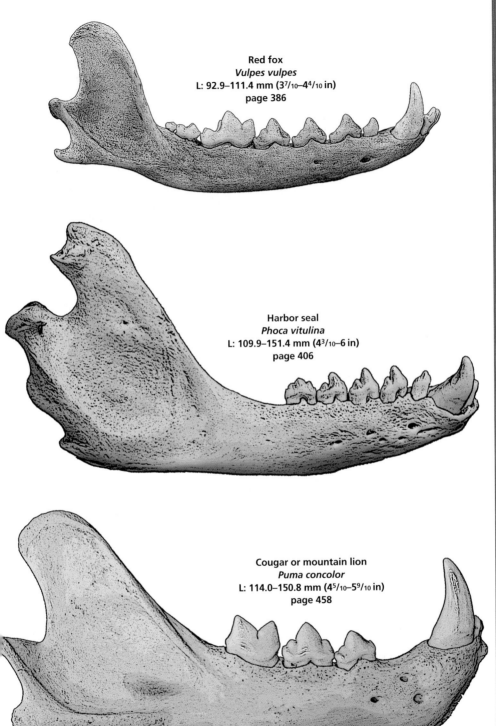

Red fox
Vulpes vulpes
L: 92.9–111.4 mm (3⁷/₁₀–4⁴/₁₀ in)
page 386

Harbor seal
Phoca vitulina
L: 109.9–151.4 mm (4³/₁₀–6 in)
page 406

Cougar or mountain lion
Puma concolor
L: 114.0–150.8 mm (4⁵/₁₀–5⁹/₁₀ in)
page 458

Coyote
Canis latrans
L: 123.8–159.6 mm
(4^9/$_{10}$–6^3/$_{10}$ in)
page 373

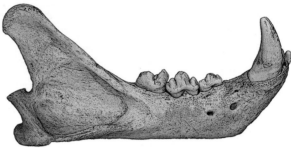

Jaguar
Panthera onca
L: 139.0–173.6 mm
(5^5/$_{10}$–6^8/$_{10}$ in)
page 471

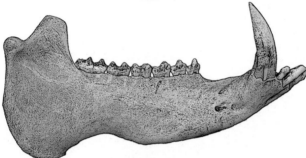

Collared peccary
or javelina
Pecari tajacu
L: 144.2–170.4 mm
(5^7/$_{10}$–6^7/$_{10}$ in)
page 485

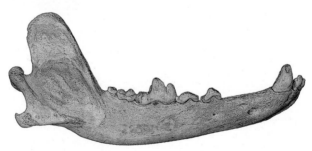

Red wolf
Canis rufus
L: 141.6–180.0 mm
(5^6/$_{10}$–7^1/$_{10}$ in)
page 379

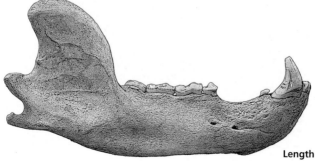

American black bear
Ursus americanus
L: 144–215.8 mm
(5^7/$_{10}$–8^5/$_{10}$ in)
page 394

Length of all jaws 50 percent
of life-size

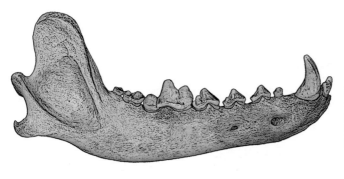

Eastern timber wolf
Canis lycaon
L: 155.0–194.4 mm
(6¹/₁₀–7⁷/₁₀ in)
page 377

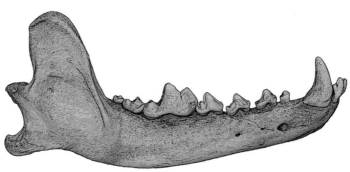

Gray wolf
Canis lupus
L: 155.0–210.3 mm
(6¹/₁₀–8³/₁₀ in)
page 375

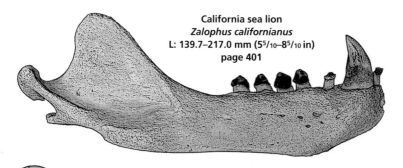

California sea lion
Zalophus californianus
L: 139.7–217.0 mm (5⁵/₁₀–8⁵/₁₀ in)
page 401

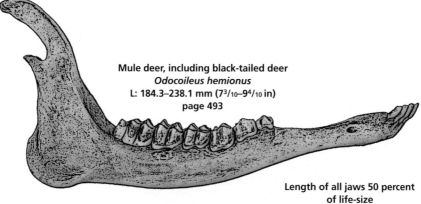

Mule deer, including black-tailed deer
Odocoileus hemionus
L: 184.3–238.1 mm (7³/₁₀–9⁴/₁₀ in)
page 493

Length of all jaws 50 percent
of life-size

Length of Mammal Jaws at 50 Percent

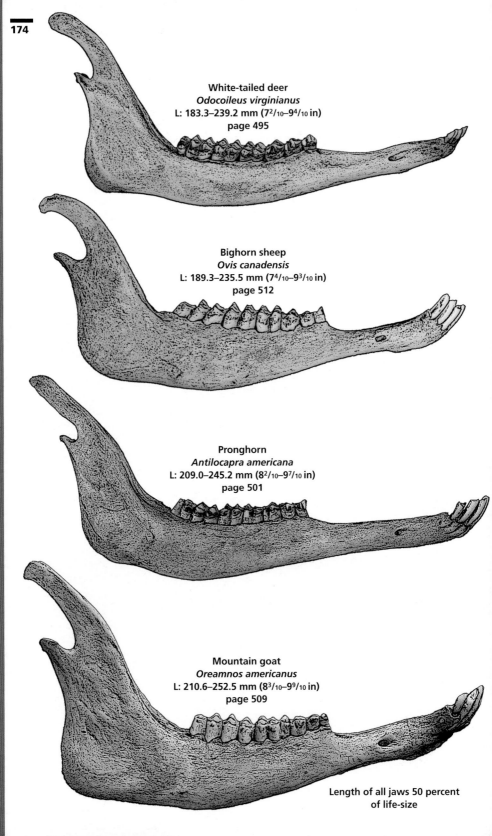

White-tailed deer
Odocoileus virginianus
L: 183.3–239.2 mm ($7^2/_{10}$–$9^4/_{10}$ in)
page 495

Bighorn sheep
Ovis canadensis
L: 189.3–235.5 mm ($7^4/_{10}$–$9^3/_{10}$ in)
page 512

Pronghorn
Antilocapra americana
L: 209.0–245.2 mm ($8^2/_{10}$–$9^7/_{10}$ in)
page 501

Mountain goat
Oreamnos americanus
L: 210.6–252.5 mm ($8^3/_{10}$–$9^9/_{10}$ in)
page 509

Length of all jaws 50 percent
of life-size

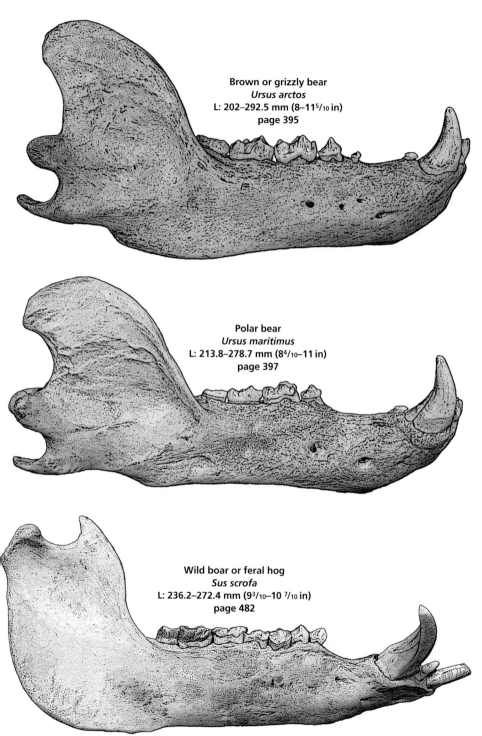

Brown or grizzly bear
Ursus arctos
L: 202–292.5 mm (8–11$^{5}/_{10}$ in)
page 395

Polar bear
Ursus maritimus
L: 213.8–278.7 mm (8$^{4}/_{10}$–11 in)
page 397

Wild boar or feral hog
Sus scrofa
L: 236.2–272.4 mm (9$^{3}/_{10}$–10 $^{7}/_{10}$ in)
page 482

Length of all jaws 50 percent
of life-size

Length of Mammal Jaws at 50 Percent

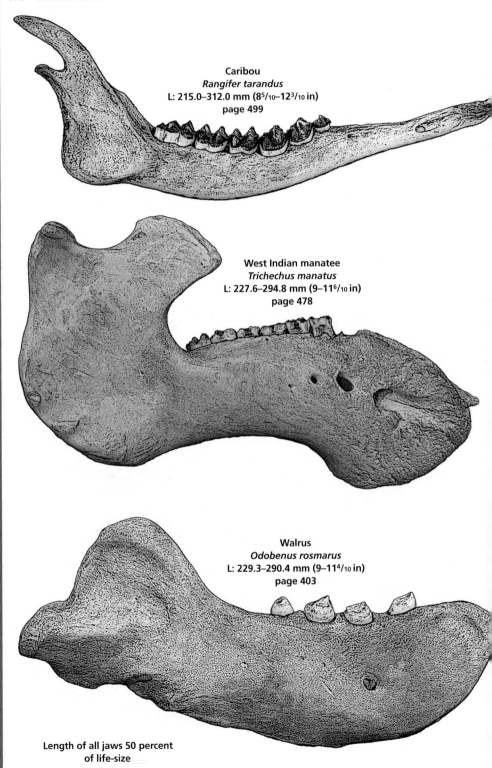

Caribou
Rangifer tarandus
L: 215.0–312.0 mm (8⁵/₁₀–12³/₁₀ in)
page 499

West Indian manatee
Trichechus manatus
L: 227.6–294.8 mm (9–11⁶/₁₀ in)
page 478

Walrus
Odobenus rosmarus
L: 229.3–290.4 mm (9–11⁴/₁₀ in)
page 403

Length of all jaws 50 percent
of life-size

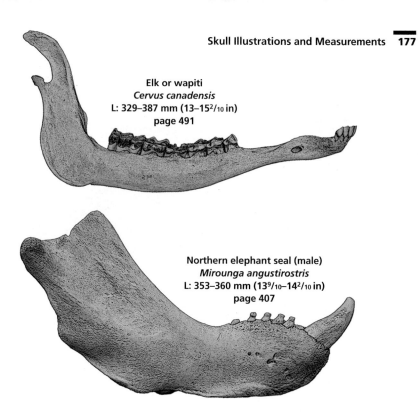

Elk or wapiti
Cervus canadensis
L: 329–387 mm (13–15²/₁₀ in)
page 491

Northern elephant seal (male)
Mirounga angustirostris
L: 353–360 mm (13⁹/₁₀–14²/₁₀ in)
page 407

Bottlenose dolphin
Tursiops truncatus
L: 360–439 mm (14²/₁₀–17³/₁₀ in)
page 475

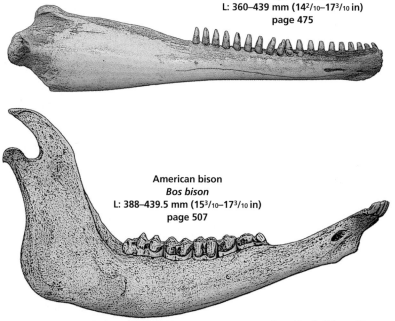

American bison
Bos bison
L: 388–439.5 mm (15³/₁₀–17³/₁₀ in)
page 507

Length of all jaws 25 percent
of life-size

Length of Mammal Jaws at 25 Percent

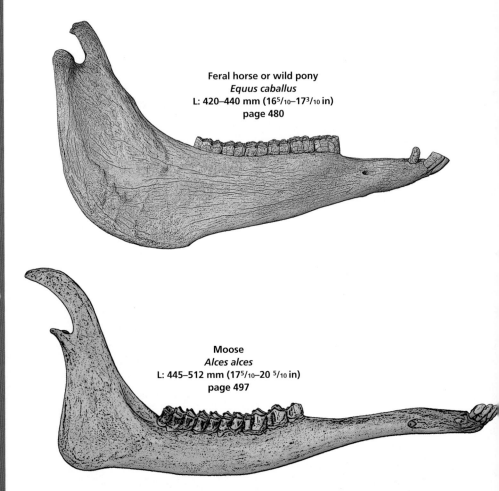

Feral horse or wild pony
Equus caballus
L: 420–440 mm (16^5/$_{10}$–17^3/$_{10}$ in)
page 480

Moose
Alces alces
L: 445–512 mm (17^5/$_{10}$–20 ^{5}/$_{10}$ in)
page 497

Length of all jaws 25 percent of life-size

Bird Skulls

American goldfinch
Carduelis tristis
GL: 21.4–26.0 mm (⁸/₁₀–1 in)
page 691

Ruby-crowned kinglet
Regulus calendula
GL: 23.8–27.2 mm (⁹/₁₀–1¹/₁₀ in)
page 675

Black-capped chickadee
Poecile atrocapillus
GL: 23.6–27.7 mm (⁹/₁₀–1¹/₁₀ in)
page 673

Cliff swallow
Petrochelidon pyrrhonota
GL: 26.6–29.0 mm (1–1¹/₁₀ in)
page 672

Yellow warbler
Dendroica petechia
GL: 26.5–30.1 mm (1–1²/₁₀ in)
page 681

Dark-eyed junco
Junco hyemalis
GL: 26.6–30.0 mm (1–1²/₁₀ in)
page 684

House wren
Troglodytes aedon
GL: 27.4–32.7 mm (1¹/₁₀–1³/₁₀ in)
page 674

Song sparrow
Melospiza melodia
GL: 26.8–31.0 mm (1¹/₁₀–1²/₁₀ in)
page 683

Northern bobwhite
Colinus virginianus
GL: 32.8–36.8 mm (1³/₁₀–1⁴/₁₀ in)
page 630

Anna's hummingbird
Calypte anna
GL: 30.9–34.5 mm (1²/₁₀–1⁴/₁₀ in)
page 661

Red crossbill
Loxia curvirostra
GL: 30.9–38.1 mm (1²/₁₀–1⁵/₁₀ in)
page 690

Eastern phoebe
Sayornis phoebe
GL: 33.2–35.0 mm (1³/₁₀–1⁴/₁₀ in)
page 665

Northern cardinal
Cardinalis cardinalis
GL: 32.2–37.2 mm (1³/₁₀–1⁵/₁₀ in)
page 685

Spotted towhee
Pipilo maculatus
GL: 31.9–35.8 mm (1³/₁₀–1⁴/₁₀ in)
page 682

Common nighthawk
Chordeiles minor
GL: 33.2–37.5 mm (1³/₁₀–1⁵/₁₀ in)
page 660

Baltimore oriole
Icterus galbula
GL: 35.8–40.0 mm (1⁴/₁₀–1⁶/₁₀ in)
page 689

Eastern kingbird
Tyrannus tyrannus
GL: 36.2–41.7 mm (1⁴/₁₀–1⁶/₁₀ in)
page 666

Evening grosbeak
Coccothraustes vespertinus
GL: 36.2–41.8 mm (1⁴/₁₀–1⁶/₁₀ in)
page 692

American kestrel
Falco sparverius
GL: 40.0–44.5 mm (1⁴/₁₀–1⁸/₁₀ in)
page 640

Mourning dove
Zenaida macroura
GL: 36.6–44.4 mm (1⁴/₁₀–1⁷/₁₀ in)
page 654

Red-winged blackbird
Agelaius phoeniceus
GL: 34.3–48.7 mm (1⁴/₁₀–1⁹/₁₀ in)
page 686

Loggerhead shrike
Lanius ludovicianus
GL: 40.5–45.3 mm (1⁴/₁₀–1⁸/₁₀ in)
page 667

Northern mockingbird
Mimus polyglottos
GL: 40.5–46.5 mm (1⁴/₁₀–1⁸/₁₀ in)
page 677

American robin
Turdus migratorius
GL: 45.3–50.1 mm (1⁸/₁₀–2 in)
page 676

Spotted sandpiper
Actitis macularia
GL: 41.7–53.8 mm (1⁶/₁₀–2¹/₁₀ in)
page 645

Killdeer
Charadrius vociferous
GL: 46.2–50.5 mm (1⁸/₁₀–2 in)
page 643

Western meadowlark
Sturnella neglecta
GL: 49.4–63.3 mm (1⁹/₁₀–2⁵/₁₀ in)
page 687

Brown thrasher
Toxostoma rufum
GL: 49.0–55.5 mm (1⁹/₁₀–2²/₁₀ in)
page 678

European starling
Sturnus vulgaris
GL: 48.2–59.1 mm (1⁹/₁₀–2³/₁₀ in)
page 680

Ruffed grouse
Bonasa umbellus
GL: 50.6–58.7 mm (2–2³/₁₀ in)
page 628

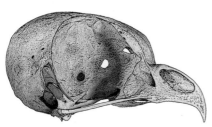

Eastern screech-owl
Otus asio
GL: 53.3–57.1 mm (2¹/₁₀–2²/₁₀ in)
page 658

Blue jay
Cyanocitta cristata
GL: 54.2–61.5 mm (2¹/₁₀–2⁴/₁₀ in)
page 668

Common grackle
Quiscalus quiscula
GL: 53.7–64.1 mm (2¹/₁₀–2⁵/₁₀ in)
page 688

Cooper's hawk
Accipiter cooperii
GL: 53.8–63.3 mm (2¹/₁₀–2⁵/₁₀ in)
page 638

California thrasher
Toxostoma redivivum
GL: 54.5–66.3 mm (2^1/$_{10}$–2^6/$_{10}$ in)
page 679

American coot
Fulica americana
GL: 59.6–68.2 mm (2^3/$_{10}$–2^7/$_{10}$ in)
page 642

Nothern flicker
Colaptes auratus
GL: 55.8–74.7 mm (2^2/$_{10}$–2^9/$_{10}$ in)
page 663

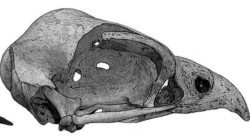

Peregrine falcon
Falco peregrinus
GL: 62.7–73.2 mm (2^5/$_{10}$–2^9/$_{10}$ in)
page 641

Bufflehead
Bucephala albeola
GL: 65.2–73.8 mm
(2^6/$_{10}$–2^9/$_{10}$ in)
page 626

Common tern
Sterna hiruno
GL: 63.6–77.9 mm
(2^5/$_{10}$–3^1/$_{10}$ in)
page 650

Black-billed magpie
Pica hudsonia
GL: 61.9–72.0 mm
(2^4/$_{10}$–2^8/$_{10}$ in)
page 669

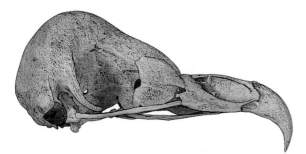

Barn owl
Tyto alba
GL: 71.8–77.4 mm
(2⁸/₁₀–3 in)
page 656

Pileated woodpecker
Dryocopus pileatus
GL: 74.3–83.8 mm
(2⁹/₁₀–3⁴/₁₀ in)
page 664

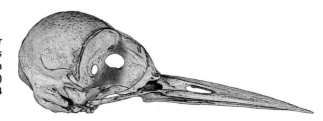

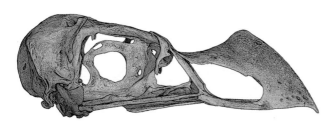

Horned puffin
Fractercula corniculata
GL: 77.7–85.3 mm
(3¹/₁₀–3⁴/₁₀ in)
page 653

Red-tailed hawk
Buteo jamaicensis
GL: 76.5–88.5 mm
(3–3⁵/₁₀ in)
page 639

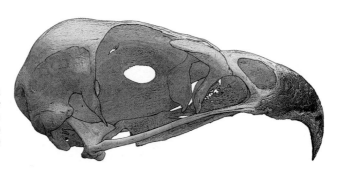

Greater roadrunner
Geococcyx californianus
GL: 72.5–99.7 mm
(2⁹/₁₀–3⁹/₁₀ in)
page 655

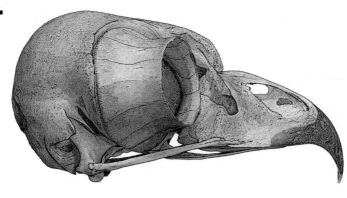

Great horned owl
Bubo virginianus
GL: 80.1–98.9 mm
(3²/₁₀–3⁹/₁₀ in)
page 659

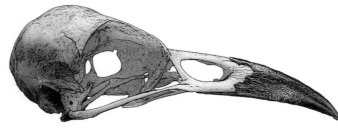

American crow
Corvus brachyrhynchos
GL: 75.1–95.1 mm
(3–3⁷/₁₀ in)
page 670

Turkey vulture
Cathartes aura
GL: 83.2–98.3 mm
(3³/₁₀–3⁹/₁₀ in)
page 636

Sooty shearwater
Puffinus griseus
GL: 90.9–97.5 mm (3⁶/₁₀–3⁸/₁₀ in)
page 631

Common snipe
Gallinago gallinago
GL: 85.4–99.8 mm (3⁵/₁₀–3⁹/₁₀ in)
page 648

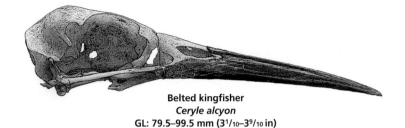

Belted kingfisher
Ceryle alcyon
GL: 79.5–99.5 mm (3^1/$_{10}$–3^9/$_{10}$ in)
page 662

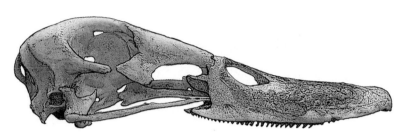

Mallard
Anas platyrhynchos
GL: 95.8–116.7 mm (3^8/$_{10}$–4^6/$_{10}$ in)
page 622

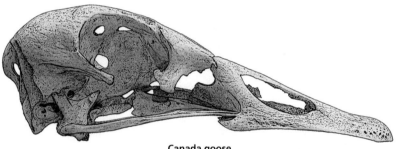

Canada goose
Branta canadensis
GL: 83.1–125.4 mm (3^3/$_{10}$–4^9/$_{10}$ in)
page 621

Northern shoveler
Anas clypeata
GL: 96.2–122.3 mm (3^8/$_{10}$–4^8/$_{10}$ in)
page 623

Common merganser
Mergus merganser
GL: 100.1–116.9 mm (3⁹/₁₀–4⁶/₁₀ in)
page 627

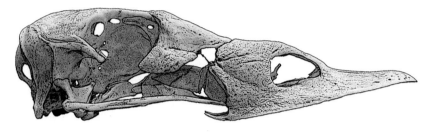

White-winged scoter
Melanitta fusca
GL: 101.1–114.3 mm (4–4⁵/₁₀ in)
page 625

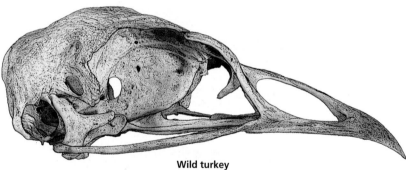

Wild turkey
Meleagris gallopavo
GL: 74.9–110.8 mm (2⁹/₁₀–4⁴/₁₀ in)
page 629

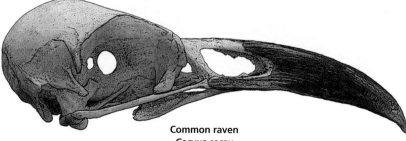

Common raven
Corvus corax
GL: 107.0–116.5 mm (4²/₁₀–4⁶/₁₀ in)
page 671

American avocet
Recurvirostra americana
GL: 107.8–141.1 mm (4^2/$_{10}$–5^6/$_{10}$ in)
page 644

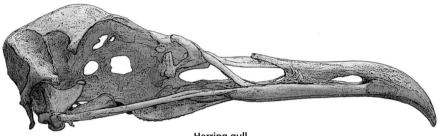

Herring gull
Larus argentatus
GL: 112.9–127.1 mm (4^4/$_{10}$–5 in)
page 649

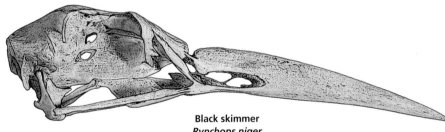

Black skimmer
Rynchops niger
GL: 101.5–138.4 mm (4–5^4/$_{10}$ in)
page 651

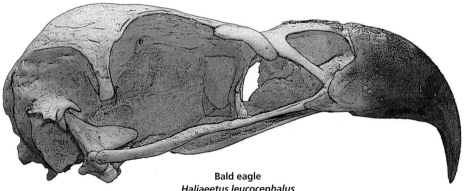

Bald eagle
Haliaeetus leucocephalus
GL: 110.3–140.0 mm (4^3/$_{10}$–5^5/$_{10}$ in)
page 637

Double-crested cormorant
Phalacrocorax auritus
GL: 118.6–138.2 mm (4⁷/₁₀–5⁴/₁₀ in)
page 633

Marbled godwit
Limosa fedoa
GL: 133.0–167.7 mm (5²/₁₀–6⁶/₁₀ in)
page 647

White-faced ibis
Plegadis chihi
GL: 138.3–184.4 mm (5⁴/₁₀–7³/₁₀ in)
page 635

Long-billed curlew
Numenius americanus
GL: 159.4–222.5 mm (6³/₁₀–8⁸/₁₀ in)
page 646

Great blue heron
Ardea herodias
GL: 193.2–222.2 mm (7⁶/₁₀–8⁷/₁₀ in)
page 634

Length of all bird skulls above at 50 percent of life-size

Brown pelican
Pelecanus occidentalis
GL: 343.0–438.0 mm (13⁵/₁₀–17²/₁₀ in)
page 632

Length of brown pelican skull 25 percent of life-size

Amphibian and Reptile Skulls

Eastern fence lizard
Sceloporus undulatus
GL: 12.08 mm ($^5/_{10}$ in)
page 700

Garter snake
Thamnophis sirtalis
GL: 15.54 mm ($^6/_{10}$ in)
page 701

Green anole
Anolis carolinensis
GL: 20.64 mm ($^8/_{10}$ in)
page 697

Pacific giant salamander
Dicamptodon ensatus
GL: 24.49 mm (1 in)
page 696

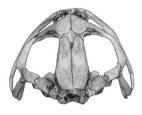

Western toad
Bufo boreas
GL: 24.56 mm (1 in)
page 694

Common chuckwalla
Sauromalus ater
GL: 37.88 mm (1$^5/_{10}$ in)
page 699

Eastern box turtle
Terrapene carolina
GL: 41.84 mm (1$^6/_{10}$ in)
page 706

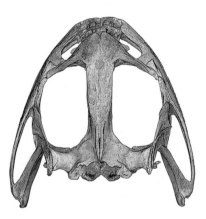

American bullfrog
Rana catesbeiana
Partial length: 43.4 mm (1$^7/_{10}$ in)
page 695

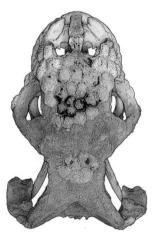

Gila monster
Heloderma suspectum
GL: 57.52 mm (2$^3/_{10}$ in)
page 698

Greatest length of skulls in millimeters and (inches)

Life-size Amphibian and Reptile Skulls

Life-size Amphibian and Reptile Skulls

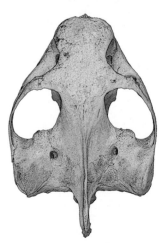

Desert tortoise
Gopherus agassizii
GL: 58.96 mm (2³/₁₀ in)
page 705

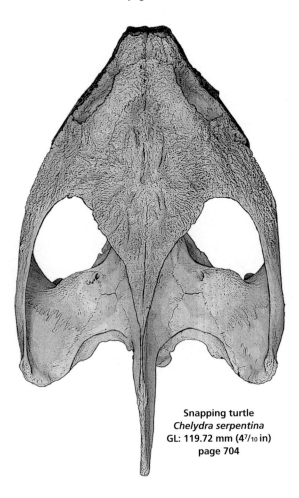

Snapping turtle
Chelydra serpentina
GL: 119.72 mm (4⁷/₁₀ in)
page 704

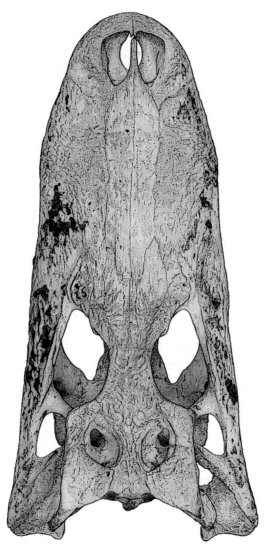

American alligator
Alligator mississippiensis
GL: 271.22 mm (10⁷/₁₀ in)
page 702

Greatest Length of Amphibian and Reptile Skulls at 50 Percent

Greatest length of skull 50 percent of life-size

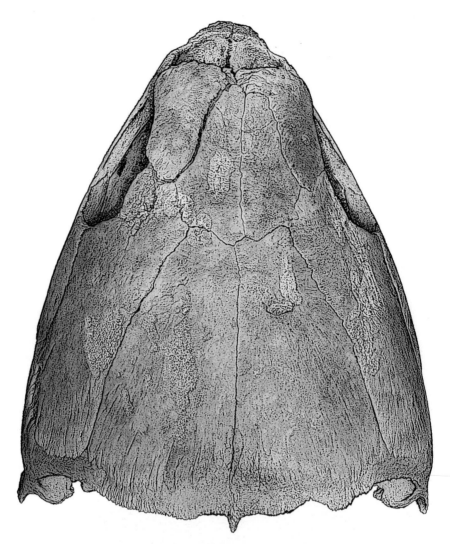

Leatherback sea turtle
Dermochelys coriacea
GL: 272.0 mm (10^{7}/$_{10}$ in)
page 703

Greatest length of skull 50 percent of life-size

Species Accounts

Order Didelphimorphia: American Marsupials

Family Didelphidae: Opossums

The Virginia opossum is the sole marsupial mammal living north of Mexico, though the occasional mouse opossum does appear in fruit boats in various harbors. The opossum skull exhibits impressive dentition and more teeth than any other North American land mammal. Adults have fifty teeth, many of them jagged and sharply cusped. Numerous teeth, a large sagittal crest, and a small braincase are characteristic of this animal.

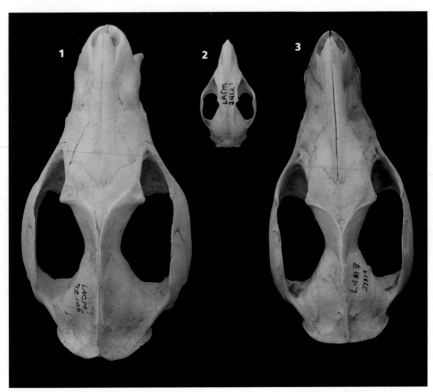

Several members of the family Didelphidae: 1. Virginia opossum *(D. virginiana)*, 2. Mexican mouse opossum *(Marmosa mexicana)*, 3. Common opossum *(D. marsupialis)*. NATURAL HISTORY MUSEUM OF LOS ANGELES COUNTY 92105, 024121, 27319.

Virginia opossum, *Didelphis virginiana*

Greatest length: 77.9–145.8 mm ($3^1/_{10}$–$5^7/_{10}$ in.) (full table of measurements page 518, life-size image page 128, life-size jaw page 168)

Specimen illustrated: Immature male, LACM 92105

Dentition: i 5/4 c 1/1 p 3/3 m 4/4, total 50 in adults.

Dorsal: Opossum skulls have a slender, triangular outline, with stout, wide-spreading zygomata and small braincases. The rostrum is long, triangular, and strong. The nasals (1) are very long and slender toward the anterior but flare widely (2) as they extend to the posterior. Heavy, wide-spreading zygomatic arches (3) are approximately parallel; zygomatic plates (4) are smaller. Postorbital processes (5) are stout and triangular. The orbits (6) are smaller and less forward facing, and the temporal fossa (7) is large. The interorbital breadth (8) is far greater than the significantly constricted postorbital breadth (9). The braincase (10) is very small and ovoid, less than one-third of the greatest length of skull; temporal ridges are well developed and converge high on the skull to form a large sagittal crest (11), which runs longer than the actual braincase. Occipital crests (12) are well developed.

Ventral: The palate (13) is exceptionally long, extending more than 50 percent of the greatest length of skull and well beyond the posterior molars; the incisive foramina (14) are large, slitlike, and well forward of the canines. Palatal fenestrae (15) occur to the posterior, and the squared posterior edge (16) of the palate is curved down. The pterygoid region (17) is very narrow. The mandibular fossae (18) are less developed. The auditory bullae (19) are tiny. The foramen magnum (20) is very small, and

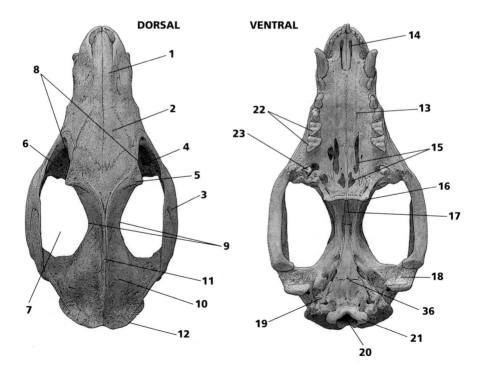

the occipital condyles (21) are reduced. The toothrows are very long; the posterior molars (22) are flattened. Premolars and molars are reduced compared with those of carnivores and omnivores. The fourth molar (23) in this animal is erupting, and the basio-occipital suture is open (36).

Lateral: From the convex sagittal crest, the dorsolateral outline slopes smoothly and gradually to the tips of the nasals. The premaxillaries (24) may extend just farther than the nasals, but they are closely aligned; the nasal vacuity (25) is small. The infraorbital foramen (26) is small and visible low on the side of the rostrum. The post-orbital processes (27) on the zygomatic arches are just bumps. The auditory meatus is obscured. The premolars and molars (28) are tightly packed together. The canines (29) are long, very slender, and slightly recurved. Note the large sagittal crest (30) from this perspective.

Mandible: The body is slender, strongly curved, and tapering to the anterior. The coronoid process (31) is large, squared, and angled to the posterior; the posterior surface (32) is concave. The condyle (33) is aligned with the toothrow, large, stout, and barrel-shaped. The angular process (34) is reduced to a small bump to the posterior but also inflected inward. Two mental foramina (35) are evident. The dentition is jagged, with little to no space between teeth.

Similar species: Foxes, raccoons, fishers.

Notes: The sutures between many bones remain open regardless of age and are therefore less useful as a gauge in estimating age. The greatest length of skull is also highly variable in adults.

Petrides (1949, in McManus 1974) created a means of estimating age in opossums by analyzing the dentition: Dentition at 3 months: i 5/2 c 1/1 p 2/2 m 0/0. Dentition at 4 months: i 5/4 c 1/1 p 3/3 m 1/2. Dentition at 5–8 months: i 5/4 c 1/1 p 3/3 m 3/4.

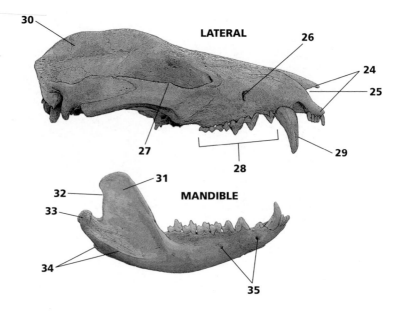

Gardner (1982) reports that the sex of adult opossums can be determined by measuring the length and width of upper canines. Using calipers, measuring at the palate from the front of the tooth to the backside: 6.4–9.8 mm for males and 4.5–6.4 mm for females. For the height of the same tooth, males measure 13.7–20.5 mm and females 9.4–12.8 mm.

Order Insectivora: Moles, Shrews

Family Soricidae: Shrews

The shrews are a large group of tiny insectivores living in nearly every environment across North America. The numerous sharp and pigmented teeth are ideally adapted for capturing and crushing insect exoskeletons and ripping into the softer bodies of worms or mammals; the two foremost incisors in both the cranium and the mandible are greatly enlarged and point forward, and are often used like forceps when apprehending and holding insect prey. The tiny skulls of shrews do not have any zygomatic arches or auditory bullae; instead, they have tympanic rings.

The long-tailed shrews are notoriously difficult to distinguish from one another, and the shape and position of the unicuspid teeth, those small teeth just behind the large procumbent first incisor and before the larger fourth premolar, become essential in identification. Their total number (three to five unicuspids), size relative to one another, and how many are visible from the lateral perspective are other useful keys (refer to page 199). The degree to which the upper incisors are separated and the presence of a median tine also differentiate among some of the smaller shrews (refer below). Here are presented visual references of the unicuspid patterns and front incisors to complement that which is provided under individual species accounts.

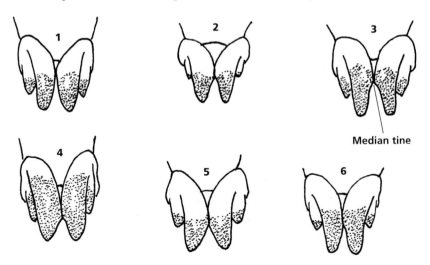

Median tine

Upper incisors of various Sorex species, viewed from the front: 1. Vagrant shrew *(S. vagrans)*, 2. Southeastern shrew *(S. longirostris)*, 3. Montane shrew *(S. monticolus)*, 4. Pygmy shrew *(S. hoyi)*, 5. Marsh shrew *(S. bendirii)*, 6. American water shrew *(S. palustris)*. Drawn after Junge and Hoffman (1981).

Small shrews of the genus *Sorex* are often described as being members of one of two large subgenera, *Otiosorex* or *Sorex*. One feature that supports this distinction is the presence or absence of a postmandibular canal, as described in Junge and Hoffmann (1981). The postmandibular canal is a tiny character visible only with a good loupe or microscope (refer to page 200). Its presence is characteristic of the subgenus *Sorex,* which includes Arizona shrew *(S. arizonae),* arctic shrew *(S. arcticus),* Merriam's shrew *(S. merriami),* Trowbridge's shrew *(S. trowbridgii),* and tundra shrew *(S. tundrensis).*

Its absence is characteristic of the subgenus *Otiosorex,* which includes marsh shrew *(S. bendirii),* American water shrew *(S. palustris),* Southeastern shrew *(S. longirostris),* smoky shrew *(S. fumeus),* rock shrew *(S. dispar),* Gaspé shrew *(S. gaspensis),* vagrant shrew *(S. vagrans),* Pacific shrew *(S. pacificus),* ornate shrew *(S. ornatus),* cinereus shrew *(S. cinereus),* and Preble's shrew *(S. preblei).*

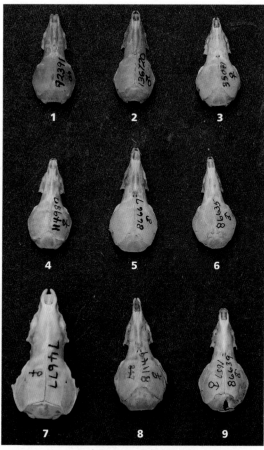

Select members of Soricidae: 1. Crawford's desert shrew, male 92391 *(Notiosorex)*, 2. Least shrew, male 136720 *(Cryptotis)*, 3. Merriam's shrew, female 35099 *(S. merriami)*, 4. Vagrant shrew, female 114980 *(S. vagrans)*, 5. Smoky shrew, male 86667 *(S. fumeus)*, 6. Cinereus shrew, male 86635 *(S. cinereus)*, 7. Northern short-tailed shrew, female 74677 *(B. brevicauda)*, 8. American water shrew, female 81149 *(S. palustris)*, 9. Arctic shrew, male 86639 *(S. arcticus)*. MUSEUM OF VERTEBRATE ZOOLOGY, UC BERKELEY.

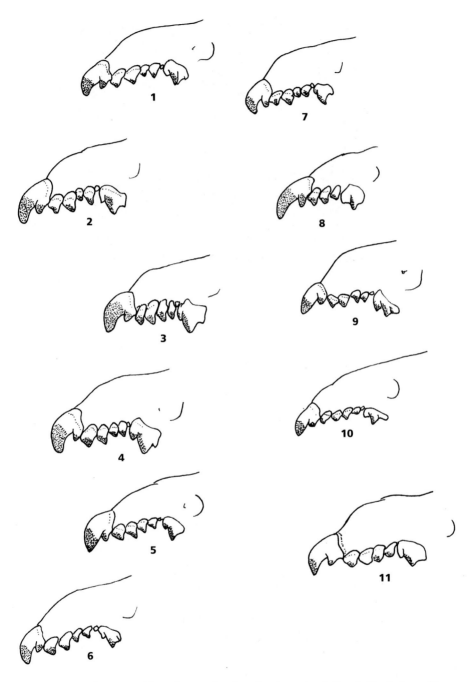

Comparison of the unicuspid toothrows of various *Sorex* species: 1. Trowbridge's shrew *(S. trowbridgii)*, 2. Ornate shrew *(S. ornatus)*, 3. Merriam's shrew *(S. merriami)*, 4. Montane shrew *(S. monticolus)*, 5. Cinereus shrew *(S. cinereus)*, 6. Marsh shrew *(S. bendirii)*, 7. American water shrew *(S. palustris)*, 8. Pygmy shrew *(S. hoyi)*, 9. Southeastern shrew *(S. longirostris)*, 10. Preble's shrew *(S. preblei)*, 11. Smoky shrew *(S. fumeus)*. Drawn after Junge and Hoffman (1981).

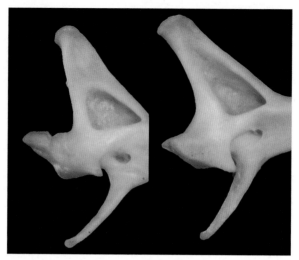

On the left is Trowbridge's shrew *(S. trowbridgii)* exhibiting the postmandibular canal (see below), and on the right the American water shrew *(S. palustris)*. Photographed with a 150 mm macro lens, cropped and enlarged. SANTA BARBARA MUSEUM OF NATURAL HISTORY VB-S213, VB-56-21.

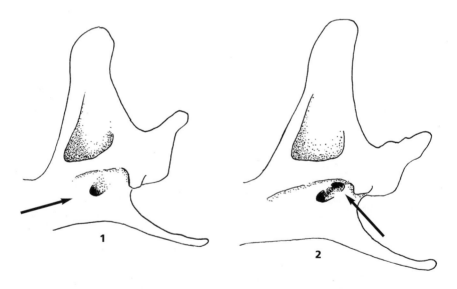

On the left (1) the postmandibular canal is absent, which is characteristic of those shrews in *Otiosorex*. On the right (2) is illustrated the postmandibular canal characteristic of shrews in the subgenus *Sorex*. Look to the main text on page 198 for a list of which species occur in which subgenus. Drawn after Junge and Hoffman (1981).

Cinereus or masked shrew, *Sorex cinereus*

Greatest length: 14.6–17.2 mm ($^6/_{10}$–$^7/_{10}$ in.) (full table of measurements page 520, life-size image page 110, life-size jaw page 159)

Specimen illustrated: Adult, SBMNH VB-135

Dentition: i 3/1 c 1/1 p 3/1 m 3/3, total 32.

Dorsal: Triangular skull overall. Rostrum (1) is elongated and more slender than in some other *Sorex* species. Braincase (2) is very round and approximately 50 percent of the greatest length of skull. The interorbital region (3) is of median breadth compared with those of other shrews. The interparietal (4) is wide and rectangular. There are no zygomatic arches, but maxillary arches (5) project outward.

Ventral: The palate (6) is long and narrow, with an abrupt posterior edge (7); it is very narrow between the anteriormost premolars (8). The foramen magnum (9) is large. There are no auditory bullae, and the tympanic bones (10) are ring-shaped. The third and fourth unicuspids (17) are about equal in size.

Lateral: Rostrum (11) is not as deep (or tall) as in other *Sorex*. The braincase (12) is only slightly elevated, and a smooth dorsal line follows the rostrum to the braincase. The posterior of the skull (13) is rounded. The nasal vacuity (14) is long and sloping, as the nasals (15) extend far short of the premaxillaries (16). The dentition is of a median weight. The first incisor is large and procumbent; the remaining teeth are unicuspid and peglike. The teeth are pigmented, and the pigment extends onto the inner ridges of the unicuspids.

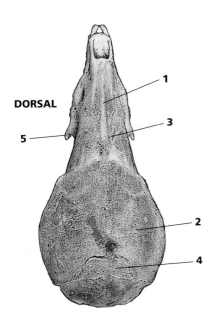

DORSAL

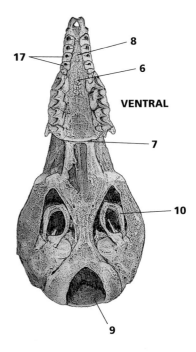

VENTRAL

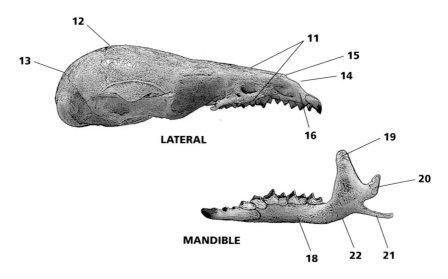

LATERAL

MANDIBLE

Mandible: The mandible is composed of a long, slender body (18). The coronoid process (19) is tall and triangular, rising straight upward from the posterior of the toothrow. The condyloid process (20) is double-faceted, having two projections, whereas moles have but one. The angular process (21) is long and very thin. The ventral curvature of the body to the angular process is a steeper curve (22), somewhat steplike.

Similar species: Other shrews, moles, and bats.

Note: The largest cinereus shrews are found in the Northeast (Whitaker 2004).

Merriam's shrew, *Sorex merriami*

Greatest length: 15.2–17.5 mm ($^6/_{10}$–$^7/_{10}$ in.) (full table of measurements page 520, life-size image page 110, life-size jaw page 159)

Specimen illustrated: Adult female, MVZ 35099

Dentition: i 3/1 c 1/1 p 3/1 m 3/3, total 32.

Dorsal: Triangular skull overall, but squatter in appearance than those of other *Sorex* species. Rostrum (1) is squatter and broader. Braincase (2) is very round and broad and less than 50 percent of the greatest length of skull. The interorbital breadth (3) is broad in comparison with those of other shrews, as is the nasal vacuity (4). The interparietal (5) is more rounded and thinner, being much wider than long. There are no zygomatic arches, but maxillary arches (6) project outward.

Ventral: The palate (7) is squatter than in other *Sorex* and broad to the posterior, with an abrupt posterior edge; the anterior of the palate constricts significantly to become narrow between anteriormost premolars (8). The foramen magnum (9) is large. There are no auditory bullae, and the tympanic bones (10) are ring-shaped.

Lateral: Rostrum (11) is deeper (or taller) than in other species. The braincase (12) is not elevated, and a smooth dorsal line follows the rostrum to the braincase. The posterior of the skull (13) is rounded. The nasal vacuity (14) is fairly steep. The dentition is of a medium weight. The first incisor (15) is large and procumbent and has a second, smaller cusp to the posterior; the remaining teeth are unicuspid and peg-like. The second unicuspid (16) is the largest, and the third (17) is larger than or equal in size to the fourth unicuspid. The teeth are pigmented.

Mandible: The mandible is composed of a long, slender body (18). The coronoid process (19) is tall and triangular, rising straight upward from the posterior of the toothrow. The condyloid process (20) is double-faceted, having two projections, whereas moles have but one. The angular process (21) is long and very thin, and the curvature of the body (22) to the angular process is shallow and smooth. The postmandibular canal is present on the inside of the mandible.

Similar species: Other shrews, moles, and bats.

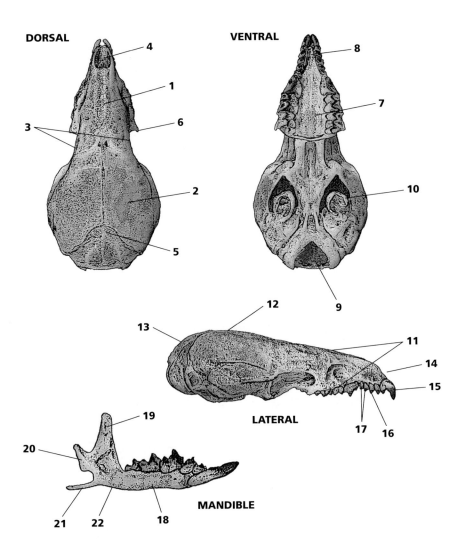

American water shrew, *Sorex palustris*

Greatest length: 18.9–22.4 mm ($^7/_{10}$–$^9/_{10}$ in.) (full table of measurements page 520, life-size image page 110, life-size jaw page 159)

Specimen illustrated: Adult male, SBMNH VB-56-21

Dentition: i 3/1 c 1/1 p 3/1 m 3/3, total 32.

Dorsal: Triangular skull overall, a more slender outline than other *Sorex* species. Rostrum (1) is longer and more slender than in other shrews. Braincase (2) is very round and smooth and significantly less than 50 percent of the greatest length of skull. The interorbital breadth (3) is narrow when compared with those of other shrews, as is the nasal vacuity (4). The interparietal (5) is more rounded and thinner, being much wider than long. There are no zygomatic arches, but maxillary arches (6) project outward.

Ventral: The palate (7) is long and narrow, with an abrupt posterior edge (8); it is very narrow between the anteriormost premolars (9), anterior to the significant constriction in the toothrows. The foramen magnum (10) is large. There are no auditory bullae, and the tympanic bones (11) are ring-shaped.

Lateral: Rostrum (12) is not as deep (or tall) as in other species. The braincase (13) is very elevated after a steep rise from the plane of the rostrum. The posterior of the skull (14) is rounded. The nasal vacuity (15) is long and sloping, as the premaxillaries (16) extend to the anterior far more than the nasals (17). The dentition is rugose. The first incisor (18) is large and procumbent and has a second, smaller cusp to the posterior; the remaining teeth are unicuspid and peglike. There are five unicuspids, and the third (19) is smaller than the fourth. The teeth are pigmented.

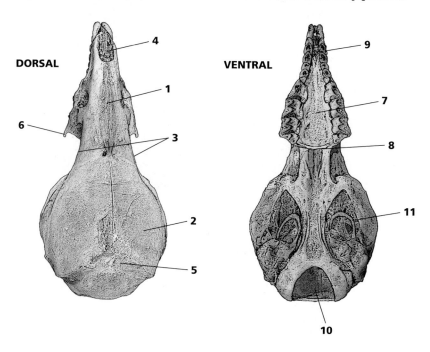

DORSAL

VENTRAL

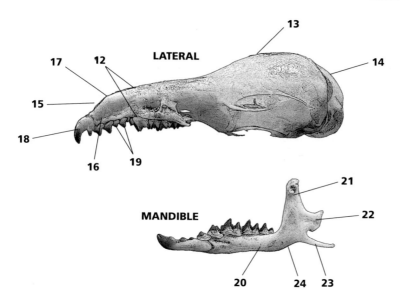

Mandible: The mandible is composed of a long, slender body (20). The coronoid process (21) is tall and triangular, rising straight upward from the posterior of the toothrow. The condyloid process (22) is double-faceted, having two projections, whereas moles have but one. The angular process (23) is long and very thin. There is a steep curve or step along the ventral outline (24) of the body to the angular process. The postmandibular canal is absent; there is a single foramen.

Similar species: Other shrews, moles, and bats.

Vagrant shrew, *Sorex vagrans*

Greatest length: 14.9–19.5 mm ($^6/_{10}$–$^8/_{10}$ in.) (full table of measurements page 522, life-size image page 110, life-size jaw page 159)

Specimen illustrated: Adult females, MVZ 114980, 114979 (mandible only)

Dentition: i 3/1 c 1/1 p 3/1 m 3/3, total 32.

Dorsal: Triangular skull overall. Rostrum (1) is long and more slender than in other shrews. Braincase (2) is very round and smooth and less than 50 percent of the greatest length of skull. The interorbital breadth (3) is narrow in comparison with those of other shrews, as is the long nasal vacuity (4). The interparietal (5) has rounded anterior sutures and is thinner, being much wider than long. There are no zygomatic arches, but maxillary arches (6) project outward.

Ventral: The palate (7) is of a medium breadth, with an abrupt posterior edge (8); it becomes very narrow between the anteriormost premolars (9) as toothrows constrict. The foramen magnum (10) is large. There are no auditory bullae, and the tympanic bones (11) are ring-shaped.

Lateral: Rostrum (12) is slightly deeper (or taller) than in other species. The braincase (13) is only slightly elevated and connects by a straight line with the rostrum.

The posterior of the skull (14) is rounded. The nasal vacuity (15) is long and slop-ing, as the premaxillaries extend to the anterior far more than the nasals. The den-tition is smaller. The first incisor (16) is large and procumbent; the remaining teeth are unicuspid and peglike. The third unicuspid (17) is much smaller than the fourth and visible. The teeth are pigmented.

Mandible: The mandible is composed of a long, slender body (18), though deeper than in other shrews, which gives the jaw a squatter appearance. The coronoid process (19) is tall, triangular, and slightly bent, rising straight upward from the posterior of the toothrow. The condyloid process (20) is double-faceted, having two projec-tions, whereas moles have but one. The angular process (21) is long and very thin and more elevated than in other shrews. The curvature of the body (22) to the angu-lar process is steep. The postmandibular canal is absent.

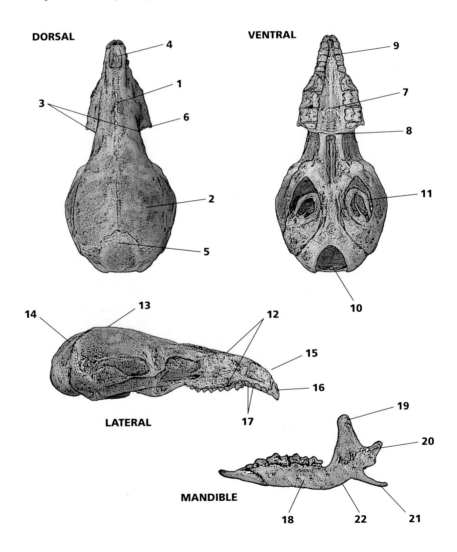

DORSAL

VENTRAL

LATERAL

MANDIBLE

Similar species: Other shrews, moles, and bats.

Note: Verts and Carraway (1998) report a method to differentiate between the craniums of *S. vagrans* and *S. trowbridgii* using the width of the interorbital breadth: greater than 3.5 mm is *S. trowbridgii,* and less than 3.5 mm is *S. vagrans.*

Northern short-tailed shrew, *Blarina brevicauda*

Greatest length: 16.9–25.2 mm (⁷/₁₀–1 in.) (full table of measurements page 522, life-size image page 111, life-size jaw page 159)

Specimen illustrated: Adult, SBMNH VB-148

Dentition: i 3/1 c 1/1 p 3/1 m 3/3, total 32.

Dorsal: Triangular skull overall, though heavier and more angular than those of *Sorex* species. Rostrum (1) and nasal vacuity (2) are both broader than in other shrews. Braincase (3) is more angular, with prominent ridges (4), smooth, and significantly less than 50 percent of the greatest length of skull. The interorbital breadth (5) is very broad in comparison with those of other shrews. The anterior sutures (6) of the interparietal are pointed, and the bone is a narrow strip much wider than long. There are no zygomatic arches, but maxillary arches (7) project outward.

Ventral: The palate (8) is broad with an abrupt posterior edge (9); it remains broad between the anteriormost premolars (10). The foramen magnum (11) is large. There are no auditory bullae, and the tympanic bones are ring-shaped (12). Note the tiny fifth unicuspid (13), which is not visible from the lateral perspective.

Lateral: Rostrum (14) is much deeper (or taller) than in other shrews. The braincase (15) is elevated compared with the line of the rostrum. The posterior of the skull (16) is angular. The nasal vacuity (17) is sloping. The dentition is very rugose. The first incisor (18) is large and procumbent; the remaining teeth are unicuspid and peglike.

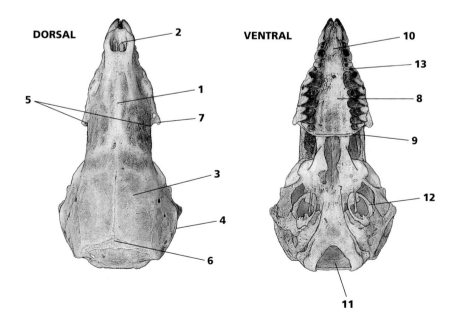

DORSAL   2

5   1

7

3

4

6

VENTRAL   10

13

8

9

12

11

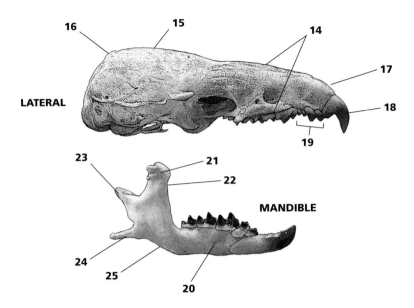

Four of the five unicuspids are visible from the lateral perspective (19), and the first two are much larger than the third and fourth. The teeth are heavily pigmented.

Mandible: The mandible is composed of a long, slender body (20), though deeper and shorter than in *Sorex*. The coronoid process (21) is thick and squared; it rises straight upward from the posterior of the toothrow, and the anterior surface (22) is concave. The condyloid process (23) is more barrel-shaped, though still with two projections, whereas moles have but one. The angular process (24) is more stout than in *Sorex* species, and there is a step (25) or steep angle following the line of the body posterior to the angular process. The dentition is heavy.

Similar species: Other shrews, moles, and bats.

Least shrew, *Cryptotis parva*

Greatest length: 14.2–18.0 mm ($^6/_{10}$–$^7/_{10}$ in.) (full table of measurements page 522, life-size image page 110, life-size jaw page 159)

Specimen illustrated: Adult, SBMNH VB-253

Dentition: i 3/1 c 1/1 p 2/1 m 3/3, total 30. One less unicuspid than *Sorex* species and unique among shrews in having thirty teeth.

Dorsal: Triangular skull overall, with a slightly squatter appearance than many *Sorex*. Rostrum (1) is broader than in many shrews. Braincase (2) is very round, smooth, and shorter, less than 50 percent of the greatest length of skull. The interorbital breadth (3) is broad in comparasion with those of other shrews, as is the nasal vacuity (4). The interparietal has pointed sutures (5) at its anterior. There are no zygomatic arches, but maxillary arches (6) project outward.

Ventral: The palate (7) is broad, with an abrupt posterior edge (8); it remains broad between the anteriormost premolars (9) as toothrows constrict. The foramen mag-

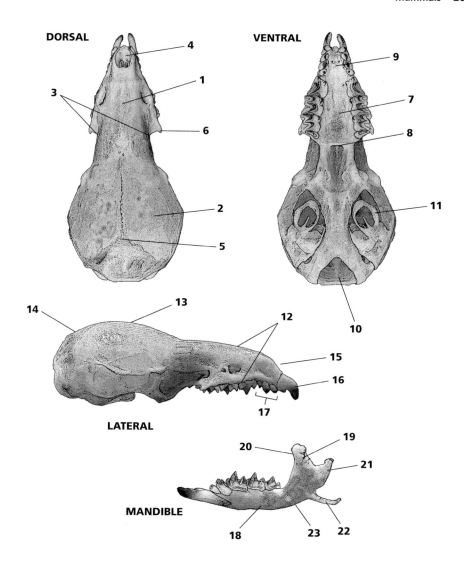

DORSAL

VENTRAL

LATERAL

MANDIBLE

num (10) is large. There are no auditory bullae, and the tympanic bones (11) are ring-shaped.

Lateral: Rostrum (12) is deeper (or taller) than in other shrews. The braincase (13) is well elevated above the line of the rostrum. The posterior of the skull (14) is rounded. The nasal vacuity (15) is steep. The dentition is smaller. The first incisor (16) is large and procumbent; the remaining teeth are unicuspid and peglike. Only three of the four unicuspids (17) are visible from lateral. The teeth are chestnut pigmented.

Mandible: The mandible is composed of a long, slender body (18). The coronoid process (19) is tall, slightly thicker, and squared, rising straight upward from the posterior of the toothrow, and then angling forward above (20). The condyloid process (21) is double-faceted, having two projections, whereas moles have but one. The angular process (22) is long and very thin. The ventral curvature of the body to the angular process (23) is a steeper curve, somewhat steplike. The dentition is heavy.

Similar species: Other shrews, moles, and bats.

Crawford's desert shrew, *Notiosorex crawfordi*

Greatest length: 15.0–17.6 mm ($^6/_{10}$–$^7/_{10}$ in.) (full table of measurements page 524, life-size image page 110, life-size jaw page 159)

Specimen illustrated: Adult female, SBMNH VB-1978

Dentition: i 3/1, c 1/1, p 1/1, m 3/3, total 28. Three upper unicuspids rather than five as in *Sorex*.

Dorsal: Triangular skull overall, with a slightly squatter appearance than those of many *Sorex*. Rostrum (1) is broader than in many shrews. Braincase (2) is slightly wider than long, smooth, and significantly less than 50 percent of the greatest length of skull. The interorbital breadth (3) is broad in comparison with those of other shrews, and there is a slight constriction. The nasal vacuity (4) is broad. The interparietal has pointed sutures (5) at its anterior. There are no zygomatic arches, but maxillary arches (6) project outward.

Ventral: The palate (7) is of median breadth at the posterior but wider than in other shrews between the anteriormost premolars (8). The foramen magnum (9) is large. There are no auditory bullae, and the tympanic bones (10) are ring-shaped.

Lateral: Rostrum (11) is deeper (or taller) than in other shrews. The braincase (12) is slightly elevated and flattened, creating a steeper dorsal outline than that of the rostrum; there is a step (13) between rostrum and braincase. The posterior of the skull (14) is more squared. The nasal vacuity (15) is steep. The dentition is medium

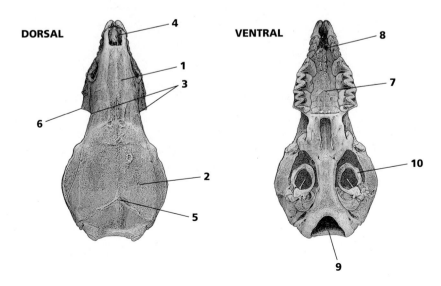

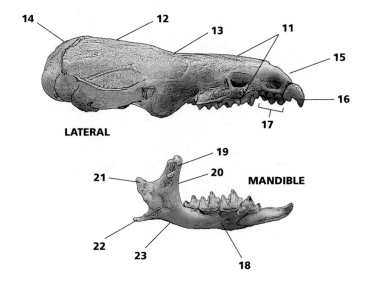

LATERAL

MANDIBLE

to rugose. The first incisor (16) is large and procumbent; the remaining teeth are unicuspid and peglike. Only three unicuspids above (17). The teeth are chestnut pigmented.

Mandible: The mandible is composed of a long, slender body (18). The coronoid process (19) is tall and triangular, rising straight upward from the posterior of the toothrow, then angling slightly forward to create a concave anterior surface (20). The condyloid process (21) is double-faceted, having two projections, though less apparent than in *Sorex* species. The angular process (22) is slightly stouter and shorter than in *Sorex*. The curvature of the body (23) is smooth and low up to the angular process.

Similar species: Other shrews, moles, and bats.

Family Talpidae: Moles

Moles are larger insectivores renowned for their subterranean existence. Their skulls are typical of insectivores, with similar-shaped teeth for the length of their toothrows, all sharply cusped or conical for crushing and tearing tough exoskeletons. Unlike shrews, moles have zygomatic arches, though weak and lacking jugal bones. Their teeth are not pigmented like shrews, but like shrews, their front incisors point forward.

The moles are split into two groups, one with completed auditory bullae and one in which they are incomplete. In the American shrew mole *(Neurotrichus gibbsii)*, star-nosed mole *(Condylura cristata)*, and hairy-tailed mole *(Parascalops breweri)*, the auditory bullae are incomplete, and there are visible openings and cracks in the ventral surface to indicate such. In the eastern mole *(Scalopus aquaticus)* and broad-footed *(Scapanus latimanus)*, coast *(Scapanus orarius)*, and Townsend's moles *(Scapanus townsendi)*, the auditory bullae are complete, and the ventral surface of the skull is smooth. Refer to the photograph on page 213 to gain a better feel for these characters.

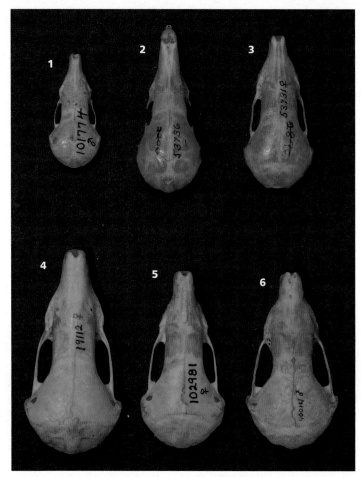

Select members of Talpidae: 1. American shrew mole, male 101774 *(Neurotrichus)*, 2. Star-nosed mole 53736 *(Condylura)*, 3. Hairy-tailed mole, female 53731 *(Parascalops)*, 4. Townsend's mole, female 19112 *(Scapanus t.)*, 5. Broad-footed mole, female 102981 *(Scapanus l.)*, 6. Eastern mole, male 40014 *(Scalopus a.)*. MUSEUM OF VERTEBRATE ZOOLOGY, UC BERKELEY.

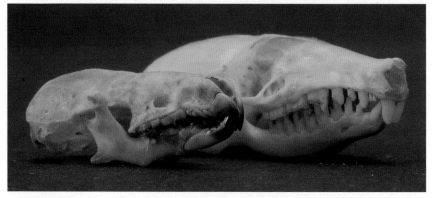

Compare the dentition of the northern short-tailed shrew *(Blarina)* on the left with that of the eastern mole *(Scalopus)*, and note colors, and the size and shape of the most anterior incisors. SANTA BARBARA MUSEUM OF NATURAL HISTORY VB-343, VB-442.

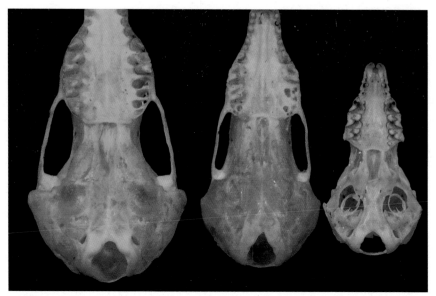

From left to right compare the complete auditory bullae in the eastern mole *(Scalopus)*, incomplete bullae in the hairy-tailed mole *(Parascalops)*, and the ringlike tympanic bones in the northern short-tailed shrew *(Blarina)*. MUSEUM OF VERTEBRATE ZOOLOGY, UC BERKELEY 40014, 53731, 74677.

American shrew mole, *Neurotrichus gibbsii*

Greatest length: 20.7–24.2 mm (8/10–1 in.) (full table of measurements page 524, lifesize image page 111, life-size jaw page 160)

Specimen illustrated: Adult female, LACM 2876

Dentition: i 3/3 c 1/1 p 2/2 m 3/3, total 36.

Dorsal: Triangular overall, with a long, slender rostrum (1); broad braincase (2) is rounded to the posterior (3); and prominent pointed mastoid processes (4). The delicate zygomatic arches (5) are without jugal bones and slightly bow outward. The orbits (6) are proportionately smaller than in other moles. The interorbital region (7) is broader than in other moles and does not constrict the braincase. The interparietal bone (8) is proportionately longer than in other moles.

Ventral: The auditory bullae (9) are incomplete (and slightly damaged in this specimen). The palate (10) is long and narrow, and the pteryroid region (11) is rounded and deep. The auditory meatus is slitlike. The molars (12) are M-shaped, which is characteristic of most insectivores, and there are bilobed basal projections on M1 and M2 (13). The foramen magnum (14) is large but narrow, with a deep ventral notch (15).

Lateral: The first incisor (16) is slightly procumbent and enlarged, and much of the dentition is well spaced; the teeth are not pigmented. The first premolar (17) is slightly larger than the canine (18). The zygomatic arches (19) sit at an angle, sloping down to the anterior. Note also the dorsal outline at the posterior of the braincase (20), which in this case is high and rounded.

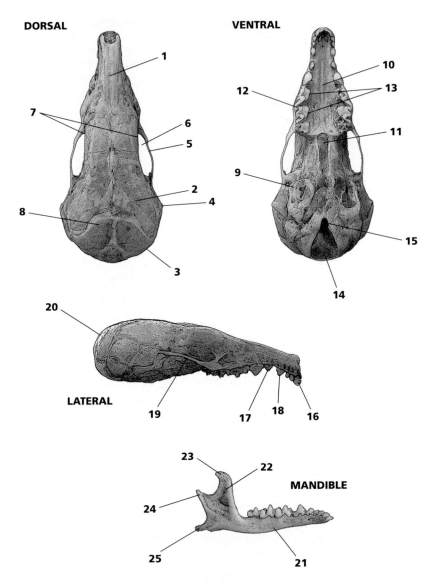

DORSAL

1

7

6

5

2

4

8

3

VENTRAL

10

13

12

11

9

15

14

LATERAL

20

19

17

18

16

MANDIBLE

23

22

24

25

21

Mandible: The body (21) of the mandible is long and slender. The coronoid process (22) is high and straight, with a tip (23) pointing to the posterior. The condyloid process (24) has a single slender point (two in shrews) and is angled upward, but the tip sits far below the coronoid process. The angular process (25) is shrewlike in that it is long and more slender than in other moles.

Similar species: Other moles, shrews, and bats.

Broad-footed mole, *Scapanus latimanus*

Greatest length: 30.5–38.1 mm ($1^2/_{10}$–$1^5/_{10}$ in.) (full table of measurements page 526, life-size image page 114, life-size jaw page 161)

Specimen illustrated: Adult female, SBMNH 112

Dentition: i 3/3 c 1/1 p 2–4/3–4 m 3/3, total 40–44.

Dorsal: Triangular overall, with a more robust, broader appearance than other moles. Long, broader rostrum (1); broad braincase (2) that is rounded to the posterior, with prominent pointed mastoid processes (3). The stouter zygomatic arches (4) are without jugal bones and do not spread widely; they are slightly convergent to the anterior. The orbits (5) are slightly forward in comparison with those of other moles.

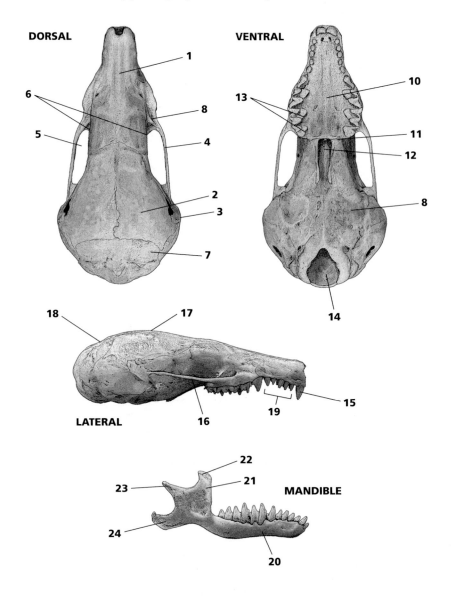

The interorbital region (6) is broader than in other moles. The interparietal bone (7) is broad and rectangular. The infraorbital foramen (8) is small but larger than in *Scalopus*.

Ventral: Auditory bullae (9) complete and flattened. The palate (10) is long and relatively broad, with an abrupt posterior edge (11); the pteryroid region (12) is rounded and deep. The molars (13) are M-shaped, which is characteristic of most insectivores, and there are bilobed basal projections on the molars. The foramen magnum (14) is proportionately very large and oval.

Lateral: The first incisor (15) is enlarged, and much of the anterior dentition is more crowded than in other moles when all six unicuspids are present; the teeth are not pigmented. It is very common to have only five unicuspids (19) above, rather than six. The zygomatic arches (16) sit at an angle, sloping down to the anterior. The braincase (17) is slightly elevated above the plane of the rostrum. The dorsal outline at the posterior of the braincase (18) is low, with a concave depression.

Mandible: The body (20) of the mandible is long and slender. The coronoid process (21) is high and straight, with a slightly squared tip (22) pointing to the posterior. The condyloid process (23) has a single slender point (two in shrews) and is angled upward at roughly 45 degrees, with the tip sitting just below the coronoid process. The angular process (24) is enlarged, thick, long, and multifaceted.

Similar species: Other moles, shrews, and bats.

Townsend's mole, *Scapanus townsendii*

Greatest length: 39.5–44.6 mm ($1^6/10$–$1^8/10$ in.) (full table of measurements page 526, life-size image page 116, life-size jaw page 161)

Specimen illustrated: Adult, SBMNH VB-1089

Dentition: i 3/3 c 1/1 p 4/4 m 3/3, total 44.

Dorsal: Triangular overall, and the skull's greater length alone can usually distinguish it from those of other moles. Long, broader rostrum (1); broad braincase (2) that is rounded to the posterior and proportionately shorter than in other moles. There are prominent pointed mastoid processes (3). The stouter zygomatic arches (4) are without jugal bones and do not spread widely; they are slightly convergent to the anterior. The orbits (5) are situated slightly behind the midpoint of the skull. The interorbital region (6) is slightly narrower comparatively; a median ridge (7) may develop along the midline of the skull. The interparietal bone is broad and rectangular (8). The infraorbital foramen (9) is small but larger than in *Scalopus*. The premaxillaries extend beyond the nasals, which forms a notch (10) when viewed from above.

Ventral: Auditory bullae (11) complete and flattened. The palate (12) is long and relatively narrower, with an abrupt posterior edge (13); the pteryroid region (14) is deep. The molars (15) are M-shaped, which is characteristic of most insectivores. The foramen magnum (16) is comparatively smaller and oval.

Lateral: The first incisor (17) is relatively smaller, and much of the dentition is well spaced; the teeth are not pigmented. The zygomatic arches (18) sit an angle, slop-

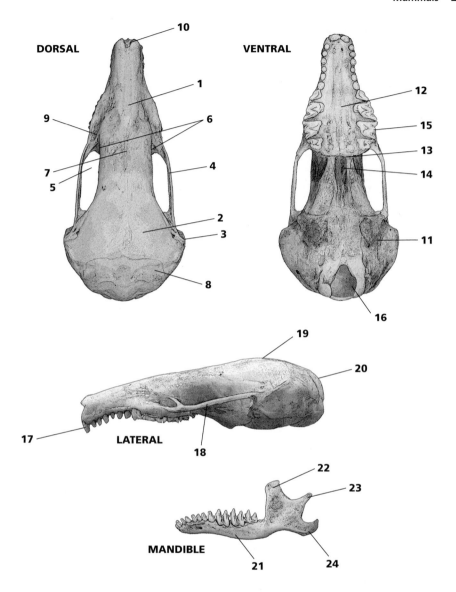

ing down to the anterior. The braincase (19) is slightly elevated above the line of the rostrum. Note also the dorsal outline at the posterior of the braincase (20), which is high, rounded, and dropping very steeply down to the posterior.

Mandible: The body (21) of the mandible is long and slender. The coronoid process (22) is high and straight, with a slightly squared tip pointing to the posterior. The condyloid process (23) has a single slender point (two in shrews) and is angled upward at roughly 45 degrees, with the tip sitting just below the coronoid process. The angular process (24) is enlarged, thick, long, and multifaceted.

Similar species: Other moles, shrews, and bats.

Hairy-tailed mole, *Parascalops breweri*

Greatest length: 30.3–35.2 mm ($1^2/_{10}$–$1^4/_{10}$ in.) (full table of measurements page 526, life-size image page 113, life-size jaw page 160)

Specimen illustrated: Adult female, MVZ 53731

Dentition: i 3/3 c 1/1 p 4/4 m 3/3, total 44.

Dorsal: Triangular overall, with a more robust, broader appearance than the skulls of other moles. Long, broader rostrum (1); broad braincase (2) that is rounded to the posterior, with prominent pointed mastoid processes (3). The nasal notch (4) is broad, formed by the premaxillaries extending far beyond the nasals. The stouter zygomatic arches (5) are without jugal bones and do not spread widely; they are slightly

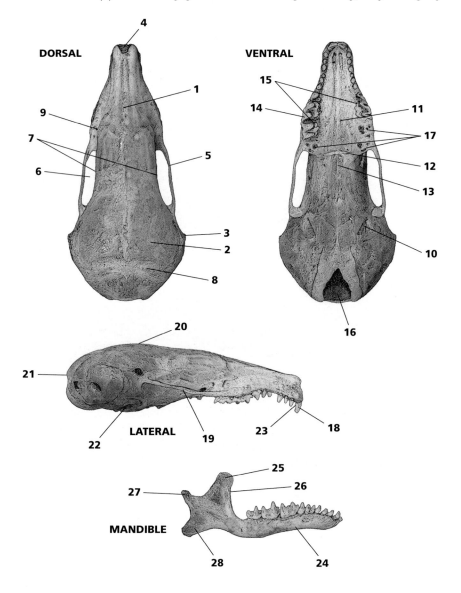

convergent to the anterior. The orbits (6) are situated approximately at the midpoint of the skull. The interorbital region (7) is broad, sometimes with a slight constriction. The interparietal bone (8) is broad and rectangular. The infraorbital foramen (9) is small but larger than in *Scalopus*.

Ventral: Auditory bullae (10) are incomplete and flattened. The palate (11) is long and relatively broad, with an abrupt posterior edge (12); the pteryroid region (13) is very shallow. The molars (14) are M-shaped, which is characteristic of most insectivores; M1 and M2 (15) have trilobed basal projections. The foramen magnum (16) is medium and oval with a narrow ventral notch. The illustrated specimen is missing three molars (17).

Lateral: The first incisor (18) is enlarged, with a distinctive accessory cusp (23), and much of the dentition is well spaced; the teeth are not pigmented. The zygomatic arches (19) sit at an angle, sloping down to the anterior. The braincase (20) is relatively flattened, and the line of the rostrum slopes downward anterior to the orbits. The dorsal outline at the posterior of the braincase (21) is concave. Incomplete bullae (22) are more visible from this angle.

Mandible: The body (24) of the mandible is long and slender. The coronoid process (25) is stout and squared, with a concave anterior surface (26). The condyloid process (27) is short and falls well below the coronoid process; the condyle is slightly upturned. The angular process (28) is thick and rounded and points downward at roughly 45 degrees.

Similar species: Other moles, shrews, and bats.

Eastern mole, *Scalopus aquaticus*

Greatest length: 29.3–40.9 mm ($1^2/10$–$1^3/10$ in.) (full table of measurements page 526, life-size image page 113, life-size jaw page 160)

Specimen illustrated: Adult male, SBMNH VB-442

Dentition: i 3/2 c 1/0 p 3/3 m 3/3, total 36.

Dorsal: Distinctly triangular overall and strongly tapering toward the pointy rostrum. Long, tapering rostrum (1), with a slender tip (2) and a narrow nasal notch (3) created by premaxillaries extending well beyond the nasals. Broad braincase (4) is larger than those of other moles, with a rounded posterior. There are prominent pointed mastoid processes (5). The stouter zygomatic arches (6) are without jugal bones, spread more widely, and are more convergent to the anterior than in other moles. The orbits (7) are situated slightly behind the midpoint of the skull. The interorbital region (8) is narrower than in other moles, constricted, and narrower than the rostrum. The interparietal bone (9) is relatively triangular and pointy. The infraorbital foramen (10) is very small.

Ventral: Auditory bullae (11) are complete and flattened. The palate (12) is long, broad at the posterior, and narrow (13) at the anterior, and it extends farther beyond the molars (14) than in other moles, with an abrupt posterior edge; the pterygoid region is of a median depth. The molars (15) are M-shaped, which is characteristic of most insectivores. The foramen magnum (16) is comparatively slightly smaller and oval, with a ventral notch (17).

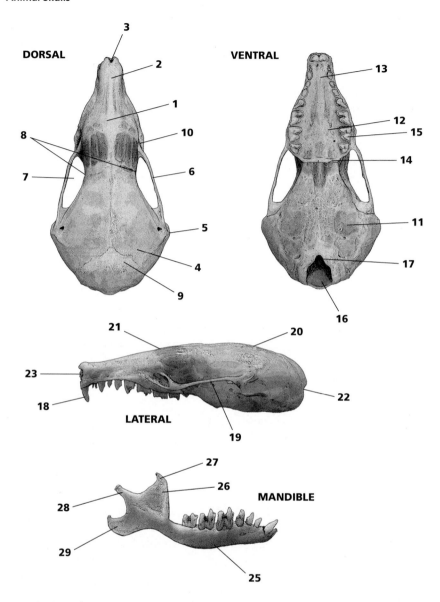

DORSAL

VENTRAL

LATERAL

MANDIBLE

Lateral: The first incisor (18) is enlarged, and much of the dentition is well spaced; the teeth are not pigmented. The zygomatic arches (19) sit at an angle, sloping down to the anterior. The braincase (20) is relatively flattened compared with the line of the rostrum; the frontal sinuses (21) are slightly swollen. The dorsal outline at the posterior of the braincase (22) is high and rounded, with a depression at the midline of the skull. The nasal notch (23) on the lateral side is deeper than in *Parascalops*.

Mandible: The body (25) of the mandible is long and slender. The coronoid process (26) is high and straight, with a slightly squared tip (27) pointing to the posterior. The condyloid process (28) has a single slender point (two in shrews) and is angled upward at roughly 45 degrees, with the tip sitting just below the coronoid process. The angular process (29) is enlarged, thick, long, and multifaceted.

Similar species: Other moles, shrews, and bats.

Note: Hartman and Yates (2003) provide a photographic guide to aging specimens by relative tooth wear.

Star-nosed mole, *Condylura cristata*

Greatest length: 32.1–35.2 mm ($1^3/_{10}$–$1^4/_{10}$ in.) (full table of measurements page 526, life-size image page 114, life-size jaw page 160)

Specimen illustrated: Adult, MCZ 36685

Dentition: i 3/3 c 1/1 p 4/4 m 3/3, total 44.

Dorsal: Distinctly long and slender skull, with very long rostrum (1). Narrow braincase (2) is slimmer than those of other moles, with a rounded posterior. Prominent pointed mastoid processes are lacking. The fragile, slender zygomatic arches (3) have a very narrow spread and often break; they are slightly convergent to the anterior. The orbits (4) are very small. The interorbital region (5) is comparatively broad. The interparietal bone (6) is very large and somewhat bowtie-shaped. The infraorbital foramen (7) is small.

Ventral: Auditory bullae are absent, and tympanic bones (8) are incomplete (somewhat damaged in this specimen). The palate (9) is long and narrow, and unlike other moles, terminates at the anterior edge of the last molar (10); the pterygoid region (11) is long and deep. The molars (12) are M-shaped, which is characteristic of most insectivores. The foramen magnum (13) is large but very narrow, with a wide ventral notch (14).

Lateral: The first incisor (15) is reduced and procumbent, the second (16) very slender, and the third (17) enlarged. The remaining dentition to the anterior is well

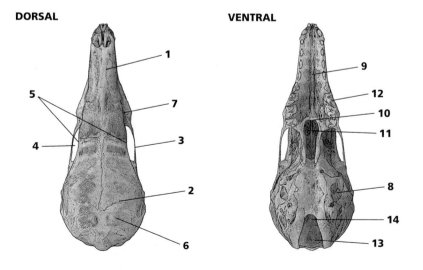

DORSAL   **VENTRAL**

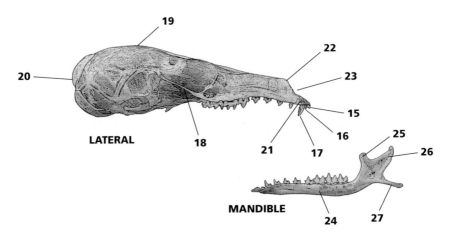

spaced and sharply tricuspid; the teeth are not pigmented. The zygomatic arches (18) sharply slope down to the anterior, more so than in other moles. The braincase (19) is elevated and bulging when compared with the line of the rostrum. The dorsal outline at the posterior of the braincase (20) appears bilobed from this perspective. The premaxillaries (21) extend well beyond the nasals (22) and create a sloping nasal vacuity (23) similar to many shrews.

Mandible: The body (24) of the mandible is very long, straight, and slender. The coronoid process (25) is squared and sits below the condyle. The condyloid process (26) is long and triangular, extending posteriorly at roughly 45 degrees to above the coronoid process; the tip of the condyle points upward. The angular process (27) is long and slender as in shrews, but the foremost tiny incisors and greater length of mandible should make it easy to distinguish from mandibles of shrews.

Similar species: Other moles, shrews, and bats.

Order Chiroptera: Bats

The bats are a large and diverse group of aerial hunters and nectar feeders. For the most part, bats are insectivores, and their jagged and sharp dentition is ideal for capturing, crushing, and tearing tough exoskeletons. Large and high braincases provide anchorage for temporalis muscles, and the wide-spreading, though often weak zygomatic arches allow ample space for their passage.

Several species have evolved unique lifestyles, dependent on living blood (vampire bats) or flower nectars, and with each change in ecology come morphological adaptations to support such endeavors. For instance in vampire bats, the incisors are highly modified, and in nectar-feeding bats, the rostrums are generally elongated.

There are a number of families of North American bats, which can be split into two large groups depending on the structure of the palate. A bat may have an incomplete palate, which is visually apparent as a significant notch at the anterior of the skull between the upper canines, or a complete palate with no notch, the structural model most other mammals share. As this is such a quick and easy way to begin to work

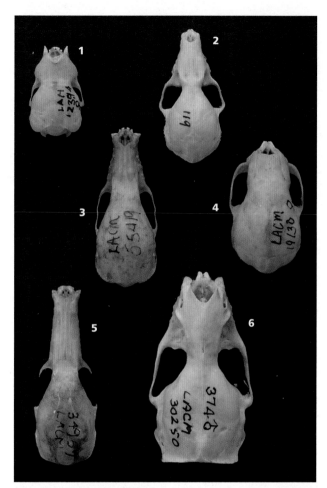

Select members of the order Chiroptera with complete palates: 1. Ghost-faced bat *(Mormoops)*, 2. California leaf-nosed bat *(Macrotus)*, 3. Southern long-tongued bat *(Leptonycteris)*, 4. Hairy-legged vampire bat *(Diphylla)*, 5. Mexican long-tongued bat *(Choeronycteris)*, 6. Western bonneted bat, *(Eumops)*. NATURAL HISTORY MUSEUM OF LOS ANGELES COUNTY.

toward species identification, representatives of all the families have been split into two photographs, one comparing bat skulls with complete palates, the other comparing those with incomplete palates.

Bat families with complete palates include Mormoopidae (genus *Mormoops*), Phyllostomidae (genera *Macrotus, Choeronycteris, Leptonycteris,* and *Diphylla*), and Molossidae (genera *Tadarida, Nyctinomops, Eumops,* and *Molossus*). Families with incomplete palates include Vespertilionidae (genera *Myotis, Lasiurus, Pipistrellus, Eptesicus, Nycticeius, Euderma, Corynorhinus, Idionycteris,* and *Antrozous*).

The shapes and structures of bat skulls are diverse enough to allow species identification without too much detailed analysis of the dentition. Nevertheless, dentition is a useful character that can be used to identify at least to a genus level. Presented

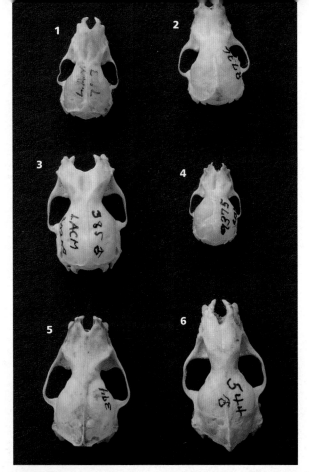

Select members of the order Chiroptera with incomplete palates: 1. Little brown bat or myotis 7138 *(M. lucifugus)*, 2. Cave myotis 8136 *(M. velifer)*, 3. Hoary bat, male 30258 *(Lasiurus)*, 4. Eastern pipistrelle, female 9375 *(Pipistrellus)*, 5. Big brown bat, male 9394 *(Eptesicus)*, 6. Pallid bat, male 944 *(Antrozous)*. NATURAL HISTORY MUSEUM OF LOS ANGELES COUNTY.

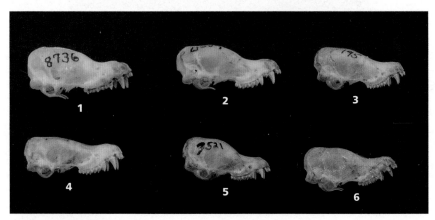

Select myotis species for comparisons: 1. Cave myotis 8136 *(M. velifer)*, 2. Fringed myotis 72871 *(M. thysanodes)*, 3. Eastern small-footed myotis 95640 *(M. leibii)*, 4. Little brown bat or myotis 7138 *(M. lucifugus)*, 5. Yuma myotis 521 *(M. yumanensis)*, 6. Long-legged myotis 91161 *(M. volans)*. NATURAL HISTORY MUSEUM OF LOS ANGELES COUNTY.

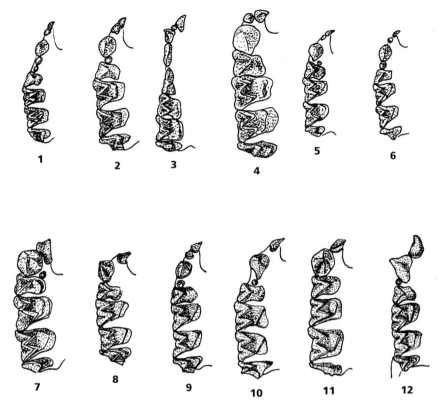

Right toothrows of various bats (genus and species), viewed from the ventral perspective. Note the number of incisors, number of small teeth posterior to the canine, and the overall shape of the teeth. 1. *Myotis* sp., 2. *Lasionycteris* (Silver-haired bat), 3. *Macrotus* (California leaf-nosed bat), 4. *Eptesicus* (Big brown bat), 5. *Pip. hesperus* (Western pipistrelle), 6. *Pip. sub-flavus* (Eastern pipistrelle), 7. *Lasiurus* sp., 8. *Nycticeius* (Evening bat), 9. *Corynorhinus* sp. (Big-eared bats), 10. *Tadarida* (Brazilian free-tailed bat), 11. *Antrozous* (Pallid bat), 12. *Eumops sp.* (Bonneted bats). Drawn after Allen (1893).

here are toothrows of various bat genera to complement the visual descriptions of skulls that follow in individual species accounts.

Differentiating among the numerous *Myotis* species is difficult, compounded by the fact that the skulls are so tiny. The greatest length of skull and the number of premolars are a good starting point in identification. The degree to which the forehead slopes from the plane of the rostrum up to the plane of the braincase is another useful character to further narrow the possibilities. Most species have a steep or abrupt slope from rostrum to braincase, but several, including the eastern small-footed myotis *(M. leibii)* and Arizona myotis *(M. occultus),* have more gradually sloping foreheads. The presence of significant sagittal crests are also useful characters in the few species that have them; cave myotis *(M. velifer)* and gray myotis *(M. grisescens)* are among the few with well-developed crests. A photograph of several *Myotis* species on page 224 shows their incredible similarities and more subtle variations.

Family *Mormoopidae:* Leaf-chinned bats

Ghost-faced bat, *Mormoops megalophylla*

Greatest length: 14.8–15.7 mm ($^5/_{10}$–$^6/_{10}$ in.) (full table of measurements page 528, life-size image page 110, life-size jaw page 159)

Specimen illustrated: Adult female, LACM 12394

Dentition: i 2/2 c 1/1 p 2/3 m 3/3, total 34.

Dorsal: Squat, wide skull. Large, squared braincase (1) is wider than long. Rostrum (2) is wider than long and as broad as braincase. Interorbital breadth (3) is narrow, and there is a significant constriction between rostrum and braincase. Narrow-spreading zygomatic arches (4) converge to anterior. Nasal vacuity is large (5).

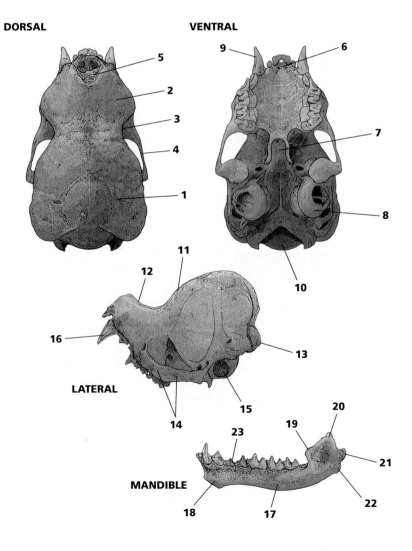

DORSAL   VENTRAL

LATERAL

MANDIBLE

Ventral: Palate (6) is complete, broad, and steeply angled, and the pterygoid region (7) is short. Auditory bullae (8) of medium size compared with those of other bats. Canines (9) exhibit outward curvature. Foramen magnum (10) is large.

Lateral: Skull is most distinctive from this lateral view: steep sloping forehead (11) to tall, flattened braincase and steeply upturned anterior of rostrum (12). Foramen magnum (13) is on a higher plane than in other bats and very high in relation to the level of the rostrum. Zygomatic arches (14) are relatively thick and follow the line of the rostrum; they are angled severely upward toward anterior. Auditory meatus (15) is relatively large. Canines (16) are large.

Mandible: Body (17) of the mandible is long and slender, though deeper at the (18) anterior tip and below the last two molars. Coronoid process (19) is reduced to a bump below the plane of the condyle when held as shown. Condyloid process (20) is triangular and the highest point when viewed as illustrated. Angular process (21) is short and trapezoidal, with blunt corners; a second process (22) sits below the larger process. Second premolar (23) is reduced in size and the smallest tooth in toothrow.

Similar species: Vampire bats and other smaller bat species.

Family Phyllostomidae: New World leaf-nosed bats

California leaf-nosed bat, *Macrotus californicus*

Greatest length: 22.4–23.9 mm ($9/10$–1 in.) (full table of measurements page 528, life-size image page 111, life-size jaw page 160)

Specimen illustrated: Adult male(?), SBMNH VB-1

Dentition: i 2/2 c 1/1 p 2/3 m 3/3, total 34.

Dorsal: The anterior of the skull is very triangular, starting with the zygomatic arches (1), which are strongly convergent to the anterior and the tapering rostrum. Long, slender, triangular rostrum (2) is shorter than the length of the braincase. The braincase (3) is large and oval. The interorbital region (6) is strongly constricted and narrow. Orbits (4) are large, and zygomatic plates (5) are especially apparent from this perspective.

Ventral: Palate (7) is complete and long and thin, narrowing (8) as it extends beyond posterior molars. Auditory bullae (9) are large. The molars (10) themselves are narrower than the breadth of the palate. The foramen magnum (12) is large. In this specimen several bones (11) that create the tongue remained attached, as is common in bats. The second premolar (22) is often in contact with the first.

Lateral: The forehead (13) is steeply sloping, and the braincase (14) is well elevated, with a rounded outline. The occipital bone (15) is angled severely to the posterior, and the posterior of the braincase (16) projects backward well beyond the auditory bullae and mastoids. Nasal vacuity (17) is large and angled, created by nasals (18) that do not extend nearly as far to the anterior as the premaxillaries (19). First premolar (20) is in contact with canine (21).

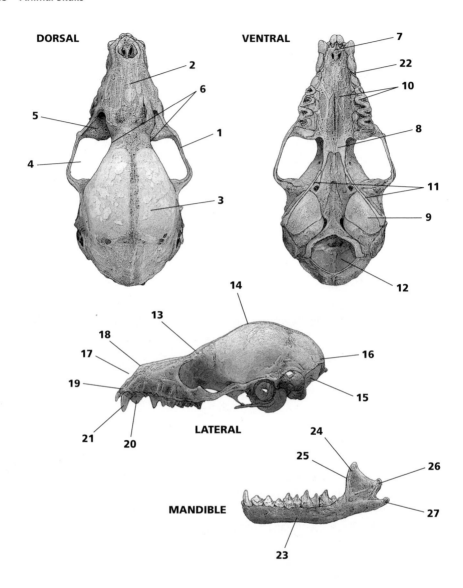

DORSAL

VENTRAL

LATERAL

MANDIBLE

Mandible: The body (23) is long, straight, and slender. Coronoid process (24) is triangular and curved, pointing slightly to posterior; the anterior edge (25) is convex. Condyloid process (26) is short, rounded, and angled upward to posterior at roughly 45 degrees. Angular process (27) is long and slender, projecting straight backward.

Similar species: Long-nosed bats, other bat species, and moles.

Note: Hoffmeister (1986) reports finding significant variation in several cranial measurements between the sexes.

Mexican long-tongued bat, *Choeronycteris mexicana*

Greatest length: 28.5–31.0 mm ($1^1/_{10}$–$1^2/_{10}$ in.) (full table of measurements page 528, life-size image page 113, life-size jaw page 161)

Specimen illustrated: Adult female, SBMNH VB-27-1971

Dentition: i 2/0 c 1/1 p 2/3 m 3/3, total 30. Molars are 2/2 in the similar long-nosed bats *(Leptonycteris)*.

Dorsal: Distinctively long and slender skull, with very long rostrum (1) that is roughly equal to or slightly longer than the braincase. The maxillary arches (2) have long projections, but zygomatic arches are incomplete, rather than complete as in the similar long-nosed bats. Interorbital breadth (3) is narrow and creates a slight constriction between braincase and rostrum. Braincase (4) is large, ovoid, and smooth.

Ventral: Palate (5) is complete, with three incisive foramina (6) at the far anterior. The palate (7) is long and slender, tapering (8) as it extends far beyond posterior molars. Pterygoid processes (9) are long and in contact with smaller auditory bullae (10). Foramen magnum (11) is large. Several of the bones (12) that create the tongue are still attached.

Lateral: The distinctive dorsolateral outline includes a steeply sloping frontal region (27), or forehead, to a well-elevated rounded braincase (13). Occipital crests (14) are developed. Premaxillaries (15) extend to anterior well beyond nasals (16), which creates a larger sloping nasal vacuity (17). Molars (18) are not in contact with each other, as they are in long-nosed bats, and all dentition posterior to the canine is well spaced. The auditory meatus (19) is small.

Mandible: The body (20) of the mandible is very long and thin, with a distinctively squared anterior edge (21). The coronoid process (22) is reduced and triangular, with a rounded point at the highest point. The condyloid process (23) is angled to posterior at roughly 45 degrees and is small and squared. The angular process (24)

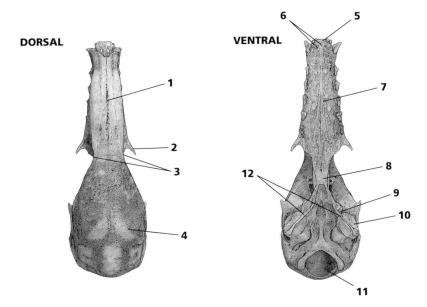

DORSAL

VENTRAL

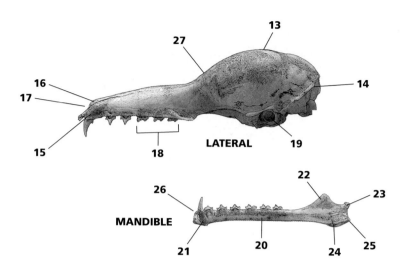

is large, with a tiny triangular projection (25) to the posterior. There are most often no lower incisors (26) in adult animals, though sometimes they persist, and remaining dentition is well spaced.

Similar species: Long-nosed bats *(Leptonycteris)*, star-nosed moles, and other mole species.

Note: The long rostrum helps this bat feed deep within nectar-producing flowers in desert regions (Liittschwager 2002).

Hairy-legged vampire bat, *Diphylla ecaudata*

Greatest length: 21.6–23.3 mm ($^9/_{10}$–1 in.) (full table of measurements page 530, life-size image page 111, life-size jaw page 159)

Specimen illustrated: Adult female, LACM 6070

Dentition: i 2/2 c 1/1 p 1/2 m 2/2, total 26.

Dorsal: An oval skull with a very short rostrum (1) and a massive rounded braincase (2). Interorbital region (3) is high, broad, and relatively long; there is a slight constriction (4) just anterior to the braincase. Zygomatic arches (5) are wide spreading and situated well forward on the skull, as are the orbits.

Ventral: Palate (6) is complete, as wide as long, and extending (7) well beyond toothrows; two large incisive foramina (8) are distinctive. Pterygoid region (9) is broad. Auditory bullae (10) are large and oval. Foramen magnum (11) also is very large. All upper cheek teeth are greatly reduced in size. First upper incisors (12) are knifelike, and the second upper incisors (13) are minute. Tiny posteriormost molars (14), absent in the common vampire bat *(Desmodus)*.

Lateral: A very deep rostrum (15), which slopes steeply to a very elevated braincase (16). Incisors (17) are procumbent. The zygomatic arches (18) are curved, and the auditory meatus (19) is medium. The ventral surface of the auditory bullae (20) is very low. Several bones (21) that contribute to the tongue remain attached.

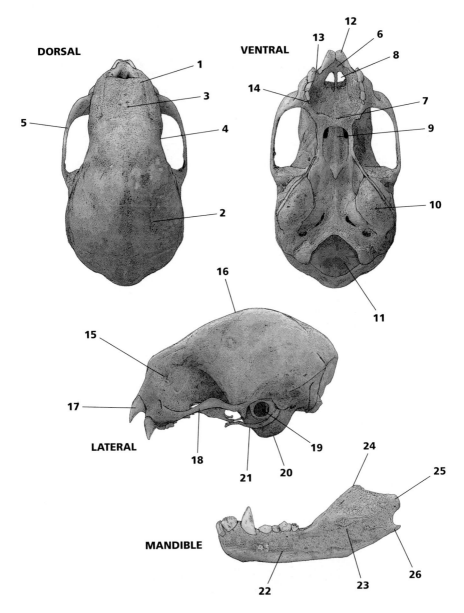

DORSAL

VENTRAL

LATERAL

MANDIBLE

Mandible: Body (22) of the mandible is relatively short, as is the accompanying toothrow. The entire ramus region (23) and associated processes are angled up toward the posterior at roughly a 45-degree angle. The coronoid process (24) is greatly reduced, a bump at the high point of the jaw (it's absent in other vampire bats). The condyloid process (25) is also reduced; it is thick and rounded and points to the posterior. The angular process (26) is also small, a slender point.

Similar species: Other vampire bats *(Desmodus)* and other bat species.

Note: Males and females are similar in size.

Family Vespertilionidae: Vesper bats

Little brown bat or myotis, *Myotis lucifugus*

Greatest length: 13.7–15.6 mm (⁵/₁₀–⁶/₁₀ in.) (full table of measurements page 532, life-size image page 110, life-size jaw page 159)

Specimen illustrated: Adult female, LACM 7138

Dentition: i 2/3 c 1/1 p 3/3 m 3/3, total 38. *Myotis* species have two upper incisors; number one is bicuspid and number two is enlarged but unicuspid. The cheek teeth are crowded.

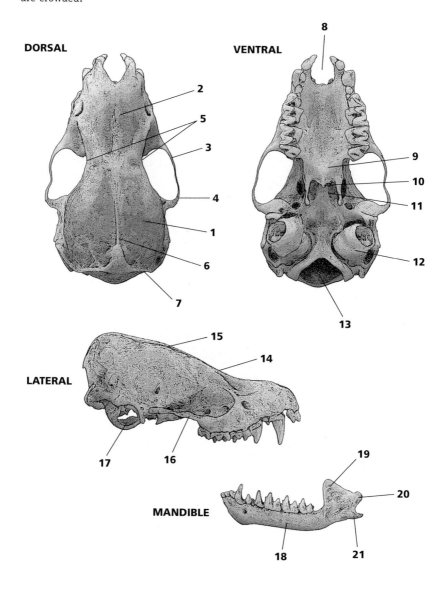

Dorsal: *Myotis* species in general have lightly constructed skulls, but this species is an even smaller, lighter variation on that model. The braincase (1) is large, rounded, and approximately 50 percent of the greatest length of skull. The rostrum (2) is broad and triangular. Weak zygomatic arches (3) spread more widely than the braincase (4) and converge to the anterior. The interorbital (5) is narrow and constricted. Small sagittal (6) and occipital crests (7) appear in this species but are more developed in other *Myotis* species.

Ventral: The palate (8) is incomplete and notched. The palate tapers (9) as it extends beyond the last molars, and at its posterior, a pointy projection (10) sticks out over the broad pterygoid region (11). The pterygoid processes are long. The toothrows are relatively long compared with those of other species. The auditory bullae (12) are smaller but inflated, and the foramen magnum (13) is large.

Lateral: A sloping forehead (14) connects the plane of the rostrum with the elevated and slightly sloping braincase (15). The zygomatic arch (16) is straight. The auditory meatus (17) is large.

Mandible: The body (18) of the mandible is straight and the ramus large. The coronoid process (19) is large, triangular, and vertical. The condyloid process (20) is reduced and rounded. The angular process (21) is a short, slim extension.

Similar species: Other *Myotis* species, other bats, and shrews.

Note: Hoffmeister (1986) was unable to find a significant difference in cranial measurements between the sexes in *Myotis* species.

Hoary bat, *Lasiurus cinereus*

Greatest length: 13.1–19.0 mm ($^5/_{10}$–$^7/_{10}$ in.) (full table of measurements page 536, life-size image page 110, life-size jaw page 159)

Specimen illustrated: Adult male, LACM 30258

Dentition: i 1/3 c 1/1 p 2/2 m 3/3, total 32. One upper incisor large; first upper premolar peglike or absent; two upper premolars, though one may be lost; second premolar single-rooted rather than double as in eastern red bat *(L. borealis);* upper incisors touch canines.

Dorsal: Members of this genus are distinctly boxy. The braincase (1) is large and squared; the rostrum (2) is short and broad, nearly equal in breadth to the braincase. The zygomatic arches (3) flare widely, creating large orbits (4). The interorbital (5) is very narrow and deeply constricted.

Ventral: The palate (6) is incomplete, with a broad and deep notch. The palate (7) is very broad and tapers (8) as it extends well beyond the last molars. The pterygoid region (9) is also broad; the pterygoid processes (10) are very long. The auditory bullae (11) are large and swollen. The foramen magnum (12) is large and wide.

Lateral: The dorsolateral outline of the rostrum and braincase sit on the same continuous angle; the braincase (13) is elevated, especially to the posterior. The foramen magnum (14) is on a higher plane than in many other bats. The zygomatic arches (15) are long, low, and straight. The auditory meatus (16) is large. The incisors (17) are procumbent.

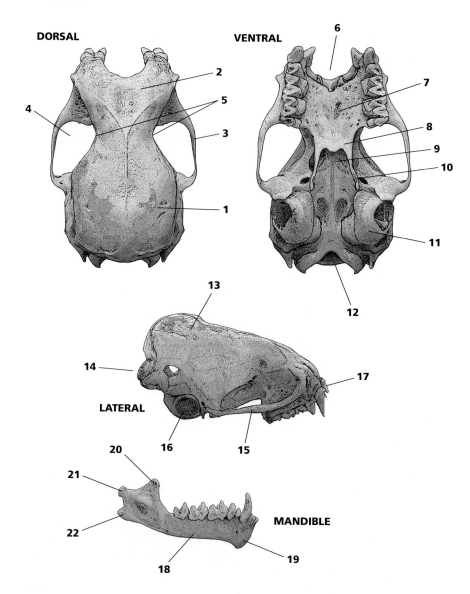

DORSAL

VENTRAL

LATERAL

MANDIBLE

Mandible: The body (18) of the mandible is long, and it is deepest (19) at the anterior. The coronoid process (20) is vertical, triangular, and rounded at its tip. The condyloid process (21) is short, slightly angled upward, and squared. The angular process (22) is reduced, triangular with blunt points.

Similar species: Red and Seminole bats, which share the same genus, and other larger vesper bats of the same family.

Note: Females are larger than males.

Big brown bat, *Eptesicus fuscus*

Greatest length: 15.1–23.0 mm (6/10–9/10 in.) (full table of measurements page 536, life-size image page 110, life-size jaw page 160)

Specimen illustrated: Adult, SBMNH 4308

Dentition: i 2/3 c 1/1 p 1/2 m 3/3, total 32. The three lower incisors are crowded and overlapping.

Dorsal: The overall outline is somewhat like a stone arrowhead, especially as the line of converging zygomatic arches continues to the anterior of the rostrum. The braincase (1) is large and oval. The zygomatic arches (2) flare very widely and converge strongly to the anterior; the orbits (3) are large and situated just anterior to the midpoint of the skull. The rostrum (4) is broad and relatively long. The interorbital (5) is narrow and deeply constricted.

Ventral: Palate (6) is incomplete, with a narrow notch. The broad palate (7) is of an equal width for the length of the toothrows, before it tapers (8) and extends beyond the last molars, ending with a pointy projection (9) over the pterygoid region. The auditory bullae (10) are relatively small but inflated. The foramen magnum (11) is large. Molars (12) are large and rugose. Several bones (13) that contribute to the tongue structure remain attached. The inner incisor (29) is much larger than the outer.

Lateral: The frontals (14) (forehead) slope gradually from the line of the rostrum to the elevated braincase (15). Sagittal crests (16) are well developed, being the highest point at the posterior of the skull. Occipital crests (17) are also apparent, and the auditory meatus (18) is large. The zygomatic arches (19) are relatively straight, and postorbital processes (20) are apparent. The canine (21) is large, and the incisors (22) are procumbent.

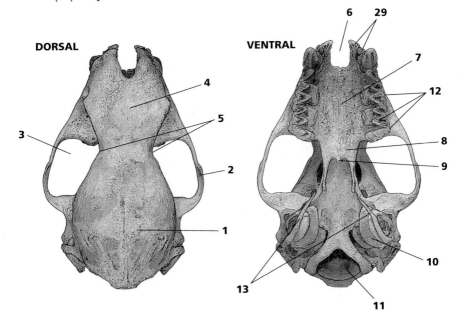

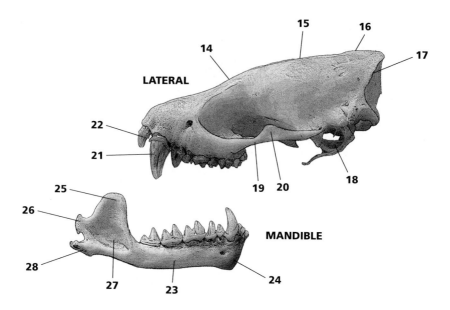

Mandible: The body (23) of the mandible is long, thin, and deepest (24) at the anterior tip. The coronoid process (25) is vertical, large, and squared. The condyloid process (26) is short but vertical, with a more barrel-shaped condyle. The masseteric fossa (27) is deep. The angular process (28) is large and multifaceted.

Similar species: Other larger vesper bats of the same family as well as other bats.

Notes: Females are larger than males in all measurements except interorbital (Hoffmeister 1986). Skull size increases with increased moisture when comparing across environments (Kurta and Baker 1990).

Pallid bat, *Antrozous pallidus*

Greatest length: 18.7–23.3 mm ($^7/_{10}$–$^9/_{10}$ in.) (full table of measurements page 538, life-size image page 111, life-size jaw page 160)

Specimen illustrated: Adult, SBMNH 3675

Dentition: i 1/2 c 1/1 p 1/2 m 3/3, total 28

Dorsal: The braincase (1) is long, oval, pointy at its posterior, and longer than 50 percent of the greatest length of the skull. The rostrum (2) is broad and long. The zygomatic arches (3) are very wide-spreading, converge slightly to the anterior, and create large orbits (4). The interorbital breadth (5) is narrow and constricted.

Ventral: Incomplete palate (6), with a deep notch. Palate narrows (7) significantly behind toothrows and terminates with a large, pointy projection (8) over the pterygoid region. Inflated auditory bullae (9) are of a medium size for bats, and the foramen magnum (10) is medium to small. The dentition is large and rugose. Several tongue bones (11) are still attached.

Lateral: The dorsolateral outline of the rostrum (12) slopes upward and smoothly connects to the moderately elevated braincase (13). Sagittal crests (14) are well developed in adults and form the high point of the skull at the posterior of the brain-case. The zygomatic arches (15) are straight. The auditory meatus (16) is large. The upper incisor (17) is procumbent, and the canine (18) large.

Mandible: The body (19) of the mandible is straight, and the ramus (20) large. The coronoid process (21) is overall triangular, large, and rounded. The condyloid process (22) is trapezoidal, small, and projects to the posterior. The angular process (23) is a thick, boxy extension equal in size to the condyloid process.

Similar species: Other large vesper bats of the same family, as well as other bats.

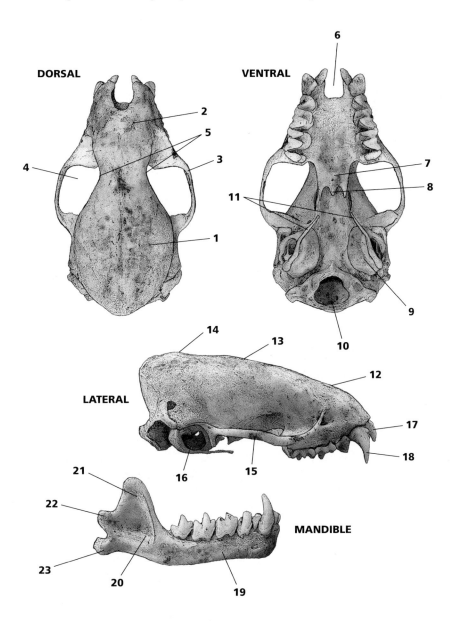

Family Molossidae: Free-tailed bats

Western bonneted bat, *Eumops perotis*

Greatest length: 29.7–33.0 mm ($1^2/_{10}$–$1^3/_{10}$ in.) (full table of measurements page 530, life-size image page 113, life-size jaw page 161)

Specimen illustrated: Adult male, SBMNH VB-15765

Dentition: i 1/2 c 1/1 p 2/1–2 m 3/3, total 28–30. Upper incisors slender and curved.

Dorsal: A large, slender, and distinctly angular skull. The braincase (1) is large and squared. The strong zygomatic arches (2) are wide-spreading, converge to the anterior, and have angular corners (3). The rostrum (4) is long and broad. The interorbital breadth (5) is very narrow, high, and constricted. Sagittal crests (6) are small, and occipital crests (7) are well developed. First incisors (8) are procumbent, curved, and distinctive.

Ventral: The palate (9) is complete and extends (10) to just beyond the toothrows; the pterygoid region (11) is broad, and the pterygoid processes (12) are very long. The auditory bullae (13) are large and swollen. The foramen magnum (14) is large. Toothrows are long; the first premolar (28) is tiny. Several tongue bones (15) still remain attached.

Lateral: The dorsolateral outline of the rostrum (16) is only just below the plane of the braincase (17), with a very nearly straight line between them. The rostrum (18) is very deep and stout. The occipital and sagittal crests are well developed. Zygomatic arches (19) are straight, and the auditory meatus (20) is very large. The canines (21) are long and large.

Mandible: The body (22) of the mandible is long and thin, and it tapers (23) in depth toward the posterior. The ramus (24) is elongated. The coronoid process (25) is

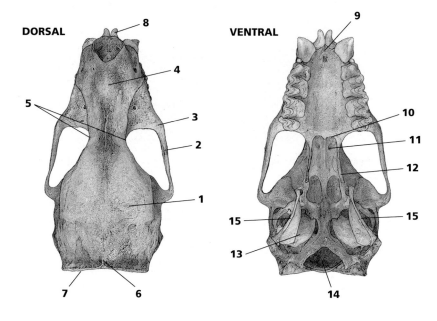

DORSAL   VENTRAL

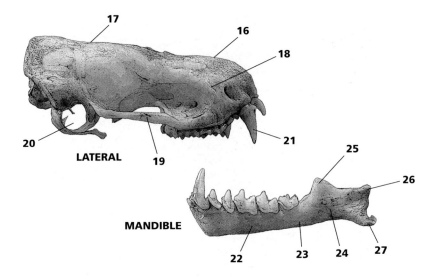

reduced and triangular, though it remains the highest point. The condyloid process (26) is a reduced, rounded bump sitting at a near 45-degree angle to the posterior, and the condyle sits just below the plane of the coronoid process. The angular process (27) is curved, multifaceted, and hooked. Dentition is rugose.

Similar species: Other large vesper bats and moles. This animal is large enough that it might be confused with a tiny weasel.

Note: Males are much larger than females, though Hoffmeister (1986) did not confirm this with cranio-morphometrics in his small sample.

Order Primates: Primates

Primate skulls are characterized by their large, forward-facing orbits and complete post-orbital bars. Large, rounded braincases to the posterior are high above the lower and smaller foramen magnum, a modification that supports the more vertical posture and balanced head. Dentition includes sharp canines and large, flattened premolars and molars, well adapted for a variety of foods. It is good to remember that we too are primates, and features of the skulls of primates presented here may be hauntingly similar to our own.

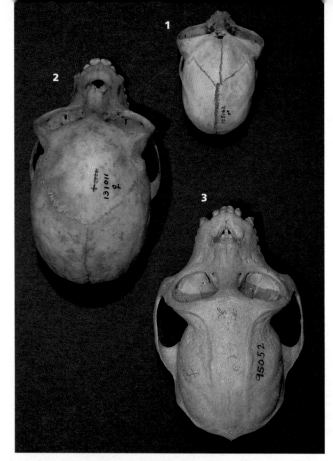

Select members of the order Primates: 1. Night monkey 155162 *(Aotus)*, 2. Spider monkey 13011 *(Ateles)*, 3. Mantled howler monkey 95052 *(Alouatta)*. MUSEUM OF VERTEBRATE ZOOLOGY, UC BERKELEY.

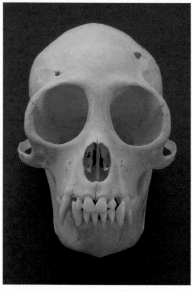

The skull of a spider monkey shares numerous characteristics with humans *(Ateles geoffroyi)*. NATURAL HISTORY MUSEUM OF LOS ANGELES COUNTY 92228.

Family Cebidae: Capuchins, Howlers, and Spider Monkeys

Mantled howler monkey, *Alouatta palliata*

Greatest length: 108.7–132.5 mm (4³/₁₀–5²/₁₀ in.) (full table of measurements page 538, life-size image page 133, life-size jaw page 169)

Specimen illustrated: Adult, MVZ 95052

Dentition: i 2/2 c 1/1 p 3/3 m 3/3, total 36.

Dorsal: A broad, flattened, and heavy skull. Large, forward-facing orbits (1). Wide-spreading, heavy zygomata (2). A large, oval braincase (3), and a long, relatively broad rostrum (4) for a North American primate. Nasals (5) are slim and constricted at their midpoints. Temporal ridges (6) are well developed and wide apart.

Ventral: The broad palate (7) ends at the midpoint of the last molar (8), and the incisive foramina (9) are small and extend to the posterior beyond the canines. The pterygoid region (10) is deep, and the pterygoid processes (11) are very large, heavy, and rounded. Auditory bullae (12) are smaller and flattened. Foramen magnum (13) is small. Toothrows are long and straight. M3 (14) is the smallest of the three molars, and the premolars (15) are also smaller than M1 and M2. Second premolar is larger than the first.

Lateral: Compared with other North American primates, howler monkeys have a flattened dorsolateral outline. The orbits are created by a heavy postorbital bar (16) and deep zygomata (17). Premaxillaries (18) extend much farther to the anterior than the tip of the nasals (19). Incisors are procumbent (20). Auditory meatus (22) is relatively large. The mandibular fossa (23) is well developed.

Mandible: A very large, heavy mandible with a deep, straight body (24) and enlarged ramus (25) and angular region (28). The coronoid process (26) is reduced, rounded,

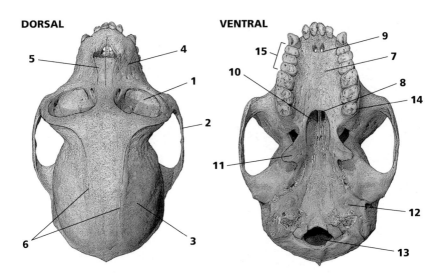

DORSAL

VENTRAL

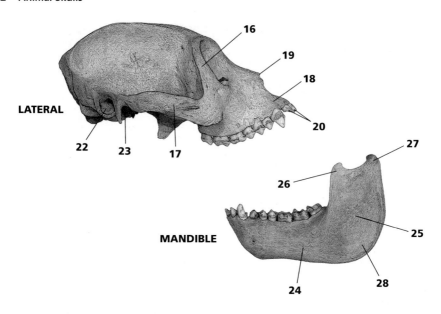

and below the condyle. The condyloid process (27) is large and rounded, and it forms the highest point on the mandible.

Similar species: Other primates. The complete postorbital bar should differentiate the mantled howler monkey from any other omnivore or carnivore.

Note: Temporal muscle coalescence occurs continuously with age, and in very old males, the temporal ridges nearly touch.

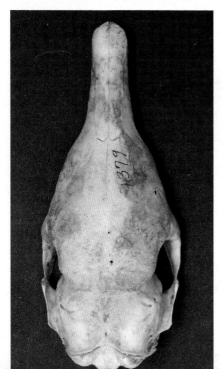

Order Xenarthra: Edentates

Family Dasypodidae: Armadillos

The armadillo is a very distinctive creature. The peglike dentition is greatly reduced and lacks enamel. The tubelike rostrum and reduced dentition are characteristic of several animals that tend to feed on social insects, including the African aardvark. Auditory bullae are incomplete and ringlike.

The sole member of this family north of Mexico is the nine-banded armadillo *(Dasypus novemcinctus).* SANTA BARBARA MUSEUM OF NATURAL HISTORY 1379.

Nine-banded armadillo, *Dasypus novemcinctus*

Greatest length: 86.1–107.3 mm ($3^4/10$–$4^2/10$ in.) (full table of measurements page 538, life-size image page 126, life-size jaw page 166)

Specimen illustrated: Adult, SBMNH 1379

Dentition: p 7/7 m 1/1, total teeth may range from 28 to 32. All but the last tooth in the row are deciduous. No incisors or canines; teeth are peglike and single rooted.

Dorsal: A distinctive rounded skull, with a long, slender, tubular rostrum (1). The zygomata (2) are short and have a narrow spread, creating small orbits that sit to the posterior of the skull. The interorbital breadth (4) is very broad, and the frontal region (5) is quite large. The nasals (6) are long and slender.

Ventral: Long palate (7), extending for much of the length of the skull. Auditory bullae (8) are ringlike and incomplete. Toothrows end before the start of the zygomatic arches. The foramen magnum (9) is large, and the occipital condyles (10) are wide apart.

Lateral: The nasals (11) are much longer than the reduced premaxillaries (12), which do not hold teeth. The zygomatic arches (13) are deep and curved. The frontal region (14) is greatly inflated.

Mandible: The entire mandible is long, slender, slightly curved, and tapering toward the anterior (15); it lacks maxillary fossae (16), the rougher structures on the inside of the mandible in most mammals where the two mandibles join. The coronoid process (17) is long, thin, and overall angled slightly to the posterior; the tip (18) is angled to the posterior. The angular process (19) is joined with the condyloid process (20) to form a thick, boxy projection; the condyle (21) is a vertical, rounded bump. The smallest teeth in the toothrow are to the posterior.

Similar species: Other armadillos in South America.

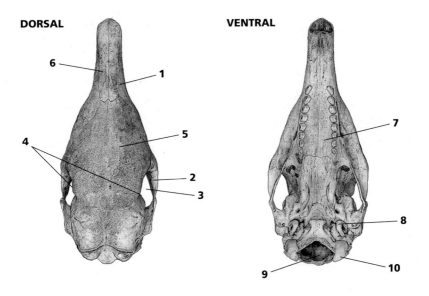

DORSAL   VENTRAL

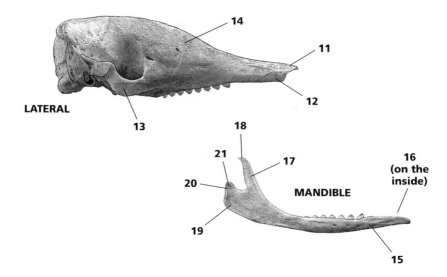

LATERAL

MANDIBLE

16
(on the
inside)

Notes: Stangl et al. (1995) could find no evidence to support sexual dimorphism in this species. They also defined three age classes based on sutures visible ventrally as follows: 1. Subadults had open basioccipital-basisphenoid and basisphenoid-presphenoid sutures. 2. Young adults had fully erupted dentition, and the basioccipital-basisphenoid had fused. 3. Old adults were characterized by the fusion and obliteration of both sutures. Refer to the photograph below.

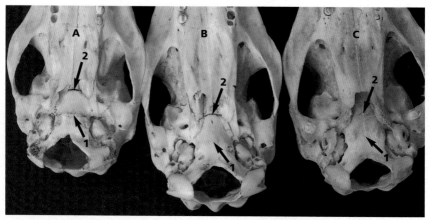

Stangl et al. (1995) defined three age classes based upon the fusion of the basisphenoid-basioccipital suture (1) and the basisphenoid-presphenoid sutures (2). In subadults (A), both sutures are open and distinctive. In young adults (B), the basisphenoid-basioccipital suture has fused and is obscured and the animal has adult dentition. In old adults (C), both sutures have fused and are obscured. MUSEUM OF COMPARATIVE ZOOLOGY, HARVARD U 30948, 61560, 998.

Order Lagomorpha: Pikas, Hares, and Rabbits

The lagomorphs are characterized by their rostral fenestra (one fenestra in pikas, family Ochotonidae; numerous in rabbits, family Leporidae), thought to aid in cooling blood vessels; massive incisive foramina that reduce the palate to a bridgelike structure; and unique dentition. Lagomorphs have four upper incisors, rather than the two that characterize all rodents. The forward pair is grooved, large, and rodent-like; the second pair, directly posterior to the first pair, is greatly reduced and peg-like. Like rodents, lagomorphs have a characteristic large diastema separating the front incisors from the remaining molariform teeth.

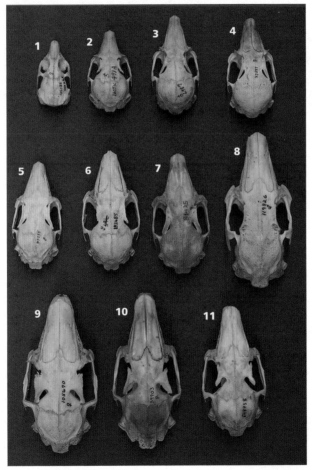

Select members of the order Lagomorpha: 1. American pika, female 135088 *(Ochotona)*, 2. Pygmy rabbit, male 165870 *(B. idahoensis)*, 3. Brush rabbit, female 6367 *(S. bachmani)*, 4. Mountain cottontail, female 27597 *(S. nuttallii)*, 5. Desert cottontail, male 95035 *(S. audubonii)*, 6. New England cottontail, male 183685 *(S. transitionalis)*, 7. Eastern cottontail, female 81425 *(S. floridanus)*, 8. Swamp rabbit, male 119826 *(S. aquaticus)*. 9. White-tailed jackrabbit, female 105670 *(L. townsendii)*, 10. Black-tailed jackrabbit, female 59903 *(L. californicus)*, 11. Snowshoe hare, female 588 *(L. americanus)*. MUSEUM OF VERTEBRATE ZOOLOGY, UC BERKELEY.

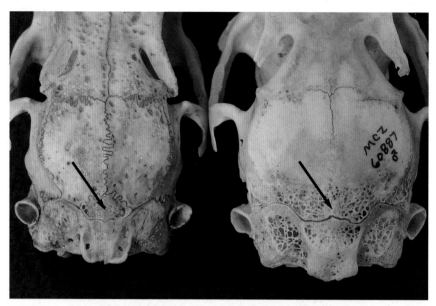

In *Sylvilagus*, such as the female eastern cottontail *(S. floridanus)* (3421) on the left, the inter-parietal bone remains distinctly separated by sutures from the parietal bones for the life of the animal. In *Lepus*, such as this male snowshoe hare *(L. americanus)* (60887) on the right, the interparietal quickly fuses with the parietals and is difficult to distinguish in mature animals.
MUSEUM OF COMPARATIVE ZOOLOGY, HARVARD U.

Eastern cottontail   **Mountain cottontail**

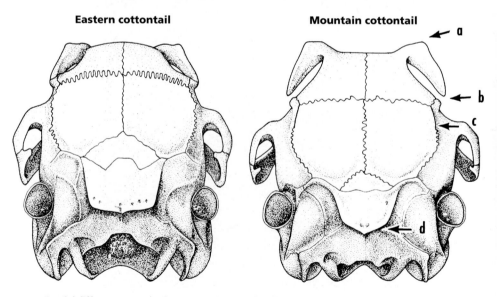

Cranial differences as seen from posterior view (Hoffmeister, 1986): (a) in eastern cottontail *(S. floridanus)* the frontal region between the supraoccipital processes is more convex than in mountain cottontail *(S. nuttallii)*; (b) the supraorbital processes are more often fused to the braincase in eastern cottontail; (c) the parieto-temporal suture is interdigitated in eastern cottontail; (d) in eastern cottontail, the supraoccipital shield is often notched or truncate, while in mountain cottontail often pointed, though sometimes rounded posteriorly. Text and illustrations used with permission of Donald Hoffmeister.

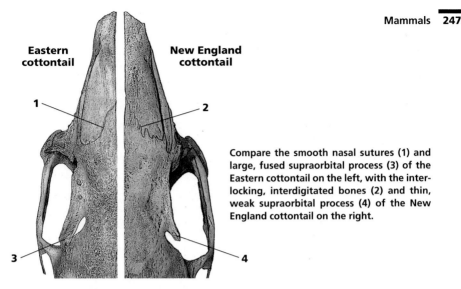

Eastern cottontail

New England cottontail

1

2

3

4

Compare the smooth nasal sutures (1) and large, fused supraorbital process (3) of the Eastern cottontail on the left, with the interlocking, interdigitated bones (2) and thin, weak supraorbital process (4) of the New England cottontail on the right.

Large rostrums are thought to indicate an excellent sense of smell. The rounded braincase and narrow spread of the zygomatic arches indicate poor development of the temporalis muscles. In lagomorphs, the masseter muscles are far larger than the temporalis muscles, supporting the grinding of foods on which they thrive; the articulation of the jaw is loose and allows for ample lateral movement in grinding and crushing.

Differentiating between cottontails and rabbits *(Sylvilagus)* and hares and jackrabbits *(Lepus)* can be done quite reliably in mature animals with a study of the interparietal bone—more specifically, the sutures between the parietal bones and the interparietal. Sutures that are visible and define interparietal distinctly are characteristic of *Sylvilagus,* whereas sutures that have fused, making the interparietal difficult to distinguish from the parietal bones, are characteristic of *Lepus* (refer to page 246). Except for the larger swamp and marsh rabbits, the greatest length of skull is often enough to differentiate between the smaller *Sylvilagus* species and larger *Lepus.* The shape of the supraoccipital shield is also useful, being much longer and more pronounced in *Lepus.*

Differentiating among the cottontails—eastern *(S. floridanus),* mountain *(S. nuttallii),* and New England *(S. transitionalis)*—is difficult. Useful characters that should be scrutinized include the shape of the supraoccipital shield, the shape and height of the supraoccipital processes, and the size and position of the auditory meatus. Each contributes much in cross-species comparisons.

Donald Hoffmeister (1986) has graciously permitted the reprinting of several illustrations (on page 246) and the accompanying text depicting the characters that distinguish between the mountain and eastern cottontails, including the following: "(a) in *S. floridanus* the frontal region between the supraoccipital processes is more convex than in *S. nuttallii;* (b) the supraoccipital processes are more often fused to the braincase [in *S. floridanus*]; (c) the parieto-temporal suture is more interdigitated [in *S. floridanus*]; (d) in *S. floridanus,* the supraoccipital shield is notched or truncated, in *S. nuttallii* often pointed or sometimes rounded posteriorly."

Eastern cottontails can be differentiated from New England cottontails through a study of the frontonasal sutures. In the eastern cottontail, the sutures are smooth lines, whereas in the New England cottontail, they are distinctly jagged, or interdigitated.

Family Ochotonidae: Pikas

American pika, *Ochotona princeps*

Greatest length: 38.8–47.3 mm (1⁵/₁₀–1⁹/₁₀ in.) (full table of measurements page 540, life-size image page 116, life-size jaw page 162)

Specimen illustrated: Adult male, SBMNH VB-S223

Dentition: i 2/1 c 0/0 p 3/2 m 2/3, total 26. Upper incisors grooved on anterior surface. One less cheek tooth than rabbits and hares in Leporidae.

Dorsal: Slender skull with relatively large, rounded orbits (1) situated well forward of the midpoint of the skull. Braincase (2) is large and ovoid, narrowing to the anterior. Interorbital region (3) is flat and relatively narrow when compared with that of rabbits. Rostrum (4) is long and slender; nasals (5) are broad and roughly rectangular, broadest at anterior. Jugals (6) extend far back beyond the squamosal arm of the zygomatic arch (7). The zygomatic plates (8) are very large. Pika lack postorbital-supraorbital processes, which are one of the distinctive characters in rabbit skulls.

Ventral: Palatal bridge (9) is very narrow, and the auditory bullae (10) are very large and swollen. Spheno-pterygoid canal (11) is large, as are the foramen ovale (12) and foramen magnum (13). Four upper incisors, two much smaller (14) are tucked behind the larger, grooved incisors. The large incisive foramen (25) in this specimen are damaged.

Lateral: Maxillaries (15) have a single large fenestra. The jugals (16) extend far back beyond the posterior zygomatic arm of the squamosal. Large diastema (17) between the incisors and molariform teeth. The auditory meatus (18) is high, at approximately half the height of the skull.

Mandible: The body (19) of the mandible is slightly curved, the diastema (20) of medium proportion and curved. The coronoid (21) and condyloid processes (22) appear as a

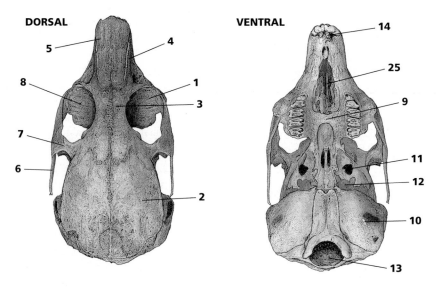

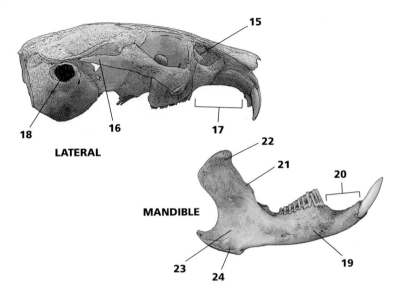

LATERAL

MANDIBLE

single large, rectangular structure. The angular process (23) is large and rounded, with a distinctive edge (24) created by the termination of the masseteric fossa.

Similar species: Pygmy rabbits and tree and ground squirrels.

Family Leporidae: Hares and rabbits

Pygmy rabbit, *Brachylagus idahoensis*

Greatest length: 46.3–52.2 mm ($1^8/10$–$2^1/10$ in.) (full table of measurements page 540, life-size image page 118, life-size jaw page 162)

Specimen illustrated: Adult male, MVZ 165870

Dentition: i 2/1 c 0/0 p 3/2 m 3/3, total 28. First upper cheek tooth (P2) with one reentrant angle on the anterior surface, which is different than in cottontails (Verts and Carraway 1998).

Dorsal: Typically rabbit in form, though much squatter in appearance than all other members. Shorter, pointed rostrum (1). Nasals (2) large, rectangular, and widest at posterior. Compared with cottontail skulls, the braincase (3) is very round and large in proportion to the overall size of the skull. Broad and high interorbital region (4). Supraorbital processes (5) are long and widest in the middle; anterior and posterior projections are often roughly equal in length. Interparietal bone (6) is not fused, a trait shared with cottontails. The supraoccipital shield (7) is small.

Ventral: Incisive foramen (8) is massive, forming a palatal bridge (9) of comparatively medium size; the palatal bridge in this specimen starts at the anterior of the second cheek tooth and terminates at the midpoint of the fourth. Massive and inflated auditory bullae (10); the width of the bullae is equal to or greater than the length of a toothrow. Foramen magnum (11) relatively large. Four upper incisors, the two

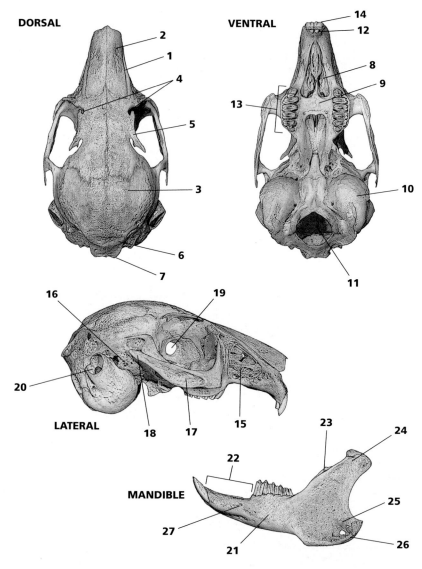

DORSAL

VENTRAL

LATERAL

MANDIBLE

smaller (12) situated behind and in contact with the larger pair. Molariform teeth (13) relatively small. Large upper incisors (14) are grooved on their anterior surface.

Lateral: Numerous fenestrae on the maxillary (15), rostrum, and squamosal (16), just posterior to the zygomatic arch. Zygomatic arches (17) are deep and stout; the projection on the jugal (18) at the posterior of zygomatic arch is much smaller than in pika. Antorbital canal (19) is large and round. Auditory meatus (20) is elevated and, compared with those of other members of the family, of medium proportions.

Mandible: The body (21) of the mandible is slightly curved, the diastema of medium proportion and curved. The coronoid (23) and condyloid (24) processes appear as a single large, rectangular structure. The angular process (25) is large and rounded, with a distinctive edge (26) created by the termination of the masseteric fossa. Mental foramen (27) on mandible just anterior to first cheek tooth.

Similar species: Cottontails and pikas. Very young cottontails often have similar proportions to pygmy rabbits; look for fused sutures to confirm age.

Note: Females often larger than males.

Desert cottontail, *Sylvilagus audubonii*

Greatest length: 61.1–74.1 mm (2⁴/₁₀–2⁹/₁₀ in.) (full table of measurements page 540, life-size image page 121, life-size jaw page 163)

Specimen illustrated: Adult female, SBMNH 3108

Dentition: i 2/1 c 0/0 p 3/2 m 3/3, total 28.

Dorsal: Long, stout, triangular rostrum (1). Nasals (2) large, rectangular, and widest at posterior. The braincase is round and relatively large. Broad and high interorbital region (3). Supraorbital processes (4) are long; anterior projections are short; posterior extension (5) is long, broad, and often upturned and fused to the braincase. Large interparietal bone (6) easily differentiated from parietal bone. The supraoccipital shield (7) is squared.

Ventral: Incisive foramen (8) is massive, forming a palatal bridge (9) of comparatively medium size; the palatal bridge in this specimen starts at the anterior of the second cheek tooth and terminates approximately one-quarter of the way into the fourth. Auditory bullae (10) are proportionately large compared with those of other family members. Foramen magnum (11) is medium. Four upper incisors, the two smaller (12) situated behind and in contact with the larger pair. Upper incisors (13) are grooved on anterior surface.

Lateral: Numerous fenestrae on the maxillary (14), rostrum, and squamosal (15), just posterior to the zygomatic arch. Zygomatic arches (16) are deep and stout; projec-

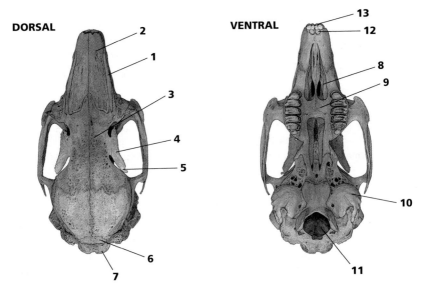

DORSAL   VENTRAL

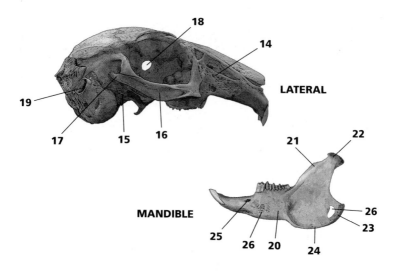

tion on jugal (17) at posterior of zygomatic arch much smaller than in pika. Antorbital canal (18) is large and round. Auditory meatus (19) is elevated and, compared with those of other members of the family, of medium proportions.

Mandible: The body (20) of the mandible is slightly curved, the diastema of medium proportion and curved. The coronoid (21) and condyloid (22) processes appear as a single large, rectangular structure; the ramus is deep. The angular process (23) is rounded, with a distinctive edge (24) created by the termination of the masseteric fossa. Mental foramen (25) on mandible just anterior to first cheek tooth. There may also be signs of fenestrae (26) along the body of the mandible or the lower ramus in rabbits.

Similar species: Other cottontails and rabbits.

Note: Females often larger than males.

Brush rabbit, *Sylvilagus bachmani*

Greatest length: 57.9–66.0 mm (2^3/10–2^6/10 in.) (full table of measurements page 540, life-size image page 119, life-size jaw page 163)

Specimen illustrated: Subadult female, SBMNH 315

Dentition: i 2/1 c 0/0 p 3/2 m 3/3, total 28.

Dorsal: Long, stout, triangular rostrum (1), though proportionately a bit shorter than in cottontails. Nasals (2) large, tapering to points at posterior (3). The braincase (4) is round and relatively large. Broad and high interorbital region (5). Supraorbital processes (6) are proportionately slimmer; anterior projections are short; posterior projection (7) is generally separate from or may just touch the braincase. Large interparietal bone (8) easily differentiated from parietal bone. The supraoccipital shield (9) is squared.

Ventral: Incisive foramen (10) is massive, forming a palatal bridge (11) of comparatively medium size; the palatal bridge in this specimen starts midline into the first

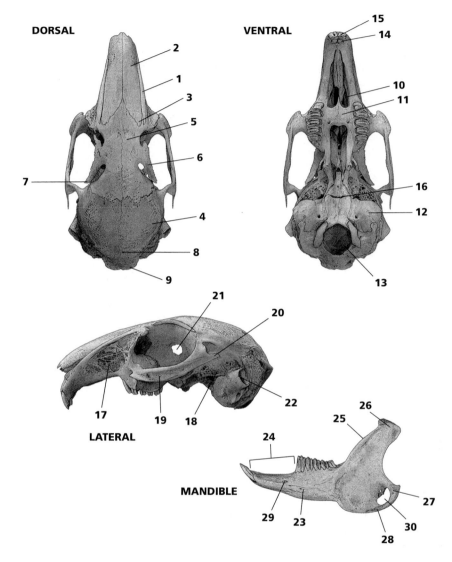

DORSAL

VENTRAL

LATERAL

MANDIBLE

cheek tooth and terminates approximately at the posterior edge of the third. Auditory bullae (12) are proportionately large and inflated compared with those of other family members. Foramen magnum (13) is large. Four upper incisors, the two smaller (14) situated behind and in contact with the larger pair. The large upper incisors (15) are grooved on anterior surface. This is a relatively young specimen, as the basioccipital suture (16) is still open.

Lateral: Numerous fenestrae on the maxillary (17), rostrum, and squamosal (18), just posterior to the zygomatic arch. Zygomatic arches (19) are deep and stout; projection on jugal (20) at posterior of zygomatic arch much smaller than in pika. Antorbital canal (21) is large and round. Auditory meatus (22) is elevated and, compared with those of other members of the family, large.

Mandible: The body (23) of the mandible is slightly curved, the diastema (24) of medium proportion and curved. The coronoid (25) and condyloid (26) processes appear as a single large, rectangular structure; the ramus is deep. The angular process (27) is rounded, with a distinctive edge (28) created by the termination of the masseteric fossa. Mental foramen (29) on mandible just anterior to first cheek tooth. There may also be signs of fenestrae (30) along the body of the mandible or the lower ramus in rabbits.

Similar species: Other cottontails and rabbits.

Note: Females often larger than males.

Eastern cottontail, *Sylvilagus floridanus*

Greatest length: 62.3–82.0 mm ($2^5/_{10}$–$3^2/_{10}$ in.) (full table of measurements page 542, life-size image page 122, life-size jaw page 164)

Specimen illustrated: Adult female, MVZ 81425

Dentition: i 2/1 c 0/0 p 3/2 m 3/3, total 28.

Dorsal: Long, stout, triangular rostrum (1). Nasals (2) large, rectangular, and widest at posterior, with smooth frontonasal sutures (3). The braincase (4) is round and relatively large. Broad and high interorbital region (5). Supraorbital processes (6) are proportionately slimmer; anterior projections (7) are short and sometimes fused to frontals; the posterior projection (8) is broad and generally fused to the braincase. Medium interparietal bone (9) easily differentiated from parietal bone. The supraoccipital shield (10) is squared.

Ventral: Incisive foramen (11) is massive, forming a palatal bridge (12) of comparatively larger size; the palatal bridge in this specimen starts approximately one-third of the way into the first cheek tooth and terminates at the posterior edge of the third. Auditory bullae (13) are proportionately small when compared with those of

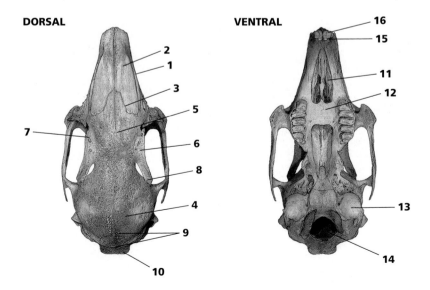

DORSAL

VENTRAL

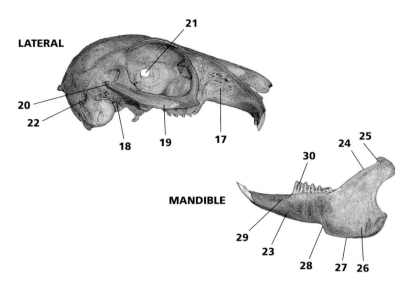

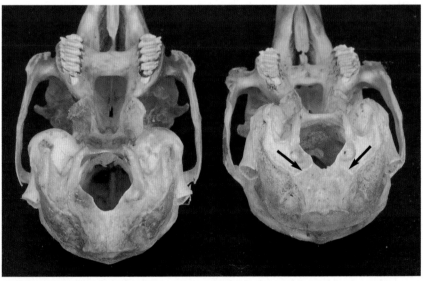

The supraoccipital-exoccipital sutures are visible in the eastern cottontail on the right, which Hoffmeister (1989) reports is indicative of subadult and young animals. When the sutures become difficult to distinguish, the animal has reached adulthood. PRIVATE COLLECTION.

other family members. Foramen magnum (14) is medium. Four upper incisors, the two smaller (15) situated behind and in contact with the larger pair. Upper incisors (16) are grooved on anterior surface.

Lateral: Numerous fenestrae on the maxillary (17), rostrum, and squamosal (18), just posterior to the zygomatic arch. Zygomatic arches (19) are deep and stout; projection on jugal (20) is small. Antorbital canal (21) is medium and round. Auditory meatus (22) is elevated and, compared with those of other members of the family, small.

Mandible: The body (23) of the mandible is slightly curved, the diastema of medium proportion and curved. The coronoid (24) and condyloid (25) processes appear as a single large, rectangular structure; the ramus is deep. The angular process (26) is large and rounded, with a distinctive edge (27) created by the termination of the masseteric fossa, and there is a significant step (28) from the ventral surface of the body to the angular process. Mental foramen (29) on mandible just anterior to first cheek tooth. There may also be signs of fenestrae along the body of the mandible or the lower ramus in rabbits. Tallest tooth (30) is at anterior, and teeth descend in size to posterior.

Similar species: Other cottontails and rabbits.

Notes: Females often larger than males. In addition to basioccipital sutures, Hoffmeister (1989) suggests a study of the supraoccipital-exoccipital suture to differentiate immature animals from adults; it is fused and indistinct in adults.

Snowshoe hare, *Lepus americanus*

Greatest length: 72.9–85.5 mm ($2^9/10$–$3^4/10$ in.) (full table of measurements page 544, life-size image page 123, life-size jaw page 164)

Specimen illustrated: Adult female, MVZ 588

Dentition: i 2/1 c 0/0 p 3/2 m 3/3, total 28.

Dorsal: Long, stout, triangular rostrum (1). Nasals (2) large, rectangular, and widest at posterior, with relatively smooth frontonasal sutures (3). The braincase (4) is round and relatively large. Broad and high interorbital region (5). Supraorbital processes (6) flare outward; the anterior projections (7) are much shorter than the posterior and may be absent altogether. The interparietal bone (8) is fused to the parietal bone and difficult to distinguish. The supraoccipital shield (9) is squared.

Ventral: Incisive foramen (10) is massive, forming a palatal bridge (11) of comparatively larger size; the palatal bridge in this specimen starts approximately one-third of the way into the first cheek tooth and terminates at the posterior edge of the third. Auditory bullae (12) are proportionately small when compared with those of other family members. Foramen magnum (13) is large. Four upper incisors, the two smaller (14) situated behind and in contact with the larger pair. Upper incisors (15) are grooved on anterior surface.

Lateral: Numerous fenestrae on the maxillary (16), rostrum, and squamosal (17), just posterior to the zygomatic arch. Zygomatic arches (18) are deep and stout; projection on jugal (19) at posterior of zygomatic arch is small. Antorbital canal (20) is large and round. Pterygoid processes (22) extend below toothrows. Auditory meatus (23) is elevated, angled at approximately 45 degrees to the posterior, and small compared with those of other members of the family.

Mandible: The body (24) of the mandible is slightly curved and tapers to the anterior; the diastema (25) is large and curved. The coronoid process (26) is greatly reduced and joins to the condyloid process (27) to appear as a single large, rectangular structure. The ramus is deep. The angular process (28) is rounded, with a dis-

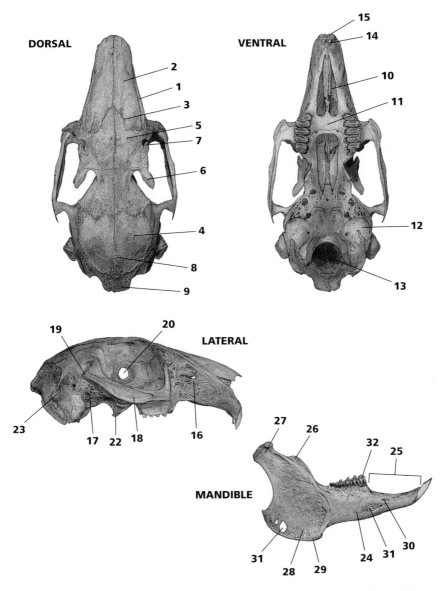

DORSAL

VENTRAL

LATERAL

MANDIBLE

tinctive edge (29) created by the termination of the masseteric fossa. Mental foramen (30) on mandible just anterior to first cheek tooth. There may also be signs of
fenestrae (31) along the body of the mandible or the lower ramus in rabbits. Tallest
tooth (32) is at anterior, and teeth descend in size to posterior.

Similar species: Other hares and jackrabbits, as well as larger cottontails and rabbits.

Note: Females often larger than males.

Black-tailed jackrabbit, *Lepus californicus*

Greatest length: 85.4–101.9 mm (3⁴/10–4 in.) (full table of measurements page 544, life-size image page 125, life-size jaw page 165)

Specimen illustrated: Adult female, SBMNH 304

Dentition: i 2/1 c 0/0 p 3/2 m 3/3, total 28.

Dorsal: Long, stout, triangular rostrum (1). Nasals (2) large, rectangular, and widest at posterior, with undulating frontonasal sutures (3). The braincase (4) is round and relatively large. Broad and high interorbital region (5). Supraorbital processes (6) flare outward but often fuse at posterior to the squamosal (7); the anterior projections (8) are much shorter than the posterior and may be absent altogether. The interparietal bone (9) is fused to the parietal bone and difficult to distinguish. The supraoccipital shield (10) is long and squared.

Ventral: Incisive foramen (11) is massive, forming a palatal bridge (12) of comparatively smaller size; the palatal bridge in this specimen starts approximately one-third of the way into the first cheek tooth and terminates at the posterior edge of the third. Auditory bullae (13) are proportionately small when compared with those of other family members. Foramen magnum (14) is large. Four upper incisors, the two smaller (15) situated behind and in contact with the larger pair. Upper incisors (16) are grooved on anterior surface.

Lateral: Numerous fenestrae on the maxillary (17), rostrum, and squamosal (18), just posterior to the zygomatic arch. Zygomatic arches (19) are deep and stout; projection on jugal (20) at posterior of zygomatic arch is small. Antorbital canal (21) is smaller and rounded. Pterygoid processes (22) extend below toothrows. Auditory meatus (23) is elevated, angled at approximately 45 degrees to the posterior, and small compared with those of other members of the family.

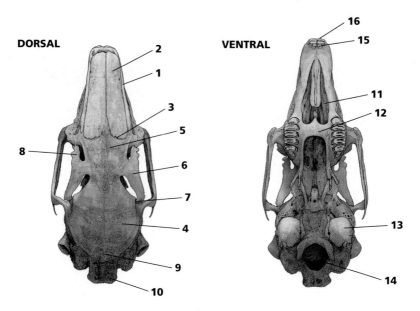

DORSAL · VENTRAL

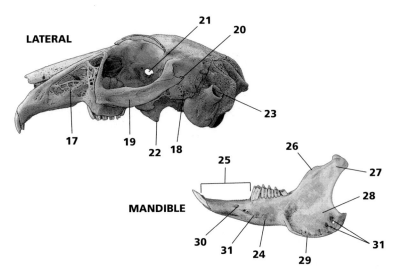

LATERAL

MANDIBLE

Mandible: The body (24) of the mandible is slightly curved and tapers to the anterior; the diastema (25) is large and straight. The coronoid process (26) is greatly reduced and joins to the condyloid process (27) to appear as a single large, rectangular structure. The ramus is deep. The angular process (28) is rounded, with a distinctive edge (29) created by the termination of the masseteric fossa. Mental foramen (30) on mandible just anterior to first cheek tooth. There may also be signs of fenestrae (31) along the body of the mandible or the lower ramus in rabbits. Tallest tooth is at anterior, and teeth descend in size to posterior.

Similar species: Other jackrabbits and hares, as well as larger cottontails and rabbits.

Note: Females often larger than males. Hoffmeister (1986) found that in Arizona, females were significantly larger in greatest length, basal length, and nasal length.

White-tailed jackrabbit, *Lepus townsendii*

Greatest length: 76.8–102.5 mm (3.0–4.0 in.) (full table of measurements page 544, life-size image page 125, life-size jaw page 165)

Specimen illustrated: Adult female, MVZ 105670

Dentition: i 2/1 c 0/0 p 3/2 m 3/3, total 28.

Dorsal: Long, stout, triangular rostrum (1). Nasals (2) large, rectangular, and widest at posterior, with smooth fronto-nasal sutures (3). The braincase (4) is round and relatively large. Broad and high interorbital region (5). Supraorbital processes (6) flare outward and rarely fuse to the squamosal at posterior; the anterior projections (7) are much shorter than the posterior. The interparietal bone (8) is fused to the parietal bone and difficult to distinguish. The supraoccipital shield (9) is squared.

Ventral: Incisive foramen (10) is massive, forming a palatal bridge (11) of comparatively larger size; the palatal bridge in this specimen starts approximately one-third of the way into the first cheek tooth and terminates at the posterior edge of the third. Auditory bullae (12) are proportionately small when compared with those of

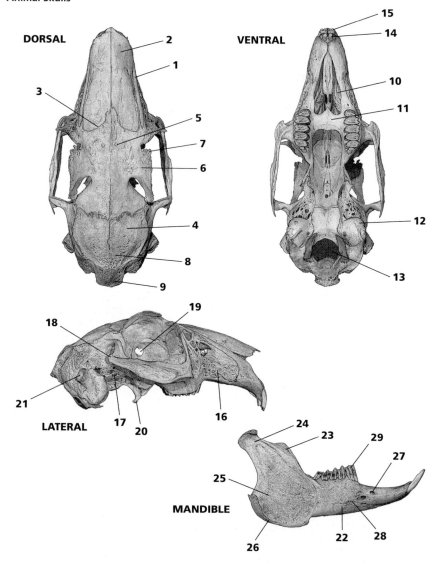

DORSAL

VENTRAL

LATERAL

MANDIBLE

other family members. Foramen magnum (13) is large. Four upper incisors, the two smaller (14) situated behind and in contact with the larger, grooved pair (15).

Lateral: Numerous fenestrae on the maxillary (16), rostrum, and squamosal (17), just posterior to the zygomatic arch. Zygomatic arches are deep and stout; projection on jugal (18) at posterior of zygomatic arch is very small. Antorbital canal (19) is smaller and round. Pterygoid processes (20) extend below toothrows. Auditory meatus (21) is elevated, angled at approximately 45 degrees to the posterior, and very small compared with those of other members of the family.

Mandible: The body (22) of the mandible is slightly curved and tapers to the anterior; the diastema is large and curved. The coronoid process (23) is greatly reduced and joins to the condyloid process (24) to appear as a single large, rectangular structure. The ramus is deep. The angular process (25) is rounded, with a distinctive edge (26) created by the termination of the masseteric fossa. Mental foramen (27) on mandible just anterior to first cheek tooth. There may also be signs of fenestrae (28) along the body of the mandible or the lower ramus in rabbits. Tallest tooth (29) is at anterior, and teeth descend in size to posterior.

Similar species: Other jackrabbits and hares, as well as larger cottontails and rabbits.

Notes: Females often larger than males. Though the shape of the supraorbital processes tends to be different in black-tailed jackrabbits *(L. californicus)*, there is variability, and Kim (1987) reports that no single feature reliably distinguishes white-tailed from black-tailed jackrabbit skulls.

Order Rodentia: Rodents

Rodents are a large and diverse group of mammals found throughout North America and the world. They are characterized by a distinctive dentition, which never exceeds twenty-two teeth and lacks canine teeth altogether. The most striking feature of the teeth and skull is the four large, sharp incisors at the anterior of the skull, separated from the remaining molariform dentition by large diastemata. The incisors are ever growing and most often coated with hard enamel only on the anterior or anterior and lateral surfaces. Softer portions of the teeth wear quickly or are chipped away by clicking the teeth together to maintain sharp and ready edges. According to W. Howard and M. Smith, in one species of pocket gophers, the top incisors grow .62 millimeters per day and the lower .99 millimeters per day (Verts and Carraway 1998).

The mandibles of rodents often are curved and loosely articulated. The curvature focuses power when closing the jaws to the far anterior, where the incisors sit. The lateral movement allows the molariform teeth to grind and crush a great diversity of foods. Rodents rely on enlarged masseter muscles to operate the grinding and crushing molariform teeth. Three common forms influence the shape and structure of the masseter muscles, and each is related to the size and shape of the infraorbital foramina. In sciuromorphs, the infraorbital foramina are very small, and no part of the masseter muscles pass through. In myomorphs, the infraorbital foramina are slitlike and allow a small portion of the masseter muscles to pass through. In hystricomorphs, the infraorbital foramina are massive, and much of the masseter muscles passes through the opening.

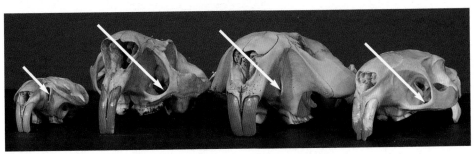

From left to right, compare the size and shape of the infraorbital foramen in muskrat, porcupine, beaver, and nutria. MUSEUM OF VERTEBRATE ZOOLOGY, UC BERKELEY 37415, 68707, 90732, 97349.

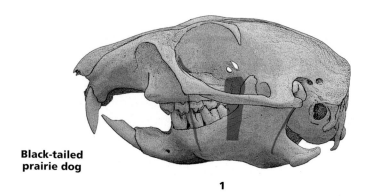

Black-tailed prairie dog

1

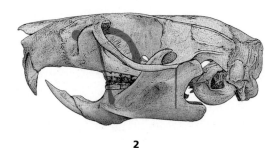

Black rat

2

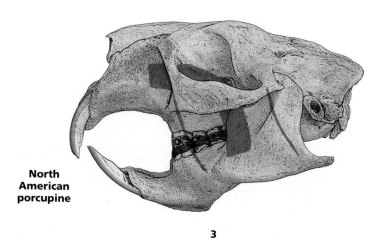

North American porcupine

3

Compare the passage of the masseter muscles in three groups of rodents: 1. In sciuromorphs, no part of the masseter medialis passes through the very small infraorbital foramen. 2. In myomorphs, a small branch of the masseter medialis passes through the slitlike infraorbital canal. 3. In hystricomorphs, the masseter medialis passes through the enlarged infraorbital canal and attaches on the side of the rostrum. Drawn after Hoffmeister (1986).

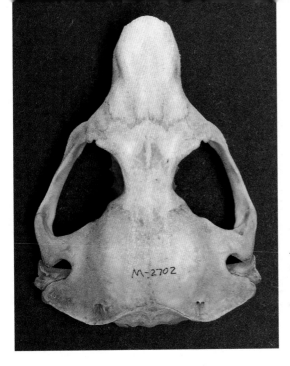

The sole member of this family is the aplodontia, or mountain beaver *(Aplodontia rufa)*. SANTA BARBARA MUSEUM OF NATURAL HISTORY, male 2702.

Family Aplodontiidae: Aplodontia

Mountain beaver or aplodontia, *Aplodontia rufa*

Greatest length: 62.7–77.1 mm ($2^4/10$–3.0 in.) (full table of measurements page 570, life-size image page 122, life-size jaw page 163)

Specimen illustrated: Adult male, SBMNH M-2702

Dentition: i 1/1 c 0/0 p 2/1 m 3/3, total 22.

Dorsal: The skull is flattened, robust, and distinctively wedge-shaped, being widest at the posterior. The rostrum (6) is large and broad. The actual braincase (1) is squared. Zygomata (2) are heavy and strongly convergent to the anterior; orbits (16) are relatively large. Interorbital breadth (3) is so narrow that one can view the maxillary bones from the dorsal perspective; postorbital processes are lacking. Mastoid processes (4) are large. Occipital crests (5) are well developed, but sagittal crests are absent.

Ventral: Very long palate (7) extends beyond posterior molars; the incisive foramina (8) are small. Auditory bullae (9) are distinctly vase-shaped, with long necks (10) that point perpendicularly to the midline of the skull. The spheno-pterygoid canals (11) are small and round, and the foramen magnum (12) is smaller. In mature animals, the maxillary molars have distinctive spikelike projections (13) from the enamel layer. Note the tiny first molar (14) and the reduced pterygoid region (15).

Lateral: The dorsolateral outline (17) is relatively straight. The zygomatic arches (18) are straight and level. The zygomatic plate (19) is small and horizontal; it can only be inferred from the corresponding illustration, as the zygomatic arm blocks the view. Nasals (20) decurve to the anterior and extend beyond the incisors. Occipital

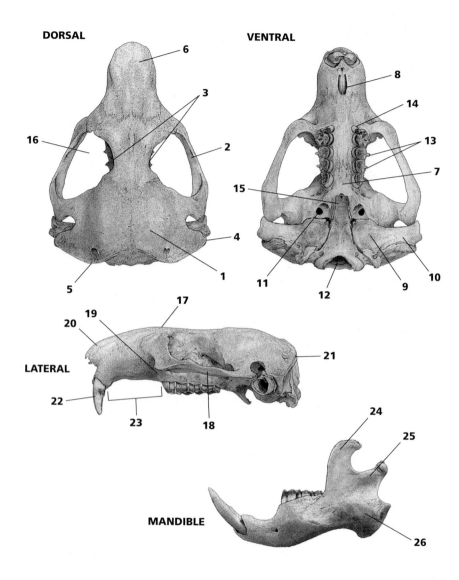

DORSAL

VENTRAL

LATERAL

MANDIBLE

crests (21) are evident. Large incisors (22) are orange and flattened, anterior to a wide diastema (23).

Mandible: The mandible is very rugose. The coronoid process (24) is high, stout, and curved to the posterior. The condyloid process (25) is angled upward to the posterior at roughly a 45-degree angle, stout, and somewhat triangular. The angular process (26) is large, multifaceted, and greatly inflected outward.

Similar species: Woodchucks, marmots, and beavers.

Family Sciuridae: Squirrels

Members of Sciuridae are rodents, further characterized by well-developed postorbital processes, small infraorbital foramina, and large zygomatic plates, which provide the lateral boundary to the large masseter muscles. No portion of the masseter muscles passes through the infraorbital foramina, characteristic of sciuromorph rodents.

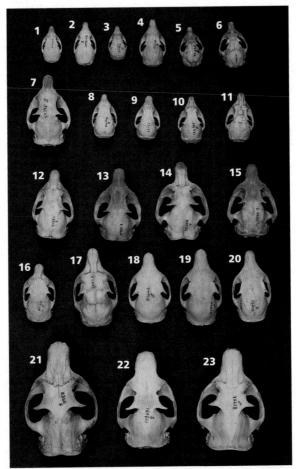

Select members of Sciuridae: 1. Yellow-pine chipmunk, female 444 *(Neo. amoenus)*, 2. Cliff chipmunk, female 109646 *(Neo. dorsalis)*, 3. Least chipmunk, male 77966 *(Neo. minimus)*, 4. Eastern chipmunk, female 90834 *(T. striatus)*, 5. Southern flying squirrel, male 95368 *(G. volans)*, 6. Northern flying squirrel, female 42540 *(G. sabrinus)*, 7. California ground squirrel, male 29375 *(Sp. beecheyi)*, 8. White-tailed antelope squirrel, female 86148 *(A. leucurus)*, 9. Thirteen-lined ground squirrel 96796 *(Sp. tridecemlineatus)*, 10. Spotted ground squirrel, female 122955 *(Sp. spilosoma)*, 11. Golden-mantled ground squirrel, female 15063 *(Sp. lateralis)*, 12. Rock squirrel, male 47883 *(Sp. variegatus)*, 13. Arctic ground squirrel, male 39720 *(Sp. parryii)*, 14. White-tailed prairie dog, male 50308 *(C. leucurus)*, 15. Black-tailed prairie dog, female 41185 *(C. ludovicianus)*, 16. Red squirrel, male 89044 *(T. hudsonicus)*, 17. Western gray squirrel, male 2087 *(S. griseus)*, 18. Abert's or tassel-eared squirrel 119563 *(S. aberti)*, 19. Eastern fox squirrel, male 160560 *(S. niger)*, 20. Eastern gray squirrel, male 53885 *(S. carolinensis)*, 21. Hoary marmot, female 8360 *(M. caligata)*, 22. Yellow-bellied marmot, female 149691 *(M. flaviventris)*, 23. Woodchuck, male 81988 *(M. monax)*. MUSEUM OF VERTEBRATE ZOOLOGY, UC BERKELEY.

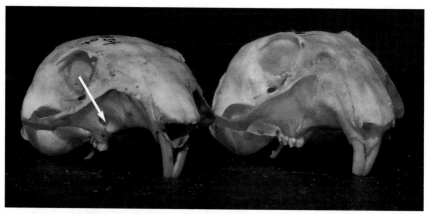

On the left is an eastern chipmunk *(Tamias striatus)* with characteristic large infraorbital foramen pierces the zygomatic plate, and on the right a thirteen-lined ground squirrel *(Spermophilus tridecemlineatus).* MUSEUM OF VERTEBRATE ZOOLOGY, UC BERKELEY 90834, 98108.

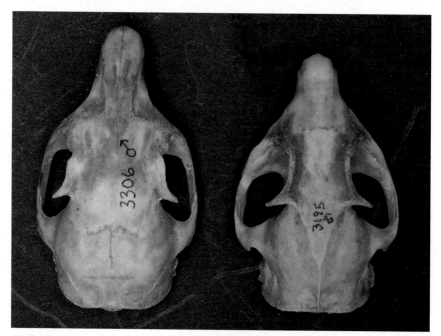

On the left, a male western gray squirrel *(Sciurus griseus)*, on the right, a male California ground squirrel *(Spermophilus beecheyi).* SANTA BARBARA MUSEUM OF NATURAL HISTORY 3306, 3195.

Small ground squirrel and chipmunk skulls are very similar in form. In general, chipmunk skulls are squatter and proportionately wider, with smaller postorbital processes and larger braincases. Small ground squirrels are proportionately more slender and have smaller braincases and larger postorbital processes. Yet this may still leave some question. The key feature to reliably separate chipmunks from ground squirrels is the infraorbital foramina. In ground squirrels, the foramina are smaller and on the side of

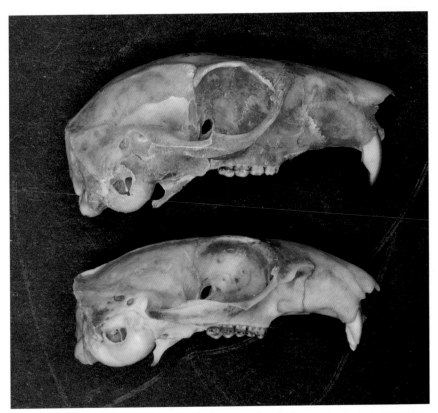

Above, western gray squirrel, below, California ground squirrel. SANTA BARBARA MUSEUM OF NATURAL HISTORY 3306, 3195.

the rostrum; in chipmunks, they are larger, round, and pierce the zygomatic plate. The photo on page 266 illustrates this perfectly.

Several characters can help differentiate ground squirrel (*Spermophilus* spp.) from tree squirrel (*Sciurus* and *Tamiasciurus*) skulls. In general, the zygomatic arches are far more convergent to the anterior in ground squirrels than in tree squirrels; the posterior edge of the zygomatics viewed from the dorsal are often curved in ground squirrels and straighter in tree squirrels. The zygomatic arches twist in ground squirrels as they move to the posterior, so that the lateral surfaces become more horizontal than in tree squirrels. Temporal ridges are often more developed in ground squirrels, as are the postorbital processes. Look for these features in the photo on page 266.

From the lateral perspective, tree squirrels have a distinctively straight dorsolateral outline from the tip of the nasals to the apex of the braincase. In ground squirrels, the entire dorsolateral outline is more convex, curving to both the anterior and the posterior (refer to the photo above). If mandibles are present, they also provide useful characters to weigh in identification. The notch that dips between the tip of the coronoid process and the condyloid process is much deeper in ground squirrels and tree squirrels.

Least chipmunk, *Neotamias minimus*

Greatest length: 27.4–33.2 mm ($1^1/10$–$1^3/10$ in.) (full table of measurements page 546, life-size image page 113, life-size jaw page 160)

Specimen illustrated: Adult female, SBMNH VB-68-197

Dentition: i 1/1 c 0/0 p 2/1 m 3/3, total 22.

Dorsal: Chipmunks have broad, smooth braincases (1), rounded zygomatic arches (2), and large zygomatic plates (3); skulls are relatively thin boned and delicate. The rostrum (4) is slender and relatively short; nasals (5) are triangular and taper to posterior. The braincase (1) is long, proportionately larger than in eastern chipmunk and some other western chipmunks. Interorbital notches (6) are small and nearly aligned with the posterior edge of the zygomatic plates (7); well-developed postorbital processes (8) point to posterior. Interorbital breadth (9) is much less than postorbital (10).

Ventral: The nasal vacuity (11) is somewhat tubular. The palate (12) extends beyond the posterior molars and terminates with a pointy projection (13) over the pterygoid region (14); incisive foramina (15) are small. Round infraorbital foramen (16) pierces zygomatic plate. Spheno-pterygoid canals (17) are large and round; foramen ovale (18) is slitlike. Auditory bullae (19) are large, round, and inflated. Foramen magnum (20) is large. Toothrows (21) are slightly convex.

Lateral: The nasals (22) extend well beyond the incisors (23). The zygomatic plate (24) is at approximately 30 degrees. The braincase (25) is high. Antorbital canal (26) is ovoid. Incisors (23) are recurved.

Mandible: The body (27) of the mandible is curved, and the ramus (28) is reduced at the center of long processes. The coronoid process (29) is slim, long, and curved to the posterior. The condyloid process (30) is long and angles up and to the posterior at roughly a 45-degree angle; the tip points to posterior. The angular process (31)

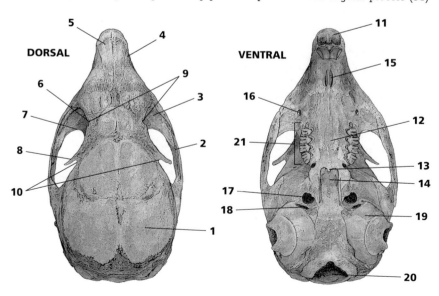

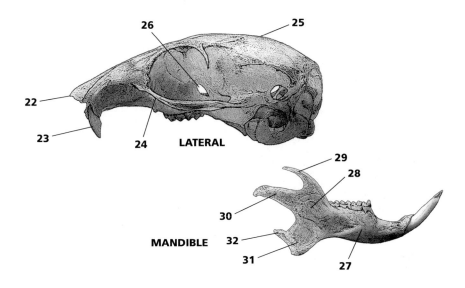

LATERAL

MANDIBLE

is wide with two points; the lower is rounded, and the upper (32) is a long projection extending to the posterior, nearly aligned with the tip of the coronoid.

Similar species: Other chipmunks, small ground squirrels, antelope squirrels, and flying squirrels.

Eastern chipmunk, *Tamias striatus*

Greatest length: 36.4–49.6 mm (1⁴/10–2 in.) (full table of measurements page 548, life-size image page 116, life-size jaw page 161)

Specimen illustrated: Adult male, SBMNH VB-67861

Dentition: i 1/1 c 0/0 p 1/1 m 3/3, total 20.

Dorsal: Chipmunks have broad, smooth braincases (1), rounded zygomatic arches (2), and large zygomatic plates (3); skulls are relatively thin boned and delicate. The rostrum (4) is slender and relatively longer than in *Neotamias;* nasals (5) are more rectangular, broadest at their anterior. The braincase (1) is oval, proportionately smaller than in *Neotamias.* Interorbital notches (6) are small and forward of the posterior edge (7) of the proportionately larger zygomatic plates, and interorbital breadth (8) is narrower than postorbital (9). Postorbital processes (10) are weak and point to posterior; occasionally there is also a very small anterior projection. Bowed zygomatic arches (2) converge to the anterior.

Ventral: The nasal vacuity (11) is somewhat tubular. The palate (12) extends beyond the posterior molars and terminates with a pointy projection (13) over the pterygoid region; incisive foramina (14) are small, but larger than in *Neotamias.* Round infraorbital foramen (15) pierces zygomatic plate. Spheno-pterygoid canals (16) are ovoid. Auditory bullae (17) are large, but proportionately smaller than in *Neotamias.* Foramen magnum (18) is large. Toothrows are slightly convex; the tiny first premolar that is characteristic in *Neotamias* is absent.

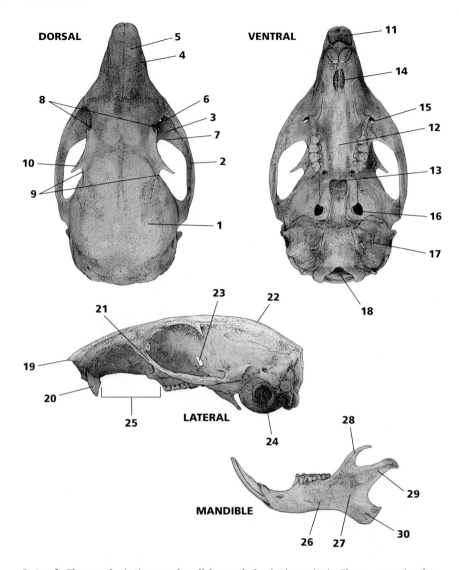

DORSAL

VENTRAL

LATERAL

MANDIBLE

Lateral: The nasals (19) extend well beyond the incisors (20). The zygomatic plate (21) is at approximately 40 degrees. The braincase (22) is high. Antorbital canal (23) is elongated, and the auditory meatus (24) is large. Incisors (20) are recurved, and the diastema (25) is wide.

Mandible: The body (26) of the mandible is curved, and the ramus (27) is larger than in the least chipmunk. The coronoid process (28) is slim, long, and curved to the posterior, though shorter than in *Neotamias*. The condyloid process (29) is long and angles up to the posterior at roughly a 45-degree angle; the tip points to posterior. The angular process (30) is large and squared, extending to posterior farther than coronoid, but short of condyle.

Similar species: Other chipmunks, flying squirrels, and smaller ground squirrels.

Yellow-bellied marmot, *Marmota flaviventris*

Greatest length: 73.2–93.4 mm ($2^9/10$–$3^7/10$ in.) (full table of measurements page 550, life-size image page 124, life-size jaw page 164)

Specimen illustrated: Adult male, LACM 3799

Dentition: i 1/1 c 0/0 p 2/1 m 3/3, total 22. Incisors smooth.

Dorsal: Skull is large, flattened, and heavy. Nasals (1) are long and triangular; posterior end of premaxillaries (2) wider than the nasals (3). The frontonasal and fronto-premaxillary sutures (4) form a distinctive arch across the rostrum, which is not the case in other members of the genus—though this is untrue in the California Sierras population of yellow-bellied marmots, where the sutures are just as illustrated with the woodchuck and hoary marmot. Heavy zygomatic arches (5) are wide-spreading, creating large orbits (6); zygomatic plates (7) are large. The interorbital region (8) may be depressed and is wider than the postorbital breadth (9); prominent, stout, and pointed postorbital processes (10) extend near perpendicular to the midline of the skull. The broad braincase (11) is wider than long. Prominent temporal ridges (12) are V-shaped and form a sagittal crest (13) at posterior; occipital crests (14) are well developed.

Ventral: Palate (15) is long and broad, and the posterior edge (16) is angled and aligned with the posterior edge of the last molar; there is a spinelike projection (17) over the relatively narrow pterygoid region (18). The incisive foramina (19) are small. The auditory bullae (20) are large and inflated. The foramen magnum (21) is of medium proportions, and the occipital condyles (22) are large. The heavy molari-form toothrows (23) are slightly divergent to the anterior.

Lateral: The dorsolateral outline is relatively straight. The rostrum (24) is deep and stout. Nasals (25) are strongly devcurved at anterior and extend to just beyond the incisors (26). Jugal bones (27) are large, and there is a short extension (28) off the

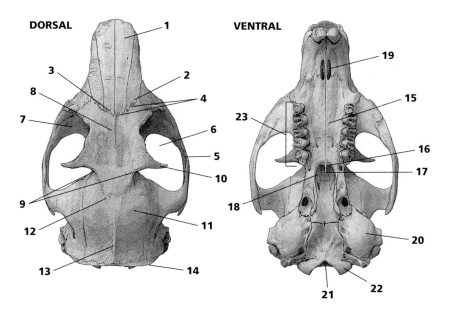

DORSAL

VENTRAL

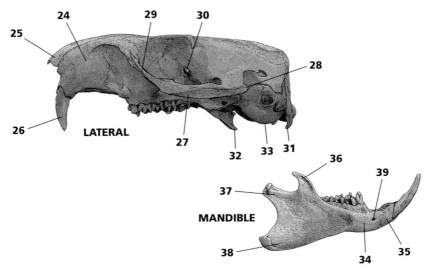

posterior beyond the squamosal arm of the zygomatic arch. The zygomatic plate (29) is at approximately 40 degrees. The antorbital canal (30) is small. Paraoccipital (31) and pterygoid (32) processes both extend below the auditory bullae (33). Incisors (26) are recurved.

Mandible: The center of the body (34) of the mandible is relatively straight, while the anterior (35) is very curved. The coronoid process (36) is small, pointed, and curved to the posterior. The condyloid process (37) is stout and squared. The angular process (38) is large and thick, forming the bulk of the ramus. There is a prominent mental foramen (39).

Similar species: Other marmots, woodchucks, aplodontia, and beavers.

Woodchuck or groundhog, *Marmota monax*

Greatest length: 73.6–102.0 mm (2⁹/10–4.0 in.) (full table of measurements page 550, life-size image page 124, life-size jaw page 164)

Specimen illustrated: Adult male, MVZ 81988

Dentition: i 1/1 c 0/0 p 2/1 m 3/3, total 22. Incisors smooth.

Dorsal: Skull is large, flattened, and heavy. Nasals (1) are long and triangular, with squared posterior edges (2); they extend to the posterior farther than the premaxillaries, and the posterior ends of premaxillaries (3) are wider than the nasals (2). Heavy zygomatic arches (4) are wide-spreading, creating large orbits (5); zygomatic plates (6) are large. The interorbital region (7) may be depressed and is wider than the postorbital breadth (8); prominent, stout, and pointed postorbital processes (9) extend nearly perpendicular to the midline of the skull. The broad braincase (10) is wider than long. Prominent temporal ridges (11) are a very narrow ∪ shape overall and form a sagittal crest (12) at posterior; occipital crests (13) are also well developed.

Ventral: Palate (14) is long and broad, and the posterior edge (15) is angled and extends beyond the posterior edge of last molar; there is a spinelike projection (16)

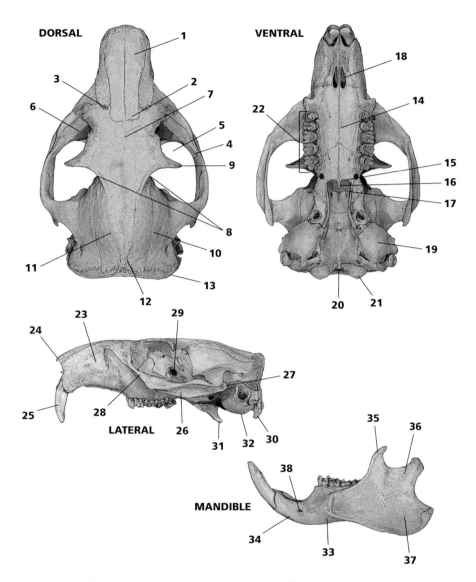

DORSAL

VENTRAL

LATERAL

MANDIBLE

over the relatively narrow pterygoid region (17). The incisive foramina (18) are small. The auditory bullae (19) are large and inflated. The foramen magnum (20) is of medium proportions, and the occipital condyles (21) are large. The heavy molariform toothrows (22) are approximately parallel, a character that differentiates woodchucks from marmots.

Lateral: The dorsolateral outline is relatively straight. The rostrum (23) is deep and stout. Nasals (24) are strongly decurved at anterior and extend to just beyond the incisors (25). Jugal bones (26) are large, and there is a short extension (27) off the posterior beyond the squamosal arm of the zygomatic arch. The zygomatic plate (28) is at approximately 40 degrees. The antorbital canal (29) is small. Paraoccipital (30) and pterygoid (31) processes both extend below the auditory bullae (32). Incisors are slightly procumbent and recurved.

Mandible: The mandible overall is more angular and heavier than in the yellow-bellied marmot. The center of the body (33) of the mandible is relatively straight, while the anterior (34) is very curved. The coronoid process (35) is small, pointed, and curved to the posterior. The condyloid process (36) is stout and squared. The angular process (37) is large and very broad, forming the bulk of the ramus. There is a prominent mental foramen (38).

Similar species: Marmots, aplodontia, and beavers.

White-tailed antelope squirrel, *Ammospermophilus leucurus*

Greatest length: 35.6–43.1 mm (1^4/10–1^7/10 in.) (full table of measurements page 552, life-size image page 116, life-size jaw page 161)

Specimen illustrated: Adult female, SBMNH VB-465

Dentition: i 1/1 c 0/0 p 2/1 m 3/3, total 22.

Dorsal: Antelope squirrels have broad, smooth braincases, straighter zygomatic arches (1) that converge strongly to the anterior, and very large zygomatic plates; skulls are relatively thin boned, delicate, and quite similar overall to those of chipmunks. Rostrum (2) is slender and relatively short; nasals (3) somewhat triangular, with squared posterior edges (4) narrower than the anterior. The premaxillaries (5) extend to the posterior farther than nasals. Braincase (6) is oval and longer than 50 percent of the greatest length. Interorbital notches (7) are small and far forward of the posterior edge of the proportionately larger zygomatic plates (8); the posterior edge of the zygomatic plates is curved. The interorbital breadth (7) is significantly narrower than the postorbital (9). Postorbital processes (10) are weak and point to posterior; occasionally there is also a very small anterior projection.

Ventral: The nasal vacuity (11) is somewhat tubular. The palate (12) extends beyond the posterior molars and terminates with a pointy projection (13) over the narrow pterygoid region (14); incisive foramina (15) are small. Spheno-pterygoid canals (16) are round. Foramen magnum (18) is large. The crowns of toothrows are slightly convex. Auditory bullae (17) are very large and swollen, approximately one and a half times the length of a toothrow. The first cheek tooth (P3) (19) is tiny and the first tooth in the molariform toothrow.

Lateral: The nasals (20) extend well beyond the incisors. Zygomatic arches (21) twist to horizontal as in ground squirrels, and their ventral surfaces (28) are below the level of the palate; the zygomatic plate (22) is at roughly 35 to 40 degrees. The braincase (23) is high. The antorbital canal (24) is elongated, with a second foramen (25) below. The auditory meatus (26) is large. Incisors (27) are recurved, and the diastema is wide.

Mandible: The body (29) of the mandible is relatively straight, except for the curving anterior (30). The coronoid process (31) is slim but shorter and curved to the posterior. The condyloid process (32) is long and triangular, with a squared tip, and

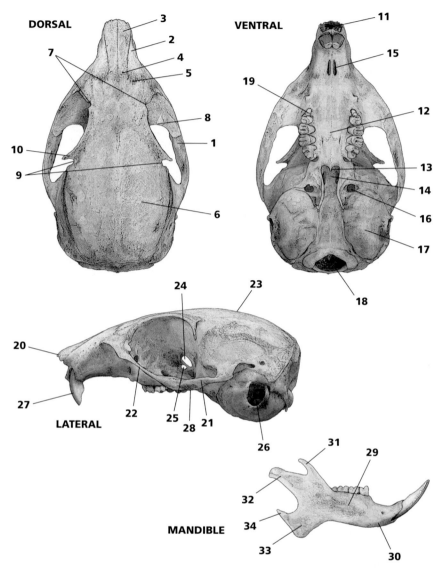

DORSAL

VENTRAL

LATERAL

MANDIBLE

extends farthest to posterior of the three processes; the tip points to posterior. The angular process (33) is large and double-faceted, with a pointy dorsal tip (34).

Similar species: Hoffmeister (1986) reports that it is difficult to distinguish this animal from *A. harrisii,* though the bullae tend to be slightly more inflated in *A. leucurus.* Small ground squirrels and chipmunks also resemble this species.

Note: There is no significant sexual dimorphism between the sexes.

California ground squirrel, *Spermophilus beecheyi*

Greatest length: 51.6–65.4 mm (2–2⁶/10 in.) (full table of measurements page 552, life-size image page 119, life-size jaw page 162)

Specimen illustrated: Adult male, SBMNH 3195

Dentition: i 1/1 c 0/0 p 2/1 m 3/3, total 22.

Dorsal: Larger ground squirrel skulls are more robust and angular than smaller species. The bowed zygomatic arches (1) are very wide and stout, converging to the anterior; the zygomatic plates (2) are very large. Rostrum (3) is slender and relatively short; nasals (4) are somewhat triangular, with narrower, squared posterior edges. The nasals and premaxillaries (5) extend to the posterior approximately equally and fall short of the anterior edge of the zygomatic plates. The interorbital breadth (6) is just slightly narrower than the postorbital (7); a small interorbital notch may be present. Postorbital processes (8) are well developed and decurved, pointing well away from the midline of the skull; occasionally there is also a very small anterior projection. The broad braincase (9) is shorter than 50 percent of the skull, and prominent temporal ridges (10) are V-shaped, forming a sagittal crest (11) for much of the posterior half of the braincase.

Ventral: The nasal vacuity (12) is somewhat tubular. The broad palate (13) extends beyond the posterior molars and terminates with a pointy projection (14) over the broader pterygoid region (15); incisive foramina (16) are small. Spheno-pterygoid canals (17) are small and round. Foramen magnum (18) is medium. Toothrows are relatively parallel. Auditory bullae (19) are comparatively medium, inflated, and slightly longer than individual toothrows.

Lateral: The dorsolateral outline (20) is very curved and convex; from the apex, the skull slopes steeply down to the occipital crests. The nasals (21) extend well beyond the incisors. Zygomatic arches (22) twist to horizontal approaching the posterior;

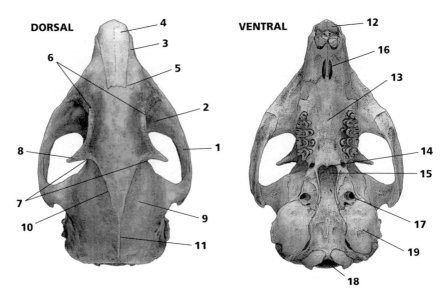

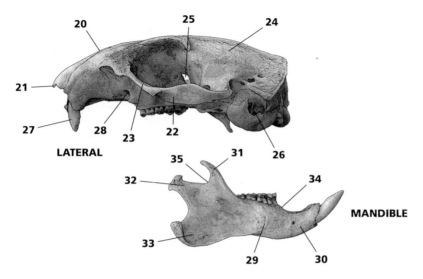

the zygomatic plate (23) is at roughly 40 degrees. The braincase (24) is high. The antorbital canal (25) is elongated, and the auditory meatus (26) is relatively small. Incisors (27) are straight, and the diastema is wide. Interorbital foramina (28) are small and oval.

Mandible: The body (29) of the mandible is relatively straight under the toothrow and then curves up sharply to the anterior (30). The coronoid process (31) is slender, high, and curved to the posterior. The condyloid process (32) is long and stout, extending at nearly a 45-degree angle to align approximately with the tip of the angular process; the notch (35) between the coronoid and condyloid processes is shallow. The angular process (33) is large and curved to the posterior. The dorsal outline of the diastema (34) is curved.

Similar species: Difficult to distinguish from rock squirrels. Also similar to other large ground squirrels and tree squirrels.

Golden-mantled ground squirrel, *Spermophilus lateralis*

Greatest length: 36.2–49.6 mm (1⁴/10–2 in.) (full table of measurements page 552, life-size image page 117, life-size jaw page 161)

Specimen illustrated: Adult female, SBMNH VB-61-8

Dentition: i 1/1 c 0/0 p 2/1 m 3/3, total 22

Dorsal: A narrower and more oval ground squirrel skull; skulls are thinner boned and similar overall to those of chipmunks. Rostrum (1) is relatively broader and a bit more squared than in chipmunks; nasals (2) are long and slender, tapering to posterior (3) and extending farther to posterior than the premaxillaries (4). Braincase (5) is round, smooth, and much less than 50 percent of the greatest length of skull. Interorbital notches (6) are very small and forward of the posterior edge of the zygomatic plates (7); the posterior edge of the zygomatic plates is curved. The interorbital breadth (8) is slightly narrower than the postorbital (9). Postorbital processes

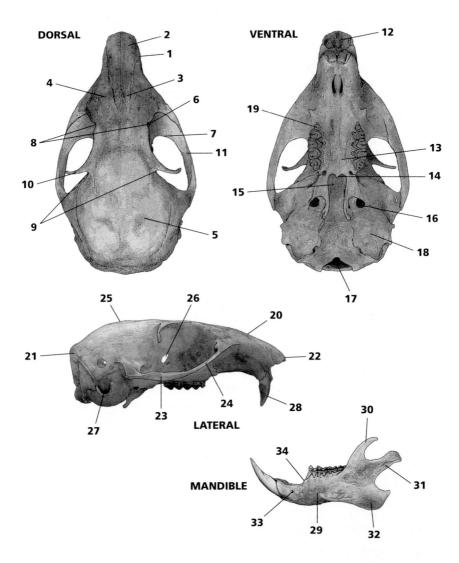

DORSAL

VENTRAL

LATERAL

MANDIBLE

(10) are situated to posterior of orbits and very long, curving to perpendicular from midline of skull and further curving to anterior at tips. Relatively straight zygomatic arches (11) converge to the anterior.

Ventral: The nasal vacuity (12) is somewhat tubular. The palate (13) extends beyond the posterior molars and terminates with a pointy projection (14) over the narrow pterygoid region (15); incisive foramina are small. Spheno-pterygoid canals (16) are round. The foramen magnum (17) is medium, and the occipital condyles are smaller. The toothrows are relatively short and slightly convergent to the posterior. Auditory bullae (18) are very large but less inflated; bullae are approximately as long as individual toothrows. The first cheek tooth (P3) (19) is small and the first tooth in the molariform toothrow.

Lateral: The dorsolateral outline (20) is very curved; from the apex, the skull slopes steeply down to the occipital crests (21). The nasals (22) are decurved and extend well beyond the incisors. Zygomatic arches (23) are low and twist to horizontal; the zygomatic plate (24) is at roughly 40 degrees. The braincase (25) is low and rounded. The antorbital canal (26) is elongated, and the auditory meatus (27) is large. Incisors (28) are long and straight. The diastema is wide.

Mandible: The body (29) of the mandible curves upward toward the anterior; the ramus is of medium dimensions. The coronoid process (30) is long, slender, and curved to the posterior. The condyloid process (31) is long, squared, and extends the farthest to posterior of the three processes. The angular process (32) is short, thick, and rounded below, and the tapered point curves upward; the angular process is smaller than in other ground squirrels. Mental foramen (33) is prominent. The posterior edge of the diastema (34) is relatively steep.

Similar species: Other medium and smaller ground squirrels, chipmunks, and smaller tree squirrels.

Thirteen-lined ground squirrel, *Spermophilus tridecemlineatus*

Greatest length: 33.2–45.8 mm (1^3/10–1^8/10 in.) (full table of measurements page 554, life-size image page 115, life-size jaw page 161)

Specimen illustrated: Adult, MVZ 96796

Dentition: i 1/1 c 0/0 p 2/1 m 3/3, total 22

Dorsal: A lighter, narrower, and more oval ground squirrel skull; skulls are relatively thin-boned and delicate and are overall similar to the skulls of chipmunks. Rostrum (1) relatively broad and long; nasals (2) are triangular, tapering to the posterior (3). The nasals extend farther to the posterior than the premaxillaries (4). Braincase (5) is round and much less than 50 percent of the greatest length of skull; temporal ridges (6) are weak and wide apart. Interorbital notches (7) are very small and far forward of the posterior edge of the proportionately larger zygomatic plates (8); the posterior edge of the zygomatic plates is curved. The interorbital breadth (7) is significantly narrower than the postorbital (9). Postorbital processes (10) are very small and weak and point to posterior; occasionally there is also a very small anterior projection. Bowed zygomatic arches (11) converge to the anterior.

Ventral: The nasal vacuity (12) is somewhat tubular. The palate (13) extends well beyond the posterior molars and terminates with a pointy projection (14) over the very narrow pterygoid region (15); incisive foramina (16) are small. Sphenopterygoid canals (17) are round. The foramen magnum (18) is medium, and the occipital condyles (19) are smaller. The toothrows are relatively short and slightly convergent to the posterior. Auditory bullae (20) are very large and swollen, though less inflated than in *S. spilosoma;* bullae are approximately as long as individual toothrows. The first cheek tooth (P3) (21) is small and the first tooth in the molariform toothrow.

Lateral: The dorsolateral outline (22) is very curved; from the apex, the skull slopes steeply down to the occipital crests. The nasals (23) are decurved and extend well

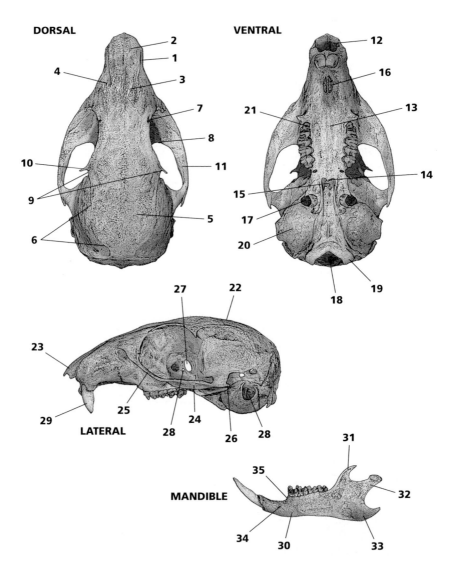

DORSAL

VENTRAL

LATERAL

MANDIBLE

beyond the incisors. Zygomatic arches (24) are low and twist to horizontal as in other ground squirrels; the zygomatic plate (25) is at roughly 40 degrees, and there is a short jugal extension (26) beyond the squamosal arm of the zygomatic arch. The braincase is high. The antorbital canal (27) is elongated, and a second small foramen (28) is anterior to it. The auditory meatus (28) is large. Incisors (29) are slightly recurved, and the diastema is wide.

Mandible: The body (30) of the mandible tapers slightly to the anterior and curves upward at tip; the ramus is large. The coronoid process (31) is of medium dimensions and curved to the posterior. The condyloid process (32) is long and squared, extending upward to posterior at approximately 45 degrees. The angular process (33) is

short and thick, and the tapered point curves upward. Mental foramen (34) is prominent. The posterior edge of the diastema (35) drops steeply from molariform teeth.
Similar species: Other small ground squirrels and chipmunks.

Rock squirrel, *Spermophilus variegatus*

Greatest length: 54.4–67.7 mm (2^1/$_{10}$–2^7/$_{10}$ in.) (full table of measurements page 556,
life-size image page 119, life-size jaw page 162)
Specimen illustrated: Adult male, MVZ 47883
Dentition: i 1/1 c 0/0 p 2/1 m 3/3, total 22.
Dorsal: Larger ground squirrel skulls are more robust and angular than smaller species.
The bowed zygomatic arches (1) are very wide and stout, converging to the anterior; the zygomatic plates (2) are very large. Rostrum (3) is slender and relatively
short; nasals (4) are somewhat triangular, with narrower, squared posterior edges
(5). They extend to the posterior farther than the premaxillaries (6) and are approximately aligned with the anterior edge (7) of the zygomatic plates. The interorbital
breadth (8) is just slightly narrower than the postorbital (9); a small interorbital
notch (8) may be present. Postorbital processes (10) are well developed and
decurved, and they point well away from the midline of the skull; occasionally there
is also a very small anterior projection. The broad braincase (11) is shorter than 50
percent of the skull, and prominent temporal ridges (12) are U-shaped (lyrelike),
forming a sagittal crest (13) at the far posterior of skull.
Ventral: The nasal vacuity (32) is somewhat tubular. The broad palate (14) extends
beyond the posterior molars and terminates with a pointy projection (15) over the
narrow pterygoid region (16); incisive foramina (17) are short slits. Spheno-pterygoid
canals (18) are small and round. The foramen magnum (19) is medium. Toothrows

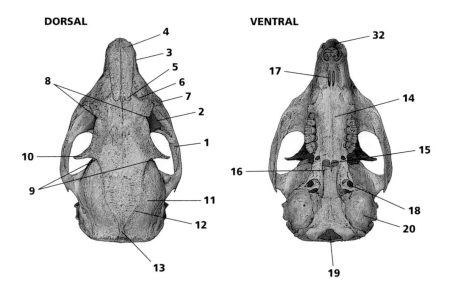

DORSAL   VENTRAL

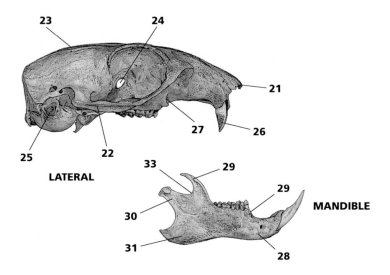

are relatively parallel. Auditory bullae (20) are comparatively medium, inflated, and slightly longer than individual toothrows.

Lateral: The nasals (21) extend well beyond the incisors. Zygomatic arches (22) twist to horizontal approaching the posterior; the zygomatic plate is at roughly 40 degrees. The braincase (23) is low. The antorbital canal (24) is ovoid, and the auditory meatus (25) is relatively small. Incisors (26) are straight, and the diastema is wide. Interorbital foramina (27) are small and oval.

Mandible: The body (28) of the mandible is relatively straight under the toothrow and then curves up sharply to the anterior. The coronoid process (29) is slender, high, and curved to the posterior. The condyloid process (30) is long and stout, extending at nearly a 45-degree angle to align approximately with the tip of the angular process; the notch (33) between the coronoid and condyloid processes is deep. The angular process (31) is large and curved to the posterior. From the anterior edge (29) of the molars, there is a steep drop into the diastema.

Similar species: Difficult to distinguish from *S. beecheyi;* similar to other large ground and tree squirrels and prairie dogs.

Black-tailed prairie dog, *Cynomys ludovicianus*

Greatest length: 60.4–67.8 mm (2⁴/10–2⁷/10 in.) (full table of measurements page 556, life-size image page 120, life-size jaw page 163)

Specimen illustrated: Adult female, LACM 6926

Dentition: i 1/1 c 0/0 p 2/1 m 3/3, total 22.

Dorsal: Prairie dog skulls are larger, more angular, and wider versions of large ground squirrel skulls. The relatively straight zygomatic arches (1) are very wide-spreading and stout, and they converge strongly to the anterior, giving a boxier overall look to the skull compared with those of ground squirrels; the zygomatic plates (2) are proportionately smaller. The orbits (3) are large. Rostrum (4) is slender and relatively longer than in ground squirrels; nasals (5) are broad and somewhat triangular, with squared posterior edges (6). The nasals and premaxillaries (7) extend to the posterior equally and are approximately aligned with the anterior edge of the zygomatic plates. The interorbital breadth (8) is approximately equal with that of the postorbital (9); a very small interorbital notch may be present. Postorbital processes (10) are well developed and decurved, and they point nearly perpendicular from the midline of the skull. The broad braincase (11) is significantly shorter than 50 percent of the greatest length of the skull, and prominent temporal ridges (12) are V-shaped, forming a sagittal crest (13) over the posterior half of the braincase. Occipital crests (14) are well developed.

Ventral: The nasal vacuity (15) is somewhat tubular. The narrow palate (16) extends beyond the posterior molars and terminates with a rounded, pointy projection (17) over the narrow pterygoid region (18); incisive foramina (19) are a bit larger than in ground squirrels, though still slitlike and small. Maxillary processes (20) anterior to the toothrows are much more developed than in other sciurids. Sphenopterygoid canals (21) are small and round. Foramen magnum (22) is small. Molariform teeth are rugose, and toothrows are strongly convergent to posterior. Auditory bullae (23) are round, comparatively smaller but inflated, and much shorter than individual toothrows.

Lateral: The nasals (24) are strongly decurved to anterior and extend well beyond the incisors. Zygomatic arches (25) are heavy and twist to horizontal approaching the posterior; the zygomatic plate (26) is at roughly 40 degrees. The jugals (26) are particularly heavy and angular at the posterior corner of the zygomatic plate. The braincase (27) sits below the apex of the skull, which is over the orbit. The antorbital canal (28) is angular, and a second, rounder foramen (29) sits below. The auditory meatus (30) is elevated and very small. Incisors (31) are long and straight. The diastema is wide. Interorbital foramina (32) are small and oval.

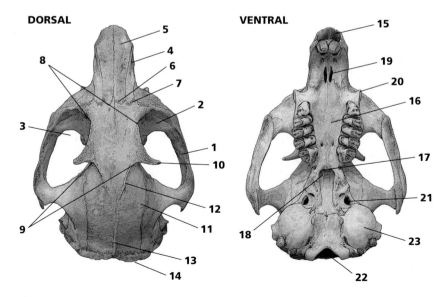

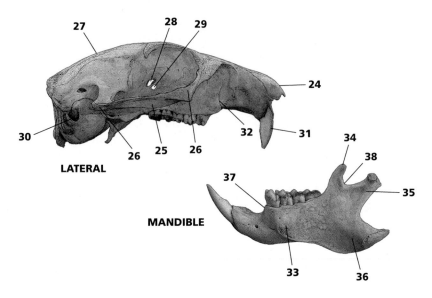

Mandible: The body (33) of the mandible is deep and curves up to the anterior. The coronoid process (34) is small, thick, and slightly curved to the posterior. The condyloid process (35) is long, stout, and squared; the notch (38) between the coronoid and condyloid processes is medium. The angular process (36) is large, rounded below, tapering and curved to the posterior. The anterior edge (37) of the molars drops steeply into the diastema.

Similar species: Other prairie dogs and large ground squirrels.

Eastern gray squirrel, *Sciurus carolinensis*

Greatest length: 53.8–66.5 mm ($2^{1}/_{10}$–$2^{6}/_{10}$ in.) (full table of measurements page 558, life-size image page 119, life-size jaw page 162)

Specimen illustrated: Adult male, MCZ 61884

Dentition: i 1/1 c 0/0 p 2/1 m 3/3, total 22.

Dorsal: Tree squirrel skulls are rounded, with slender, laterally compressed rostrums, very wide interorbital regions, and depressed braincases. The bowed zygomatic arches (1) converge to the anterior; the posterior edge of the large zygomatic plates (2) is straighter and nearly perpendicular to the midline of the skull. Rostrum (3) is long and slender; nasals (4) are long, slender, and somewhat triangular, with pointed posterior edges (5) narrower than the anterior. The nasals and premaxillaries (6) extend to the posterior approximately equally, which is not true in western gray squirrels. The interorbital region (7) is inflated and broad, making the orbits (8) appear smaller than in ground squirrels. The interorbital breadth (9) is approximately equal to the postorbital (10); a small interorbital notch may be present. Postorbital processes (11) have small tips and point to the posterior; occasionally there is also a very small anterior projection. The braincase (12) is large and rounded, and temporal ridges are weak to absent. Occipital crests (13) are developed.

Ventral: The nasal vacuity (14) is somewhat tubular. The broad palate (15) extends beyond the posterior molars and terminates with a pointy projection (16) over the narrow pterygoid region (17); incisive foramina are small. Spheno-pterygoid canals (18) are large and round. The foramen magnum (19) is large. Auditory bullae (20) are comparatively medium and somewhat deformed. Toothrows are slightly convex; upper premolar three (21) is tiny and may be absent, and P4 (22) is usually longer than wide.

Lateral: The dorsolateral outline in tree squirrels from the apex of the skull to the anterior tips of the nasals is straight (23), rather than curved as in ground squirrels, and from the apex back to the occipital crests is a steeper curvature (24). The

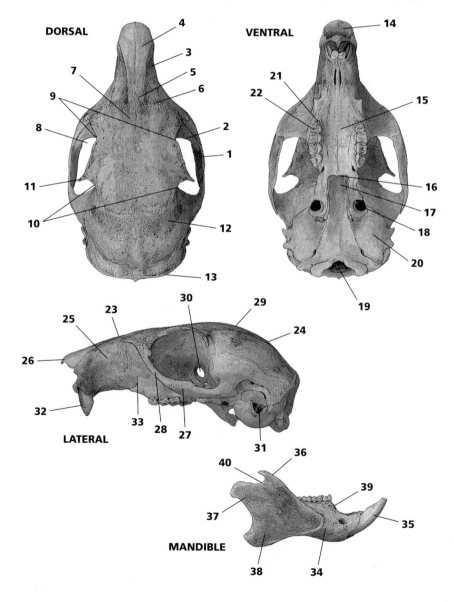

rostrum (25) is very deep and stout; the nasals (26) extend beyond the incisors. Zygomatic arches (27) do not twist as in ground squirrels; the zygomatic plate (28) is steep, at roughly 50 degrees. The braincase (29) is high. The antorbital canal (30) is oval, and the auditory meatus (31) is relatively small. Incisors (32) are straight, and the diastema is wide. Interorbital foramina (33) are small and oval.

Mandible: The body (34) of the mandible curves to the anterior; the incisor (35) is stout. The coronoid process (36) is small, pointed, and curved to the posterior; the notch (40) between the coronoid and condyloid processes is shallow. The condyloid process (37) is stout and somewhat rounded, extending at nearly a 45-degree angle to the posterior. The angular process (38) is large and squared. The anterior edge (39) of the molars curves into the diastema.

Similar species: Other large tree squirrels of the genus *Sciurus* and large ground squirrels.

Western gray squirrel, *Sciurus griseus*

Greatest length: 63.1–70.4 mm ($2^5/_{10}$–$2^8/_{10}$ in.) (full table of measurements page 558, life-size image page 121, life-size jaw page 162)

Specimen illustrated: Adult male, SBMNH 440

Dentition: i 1/1 c 0/0 p 2/1 m 3/3, total 22.

Dorsal: Tree squirrel skulls are rounded, with slender, laterally compressed rostrums, very wide interorbital regions, and depressed braincases. The straight zygomatic arches (1) converge to the anterior; the posterior edge of the large zygomatic plates (2) is straighter and nearly perpendicular to the midline of the skull. Rostrum (3) is long and slender; nasals (4) are long, slender, and somewhat triangular, with more narrow, squared posterior edges (5). The nasals extend to the posterior just beyond the premaxillaries (6), which is not true in eastern gray squirrels. The interorbital region (7) is inflated and broad, making the orbits (8) appear smaller than in ground squirrels. The interorbital breadth (9) is approximately equal to the postorbital (10); a small interorbital notch may be present. Postorbital processes (11) have small tips and point to the posterior; occasionally there is also a very small anterior projection. The braincase (12) is large and rounded, and temporal ridges are weak to absent. Occipital crests (13) are developed.

Ventral: The nasal vacuity (14) is somewhat tubular. The broad palate (15) extends beyond the posterior molars and terminates with a pointy projection (16) over the narrow pterygoid region (17); incisive foramina (18) are small. In this specimen, the maxillary processes (19) anterior to the toothrows are absent, but they are present in other sciurids. Spheno-pterygoid canals (20) are smaller and oval. The foramen magnum (21) is large. Auditory bullae (22) are comparatively medium and somewhat deformed. Toothrows are slightly convex; upper premolar three (23) is tiny, and P4 (24) is wider than long.

Lateral: The dorsolateral outline in tree squirrels from the apex of the skull to the anterior tips of the nasals is straight (25), rather than curved as in ground squirrels, and from the apex back to the occipital crests is a steeper curvature (26). The rostrum (27) is very deep and stout; the nasals (28) extend beyond the incisors. Zygomatic

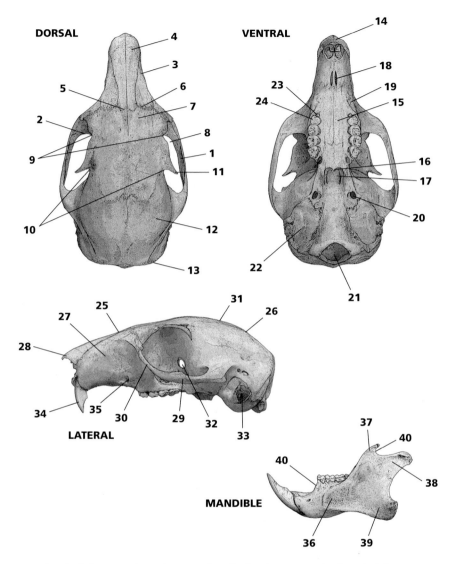

DORSAL

VENTRAL

LATERAL

MANDIBLE

arches (29) do not twist as in ground squirrels; the zygomatic plate (30) is steep, at roughly 50 degrees. The braincase (31) is high. The antorbital canal (32) is large and oval, and the auditory meatus (33) is relatively small. Incisors (34) are slightly recurved, and the diastema is wide. Interorbital foramina (35) are small and oval.

Mandible: The body (36) of the mandible curves to the anterior; the incisor is stout. The coronoid process (37) is small, pointed, and curved to the posterior; the notch (40) between the coronoid and condyloid processes is shallow. The condyloid process (38) is stout and somewhat rounded, extending at nearly a 45-degree angle to the posterior. The angular process (39) is large and squared. From the anterior edge (40) of the molars there is a steep drop into the diastema.

Similar species: Other large tree squirrels of the genus *Sciurus* and large ground squirrels.

Eastern fox squirrel, *Sciurus niger*

Greatest length: 47.1–71.8 mm (1^9/$_{10}$–2^8/$_{10}$ in.) (full table of measurements page 558, life-size image page 120, life-size jaw page 162)

Specimen illustrated: Adult male, MVZ 160560

Dentition: i 1/1 c 0/0 p 1/1 m 3/3, total 20.

Dorsal: Tree squirrel skulls are rounded, with slender, laterally compressed rostrums, very wide interorbital regions, and depressed braincases. The slightly bowed zygomatic arches (1) are relatively parallel; the posterior edge of the large zygomatic plates (2) is not as perpendicular to the midline of the skull as in gray squirrels. Rostrum (3) is long and broader than in other tree squirrels; nasals (4) are long, slender, and somewhat triangular, with squared posterior edges (5). The nasals extend to the posterior just beyond the premaxillaries (6). The interorbital region (7) is inflated and broad, making the orbits (8) appear smaller than in ground squirrels. The interorbital breadth is approximately equal to the postorbital (9); the interorbital notch (10) is deeper than in other tree squirrels. Postorbital processes (11) are stout and point to the posterior; occasionally there is also a very small anterior projection. The braincase (12) is large and rounded, and temporal ridges (13) are better developed, U-shaped lyre-like, and form a small sagittal crest (14) at the posterior. Occipital crests (15) are developed.

Ventral: The nasal vacuity (16) is somewhat tubular. The broad palate (17) extends beyond the posterior molars and lacks a pointy projection over the narrow pterygoid region (18); incisive foramina (19) are small. Spheno-pterygoid canals (20) are large and round. The foramen magnum (21) is large. Auditory bullae (22) are comparatively smaller, rounder, and more inflated. Toothrows are slightly convex; upper premolar three is generally absent, whereas it is generally present in gray squirrels.

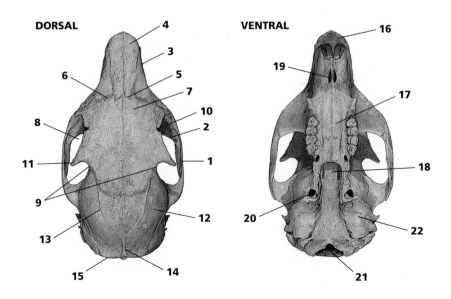

DORSAL   VENTRAL

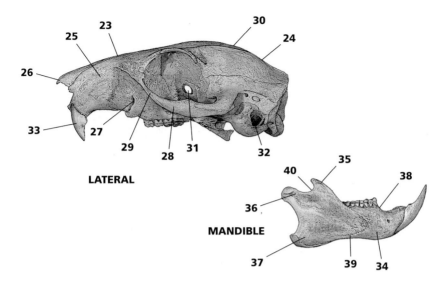

LATERAL

MANDIBLE

Lateral: The dorsolateral outline in tree squirrels from the apex of the skull to the anterior tips of the nasals is straight (23), rather than curved as in ground squirrels, and from the apex back to the occipital crests is a steeper curvature (24). The rostrum (25) is very deep and stout; the nasals (26) extend beyond the incisors. Infraorbital foramina (27) are small and low on rostrum. Zygomatic arches (28) do not twist as in ground squirrels; the zygomatic plate (29) is steep, at roughly 45 degrees. The braincase (30) is high. The antorbital canal (31) is oval, and the auditory meatus (32) is relatively small. Incisors (33) are recurved, and the diastema is wide.

Mandible: The body (34) of the mandible curves to the anterior; the incisor is stout. The coronoid process (35) is small, pointed, and curved to the posterior. The condyloid process (36) is stout and somewhat rounded, extending at nearly a 45-degree angle to the posterior; the notch (40) between the coronoid and condyloid processes is shallow. The angular process (37) is large and squared. The posterior edge of the diastema (38) is curved. The masseteric fossa (39) extends far to the anterior in *Sciurus* species.

Similar species: Other large tree squirrels of the genus *Sciurus* and large ground squirrels.

Notes: The bones of this species have a distinctive pinkish tint that may or may not be obvious; under ultraviolet lights, the bones appear bright red (Flyger and Gates 1982).

Red squirrel, *Tamiasciurus hudsonicus*

Greatest length: 42.4–51.3 mm (1⁷/₁₀–2 in.) (full table of measurements page 560, life-size image page 117, life-size jaw page 161)

Specimen illustrated: Adult male, SBMNH VB-12

Dentition: i 1/1 c 0/0 p 1/1 m 3/3, total 20.

Dorsal: *Tamiasciurus* skulls are rounded, with slender, laterally compressed rostrums, very wide interorbital regions, and depressed braincases. The bowed zygomatic arches (1) converge slightly to the anterior; the posterior edge of the proportionately larger zygomatic plates (2) is relatively curved. Rostrum (3) is shorter than in *Sciurus* species; nasals (4) are shorter, broader, and triangular. The nasals and premaxillaries (5) extend to the posterior approximately equally. The interorbital region (6) is inflated and broad, making the orbits (7) appear smaller than in ground squirrels. The interorbital breadth is approximately equal to the postorbital (8); a small interorbital notch (9) may be present. Postorbital processes (10) have small tips and point to the posterior; occasionally there is also a very small anterior projection. The braincase (11) is very large and round, much larger in proportions than members of *Sciurus*. Temporal ridges are weak to absent. Occipital crests are less developed.

Ventral: The nasal vacuity (12) is somewhat tubular. The broad palate (13) extends beyond the posterior molars and terminates with a pointy projection (14) over the broader pterygoid region (15); incisive foramina are small. The maxillary processes (16) anterior to the toothrows are small. Spheno-pterygoid canals (17) are small and ovoid. The foramen magnum (18) is large. Auditory bullae (19) are comparatively large, deformed, and swollen. Toothrows are slightly convex; P3 is absent, whereas it is present in gray squirrels.

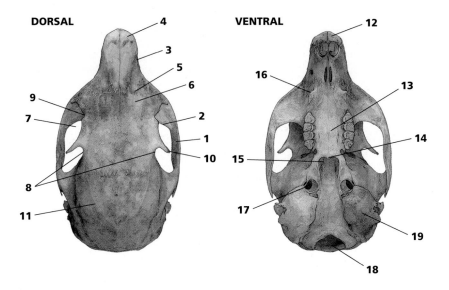

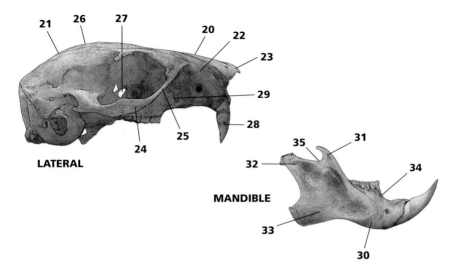

LATERAL

MANDIBLE

Lateral: The dorsolateral outline in tree squirrels from the apex of the skull to the anterior tips of the nasals is straight (20), rather than curved as in ground squirrels, and from the apex back to the occipital crests is a steeper curvature (21). The rostrum (22) is very deep and stout; the nasals (23) extend beyond the incisors. Zygomatic arches (24) do not twist as in ground squirrels; the zygomatic plate (25) is steep, at roughly 50 degrees. The braincase (26) is high. The antorbital canal (27) is ovoid, and the auditory meatus is relatively small. Incisors (28) are straight, and the diastema is wide. Interorbital foramina are (29) small and oval.

Mandible: The body (30) of the mandible curves to the anterior; the incisor is stout. The coronoid process (31) is small, pointed, and curved to the posterior. The condyloid process (32) is stout and somewhat rounded, extending at nearly a 45-degree angle to the posterior; the notch (35) between the coronoid and condyloid processes is medium. The angular process (33) is large and squared. It is a steep drop from the anterior edge (34) of the molars into the diastema.

Similar species: Larger tree squirrels (*Sciurus* spp.), chipmunks, and ground squirrels.

Notes: Hoffmeister (1986) reports that sexual dimorphism is minimal. Verts and Carraway (1998) were unable to distinguish with certainty the skulls of Douglas's squirrel *(T. douglasii)* and red squirrel *(T. hudsonicus)*, though some morphometric comparisons based on five measurements were able to separate 78 percent of the specimens from one region of Oregon.

Northern flying squirrel, *Glaucomys sabrinus*

Greatest length: 36.0–44.2 mm (1⁴/₁₀–1⁷/₁₀ in.) (full table of measurements page 560, life-size image page 116, life-size jaw page 161)
Specimen illustrated: Adult female, MVZ 42540
Dentition: i 1/1 c 0/0 p 2/1 m 3/3, total 22
Dorsal: Flying-squirrel skulls are more delicate and rounded, with slender, laterally compressed rostrums, notched interorbital regions, and large, depressed braincases.

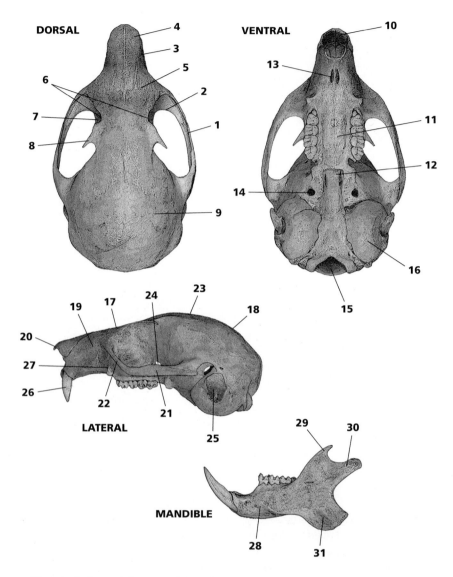

DORSAL

VENTRAL

LATERAL

MANDIBLE

The relatively straight zygomatic arches (1) converge strongly to the anterior; the posterior edge of the large zygomatic plates (2) is curved. Rostrum (3) is of medium proportions; nasals (4) are long, broad, and somewhat triangular, with squared posterior edges. The nasals and premaxillaries (5) extend to the posterior approximately equally. The interorbital region (6) is proportionately much narrower than in other tree squirrels and slightly narrower than the postorbital; the interorbital notch (6) is large. From the dorsal perspective, looking through the interorbital notches, the maxillary bones (7) are visible, which is also the case in the southern flying squirrel, but to a lesser degree. Postorbital processes (8) are more forward than in other tree squirrels, have small depressed tips, and point to the posterior; occasionally there is also a very small anterior projection. The braincase (9) is very large and oval, equal to 50 percent or more of the greatest length of the skull; temporal ridges are weak to absent.

Ventral: The nasal vacuity (10) is somewhat tubular. The broad palate (11) extends beyond the posterior molars; the pterygoid region (12) is narrow, and the incisive foramina (13) are small slits. Spheno-pterygoid canals (14) are small and round. The foramen magnum (15) is large. Auditory bullae (16) are comparatively large, oval, and inflated. Toothrows are relatively parallel.

Lateral: The dorsolateral outline in tree squirrels from the apex of the skull to the anterior of the nasals is straight (17), rather than curved as in ground squirrels, and from the apex back to the occipital crests is a steeper curvature (18); the anterior tips of the nasals are decurved. The rostrum (19) is not as deep as in larger tree squirrels; the nasals (20) extend beyond the incisors. Zygomatic arches (21) do not twist as in ground squirrels; the zygomatic plate (22) is steep, at roughly 50 degrees. The braincase (23) is high. The antorbital canal (24) is smaller, and the auditory meatus (25) is relatively large. Incisors (26) are slender and straight; the diastema is wide. Interorbital foramina (27) are small and oval.

Mandible: The body (28) of the mandible curves to the anterior; the incisor is stout. The coronoid process (29) is small, pointed, and curved to the posterior. The condyloid process (30) is stout and somewhat rounded, extending at nearly a 45-degree angle to the posterior. The angular process (31) is large and squared.

Similar species: Small ground squirrels and chipmunks.

Note: Sexual dimorphism is not evident.

Southern flying squirrel, *Glaucomys volans*

Greatest length: 32.0–37.2 mm (1³/₁₀–1⁵/₁₀ in.) (full table of measurements page 560, life-size image page 114, life-size jaw page 160)

Specimen illustrated: Adult male, MVZ 95368

Dentition: i 1/1 c 0/0 p 2/1 m 3/3, total 22.

Dorsal: Flying-squirrel skulls are more delicate and rounded, with slender, laterally compressed rostrums, notched interorbital regions, and large, depressed braincases. The curved zygomatic arches (1) converge strongly to the anterior; the posterior edge of the large zygomatic plates (2) is curved. Rostrum (3) is of medium proportions; nasals (4) are short, broad, and triangular, with squared posterior edges. The premaxillaries (5) extend to the posterior farther than the nasals. The interorbital region is proportionately much narrower than in other tree squirrels and slightly narrower than the postorbital; the interorbital notch (6) is large. From the dorsal perspective, looking through the interorbital notches, the maxillary bones are just visible; in the northern flying squirrel, they are very visible. Postorbital processes (7) are more forward on the skull than in other tree squirrels, have small depressed tips, and point to the posterior; occasionally there is also a very small anterior projection. The braincase (8) is very large and oval, equal to 50 percent or more of the greatest length of skull; temporal ridges are weak to absent.

Ventral: The nasal vacuity (9) is somewhat tubular. The broad palate (10) extends beyond the posterior molars. The pterygoid region (11) is narrow, and the incisive

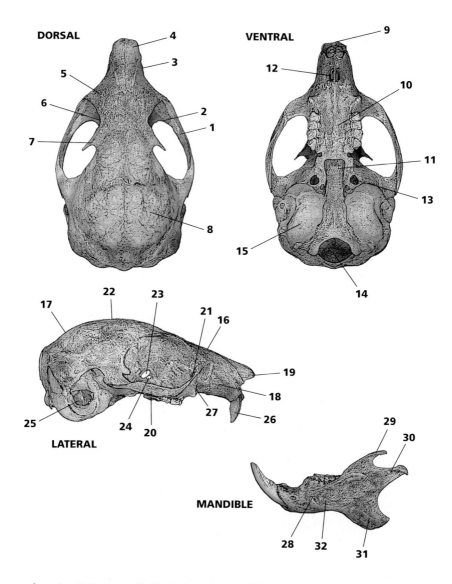

DORSAL

VENTRAL

LATERAL

MANDIBLE

foramina (12) are small slits. Spheno-pterygoid canals (13) are small and round. The foramen magnum (14) is large. Auditory bullae (15) are comparatively large, oval, and inflated. Toothrows are relatively parallel.

Lateral: The dorsolateral outline in tree squirrels from the apex of the skull to the anterior of the nasals is straight (16), rather than curved as in ground squirrels, and from the apex back to the occipital crests is a steeper curvature (17); the anterior tips of the nasals are decurved. The rostrum (18) is not as deep as in other tree squirrels; the nasals (19) extend beyond the incisors. Zygomatic arches (20) do not twist as in ground squirrels; the zygomatic plate (21) is steep, at roughly 50 to 60 degrees. The braincase (22) is high. The antorbital canal (23) is oval, and a second, smaller foramen (24) is below. The auditory meatus (25) is medium. Incisors (26) are slender and straight, and the dentition overall is more delicate than in the northern flying squirrel; the diastema is wide. Interorbital foramina (27) are small and oval.

Mandible: The body (28) of the mandible curves to the anterior; the incisor is stout. The coronoid process (29) is longer, pointed, and curved farther to the posterior than in other tree squirrels. The condyloid process (30) is stout, somewhat rounded, and extends at nearly a 45-degree angle to the posterior. The angular process (31) is large and squared. The masseteric fossa (32) extends far to the anterior, as in all tree squirrels.

Similar species: Northern flying squirrel, smaller ground squirrels, and chipmunks.

Note: Sexual dimorphism is not evident.

Family Geomyidae: Pocket gophers

Pocket gophers are rodents that are characterized by their rootless, fragile molariform teeth; flattened, squared skulls; and strong, wide-spreading zygomata. Temporal ridges and sagittal crests are developed further in pocket gophers than in other rodents, indicative of stronger temporalis muscles.

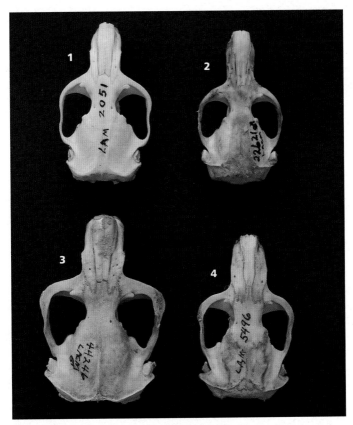

Select members of Geomyidae, all are males: 1. Botta's pocket gopher *(T. bottae)*, 2. Northern pocket gopher 22621 *(T. talpoides)*, 3. Yellow-faced pocket gopher 44246 *(C. castanops)*, 4. Plains pocket gopher 5496 *(G. bursarius)*. NATURAL HISTORY MUSEUM OF LOS ANGELES COUNTY.

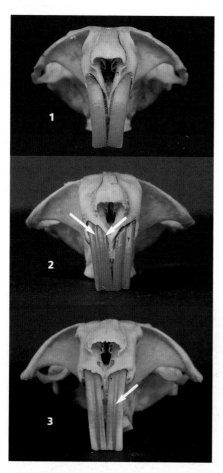

There are three North American pocket gopher genera, and each has its own distinctive anterior surface to the upper incisors. *Thomomys* are characterized by smooth anterior surfaces, *Geomys* by two deep grooves per tooth, and *Cratogeomys* by a single deep groove per tooth.

Compare the teeth in the three genera of pocket gophers: 1. The incisors of *Thomomys* are not grooved, as represented by this male northern pocket gogher 6954. 2. The incisors of *Geomys* are twice grooved, the wider, deeper groove centrally and a second slender groove to the inside close to the midline of the skull (note arrows). This is a male plains pocket gopher, 5490. 3. In *Cratogeomys* the insicors hold a single deep groove, yet each often appears more like two smaller grooves right next to each other. This is a male yellow-faced pocket gopher 5546. NATURAL HISTORY MUSEUM OF LOS ANGELES COUNTY.

Botta's pocket gopher, *Thomomys bottae*

Greatest length: 34.0–46.4 mm ($1^3/_{10}$–$1^8/_{10}$ in.) (full table of measurements page 562, life-size image page 115, life-size jaw page 161)

Specimen illustrated: Adult, SBMNH M-3528

Dentition: i 1/1 c 0/0 p 1/1 m 3/3, total 20. The anterior surfaces of the upper incisors are smooth.

Dorsal: Pocket gopher skulls are robust and angular, with wide-spreading zygomatic arches, small lacrimal processes (1), and large orbits (2). Rostrum is long, laterally compressed, and stout; nasals (3) are long, broad, and somewhat triangular. The nasals do not extend to the posterior as far as the premaxillaries (4). The angular, wide-spreading zygomatic arches (5) are parallel. The interorbital region (6) is narrow. Postorbital processes are rudimentary or absent. The braincase (7) is large and squared, less than 50 percent of the greatest length of skull; temporal ridges (8) are weak and do not make contact. Occipital crests (9) are developed. The interparietal (23) is small, narrow, and well forward of the occipital crests.

Ventral: The palate (10) is distinctive, two-tiered, and very narrow; the pterygoid region (11) is very narrow, and pterygoid processes (12) are relatively thin and long. The incisive foramina (13) are very small slits, situated closer to the molariform toothrows than the large incisors, and behind the anterior edge of the infraorbital foramina (24). The foramina ovale (14) are apparent. The foramen magnum (15) is large. Auditory bullae (16) are large and inflated, with long necks or extensions to the auditory meatus. Toothrows are very close together and convergent to the anterior. The first cheek tooth (17) is constricted in the middle and hourglass-shaped.

Lateral: The dorsolateral outline is relatively flat, though worth comparing across the three genera of pocket gophers. The anterior tips of the nasals (18) are

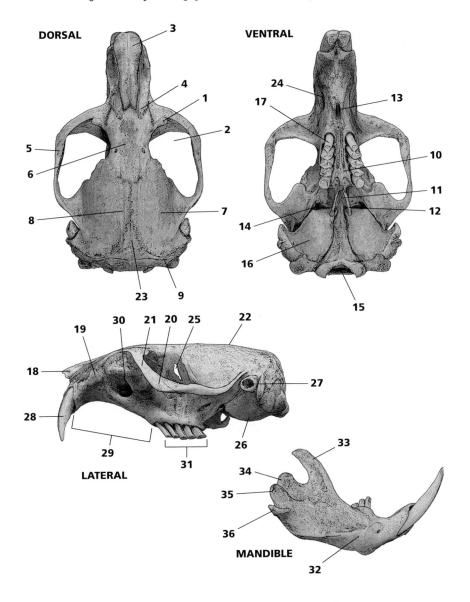

decurved and extend to the anterior approximately in line with the anterior of the incisors. The rostrum (19) is deep and stout. Zygomatic arches (20) are comparatively elevated; the zygomatic plate (21) is steep, at roughly 55 to 60 degrees. The braincase (22) is not elevated. The sphenoidal fissure (25) is well open. The auditory bullae (26) and auditory meatus (27) are well elevated; the auditory meatus is above the midpoint of skull and small. Incisors (28) are stout, procumbent, and recurved; the diastema (29) is exceptionally wide. Interorbital foramina (30) are very large and low on the side of the rostrum. The toothrows (31) are distinctly angled to the posterior.

Mandible: The body (32) of the mandible is deep, heavy, and curved; the incisor is stout. The coronoid process (33) is long, thick, and curved to the posterior, the tip well short of the condyle; the coronoid is more slender than those of yellow-faced pocket gophers and more curved to the posterior than those of plains pocket gophers. The condyloid process (34) is thick, rounded, and short. The angular process (35) is large and multifaceted, flaring outward on a separate plane from the others; the secondary process (36) is flatter and pointed.

Similar species: Other pocket gophers and muskrats.

Note: Males are larger than females, and their skulls are overall more robust, with more angular zygomata.

Plains pocket gopher, *Geomys bursarius*

Greatest length: 40.5–60.0 mm (1⁶/10–2⁴/10 in.) (full table of measurements page 562, life-size image page 117, life-size jaw page 161)

Specimen illustrated: Adult male, LACM 5496

Dentition: i 1/1 c 0/0 p 1/1 m 3/3, total 20. The anterior surfaces of the upper incisors each have two deep grooves.

Dorsal: Pocket gopher skulls are robust and angular, with wide-spreading zygomatic arches, small lacrimal processes (1), and large orbits (2). Rostrum (3) is long, laterally compressed, and broader than in other pocket gophers; nasals (4) are long and more slender than in other species. The nasals extend to the posterior much less than the premaxillaries (5). The angular, wide-spreading zygomatic arches (6) are near parallel in subadults and converge to the posterior in mature specimens. The interorbital region (7) is narrow. Postorbital processes are rudimentary or absent. The braincase (8) is large and squared, less than 50 percent of the greatest length of skull; temporal ridges are less developed and may form a small sagittal crest at the posterior of the skull. Occipital crests (9) are developed. The interparietal (10) is wider than long and just forward of the occipital crests.

Ventral: The palate (11) is distinctive, two-tiered, and very narrow; the pterygoid region (12) is very narrow, and pterygoid processes (13) are of medium width. The incisive foramina (14) are very small slits, situated closer to the molariform toothrows than the large incisors. The foramina ovale (15) are apparent and wide. The foramen magnum (16) is smaller. Auditory bullae (17) are large and inflated, with long necks or extensions (18) to the auditory meatus. Toothrows are very close

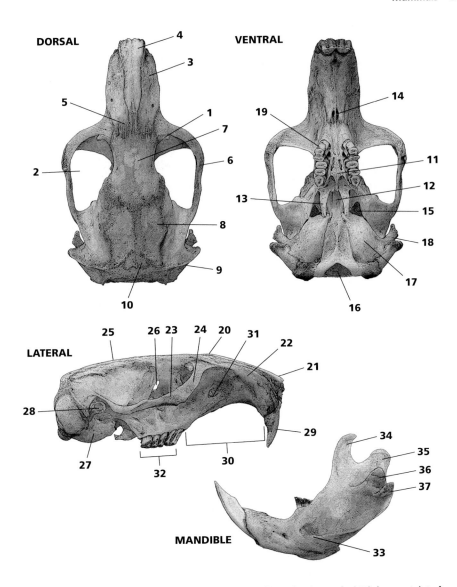

DORSAL

VENTRAL

LATERAL

MANDIBLE

together and convergent to the anterior. The first cheek tooth (19) is constricted in the middle and hourglass-shaped.

Lateral: The dorsolateral outline is relatively flat, with the apex of the skull (20) at the posterior of the rostrum. The anterior tips of the nasals (21) are decurved and extend to the anterior approximately in line with the anterior of the incisors. The rostrum (22) is deep and stout. Zygomatic arches (23) are comparatively elevated; the zygomatic plate (24) is steep, at roughly 50 degrees. The braincase (25) is low. The sphenoidal fissure (26) is open. The auditory bullae (27) and auditory meatus (28) are well elevated; the auditory meatus is above the midpoint of skull and very small. Incisors (29) are stout and recurved; the diastema (30) is exceptionally wide.

Interorbital foramina (31) are small and low on the side of the rostrum. The toothrows (32) are less angled to the posterior than in other pocket gophers.

Mandible: The body (33) of the mandible is deep, heavy, and curved; the incisor is stout. The coronoid process (34) is long, thick, and curved to the posterior, the tip well short of the condyle. The condyloid process (35) is thick, rounded, and short. The angular process (36) is large and multifaceted, extending on a separate plane from the others; the secondary process (37) is more vertical and triangular.

Similar species: Other pocket gophers and muskrats.

Yellow-faced pocket gopher, *Cratogeomys castanops*

Greatest length: 41.5–58.3 mm ($1^6/10$–$2^3/10$ in.) (full table of measurements page 562, life-size image page 117, life-size jaw page 162)

Specimen illustrated: Adult male, LACM 44244

Dentition: i 1/1 c 0/0 p 1/1 m 3/3, total 20. The upper incisors each have a single groove.

Dorsal: Pocket gopher skulls are robust and angular, with wide-spreading zygomatic arches, small lacrimal processes (1), and large orbits (2). Rostrum (3) is long, laterally compressed, and stout; nasals (4) are long, broad, and somewhat triangular. The nasals do not extend to the posterior as far as the premaxillaries (5). The angular, wide-spreading zygomatic arches (6) are nearly parallel in subadults and converge strongly to the posterior in mature specimens (see page 302). The interorbital region (7) is narrow. Postorbital processes are rudimentary or absent. The braincase (8) is large and squared, less than 50 percent of the greatest length of skull; temporal ridges (9) join high on the skull and form a sagittal crest (10) for much of the posterior of the skull. Occipital crests (11) are developed.

Ventral: The palate (12) is distinctive, two-tiered, and very narrow; the pterygoid region (13) is very narrow, and pterygoid processes (14) are distinctly thickened. The incisive foramina (15) are very small slits, situated closer to the molariform toothrows than the large incisors. The foramina ovale (16) are wide. The foramen magnum (17) is large. Auditory bullae (18) are large and inflated, with long necks or extensions (19) to the auditory meatus. Toothrows are very close together and convergent to the anterior. The last upper molar (21) is the largest of the molars, and the first cheek tooth (20) is constricted in the middle, and hourglass-shaped.

Lateral: The dorsolateral outline (22) is relatively flat. The anterior tips of the nasals (23) are decurved and extend to the anterior approximately in line with the anterior of the incisors. The rostrum (24) is deep and stout. Zygomatic arches (25) are comparatively elevated and deep; the zygomatic plate (26) is steep, at roughly 60 degrees. The braincase (27) is low. The sphenoidal fissure (28) is closed. The auditory bullae (29) and auditory meatus (30) are well elevated; the auditory meatus sits at the midpoint of skull and is small. Incisors (31) are stout and recurved; the diastema (32) is exceptionally wide. Interorbital foramina (33) are smaller and slightly more elevated on the side of the rostrum than in other pocket gophers. The toothrows are distinctly angled to the posterior.

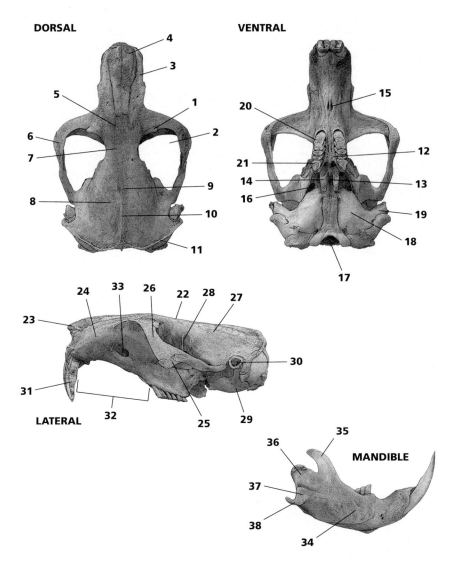

DORSAL

VENTRAL

LATERAL

MANDIBLE

Mandible: The body (34) of the mandible is deep, heavy, and curved; the incisor is stout. The coronoid process (35) is long, thick, and curved to the posterior, the tip well short of the condyle. The condyloid process (36) is thick, rounded, and short. The angular process (37) is large and multifaceted, extending on a separate plane from the others; the secondary process (38) is long and decurved, and then curved to the posterior.

Similar species: Other pocket gophers and muskrats.

(Continued on next page.)

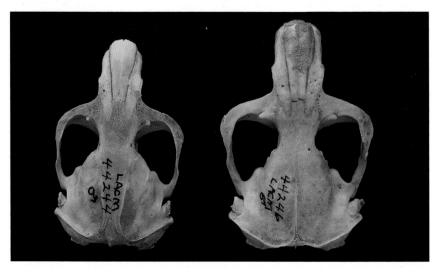

Compare the parallel zygomatic arches in the subadult male on the left with the mature male on the right, in which the zygomata converge to the posterior. NATURAL HISTORY MUSEUM OF LOS ANGELES COUNTY 44244, 44246.

Family Heteromyidae: Pocket mice and kangaroo rats

Heteromyids are rodents that are distinguished by their thin grooved upper and smooth lower incisors and incredibly enlarged, swollen mastoids and auditory bullae. In 1962, D. B. Webster studied the enlarged auditory bullae and swollen mastoid regions in kangaroo rats (Ewer 1973). The enlargement increases the air space behind the tympanic membrane, which then resonates with specific frequencies. The frequencies causing the greatest resonance were those created by an owl swooping in for a kill and a rattlesnake making a strike. Thus the kangaroo rat is thought to have adapted to hear and then react quickly enough to make last-moment escapes from threats on its life.

The shape and size of the interparietal bone at the posterior of the skull are particularly important in differentiating among the many species that belong to this family. Always note this bone's form in the illustrations of the dorsal perspective.

The mandible is distinctive in form, though similar to those of the closely

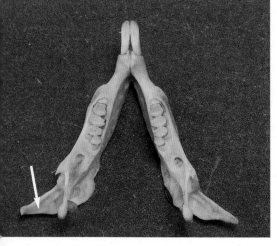

The complete mandibles of Ord's kangaroo rat show the characteristic flaring angular processes of all members of the family except the spiny pocket mouse. Male, SANTA BARBARA MUSEUM OF NATURAL HISTORY VB-71.

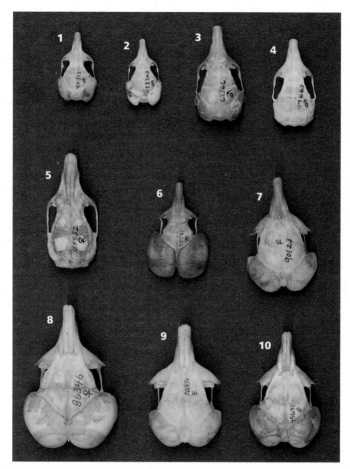

Select members of Heteromyidae: 1. Silky pocket mouse, male 91312 *(P. flavus)*, 2. Little pocket mouse, male 123340 *(P. longimembris)*, 3. Bailey's pocket mouse, male 6216 *(C. baileyi)*, 4. Sonoran desert pocket mouse, male 77663 *(C. penicillatus)*, 5. Mexican spiny pocket mouse, female 155552 *(Liomys irroratus)*, 6. Dark kangaroo mouse, male 52781 *(Microdipodops megacephalus)*, 7. Merriam's kangaroo rat, female 90123 *(D. merriami)*, 8. Desert kangaroo rat, female 86346 *(D. deserti)*, 9. California kangaroo rat, female 70331 *(D. californicus)*, 10. Ord's kangaroo rat, male 4564 *(D. ordii)*. MUSEUM OF VERTEBRATE ZOOLOGY, UC BERKELEY.

Compare the lateral edges of the occiput. On the left, a female Sonoran desert pocket mouse *(Chaetodipus penicillatus)*, and on the right a male little pocket mouse *(Perognathus longimembris)*. SANTA BARBARA MUSEUM OF NATURAL HISTORY VB 64-745, VB 1403.

related pocket gophers and the more distantly related aplodontia. The angular process flares outward and is often on a separate plane from the condyloid and coronoid processes. This is difficult to appreciate from the lateral perspective, so a photo of both mandibles of the Ord's kangaroo rat *(Dipodomys ordii)* is provided on page 302 to help you better visualize this feature of heteromyids.

The occipital sutures can be used to differentiate among pocket mice. The shape of the suture separating the occiput and mastoids is a good start to narrowing down possibilities (Ingles 1965). Pocket mice in the genus *Perognathus* have relatively straight sutures, whereas those in the genus *Chaetodipus* have curved sutures where the mastoid swells to fill the concave occiput. The photo on page 303 will help you better visualize this character.

Little pocket mouse, *Perognathus longimembris*

Greatest length: 20.2–22.6 mm ($^8/_{10}$–$^9/_{10}$ in.) (full table of measurements page 564, life-size image page 111, life-size jaw page 159)

Specimen illustrated: Adult male, SBMNH VB-1906

Dentition: i 1/1 c 0/0 p 1/1 m 3/3, total 20.

Dorsal: Pocket mouse skulls are long and slender, with long, thin rostrums (1), fragile zygomatic arches, and swollen mastoids (2) visible at the posterior corners of the braincase; they are thin-boned and fragile. Nasals (3) are long and slender, like the rostrum, and extend to the posterior less than the premaxillaries (4). The maxillary arms (5) of the zygomatics are well developed and include small lacrimal projections (6) or wings dorsally. Zygomatic arches (7) are very fragile and often concave. The interorbital breadth (8) is relatively broad and much wider than the rostrum. The braincase (9) is very large, longer than wide, and approximately 50 percent of the greatest length of skull. The interparietal bone (10) is smaller, slightly wider

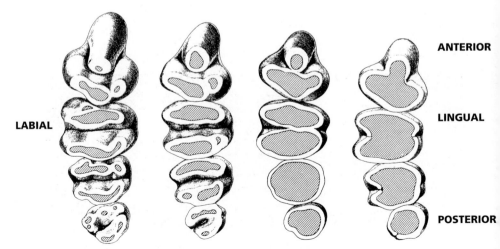

ANTERIOR

LINGUAL

POSTERIOR

LABIAL

From left to right, visual changes in the teeth of the little pocket mouse *(P. longimembris)*, which occur with increased age and wear. Used with permission of Donald Hoffmeister.

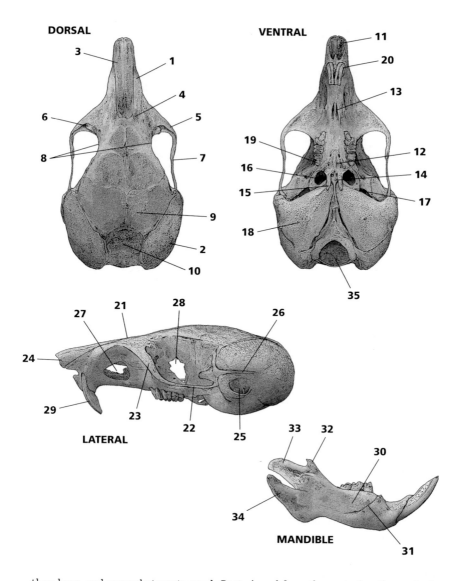

DORSAL

VENTRAL

LATERAL

MANDIBLE

than long, and somewhat pentagonal. Best viewed from the posterior, the occiput-mastoid suture is relatively straight.

Ventral: Nasal vacuity (11) is tubular. The palate (12) extends beyond the posterior molars; incisive foramina (13) are small and situated closer to the molariform teeth than the front incisors. Pterygoid region (14) is very small, as are the pterygoid processes (15). Spheno-pterygoid canals (16) are large and ovoid; the foramina ovale (17) are apparent. Auditory bullae (18) are very large and swollen and somewhat triangular, their anterior tips converging near to contact. The foramen magnum (35) is large. Very short toothrows converge to the anterior; the last cheek tooth (19) is the smallest in row. Slender upper incisors (20) are grooved.

Lateral: The dorsolateral outline from the tips of the nasals to the apex of the skull midway above the orbits is very straight (21), and then curves gradually down to the posterior. Zygomatic arches (22) are flat and straight, and the zygomatic plates (23) are steep. Nasals (24) extend far beyond the incisors. The auditory meatus (25) is large and elevated, approximately one-third up the height of the skull. There is a separation (26) between the swollen mastoid and bullae. Infraorbital foramina (27) are very large and create a hole straight through the rostrum anterior to the zygomatic arches. The antorbital canal (28) is large. Incisors (29) are strongly recurved.

Mandible: The structure of the mandible is similar for almost all pocket mice and kangaroo rats, as well as the related pocket gophers. The body (30) of the mandible is deep, with an obvious ridge (31) where masseter muscles attach. The coronoid process (32) is reduced, a small tapering point to posterior. The condyloid process (33) is long, stout, and rounded, pointing to posterior. The angular process (34) is large, multifaceted, and flaring, extending on a separate plane from the others.

Similar species: Other pocket mice and all other mouse species, including jumping and white-footed.

Notes: A visual representation of the toothrow wear patterns in this species as it ages is presented on page 305.

Great basin pocket mouse, *Perognathus parvus*

Greatest length: 23.2–29.0 mm ($^9/_{10}$–1$^1/_{10}$ in.) (full table of measurements page 564, life-size image page 112, life-size jaw page 159)

Specimen illustrated: Adult female, SBMNH VB-61-21

Dentition: i 1/1 c 0/0 p 1/1 m 3/3, total 20.

Dorsal: Pocket mouse skulls are long and slender, with long, thin rostrums (1), fragile zygomatic arches, and swollen mastoids (2) visible at the posterior corners of the braincase; they are thin-boned and fragile. Nasals (3) are long and slender, like the rostrum, and extend to the posterior approximately equally to the premaxillaries (4). The maxillary arms (5) of the zygomatics are well developed and include small lacrimal projections (6) or wings dorsally, which do not remain in contact with the maxillaries for their entire length, as they do in some pocket mice. Zygomatic arches (7) are very fragile and often concave. The interorbital breadth (8) is relatively broad and much wider than the rostrum. The braincase (9) is very large, longer than wide, and approximately 50 percent of the greatest length of skull. Mastoids (2) are swollen and large, but less so than in some pocket mice. The interparietal bone (10) is larger, much wider than long, and somewhat pentagonal. Best viewed from the posterior, the occiput-mastoid suture is relatively straight.

Ventral: Nasal vacuity (11) is tubular. The palate (12) extends beyond the posterior molars; incisive foramina (13) are small and situated closer to the molariform teeth than the front incisors. Pterygoid region (14) is very small, as are the pterygoid processes (15). Spheno-pterygoid canals (16) are larger and ovoid; the foramina ovale (17) are apparent. Auditory bullae (18) are very large and swollen and somewhat triangular, their anterior tips converging, but not to the degree as in

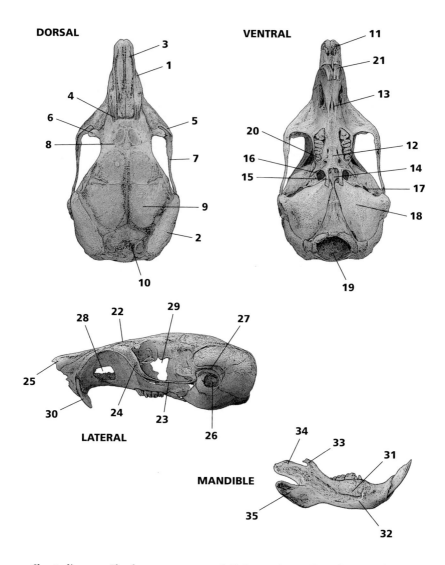

DORSAL

VENTRAL

LATERAL

MANDIBLE

Chaetodipus sp. The foramen magnum (19) is very large. Very short toothrows converge to the anterior; the last cheek tooth (20) is the smallest in row. Slender incisors (21) are grooved.

Lateral: The dorsolateral outline from the tips of the nasals to the apex of the skull midway above the orbits is very straight (22), and then curves to the posterior. Zygomatic arches (23) are flat and straight, and the zygomatic plates (24) are steep. Nasals (25) extend far beyond the incisors. The auditory meatus (26) is large and elevated, approximately one-third up the height of the skull. There is a separation (27) between the swollen mastoids and bullae. Infraorbital foramina (28) are very large and create a hole straight through the rostrum anterior to the zygomatic arches. The antorbital canal (29) is very large. Incisors (30) are strongly recurved.

Mandible: The structure of the mandible is similar for almost all pocket mice and kangaroo rats, as well as the related pocket gophers. The body (31) of the mandible is deep, with an obvious ridge (32) where masseter muscles attach. The coronoid process (33) is reduced, a small tapering point to posterior. The condyloid process (34) is long, stout, and rounded, pointing to posterior. The angular process (35) is large and multifaceted, extending on a separate plane from the others.

Similar species: Other pocket mice and all other mouse species, including jumping and white-footed.

Sonoran desert pocket mouse, *Chaetodipus penicillatus*

Greatest length: 22.6–27.1 mm ($9/10$–$1^1/10$ in.) (full table of measurements page 564, life-size image page 111, life-size jaw page 159)

Specimen illustrated: Adult female, SBMNH VB-64-387

Dentition: i 1/1 c 0/0 p 1/1 m 3/3, total 20.

Dorsal: Pocket mouse skulls are long and slender, with long, thin rostrums (1), fragile zygomatic arches, and swollen mastoids (2) visible at the posterior corners of the braincase; they are thin-boned and fragile. Nasals (3) are long and slender, like the rostrum, and extend to the posterior less than the premaxillaries (4). The maxillary arms (5) of the zygomatics are well developed and include small lacrimal projections (6) or wings dorsally, which do not remain in contact with the maxillaries for their entire length, as in some pocket mice. Zygomatic arches (7) are stouter and more parallel, or slightly converging to the anterior, than those of *Perognathus*. The interorbital breadth (8) is broad and much wider than the rostrum. The braincase (9) is very large, longer than wide, and approximately 50 percent of the greatest length of skull. Mastoids (2) are swollen but proportionately smaller than in many pocket mice. The interparietal bone (10) is very large, wider than long, and somewhat pentagonal. Best viewed from the posterior, the occiput-mastoid suture is relatively curved (see figure on page 303).

Ventral: Nasal vacuity (11) is tubular. The palate (12) extends beyond the posterior molars; incisive foramina (13) are small and situated closer to the molariform teeth than the front incisors. Pterygoid region (14) is very small, as are the thicker pterygoid processes (15). Spheno-pterygoid canals (16) are large and ovoid; the foramina ovale (17) are apparent. Auditory bullae (18) are very large and swollen and somewhat triangular, their anterior tips converging near to contact. The foramen magnum (19) is large. Very short toothrows converge to the anterior. Slender upper incisors (20) are grooved.

Lateral: The dorsolateral outline from the tips of the nasals to the apex of the skull midway above the orbits is very straight (21), and then curves gradually down to the posterior (22). Zygomatic arches (23) are flat and straight, and the zygomatic plates (24) are steep. Nasals (25) extend far beyond the incisors. The auditory meatus (26) is large and elevated, approximately one-third up the height of the skull. There is a separation (27) between the swollen mastoids and bullae. Infraorbital foramina (28) are very large and create a hole straight through the rostrum anterior

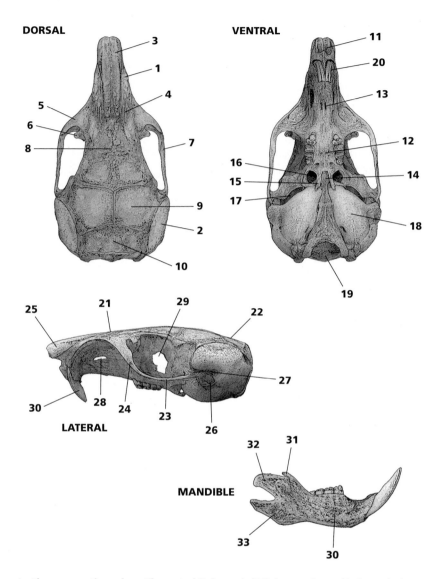

DORSAL

VENTRAL

LATERAL

MANDIBLE

to the zygomatic arches. The antorbital canal (29) is very large. Incisors (30) are strongly recurved.

Mandible: The structure of the mandible is similar for almost all pocket mice and kangaroo rats, as well as the related pocket gophers. The body (30) of the mandible is deep, with an obvious ridge where masseter muscles attach. The coronoid process (31) is reduced, a small tapering point to posterior. The condyloid process (32) is long, stout, and rounded, pointing to posterior. The angular process (33) is large and multifaceted, extending on a separate plane from the others.

Similar species: Other pocket mice and all other mouse species, including jumping and white-footed.

Dark kangaroo mouse, *Microdipodops megacephalus*

Greatest length: 25.2–29.3 mm (1–1²/₁₀ in.) (full table of measurements page 566, life-size image page 112, life-size jaw page 159)

Specimen illustrated: Adult male, MVZ 52781

Dentition: i 1/1 c 0/0 p 1/1 m 3/3, total 20.

Dorsal: Kangaroo mouse skulls closely resemble those of kangaroo rats, with their long, slender rostrums, fragile zygomatic arches, and exceptionally swollen mastoids (1), very visible as two balloons at the posterior corners of the braincase; they are thin-boned and fragile. Nasals (2) are very long and slender, as is the rostrum (3), and the squared posterior sutures fall well short of the ends of the premaxillaries (4). The maxillary arms (5) of the zygomatics are distinctively narrower than in kangaroo rats, and the zygomatic arches converge at their tips. Small outward lacrimal projections (6) or wings on the dorsal surface do not remain in contact with the maxillaries for their entire length. Zygomatic arches (7) are very fragile and straight, and they are often lost in skulls recovered in the field. The interorbital breadth (8) is very broad, but slightly narrower and more curved than in kangaroo rats. The braincase (9) is very large, longer than wide, and approximately 50 percent of the greatest length of skull. Mastoids are remarkably swollen and large, more so than in any kangaroo rat species. The interparietal bone (10) is absent, squeezed away between the mastoids; the supraoccipital (11) is absent as well.

Ventral: Nasal vacuity (12) is tubular. The palate (13) extends beyond the posterior molars; incisive foramina (14) are relatively longer and situated closer to the molariform teeth than to the front incisors. Pterygoid region (15) is very small, as are the pterygoid processes. Spheno-pterygoid canals (16) are large and round; the foramina ovale (17) apparent. Auditory bullae (18) are massive and swollen, larger than in kangaroo rats, with the inner triangular portions converging near to contact. The foramen magnum (19) is medium. Very short toothrows are approximately parallel; the last cheek tooth is the smallest in row. Slender incisors (20) are grooved.

Lateral: The dorsolateral outline from the tips of the nasals to the apex of the skull midway above the orbits is very straight (21), and then curves gradually down to the posterior (22). Zygomatic arches (23) slope to posterior, and the zygomatic plates (24) are very steep. Nasals (25) extend far beyond the incisors. The auditory meatus (26) is very large and low on the posterior of the skull. There is a separation (27) between the swollen mastoids and bullae; the ventral surface of the auditory bullae (38) is very low. Infraorbital foramen (28) is very large and creates a hole straight through the rostrum anterior to the zygomatic arches. The antorbital canal (29) is large, and a second foramen (30) sits below. Incisors (31) are strongly recurved anterior to a large diastema.

Mandible: The structure of the mandible is similar for almost all pocket mice and kangaroo rats, as well as the related pocket gophers. The body (32) of the mandible is deep, with an obvious ridge where masseter muscles attach and a distinctive process (33) that projects above the diastema. The coronoid process (34) is reduced, a small,

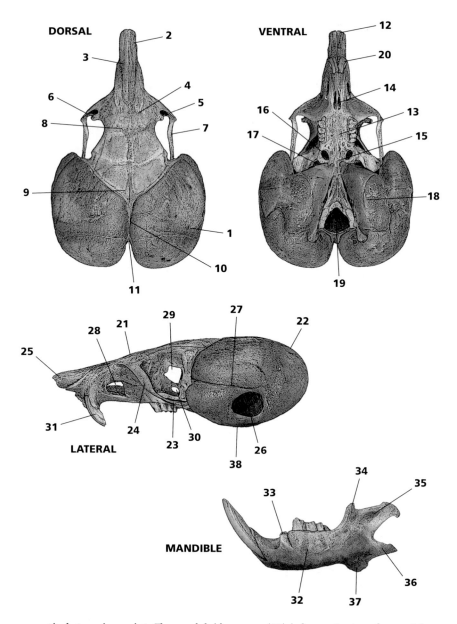

vertical, tapering point. The condyloid process (35) is long, stout, and more triangular, pointing to posterior. The angular process is large and multifaceted, a rounded corner (37) below and a slender, sharp projection (36) above.

Similar species: Pale kangaroo mouse *(M. pallidus)* and kangaroo rats.

Desert kangaroo rat, *Dipodomys deserti*

Greatest length: 41.5–46.7 mm ($1^6/_{10}$–$1^8/_{10}$ in.) (full table of measurements page 566, life-size image page 117, life-size jaw page 160)

Specimen illustrated: Adult male, SBMNH VB-24

Dentition: i 1/1 c 0/0 p 1/1 m 3/3, total 20.

Dorsal: Kangaroo rat skulls are incredibly distinctive, with their long, slender rostrums (1), fragile zygomatic arches, and exceptionally swollen mastoids (2), very visible as two balloons at the posterior corners of the braincase; they are thin-boned and fragile. The desert kangaroo rat skull has a comparatively broad outline, with the posterior corners rounded. Nasals (3) are very long and slender, as is the rostrum, and the posterior sutures along with those of the premaxillaries form a distinctive V (4). The maxillary arms of the zygomatics (5) are well developed and include small lacrimal projections (6) or wings dorsally. Zygomatic arches (7) are very fragile and straight, and they are often lost in skulls recovered in the field. The interorbital breadth (8) is very broad and significantly wider than the rostrum. The braincase (9) is very large, longer than wide, and approximately 50 percent of the greatest length of skull. Mastoids (2) are remarkably swollen and large and are directly posterior to the parietal bones. The interparietal bone (10) is absent, squeezed away between the mastoids; the supraoccipital (11) is barely visible and only as wide as 1 millimeter.

Ventral: Nasal vacuity (12) is tubular. The palate (13) extends beyond the posterior molars; incisive foramina (14) are relatively longer and situated closer to the molariform teeth than to the front incisors. Pterygoid region (15) is very small, as are the thick pterygoid processes (16). Spheno-pterygoid canals (17) are large and round; the foramina ovale (18) are apparent. Auditory bullae (19) are massive and swollen, the largest of all kangaroo rats, the inner triangular portions converging

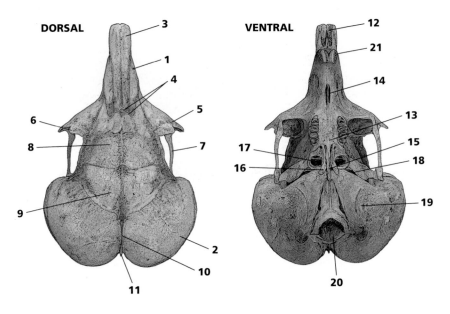

DORSAL   VENTRAL

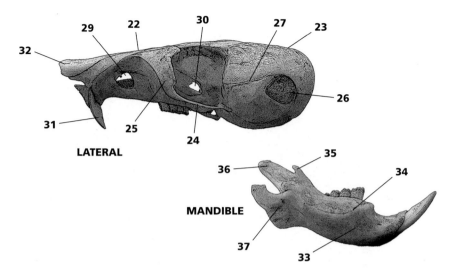

29 22 30 27 23

32

26

31 25

24

LATERAL

35

36 34

MANDIBLE

37 33

near to contact. The foramen magnum (20) is medium. Very short toothrows converge slightly to the anterior; the last cheek tooth is the smallest in row. Slender incisors (21) are grooved.

Lateral: The dorsolateral outline from the tips of the nasals to the apex of the skull midway above the orbits is very straight (22), and then curves gradually down to the posterior (23). Zygomatic arches (24) are straight and nearly flat, and the zygomatic plates (25) are very steep. Nasals (32) extend far beyond the incisors. The auditory meatus (26) is very large and elevated, approximately midway up the height of the skull. There is a separation (27) between the swollen mastoids and bullae. Infraorbital foramen (29) is very large and creates a hole straight through the rostrum anterior to the zygomatic arches. The antorbital canal (30) is small. Incisors (31) are strongly recurved anterior to a large diastema.

Mandible: The structure of the mandible is similar for almost all pocket mice and kangaroo rats, as well as the related pocket gophers. The body (33) of the mandible is deep, with an obvious ridge (34) where masseter muscles attach. The coronoid process (35) is reduced, a small, tapering point to posterior. The condyloid process (36) is long, stout, and rounded, pointing to posterior. The angular process (37) is large and multifaceted, extending on a separate plane from the others.

Similar species: Giant kangaroo rat *(D. ingens)* and other larger kangaroo rat species.

Merriam's kangaroo rat, *Dipodomys merriami*

Greatest length: 33.5–37.9 mm ($1^{3}/_{10}$–$1^{5}/_{10}$ in.) (full table of measurements page 568, life-size image page 114, life-size jaw page 160)

Specimen illustrated: Adult female, SBMNH VB-68-356

Dentition: i 1/1 c 0/0 p 1/1 m 3/3, total 20.

Dorsal: Kangaroo rat skulls are incredibly distinctive, with their long, slender rostrums (1), fragile zygomatic arches, and exceptionally swollen mastoids (2), very visible

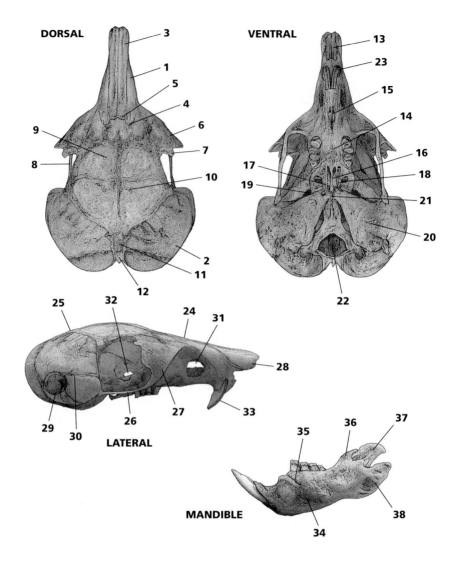

DORSAL

VENTRAL

LATERAL

MANDIBLE

as two balloons at the posterior corners of the braincase; they are thin-boned and fragile. The Merriam's kangaroo rat skull has a comparatively broad outline, with the posterior corners rounded. Nasals (3) are very long and slender, as is the rostrum, and the squared posterior sutures (5) do not extend as far as the premaxillaries (4). The maxillary arms of the zygomatics (6) are very long and well developed, and their shape and length may be useful in cross-species comparisons. There are small lacrimal projections (7) or wings dorsally, which are fused with the maxillaries for their entire length. Zygomatic arches (8) are very fragile and straight, and they are often lost in skulls recovered in the field. The interorbital breadth (9) is very broad and significantly wider than the rostrum. The braincase (10) is very large, longer than wide, and approximately 50 percent of the greatest length of skull. Mastoids (2) are remarkably swollen and large. The interparietal bone (11) is small, narrow, and rectangular; the supraoccipital (12) is visible and narrow.

Ventral: Nasal vacuity (13) is tubular. The palate (14) extends beyond the posterior molars; incisive foramina (15) are relatively longer and situated closer to the molariform teeth than to the front incisors. Pterygoid region (16) is very small, as are the slender pterygoid processes (17). Spheno-pterygoid canals (18) are medium and round; the foramina ovale (19) are apparent. Auditory bullae (20) are massive and swollen, the inner triangular portions converging to contact (21). The foramen magnum (22) is medium. Very short toothrows converge slightly to the anterior; the last cheek tooth is the smallest in row. Slender incisors (23) are grooved.

Lateral: The dorsolateral outline from the tips of the nasals to the apex of the skull midway above the orbits is very straight (24), and then curves more steeply down to the posterior than in other species (25). Zygomatic arches (26) are flat and straight, and the zygomatic plates (27) are very steep. Nasals (28) extend far beyond the incisors. The auditory meatus (29) is very large and low on the posterior of the skull. There is a separation (30) between the swollen mastoids and bullae. Infraorbital foramen (31) is very large and creates a hole straight through the rostrum anterior to the zygomatic arches. The antorbital canal (32) is small. Incisors (33) are strongly recurved anterior to a large diastema.

Mandible: The structure of the mandible is similar for almost all pocket mice and kangaroo rats, as well as the related pocket gophers. The body (34) of the mandible is deep, with an obvious ridge (35) where masseter muscles attach. The coronoid process (36) is reduced, a small, tapering point to posterior. The condyloid process (37) is long, stout, and rounded, pointing to posterior. The angular process (38) is large and multifaceted, extending on a separate plane from the others.

Similar species: Fresno kangaroo rat and other medium-size kangaroo rats and kangaroo mice.

Ord's kangaroo rat, *Dipodomys ordii*

Greatest length: 34.9–42.4 mm (1^4/10–1^7/10 in.) (full table of measurements page 568, life-size image page 115, life-size jaw page 160)

Specimen illustrated: Adult male, SBMNH VB-71

Dentition: i 1/1 c 0/0 p 1/1 m 3/3, total 20.

Dorsal: Kangaroo rat skulls are incredibly distinctive, with their long, slender rostrums (1), fragile zygomatic arches, and exceptionally swollen mastoids (2), very visible as two balloons at the posterior corners of the braincase; they are thin-boned and fragile. The Ord's kangaroo rat skull has a comparatively slender outline, with the posterior corners straighter and angular. Nasals (3) are very long and slender, as is the rostrum, and the squared posterior sutures (4) do not extend as far as the premaxillaries (5). The maxillary arms of the zygomatics (6) are well developed, and their shape and length may be useful in cross-species comparisons. There are small lacrimal projections (7) or wings dorsally. Zygomatic arches (8) are very fragile and straight, and they are often lost in skulls recovered in the field. The interorbital

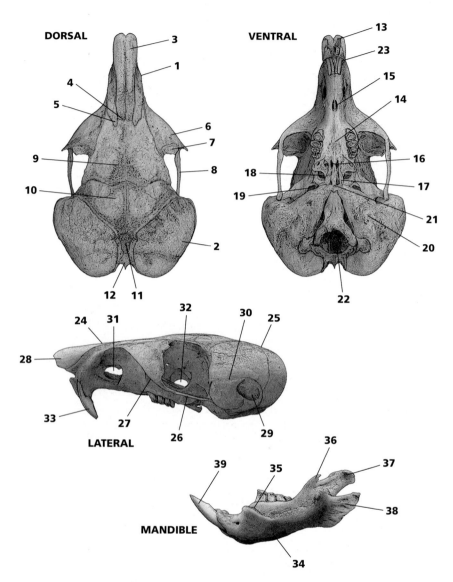

DORSAL

VENTRAL

LATERAL

MANDIBLE

breadth (9) is very broad and significantly wider than the rostrum. The braincase (10) is very large, longer than wide, and approximately 50 percent of the greatest length of skull. Mastoids (2) are remarkably swollen and large. The interparietal bone (11) is small, narrow, and tapering to the posterior; the supraoccipital (12) is visible and wider.

Ventral: Nasal vacuity (13) is tubular. The palate (14) extends beyond the posterior molars; incisive foramina (15) are comparatively very small and situated closer to the molariform teeth than to the front incisors. Pterygoid region (16) is very small, as are the thicker pterygoid processes (17). Spheno-pterygoid canals (18) are medium and round; the foramina ovale (19) are apparent. Auditory bullae (20) are massive and swollen, the inner triangular portions converging to contact (21). The foramen magnum (22) is medium. Very short toothrows converge slightly to the anterior; the last cheek tooth is the smallest in row. Slender incisors (23) are grooved.

Lateral: The dorsolateral outline from the tips of the nasals to the apex of the skull midway above the orbits is very straight (24), and then curves gradually down to the posterior (25). Zygomatic arches (26) are sloping and straight, and the zygomatic plates (27) are very steep. Nasals (28) extend far beyond the incisors. The auditory meatus (29) is very large and slightly elevated, approximately one-third up the height of the skull. There is a separation (30) between the swollen mastoids and bullae. Infraorbital foramen (31) is very large and creates a hole straight through the rostrum anterior to the zygomatic arches. The antorbital canal (32) is small. Incisors (33) are strongly recurved anterior to a large diastema.

Mandible: The structure of the mandible is similar for almost all pocket mice and kangaroo rats, as well as the related pocket gophers. The body (34) of the mandible is deep, with an obvious ridge (35) where masseter muscles attach. The coronoid process (36) is reduced, a small, tapering point to posterior. The condyloid process (37) is long, stout, and rounded, pointing to posterior. The angular process (38) is large and multifaceted, extending on a separate plane than from the others.

Similar species: Chisel-toothed kangaroo rats *(D. microps)* and other medium-size kangaroo rats.

Note: The lower incisors (39) are rounded on the anterior surfaces, rather than flattened, which is a character useful in differentiating this species from *D. microps.* Admittedly, though, this character is a difficult feature to see without skulls of both species in hand for comparison.

Mexican spiny pocket mouse, *Liomys irroratus*

Greatest length: 29.8–37.8 mm (1²/10–1⁵/10 in.) (full table of measurements page 566, life-size image page 113, life-size jaw page 160)

Specimen illustrated: Adult female, MVZ 155552

Dentition: i 1/1 c 0/0 p 1/1 m 3/3, total 20.

Dorsal: Spiny pocket mouse skulls are long and very slender, with exceptionally long, thin rostrums (1), straight zygomatic arches, and swollen mastoids visible at the posterior corners of the braincase; they are thin-boned and fragile. Nasals (2) are very long and slender, like the rostrum, and their posterior sutures (3) along with those of the premaxillaries (4) form a V. The maxillary arms of the zygomatics (5) and the zygomatic plates are smaller than in other pocket mice and include small lacrimal projections (6) or wings dorsally. Zygomatic arches (7) are straight, parallel, and stouter than in other pocket mice. The interorbital breadth (8) is relatively broad and wider than the rostrum. The braincase (9) is large, oval, and less than 50 percent of the greatest length of skull. Mastoids (10) are swollen and just visible from the dorsal perspective. The interparietal bone (11) is large and rectangular.

Ventral: Nasal vacuity (12) is tubular. The palate (13) extends beyond the posterior molars; incisive foramina (14) are tiny and situated approximately midway between the molariform teeth and the incisors. Pterygoid region (15) is very small, as are the pterygoid processes (16). The foramina ovale (17) are large and distinctive. Audi-

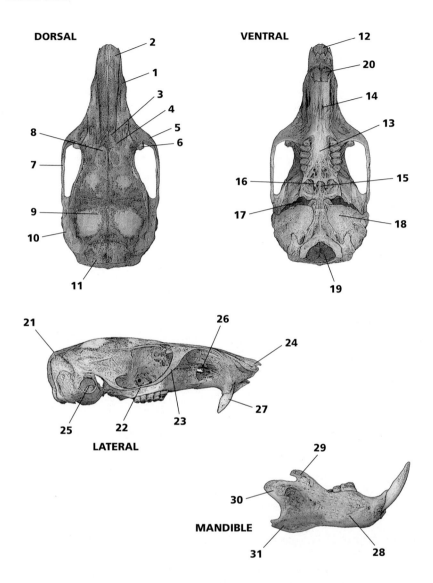

DORSAL

VENTRAL

LATERAL

MANDIBLE

tory bullae (18) are very large and swollen and somewhat triangular, their anterior tips converging, but much more widely spaced than in other pocket mice. The foramen magnum (19) is large. Very short toothrows converge to the anterior; the last cheek tooth is the smallest in row. Slender incisors (20) are not grooved.

Lateral: The overall dorsolateral outline is relatively straight; the posterior of the skull (21) is angular rather than rounded. Zygomatic arches (22) are nearly flat and straight, and the zygomatic plates (23) are steep. Nasals (24) extend far beyond the incisors. The auditory meatus (25) is medium and only slightly elevated. Infraorbital foramina (26) are very large and create a hole straight through the rostrum anterior to the zygomatic arches. Incisors (27) are strongly recurved anterior to a very large diastema.

Mandible: The structure of the mandible is not like those of the other pocket mice and kangaroo rats. The body (28) of the mandible is deep and curved upward at the anterior. The coronoid process (29) is small, blunt, and angled to posterior. The condyloid process (30) is long, rounded, and the longest and widest of the three processes. The angular process (31) is reduced and rounded, with a squared tip pointing to posterior.

Similar species: Pocket mice, jumping mice, Florida mouse, and all other mouse species.

Family Castoridae: Beavers

There is but one member in this family, the American beaver. The beaver is a rodent that is characterized by a large, heavy skull but tiny infraorbital foramina. The orbits are small and elevated, and they are visible above the waterline in partially submerged animals. The auditory meatus too is elevated to accomodate an aquatic lifestyle.

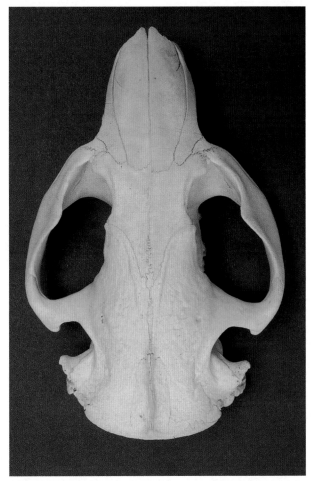

The sole member of this family is the American beaver *(Castor canadensis)*. SANTA BARBARA MUSEUM OF NATURAL HISTORY 3691.

American beaver, *Castor canadensis*

Greatest length: 100.8–158.6 mm (4–6^2/10 in.) (full table of measurements page 570, life-size image page 137, life-size jaw page 170)

Specimen illustrated: Adult, SBMNH 3691

Dentition: i 1/1 c 0/0 p 1/1 m 3/3, total 20. Incisors massive, with yellow enamel evident on the anterior edges. The cheek teeth are high-crowned and rooted.

Dorsal: Large, heavy skull. Rostrum (1) is broad and stout. Nasals (2) are broad and long, widest at their midpoints and tapering to points at the anterior. The sutures at the posterior of the nasals (3) and premaxillaries (4) form an arch over the rostrum. Large, heavy zygomatic arches (5) are slightly curved and converge to the anterior. The frontals lack true postorbital processes, yet the orbit is enclosed by bony "corners" (6) at the posterior of the frontal bones. Postorbital processes are well developed on the zygomatic arches (7). The zygomatic plates (8) are very large and concave to accommodate large masseter muscles. The orbits (9) are small, and the temporal fossa (10) is large. The braincase (11) is long and narrow; temporal ridges (12) are well developed in a narrow V shape, converging to form a well-developed sagittal crest (13) on the posterior half of the braincase. Occipital crests (14) are developed. The auditory meatus (15) is visible from the dorsal view.

Ventral: Palate (16) is narrow and terminates approximately in line with the posterior edge of the last molar; a stout, pointy projection (17) extends over the relatively narrow pterygoid region (18). The pterygoid processes (19) are relatively long. The incisive foramina (20) are small and slitlike, situated closer to the toothrows than to the incisors, and relatively aligned with the small, slitlike infraorbital foramina (21) that are situated on the sides of the rostrum anterior to the zygomatic plates. Auditory bullae (22) are medium and inflated, and auditory canals form large extensions or necks, angled dorsally. There is a distinctive depression or pit in the basioccipital region (23).

Lateral: The dorsolateral outline is relatively straight, the deepest point above the anterior of the orbits (24). The rostrum (25) is very deep and strong; the braincase (26) is not elevated. The stout zygomatic arches (27) are elevated, as are the orbits, to allow the beaver to see while swimming with the head partially submerged. The jugal bones (28) are exceptionally broad and heavy. The small auditory meatus (29) is also elevated and is above the midpoint of the skull; the long auditory canal (30) is better viewed from this perspective as well.

Mandible: The body (31) of the mandible is very deep, and at the anterior is a distinctive bone extension (32) below the ventral outline of the bone, just where the body curves strongly up to the anterior. The coronoid process (33) is near vertical, long, and curved slightly to the posterior; the tip points to the posterior. The condyloid process (34) is reduced and stout; the condyle sits below the apex of the coronoid. The angular process (35) is broad and rounded at the posterior.

Similar species: Other larger rodents such as nutrias, porcupines, woodchucks, and marmots.

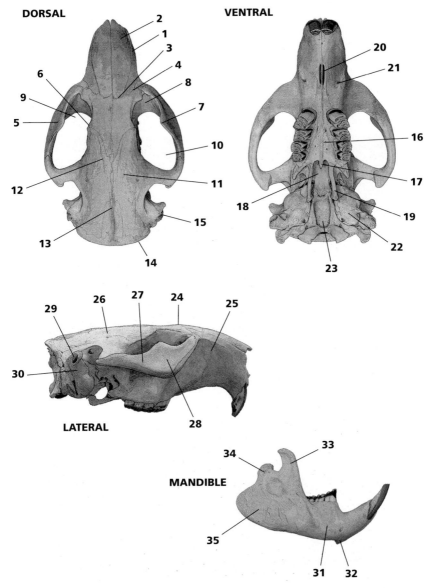

DORSAL

VENTRAL

LATERAL

MANDIBLE

Notes: Bond (1956) reports finding no apparent sexual dimorphism when comparing cranial measurements. Baker and Hill (2003) state that the deciduous premolars are replaced by eleven months of age, which helps differentiate young from adult animals.

Robertson and Shadle (1954) provide detailed descriptions of several cranial features which change with age, including fusing of sutures associated with the frontals, interparietal and occipital bones, as well as greatest length of skull and zygomatic width.

Family Muridae: Mice, rats, and voles

Murids are a large and diverse group of rodents. This family includes numerous smaller species that are difficult to distinguish. They have only three molariform teeth on each side and lack postorbital processes. Murids are also characterized by their slitlike infra-orbital foramina, through which a portion of the masseter muscles pass; rodents in which a portion of the masseter passes through the infraorbital are called myomorphs. Rodents are further characterized by their molars: crowned in mice and rats, prisms in voles and muskrats. Gilbert (1980) provides detailed descriptions of these and other features.

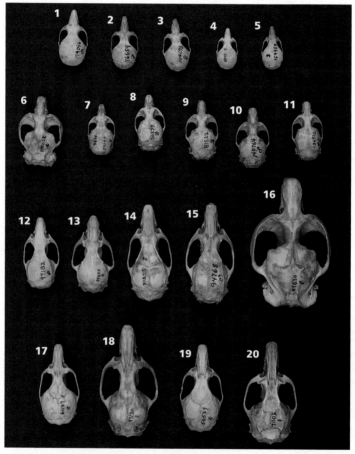

Select members of Muridae: 1. Northern grasshopper mouse, male 79081 *(Onychomys)*, 2. Deer mouse, female 104073 *(P. maniculatus)*, 3. White-footed mouse, female 104073 *(P. leucopus)*, 4. Western harvest mouse, female 28807 *(Reithrodontomys)*, 5. House mouse, female 169950 *(Mus)*, 6. Brown lemming, female 14032 *(Lemmus)*, 7. Southern red-backed vole, male 54199 *(Clethrionomys)*, 8. Long-tailed vole, male 30879 *(M. longicaudus)*, 9. Montane vole, female 81522 *(M. montanus)*, 10. California vole, male 149764 *(M. californicus)*, 11. Meadow vole, male 136972 *(M. pennsylvanicus)*, 12. Marsh rice rat, male 97182 *(Oryzomys)*, 13. Hispid cotton rat, male 50853 *(Sigmodon)*, 14. Black rat, male 29223 *(R. rattus)*, 15. Norway rat, male 94768 *(R. norvegicus)*, 16. Common muskrat, male 97830 *(Ondatra)*, 17. Desert woodrat, male 61189 *(N. lepida)*, 18. Eastern woodrat, female 97130 *(N. floridana)*, 19. White-throated woodrat, male 56589 *(N. albigula)*, 20. Bushy-tailed woodrat, female 71105 *(N. cinerea)*. MUSEUM OF VERTEBRATE ZOOLOGY, UC BERKELEY.

Marsh rice rat, *Oryzomys palustris*

Greatest length: 26.2–35.3 mm (1–1⁴/₁₀ in.) (full table of measurements page 578, life-size image page 112, life-size jaw page 160)

Specimen illustrated: Subadult–adult female, SBMNH VB-192

Dentition: i 1/1 c 0/0 p 0/0 m 3/3, total 16. Upper molar cusps alternate, rather than opposite in others.

Dorsal: The skulls of marsh rice rats are smaller, smoother versions of cotton rat skulls, with long, slender zygomatic arches, slender triangular rostrums, and large orbits. The rostrum (1) is slender and triangular; the nasals (2) are long, slender, and triangular. Zygomatic notches (3) are deep and distinctive. The zygomatic arches (4) are slim and converge to the anterior; the maxillary arms (5) of the zygomatic arches spread wider than the braincase. Lacrimal bone projections (6) are very small and in the dorsal corner of the maxillary arm (one is missing [7] in this specimen). The orbits (8) are large, and the interorbital breadth (9) is narrow and constricted, the maxillary bones just visible below. The braincase (10) is large, roughly as long as wide, and less than 50 percent of the greatest length of skull; temporal ridges (11) are less developed and bow outward toward the posterior of the skull. The interparietal (12) is smaller and not as wide as the braincase.

Ventral: The relatively broad palate (13) terminates well beyond the posterior molars; the incisive foramina (14) are large and broad, tapering slightly toward the anterior; their posterior edges (15) are approximately aligned with the anterior edge of the first cheek tooth. The pterygoid region (16) is narrow and small. The sphenopterygoid canals (17) are small and oval; the foramina ovale (18) are wide. Auditory bullae (19) are smaller and inflated. The foramen magnum (20) is large, with smaller occipital condyles (21). Toothrows are short and roughly parallel; the largest of three teeth (22) is at the anterior, descending in size to posterior. Palatal pits (23) are prominent at the posterior of the palate.

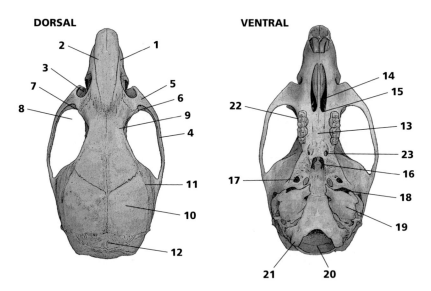

DORSAL   VENTRAL

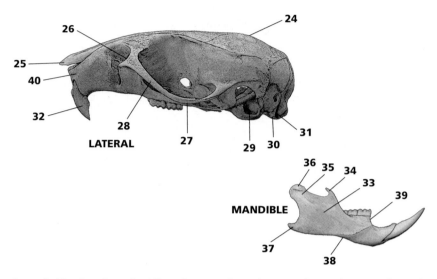

Lateral: The dorsolateral outline slopes up from the posterior to the apex above the inflated braincase (24), and then gradually curves to the tips of the nasals (25), which extend well beyond the premaxillaries (40) and incisors. The infraorbital foramina (26) are slitlike and high on the rostrum. Zygomatic arches (27) are low; the zygomatic plates (28) are angled at approximately 40 degrees. The auditory meatus (29) is low and medium. The paraoccipital processes (30) do not extend below the occipital condyles (31), as they do in the hispid cotton rat. The incisors (32) are recurved; the diastema is wide.

Mandible: The mandible is long and curved; the ramus region (33) is large. The coronoid process (34) is short, slender, tapering, and curved strongly to the posterior. The condyloid process (35) is long and broad, pointing to the posterior at near 45 degrees; the condyle (36) sits above the tip of the coronoid. The angular process (37) is well developed, tapers, and points to the posterior; note the ventral step (38) from the body of the mandible to the sloping angular process below the posterior teeth. There is a steep drop (39) from the anterior of the cheek teeth into the diastema.

Similar species: Cotton rats, black and Norway rats, and woodrats.

Western harvest mouse, *Reithrodontomys megalotis*

Greatest length: 18.4–22.8 mm (⁷/₁₀–⁹/₁₀ in.) (full table of measurements page 574, life-size image page 111, life-size jaw page 159)

Specimen illustrated: Adult (?) male, SBMNH VB-72

Dentition: i 1/1 c 0/0 p 0/0 m 3/3, total 16. Upper incisors grooved.

Dorsal: The skulls of mice are slender and fragile, with weak zygomatic arches, slender triangular rostrums, large orbits, and large, rounded braincases. The rostrum (1) is slender, triangular, and shorter than in white-footed mice *(Peromyscus);* the nasals (2) are very long and relatively broader, tapering toward the posterior. The zygomatic

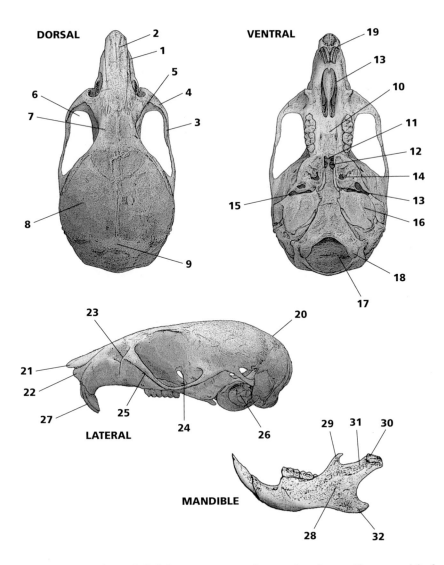

DORSAL

VENTRAL

LATERAL

MANDIBLE

arches (3) are slim and slightly convergent to the anterior; the maxillary arms (4) of the zygomatic arches do not spread as wide as the braincase. Lacrimal bone projections (5) are tiny in the dorsal corner of the maxillary arm. The orbits (6) are large, and the interorbital breadth (7) is relatively narrow, with the maxillary bones just visible below. The braincase (8) is very large, very round, and more than 50 percent of the greatest length of skull; ridges are not developed, and the braincases of mice are smooth. The interparietal (9) is smaller and much wider than long.

Ventral: The relatively broad palate (10) terminates just beyond the last molars and has a small projection (11) extending over the pterygoid region (12); the incisive foramina (13) are very large, long, and slender, tapering slightly toward the posterior. The pterygoid region is extremely narrow (12), and the pterygoid processes

(13) are relatively long. The spheno-pterygoid canals (14) are very small and round; foramina ovale (15) are apparent. Auditory bullae (16) are medium and less inflated. The foramen magnum (17) is very large, with fairly stout occipital condyles (18). Toothrows are short and may be roughly parallel or slightly divergent to the anterior. Incisors are grooved (19); the largest of three cheek teeth is at the anterior, descending in size to posterior.

Lateral: The dorsolateral outline slopes down toward the anterior, and the posterior (20) is rounded. The nasals (21) extend beyond the premaxillaries (22). The infraorbital foramina (23) are slitlike and high on the rostrum. Zygomatic arches (24) dip low to the level of the palate; thin zygomatic plates (25) are angled at approximately 45 degrees. The auditory meatus (26) is very low and large. The incisors (27) are strongly recurved.

Mandible: The mandible is long, squatter, and curved; the ramus region (28) is large. The coronoid process (29) is short, slender, and curved to the posterior, and it sits well below the condyle (30). The condyloid process (31) is long and high, pointing to the posterior at nearly 45 degrees. The angular process (32) is well developed, tapers, and points to the posterior.

Similar species: Other harvest mice, house mice, and other small mouse species. The length of the braincase seems to be the most reliable measurement to distinguish from the salt marsh harvest mouse, *R. raviventris;* for *R. megalotis,* the mean is approximately 9.5 mm (8.7–10.4 mm), and for *R. raviventris,* slightly more than 10 mm (9.5–10.9 mm) (Fisler 1965). House mice have notched upper incisors when viewed laterally.

Notes: Hoffmeister (1986) reports that he could find no significant variation between males and females.

White-footed mouse, *Peromyscus leucopus*

Greatest length: 23.8–28.7 mm ($9/10$–$1^1/10$ in.) (full table of measurements page 574, life-size image page 112, life-size jaw page 159)

Specimen illustrated: Adult male, MCZ 59232

Dentition: i 1/1 c 0/0 p 0/0 m 3/3, total 16.

Dorsal: The skulls of white-footed mice are slender and fragile, with weak zygomatic arches, slender triangular rostrums, large orbits, and large, rounded braincases. The rostrum (1) is slender, triangular, and shorter than in many other *Peromyscus* species; the nasals (2) are very long and slender, tapering toward the posterior. The zygomatic arches (3) are slim and roughly parallel; lacrimal bone projections (4) are very small in the dorsal corner of the maxillary arm. The orbits (5) are very large, and the interorbital breadth (6) is relatively broad, with the maxillary bones just visible below. The braincase (7) is large, round, and less than 50 percent of the greatest length of skull; ridges are not developed, and the braincases of mice are smooth. The interparietal (8) is large and much wider than long.

Ventral: The relatively broad palate (9) terminates at the posterior edge of the last molars; the incisive foramina (10) are very large, long, and slender, tapering slightly toward the anterior. The pterygoid region (11) is narrow, and the pterygoid processes

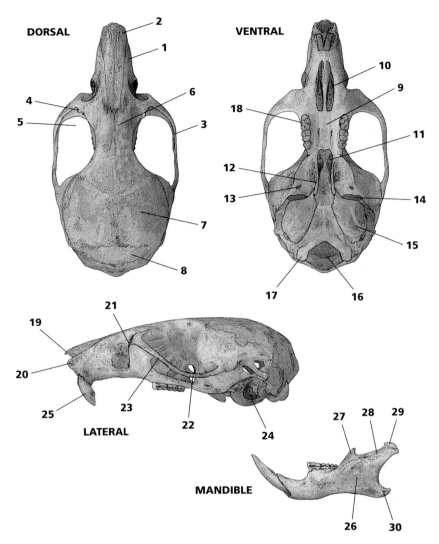

DORSAL

VENTRAL

LATERAL

MANDIBLE

(12) are relatively long. The spheno-pterygoid canals (13) are very small and round; foramina ovale (14) are apparent. Auditory bullae (15) are medium and less inflated. The foramen magnum (16) is large, with fairly stout occipital condyles (17). Toothrows are short and may be roughly parallel or slightly divergent to the anterior. The largest of three teeth (18) is at the anterior, descending in size to posterior.

Lateral: The dorsolateral outline slopes down toward the anterior, and the posterior is rounded. The nasals (19) extend just beyond the premaxillaries (20). The infraorbital foramen (21) is slitlike and high on the rostrum. Zygomatic arches (22) are relatively short; thin zygomatic plates (23) are angled at approximately 35 degrees. The auditory meatus (24) is very low and large. The incisors (25) are strongly recurved.

Mandible: The mandible is long, slender, and curved; the ramus region is large (26). The coronoid process (27) is greatly reduced to a blunt projection pointing to the posterior and sits well below the condyle (29). The condyloid process (28) is long and high, pointing to the posterior at nearly 45 degrees. The angular process (30) is well developed, tapers, and points to the posterior.

Similar species: Other *Peromyscus* species, grasshopper mice, and other mouse species.

Notes: Hoffmeister (1989) provides several cranial features to consider when differentiating deer mice *(P. maniculatus)* from white-footed mice *(P. leucopus)*. Deer mice are smaller, and if you multiply the greatest length of skull by the length of a single toothrow, a product between 65 and 80 millimeters is characteristic of deer mice, and 82 or more of white-footed mice. The zygomatic arches are pinched in deer mice but parallel in white-footed, and a zygomatic width taken just posterior to the zygomatic plates is usually less than 12 millimeters in deer mice but more in white-footed mice.

Deer mouse, *Peromyscus maniculatus*

Greatest length: 23.3–28.0 mm ($9/10$–$1 1/10$ in.) (full table of measurements page 576, life-size image page 112, life-size jaw page 159)

Specimen illustrated: Adult (?) male, SBMNH VB-120

Dentition: i 1/1 c 0/0 p 0/0 m 3/3, total 16.

Dorsal: The skulls of *Peromyscus* are slender and fragile, with weak zygomatic arches, slender triangular rostrums, large orbits, and large, rounded braincases. The rostrum (1) is slender, triangular, and shorter than in many other *Peromyscus* species; the nasals (2) are very long and slender, tapering toward the posterior. The zygomatic arches (3) are slim and distinctly pinched (4) inward, a character which separates this species from *P. leucopus*; lacrimal bone projections (5) are very small in the dorsal corner of the maxillary arm. The orbits (6) are very large, and the interorbital breadth (7) is slightly broader than in white-footed mice, with the maxillary bones just visible below. The braincase (8) is large, round, and less than 50 percent of the greatest length of skull; ridges are not developed, and the braincases of mice are smooth. The interparietal (9) is large and much wider than long.

Ventral: The relatively broad palate (10) terminates at the posterior edge of the last molars; the incisive foramina (11) are very large, long, and slender, tapering slightly toward the anterior. The pterygoid region (12) is narrow, and the pterygoid processes (13) are relatively long. The spheno-pterygoid canals (14) are very small. Auditory bullae (15) are medium and less inflated. The foramen magnum (16) is large, with fairly stout occipital condyles (17). Toothrows are short and may be roughly parallel or slightly divergent to the anterior. The largest of three teeth is at the anterior (18), descending in size to posterior. The anterior surface of the incisors (19) is smooth.

Lateral: The dorsolateral outline slopes down toward the anterior (20), and the posterior is rounded. The nasals (21) extend beyond the premaxillaries (22). The infraorbital foramen (23) is slitlike and high on the rostrum. Zygomatic arches (24) are relatively short; thin zygomatic plates (25) are angled at approximately 35 degrees. The auditory meatus (26) is very low and large. The incisors (27) are shorter and less recurved.

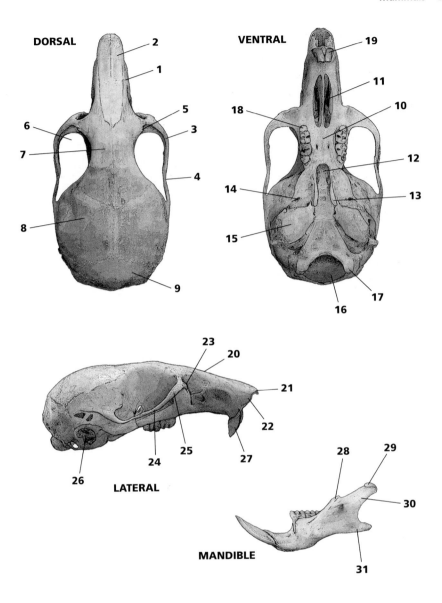

DORSAL

VENTRAL

LATERAL

MANDIBLE

Mandible: The mandible is long, slender, and more curved than in the white-footed mouse; the ramus region is smaller. The coronoid process (28) is greatly reduced to a bump and sits well below the condyle (29). The condyloid process (30) is long and slender, pointing to the posterior at nearly 45 degrees. The angular process (31) is well developed and rounded, pointing to the posterior.

Similar species: Other *Peromyscus* species, grasshopper mice, and other mouse species.

Note: Refer to notes on white-footed mouse *(P. leucopus)* for how to differentiate the two species.

Northern grasshopper mouse, *Onychomys leucogaster*

Greatest length: 25.0–27.9 mm (1–1²/10 in.) (full table of measurements page 576, life-size image page 112, life-size jaw page 160)

Specimen illustrated: Adult female, LACM 5729

Dentition: i 1/1 c 0/0 p 0/0 m 3/3, total 16. Labial projections on molariform teeth. Hypsodont (sharply cusped) molars distinguish from *Peromyscus* species.

Dorsal: The skulls of mice are slender and fragile, with weak zygomatic arches, slender triangular rostrums, large orbits, and large, rounded braincases. The rostrum (1) is slender and triangular; the nasals (2) are very long and slender, tapering toward their distinctly pointed posteriors (3). The zygomatic arches (4) are very slim and roughly parallel; the maxillary arms (5) are proportionately smaller than in *Peromyscus* species. Lacrimal bone projections (6) are very small in the dorsal corner of the maxillary arm. The orbits (7) are very large, and the interorbital breadth (8) is relatively broad, with the maxillary bones just visible below. The braincase (9) is large, round, and less than 50 percent of the greatest length of skull; ridges are not developed, and the braincases of mice are smooth. The interparietal (10) is large and much wider than long.

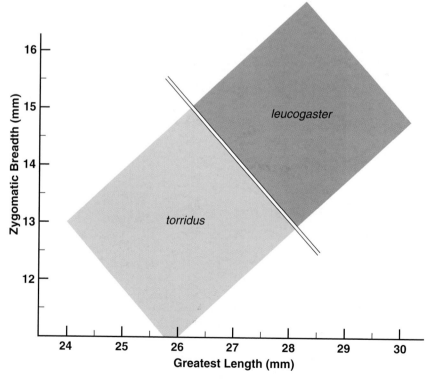

Donald Hoffmeister (1986) created this scattergram using the greatest length and zygomatic breadths of individual skulls to aid in distinguishing northern *(O. leucogaster)* from southern *(O. torridus)* grasshopper mice in Arizona. Adult specimens should fall within the designated ranges for each species. Used with permission of Donald Hoffmeister.

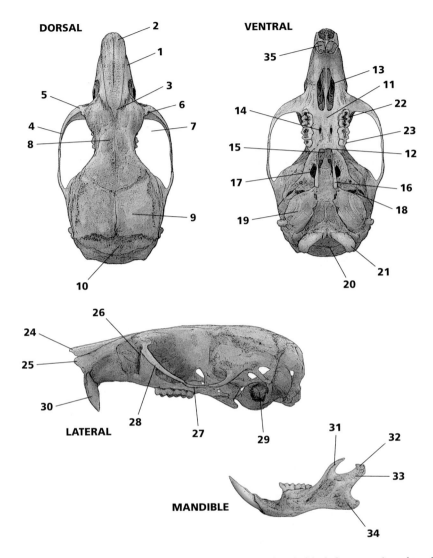

DORSAL

VENTRAL

LATERAL

MANDIBLE

Ventral: The relatively broad palate (11) terminates just behind the posterior edge of the last molars, and there is a small projection (12) over the pterygoid region. The incisive foramina (13) are slightly shorter and wider than in *Peromyscus* species, tapering toward the anterior, and palatal pits (14) are prominent. The pterygoid region (15) is narrow, and the pterygoid processes (16) are relatively long. The spheno-pterygoid canals (17) are larger and ovoid; foramina ovale (18) are apparent. Auditory bullae (19) are medium and less inflated. The foramen magnum (20) is larger, with fairly stout occipital condyles (21). Toothrows are short and may be roughly parallel or slightly divergent to the anterior. The largest of three sharply cusped teeth (22) is at the anterior, descending in size to posterior; M3 (23) is usually longer than wide. Anterior surfaces of incisors are smooth (35).

Lateral: The dorsolateral outline slopes down toward the anterior, and the posterior is rounded. The nasals (24) extend beyond the premaxillaries (25). The infraorbital foramen (26) is slitlike and high on the rostrum. Zygomatic arches (27) are relatively short and low; thin zygomatic plates (28) are angled at approximately 35 degrees. The auditory meatus (29) is low and large. The incisors (30) are straighter than in *Peromyscus* species.

Mandible: The mandible is long, slender, and curved; the ramus region is large. The coronoid process (31) is long and slender, curves to the posterior, and sits above the condyle (32). The condyloid process (33) is long and high, pointing to the posterior at nearly 45 degrees. The angular process (34) is well developed and rounded, pointing to the posterior.

Similar species: Southern grasshopper mice and other mice of similar size in the genus *Peromyscus*.

Notes: Can be differentiated from southern grasshopper mouse (page 330) by its longer mandible, wider zygomatic breadth, and larger braincase (Hoffmeister 1986). Sharply cusped teeth distinguish grasshopper mice from white-footed mice, *Peromyscus* species.

Hispid cotton rat, *Sigmodon hispidus*

Greatest length: 30.5–40.6 mm ($1^2/_{10}$–$1^6/_{10}$ in.) (full table of measurements page 578, life-size image page 115, life-size jaw page 160)

Specimen illustrated: Adult (?) male, SBMNH VB-1269

Dentition: i 1/1 c 0/0 p 0/0 m 3/3, total 16.

Dorsal: The skulls of hispid cotton rats are relatively triangular, with deep zygomatic notches and broad braincases. The rostrum (1) is relatively short and broad compared with those of other rodents of similar size; the nasals (2) are long and slender, extending to the posterior equally to the premaxillaries (3). Zygomatic notches (4) are deep and distinctive, and anterior maxillary extensions (5) are long. The zygomatic arches (6) are slim and convergent to the anterior; the squamosal arms (7) of the zygomatic arches spread much wider than the braincase. Lacrimal bone projections (8) are small and in the dorsal corner of the maxillary arm. The orbits (9) are large, and the interorbital breadth (10) is narrow and constricted, allowing views of the maxillary bones below. The braincase (11) is broad, rectangular, and short; temporal ridges (12) are well developed and distinctive, bowing outward toward the posterior of the skull. The interparietal (13) is short and wide.

Ventral: The relatively narrow palate (14) terminates just beyond the posterior molars and has a small projection (15) extending over the pterygoid region; palatal pits (20) are deep. The incisive foramina (16) are large and broad, tapering slightly toward the posterior; their posterior edges (17) extend beyond the anterior edge of the first cheek tooth. The pterygoid region (18) is small and narrow. The sphenopterygoid canals (19) are small and oval; foramina ovale (24) are apparent. Auditory bullae (21) are smaller and inflated. The foramen magnum (22) is medium, with a rounded ventral edge and fairly stout occipital condyles (23). Toothrows are short

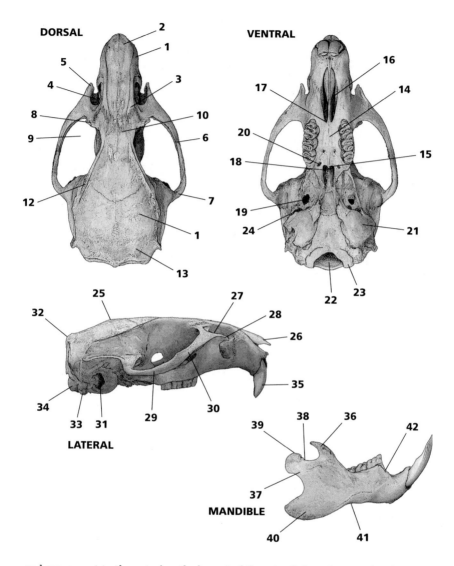

DORSAL

VENTRAL

LATERAL

MANDIBLE

and convergent to the anterior; the largest of three teeth is at the anterior, descending in size to posterior.

Lateral: The dorsolateral outline slopes up from the posterior to the apex (25) above the braincase, and then is relatively level over much of the skull before curving down with the nasals. The nasals (26) extend beyond the premaxillaries and incisors. The infraorbital foramen (27) is slitlike and high on the rostrum; there are long extensions (28) on the anterior arm of the zygomatic arch. Zygomatic arches (29) are low; zygomatic plates (30) are angled at approximately 40 degrees. The auditory meatus (31) is low and large, and the posterior of the skull (32) is squared. The paraoccipital processes (33) extend below the occipital condyles (34), which is not the case in marsh rice rats. The incisors (35) are recurved; the diastema is wide.

Mandible: The mandible is long and curved; the ramus region is large. The coronoid process (36) is shorter, slender, tapering, and curved strongly to the posterior. The condyloid process (37) is long, broad, and with concave dorsal (38) and ventral surfaces; the condyle (39) sits below the tip of the coronoid. The angular process (40) is well developed, tapers, and points to the posterior; there is a ventral step (41) from the body of the mandible to the sloping angular process below the posterior teeth. There is a steep drop (42) from the anterior of the cheek teeth into the diastema.

Similar species: Other cotton rats, marsh rice rats, Norway and black rats, and woodrats. Hoffmeister (1986) provides differentiation from *S. arizonae*.

White-throated woodrat, *Neotoma albigula*

Greatest length: 37.2–46.3 mm ($1^5/_{10}$–$1^8/_{10}$ in.) (full table of measurements page 580, life-size image page 117, life-size jaw page 161)

Specimen illustrated: Adult (?) female, SBMNH VB-64-510

Dentition: i 1/1 c 0/0 p 0/0 m 3/3, total 16.

Dorsal: Woodrat skulls are larger versions of mouse skulls, with slim zygomatic arches, slender rostrums, and large orbits. The rostrum (1) is slender but stout. The nasals (2) are very long and slender, tapering to sharp points (3) to the posterior; the posterior portions of the premaxillaries (4) are broad and extend to the posterior much farther than the nasals. The zygomatic arches (5) are slim and converge to the anterior; lacrimal bone projections (6) are very small in the dorsal corner of the maxillary arm. The orbits (7) are very large, and the interorbital breadth (8) is relatively narrow, allowing good views of the maxillary bones below. The braincase (9) is large, round, and approaching 50 percent of the greatest length of skull; temporal ridges are weak, and the braincase of this species is comparatively smooth. The interparietal (10) is large, much wider than long, and tapering to either side.

Ventral: The relatively narrow palate (11) terminates just beyond the anterior edge of the last molar; the incisive foramina (12) are very large, long, and relatively broad, tapering slightly toward the anterior; their posterior edges (13) are aligned with the anterior edges of the first cheek teeth. Sphenopalatine vacuities (14) are large. The pterygoid region (15) is narrow, and the pterygoid processes (16) are relatively long. The spheno-pterygoid canals (17) are very small and round. Auditory bullae (18) are medium and inflated. The foramen magnum (19) is large, with fairly small occipital condyles. (20) Toothrows are longer and slightly convergent to the anterior. The largest of three teeth is at the anterior, descending in size to posterior.

Lateral: The dorsolateral outline is convex, with a gradual slope toward the anterior and a more rounded posterior. The nasals (21) extend just beyond the premaxillaries (22). The infraorbital foramen (23) is slitlike and high on the rostrum. Zygomatic arches (24) are relatively low; thin zygomatic plates (25) are angled at approximately 35 to 40 degrees. The auditory meatus (26) is very low and large; the midline of the auditory meatus is aligned with the grinding surface of the molars (27). The incisors (28) are recurved.

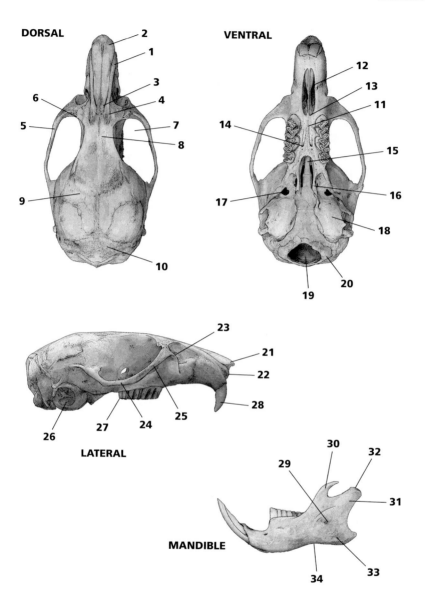

DORSAL

VENTRAL

LATERAL

MANDIBLE

Mandible: The mandible is long and curved; the ramus region is large (29). The coronoid process (30) is shorter, slender, and strongly curved to the posterior. The condyloid process (31) is long and broad, pointing to the posterior at nearly 45 degrees; the condyle (32) sits below the tip of the coronoid. The angular process (33) is well developed, tapers, and points to the posterior; note the concave ventral outline (34) of the body below the posterior teeth.

Similar species: Other woodrats, cotton rats, and black and Norway rats.

Bushy-tailed woodrat, *Neotoma cinerea*

Greatest length: 43.0–55.6 mm ($1^7/10$–$2^2/10$ in.) (full table of measurements page 580, life-size image page 118, life-size jaw page 161)
Specimen illustrated: Adult female, MVZ 71105
Dentition: i 1/1 c 0/0 p 0/0 m 3/3, total 16.
Dorsal: Woodrat skulls are larger versions of mouse skulls, with slim zygomatic arches, slender rostrums, and large orbits. The rostrum (1) is slender, longer, and more laterally flattened. The nasals (2) are very long and slender, taper, and have squared posterior edges (3); the posterior portions of the premaxillaries (4) are slim and extend to the posterior much farther than the nasals. The zygomatic arches (5) are slightly stouter than in smaller *Neotoma* species, wider-spreading, and converging to the anterior; lacrimal bone projections (6) are very small in the dorsal corner of the maxillary arm. The orbits (7) are very large, and the interorbital breadth is relatively narrow, allowing good views of the maxillary bones below. The braincase (8) is shorter than in other *Neotoma* species, more angular, and less than 50 percent of the greatest length of skull; temporal ridges (9) are more developed, and the braincase of this species is comparatively more rugged. The interparietal (10) is large, with a distinctive shape: a wide, thin rectangle with a half circle on top of the anterior edge, the squared extensions of the rectangle evident to either side.
Ventral: The relatively narrow palate (11) terminates near the midpoint of the last molar; the incisive foramina (12) are very large, longer, and relatively broad, tapering slightly toward the anterior; their posterior edges (13) are aligned with the anterior edges of the first cheek teeth. The pterygoid region (14) is narrow, and the pterygoid processes (15) are relatively long. The spheno-pterygoid canals (16) are very small and round. Auditory bullae (17) are medium and inflated. The foramen magnum (18) is large, with fairly small occipital condyles (19). Toothrows are longer and slightly convergent to the anterior. The largest of three teeth in the toothrow is at the anterior, descending in size to posterior.
Lateral: The dorsolateral outline is less convex than in smaller *Neotoma* species, relatively level, and with a more angular posterior (20). The nasals (21) extend just beyond the premaxillaries (22). The infraorbital foramen (23) is slitlike and high on the rostrum. Zygomatic arches (24) are relatively low; thin zygomatic plates (25) are angled at approximately 35 to 40 degrees. The auditory meatus (26) is medium, and the midline of the auditory meatus is above the grinding surface (27) of the molars. The paraoccipital processes (28) extend well below the occipital condyles (29). The incisors (30) are recurved.
Mandible: The mandible is more slender and curved than in smaller *Neotoma* species; the ramus region is large. The coronoid process (31) is slightly shorter, broader, and strongly curved to the posterior. The condyloid process (32) is long and broad, pointing to the posterior at nearly 45 degrees; the condyle (33) is nearly level with the tip of the coronoid. The angular process (34) is smaller and rounded, pointing to the posterior; note the concave ventral outline (35) of the body below the posterior molars.

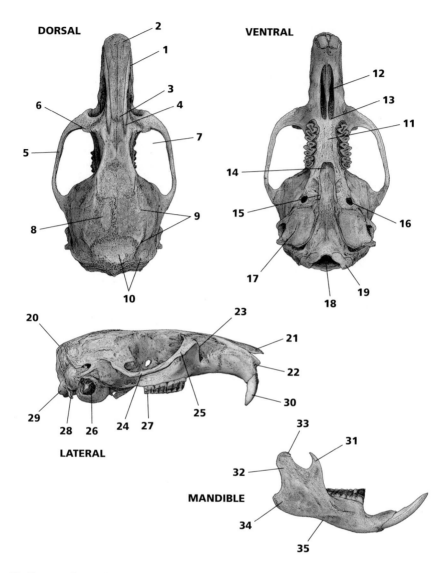

DORSAL

VENTRAL

LATERAL

MANDIBLE

Similar species: Other woodrats, cotton rats, and black and Norway rats.

Note: Verts and Carraway (1998) report that males are as much as 15 percent larger than females in inland populations in Oregon, less in coastal populations.

Desert woodrat, *Neotoma lepida*

Greatest length: 33.3–46.0 mm ($1^3/_{10}$–$1^8/_{10}$ in.) (full table of measurements page 582, life-size image page 115, life-size jaw page 161)

Specimen illustrated: Adult (?) female, SBMNH VB-68-3

Dentition: i 1/1 c 0/0 p 0/0 m 3/3, total 16.

Dorsal: Woodrat skulls are larger versions of mouse skulls, with slim zygomatic arches, slender rostrums, and large orbits. The rostrum (1) is slender but stout. The nasals (2) are very long and slender, taper, and have squared edges (3) to the posterior; the posterior portions of the premaxillaries (4) are slim and extend to the posterior much farther than the nasals. The zygomatic arches (5) are slim, converge to the anterior, and may be slightly pinched (6) at their midpoints; lacrimal bone projections (7) are very small in the dorsal corner of the maxillary arm. The orbits (8) are very large, and the interorbital breadth (9) is relatively narrow, allowing good views of the maxillary bones below. The braincase (10) is large, round, and approaching 50 percent of the greatest length of skull; temporal ridges are weak, and the braincase of this species is comparatively smooth. The interparietal (11) is larger and boxier than in *N. albigula*, with tiny tapering extensions (12) to either side.

Ventral: The relatively narrow palate (13) terminates just beyond the anterior edge of the last molar; the incisive foramina (14) are very large, long, and broad to the anterior, tapering slightly toward the posterior (15); their posterior edges are aligned with the anterior edges of the first cheek teeth. The pterygoid region (16) is narrow, and the pterygoid processes (17) are relatively long. The spheno-pterygoid canals (18) are very small and round. Auditory bullae (19) are medium and inflated. The foramen magnum (20) is large, with fairly small occipital condyles (21). Toothrows are longer and slightly convergent to the anterior. The largest of three teeth in the toothrow is at the anterior, descending in size to posterior.

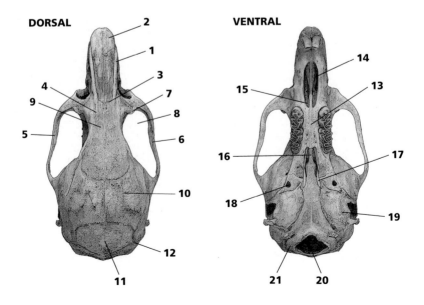

DORSAL   VENTRAL

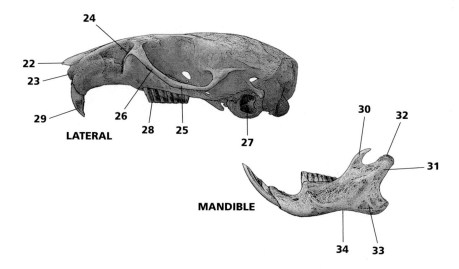

LATERAL

MANDIBLE

Lateral: The dorsolateral outline is convex, with a gradual slope toward the anterior and a more rounded posterior. The nasals (22) extend just beyond the premaxillaries (23). The infraorbital foramen (24) is slitlike and high on the rostrum. Zygomatic arches (25) are relatively low; thin zygomatic plates (26) are angled at approximately 35 to 40 degrees. The auditory meatus (27) is medium, and the midline of the auditory meatus is aligned with the grinding surface (28) of the molars. The incisors (29) are recurved.

Mandible: The mandible is long and curved; the ramus region is large. The coronoid process (30) is shorter, slender, and strongly curved to the posterior. The condyloid process (31) is long and broad, pointing to the posterior at nearly 45 degrees; the condyle (32) sits below the tip of the coronoid. The angular process (33) is well developed, tapers, and points to the posterior; note the concave ventral outline (34) of the body below the posterior teeth.

Similar species: Other woodrats, cotton rats, and black and Norway rats.

Norway rat, *Rattus norvegicus*

Greatest length: 43.0–51.5 mm ($1^7/_{10}$–2 in.) (full table of measurements page 582, life-size image page 117, life-size jaw page 161)

Specimen illustrated: Adult female, SBMNH VB-481

Dentition: i 1/1 c 0/0 p 0/0 m 3/3, total 16. Three longitudinal rows of cusps.

Dorsal: The skulls of rats are slender and relatively fragile, with long, slender zygomatic arches, slender triangular rostrums, and large orbits. The rostrum (1) is slender and long; the nasals (2) are long and slender, tapering toward the posterior. Zygomatic notches (3) are deep and distinctive. The zygomatic arches (4) are slim and slightly convergent to the anterior; the maxillary arms (5) of the zygomatic arches spread wider than the braincase. Lacrimal bone projections (6) are larger than in woodrats and are in the dorsal corner of the maxillary arm. The orbits (7) are

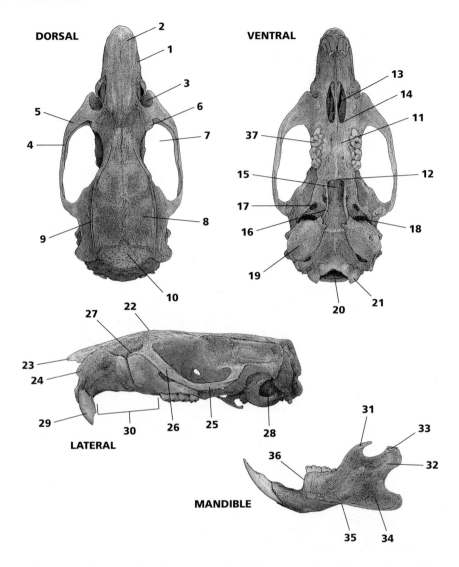

DORSAL

VENTRAL

LATERAL

MANDIBLE

large, and the interorbital breadth is relatively narrow, allowing good views of the maxillary bones below. The braincase (8) is large, squared, and less than 50 percent of the greatest length of skull; temporal ridges (9) are well developed and distinctive, roughly paralleling each other to the posterior of the skull (more bowed out in black rats). The interparietal (10) is smaller and much wider than long.

Ventral: The relatively broad palate (11) terminates well beyond the posterior molars and has a small projection (12) extending over the pterygoid region; the incisive foramina (13) are shorter than in woodrats, wider, and tapering slightly toward the anterior; their posterior edges (14) are forward of the toothrows. The pterygoid region (15) is narrow, and the pterygoid processes (16) are relatively long. The spheno-pterygoid canals (17) are small and oval; the foramina ovale (18) are wide. Auditory bullae (19) are medium and inflated. The foramen magnum (20) is medium, with fairly stout occipital condyles (21). Toothrows are short and roughly parallel; the largest of three teeth is at the anterior, descending in size to posterior. The toothrows have two longitudinal rows of cusps (37).

Lateral: The dorsolateral outline slopes up from the posterior to the apex (22) above the zygomatic plate, and then down more steeply to the tips of the nasals; it is more level in black rats. The nasals (23) extend beyond the premaxillaries (24) and incisors. The infraorbital foramen (27) is slitlike and high on the rostrum. Zygomatic arches (25) are low; zygomatic plates (26) are angled at approximately 35 degrees. The auditory meatus (28) is low and large. The incisors (29) are recurved; the diastema (30) is very wide.

Mandible: The mandible is long and curved; the ramus region is large. The coronoid process (31) is shorter, slender, tapering, and curved strongly to the posterior. The condyloid process (32) is long and broad, pointing to the posterior at nearly 45

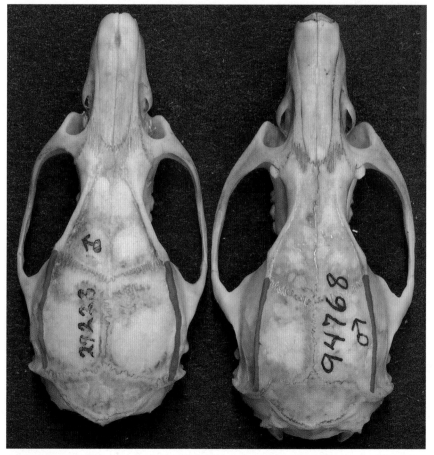

On the left, a male black rat *(R. rattus)* 29223, and on the right, a male Norway rat *(R. norvegicus)* 94768. The red lines denote the temporal ridges along the parietal bones. MUSEUM OF VERTEBRATE ZOOLOGY, UC BERKELEY.

degrees; the condyle (33) sits below the tip of the coronoid. The angular process (34) is well developed, tapers, and points to the posterior; there is a ventral step (35) from the body of the mandible to the sloping angular process below the posterior teeth. There is a steep drop (36) from the anterior of the cheek teeth into the diastema.

Similar species: Black rats, wood rats, and cotton rats. Chipmunks, pocket gophers, and flying squirrels.

Notes: Differentiating black rat from Norway rat skulls can be a considerable challenge. Compare all the features described in the table below and refer to the figure on page 341 before making a diagnosis.

Black rat	Norway rat
Skull is deepest above braincase	Skull is deepest above zygomatic plate
Temporal ridges bow outward	Temporal ridges more parallel
Greatest distance between ridges 13 mm or more (Hoffmeister 1986)	Distance less than 13 mm
Length of parietal along temporal ridge much shorter than distance between temporal ridges	Distance along parietal roughly equal to or less than distance between ridges
First row of cusps on M1 notched	Cusps not notched
Anterior edge of infraorbital plate slopes posteriorly	Anterior edge of infraorbital plate projects anteriorly

House mouse, *Mus musculus*

Greatest length: 19.5–23.5 mm ($8/10$–$9/10$ in.) (full table of measurements page 578, life-size image page 111, life-size jaw page 159)

Specimen illustrated: Adult male, SBMNH VB-481

Dentition: i 1/1 c 0/0 p 0/0 m 3/3, total 16. Notched upper incisors.

Dorsal: The skulls of mice are slender and fragile, with weak zygomatic arches, slender triangular rostrums, large orbits, and large, rounded braincases. The rostrum (1) is slender, triangular, and shorter than in *Peromyscus* species; the nasals (2) are very long and slender, tapering toward the posterior. The zygomatic arches (3) are slim and slightly convergent to the anterior; the maxillary arms (4) of the zygomatic arches spread equally with the braincase, which is not the case in harvest mice. Lacrimal bone projections (5) are larger in the dorsal corner of the maxillary arm. The orbits are large, and the interorbital breadth (6) is relatively broad, with the maxillary bones just visible below. The braincase (7) is very large, very round, and less than 50 percent of the greatest length of skull; ridges are not developed, and the braincases of mice are smooth. The interparietal (8) is large and much wider than long.

Ventral: The relatively broad palate (9) terminates well beyond the last molars and has a small projection (10) extending over the pterygoid region; the incisive foramina (11) are very large, long, and broad, tapering slightly toward the posterior; their posterior edges (12) are at the midpoint of the first cheek tooth. The pterygoid region (13) is extremely narrow, and the pterygoid processes (14) are relatively

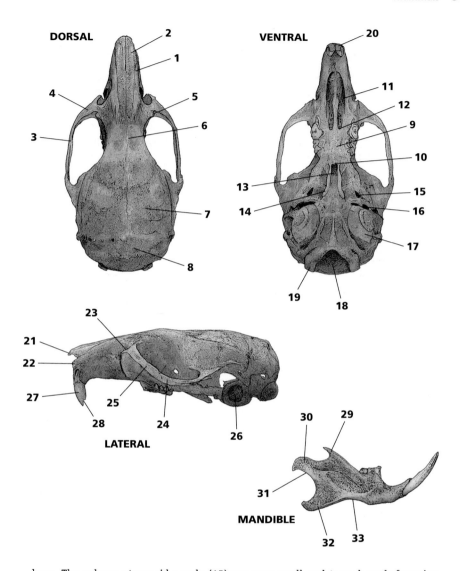

DORSAL

VENTRAL

LATERAL

MANDIBLE

long. The spheno-pterygoid canals (15) are very small and tear-shaped; foramina ovale (16) are apparent. Auditory bullae (17) are medium and less inflated. The foramen magnum (18) is very large, with fairly stout occipital condyles (19). Toothrows are very short and divergent to the anterior. Incisors (20) are smooth; the largest of three cheek teeth is at the anterior, descending in size to posterior.

Lateral: The dorsolateral outline slopes down toward the anterior, and the posterior is rounded. The nasals (21) extend beyond the premaxillaries (22). The infraorbital foramen (23) is slitlike and high on the rostrum. Zygomatic arches (24) dip low to the level of the palate; thin zygomatic plates (25) are angled at approximately 45 degrees. The auditory meatus (26) is very low and large. The incisors (27) are straight and distinctly notched (28), a quick character for identification.

Mandible: The mandible is long and curved; the ramus region is large. The coronoid process (29) is longer and slender, tapers, and points to the posterior. The condyloid process (30) is long and broad, extending the farthest to the posterior; its ventral surface (31) is concave. The angular process (32) is well developed, tapers, and points to the posterior; there is a ventral step (33) when the body transitions to the angular process.

Similar species: Harvest mice, pocket mice, grasshopper mice, and white-footed mice (*Peromyscus* species). In harvest mice, the upper incisors are grooved but not notched, discussed under the "Lateral" perspective.

Southern red-backed vole, *Clethrionomys gapperi*

Greatest length: 21.5–26.4 mm (⁸/10–1 in.) (full table of measurements page 584, life-size image page 111, life-size jaw page 160)

Specimen illustrated: Adult, MCZ 47214

Dentition: i 1/1 c 0/0 p 0/0 m 3/3, total 16. Cheek teeth with prisms.

Dorsal: The skulls of voles are robust and angular compared with those of other small rodents, with wide-spreading strong zygomatic arches, shorter slender rostrums, and large squared braincases. Those of red-backed voles are less angular, more slender, and rounder. The rostrum (1) is slender and shorter; the nasals (2) are wider toward the anterior and taper toward the posterior. The zygomatic arches (3) are slimmer and more rounded than in *Microtus* species and spread wider than the braincase. Small lacrimal bone projections (4) occur on the dorsal corner of the maxillary arm. The orbits (5) and interorbital breadth (6) are relatively broader, allowing only the edges of the maxillary bones to be viewed. The anterior edge of the squamosal (7) has an angular projection, which contributes to the braincase having a squared appearance. The braincase (8) is very large and more than 50 percent of the greatest length of skull; temporal ridges are less developed, giving the red-backed vole a smoother appearance than many members of *Microtus* species. The interparietal (9) is very large, covering the width of the entire braincase.

Ventral: The palate (10) is simpler, with an abrupt emarginated edge (11), rather than multitiered as in *Microtus* species; the palate is also not perforated as it is in *Microtus*. The incisive foramina (12) are very long, relatively wide, and constricted only at the anterior tips; they are positioned farther from the toothrows than in *Microtus*. The spheno-pterygoid canals are smaller; foramina ovale (13) are evident. Auditory bullae (14) are large and inflated. The foramen magnum (15) is large. Toothrows are long and slightly convergent to the anterior, and the dentition is reduced compared with that of *Microtus*; the posterior extension of M3 (16), the last tooth in the toothrow, is much shorter than in *Microtus*.

Lateral: The dorsolateral outline is relatively level. The nasals (17) do not extend beyond the premaxillaries (18). The infraorbital foramen (19) is slitlike and high on the rostrum. Zygomatic arches (20) are elevated to approximately the midline of the skull. The ventral surface of the auditory bullae (21) is well below the toothrows; the auditory meatus (22) is very large. The incisors (23) are relatively straight.

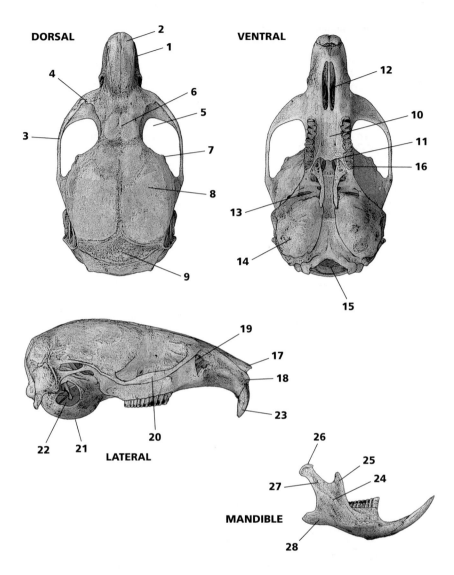

DORSAL

VENTRAL

LATERAL

MANDIBLE

Mandible: The mandible is stout and the body curved; the ramus region (24) is smaller than in mice. The coronoid process (25) is reduced and blunt, sitting well forward and below the condyle (26). The condyloid process (27) is long, slender, and high; the condyle (26) sits far above the toothrow. The angular process (28) is shorter and thick, and it points to the posterior. Roots of the lower incisors extend behind and to the outside of molars.

Similar species: Northern and western red-backed voles, other voles, and lemmings.

Montane vole, *Microtus montanus*

Greatest length: 25.4–30.2 mm (1–1²/₁₀ in.) (full table of measurements page 584, life-size image page 112, life-size jaw page 160)

Specimen illustrated: Adult (?) female, SBMNH VB-68-108

Dentition: i 1/1 c 0/0 p 0/0 m 3/3, total 16. Cheek teeth with prisms.

Dorsal: The skulls of voles are robust and angular compared with those of other small rodents, with wide-spreading strong zygomatic arches, shorter slender rostrums, and large squared braincases. The rostrum (1) is slender and stout; the nasals (2) are wider toward the anterior and taper toward the posterior. The zygomatic arches (3) are heavy and spread wider than the braincase. Small lacrimal bone projections (4) occur on the dorsal corner of the maxillary arm (the bone is missing on the left). The orbits (5) are large, and the interorbital breadth (6) is very narrow, allowing a view of the maxillary bones; a midline ridge (7) may also be apparent. The anterior edge of the squamosal has an angular projection (8), which contributes to the braincase having a squared appearance. The braincase (9) is large and approximately 50 percent of the greatest length of skull; temporal ridges are less developed, giving the montane vole's skull a smoother appearance than those of many other members of *Microtus*. The interparietal (10) is very large and much wider than long.

Ventral: The palate (11) is multitiered, complex, and perforated; the notch (12) along the midline is well into the toothrows. The incisive foramina (13) are long, thin, and constricted to their posterior (14); their posterior edges are very close to the toothrows. The spheno-pterygoid canals (15) are larger and round. Auditory bullae (16) are large and inflated. The foramen magnum (17) is large. Toothrows are long, and the middle upper molar (18) is characterized by four closed triangles. The cheek teeth are not rooted.

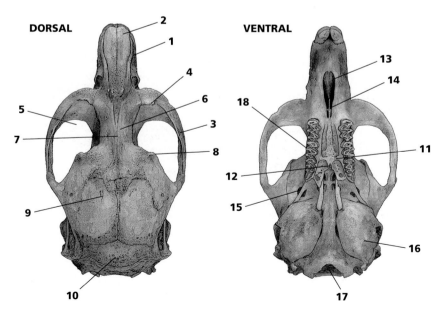

DORSAL

VENTRAL

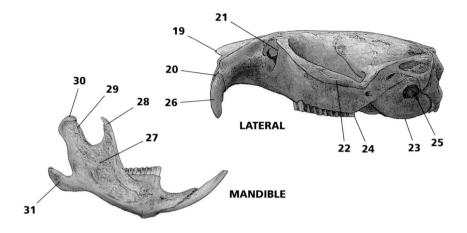

LATERAL

MANDIBLE

Lateral: The dorsolateral outline is relatively level. The nasals (19) do not extend beyond the premaxillaries (20). The infraorbital foramen (21) is slitlike and high on the rostrum. Zygomatic arches (22) are elevated to approximately the midline of the skull. The ventral surface of the auditory bullae (23) is approximately aligned with the grinding surface of the molars (24); the auditory meatus (25) is higher than in mice and smaller. The incisors (26) are procumbent.

Mandible: The mandible is stout and the body curved; the ramus region (27) is smaller than in mice. The coronoid process (28) is slender and pointed, with a tip that points to the posterior; the coronoid sits well forward and just below the condyle. The condyloid process (29) is large, high, thick, and rectangular; the condyle (30) sits far above the toothrow. The angular process (31) is long and slender, and it points upward. Roots of the lower incisors extend behind and to the outside of molars.

Similar species: Other voles, lemmings, and pocket gophers.

Meadow vole or field mouse, *Microtus pennsylvanicus*

Greatest length: 23.8–31.0 mm ($^9/_{10}$–$1^2/_{10}$ in.) (full table of measurements page 586, life-size image page 113, life-size jaw page 160)

Specimen illustrated: Adult female, MVZ 96877

Dentition: i 1/1 c 0/0 p 0/0 m 3/3, total 16. M2 with five loops.

Dorsal: The skulls of voles are robust and angular compared with those of other small rodents, with wide-spreading strong zygomatic arches, shorter slender rostrums, and large squared braincases. The rostrum (1) is slender and stout; the nasals (2) are wider toward the anterior and taper toward the posterior. The zygomatic arches (3) are heavy and spread wider than the braincase. Small lacrimal bone projections (4) occur on the dorsal corner of the maxillary arm. The orbits (5) are large, and the interorbital breadth (6) is narrow, allowing a view of the maxillary bones. The anterior edge of the squamosal has an angular projection (7), which contributes to the braincase having a squared appearance. The braincase (8) is large and more than 50 percent of the greatest length of skull; temporal ridges are more developed, and

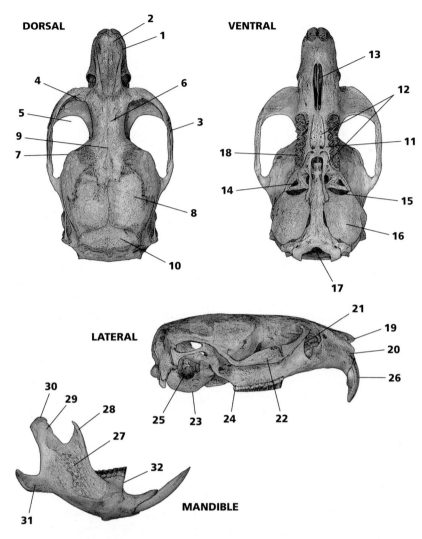

DORSAL

VENTRAL

LATERAL

MANDIBLE

ridges along the midline of the skull (9) are common. The interparietal (10) is very large and much wider than long.

Ventral: The palate (11) is multitiered, complex, and perforated (12). The incisive foramina (13) are long, thin, and not noticeably constricted; the posterior edges are nearly aligned with the anterior of the toothrows. The spheno-pterygoid canals (14) are smaller; foramina ovale (15) evident. Auditory bullae (16) are medium and inflated. The foramen magnum (17) is large. Toothrows are long, and M3 (18) has three closed triangles.

Lateral: The dorsolateral outline is relatively level. The nasals (19) do not extend beyond the premaxillaries (20). The infraorbital foramen (21) is larger, slitlike, and high on the rostrum. Zygomatic arches (22) are deeper and elevated to approximately the midline of the skull. The ventral surface of the auditory bullae (23) is approximately aligned with the grinding surface (24) of the molars; the auditory meatus (25) is larger. The incisors (26) are procumbent.

Mandible: The mandible is stout and the body curved; the ramus region (27) is smaller than in mice. The coronoid process (28) is slender and pointed, with a tip that points to the posterior; the coronoid sits well forward and just below the condyle (30). The condyloid process (29) is large, high, thick, and rectangular; the condyle (30) sits far above the toothrow. The angular process (31) is long and slender, and it points upward. Roots of the lower incisors extend behind and to the outside of molars. The drop from the anterior edge of the molars (32) into the diastema is vertical.

Similar species: Other voles, bog lemmings, mice, and pocket gophers.

Common muskrat, *Ondatra zibethicus*

Greatest length: 58.2–72.3 mm ($2^3/10$–$2^8/10$ in.) (full table of measurements page 570, life-size image page 121, life-size jaw page 163)

Specimen illustrated: Adult (?) male, MVZ 97830

Dentition: i 1/1 c 0/0 p 0/0 m 3/3, total 16.

Dorsal: Muskrat skulls are larger versions of vole skulls, rugose, angular, and with strong, wide-spreading zygomatic arches. The rostrum (1) is shorter, slender, and stout; the nasals (2) are triangular, tapering toward the posterior. The zygomatic arches (3) are heavy and spread much wider than the braincase. Tiny lacrimal bone projections (4) occur on the dorsal corner of the maxillary arm. The orbits (5) are large, and the interorbital breadth (6) is extremely narrow and high, allowing ample view of the maxillary bones; there is often a sharp crest (7) following the midline of the frontal bones. The anterior edge of the squamosal has a strong angular projection (8), which contributes to the braincase having a squared appearance. The braincase (9) is large, constricted (10) to the posterior, and approximately 50 percent of the greatest length of skull; temporal ridges (11) are developed. The interparietal (12) is small and rectangular.

Ventral: The palate (13) is multitiered, complex, and perforated (14); there is a spine-like projection (15) over the pterygoid region. The incisive foramina (16) are long and thin, and the posterior edges are aligned with the anterior of the toothrows. The spheno-pterygoid canals are small (33) and compressed; foramina ovale (17) evident. Auditory bullae (18) are medium and inflated. The foramen magnum (19) is medium. Toothrows are long, and the teeth descend in size to the posterior; the first lower molar (20) has five closed triangles (loops).

Lateral: The dorsolateral outline is relatively level, gradually sloping up to the apex (21) above the jugal bones from either end. The nasals (22) are approximately aligned with the premaxillaries. The infraorbital foramen (23) is small, slitlike, and high on the rostrum. Zygomatic arches (24) are elevated to approximately the midline of the skull. The auditory meatus (25) is high and small. The incisors (26) are large, procumbent, and slightly recurved.

Mandible: The mandible is very stout and the body deep and curved; the ramus region (27) is large. The coronoid process (28) is long, slender, tapering, and curved to the

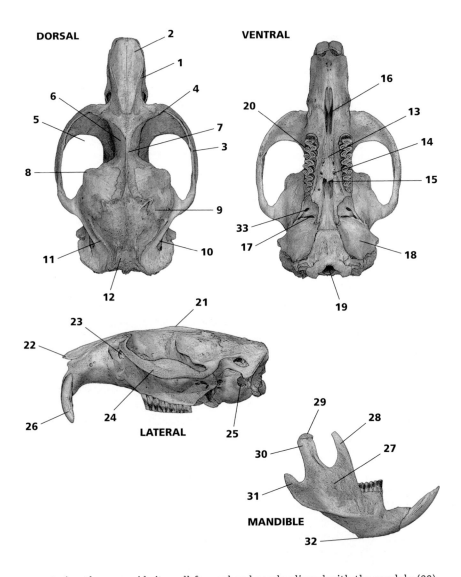

DORSAL

VENTRAL

LATERAL

MANDIBLE

posterior; the coronoid sits well forward and nearly aligned with the condyle (29). The condyloid process (30) is long, stout, and nearly vertical, approximately aligned with the coronoid. The angular process (31) is stout, blunt, and curved upward. At the anterior of the jaw is a small bone protrusion (32) along the vertical surface, a smaller version of what is characteristic in beaver mandibles.

Similar species: Pocket gophers, round-tailed muskrats *(Neofiber),* lemmings, and water voles.

Brown lemming, *Lemmus trimucronatus*

Greatest length: 27.6–35.1 mm ($1^1/_{10}$–$1^4/_{10}$ in.) (full table of measurements page 586, life-size image page 113, life-size jaw page 161)

Specimen illustrated: Adult male, LACM 23112

Dentition: i 1/1 c 0/0 p 0/0 m 3/3, total 16.

Dorsal: Brown lemming skulls are volelike but more robust and angular, with wider-spreading, heavier zygomatic arches. The rostrum (1) is slender and stout; the nasals (2) are wider toward the anterior and taper toward the posterior. The zygomatic arches (3) are very heavy and rugose, spreading much wider than the braincase. Small lacrimal bone projections (4) occur on the dorsal corner of the maxillary arm. The orbits (5) are large, and the interorbital breadth (6) is very narrow, allowing a view of the maxillary bones; there is a sharp median ridge (7) along the midline of the frontals. The anterior edge of the squamosal (8) is very angular, which contributes to the braincase having a squared appearance. The braincase (9) is large, constricted to the posterior (10), and nearing 50 percent of the greatest length of skull; temporal ridges (11) are developed. The interparietal (12) is smaller and rectangular.

Ventral: The palate (13) is simpler than in *Microtus*, terminating toward the anterior of the last molar, and with a pointy projection (14) over the pterygoid region (15). The incisive foramina (16) are long, thin, and constricted posteriorly (17); they are situated farther from the anterior of the toothrows than in *Microtus*. The spheno-pterygoid canals are not visible; foramina ovale (18) evident. Auditory bullae (19) are more triangular, large, and inflated. The foramen magnum (20) is large. Toothrows are long and convergent to the anterior.

Lateral: The dorsolateral outline is relatively level from the anterior of the zygomatic arches to the posterior (21) but steeply sloping at the anterior (22). The nasals (23) are approximately aligned with the premaxillaries (24). The infraorbital foramen (25)

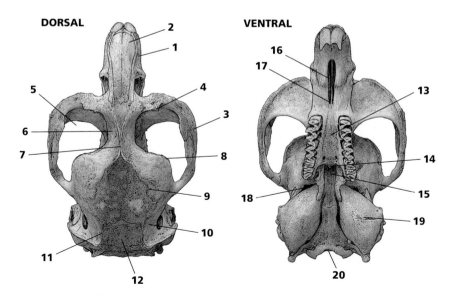

DORSAL

VENTRAL

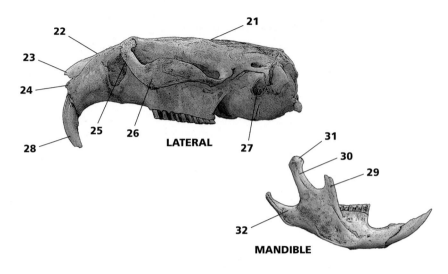

is slitlike and high on the rostrum. Zygomatic arches (26) are very deep, with large jugals, and elevated to approximately the midline of the skull. The auditory meatus (27) is small and well elevated. The incisors (28) are procumbent and recurved.

Mandible: The mandible is stout and the body curved; the ramus region is smaller than in mice. The coronoid process (29) is reduced, squared, and pointing slightly to the posterior; the coronoid sits well forward and below the condyle (31). The condyloid process (30) is very long, very high, and slender; the condyle sits far above the toothrow. The angular process (32) is very long, slender, tapering, and angled slightly upward. Roots of the lower incisors extend behind and to the outside of molars.

Similar species: Other lemmings, large voles, pocket gophers, and muskrats.

Family Zapodidae: Jumping mice

Jumping mice are rodents whose skulls are characterized by their two infraorbital foramina. The first is large, with a second, smaller one below; as a portion of the masseter muscles pass through the infraorbital foramina, jumping mice are characterized as myomorph rodents. The two genera in this family are easily differentiated by the number of upper cheek teeth present on a given side: four in *Zapus* and three in *Napaeozapus*.

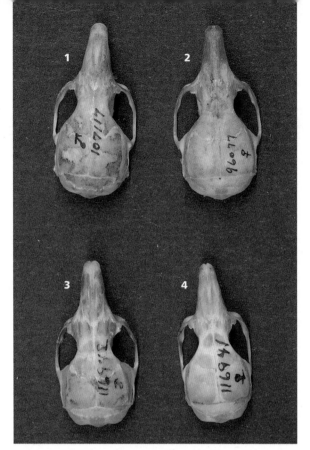

Members of Zapodidae: 1. Western jumping mouse, male 107117 *(Z. princeps)*, 2. Pacific jumping mouse, female 96077 *(Z. trinotatus)*, 3. Woodland jumping mouse, male 116942 *(Napaeozapus insignis)*, 4. Meadow jumping mouse, female 116941 *(Z. hudsonius)*. MUSEUM OF VERTEBRATE ZOOLOGY, UC BERKELEY.

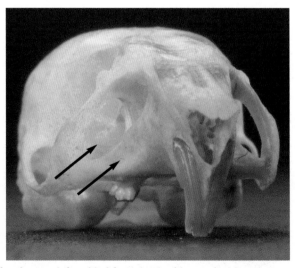

Look closely for the two infraorbital foramina in this meadow jumping mouse *(Z. hudsonius)*. The larger is obvious, and the much smaller sits below. MUSEUM OF COMPARATIVE ZOOLOGY, HARVARD U 60174.

Meadow jumping mouse, *Zapus hudsonius*

Greatest length: 20.8–23.8 mm ($^8/_{10}$–$^9/_{10}$ in.) (full table of measurements page 588, life-size image page 111, life-size jaw page 159)

Specimen illustrated: Adult female, MCZ 60174

Dentition: i 1/1 c 0/0 p 1/0 m 3/3, total 18. Incisors grooved and deep yellow to orange. First molar has one reentrant fold lingually and four labially.

Dorsal: The skulls of mice are slender and fragile, with weak zygomatic arches, slender triangular rostrums, large orbits, and large, rounded braincases. The rostrum (1) is long, slender, and triangular; the nasals (2) are very long and broad, with squared posterior edges (3). The zygomatic arches (4) are very slim and roughly parallel; the maxillary arms (5) and zygomatic plates are proportionately smaller than in *Peromyscus*. Lacrimal bone projections (6) are larger in the dorsal corner of the maxillary arm. The orbits (7) are large, and the interorbital breadth (8) is slightly narrower than in *Napaeozapus*, with the maxillary bones just visible below. The braincase (9) is large, round, and approaching 50 percent of the greatest length of skull; ridges are not developed, and the braincases of mice are smooth. The interparietal (10) is large, but very slim, and as wide as the braincase, tapering to either side.

Ventral: The relatively broad palate (11) terminates at approximately the midpoint of the posterior molar (12), with a pointed projection (13) over the pterygoid region; palatal pits (14) are evident. The incisive foramina (15) taper toward the anterior and are slightly shorter and wider than in *Peromyscus* and shorter than in the western jumping mouse *(Z. princeps)*; the posterior edge (16) of the incisive foramina is aligned with the anterior edge of the tiny first cheek tooth. The pterygoid region (17) is narrow, and the pterygoid processes (18) are relatively long. The spheno-pterygoid canals are obscured; foramina ovale (19) are wide. Auditory bullae (20) are medium

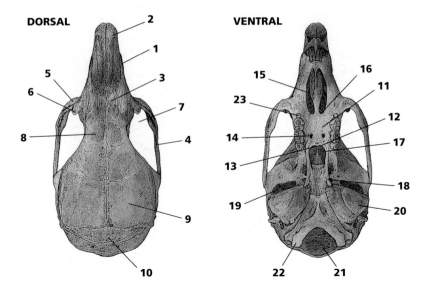

DORSAL   2

VENTRAL

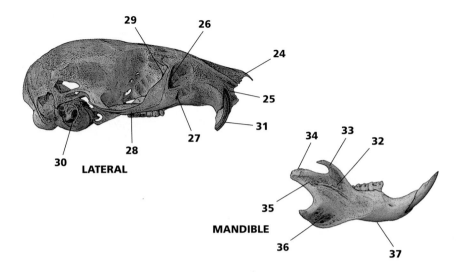

and triangular. The foramen magnum (21) is larger, with smaller occipital condyles (22). Toothrows are short and slightly divergent to the anterior. The first cheek tooth (23) is tiny and the second is the largest, descending in size to posterior.

Lateral: The dorsolateral outline slopes down toward the anterior, and the posterior is rounded. The nasals (24) extend well beyond the premaxillaries (25) and incisors. The first infraorbital foramen (26) is round and as large as the nasal vacuity; a second, smaller infraorbital foramen (27) sits below the first. Zygomatic arches (28) are relatively straight and extend below the level of the palate; the vertical process of the jugal bone (29) extends up to near the lacrimal, and the small zygomatic plate is at or near level. The auditory meatus (30) is low and large. The incisors (31) are grooved and recurved.

Mandible: The mandible is deep, stout, and curved; the ramus region (32) is large. The coronoid process (33) is slightly longer than in *Napaeozapus,* slender, curved to the posterior, and located above the condyle (34). The condyloid process (35) is long and thick, pointing to the posterior at nearly 45 degrees. The angular process (36) is large and angular, points to the posterior, and sits below the ventral surface of the body (37) below the first cheek tooth.

Similar species: Other jumping mice, pocket mice, and other mouse species.

Woodland jumping mouse, *Napaeozapus insignis*

Greatest length: 22.2–24.5 mm (⁹/₁₀–1 in.) (full table of measurements page 588, life-size image page 111, life-size jaw page 159)

Specimen illustrated: Adult female, MCZ 56512

Dentition: i 1/1 c 0/0 p 0/0 m 3/3, total 16. Incisors deep yellow to orange. First molar has one reentrant fold lingually and three labially.

Dorsal: The skulls of mice are slender and fragile, with weak zygomatic arches, slender triangular rostrums, large orbits, and large, rounded braincases. The rostrum (1)

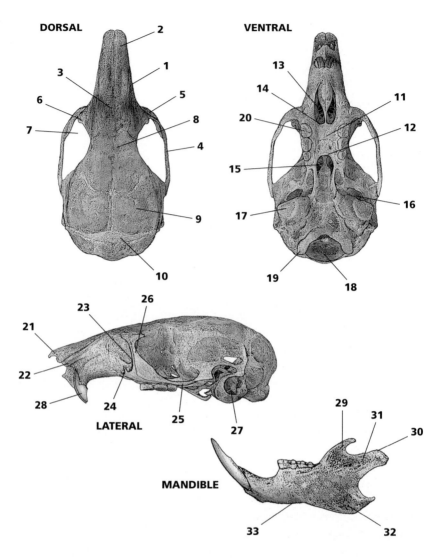

is long, slender, and triangular; the nasals (2) are very long and broad, tapering toward the posterior (3). The zygomatic arches are very slim (4) and roughly parallel; the maxillary arms (5) and zygomatic plates are proportionately smaller than in *Peromyscus*. Lacrimal bone projections (6) are larger in the dorsal corner of the maxillary arm. The orbits (7) are large, and the interorbital breadth (8) is broad; the maxillary bones are not visible below. The braincase (9) is large, round, and less than 50 percent of the greatest length of skull; ridges are not developed, and the braincases of mice are smooth. The interparietal (10) is large, but very slim, and as wide as the braincase, tapering to either side.

Ventral: The relatively broad palate (11) terminates at approximately the midpoint of the posterior molar (12); the incisive foramina (13) are slightly shorter and wider than in *Peromyscus,* tapering toward the anterior; the posterior edge of the incisive foramina (14) is aligned with the anterior edge of the first cheek tooth. The pterygoid region (15) is narrow, and the pterygoid processes are relatively long. The spheno-pterygoid canals are not visible; foramina ovale (16) are wide. Auditory bullae (17) are medium and triangular. The foramen magnum (18) is larger, with smaller occipital condyles (19). Toothrows are short and slightly divergent to the anterior. The largest of the cheek teeth (20) is at the anterior, descending in size to posterior.

Lateral: The dorsolateral outline slopes down toward the anterior, and the posterior is rounded. The nasals (21) extend well beyond the premaxillaries (22) and incisors. The first infraorbital foramen (23) is round and as large as the nasal vacuity; a second, smaller infraorbital foramen (24) sits below the first. Zygomatic arches (25) are relatively straight and low; the vertical process of the jugal bone (26) extends up to near the lacrimal, and the small zygomatic plate is at or near level. The auditory meatus (27) is low and large. The incisors (28) are grooved and recurved.

Mandible: The mandible is deep, stout, and curved; the ramus region is large. The coronoid process (29) is long, slender, curved to the posterior, and located above the condyle (30). The condyloid process (31) is long and thick, pointing to the posterior at nearly 45 degrees. The angular process (32) is large and angular, points to the posterior, and sits below the ventral surface of the body (33) below the first cheek tooth.

Similar species: Other jumping mice, pocket mice, and other mouse species.

Family Erethizontidae: New World porcupines

Porcupines are rodents whose skulls are characterized by their very large infraorbital foramina through which the masseter muscles pass; rodents that share these characteristics are called hystricomorphs. Many rodents in Central and South America are hystricomorphs, yet the only native animal north of Mexico with these characteristics is the North American porcupine.

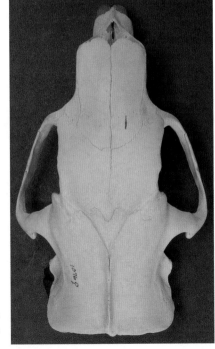

The sole member of this family living north of Mexico is the North American porcupine (*Erethizon dorsatum*). Female, SANTA BARBARA MUSEUM OF NATURAL HISTORY 1076.

North American porcupine, *Erethizon dorsatum*

Greatest length: 91.8–120.1 mm (3⁶/10–4⁷/10 in.) (full table of measurements page 570, life-size image page 131, life-size jaw page 165)

Specimen illustrated: Adult female, SBMNH 1076

Dentition: i 1/1 c 0/0 p 1/1 m 3/3, total 20. Incisors massive, and deep yellow to orange enamel is evident on the anterior edges.

Dorsal: The porcupine skull is large and triangular, with narrow, low zygomatic arches. The rostrum (1) is relatively broad and long, and the premaxillaries (2) project far to the anterior. Nasals (3) are very broad and rectangular. Slim zygomatic arches (4) converge strongly to the anterior; postorbital processes (5) on the frontals are reduced to bumps. The orbits (6) are relatively small, and the temporal fossae (7) are reduced. The angular processes (8) on the squamosals are not found in the similar nutria *(Myocastor)* and contribute to the squared appearance of the braincase; the braincase (9) is greater than one-third the greatest length of skull, which is larger than in nutria; temporal ridges (10) are well developed and converge in a V shape to form a well-developed sagittal crest (11), which extends for much of the length of the braincase. Occipital crests (12) are developed. Mastoid processes (13) are well developed and visible.

Ventral: The palate (14) is very narrow and triangular, terminating approximately aligned with the anterior edge of the last molar (15). The pterygoid processes (16) are relatively short. The incisive foramina (17) are larger and slitlike, situated approximately midway between the toothrows and incisors. Auditory bullae (18) are medium and inflated, and lack auditory canals. The toothrows strongly converge toward the anterior; the first cheek tooth (P4) (19) is the largest in the row. The pterygoid fossae (36) are open.

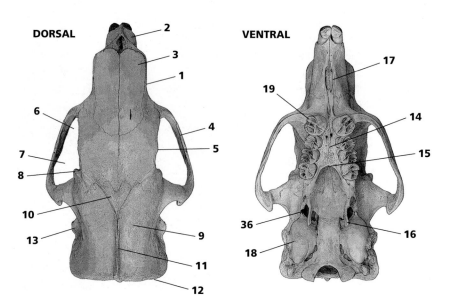

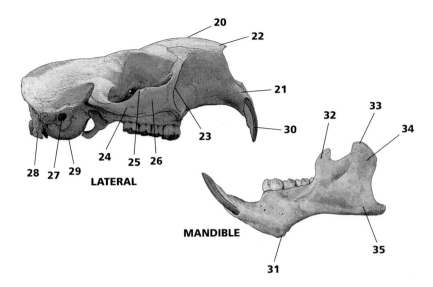

20
22
21
33
32
34
30
23
24 25 26
28 27 29
LATERAL
MANDIBLE
35
31

Lateral: The dorsolateral outline of the skull slopes upward toward the anterior; the deepest part of the skull (20) is the robust, curved rostrum. The premaxillaries (21) extend to the anterior far forward of the nasals (22). Porcupines are hystricomorph mammals, with very large infraorbital canals (23) through which the masseter muscles pass. The stout and deep zygomatic arches (24) have rounded postorbital processes (25). The jugal bones (26) are exceptionally broad and heavy. The very small auditory meatus (27) is slightly elevated. The paraoccipital processes (28) do not extend below the ventral surface of the auditory bullae (29). Stout incisors (30) are procumbent and recurved.

Mandible: The body is curved and slender, and the anterior has a distinctive step (31) along the ventral surface; as in beavers, there is a bone projection (31) on the ventral surface where the body curves steeply upward. The coronoid process (32) is reduced, blunt, and located below the condyle (33). The condyloid process (34) is large, thick, and angular. The angular process (35) is long and rounded.

Notes: Aging up to twenty-six months through an analysis of molar eruption is quite reliable and beautifully illustrated in Dodge (1982). At birth, the porcupine has four incisors and four premolars. At four months, the first molars are in place and the second are erupting. At one year of age, the third molar erupts. At two years, the premolars are completely replaced by permanent dentition. Roze and Ilse (2003) report that in fifty skulls and five hundred live captures, they had never seen an instance of malocclusion, a misalignment of the incisors when the jaw is closed.

Similar species: Nutrias, agoutis, pacas, and beavers.

Family Myocastoridae: Nutrias

Nutrias are rodents whose skulls are characterized by their very large infraorbital foramina through which the masseter muscles pass; rodents that share these characteristics are called hystricomorphs. Nutrias are native to South America, where many rodents are hystricomorphs.

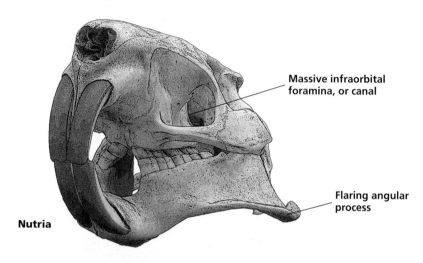

Massive infraorbital foramina, or canal

Flaring angular process

Nutria

Nutria or coypu, *Myocastor coypus*

Greatest length: 109.6–125.6 mm (4³/₁₀–4⁹/₁₀ in.) (full table of measurements page 572, life-size image page 132, life-size jaw page 167)

Specimen illustrated: Adult, private collection

Dentition: i 1/1 c 0/0 p 1/1 m 3/3, total 20. Incisors massive, and yellow enamel is evident on the anterior edges.

Dorsal: The nutria skull is large, with a relatively broad and long rostrum (1). Nasals (2) are broad and rectangular. Stout zygomatic arches (3) converge strongly to the anterior; postorbital processes on the frontals (4) are small, but they are larger and rounded on the zygomatic arches (5), better viewed from the lateral. The orbits (6) are relatively large, and the temporal fossae (7) are reduced. The braincase (8) is smaller and narrow, approximately one-third the greatest length of skull; temporal ridges (9) are very well developed and converge in a V shape to form a well-developed sagittal crest (10) on the posterior half of the braincase. Occipital crests (11) are developed. Mastoid processes are less developed.

Ventral: The palate (12) is very narrow and triangular, terminating approximately in line with the posterior edge of the last molar (13). The pterygoid processes (14) are relatively short. The incisive foramina (15) are wider and slitlike, situated much closer to the toothrows than to the incisors. Auditory bullae (16) are small and inflated, and the short auditory canals are angled toward the dorsal surface. The toothrows strongly converge toward the anterior; the last molar (17) is the largest in the row, and teeth descend in size toward the anterior. The foramen magnum (18) is small.

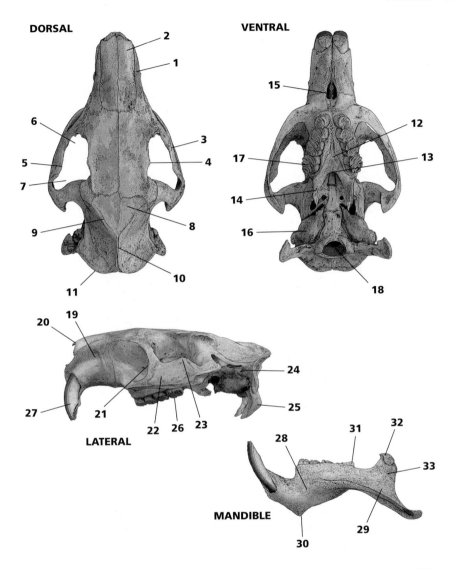

DORSAL

VENTRAL

LATERAL

MANDIBLE

Lateral: The dorsolateral outline of the skull is relatively straight. The rostrum (19) is deep and stout; the nasals (20) do not extend to the anterior of the skull. Nutrias are hystricomorph mammals, with very large infraorbital canals (21) through which the masseter muscles pass. The stout and deep zygomatic arches (22) have rounded postorbital processes (23). The jugal bones (22) are exceptionally broad and heavy. The very small auditory meatus (24) is elevated to approximately the midpoint of the skull. One of the most distinctive features of the nutria skull is the very long paraoccipital processes (25), which extend down at the posterior of the skull and then slightly forward. Note also the angle of the grinding surfaces of the toothrows (26). Stout incisors (27) are slightly procumbent and recurved.

Mandible: The mandible is very distinctive. The body (28) is curved, and the angular process (29) flares out and is flattened, somewhat winglike. Like the beaver, there is a bump or bone projection (30) at the anterior of the mandible on the ventral surface, where the body curves steeply upward. The coronoid process (31) is greatly reduced to a mere bump and sits far forward of the condyle (32). The condyloid process (33) is squared and near vertical.

Similar species: Porcupines, agoutis, pacas, and beavers.

Family Dasyproctidae: Agoutis

Agoutis are rodents whose skulls are characterized by their very large infraorbital foramina through which the masseter muscles pass; rodents that share these characteristics are called hystricomorphs. Agoutis are among the many hystricomorph rodents in Central and South America.

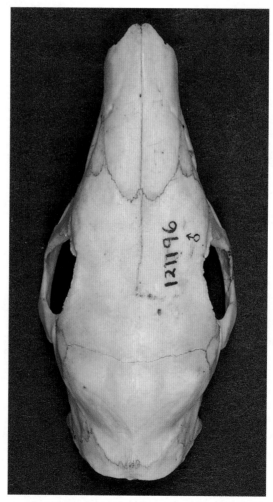

The northernmost member of this family is the Mexican black agouti *(Dasyprocta mexicana)*.
Male, MUSEUM OF VERTEBRATE ZOOLOGY, UC BERKELEY 121196.

Mexican black agouti, *Dasyprocta mexicana*

Greatest length: 106.7 mm ($4^2/_{10}$ in.) (full table of measurements page 572, life-size image page 128, life-size jaw page 164)

Specimen illustrated: Adult male, MVZ 121196

Dentition: i 1/1 c 0/0 p 1/1 m 3/3, total 20.

Dorsal: The agouti skull is very slender, with a long, broad rostrum and narrow zygomatic arches. The rostrum (1) is broad and very long; nasals (2) are broad and taper to the posterior. Slim zygomatic arches (3) are short and have a very narrow spread; postorbital processes on the frontals are absent, and lacrimal projections (4) are small. The orbits (5) are relatively large, facing to either side, and the temporal fossae (6) are greatly reduced. The braincase (7) is rounded and constricted to posterior (8); temporal ridges (9) are less developed and converge in a V shape to form a very small sagittal crest (10) at the far posterior of the braincase in old animals. Occipital crests (11) are developed.

Ventral: The palate (12) is broader than in nutrias and rectangular, terminating approximately in line with the anterior edge of the last molar (13). The pterygoid region is broad. The incisive foramina (14) are tiny, slitlike, and situated much closer to the incisors than to the toothrows. Auditory bullae (15) are medium and inflated. The toothrows are relatively parallel, and the first three cheek teeth are of similar proportions; the last molar (16) is the smallest. Other agoutis have only three cheek teeth.

Lateral: The dorsolateral outline of the skull is convex. The rostrum (17) is very deep and stout; the nasals (18) extend to the anterior just beyond or aligned with the premaxillaries (19); the nasal vacuity (20) is large. Agoutis are hystricomorph mammals, with very large infraorbital canals (21) through which the masseter muscles pass. The slim zygomatic arches (22) extend low to the level of the palate. The very small auditory meatus (23) is slightly elevated. Smaller incisors (24) are recurved.

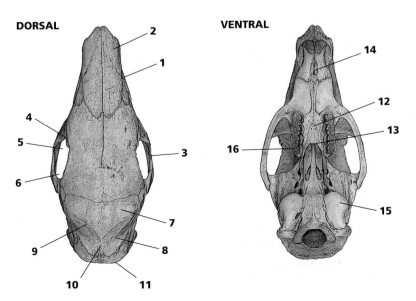

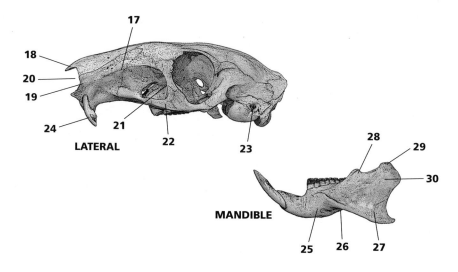

Mandible: The body (25) of the mandible is curved, with a distinctive step (26) to the large angular process (27), which slopes down and out before curving to the posterior. The coronoid process (28) is greatly reduced to a bump and sits far forward of the condyle (29). The condyloid process (30) is squared and thick, pointing to the posterior at roughly 45 degrees.

Similar species: Other agoutis, pacas, nutrias, and porcupines.

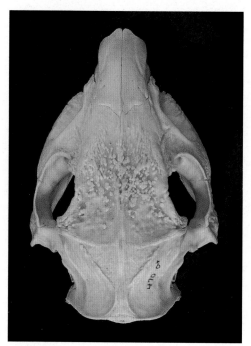

Family Agoutidae: Pacas

Pacas are rodents whose skulls are characterized by their large infraorbital foramina through which the masseter muscles pass; rodents that share these characteristics are called hystricomorphs. Pacas are among the many hystricomorph rodents in Central and South America. They also have incredibly distinctive cheek plates, which are extensions from the zygomatic arches.

A Central American member of this family is the paca *(Agouti paca)*. Male, SANTA BARBARA MUSEUM OF NATURAL HISTORY 470.

Paca, *Agouti paca*

Greatest length: 141.0–160.2 mm ($5^5/_{10}$–$6^3/_{10}$ in.) (full table of measurements page 572, life-size image page 137, life-size jaw page 166)

Specimen illustrated: Adult male, SBMNH 470

Dentition: i 1/1 c 0/0 p 1/1 m 3/3, total 20. Incisors massive, and yellow enamel is evident on the anterior edges.

Dorsal: The paca skull is broad and triangular, with a slender rostrum and large, distinctive cheek bones. The rostrum (1) is relatively short and slender; nasals (2) are short, broad, and rectangular. Stout zygomatic arches (3) converge strongly to the anterior; postorbital processes (29) on the frontals are far to the posterior, but larger lacrimal projections (4) exist in the dorsal corner of the zygomatic arches. The orbits (5) are medium, and the temporal fossae (6) are much reduced. The braincase (7) is short and broad, approximately one-third the greatest length of skull; temporal ridges (8) are very well developed and converge in a V shape to form a small sagittal crest (9) on the posterior half of the braincase. Occipital crests (10) are developed. The frontal and temporal regions become more textured, pitted (11), and rugose with age.

Ventral: The palate (12) is long, with a distinctive narrow extension to the anterior of the toothrows, and extending to the posterior to approximately in line with the anterior edge of the last molar (14). The pterygoid processes (15) are relatively short. The incisive foramina (16) are tiny, situated much closer to the incisors than to the toothrows. Auditory bullae (17) are small and round. The toothrows converge toward the anterior; the last molar (18) is the largest in the row, and teeth descend in size toward the anterior. The foramen magnum (19) is small.

Lateral: The dorsolateral outline of the skull is slightly convex. The rostrum (20) is deep and stout; the nasals (21) do not extend to the anterior as far as the premax-

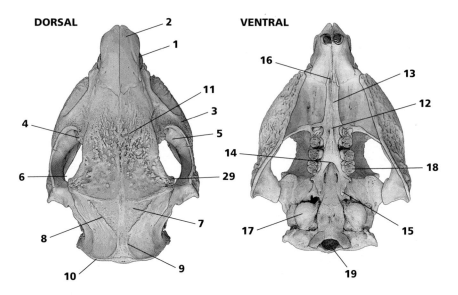

DORSAL · VENTRAL

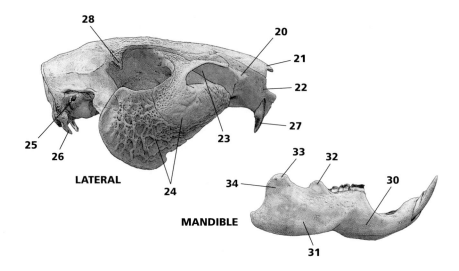

LATERAL
MANDIBLE

illaries (22). Paca are hystricomorph mammals, with very large infraorbital canals (23) through which the masseter muscles pass. The zygomatic arches are incredibly distinctive, with very large extensions of the maxillaries and jugals forming pitted plates (24) that cover much of the mandible. The very small auditory meatus (25) is slightly elevated. The longer paraoccipital processes (26) extend well below the auditory bullae. The incisors (27) are small and straight. The postorbital process (28) is small.

Mandible: The body (30) is curved, and the angular process (31) is very large, curving to the posterior. The coronoid process (32) is greatly reduced to a rounded projection far forward of the condyle (33). The condyloid process (34) is bulbous, rounded, and only slightly taller than the coronoid.

Similar species: Agoutis, nutrias, porcupines, and beavers.

Notes: Aging by tooth development can be found in Nelson and Shump (1978).

Order Carnivora: Carnivores

Family Canidae: Dogs, coyotes, foxes, and wolves

Canids have large canine teeth, which are slightly blunted for grabbing and holding prey. The lower canines are slightly anterior to the upper ones, and this together with a small diastema posterior to the lower canines allows the teeth to interlock when the mouth is closed. The incisors are well developed and work in unison with the canines to allow for excellent gripping and tearing. The anterior half of canid dentition seems to be focused on the capturing and killing of live prey and includes well-developed carnassials. The laterally flattened and W-shaped configuration of the cusps allows for foods to be trapped and then sliced or sheared.

Approaching the posterior of the mouth, the function of the teeth changes from gripping and shearing to holding and crushing, which is more characteristic of a vege-

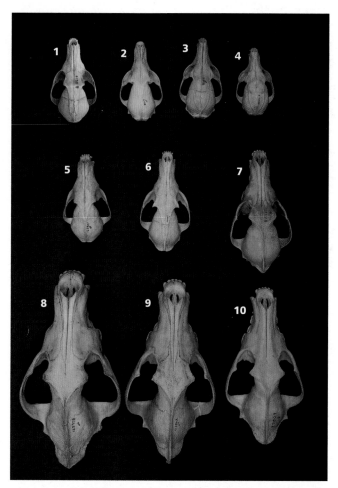

Wild members of Canidae: 1. Swift fox, MCZ B8610 *(V. velox)*, 2. Kit fox, male 185243 *(V. macrotis)*, 3. Common gray fox, male 90627 *(U. cinereoargenteus)*, 4. Island fox, male 38353 *(U. littoralis)*, 5. Arctic fox, male 123978 *(V. lagopus)*, 6. Red fox, female 129307 *(V. vulpes)*, 7. Coyote, male 81536 *(C. latrans)*, 8. Gray wolf, male 123978 *(C. lupus)*, 9. Eastern timber wolf, male 123562 *(C. lycaon)*, 10. Red wolf, female 95809 *(C. rufus)*. MUSEUM OF VERTEBRATE ZOOLOGY, UC BERKELEY.

tarian or specialized diet, such as the crushing of large bones as done by wolves. The posterior of the lower carnassials and all teeth posterior to them are somewhat flattened, with smaller, rounded cusps. Crushing also requires more lateral movement of the mandible, and in canids, this is allowed by the articulation of mandible and cranium. Canine skulls tend to have well-developed sagittal crests and wide zygomata, structures to support muscles which provide tremendous power for closing the mouth to make the kill and tear chunks from prey. Yet there is also some lateral movement so that canids can kill, shear, as well as crush a great variety of foods.

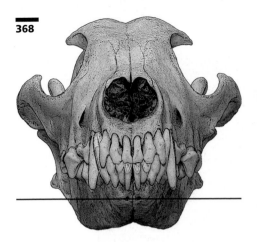

Domestic dog, of coyote proportions

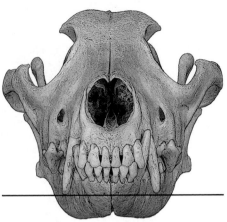

Red wolf

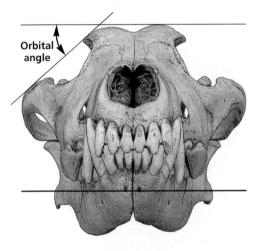

Orbital
angle

Gray wolf

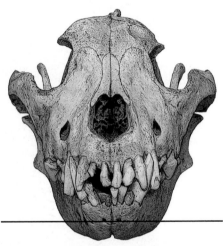

Domestic dog, of near wolf proportions

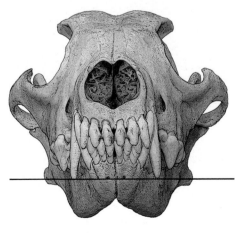

Eastern coyote

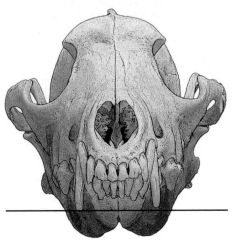

Western coyote

Following are useful references and descriptions to help differentiate among the large canids: the coyote *(Canis latrans)*, gray wolf *(C. lupus)*, eastern timber wolf *(C. lycaon)*, red wolf *(C. rufus)*, and domestic dogs *(C. familiaris)*. Further descriptive characters are in accounts and the essay "Cranial Traits Separating Canids" (Gilbert 1980).

To differentiate between domestic dog and coyote skulls, a useful character is the length of the upper canines in relation to a line drawn across the mandibular mental foramina (refer to illustrations). Should the canines extend below this line when the jaw is closed, the skull is likely that of a coyote; the majority of dog canines will not reach the line. Another method, used by Howard in 1949, is to compare the width of the palate between the first premolars with the length of the toothrow, measured from the anterior of the first premolar to the posterior of the last molar (refer to illustration on page 373). If the length of the toothrow is approximately 3.1 times the width of the palate, you have a coyote skull. If it is 2.7 times or less the width of the palate, you've found a domestic dog. This ratio proved 95 percent accurate (Bekoff 1977). There are additional excellent characters described to differentiate coyotes from dogs and coyotes from coyote-dog hybrids described in *Mammals of Illinois* by Donald Hoffmeister (1989).

To differentiate between coyotes and gray wolves, the greatest length of skull and the zygomatic width are often sufficient. Ingles (1965) measured the length of the upper canine at the gum line from front to back. In coyotes, this measurement was 11 millimeters or less, whereas in gray wolves, it was 12 millimeters or more. He also measured the upper carnassial, which in coyotes was up to 20 millimeters long and in wolves about 25 millimeters long. The posterior edge of the palate may be another distinguishing character. In coyotes, both east and west, the palate terminates either aligned with the anterior edge of the last molar or as far back as the midpoint of that molar. In wolves, the termination of the palate is aligned with the posterior of the last molar.

To differentiate between coyotes and red wolves, a very useful clue is the greatest length of skulls, where there is almost no overlap. The red wolf also has a higher cranium, often with a larger sagittal crest, deeper rostrum, more spreading zygomata, a supraoccipital shield that extends farther posteriorly, more robust jugal, more deeply inserted maxillaries, thicker orbital border that bows out, proportionately smaller M2, and usually larger auditory bullae (Young and Goldman 1944).

To differentiate between red wolves and gray or eastern timber wolves, look at M2, which is proportionately larger in red wolves than in gray wolves. When the jaw is closed and a line is drawn across the anterior mental foramina, the canines in red wolves often extend below the line, but not in gray wolves (Paradiso and Nowak 1972). Red wolves also have a prominent cingulum on the outer side of the first upper molar and more deeply cleft crowns and laterally compressed cusps on large molars, all of which helps distinguish them from both gray and eastern timber wolves (Paradiso and Nowak 1972). The eastern timber wolf has a broader skull than the red wolf, with a higher braincase, more widely spreading zygomata, and the posterior of postorbital processes turned inward less abruptly (Young and Goldman 1944).

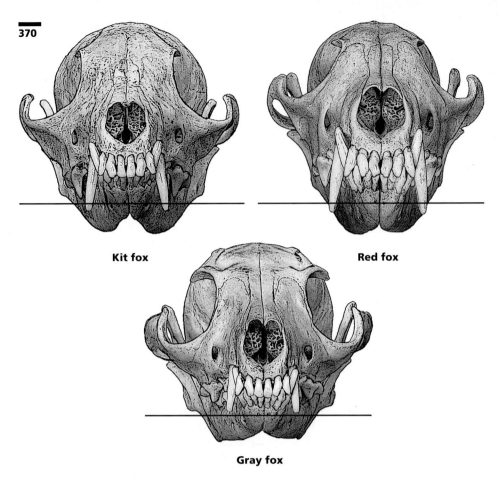

Kit fox

Red fox

Gray fox

Compare the size and shape of the incisors and relative length of canines in these three fox species.

To differentiate between eastern timber wolves and gray wolves, consider the following characters: The skull of the eastern timber wolf is smaller, with a more slender rostrum, and the supraoccipital shield projects less to the posterior over the foramen magnum and occipital condyles. The nasals of eastern timber wolves tend to be more deeply emarginated to the anterior, and they have proportionately smaller upper carnassials (Young and Goldman 1944).

To differentiate among gray wolves, wolf-dog hybrids, and domestic dogs, first consider the size, as the majority of domestic dog skulls will be smaller. Yet there are larger breeds that attain wolflike proportions, and in these instances, you'll need to look for other characters. Dogs tend to have broader, steeper forehead regions and proportionately much smaller teeth; the carnassials are often much larger and stouter in gray wolves than in domestic breeds. The auditory bullae of wolves are convex and large, whereas in domestic dogs they tend to be less inflated and misshapen.

In 1941, Iljin described using the orbital angle to differentiate among these large canids (Mech 1974). (Refer to the illustration on page 368 to note how the orbital angle is measured.) Iljin recorded orbital angles of 40 to 45 degrees in gray wolves and

53 to 60 in large domestic dogs; in wolf hybrids, orbital angles fell in between these two ranges.

To differentiate foxes from the other canids, the anterior perspective of the skull provides clues. Consider the shape and size of the incisors, as well as the length of the canines in relation to a line drawn through the mandibular mental foramina (refer to the illustration on page 370).

Domestic dog, *Canis familiaris*

Specimens illustrated: LACM 30129, 30124, 30371, chihuahua (unknown #)
It is difficult to describe the domestic dog skull, as the great diversity of breeds living today have equally varied bone forms, though a great many follow the basic form described for the coyote and wolves. Features that are useful in determining whether you've found a wild or domestic canid skull are described in the introduction to the

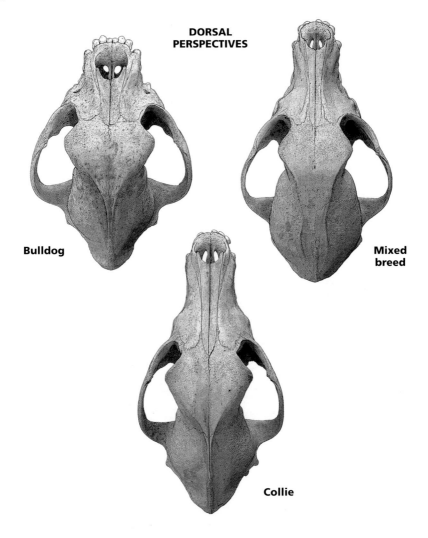

DORSAL PERSPECTIVES

Bulldog

Mixed breed

Collie

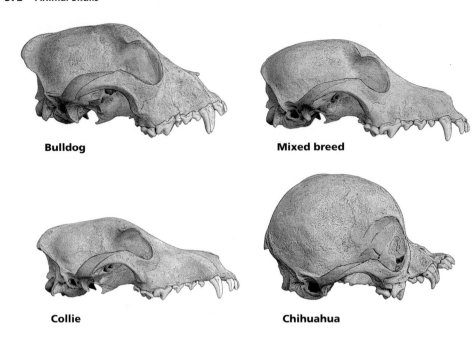

Bulldog **Mixed breed**

Collie **Chihuahua**

LATERAL PERSPECTIVES

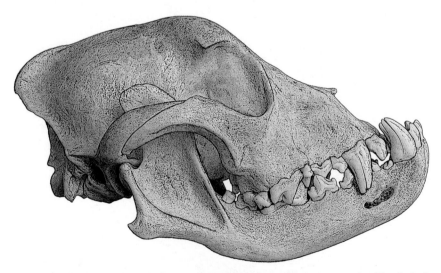

An English bulldog, bred to be able to breathe while attached by its jaws to the side of a bull.
NATURAL HISTORY MUSEUM OF LOS ANGELES COUNTY 30129.

canid family and in the species accounts of their wild counterparts. The skulls illustrated here only hint at the diversity of forms that dog skulls may take.

Note: English bulldogs were bred to bait bulls, and the longer mandibles allow them to breathe while latched on to an animal for a very long time (Liittschwager 2002).

Coyote (northeast), *Canis latrans*

Greatest length: 173.8–220.3 mm (6$^{7}/_{10}$–8$^{7}/_{10}$ in.) (full table of measurements page 590, life-size image page 138, life-size jaw page 172)

Specimen illustrated: Western adult male, MVZ 81536

Dentition: i 3/3 c 1/1 p 4/4 m 2/3, total 42.

Dorsal: Canine skulls have a somewhat slender, triangular outline, especially from the posterior of the zygomatic arches forward. The rostrum (1) is long and slender, but strong. The nasals (2) are very long and slender, extending to the posterior into the orbit and just beyond the maxillaries (3). Heavy, wide-spreading zygomatic arches (4) strongly converge to the anterior and are positioned to the posterior of the skull. Postorbital processes from the frontals (5) are stout, triangular, and convex on their dorsal surfaces; postorbital processes are stout and triangular from the zygomatic arches (6) as well. The orbits (7) point forward and are medium for a carnivore, and the temporal fossa (8) is large; the position of the orbits is approximately midway along the length of the skull. The interorbital (9) and postorbital breadths (10) are near equal, and the postorbital breadths tend to be wider than in dogs of similar size. The braincase (11) is large and rounded, forming much less than 50 percent of the greatest length of skull; temporal ridges (12) are well developed and converge at the anterior of the braincase in a V shape to form a long and large sagittal crest (13). Occipital crests (14) are well developed and contribute to a triangular supraoccipital shield (15).

Ventral: The long palate (16) terminates at the anterior edge (or the midpoint in eastern animals) of the last molar (17); the incisive foramina (18) are medium and well forward on the palate. The pterygoid region (19) is broad, and the pterygoid processes (20) are long. The mandibular fossa (21) is well developed. The auditory bullae (22) are medium, oval, and inflated. The foramen magnum (23) is medium, and the occipital condyles (24) are stout. The toothrows are very long, the carnassial (25) is thin, and the posterior molars (26) are flattened. The front incisors (27) are distinctly lobed and smaller than in domestic dogs of similar proportions.

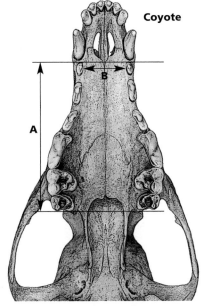

Coyote

Lateral: From the elevated braincase, the dorsolateral outline curves smoothly and relatively gradually down to the plane of the rostrum. The premaxillaries (28) extend farther than the nasals (29). The infraorbital foramina (30) are small and visible low on the side of the rostrum. The postorbital processes on

Howard (1949) used two measurements to differentiate dog from coyote skulls with 95% accuracy. If "A" is 2.7 times or less the distance of "B" then it is a domestic dog. If "A" divided by "B" is approximately 3.1, you have a coyote.

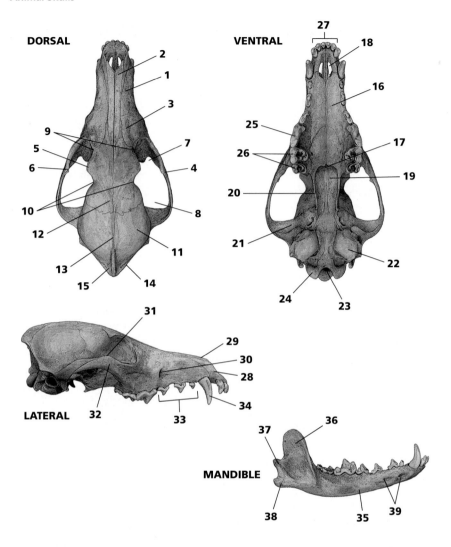

DORSAL

VENTRAL

LATERAL

MANDIBLE

the zygomatic arches (31) are small; the jugals (32) are stout. The auditory meatus is medium. The carnassial is large and well developed. The premolars (33) are well spaced, which is rarely the case in domestic breeds of similar size. The canines (34) are long, slender, and recurved.

Mandible: The body (35) is long and curved, tapering slightly to the anterior. The coronoid process (36) is near vertical, large, and rounded. The condyle (37) is aligned with the toothrow, stout, and barrel-shaped. The angular process (38) is small, stout, and rounded. Two mental foramina (39) are evident.

Similar species: Wolves, red foxes, and domestic dogs.

Notes: Sagittal crests are larger on mature males than mature females. Coyotes are sexually dimorphic, and according to Hoffmeister (1986), the three measurements most useful in determining the sex of a skull are greatest length, zygomatic breadth, and length of the nasals.

Gray wolf, *Canis lupus*

Greatest length: 213.6–293.7 mm (8⁴/₁₀–11⁶/₁₀ in.) (full table of measurements page 590, life-size image page 142, life-size jaw page 173)

Specimen illustrated: Adult male, MVZ 123978

Dentition: i 3/3 c 1/1 p 4/4 m 2/3, total 42.

Dorsal: Canine skulls have a somewhat slender, triangular outline, especially from the posterior of the zygomatic arches forward. The rostrum (1) is long and slender, but strong. The nasals (2) are very long and very slender, extending to the posterior into the orbit and just beyond the maxillaries (3). Heavy, wide-spreading zygomatic arches (4) strongly converge to the anterior. Postorbital processes from the frontals (5) are stout, triangular, and convex on their dorsal surfaces; postorbital processes

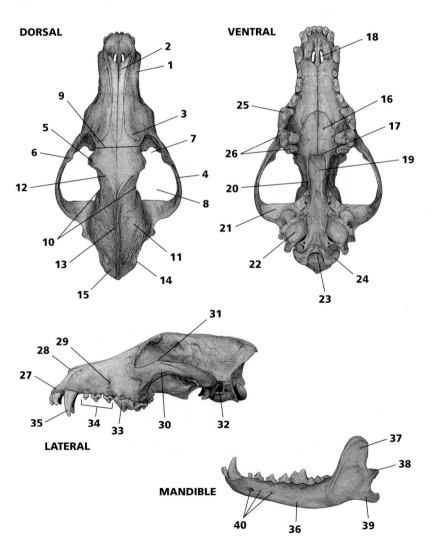

are stout and triangular from the zygomatic arches (6) as well. The orbits (7) are forward and proportionately smaller than in coyotes, and the temporal fossa (8) is larger. The interorbital breadth (9) is wider than the postorbital (10). The braincase (11) is proportionately smaller and oval, forming approximately one-third of the greatest length of skull; temporal ridges (12) are well developed and converge at the anterior of the braincase in a V shape to form a long and very large sagittal crest (13). Occipital crests (14) are very well developed, contributing to a large, triangular supraoccipital shield (15).

Ventral: The long palate (16) terminates at the posterior edge of the last molar (17); the incisive foramina (18) are proportionately smaller than in coyotes and well forward on the palate. The pterygoid region (19) is narrower, and the pterygoid processes (20) are stouter and longer. The mandibular fossa (21) is larger and well developed. The auditory bullae (22) are smaller, oval, and inflated. The foramen magnum (23) is medium, and the occipital condyles (24) are stout. The toothrows are very long, the carnassial (25) is large and stout, and the posterior molars (26) are flattened.

Lateral: From the elevated braincase, the dorsolateral outline curves smoothly and relatively gradually down to the plane of the rostrum. The premaxillaries (27) extend farther than the nasals (28). The infraorbital foramen (29) is small and visible low

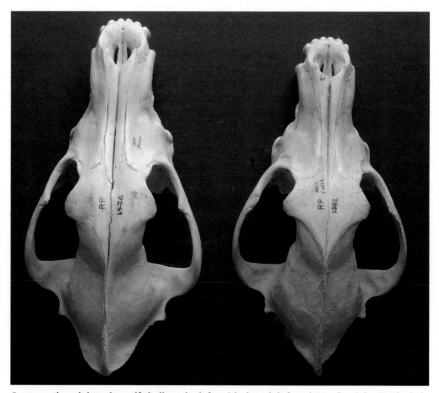

Compare the adult male wolf skull on the left, with the adult female on the right. Particularly useful in sexing gray wolf skulls is the width of rostrum. MUSEUM OF COMPARATIVE ZOOLOGY, HARVARD U 50511, 50512.

on the side of the rostrum. Zygomatic arches (30) are more stout, and the postorbital processes on the zygomatic arches (31) are small; the jugals (30) are large. The auditory meatus (32) is medium. The carnassial (33) is large and well developed. The premolars (34) are well spaced, which is rarely the case in domestic breeds of similar size. The canines (35) are stout, the dentition heavy.

Mandible: The mandible is a larger, more robust version of the coyote's, and the body (36) is long and curved, tapering slightly to the anterior. The coronoid process (37) is near vertical, large, and rounded. The condyle (38) is aligned with the toothrow, stout, and barrel-shaped. The angular process (39) is small, stout, and rounded. Three mental foramina (40) are evident.

Similar species: Other wolves, large domestic dogs, and coyotes. See family notes.

Eastern timber wolf, *Canis lycaon*

Greatest length: 213.6–267.0 mm ($8^4/10$–$10^5/10$ in.) (full table of measurements page 590, life-size image page 141, life-size jaw page 173)

Specimen illustrated: Adult male, MVZ 123562

Dentition: i 3/3 c 1/1 p 4/4 m 2/3, total 42.

Dorsal: Canine skulls have a somewhat slender, triangular outline, especially from the posterior of the zygomatic arches forward; the eastern timber wolf skull is a smaller version of the gray wolf's. The rostrum (1) is long and slender, but strong. The nasals (2) are very long and very slender, extending to the posterior into the orbit and just beyond the maxillaries (3). Heavy, wide-spreading zygomatic arches (4) strongly converge to the anterior. Postorbital processes from the frontals (5) are stout, triangular, and convex on their dorsal surfaces; postorbital processes are stout and triangular from the zygomatic arches (6) as well. The orbits (7) are forward and proportionately smaller than in coyotes, but a bit larger than in gray wolves, and the temporal fossa (8) is larger. The interorbital breadth (9) is wider than the postorbital (10). The braincase (11) is proportionately smaller and oval, forming approximately one-third of the greatest length of skull; temporal ridges (12) are well developed and converge at the anterior of the braincase in a V shape to form a long and very large sagittal crest (13). Occipital crests (14) are very well developed and contribute to the triangular supraoccipital shield (15).

Ventral: The long palate (16) terminates at the posterior edge of the last molar (17); the incisive foramina (18) are proportionately smaller than in coyotes and well forward on the palate. The pterygoid region (19) is narrower, and the pterygoid processes (20) are stouter and longer. The mandibular fossa (21) is larger and well developed. The auditory bullae (22) are smaller, oval, and inflated. The foramen magnum (23) is medium, and the occipital condyles are stout (24). The toothrows are very long, the carnassial (25) is large and stout, and the posterior molars (26) are flattened.

Lateral: From the elevated braincase, the dorsolateral outline curves smoothly and relatively gradually down to the plane of the rostrum. The premaxillaries (27) extend farther than the nasals (28). The infraorbital foramina (29) are small and visible low on the side of the rostrum. Zygomatic arches are more stout, and the postorbital

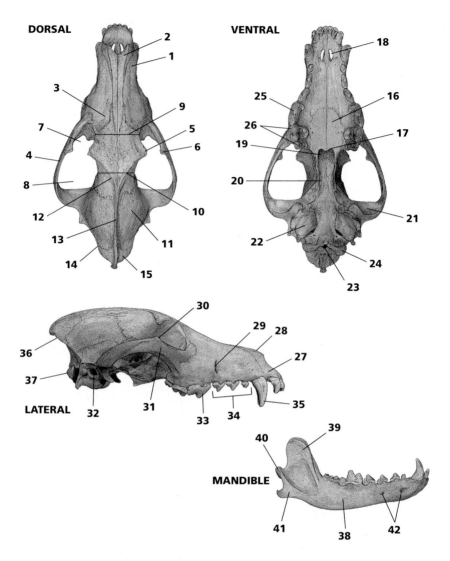

DORSAL

VENTRAL

LATERAL

MANDIBLE

processes on the zygomatic arches (30) are small; the jugals (31) are large. The auditory meatus (32) is medium. The carnassial (33) is large and well developed. The premolars (34) are well spaced, which is rarely the case in domestic breeds of similar size. The canines (35) are stout, the dentition heavy. Note the length to which the supraoccipital shield (36) extends over the occipital condyles (37).

Mandible: The mandible is a larger, more robust version of the coyote's, and the body (38) is long and curved, tapering slightly to the anterior. The coronoid process (39) is near vertical, large, and rounded. The condyle (40) is aligned with the toothrow, stout, and barrel-shaped. The angular process (41) is small, stout, and rounded. Two mental foramina (42) are evident.

Similar species: Other wolves, large domestic dogs, and coyotes. See family notes.

Red wolf, *Canis rufus*

Greatest length: 198.5–261.0 mm ($7^8/_{10}$–$10^3/_{10}$ in.) (full table of measurements page 592, life-size image page 140, life-size jaw page 172)

Specimen illustrated: Adult female, MVZ 95809

Dentition: i 3/3 c 1/1 p 4/4 m 2/3, total 42.

Dorsal: Canine skulls have a somewhat slender, triangular outline, especially from the posterior of the zygomatic arches forward; red wolf skulls provide the middle ground between coyote and gray wolf skulls. The rostrum (1) is long and slender, but strong. The nasals (2) are very long and slender, extending to the posterior into the orbit and well beyond the maxillaries (3). Heavy, wide-spreading zygomatic arches (4) strongly converge to the anterior. Postorbital processes from the frontals (5) are stout, triangular, and convex on their dorsal surfaces; postorbital processes are stout and triangular from the zygomatic arches (6) as well. The orbits (7) are forward and medium for a carnivore, and the temporal fossa (8) is large; the proportions of orbit and temporal fossa are more similar to those in coyotes than in other wolves. The interorbital (9) and postorbital (10) breadths are near equal, and the postorbital breadths tend to be wider than in dogs of similar size. The braincase (11) is proportionately between coyotes and gray wolves; temporal ridges (12) are well developed and converge at the anterior of the braincase in a V shape to form a long and large sagittal crest (13). Occipital crests are well developed, and the supraoccipital shield (42) extends far to the posterior.

Ventral: The long palate (13) terminates at the posterior edge of the last molar (14) as in other wolves; in this specimen, however, there is an anomaly in the form of a tiny extra molar (15) at the far posterior on the left and behind the edge of the palate. The incisive foramina (16) are medium and well forward on the palate. The pterygoid region (17) is narrower as in other wolves, and the pterygoid processes

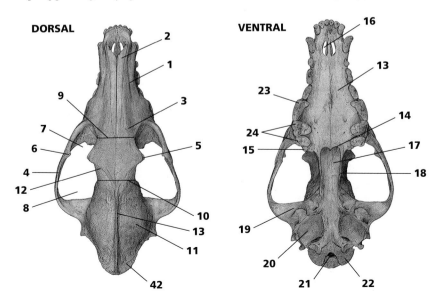

DORSAL

VENTRAL

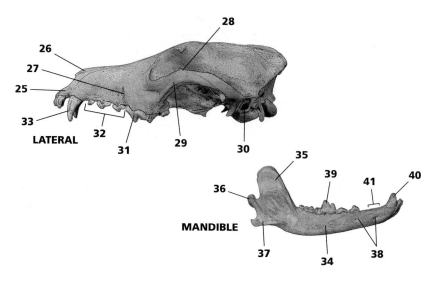

(18) are long. The mandibular fossa (19) is well developed. The auditory bullae (20) are medium, oval, and inflated, proportionately similar to coyotes. The foramen magnum (21) is medium, and the occipital condyles (22) are stout. The toothrows are very long, the carnassial (23) is thin, and the posterior molars (24) are flattened.

Lateral: From the elevated braincase, the dorsolateral outline curves smoothly and relatively gradually down to the plane of the rostrum. The premaxillaries (25) extend farther than the nasals (26). The infraorbital foramina (27) are small and visible low on the side of the rostrum. The postorbital processes on the zygomatic arches (28) are small; the jugals (29) are stout. The auditory meatus (30) is medium. The carnassial (31) is large and well developed. The premolars (32) are well spaced, which is rarely the case in domestic breeds of similar size. The canines (33) are stout and recurved. The proportions in size of zygomatic arches and teeth are a middle ground between the larger wolves and the smaller coyote.

Mandible: The body (34) is long and curved, tapering slightly to the anterior. The coronoid process (35) is near vertical, large, and rounded. The condyle (36) is aligned with the toothrow, stout, and barrel-shaped. The angular process (37) is small, stout, and rounded. Two mental foramina (38) are evident. The carnassial (39) is larger than that of coyotes. This specimen is an older animal, evident in the broken and smoother canine (40) and missing premolars (41).

Similar species: Other wolves, large domestic dogs, and coyotes. See family notes.

Arctic fox, *Vulpes lagopus*

Greatest length: 121.8–134.9 mm (4⁸/10–5³/10 in.) (full table of measurements page 592, life-size image page 134, life-size jaw page 170)

Specimen illustrated: Adult male, MVZ 123987

Dentition: i 3/3 c 1/1 p 4/4 m 2/3, total 42.

Dorsal: Canine skulls have a somewhat slender, triangular outline, especially from the posterior of the zygomatic arches forward. The rostrum (1) is very broad for the family and strong. The nasals (2) are long and slender, extending to the posterior to align with the anterior edge of the orbit as well as with the maxillaries (3). Heavy, wide-spreading zygomatic arches strongly converge to the anterior. Postorbital processes from the frontals (4) are stout, blunt, and convex on their dorsal surfaces; postorbital processes are stout and triangular from the zygomatic arches (5) as well. The orbits (6) are forward and proportionately larger for a canine, and the temporal fossa (7) is smaller. The interorbital breadth (8) is wider than the postorbital (9). The braincase (10) is very large and ovoid, forming less than 50 percent of the greatest length of skull; temporal ridges (11) are less developed and converge at the far posterior of the braincase in a V shape to form a very small sagittal crest (12), if one is present at all. Occipital crests are less developed; the supraoccipital shield (13) is very small. Mastoid processes often do not show from this perspective and are less developed than in the red fox.

Ventral: The long palate (14) terminates at the midpoint of the last molar; the incisive foramina (15) are medium and well forward on the palate. The pterygoid region (16) is broad, and the pterygoid processes (17) are long. The mandibular fossa (18) is well developed. The auditory bullae (19) are medium, oval, and inflated. The foramen magnum (20) is medium, and the occipital condyles (21) are stout. The

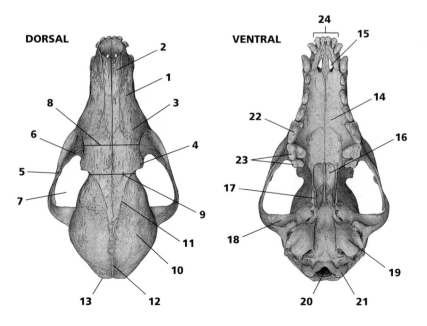

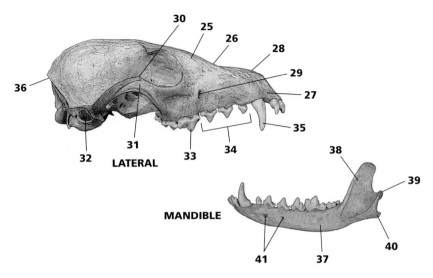

toothrows are very long, the carnassial (22) is thin, and the posterior molars (23) are flattened. The front incisors (24) are distinctly lobed.

Lateral: From the elevated braincase, the dorsolateral outline curves quite steeply down to the plane of the rostrum; the inflated frontal region (25) creates a relative step (26) and the appearance of a shortened rostrum. The premaxillaries (27) extend farther than the nasals (28). The infraorbital foramina (29) are small and visible low on the side of the rostrum. The postorbital processes on the zygomatic arches (30) are small; the jugals (31) are stout. The auditory meatus (32) is medium. The carnassial (33) is large and well developed. The premolars (34) are well spaced, which is rarely the case in domestic breeds of similar size. The canines (35) are slightly shorter and stouter than other foxes, and the incisors are procumbent. The supraoccipital shield (36) is shorter than in the red fox.

Mandible: The body (37) is long and curved, tapering slightly to the anterior. The coronoid process (38) is more slender and points more to the posterior. The condyle (39) is aligned with the toothrow, stout, and barrel-shaped. The angular process (40) is small, stout, and rounded. Two mental foramina (41) are evident.

Similar species: Red foxes, other foxes, domestic dogs, and coyotes.

Kit fox, *Vulpes macrotis*

Greatest length: 101.0–120.3 mm (4–4^{7}/$_{10}$ in.) (full table of measurements page 592, life-size image page 129, life-size jaw page 168)

Specimen illustrated: Adult male, MVZ 185243

Dentition: i 3/3 c 1/1 p 4/4 m 2/3, total 42.

Dorsal: Canine skulls have a somewhat slender, triangular outline, especially from the posterior of the zygomatic arches forward. The rostrum (1) is long and more slender, but strong. The nasals (2) are very long and slender, extending to the posterior to align with the anterior edge of the orbit, and just short of the maxillaries (3).

Heavy, wide-spreading zygomatic arches (4) converge to the anterior; kit and swift foxes have proportionately larger zygomatic plates (5). Postorbital processes from the frontals (6) are narrower and triangular, pointing to the posterior; postorbital processes are stout and triangular from the zygomatic arches (7) as well. The orbits (8) are forward and large for a canine, and the temporal fossa (9) is smaller. The interorbital and postorbital breadths are near equal. The braincase (10) is large and ovoid, approaching 50 percent of the greatest length of skull; temporal ridges (11) are weaker and converge at the far posterior of the braincase in a V shape (more U-shaped in swift foxes) to form a short sagittal crest (12), if one is present at all.

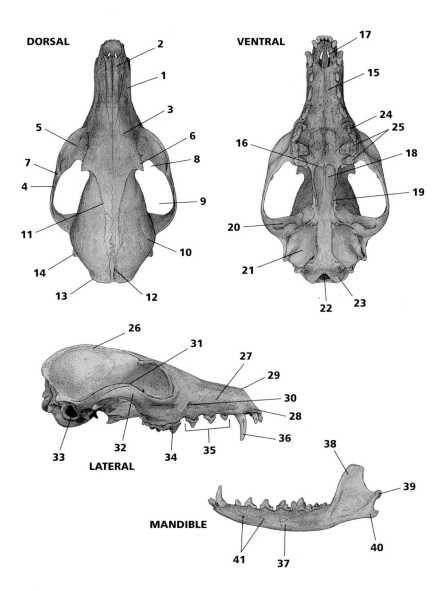

Occipital crests (13) are well developed. Mastoid processes (14) are just visible from this perspective.

Ventral: The long, narrow palate (15) terminates at the posterior edge of the last molar (16); the incisive foramina (17) are longer and well forward on the palate. The pterygoid region (18) is broad, and the pterygoid processes (19) are long. The mandibular fossa (20) is well developed. The auditory bullae (21) are larger, oval, and inflated. The foramen magnum (22) is medium, and the occipital condyles (23) are stout. The toothrows are very long, the carnassial (24) is thin, and the posterior molars (25) are flattened. The dentition as a whole is reduced compared with those of other wild canines.

Lateral: From the elevated braincase (26), the dorsolateral outline curves smoothly and gradually down to the plane of the rostrum; the rostrum (27) is less deep than in other family members. The premaxillaries (28) extend farther than the nasals (29). The interorbital foramina (30) are small and visible low on the side of the rostrum. The postorbital processes (31) on the zygomatic arches are small; the jugals (32) are stout. The auditory meatus (33) is medium. The carnassial (34) is less developed and proportionately smaller than in many canines. The premolars (35) are well spaced, which is rarely the case in domestic breeds of similar size. The canines (36) are long, very slender, and recurved.

Mandible: The body (37) is more slender and less deep, tapering slightly to the anterior. The coronoid process (38) is near vertical, large, and more squared. The condyle (39) is just above the toothrow, stout, and barrel-shaped. The angular process (40) is small, stout, and rounded. Two mental foramina (41) are evident. The dentition is reduced.

Similar species: Swift foxes, other foxes, and domestic dogs. See family notes.

Swift fox, *Vulpes velox*

Greatest length: 111.4–116.8 mm ($4^4/10$–$4^6/10$ in.) (full table of measurements page 592, life-size image page 131, life-size jaw page 168)

Specimen illustrated: Adult, MCZ B8610

Dentition: i 3/3 c1/1 p 4/4 m 2/3, total 42.

Dorsal: Canine skulls have a somewhat slender, triangular outline, especially from the posterior of the zygomatic arches forward. The rostrum (1) is long and more slender, but strong. The nasals (2) are very long and slender, extending to the posterior to align with the anterior edge of the orbit, and just short of the maxillaries (3). Heavy, wide-spreading zygomatic arches (4) converge to the anterior; kit and swift foxes have proportionately larger zygomatic plates (5). Postorbital processes from the frontals (6) are narrower and triangular, pointing to the posterior; postorbital processes are stout and triangular from the zygomatic arches (7) as well. The orbits (8) are forward and large for a canine, and the temporal fossa (9) is smaller. The interorbital and postorbital breadths are near equal. The braincase (10) is large and ovoid, approaching 50 percent of the greatest length of skull; temporal ridges (11) are weaker and converge at the far posterior of the braincase in a U shape (more V-shaped in kit foxes) to form a short sagittal crest (12), if one is present at all. Occipital crests (13) are well developed. Mastoid processes are not visible in this animal from this perspective.

Ventral: The long, narrow palate (14) terminates at the midpoint of the last molar (15); the incisive foramina (16) are medium and well forward on the palate. The pterygoid region (17) is broad, and the pterygoid processes (18) are long. The mandibular fossa (19) is well developed. The auditory bullae (20) are larger, oval, and inflated. The foramen magnum (21) is medium, and the occipital condyles (22) are stout. The toothrows are very long, the carnassial (23) is thin, and the posterior molars (24) are flattened. The dentition as a whole is reduced compared with those of other wild canines.

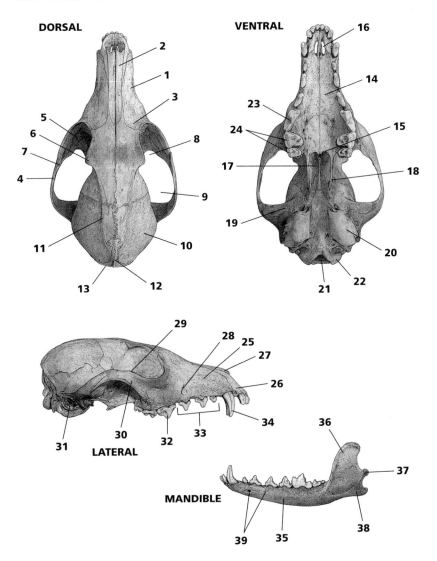

Lateral: From the elevated braincase, the dorsolateral outline curves smoothly and gradually down to the plane of the rostrum; the rostrum (25) is less deep than in other family members. The premaxillaries (26) extend farther than the nasals (27). The infraorbital foramina (28) are small and visible low on the side of the rostrum. The postorbital processes on the zygomatic arches (29) are small; the jugals (30) are stout. The auditory meatus (31) is medium. The carnassial (32) is well developed, though proportionately smaller than in many canines. The premolars (33) are well spaced, which is rarely the case in domestic breeds of similar size. The canines (34) are long, very slender, and recurved.

Mandible: The body (35) is more slender and less deep, tapering slightly to the anterior. The coronoid process (36) is near vertical, large, and more squared. The condyle (37) is aligned with the toothrow, stout, and barrel-shaped. The angular process (38) is small, stout, and rounded. Two mental foramina (39) are evident. The dentition is reduced.

Similar species: Kit foxes, other foxes, and domestic dogs.

Red fox, *Vulpes vulpes*

Greatest length: 124.5–157.2 mm ($4^9/_{10}$–$6^2/_{10}$ in.) (full table of measurements page 592, life-size image page 137, life-size jaw page 171)

Specimen illustrated: Adult male, MCZ 39038

Dentition: i 3/3 c 1/1 p 4/4 m 2/3, total 42.

Dorsal: Canine skulls have a somewhat slender, triangular outline, especially from the posterior of the zygomatic arches forward. The rostrum (1) is long and more slender than in coyotes. The nasals (2) are very long and slender, extending to the posterior into the orbit and just short of the maxillaries (3). Heavy, wide-spreading zygomatic arches (4) strongly converge to the anterior. Postorbital processes from the frontals (5) are more slender and triangular, pointing to the posterior; there is a depression (6) above the postorbital processes. Postorbital processes are stout and triangular from the zygomatic arches (7) as well. The orbits (8) are forward and medium for a canine, and the temporal fossa (9) large. The interorbital and postorbital breadths are near equal. The braincase (10) is large and rounded, forming much less than 50 percent of the greatest length of skull; temporal ridges (11) are well developed and converge at the anterior of the braincase in a V shape to form a sagittal crest (12) at the posterior of the skull. Occipital crests are well developed; supraoccipital shield (13) is short but broad.

Ventral: The long, narrow palate (14) terminates at the midpoint of the last molar; the incisive foramina (15) are medium and more forward on the palate than in arctic foxes; there may be a small, pointed projection (16) over the pterygoid region. The pterygoid region (17) is broad, and the pterygoid processes (18) are long. The mandibular fossa (19) is well developed. The auditory bullae (20) are proportionately larger than those of coyotes, oval, and inflated. The foramen magnum (21) is medium, and the occipital condyles (22) are stout. The toothrows are very long, the carnassial (23) is thin, and the posterior molars (24) are flattened.

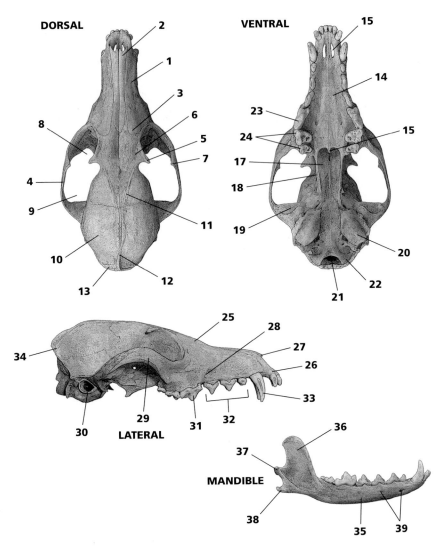

DORSAL

VENTRAL

LATERAL

MANDIBLE

Lateral: From the elevated braincase, the dorsolateral outline curves smoothly and relatively gradually down to the plane of the rostrum; the frontals (25) are slightly inflated, though less than in arctic foxes. The premaxillaries (26) extend farther than the nasals (27). The infraorbital foramina (28) are small and visible low on the side of the rostrum. The postorbital processes on the zygomatic arches are small; the jugals (29) are stout. The auditory meatus (30) is medium. The carnassial (31) is large and well developed. The premolars (32) are well spaced, which is rarely the case in domestic breeds of similar size. The canines (33) are long, slender, and recurved. The supraoccipital shield (34) extends to the posterior farther than in the arctic fox.

Mandible: The body (35) is overall more slender than in coyotes, long, and curved, tapering slightly to the anterior. The coronoid process (36) is more curved to the posterior, large, and rounded. The condyle (37) is aligned with the toothrow, stout, and barrel-shaped. The angular process (38) is small, stout, and slightly hooked. Two mental foramina (39) are evident.

Similar species: Arctic foxes, other foxes, coyotes, and domestic dogs. See family notes.

Notes: Grinnell et al. (1937) write that with age, the postorbital processes develop further from pointy in young animals to more rounded in adults; the sagittal and occipital crests also develop further, and the zygomata spread wider. Samuel and Nelson (1982) provide some clues in aging skulls: "The presphenoidal-basisphenoid suture closes in the first and second years, and the palatal portion of the premaxillary-maxillary suture closes during years four to six."

Common gray fox, *Urocyon cinereoargenteus*

Greatest length: 111.6–131.9 mm ($4^4/10$–$5^2/10$ in.) (full table of measurements page 594, life-size image page 132, life-size jaw page 169)

Specimen illustrated: Adult male, LACM 45017

Dentition: i 3/3 c 1/1 p 4/4 m 2/3, total 42.

Dorsal: Canine skulls have a somewhat slender, triangular outline, especially from the posterior of the zygomatic arches forward. The rostrum (1) is shorter and very slender. The nasals (2) are very long and slender, extending into the anterior of the orbit and just beyond the maxillaries (3). Heavy, wide-spreading (though less than in other canines) zygomatic arches (4) strongly converge to the anterior; zygomatic plates (5) are proportionately larger. Postorbital processes from the frontals (6) are stout and triangular, and there is a significant depression (7) just behind them in the frontal bones; postorbital processes are slender and triangular from the zygomatic arches (8) as well. The orbits (9) are forward and are larger for a canine; the temporal fossa (10) is smaller. The interorbital breadth (11) is less than the postorbital. The braincase is proportionately very large and oval, approaching 50 percent of the greatest length of skull; temporal ridges (12) are well developed, widely separate, and distinctively U-shaped, or lyre-shaped, when they converge at the posterior of the braincase to form a small sagittal crest (13) (this is unique to the gray and island foxes). Between the ridges, the braincase is relatively smooth, while outside the cranium is pitted (15). Occipital crests are developed; the supraoccipital shield (14) is small.

Ventral: The long palate (15) terminates at the posterior edge of the last molar (16); the incisive foramina (17) are medium and well forward on the palate. The pterygoid region (18) is broad, and the pterygoid processes (19) are proportionately longer. The mandibular fossa (20) is well developed. The auditory bullae (21) are larger, oval, and inflated. The foramen magnum (22) is medium, and the occipital condyles (23) are stout. Compared with those of other wild canines, the toothrows are proportionately shorter, the carnassial (24) is reduced and thin, and the posterior molars (25) are proportionately wider and flatter.

Lateral: From the elevated braincase, the dorsolateral outline curves smoothly and relatively gradually down to the plane of the rostrum; the height of the rostrum is less than in other canines. Importantly, the braincase does not rise significantly above the temporal ridges (26) from this perspective, a character of island foxes. The premaxillaries (27) extend farther than the nasals (28). The infraorbital foramina are small and visible low on the side of the rostrum. The postorbital processes on the zygomatic arches (29) are small; the jugals (30) are stout. The auditory meatus (31) is medium. The carnassial (32) is smaller. The premolars (33) are well spaced, which is rarely the case in domestic breeds of similar size. The canines are shorter, slender, and recurved.

Mandible: The body (34) is thin, long, and straighter, tapering slightly to the anterior. The coronoid process (35) is near vertical, large, and squared. The condyle (36)

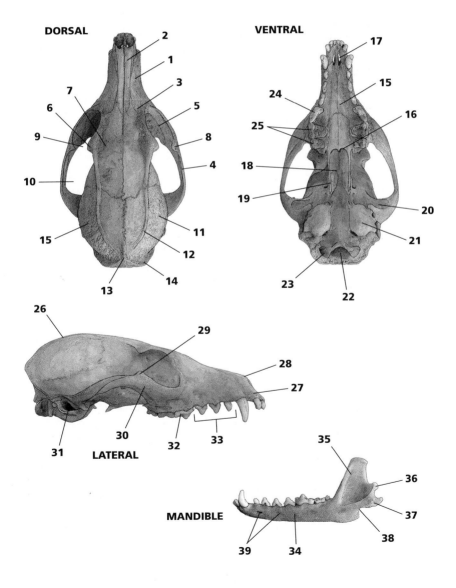

sits slightly above the toothrow and is stout and barrel-shaped. The angular process (37) is small, stout, and rounded, and there is a distinctive step (38) at the posterior, unique to the gray and island foxes. Two mental foramina (39) are evident.

Similar species: Island foxes, kit and swift foxes, and domestic dogs. See family notes.

Notes: Males are larger than females. For more details on differentiating between gray and island foxes, see the notes in the species account for the island fox.

Island gray fox, *Urocyon littoralis*

Greatest length: 96.8–110.3 mm ($3^8/10$–$4^3/10$ in.) (full table of measurements page 594, life-size image page 127, life-size jaw page 166)

Specimen illustrated: Adult male, LACM 7962

Dentition: i 3/3 c 1/1 p 4/4 m 2/3, total 42.

Dorsal: The island gray fox is a smaller version of the gray fox, with a few distinctive characters. Canine skulls have a somewhat slender, triangular outline, especially from the posterior of the zygomatic arches forward. The rostrum (1) is shorter and very slender. The nasals (2) are very long and slender, extending into the anterior of the orbit and aligned with the maxillaries (3). Heavy, wide-spreading (though less than in other canines) zygomatic arches (4) strongly converge to the anterior; zygomatic plates (5) are proportionately larger. Postorbital processes from the frontals (6) are stout and triangular, and there is a significant depression (7) just behind them in the frontal bones; postorbital processes are slender and triangular from the zygomatic arches (8) as well. The orbits (9) are forward and are larger for a canine; the temporal fossa (10) is smaller. The interorbital breadth is less than the postorbital. The braincase (11) is proportionately very large and oval, approaching 50 percent of the greatest length of skull; temporal ridges (12) are well developed, widely separate, and distinctively U-shaped, or lyre-shaped, when they converge at the posterior of the braincase to form a small sagittal crest (13) (this is unique to the island and gray foxes). Between the ridges, the braincase is relatively smooth, while outside the cranium is pitted (14). Occipital crests are developed; supraoccipital shield (15) is small.

Ventral: The long palate (16) terminates at the posterior edge of the last molar (17); the incisive foramina (18) are medium and well forward on the palate. The pterygoid region (19) is broad, and the pterygoid processes (20) are proportionately longer. The mandibular fossa (21) is well developed. The auditory bullae (22) are larger, oval, and inflated. The foramen magnum (23) is medium, and the occipital condyles (24) are stout. Compared with those of other wild canines, the toothrows are proportionately shorter, the carnassial (25) is thin, and the posterior molars (26) are proportionately wider and flatter.

Lateral: From the elevated braincase, the dorsolateral outline curves smoothly and relatively gradually down to the plane of the rostrum; the height of the rostrum (27) is less than in other canines. Importantly, the braincase (28) rises significantly above the temporal ridges (29) from this perspective, a character different from the gray fox. The premaxillaries (30) extend farther than the nasals (31). The infraorbital foramina (32) are small and visible low on the side of the rostrum. The post-

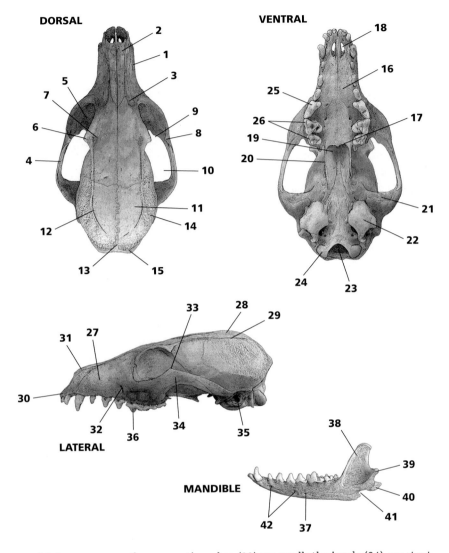

DORSAL

VENTRAL

LATERAL

MANDIBLE

orbital processes on the zygomatic arches (33) are small; the jugals (34) are stout. The auditory meatus (35) is medium. The carnassial (36) is smaller. The premolars are well spaced, which is rarely the case in domestic breeds of similar size. The canines are short, slender, and recurved.

Mandible: The body (37) is long and straighter, tapering slightly to the anterior. The coronoid process (38) is near vertical, large, and rectangular. The condyle (39) sits slightly above the toothrow and is stout and barrel-shaped. The angular process (40) is small, stout, and rounded, and there is a distinctive step (41) at the posterior, unique to the island and gray foxes. Two mental foramina (42) are evident.

Similar species: The gray fox, kit and swift foxes, and domestic dogs.

(Continued on next page.)

Notes: Males are larger than females. Moore and Collins (1995) explain how to differentiate between island and gray foxes: "Cranial characters that differentiate island foxes from gray foxes include: smaller size, approximately 83% as large (Collins, 1982); nasal bones that are wider relative to their lengths; lack of bifurcation along the anterior base of the malar; lyre-shaped temporal ridges that are less developed and more widely separated; and a more convex roof to the cranium between the temporal ridges (Grinnell et al., 1937)." Collins (1982) and Moore and Collins (1995) also provide clues to determine the relative age of skulls: Juveniles and subadults show no wear on the upper first molar, and the basisphenoid-basioccipital and basisphenoid-presphenoid sutures are open; young adults have closed sutures but little wear on the molar; adults have considerable wear on M1. In addition, Collins (1993) provides a diagram to aging specimens using molar tooth wear.

Family Ursidae: Bears

The canines of bears are impressive in size but blunt. The molars are broad and flattened for crushing, and carnassials are poorly developed for shearing; yet the dentition of bears allows for diverse application, from limited shearing to powerful crushing. The temporalis muscles are reduced, along with the related sagittal crests and postorbital processes. Zygomata are heavy, providing solid anchorage for larger masseter muscles and evidence of the balancing of power between the anterior and posterior of the jaws, a characteristic of omnivores. Mandibles allow for some lateral movement for crushing, as well as solid closing of the mouth for power.

The polar bear exhibits a number of modifications to support a more carnivorous diet. Sagittal crests are better developed, and the canines and incisors are well developed, for tearing chunks of flesh from a carcass. The carnassials are also more sharply cusped.

Differentiating between black *(Ursus americanus)* and brown bear *(U. arctos)* skulls is a much more difficult task than might be assumed, because of the great variability in size and shape of black and brown bears across North America. Various descriptions have been issued: Grinnell et al. (1937) write that the skull of the brown bear is narrower than that of the black, and the highest point of the skull is farther to the posterior than in blacks. Others report that the curvature of the braincase, from the lateral perspective, is more gradual in brown bears than in blacks. Hoffmeister (1986) writes that the fourth upper premolar (P4) has median accessory cusps in the brown bear, but they are absent in the black bear.

The most reliable means to differentiate between these two closely related species seems to be to measure the upper molar teeth in the cranium. Gordon (1977) suggests measuring the first molar (the second to last tooth in the row); this is greater than 20.4 millimeters long and 10.5 millimeters wide for brown bears and less for black bears. In 1955, Storer and Tevis (Craighead and Mitchell 1982) suggested measuring the posteriormost molar, which they found was rarely in brown bears less than 38 millimeters, whereas in the black bear, it was less than 31 millimeters. I have measured a number of brown bear molars less than 38 millimeters, yet the 31-millimeters cutoff

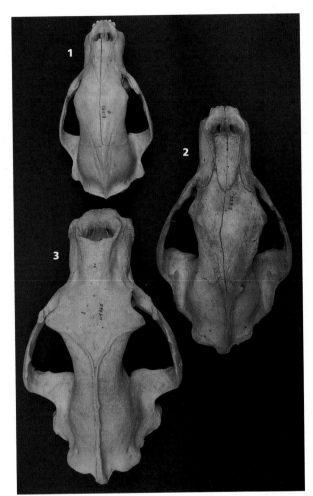

Members of the family Ursidae: 1. American black bear, male 81581 *(U. americanus)*, **2. Brown or grizzly bear, male 323** *(U. arctos)*, **3. Polar bear, male 119065** *(U. maritimus).* MUSEUM OF VERTEBRATE ZOOLOGY, UC BERKELEY.

has held firm. Grinnell et al. (1937) measured the same posterior molar and provide the cutoff point of $1^{1}/_{4}$ inches (31.5 millimeters), which is almost identical.

The shape of the posterior molar is also a useful character. The tooth is generally widest at the anterior in brown bears but widest at the midpoint in black bears.

American black bear, *Ursus americanus*

Greatest length: 235.0–349.0 mm (9³/₁₀–13⁷/₁₀ in.) (full table of measurements page 594, life-size image page 146, life-size jaw page 172)

Specimen illustrated: Subadult (?) male, SBMNH 2049

Dentition: i 3/3 c 1/1 p 4/4 m 2/3, total 42. Premolars are often lost in life, and carnassials are absent.

Dorsal: Bear skulls are massive, with wide-spreading zygomatics; large, broad frontals; and broad rostrums. The rostrum (1) is shorter than in canines but longer than in felines, very broad and strong; the nasals (2) are shorter, stout, and triangular, extending to the posterior to the midline of the orbits. The nasal vacuity (3) is broad. The zygomatic arches (4) are heavy, wide-spreading, and curved, converging to the anterior; postorbital processes from the frontals (5) are thickened and triangular, and from the zygomatics (6) more slender and longer. The orbits (7) are small and well forward of the midline of the skull; the temporal fossa (8) is very large. The frontal region (9) and interorbital breadth are very large and swollen, one of the distinctive features of bear skulls. The braincase (10) is large and narrower than the postorbital processes; smaller temporal ridges (11) coalesce with age, converging to form a sagittal crest (12) at the posterior of the skull. Occipital crests (13) are well developed. The mastoid processes (14) are very large and, together with the squamosal arm of the zygomatic arch (15), form a shelf at the posterior of the skull.

Ventral: The long, broad palate (16) extends well beyond the posterior molars. Toothrows are long, though proportionately shorter than those of canines. The incisive foramina (17) are a bit larger. The pterygoid region (18) is narrow, and the pterygoid processes (19) are shorter. The mandibular fossa (20) is well developed. Auditory bullae (21) are small, deformed, and flattened. Molars are broad and flattened; the posterior molar (22) is broadest at its midpoint.

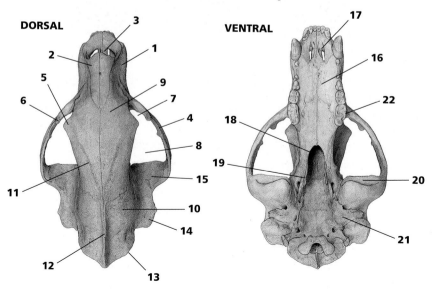

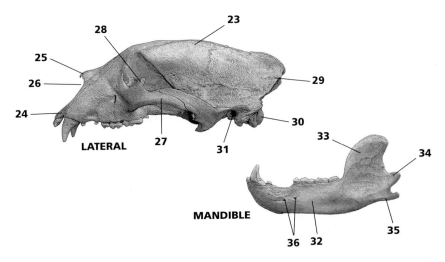

Lateral: The dorsolateral outline is strongly curved, the braincase (23) is well elevated, and the skull as a whole is very deep. The premaxillaries (24) extend well beyond the nasals (25), and the nasal vacuity (26) is very large and sloping. The zygomatics (27) are stout, with narrow postorbital projections (28) far to the anterior. The supraoccipital shield (29) extends far beyond the occipital condyles (30), which is not the case in polar bears. The auditory meatus (31) is small.

Mandible: The mandible is heavy; the body (32) is deep and straight, and then curves at the anterior. The coronoid process (33) is large, stout, and rounded, curving to the posterior. The condyle (34) is stout and barrel-shaped. The angular process (35) is slender and longer, pointing to the posterior. Two mental foramina (36) are evident.

Similar species: Brown and polar bears (family notes), gray wolves, and large domestic dogs.

Notes: Sexing skulls by the size of the canine teeth is described in Sauer (1966).

Brown or grizzly bear, *Ursus arctos*

Greatest length: 230.3–422.0 mm (9^1/$_{10}$–16^6/$_{10}$ in.) (full table of measurements page 596, life-size image page 149, life-size jaw page 175)

Specimen illustrated: Adult male, MVZ 223

Dentition: i 3/3 c 1/1 p 4/4 m 2/3, total 42. Premolars are often lost in life, and carnassials are lacking.

Dorsal: Bear skulls are massive, with wide-spreading zygomatics; large, broad frontals; and broad rostrums. The rostrum (1) is shorter than in canines but longer than in felines, very broad and strong; the nasals (2) are shorter, stout, and triangular, extending to the posterior to the midline of the orbits. The nasal vacuity (3) is broad. The zygomatic arches (4) are heavy, wide-spreading, and curved, converging to the anterior; postorbital processes from the frontals (5) are thickened and triangular, and from the zygomatics (6) more slender and longer. The orbits (7) are small and well forward of the midline of the skull; the temporal fossa (8) is very large. The frontal region (9) and interorbital breadth are very large and swollen, one of the distinctive features of bear skulls. The braincase (10) is large and as wide as the postorbital processes; smaller temporal ridges (11) coalesce with age, converging to form a sagittal crest (12) at the posterior of the skull. Occipital crests (13) are well developed. The mastoid processes (14) are very large and, together with the squamosal arm of the zygomatic arch (15), form a shelf at the posterior of the skull. Note also the incredible asymmetry of the temporal ridges and crests in this animal.

Ventral: The long, broad palate (16) extends well beyond the posterior molars. Toothrows are long, though proportionately shorter than those of canines. The incisive foramina (17) are a bit larger. The pterygoid region (18) is narrow, and the pterygoid processes (19) are shorter. The mandibular fossa (20) is well developed.

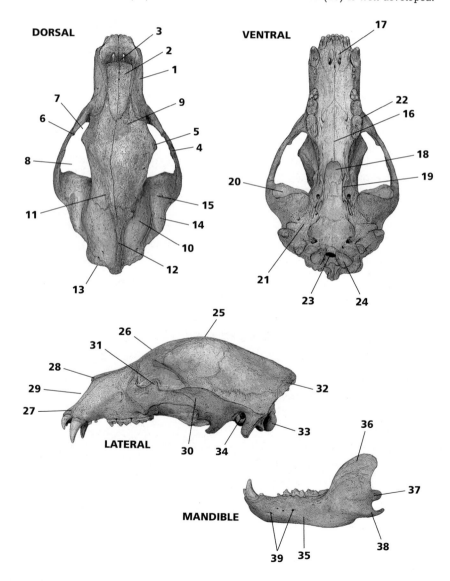

Auditory bullae (21) are small, deformed, and flattened. Molars are broad and flattened; the posterior molar (22) is broadest at the anterior. The foramen magnum (23) is small, and occipital condyles (24) are stout.

Lateral: The dorsolateral outline is strongly curved, the braincase (25) is well elevated, and the skull as a whole is very deep. The domed forehead (26) in this animal is characteristic of coastal brown bears on and near Kodiak Island, Alaska; interior brown bears and southern populations have a dorsolateral outline more similar to that of the black bear. The premaxillaries (27) extend beyond the nasals (28), and the nasal vacuity (29) is very large and sloping. The zygomatics (30) are stout, with narrow postorbital projections (31) far to the anterior. The supraoccipital shield (32) extends far beyond the occipital condyles (33), which is not the case in polar bears. The auditory meatus (34) is small.

Mandible: The mandible is heavy; the body (35) is deep and straight, and then curves at the anterior. The coronoid process (36) is large, stout, and rounded, curving to the posterior. The condyle (37) is stout and barrel-shaped. The angular process (38) is slender and longer, pointing to the posterior. Mental foramina (39) are evident.

Similar species: Black and polar bears (family notes), gray wolves, and large domestic dogs.

Notes: There is tremendous size variation in brown bears depending on geographic range, so much so that specimens of unknown origin are difficult to sex based on cranial measurements (Rausch 1953). The largest Alaska brown bear skull to be recorded measured 455.6 millimeters long and 325.4 millimeters wide (Schartz et al. 2003).

Polar bear, *Ursus maritimus*

Greatest length: 318.0–410.0 mm (12^5/10–16^1/10 in.) (full table of measurements page 596, life-size image page 154, life-size jaw page 175)

Specimen illustrated: Adult male, MVZ 119065

Dentition: i 3/3 c 1/1 p 2–4/2–4 m 2/3, total 34–42. Premolars are often lost in life.

Dorsal: Bear skulls are massive, with wide-spreading zygomatics; large, broad frontals; and broad rostrums. The rostrum (1) is broader and more robust than in black and brown bears; the nasals (2) are short, stout, and triangular, extending to the posterior to the midline of the orbits. The nasal vacuity (3) is broad. The zygomatic arches (4) are heavy, wide-spreading, and curved, converging to the anterior; postorbital processes from the frontals (5) are thickened and triangular, and from the zygomatics (6) more slender and longer. The orbits (7) are very small and well forward of the midline of the skull; the temporal fossa (8) is larger than in other bears. The frontal region (9) and interorbital breadth are proportionately larger than in other bears; the postorbital is narrower. The braincase (10) is large and narrower than the postorbital processes; well-developed temporal ridges (11) coalesce with age, converging to form a large sagittal crest (12) for the length of the braincase. Occipital crests are well developed; the supraoccipital shield (13) is wider. The mastoid processes (16) are very large and, together with the squamosal arm of the zygomatic arch (17), form a shelf at the posterior of the skull.

Ventral: The long, broad palate (18) extends well beyond the posterior molars. Toothrows are long, though proportionately shorter than those of canines. The incisive foramina (19) are a bit larger. The pterygoid region (20) is narrow, and the pterygoid processes (21) are shorter. The mandibular fossa (22) is well developed. Auditory bullae (23) are small, deformed, and flattened. Molars are flattened, though a small shearing surface (24) is developed. The molars as a whole are reduced compared with those of black and brown bears; polar bear teeth are primarily used for tearing.

Lateral: The dorsolateral outline is flatter than in the other bears, the braincase (25) less elevated, and the rostrum (26) longer and deeper. The premaxillaries (27)

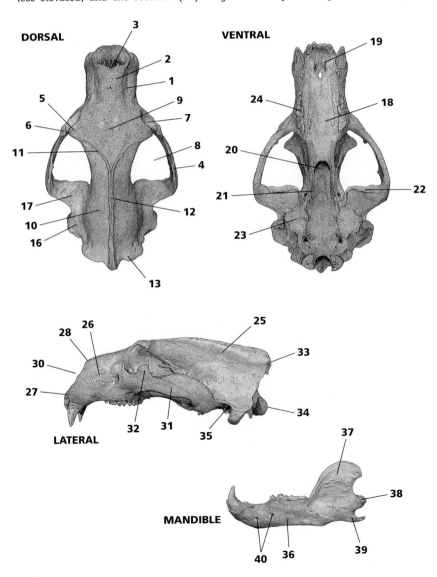

extend beyond the nasals (28), and the nasal vacuity (30) is very large and sloping. The zygomatics (31) are stouter and deeper than in black and brown bears, with stouter postorbital projections (32) far to the anterior. The posterior edge of the supraoccipital crest (33) is aligned with the posterior of the condyles (34), which is not the case in black and brown bears. The auditory meatus (35) is small.

Mandible: The mandible is heavy; the body (36) is more slender and straight, and then curves at the anterior. The coronoid process (37) is large, stout, and rounded, curving to the posterior. The condyle (38) is stout and barrel-shaped. The angular process (39) is slender and longer, pointing to the posterior. Two mental foramina (40) are evident.

Notes: Sexual dimorphism is the most pronounced of any bear (Amstrup 2003). Premolars are small, creating a larger gap between canines and molars, an adaptation believed to aid in holding large prey. Amstrup includes a means of determining age in polar bears using tooth replacement and wear. Bears in their first fall and winter have small, cone-shaped canines; early in their second year, the teeth are still conical in cross section, meaning they are not fully erupted; and in their second winter, just before their second birthday, their canines finally reach adult status and have distinctive bases and crowns. Larsen (1971) provides research that differentiated males from females in one population by the length of the toothrows, measured from the anterior of P4 to the posterior of M2, and on the mandible from the anterior of p4 to the posterior of m3. Upper toothrows: males 58 to 70 millimeters, females 50 to 60. Mandibular toothrow: males 68 to 78 millimeters, females 60 to 70.

Similar species: Brown bears, black bears, elephant seals, sea lions, and wolves.

Family Otariidae: Sea lions and fur seals

Eared seals are characterized by their large orbits and large postorbital processes. Their teeth are simple and conical, ideal for capturing, holding, and tearing slippery fish and squid, which constitute much of their diet. The mandible is afforded considerable lateral movement as well.

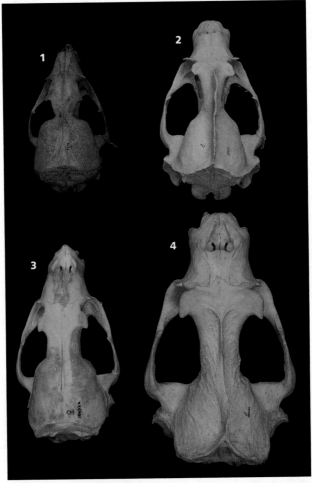

Select members of Otariidae: Female (1) and male (2) California sea lions *(Zalophus californianus)* 4103 and 139211, and below female (3) and male (4) Steller's sea lions *(Eumetopias jubatus)* 186326 and 13680. MUSEUM OF VERTEBRATE ZOOLOGY, UC BERKELEY.

California sea lion, *Zalophus californianus*

Greatest length: 232.9–304.8 mm ($9^2/10$–12 in.) (full table of measurements page 596, life-size image pages 140 and 145, life-size jaw page 173)

Specimen illustrated: Adult male, SBMNH 941, adult female, dorsal only, private collection.

Dentition: i 3/2 c 1/1 p 4/4 m 2/1, total 36.

Dorsal: California sea lion skulls are large, slender, and triangular, with well-developed postorbital processes and peglike teeth. The rostrum (1) is relatively long and slender; the nasals (2) are shorter and triangular, tapering to the posterior. The zygomatic arches (3) are long and wide-spreading, and they strongly converge to the anterior. Postorbital processes (4) are large, well developed, triangular, and situated far forward on the skull; the orbits (5) are relatively large and forward facing, and the temporal fossa (6) is large. The interorbital region (7) is broad, and the interorbital breadth is much wider than the very constricted postorbital breadth. The braincase (8) is squared and less than 50 percent of the greatest length of skull; temporal ridges (9) are well developed, coalesce with age, and converge on the frontals in adult males to form a large sagittal crest (10) that extends for more than half the length of the skull. Occipital crests (11) are less developed. The mastoid processes (12) are large and visible.

Ventral: The broad palate (13) extends well beyond the posterior teeth. The incisive foramina (14) are relatively long and extend to the posterior beyond the canines. The pterygoid region (15) is broad. The mandibular fossa (16) is well developed. Auditory bullae (17) are small and flattened. The foramen magnum (18) is large, and the occipital condyles (19) are stout. The posterior lacerate foramina (20) are large and distinctive, located just anterior to the smaller condylar foramen (21), which is also very large and distinctive when compared with other carnivores.

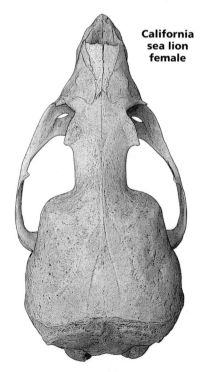

California sea lion female

Lateral: The dorsolateral outline varies with sex and age, from relatively level in females and immature males to significantly convex in older males. The anterior edges of the premaxillaries (22) extend much farther than the nasals (23); the nasal vacuity (24) is large and sloping. The zygomatics (25) are curved, and postorbital processes (26) are developed on the jugals. The pterygoid processes (27) are short. The auditory meatus is obscured. The canine (28) is long and stout, the outermost

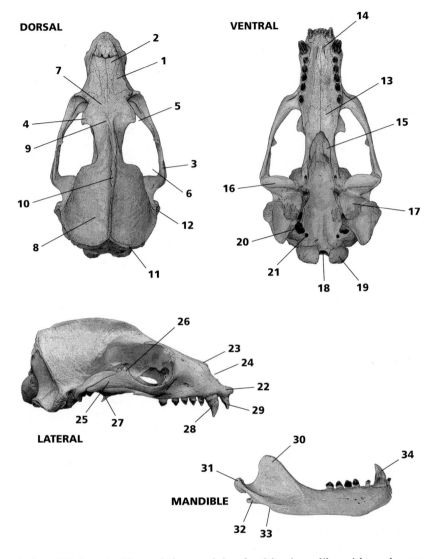

DORSAL

VENTRAL

LATERAL

MANDIBLE

incisor (29) is caninelike, and the remaining dentition is peglike, with mushroom-like tops. Teeth are colored with brown pigment.

Mandible: The mandible is long, strong, and slender. The coronoid process (30) is large, high, and rounded. The condyle (31) is long, stout, and barrel-shaped, and it sits aligned with the toothrow. The angular process (32) is reduced and pointed, and there is a distinctive step (33) in the ventral outline at the posterior of the mandible. The canine (34) is large. On the inside of the mandible, the mandibular symphysis does not fuse with the paired mandible.

Similar species: Northern fur seal, Steller's sea lion, harbor seal, bears, and wolves. Nasals are longer and more slender than in northern fur seal. The spacing of the last upper molar can be used to distinguish between sea lion species: In California sea lions, the last upper molar is spaced roughly evenly with the other molars; in Steller's sea lions *(Eumetopias jubatus)*, it is farther back, creating a larger, disproportionate space between them.

Notes: Males are much larger than females, as seen in the photograph on page 400.

Family Odobenidae: Walruses

The walrus skull is very distinctive, heavy and solid. The great weight of a walrus's skull is thought to aid the animal when breaking through ice flows to create breathing holes in winter. The ivory tusks are also distinctive, modified upper canines that grow larger in males than in females. During the breeding season, males use their tusks to attract females, and in defense. The skull is also accentuated to the posterior by massive mastoid processes and very large occipital condyles, both adaptations that allow these rotund beasts to haul themselves onto ice flows using only their tusks as anchorage and leverage. The orbits of the walrus are also high and relatively unobstructed by surrounding bones, allowing this pinniped to look directly upward, an adaptation researchers believe aids it while plowing through ice and other debris. (Kastelein 2002)

Walrus, *Odobenus rosmarus*

Greatest length: 319.0–396.0 mm (12⁵/10–15⁶/10 in.) (full table of measurements page 598, life-size image page 150, life-size jaw page 176)
Specimen illustrated: Adult male, MVZ 119066
Dentition: i 1/0 c 1/1 p 3/3 m 0/0, total 18.
Dorsal: Walrus skulls are distinctively dense, incredibly heavy, and rectangular in outline. The rostrum (1) is very broad and strong because of enlarged maxillaries to accommodate the tusks; the nasals (2) are broad and rectangular. The zygomatic arches (3) are short, stout, and bowed outward. Postorbital processes (4) are well developed and far forward on the frontal bones; the orbits (5) are medium and forward facing, and the temporal fossa (6) is large. The interorbital region (7) is very broad, and the interorbital breadth is considerably wider than the very constricted postorbital breadth (8). The braincase (9) is large, short, and very broad; temporal ridges are weak, coalescing with age, and occipital crests (10) are developed. The mastoid processes (11) are large and swollen.
Ventral: The very large and broad palate (12) extends well beyond the posterior molars and is over half the greatest length of the skull. The incisive foramina are obscured. The pterygoid region (13) is short and broad. The mandibular fossa (14) is poorly developed. Auditory bullae (15) are small and flattened. The foramen magnum (16) is large, and the occipital condyles (17) are stout. The teeth posterior to the tusks are all simple and peglike; the first tooth (18) in each row is an incisor.
Lateral: The modified canines, or tusks, (19) of the walrus dominate the skull structure and make their skulls quite distinctive. The anterior edges of the premaxillaries (20) extend farther than the nasals (21), and the nasal vacuity (22) is large and rounded. The zygomatics are thick, and the jugals have well-developed postorbital

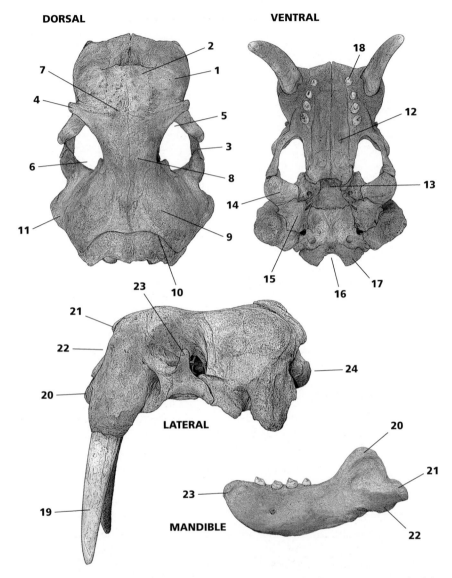

DORSAL

VENTRAL

LATERAL

MANDIBLE

processes (23). The auditory meatus is obscured, and the foramen magnum (24) is elevated to the midpoint of the skull.

Mandible: The mandible is heavy and rounded. The coronoid process (20) is vertical, triangular, and rounded. The condyle (21) is stout and blunt, and it sits aligned with the toothrow. The angular process (22) is much reduced, and there is a step along the ventral surface at the posterior of the mandible. Mandibular symphysis is deep, fused in adults, and a small anterior process projects from each mandible (23).

Notes: Tusks occur in both sexes; male tusks are more elliptical, more robust, and straighter.

Similar species: Steller's sea lions and manatees.

Family Phocidae: Earless or hair seals

Hair seals are characterized by their large orbits and lack of postorbital processes. Their teeth are cusped and conical, ideal for capturing, holding, gulping, and tearing slippery fish and squid, which constitute much of their diet. Conical teeth are also ideal for crushing and piercing tough mollusk shells, much like shrews do insect exoskeletons. The mandible is afforded considerable lateral movement as well.

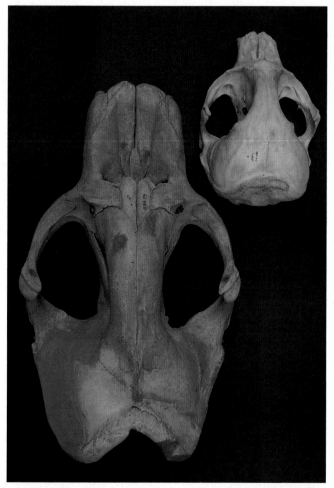

The incredible sexual dimorphism in Northern elephant seals *(Mirounga angustirostris)* is apparent when comparing the massive male's skull and much smaller female's. MUSEUM OF VERTEBRATE ZOOLOGY, UC BERKELEY 113479, 184140.

Harbor seal, *Phoca vitulina*

Greatest length: 174.9–221.0 mm (6⁹/₁₀–8⁷/₁₀ in.) (full table of measurements page 598, life-size image page 139, life-size jaw page 171)

Specimen illustrated: Adult female, SBMNH 1683

Dentition: i 3/2 c 1/1 p 4/4 m 1/1, total 34.

Dorsal: Harbor seal skulls are flattened, with slender rostrums, large orbits, and rounded braincases. The rostrum (1) is slender and triangular; the nasals (2) are long and slender, tapering to the posterior, where they extend between the frontal bones (3); their anterior edges are notched (4). The zygomatic arches (5) are wide-spreading and converge to the anterior. Postorbital processes on the frontals are absent or very small, but better developed on the zygomatic arches (6); the orbits (7) are large and forward facing, and the temporal fossa (8) is reduced. The interorbital region (9) is very narrow and constricted. The braincase (10) is large, round, and less than 50 percent of the greatest length of skull; temporal ridges are weak, coalescing with age, though the surface of the braincase becomes more textured and rugose with age. Occipital crests (11) are weak. The mastoid processes (12) are large and swollen, forming a shelf with the squamosal arm of the zygomatic arch (13).

Ventral: The broad, triangular palate (14) extends well beyond the posterior molars; the posterior edge is V-shaped (15). The incisive foramina (16) extend to the posterior farther than the canines. The pterygoid region (17) is very broad. The mandibular fossa (18) is well developed. Auditory bullae (19) are larger, slightly more inflated, and spaced well apart. The foramen magnum (20) is medium, and the occipital condyles (21) are stout. The jugular foramen (23) is wide.

Lateral: The dorsolateral outline is relatively straight, and then drops down steeply from the tip of the nasals to the tip of the rostrum. The anterior edges of the premaxillaries (24) extend much farther than the nasals (25), and the upper end of the

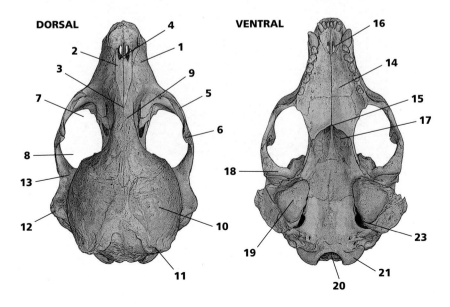

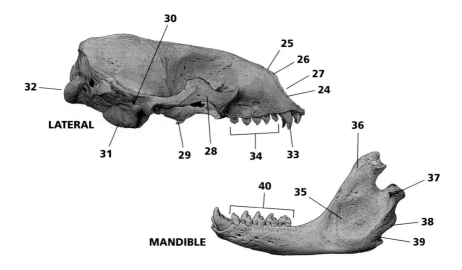

premaxillaries (26) makes contact with the nasals; the nasal vacuity (27) is large and sloping. The zygomatics are thick, and the jugal (28) is shorter. The pterygoid processes (29) are short. The auditory meatus (30) is very small, and the auditory bullae (31) are low. The foramen magnum (32) is slightly elevated. The canines (33) are relatively reduced, and the cheek teeth (34) have two to three cusps each, giving them a serrated appearance, whereas gray seals have simple peglike teeth.

Mandible: The mandible is long and slender, with a large ramus (35). The coronoid process (36) is tall and angular, pointing to the posterior. The condyle (37) is thick, stout, and barrel-shaped, and it sits well above the toothrow. The angular process (38) is reduced and rounded, with a distinctive step (39) low down on the posterior edge. The dentition is serrated (40).

Similar species: Gray seals, other seals, sea lions, coyotes, wolves.

Note: Harbor seals are less sexually dimorphic than other pinnipeds.

Northern elephant seal, *Mirounga angustirostris*

Greatest length: 232.6–525.0 mm (9²/10–20⁷/10 in.) (full table of measurements page 598, life-size image pages 146 and 157, life-size jaw page 177)

Specimens illustrated: Adult male, SBMNH 1854; adult female (dorsal only), MVZ 184140

Dentition: i 2/1 c 1/1 p 4/4 m 1/1, total 30.

Dorsal: It is more difficult to describe a species in which the skulls of males and females are so radically disproportionate. Yet many features are shared by both sexes, and only the proportions are different. The rostrum (1) is short and broad, much broader in the male; the nasals (2) are tiny, tapering to the posterior, where they extend between the frontal bones (3); the nasal vacuity (4) is enlarged, massive in males. The zygomatic arches (5) are bowed and stout. Postorbital processes are absent; the orbits (6) are relatively large and forward facing, and the temporal fossa (7) is reduced. The interorbital region (8) is long, very narrow, high, and constricted. The braincase (9) is broad, proportionately much larger and rounder in the female (9); the male's is distinctively notched at the posterior; temporal ridges are weak in the female but form a small sagittal crest in males. Occipital crests (10) are developed. The mastoid processes (11) are large and swollen, forming a shelf with the squamosal arm of the zygomatic arch (12).

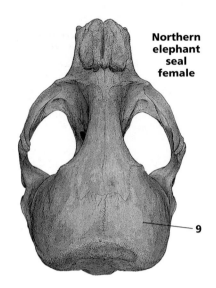

Northern elephant seal female

Ventral: The broad palate (13) extends well beyond the posterior molars. The incisive foramina are obscured. The pterygoid region (14) is very broad. The mandibular fossa (15) is developed. Auditory bullae (16) are large and flattened. The foramen magnum (17) is large, and the occipital condyles (18) are stout, more so in males than females. There are only four incisors, the outer two (19) somewhat canine-shaped.

Lateral: The dorsolateral outline is disrupted in both sexes by the steep drop (20) from the tips of the nasals to the anterior of the premaxillaries (21), creating a very large shelf and nasal vacuity (22). In males, the occipital bone (23) extends above the braincase. The zygomatics are thick and the jugals are short (24) but contribute to the large postorbital processes (25). The auditory meatus is obscured, and the foramen magnum (26) is slightly elevated. The canines (27) are stout, and the remaining dentition (28) is reduced and peglike.

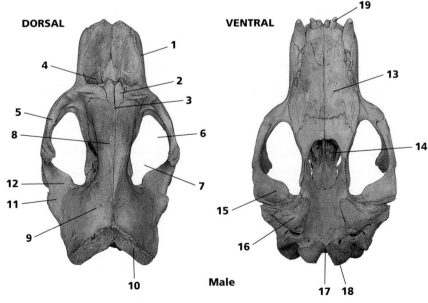

DORSAL

VENTRAL

Male

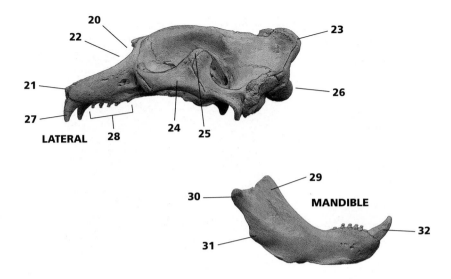

Mandible: The mandible is large and curved. The coronoid process (29) is high and tri-angular. The condyle (30) is stout and barrel-shaped, sitting well above the toothrow. The angular process (31) is greatly reduced and rounded. The canines (32) are large, and there is only one incisor, hidden from view.

Similar species: Mature males: Steller's sea lions and bears. Young males and females: California sea lions, seals, and bears.

Notes: Males are much larger than females, as compared in the photograph on page 405.

Family Procyonidae: Ringtails, raccoons, and coatis

Raccoons are likely the best-known procyonid, and family descriptions generally fol-low the raccoon model. In general, the canines are blunter and shorter; they are larger and bladelike in the coati and slightly more slender in the more carnivorous ringtail. In general, molars are broad and flattened for crushing, yet the dentition of ringtails is more sharply cusped. In general, the carnassials are poorly developed for shearing, but they are more developed in the ringtail. Temporalis muscles are not large, and sagittal crests and postorbital processes are generally small, though they are excep-tionally large in male coatis. The dentition overall supports an omnivorous diet, though the ringtail's modifications support its more carnivorous diet. There is some lateral movement in the mandibles, which aids in crushing, yet the articulation is strong enough to also provide good power when closing the mouth.

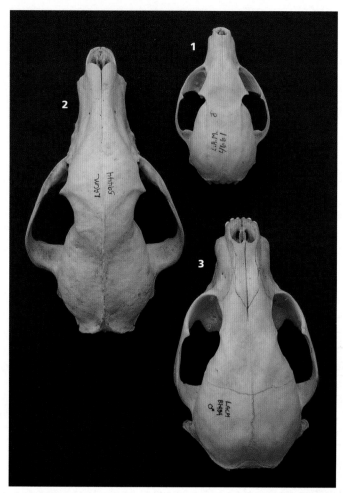

Members of Procyonidae, all males: 1. Ringtail 4661 *(Bassariscus)*, 2. White-nosed coati 59444 *(Nasua)*, 3. Northern raccoon 87484 *(Procyon)*. NATURAL HISTORY MUSEUM OF LOS ANGELES COUNTY.

Ringtail, *Bassariscus astutus*

Greatest length: 70.4–84.8 mm ($2^8/_{10}$–$3^3/_{10}$ in.) (full table of measurements page 598, life-size image page 123, life-size jaw page 164)

Specimen illustrated: Adult male, LACM 9368

Dentition: i 3/3 c 1/1 p 3/4 m 3/2, total 40.

Dorsal: The ringtail skull is small and rounded, with very wide-spreading yet very slim zygomatic arches, a slender rostrum, and a large braincase. The rostrum (1) is very slender. The nasal sutures (2) are fused and obscured in adult animals. Slender, wide-spreading zygomatic arches (3) strongly converge to the anterior; zygomatic plates (4) are proportionately larger than in other carnivores. Postorbital processes from the frontals (5) are large and triangular, and from the zygomatic arches (6) are slender and triangular. The orbits (7) are large and face forward, and the temporal fossa (8) is large. The interorbital breadth (9) is approximately equal to the constricted postorbital breadth. The braincase (10) is very large, flattened, oval, and approximately 50 percent of the greatest length of skull; temporal ridges (11) are small, widely separate, and distinctively U-shaped, or lyre-shaped, when they converge at the posterior of the braincase in some animals to form a small sagittal crest; the braincase is relatively smooth. Occipital crests (12) are developed, and the mastoid processes (13) are larger and visible, forming a shelf with the squamosal arm of the zygomatic arch (14).

Ventral: The narrow palate (15) terminates with the posterior edge of the last molar (16), and a pointy projection (17) extends over the pterygoid region; the incisive foramina (18) are large and situated at the far anterior edge of the palate. The pterygoid region (19) is narrow, and the pterygoid processes (20) are long. The mandibular fossae (21) are well developed. The auditory bullae (22) are medium, oval, and inflated. The foramen magnum (23) is large, and the occipital condyles (24) are smaller. The toothrows are proportionately shorter than in wild canines, and the carnassial (25) is more developed than in other procyonids; the posterior molars (26) are wider than long, and flattened.

Lateral: From the elevated braincase (40), the dorsolateral outline curves smoothly and relatively gradually down to the plane of the rostrum. The premaxillaries (27) extend farther than the nasals (28); the nasal vacuity (29) is relatively large and angled. The infraorbital foramina (30) are larger and visible low on the side of the rostrum. The postorbital processes on the zygomatic arches (31) are small. The auditory meatus (32) is medium. The premolars are well spaced, and the canines (33) are long and slender.

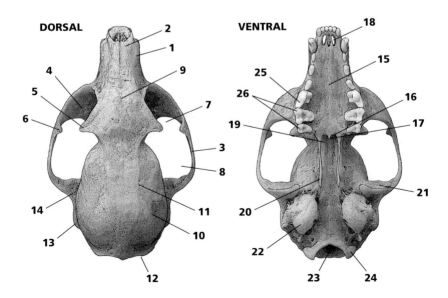

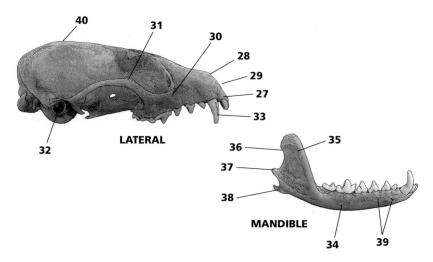

Mandible: The body (34) is long, slender, and curved. The coronoid process (35) is high and slender, pointing to the posterior; the posterior edge (36) is concave. The condyle (37) sits just above the toothrow and is stout and barrel-shaped. The angular process (38) is small, slender, and pointed, and it curves to the posterior. Two mental foramina (39) are evident. The dentition is sharp.

Similar species: River otters, small foxes, and domestic cats.

Notes: Grinnell et al. (1937) describe the following changes in the skull with increased age: increased zygomatic breadth, sharper and wider-spreading postorbital processes, a closer approach of temporal ridges, and a narrowing of the postorbital constriction. They also write that when females and males of corresponding age are compared, males have larger skulls and more developed temporal and occipital ridges. Gilbert (1980) provides a visual means to determine males from females—in females the temporal ridges are much closer together.

Northern raccoon, *Procyon lotor*

Greatest length: 93.6–135.5 mm (3^7/10–5^5/10 in.) (full table of measurements page 598, life-size image page 130, life-size jaw page 167)

Specimen illustrated: Adult female, SBMNH 875

Dentition: i 3/3 c 1/1 p 4/4 m 2/2, total 40. Variation in the number of premolars has been recorded. Teeth are for crushing—flattened, broad, and without deep cusps.

Dorsal: The raccoon skull is triangular in outline, with a short, broad rostrum; long, wide-spreading zygomatic arches, and a large braincase. The rostrum (1) is shorter and broad. The nasals (2) are long and constricted (3) at their midpoints; sutures obscure with old age. Strong, wide-spreading zygomatic arches (4) converge to the anterior; zygomatic plates (5) are larger. Postorbital processes from the frontals (6) are small and triangular, and from the zygomatic arches (7) are slender and triangular. The orbits (8) are medium and face forward, and the temporal fossa (9) is large. The interorbital breadth is approximately equal to the postorbital. The braincase (10) is very large, oval, relatively smooth, and approaching 50 percent of the greatest length of skull; temporal ridges (11) are well developed, converging high on the skull in a V shape to form a long sagittal crest (12). Occipital crests are developed, and the supraoccipital shield (13) is small. Mastoid processes (14) are large but not inflated.

Ventral: The very long palate (15) narrows considerably as it extends beyond the posterior molars, and it terminates with a large, pointy projection (16) over the pterygoid region; the incisive foramina (17) are small and forward of the canines. The pterygoid region (18) is small, and the pterygoid processes (19) are short. The mandibular fossae (20) are well developed. The auditory bullae (21) are medium, oval, and inflated. The foramen magnum (22) is medium, and the occipital condyles

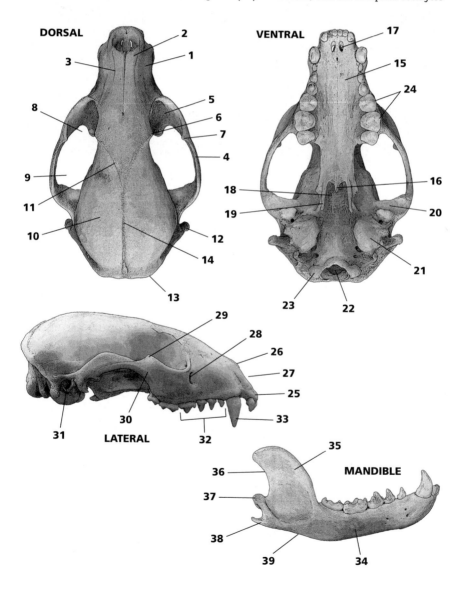

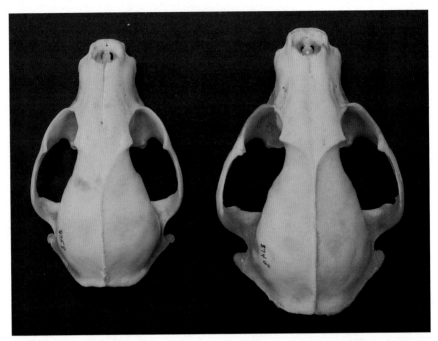

Adult female on the left, and an adult male on the right. SANTA BARBARA MUSEUM OF NATURAL HISTORY 874, 875.

(23) are stout. The posterior molars are all flattened and blunt, and a developed carnassial is absent; the fourth and fifth cheek teeth (24) are larger than sixth (last molar).

Lateral: From the elevated braincase, the dorsolateral outline curves smoothly down to the plane of the rostrum. The premaxillaries (25) extend farther than the nasals (26); the nasal vacuity (27) is medium and sloping. The infraorbital foramina (28) are small and visible low on the side of the rostrum. The postorbital processes (29) on the zygomatic arches are small; the jugals (30) are stout. The auditory meatus (31) is medium. The premolars (32) are tightly spaced. The canine (33) is large and straight.

Mandible: The body (34) is long and curved. The coronoid process (35) is large, rounded, and curved strongly to the posterior; the posterior edge (36) is concave. The condyle (37) is aligned with the toothrow, stout, and barrel-shaped. The angular process (38) is small, slender, and pointed, pointing to the posterior; there is a steep incline (39) to the posterior just beyond the last molar.

Similar species: Often confused with badgers. Also, coatis, otters, fishers, and foxes.

Notes: Males have more developed sagittal crests, larger canines, and reach a larger overall size than females (see above image). Individual variation is great when comparing across geographic populations and age classes. Gehrt (2003) reports that the largest raccoons are found in the U.S. Northwest and the smallest in the Southeast.

White-nosed coati, *Nasua narica*

Greatest length: 119.4–138.0 mm ($4^7/_{10}$–$5^4/_{10}$ in.) (full table of measurements page 600, life-size image page 135, life-size jaw page 169)

Specimen illustrated: Adult male, LACM 59444

Dentition: i 3/3 c 1/1 p 4/4, m 2/2, total 40.

Dorsal: The coati skull is somewhat doglike, with a triangular outline and long, slender rostrum. Yet confusion should be short-lived. The rostrum (1) is long, slender, and distinctly constricted (2) at its midpoint. The nasals (3) are long, but sutures are obscured in adult animals. Heavy, wide-spreading zygomatic arches (4) strongly converge to the anterior; zygomatic plates (5) are small. Postorbital processes from the frontals (6) are stout and pointed. The orbits (7) are medium, and the temporal fossa (8) is large. The interorbital breadth (9) is greater than the postorbital. The braincase (10) is medium, oval, and much less than 50 percent of the greatest length of skull; temporal ridges (11) are well developed, converging high on the skull to form a sagittal crest (12). (Males develop large crests with age, whereas younger males and females may have relatively smooth craniums.) Occipital crests are developed, and the supraoccipital shield (13) is narrow.

Ventral: The exceptionally long palate (14) is depressed along the midline (15), and it terminates near the squamosal arm of the zygomatic arches; three incisive foramina (16) are well forward on the palate. The pterygoid region (17) is small and narrow. The mandibular fossa (18) are well developed. The auditory bullae (19) are medium, round, and very inflated. The foramen magnum (20) is medium, and the occipital condyles are stout. There is a significant gap (21) between the slender canine and first premolar; the posterior molars are wide and flattened, and the fourth cheek tooth (M1) (22) is as long as wide.

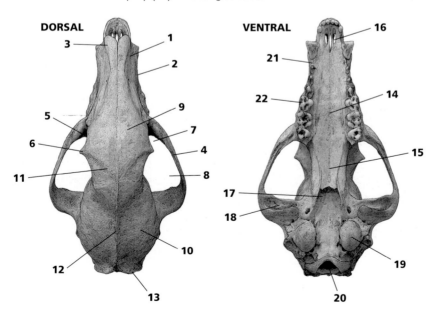

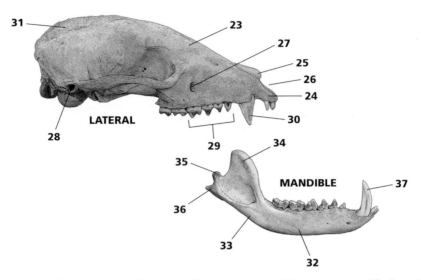

Lateral: From the elevated braincase, the dorsolateral outline curves smoothly down the swollen frontals (23) to the plane of the rostrum; the premaxillaries (24) extend to the anterior far beyond the nasals (25), and the nasal vacuity (26) is low and long. The infraorbital foramina (27) are small and visible low on the side of the rostrum.

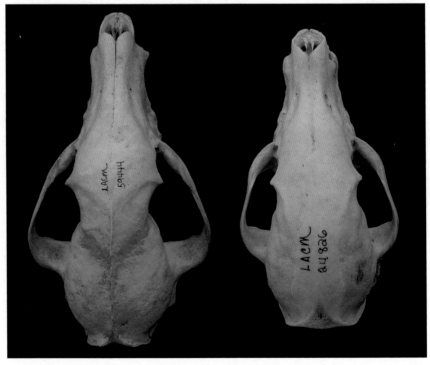

Adult male coati on the left, and adult female on the right. NATURAL HISTORY MUSEUM OF LOS ANGELES COUNTY 59444, 24826.

The postorbital processes on the zygomatic arches are absent. The auditory meatus (28) is small. The premolars (29) are tight together, and the canines (30) are triangular, knifelike, and very distinctive. Note also the development of the sagittal crest (31).

Mandible: The body (32) is long and straighter, but the mandible curves steeply up (33) posterior to the last molar. The coronoid process (34) is vertical, rounded, and shorter. The condyle (35) sits above the toothrow and is stout and barrel-shaped. The angular process (36) is small, slender, and pointed. The canines (37) are large, knifelike, and distinctive.

Similar species: Foxes, coyotes, raccoons, badgers, and opossums.

Notes: Males are larger and have a more developed sagittal crest than females (see page 416).

Family Mustelidae: Weasels, otters, and badgers

Mustelids are a diverse group in size and form, from the tiny least weasel to the massive sea otters. In general, the family is characterized by their long and slender canines, well-developed carnassials, and short, rounded mandibles. Temporalis muscles attach to longer, larger braincases and well-developed sagittal crests. Smaller zygomatics reveal the much lesser development of the masseter muscles.

In otters, 80 percent of the muscle weight attached to the mandibles is in the temporalis muscles (Ewer 1973). Longer braincases provide ample area for temporalis muscles to expand and attach, which allows them to pull the short jaws from farther to the posterior than in other carnivores. This shift in angles and physics allows for power to be delivered at the anterior of the mouth to drive canines home when biting to kill, as well as to be shared with the area of the dentition where the carnassials sit. Whereas greater development of the masseter muscles is the more common means to ensure strong shearing capabilities, the longer braincase and shortened dentition and mandibles of mustelids provide an alternate means to the same end. In addition, mustelids have a more tightly articulated mandible, allowing for little lateral movement and the focusing of power when closing the mouth—characteristics of a true carnivore.

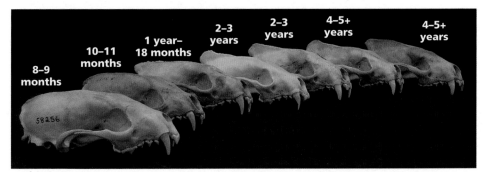

From left to right, note the development of the sagittal crest in male fishers *(Martes pennanti)* with age. Using Powell et al. (2004) as a guide and several known specimens, I've labeled the approximate age of the specimens photographed. These are not definite ages, but best guesses. MUSEUM OF COMPARATIVE ZOOLOGY, HARVARD U 58256, 7437, 59142, 62223, 62615, 62033, 58265.

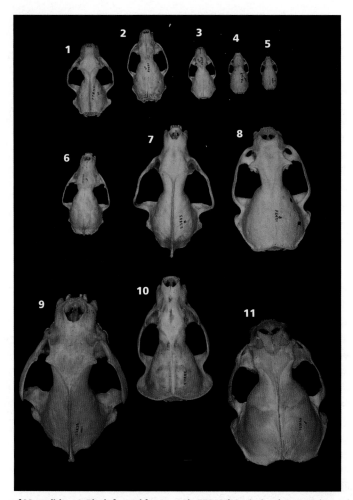

Members of Mustelidae: 1. Black-footed ferret, male 77840 *(M. nigripes)*, **2.** American mink, male 12904 *(M. vison)*, **3.** Long-tailed weasel, male 13778 *(M. frenata)*, **4.** Ermine, male 78129 *(M. erminea)*, **5.** Least weasel, male 71641031 *(M. nivalis)*, **6.** American marten, male 134566 *(Martes americana)*, **7.** Fisher, male 23883 *(Martes pennanti)*, **8.** Northern river otter, female 12475 *(Lontra canadensis)*, **9.** Wolverine, male 12223 *(Gulo gulo)*, **10.** American badger 44202 *(Taxidea taxus)*, **11.** Sea otter, male 16330 *(Enhydra lutris)*. MUSEUM OF VERTEBRATE ZOOLOGY, UC BERKELEY.

Several mustelids are variations on the model above, having specialized in various ways to succeed in niches where other animals cannot. The flattened dentition of badgers and sea otters provides excellent surfaces for crushing vegetation, sea urchins, crabs, and bones. Like Africa's hyenas, wolverines have stout and strong carnassials, and the musculature to work them, allowing them to break bones that most animals cannot. Thus the wolverine can scavenge at carcasses long since abandoned by other animals.

Adult male fishers have exceptional sagittal crests. The male's sagittal crest has begun developing by nine months of age, and by eleven months it is well developed, though not yet extending beyond the supraoccipital bones. In adult males, the sagittal crest continues to enlarge both vertically and to the posterior, extending over the occiput. Small sagittal crests may or may not be present in females. A visual presentation of the development of sagittal crests in males can be seen on page 417, and in both males and females of various ages in Powell et al. (2003).

American marten, *Martes americana*

Greatest length: 67.7–87.9 mm ($2^{7}/_{10}$–$3^{5}/_{10}$ in.) (full table of measurements page 600, life-size image page 124, life-size jaw page 163)

Specimen illustrated: Adult male, SBMNH 3948

Dentition: i 3/3 c 1/1 p 4/4 m 1/2, total 38. Fisher and marten have four upper and lower premolars.

Dorsal: Skulls of the *Martes* species are long and slender, with wide-spreading, slender zygomatics; shorter rostrums; and large, long braincases. The rostrum (1) is short and stout; the nasal sutures (2) are visible only in immature specimens. The zygomatic arches (3) are wide-spreading and very slender, strongly converging to the anterior. Postorbital processes (4) are well developed and sharp; the orbits (5) are relatively large, forward facing, and less than half the size of the massive temporal fossae (6). The interorbital region (7) is broad, and the interorbital breadth is wider than the constricted postorbital breadth (8). The braincase is very long, oval, and more than 50 percent of the greatest length of skull; temporal ridges (9) are well developed, coalesce with age, and converge high on the skull in adult males to form a sagittal crest (10). Occipital crests (11) are also well developed. The mastoid processes (12) are just visible from this perspective.

Ventral: The triangular palate (13) abruptly narrows as it extends well beyond the posterior molars. Toothrows are longer than in *Mustela* species. The incisive foramina (14) are wider and completely forward of the posterior edge of the canines (15). The

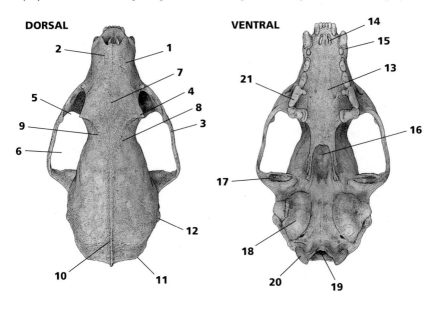

DORSAL   VENTRAL

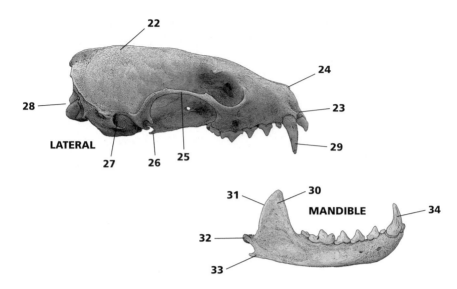

pterygoid region (16) is broad. The mandibular fossa (17) is well developed. Auditory bullae (18) are large and somewhat flattened. The foramen magnum (19) is large, and the occipital condyles (20) are stout. The carnassial (21) is thin and strong.

Lateral: The dorsolateral outline curves gradually down from the elevated braincase (22), and then more steeply drops down the frontals to the rostrum. The anterior

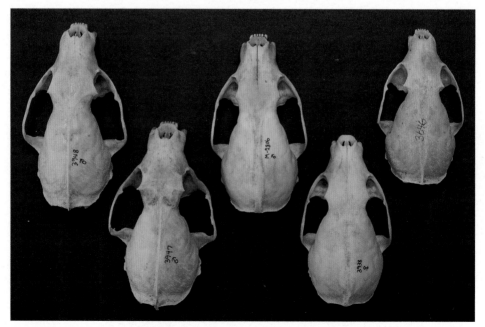

The two left most skulls are older males, the central skull an immature male, and the remaining two skulls are mature females. SANTA BARBARA MUSEUM OF NATURAL HISTORY 3948, 3947, 2806, 3938, 3646.

edges of the premaxillaries (23) extend farther than the nasals (24). The zygomatics (25) are thin, curved, and elevated at their midpoints. The pterygoid processes (26) are short. The auditory meatus (27) is medium, and the foramen magnum (28) is elevated. The canines (29) are long and slender, the dentition jagged.

Mandible: The mandible is strong and curved. The coronoid process (30) is vertical, high, and triangular; the posterior edge (31) is convex in outline. The condyle (32) is stout and barrel-shaped, and it sits aligned with the toothrow. The angular process (33) is reduced and pointed. The canines (34) are large, the dentition jagged.

Similar species: Fishers, black-footed ferrets, striped skunks, and mink.

Notes: There are a number of ways to determine age and sex. Adult dentition is reached within eighteen weeks of age (Strickland et al. 1982). Grinnell et al. (1937) describe changes with age as follows: "actual decrease in gross size of brain case; spreading of zygomatic arches; development (in males) of well-marked sagittal and lambdoidal ridges; lengthening and narrowing of rostrum; development of prominent postorbital processes; narrowing of postorbital constriction in cranium." Sagittal crests develop with age in males, but they may or may not do so in females (see page 420). Strickland et al. (1982) write that though a sagittal crest in a female indicates she is an adult, its absence does not mean she is an immature animal. Poole et al. (1994) compare several methods for aging and sexing specimens and find that the greatest length of skull correctly identifies the sex 99.3 to 100 percent of the time. Relative aging can also be done using temporal muscle coalescence, as described on page 69.

Fisher, *Martes pennanti*

Greatest length: 98.7–135.0 mm ($3^9/_{10}$–$5^3/_{10}$ in.) (full table of measurements page 600, life-size image pages 127 and 135, life-size jaw page 166)

Specimens illustrated: Adult male, MCZ 62033; adult female, MCZ 60626

Dentition: i 3/3 c 1/1 p 4/4 m 1/2, total 38. Fishers and martens have four upper and lower premolars.

Dorsal: Skulls of the *Martes* species are long and slender, with wide-spreading, slender zygomatics; shorter rostrums; and large, long braincases. The rostrum (1) is short and stout; the nasal sutures (2) are visible only in immature specimens. The zygomatic arches (3) are wide-spreading (compare differences between the male and female) and very slender, strongly converging to the anterior. Postorbital processes (4) are developed and trian-

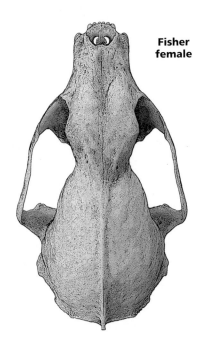

Fisher female

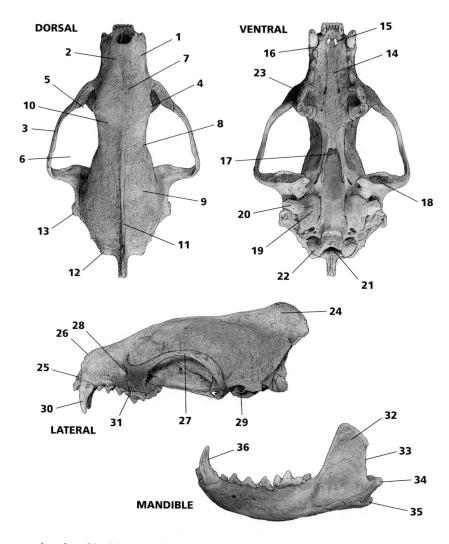

DORSAL

VENTRAL

LATERAL

MANDIBLE

gular; the orbits (5) are smaller, forward facing, and less than half the size of the massive temporal fossae (6). The interorbital region (7) is broad, and the interorbital breadth is wider than the constricted postorbital breadth (8). The braincase (9) is very long, oval, and approximately 50 percent of the greatest length of skull; temporal ridges (10) are well developed, coalesce with age, and converge high on the skull in adult specimens to form a sagittal crest (11). Occipital crests (12) are also well developed. The mastoid processes (13) are larger than in martens and larger in males than females.

Ventral: The triangular palate (14) abruptly narrows as it extends well beyond the posterior molars. Toothrows are longer than in *Mustela* species. The incisive foramina (15) are wider and completely forward of the posterior edge of the canines (16). The pterygoid region (17) is narrow. The mandibular fossa (18) is well developed. Auditory bullae (19) are large and somewhat flattened, with long auditory canals (20). The foramen magnum (21) is smaller, and the occipital condyles (22) are stout. The carnassial (23) is thin and strong.

Lateral: The dorsolateral outline curves gradually down from the elevated braincase, and then more steeply drops down the frontals to the rostrum. In old males, the sagittal crest (24) is massive and a dominant feature at the posterior of the skull. The anterior edges of the premaxillaries (25) extend just past the nasals with which they (26) are nearly aligned. The zygomatics (27) are thin, curved, and elevated at their midpoints. The infraorbital foramen (28) is oval. The auditory meatus (29) is small. The canines (30) are long and slender, the dentition jagged. The fisher has an external median rootlet (31) above the upper carnassial, which is absent in martens.

Mandible: The mandible is strong and curved. The coronoid process (32) is vertical, high, and squared; the posterior edge (33) is straight. The condyle (34) is stout and

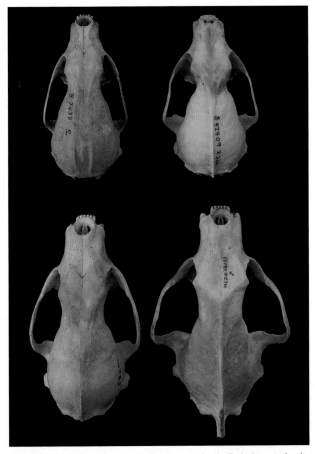

Compare the two female skulls above, with the two male skulls below. In both rows, the left skull is an immature animal and the right a full adult. MUSEUM OF COMPARATIVE ZOOLOGY, HARVARD U 7438, 60626, 58256, 62033.

barrel-shaped, and it sits aligned with the toothrow. The angular process (35) is reduced and pointed. The canines (36) are large, the dentition jagged.

Similar species: Racoons, coatis, martens, tayras, foxes, badgers, and wolverines.

Notes: With age, males exhibit a dramatic increase in the sagittal crest and a bowing out of the zygomatics (refer to the photographs on pages 71 and 417). Zygomatic-temporal, naso-maxillary, and nasofrontal sutures do not fuse in males and females until after one year and are useful in differentiating juveniles from adults. Poole et al. (1994) write: "Because fishers have more sexual dimorphism than martens, techniques involving skull or canine measurements generally have proven to be 100% accurate in determining sex of fishers." Skulls of males are longer than females.

Ermine or short-tailed weasel, *Mustela erminea*

Greatest length: 33.9–46.0 mm ($1^3/10$–$1^8/10$ in.) (full table of measurements page 600, life-size image page 115, life-size jaw page 160)

Specimen illustrated: Adult female, MCZ 50555

Dentition: i 3/3 c 1/1 p 3/3 m 1/2, total 34.

Dorsal: Skulls of the *Mustela* species are long and slender, with short, wide-spreading, and thin zygomatics; very short, broad rostrums; and massive, oval braincases. The rostrum (1) is very short and triangular; the nasal sutures (2) are visible only in immature specimens. The zygomatic arches (3) are wide-spreading and very thin, with large zygomatic plates (4) and large infraorbital foramina (5). Postorbital processes (6) are small and triangular; the orbits (7) are relatively large, forward facing, and approximately 50 percent of the size of the temporal fossae (8). The interorbital breadth (9) may be approximately equal to or slightly wider than the postorbital. The braincase (10) is massive, oval, and approaching two-thirds the greatest length of skull; temporal ridges are weak to developed, depending on geographic population and sex, and sagittal crests are absent or very small. The mastoid processes often are not visible from this perspective. Occipital crests (11) are developed.

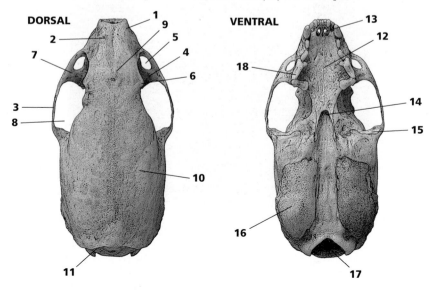

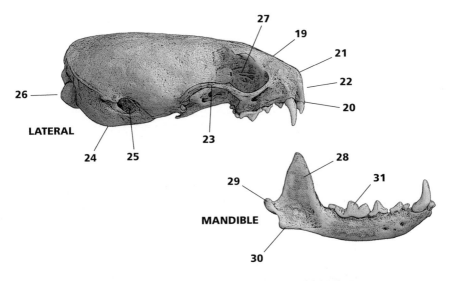

LATERAL

MANDIBLE

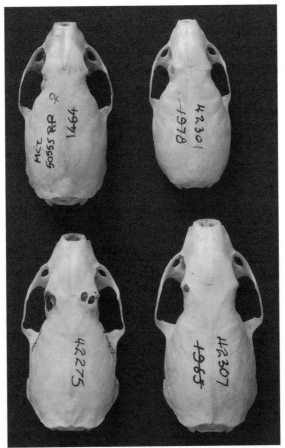

Above, two females, and below two males. Note the damage caused by parasites to the frontal sinuses. MUSEUM OF COMPARATIVE ZOOLOGY, HARVARD U 50555, 1978, 42275, 42307.

Ventral: The triangular palate (12) abruptly narrows as it extends well beyond the posterior molars. Toothrows are relatively short. The incisive foramina (13) are wider and completely forward of the posterior edge of the canines. The pterygoid region (14) is narrow. The mandibular fossa (15) is well developed. Auditory bullae (16) are large, very long, and somewhat flattened; they are closer together than in long-tailed weasels. The foramen magnum (17) is large. The toothrows are short, and the carnassial (18) is thin and strong.

Lateral: The dorsolateral outline is dominated by the braincase, sloping steeply at the anterior (19) to the tip of the rostrum. The anterior edges of the premaxillaries (20) and nasals (21) are aligned, and the nasal vacuity (22) is large and vertical. The zygomatics (23) are thin and curved. The pterygoid processes are short, and less-inflated auditory bullae (24) do not extend ventrally to the level found in long-tailed weasels. The auditory meatus (25) is medium, and the foramen magnum (26) is elevated. From this perspective, the orbit (27) appears large.

Mandible: The mandible is strong and curved. The coronoid process (28) is vertical, high, and triangular. The condyle (29) is stout and barrel-shaped, and it sits aligned with the toothrow. The angular process (30) is reduced and rounded. The carnassial (31) is large, the dentition jagged.

Similar species: Other weasels, mink, and bonnetted bats.

Note: Ermines exhibit pronounced sexual dimorphism (page 425); males are larger and approximately 40 to 80 percent heavier than females (Verts and Carraway 1998).

Long-tailed weasel, *Mustela frenata*

Greatest length: 38.4–53.6 mm ($1^5/_{10}$–$2^1/_{10}$ in.) (full table of measurements page 602, life-size image page 118, life-size jaw page 161)

Specimens illustrated: Adult male, SBMNH 3223; adult male from Maine, MCZ 55501

Dentition: i 3/3 c 1/1 p 3/3 m 1/2, total 34.

Dorsal: Skulls of the *Mustela* species are long and slender, with short, wide-spreading, and thin zygomatics; very short, broad rostrums; and massive, oval braincases. The rostrum (1) is very short, broad, and triangular; the nasal sutures (2) are visible only in immature specimens. The zygomatic arches (3) are wide-spreading and very thin, with large zygomatic plates (4) and large infraorbital foramina (5). Postorbital processes (6) are well developed and

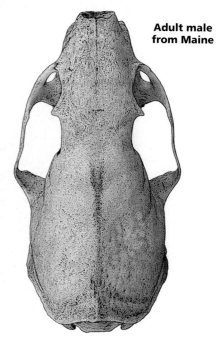

Adult male from Maine

triangular; the orbits (7) are relatively large, forward facing, and approximately 30–50 percent of the size of the massive temporal fossae (8) (depending on location). The interorbital breadth (9) may be approximately equal to or wider than the postorbital, varying across individuals and geographic populations. The braincase (10) is massive, oval, and approaching two-thirds the greatest length of skull; temporal ridges (11) are developed, varying with geographic population and sex, and sagittal (12) and occipital (13) crests are present in mature specimens. Mastoid processes (14) are larger and often visible at the posterior of the skull.

Ventral: The triangular palate (15) abruptly narrows as it extends well beyond the posterior molars. Toothrows are relatively larger than in the ermine. The incisive foram-

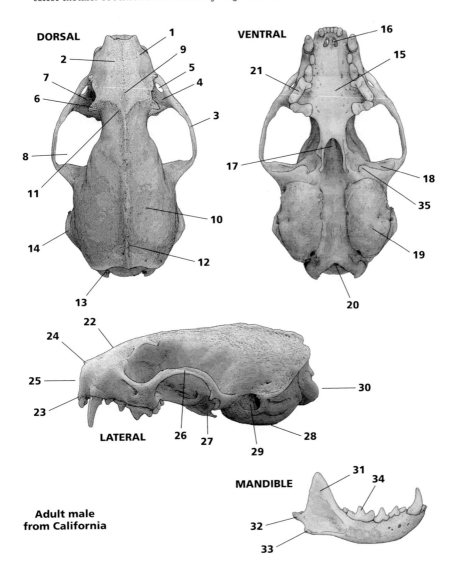

DORSAL

VENTRAL

LATERAL

MANDIBLE

**Adult male
from California**

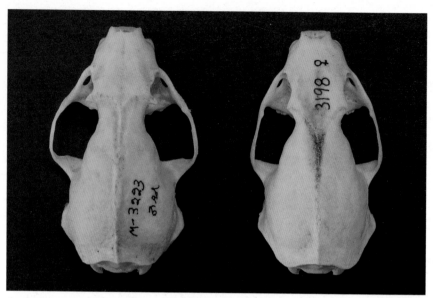

On the left, a mature male, and on the right, a mature female, both from southern California.
SANTA BARBARA MUSEUM OF NATURAL HISTORY 3223, 3198.

ina (16) are wider and completely forward of the posterior edge of the canines. The pterygoid region (17) is narrow. The mandibular fossa (18) is deep and the squamosal process (35) is well developed. Auditory bullae (19) are large, very long, and somewhat flattened; they are situated farther apart than in ermines. The foramen magnum (20) is large. The toothrows are short, and the carnassial (21) is thin and strong.

Lateral: The dorsolateral outline is dominated by the braincase, sloping more steeply at the anterior (22) to the tip of the rostrum. The anterior edges of the premaxillaries (23) and nasals (24) are aligned, and the nasal vacuity (25) is large and vertical. The zygomatics (26) are thin and curved. The pterygoid processes (27) are short, and more-inflated auditory bullae (28) extend lower than the level found in ermines. The auditory meatus (29) is medium, and the foramen magnum (30) is elevated.

Mandible: The mandible is strong and curved, and the body is deeper than in ermines. The coronoid process (31) is vertical, high, and triangular. The condyle (32) is stout and barrel-shaped, and it sits aligned with the toothrow. The angular process (33) is reduced and rounded. The carnassial (34) is large, the dentition jagged.

Similar species: Other weasels, mink, ferrets, and bonnetted bats.

Notes: Hall (1951) describes three age classes: Young animals up to seven and a half months old exhibit visible naso-maxillary and naso-premaxillary sutures. Subadults, from seven and a half to ten months old, have naso-maxillary sutures that are visible but indistinct. Animals over ten months old are considered adults, and sutures are no longer visible. In 1985, K. Ralls and P. Harvey described three different geographic populations: a western population with small males and females and intermediate sexual dimorphism; a central population with large males and females and lower sexual dimorphism; and an eastern population with medium males, small females, and high sexual dimorphism (Sheffield and Thomas 1997).

Black-footed ferret, *Mustela nigripes*

Greatest length: 62.5–70.0 mm ($2^5/_{10}$–$2^8/_{10}$ in.) (full table of measurements page 602, life-size image page 122, life-size jaw page 162)

Specimen illustrated: Adult male, MVZ 77840

Dentition: i 3/3 c 1/1 p 3/3 m 1/2, total 34.

Dorsal: I've seen only male skulls of this species, which are rugose, robust, and angular, with very wide-spreading zygomatics; short, broad rostrums; and well-developed crests. The rostrum (1) is very short and very broad; the nasal sutures (2) are visible only in immature specimens. The zygomatic arches (3) are very wide-spreading and slightly stouter. Postorbital processes (4) are larger and triangular; the orbits (5) are relatively large, forward facing, and approximately 50 percent of the size of the massive temporal fossae (6). The interorbital breadth (7) is much wider than the very constricted postorbital breadth (8). The braincase (9) is large, approximately 50 percent of the greatest length of skull; temporal ridges (10) are very developed, and sagittal crests (11) are large, running the entire length of the braincase. Occipital crests (12) are also well developed. The mastoid processes (13) are swollen and large.

Ventral: The triangular palate (14) abruptly narrows to a greater degree (15) than any other *Mustela* species as it extends well beyond the posterior molars. Toothrows are relatively longer. The incisive foramina (16) are much wider and completely forward of the posterior edge of the canines. The pterygoid region (17) is very narrow. The mandibular fossa (18) is deep and the process on the squamosal (34) is exceptionally developed. Auditory bullae (19) are large, broad, and somewhat flattened. The foramen magnum (20) is large. The carnassial (21) is thin and strong.

Lateral: The dorsolateral outline is dominated by the braincase and sagittal crest, sloping more steeply at the anterior (22) to the tip of the rostrum. The anterior edges of the premaxillaries (23) and nasals (24) are aligned, and the nasal vacuity

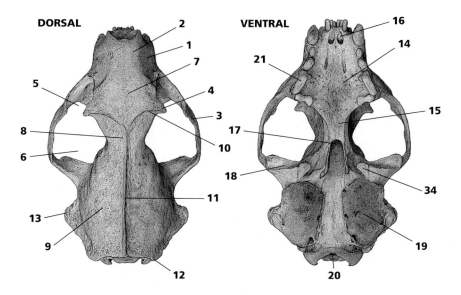

DORSAL   VENTRAL

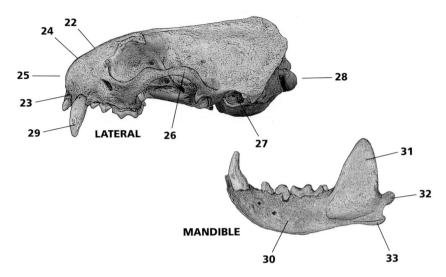

(25) is smaller and vertical. The zygomatics (26) are thin and curved. The ptery-goid processes are short. The auditory meatus (27) is smaller, and the foramen magnum (28) is elevated. The canines (29) are large and straight.

Mandible: The mandible is very robust and curved; the body (30) is very deep. The coronoid process (31) is vertical, high, and triangular. The condyle (32) is stout and barrel-shaped, and it sits aligned with the toothrow. The angular process (33) is reduced and rounded. The dentition is jagged.

Similar species: Mink, long-tailed weasels, martens, and domestic ferrets.

Least weasel, *Mustela nivalis*

Greatest length: 29.0–32.8 mm (1^1/$_{10}$–1^3/$_{10}$ in.) (full table of measurements page 602, life-size image page 113, life-size jaw page 160)

Specimen illustrated: Adult male, MVZ 41031

Dentition: i 3/3 c 1/1 p 3/3 m 1/2, total 34.

Dorsal: Skulls of the *Mustela* species are long and slender, with short, wide-spreading, and thin zygomatics; very short, broad rostrums; and massive, oval braincases. The rostrum (1) is very short and triangular; the nasal sutures (2) are visible only in immature specimens. The zygomatic arches (3) are wide-spreading and very thin, with large zygomatic plates (4) and large infraorbital foramina (5). Postorbital processes are small and triangular; the orbits (6) are relatively large, forward facing, and approximately 50 percent of the size of the temporal fossae (7). The interorbital breadth (8) may be approximately equal to or slightly wider than the postorbital. The braincase (9) is massive, oval, and approaching two-thirds the greatest length of skull; temporal ridges (10) are more developed, depending on geographic population and sex; and sagittal (11) and occipital crests (12) are often more visible and developed than in ermines. Mastoid processes (13) are slightly larger than in ermines and often visible at the posterior of the skull.

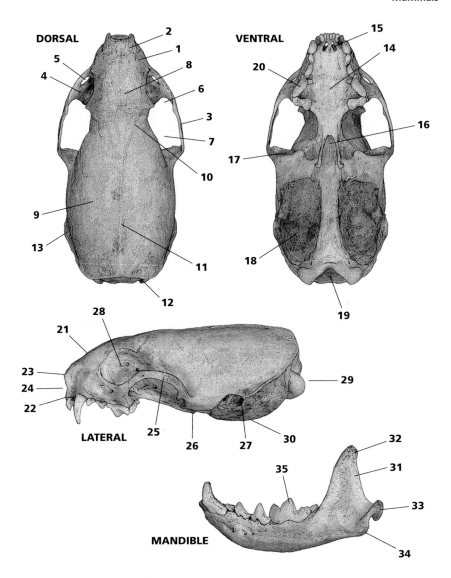

DORSAL

VENTRAL

LATERAL

MANDIBLE

Ventral: The triangular palate (14) abruptly narrows as it extends well beyond the posterior molars. Toothrows are relatively short. The incisive foramina (15) are wider and completely forward of the posterior edge of the canines. The pterygoid region (16) is narrow. The mandibular fossa (17) is well developed. Auditory bullae (18) are large, very long, and somewhat flattened. The foramen magnum (19) is large. The toothrows are short, and the carnassial (20) is thin and strong.

Lateral: The dorsolateral outline is dominated by the braincase, sloping steeply at the anterior (21) to the tip of the rostrum. The anterior edges of the premaxillaries (22) and nasals (23) are aligned, and the nasal vacuity (24) is smaller and vertical. The zygomatics (25) are thin and curved. The pterygoid processes (26) are short. The

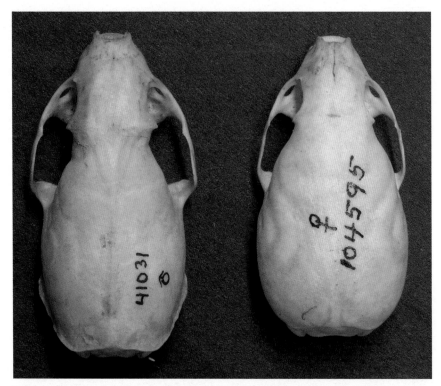

The larger male is on the left, and the female is on the right. MUSEUM OF VERTEBRATE ZOOLOGY, UC BERKELEY 41031, 104595.

auditory meatus (27) is medium, and the foramen magnum (29) is elevated. From this perspective, the orbit (28) appears large. The auditory bullae (30) are low.

Mandible: The mandible is strong and curved. The coronoid process (31) is vertical, triangular, and more slender, with the tip (32) curving to the posterior. The condyle (33) is stout and barrel-shaped, and it sits aligned with the toothrow. The angular process (34) is reduced and rounded. The carnassial (35) is large, the dentition jagged.

Similar species: Other weasels and bonnetted bats.

American mink, *Mustela vison*

Greatest length: 53.3–70.6 mm ($2^1/_{10}$–$2^8/_{10}$ in.) (full table of measurements page 602, life-size image page 120, life-size jaw page 162)

Specimen illustrated: Adult male, MVZ 12904

Dentition: i 3/3 c 1/1 p 3/3 m 1/2, total 34.

Dorsal: Skulls of the *Mustela* species are long and slender, with short, wide-spreading, and thin zygomatics; short, broad rostrums; and massive, oval braincases. The rostrum (1) is short and stout; the nasal sutures (2) are visible only in immature specimens. The zygomatic arches (3) are wide-spreading and very thin, with large zygomatic plates (4) and large infraorbital foramina (5). Postorbital processes are small and triangular; the orbits (6) are relatively large, forward facing, and smaller than 50 percents of the size of the massive temporal fossae (7). The interorbital breadth (8) may be approximately equal to or just wider than the constricted post-orbital breadth. The braincase (9) is massive, oval, and well over 50 percent of the greatest length of skull; temporal ridges are developed, varying with sex, and sagittal (10) and occipital crests are very evident; the supraoccipital shield (11) is pronounced and broad. The mastoid processes (12) are large and visible.

Ventral: The triangular palate (13) abruptly narrows substantially as it extends well beyond the posterior molars. The incisive foramina (14) are wider and completely forward of the posterior edge of the canines. The pterygoid region (15) is very nar-

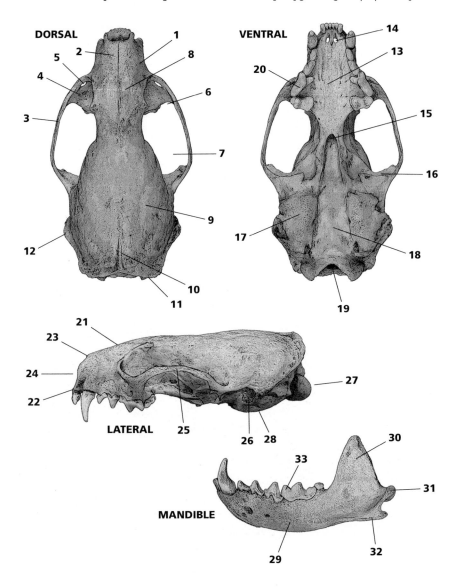

DORSAL

VENTRAL

LATERAL

MANDIBLE

row. The mandibular fossa (16) is well developed. Auditory bullae (17) are large, deformed, flattened, and spaced well apart (18). The foramen magnum (19) is large. The toothrows are short, and the carnassial (20) is thin and strong.

Lateral: The dorsolateral outline slopes gently (21) from the slightly elevated braincase to the tip of the rostrum; the overall outline is more slender than in other *Mustela* species. The anterior edges of the premaxillaries (22) extend just beyond the nasals (23), and the nasal vacuity (24) is larger and steep. The zygomatics (25) are thin and curved. The pterygoid processes are short. The auditory meatus (26) is medium, and the foramen magnum (27) is elevated. The ventral surface of the auditory bullae (28) is high.

Mandible: The mandible is stouter and curved, and the body (29) is relatively deeper than in smaller *Mustela* species. The coronoid process (30) is vertical, high, triangular, and broader than in other *Mustela* species. The condyle (31) is stout and barrel-shaped, and it sits aligned with the toothrow. The angular process (32) is slightly longer and rounded. The carnassial (33) is large, the dentition jagged.

Notes: Sagittal and occipital crests further develop with greater age, especially in males. According to Linscombe et al. (1982), deciduous teeth erupt between sixteen and forty-nine days from birth, and permanent teeth between forty-four and seventy-one days. They also report that determining the sex of a mink skull using basilar length and the length of the upper toothrow is 99 percent accurate. Males have a length cutoff of 63 millimeters or more and a toothrow cutoff of 25 millimeters or more. Birney and Fleharty (1966) found condyle-premaxillary length the most useful in determining sex, and zygomatic breadth to a lesser degree, though parameters for zygomatic widths showed no overlap at all between males and females. Lynch and Hayden (1995) compared the skulls of ranch-raised and wild mink and found that sexual dimorphism was reduced in captive-bred populations, and several

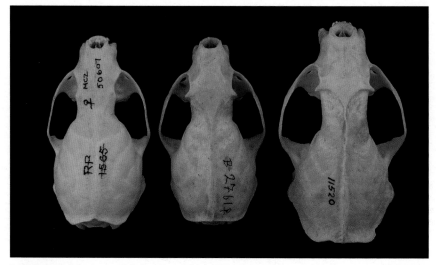

From left to right, two adult female mink and an adult male. MUSEUM OF COMPARATIVE ZOOLOGY, HARVARD U 50607, B2761, 11520.

other morphological changes were evident as well. Females showed proportionately greater degrees of change than males, but both ranch populations exhibited increased size; narrower interorbital, mastoidal, and zygomatic widths; broader postorbital widths; and shorter palates.

Wolverine, *Gulo gulo*

Greatest length: 135.8–173.4 mm (5³/₁₀–6⁸/₁₀ in.) (full table of measurements page 604, life-size image page 138, life-size jaw page 170)

Specimen illustrated: Adult male, SBMNH 4339

Dentition: i 3/3 c 1/1 p 4/4 m 1/2, total 38.

Dorsal: The skulls of wolverines are dense, heavy, and wedge-shaped, with wide-spreading zygomata, short rostrums, and prominent crests. The rostrum (1) is very short, very broad, and stout; complete nasal sutures (2) are visible only in younger animals. The zygomatic arches (3) are wide-spreading and stout, strongly converging to the anterior. Postorbital processes (4) are well developed and blunt; the orbits (5) are relatively small, forward facing, and less than one-third the size of the massive temporal fossae (6). The interorbital region (7) is very broad, and the interorbital breadth is wider than the constricted postorbital breadth. The braincase (8) is very long, ovoid, widest at the mastoids, and approaching 50 percent of the greatest length of skull; temporal ridges (9) are well developed, coalesce with age, and converge high on the skull in adult specimens to form a large, long sagittal crest (10). Occipital crests (11) are also well developed. The mastoid processes (12) are large and well developed.

Ventral: The very broad, triangular palate (13) abruptly narrows as it extends well beyond the posterior molars. The incisive foramina (14) are wider and completely forward of the posterior edge of the canines. The pterygoid region (15) is broad. The

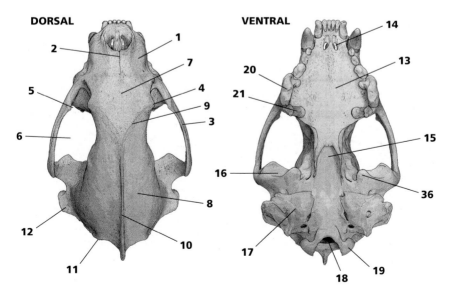

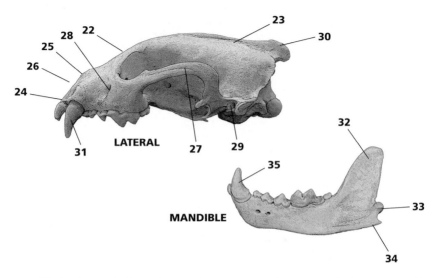

mandibular fossae (16) are deep and the squamosal processes (36) are very well developed. Auditory bullae (17) are large, deformed, and inflated on the sides closest to each other. The foramen magnum (18) is medium, and the occipital condyles (19) are stout. Dentition is robust and blunt; the carnassial (20) is large and stout, and the posterior molar (21) has a flattened surface.

Lateral: The dorsolateral outline is rounded, with a relatively steep slope from the apex down the frontals (22) to the rostrum, and a lower braincase (23) to the pos-

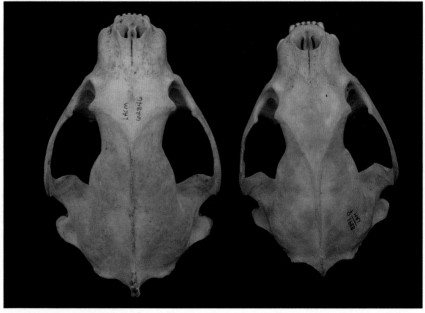

Compare the size and length of the male wolverine on the left with the female on the right.
NATURAL HISTORY MUSEUM OF LOS ANGELES COUNTY 62846, 8391.

terior. The anterior edges of the premaxillaries (24) extend farther than the nasals (25), and the nasal vacuity (26) is large and angled. The zygomatics (27) are deep, curved, and elevated at their midpoints; the large infraorbital foramina (28) are anterior to the zygomatic arches above P4. The pterygoid processes are short. The auditory meatus (29) is small. The sagittal crest (30) extends to the posterior over the occipital region and continues to lengthen with age. The canines (31) are large and stout, the dentition jagged.

Mandible: The mandible is strong and curved. The coronoid process (32) is robust, high, rounded, and slightly angled to the posterior. The condyle (33) is stout and barrel-shaped, and it sits aligned with the toothrow. The angular process (34) is reduced and pointed. The canines (35) are large, and the dentition jagged.

Similar species: Badgers, fishers, sea otters, and raccoons.

Notes: Grinnell et al. (1937) write that southern wolverines have "lighter" (meaning smaller) carnassials and dentition than far northern counterparts. Articulation of the lower jaw is so tight that it may be difficult to separate from the cranium without damaging the specimen. Males are larger than females (see page 436). The lengthening of the sagittal crest is much more dramatic in males than females; in a female that was so old that nearly all her teeth were worn completely to the gums, the sagittal crest extended over the occipital region only to the degree of the relatively young male illustrated here.

American badger, *Taxidea taxus*

Greatest length: 108.0–131.6 mm ($4^3/_{10}$–$5^2/_{10}$ in.) (full table of measurements page 604, life-size image page 133, life-size jaw page 169)

Specimen illustrated: Adult female, LACM 45012

Dentition: i 3/3 c 1/1 p 3/3 m 1/2, total 34.

Dorsal: Badger skulls are dense, heavy, and triangular, with stout, wide-spreading zygomatics; shorter rostrums; and triangular braincases. The rostrum (1) is very short, broad, and stout; the nasal sutures (2) are visible only in immature specimens. The zygomatic arches (3) are wide-spreading, curved, and stout, converging to the anterior. Postorbital processes (4) are well developed and blunt; the orbits (5) are medium, forward facing, and less than 50 percent of the massive temporal fossae (6). The interorbital region (7) is broad, and the interorbital breadth is approximately equal to the slightly constricted postorbital breadth. The braincase (8) is very long, triangular, and approximately 50 percent of the greatest length of skull; temporal ridges (9) are developed and coalesce with age, but sagittal crests (10) are low and poorly developed or absent altogether. Occipital crests (11) are well developed. The mastoid processes (12) are wide and distinctive, contributing to the wedge-shaped outline.

Ventral: The broad, rectangular palate (13) narrows as it extends well beyond the posterior molars and is longer than half the length of skull. The incisive foramina (14) are wider and completely forward of the canines. The pterygoid region (15) is narrower. The mandibular fossa (16) is well developed. Auditory bullae (17) are large and more inflated than in many mustelids. The foramen magnum (18) is large, and

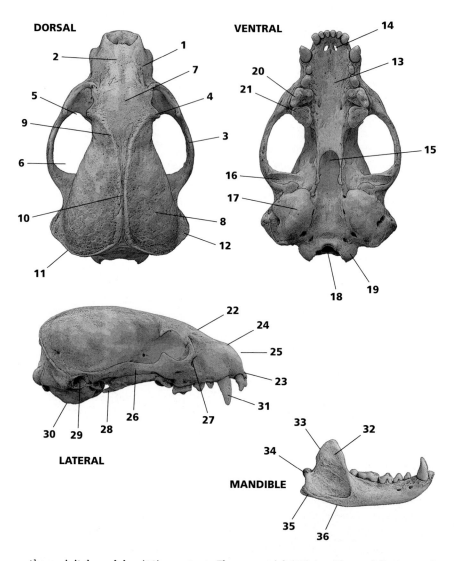

DORSAL

VENTRAL

LATERAL

MANDIBLE

the occipital condyles (19) are stout. The carnassial (20) is wider and flatter, and the triangular posterior molar (21) is distinctive.

Lateral: The dorsolateral outline curves gradually down from the elevated braincase, and then more steeply drops down the frontals (22) to the rostrum. The anterior edges of the premaxillaries (23) extend farther than the nasals (24); the nasal vacuity (25) is sloping. The zygomatics (26) are thick and relatively straight; the infraorbital foramina (27) sit anterior to the zygomatic arches and are larger than in raccoons, whose skulls are often confused with badgers'. The pterygoid processes (28) are larger. The auditory meatus (29) is medium, and the auditory bullae (30) extends below the molars. The canines (31) are long, the remaining dentition jagged but reduced in comparison with those of other mustelids.

Mandible: The mandible is strong and curved. The coronoid process (32) is vertical, much shorter, and triangular; the posterior edge (33) is convex in outline. The condyle (34) is stout, slightly elevated, and barrel-shaped, and it sits aligned with the toothrow. The angular process (35) is reduced and blunt. The ventral outline has a distinctive bend (36) upward just posterior to the last molar.

Similar species: Often confused with raccoons. Also, otters, wolverines, and foxes.

Notes: Well-developed lambdoidal crest and lightly developed sagittal crest, which is the opposite of many mammals. Raccoons have similar palates, dentition, and infraorbital foramina. In Hoffmeister (1986), Long divided specimens into two age categories: Subadults exhibit no wear of the teeth, and sutures associated with nasals are visible. Adults show at least some tooth wear, and the sutures associated with the nasals have fused. Male specimens are longer than female (Lindzey 2003), yet there is greater overlap in cranial measurements than in other mustelids.

Northern river otter, *Lontra canadensis*

Greatest length: 101.5–129.9 mm (4–5^{1}/$_{10}$ in.) (full table of measurements page 604, life-size image page 129, life-size jaw page 165)

Specimen illustrated: Adult female, MCZ 62026

Dentition: i 3/3 c 1/1 p 4/3 m 1/2, total 36. Dentition for holding and crushing.

Dorsal: Otter skulls are flattened and rounded, with wide-spreading, slender zygomatics; very short rostrums; and very large braincases. The rostrum (1) is very short and broad; the nasal sutures (2) are visible only in immature specimens. The zygomatic arches (3) are very wide-spreading and slender, converging to the anterior; the oblong infraorbital foramina (4) are large. Postorbital processes (5) are well developed and sharp; the orbits (6) are medium, forward facing, and less than half the size of the massive temporal fossae (7). The interorbital region (8) is broad, and the

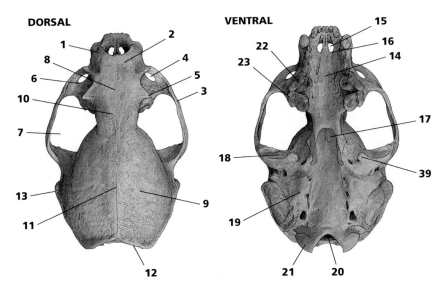

DORSAL   VENTRAL

LATERAL

MANDIBLE

interorbital breadth is wider than the very constricted postorbital breadth. The braincase (9) is long, wide, and much more than 50 percent of the greatest length of skull; temporal ridges (10) are poorly developed and converge high on the skull in adult specimens to form a low sagittal crest (11). Occipital crests (12) are well developed. The mastoid processes (13) are large and distinctive.

Ventral: The relatively narrow, rectangular palate (14) abruptly narrows as it extends beyond the posterior molars. Toothrows are relatively short. The incisive foramina (15) are large and extend to the posterior (16) beyond the canines. The pterygoid region (17) is broad. The mandibular fossa (18) is deep and the squamosal process (39) is well developed. Auditory bullae (19) are medium and flattened. The foramen magnum (20) is large, and the occipital condyles (21) are stout. The carnassial (22) and posterior molars (23) have sharp cutting edges and broad bases for crushing.

Lateral: The dorsolateral outline is relatively straight, curving gradually down from the slightly elevated braincase (24). The anterior edges of the premaxillaries (25) extend much farther than the nasals (26); the nasal vacuity (27) is large and angled. The zygomatics (28) are thicker, curved, and elevated at their midpoints. The pterygoid processes (29) are large. The auditory meatus (30) is small, and the foramen

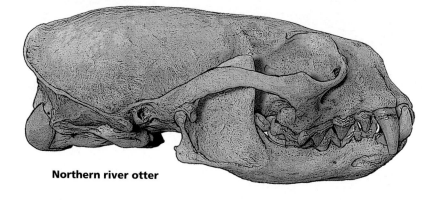

Northern river otter

magnum (31) is low. The canines (32) are long and slender, the dentition jagged. Well-developed occipital crests (33) project to the posterior.

Mandible: The mandible is strong and curved. The coronoid process (34) is vertical, high, and triangular; the anterior edge (35) is straight, and the posterior edge (36) is rounded. The condyle (37) is stout and barrel-shaped, and it sits aligned with the toothrow. The angular process (38) is reduced and rounded. The dentition is jagged.

Similar species: Sea otters, raccoons, fishers, and domestic cats.

Notes: Sexual dimorphism is less pronounced than in many other mustelids, and males are only slightly larger than females. In mature animals, the hook-shaped process on the anterior edge of the mandibular fossa is so well developed that the jaws often cannot be disarticulated from the cranium.

Sea otter, *Enhydra lutris*

Greatest length: 125.1–148.6 mm ($4^9/_{10}$–$5^9/_{10}$ in.) (full table of measurements page 604, life-size image page 137, life-size jaw page 168)

Specimen illustrated: Adult male, SBMNH 3377

Dentition: i 3/2 c 1/1 p 3/3 m 1/2, total 32. Two pairs of lower incisors, four total, unique among North American carnivores.

Dorsal: Otter skulls are flattened and rounded, with wide-spreading, slender zygomatics; very short rostrums; and very large braincases. In addition, sea otter skulls are heavy, dense, and boxy. The rostrum (1) is very short and very broad; the nasal sutures (2) are often very obscured. The zygomatic arches (3) are very wide-spreading and slender, converging to the anterior; the oblong infraorbital foramina (4) are very large. Postorbital processes (5) are small and sharp; the orbits (6) are smaller, forward facing, and less than half the size of the massive temporal fossae (7). The interorbital region (8) is very broad, and the interorbital breadth is wider than the very constricted postorbital breadth. The postorbital constriction may or may not have an obvious constricted notch, which is more characteristic of far northern populations (Roest 1973). The braincase (10) is long, wide, and much more than 50 percent of the greatest length of the skull; temporal ridges (11) are well developed and converge high on the skull in adult specimens to form a sagittal crest (12) that extends the full length of the braincase. Occipital crests (13) are well developed. The mastoid processes (14) are large and distinctive.

Ventral: The relatively broad, rectangular palate (15) extends beyond the posterior molars. Toothrows are relatively short. The incisive foramina (16) are large and extend to the posterior beyond the canines. The pterygoid region (17) is broad. The mandibular fossa (18) is very deep and the hook-shaped process (38) is well developed. Auditory bullae (19) are medium and flattened. The foramen magnum (20) is medium, and the occipital condyles (21) are stout. The posteriormost two teeth (22) are large, broad, and flattened. The posterior lacerate foramina (23) are very large and round, approximately 8 millimeters in diameter.

Lateral: The dorsolateral outline is relatively straight, curving gradually down from the slightly elevated braincase; it is the height of the skull that is distinctive, with the depth continuous through its entire length. The anterior edges of the premax-

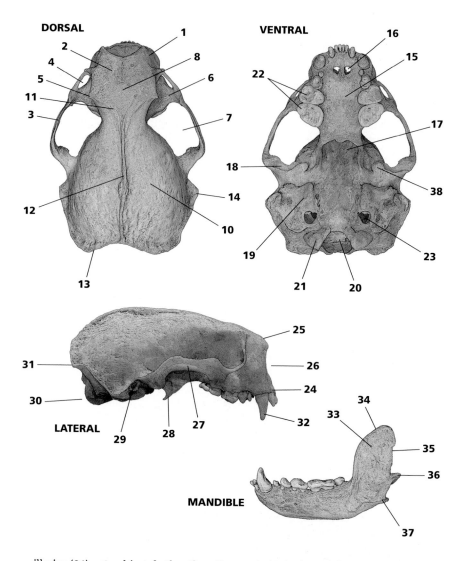

illaries (24) extend just farther than the nasals (25); the nasal vacuity (26) is very large and vertical. The zygomatics (27) are thicker, curved, and elevated at their midpoints. The pterygoid processes (28) are large. The auditory meatus (29) is small, and the foramen magnum (30) is low; the occipital crests (31) extend to the posterior over the foramen magnum. The canines (32) are long and blunt, and the remaining dentition is also blunt.

Mandible: The mandible is strong and curved. The coronoid process (33) is vertical, thick, and somewhat triangular. The coronoid process varies in shape among geographic populations (Roest 1973): in California, it curves strongly to the posterior (34) and often has concave posterior edges (35); whereas in the northern populations around the Aleutians, it is more vertical, often with the apex forward of the

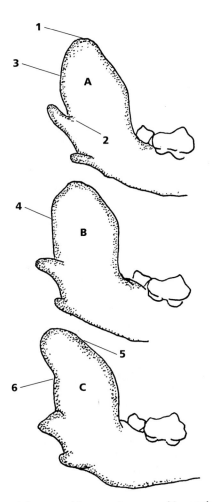

Variation in the form of the coronoid process in geographic populations of sea otters: A. Typical Aleutian mandible with highest point of coronoid (1) anterior to base of condyloid process (2), and a convex posterior edge (3). B. Aleutian mandible variation, with posterior edge straight (4). C. Typical California mandible, with coronoid process angled to posterior (5) and concave posterior edge (6). Drawn after Roest (1973).

entire condyloid process, and has straight or slightly convex posterior edges (above). The condyle (36) is stout and barrel-shaped, and it sits aligned with the toothrow. The angular process (37) is reduced and pointed. The dentition is flattened.

Similar species: River otters, wolverines, harbor seals, badgers, and bobcats.

Notes: The color of bones and teeth are related to diet: purplish from eating purple sea urchins, maroon from red sea urchins, and white often from crabs and squid (Liittschwager 2002). Often the left side of the skull is noticeably larger than the right (Verts and Carraway 1998).

Family Mephitidae: Skunks

Skunks were until quite recently included with weasels and companions in the family Mustelidae. Skunk skulls are characterized by dentition more supportive of an omnivorous and varied diet: The blades of the carnassials are reduced, and the carnassials overall are slightly wider to accommodate a greater degree of crushing. The articulation of the mandible is also looser than in mustelids, which further supports crushing in addition to a reduced shearing capability. Spotted skunks are the most carnivorous of the skunks, and their carnassials are the most developed. Hog-nosed skunks are the least predaceous, and their carnassials are poorly developed and more flattened.

There are several nematodes that can infest and damage the frontal sinuses in skunks and weasels; the best studied and recorded is *Skrjabingylus nasicola,* and

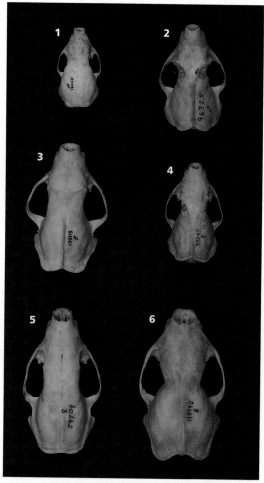

Members of Mephitidae. 1. Pygmy spotted skunk, male 155581 *(S. pygmaea)*, 2. Western spotted skunk, male 96325 *(S. gracilis)*, 3. Hooded skunk, male 10015 *(M. macroura)*, 4. Eastern spotted skunk, female 97347 *(S. putorius)*, 5. Striped skunk, female 59709 *(M. mephitis)*, 6. White-backed hog-nosed skunk, female 114940 *(Conepatus leuconotus)*. MUSEUM OF VERTEBRATE ZOOLOGY, UC BERKELEY.

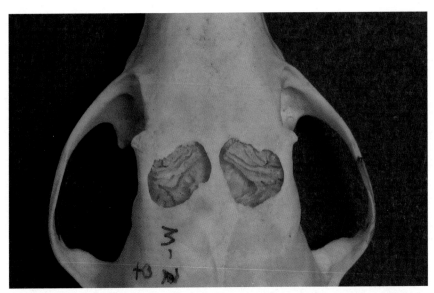

Sinus damage in a female western spotted skunk *(Spilogale gracilis)* from southern California.
SANTA BARBARA MUSEUM OF NATURAL HISTORY M-2503.

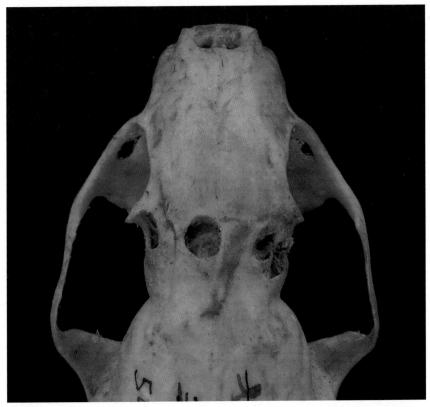

Sinus damage in a male long-tailed weasel *(Mustela frenata)* from New Hampshire. MUSEUM OF COMPARATIVE ZOOLOGY, HARVARD U 54075.

another is *Troglotrema acutum* (Walker 1987; Duncan 1976). Though these nematodes also infest larger mustelids, damage is more easily detected and even dramatic in the smaller mustelids and skunks, in which proportionately greater damage occurs. A photograph of very dramatic signs of infestation in hooded skunk skulls appears in chapter 2. Infestations are perhaps most common in spotted skunks, and to lesser degrees in all the small weasels (*Mustela* spp.) and the other skunks; as many as seventy-seven tiny worms have been removed from a single weasel (Duncan 1976). Infestations are evident in skulls by the inflation or bubbling of the sinuses or actual holes in the bone that reveal the inner sinus structures (see page 445).

How *S. nasicola* is transmitted is unclear though a mollusk appears to serve as an intermediate host (Duncan 1976). Infected weasels housed with noninfected weasels do not transmit the parasites. It is thought that the varied diets of mustelids and skunks make them particularly vulnerable; skunks and weasels may eat infected snails or mollusks, or they may eat shrews, mice, or chipmunks that were infected by eating snails or mollusks. There also seems to be a correlation between increased stress and greater infection within a population: In times of food shortage, it is thought that skunks and weasels increase the variety of foods they ingest, and thus increase the likelihood of being infected. Shrews in particular, which are often hosts for the nematodes, are thought not to be preferred foods, yet they will be eaten when other foods are less available.

Western spotted skunk, *Spilogale gracilis;* Eastern spotted skunk, *Spilogale putorius*

Greatest length: 49.4–63.6 mm ($1^9/10$–$2^5/10$ in.) (full table of measurements pages 604 and 606, life-size image page 118, life-size jaw page 162)

Specimen illustrated: Adult male *(S. gracilis),* SBMNH 145

Dentition: i 3/3 c 1/1 p 3/3 m 1/2, total 34.

Dorsal: Spotted skunk skulls are distinctively flattened, with wide-spreading zygomatic arches and broad, swollen mastoids. The rostrum (1) is short, broad, and wedge-shaped; the nasal sutures (2) are visible only in immature specimens. The zygomatic arches (3) are bowed, wide-spreading, and thin, converging to the anterior. The postorbital processes (4) are well developed and pointed; the orbits (5) are medium and forward facing; the temporal fossa (6) is large. The interorbital breadth (7) is wider than the constricted postorbital breadth. The braincase (8) is large, as broad as long, and approximately 50 percent of the greatest length of skull; temporal ridges (9) are developed and converge to form sagittal crests (10) that may extend the length of the braincases; occipital crests are very well developed, and the supraoccipital shield (11) is broad. The mastoid processes (13) are large and swollen, more so in males, and often approach the width of the zygomatic arches. The holes in the frontals (14) are caused by parasitic nematodes.

Ventral: The broad, rectangular palate (15) terminates just beyond the last molar (16). Toothrows are relatively short. The incisive foramina (17) are very small and forward of the canines. The pterygoid region (18) is narrow. The mandibular fossa (19) is

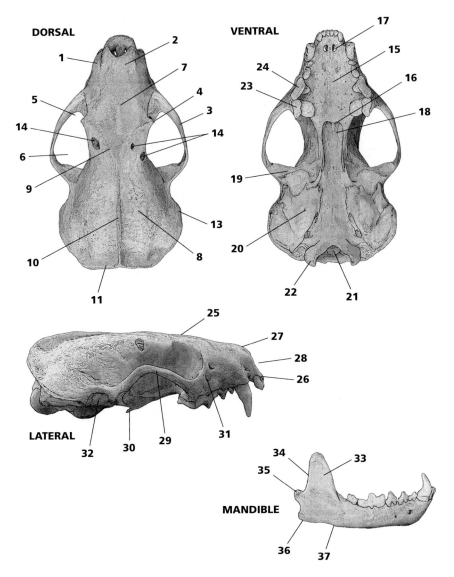

DORSAL

VENTRAL

LATERAL

MANDIBLE

well developed. Auditory bullae (20) are medium and inflated. The foramen magnum (21) is large, and the occipital condyles (22) are strong. The toothrows are relatively short, and the posterior molar (23) is wide and flattened; the carnassial (24) is more developed than in other skunks.

Lateral: The dorsolateral outline of the skull is nearly straight (25), an important character in spotted skunks. The anterior edges of the premaxillaries (26) extend beyond the nasals (27), and the nasal vacuity (28) is medium and angled. The zygomatics (29) are thin and curved, the midpoints well elevated as in mustelids. The pterygoid processes (30) are short, and the infraorbital foramen (31) appears as a single hole just anterior to the zygomatic arch, but it is separated into two chambers by

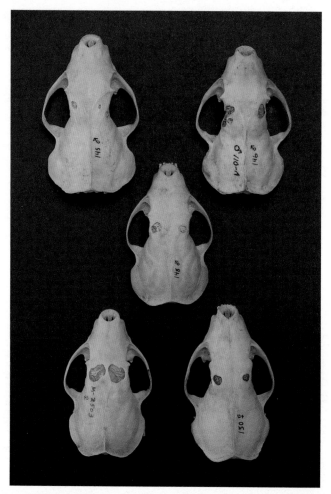

The topmost pair of Western spotted skunks are adult males, the central skull an immature male, and the lower pair adult females. SANTA BARBARA MUSEUM OF NATURAL HISTORY 145, 146, 148, 2503, 150.

a wafer-thin bone often lost in specimens; it is much smaller than in mustelids of similar size. The auditory meatus (32) is medium, and the foramen magnum is low.

Mandible: The mandible is strong, and the body is curved. The coronoid process (33) is vertical, high, and rounded; the anterior edge is sloping and the posterior edge (34) straight. The condyle (35) is stout and barrel-shaped, and it sits aligned with the toothrow. The angular process (36) is reduced and rounded, and the ventral outline at the posterior (37) is straighter than in striped skunks. The dentition is jagged.

Similar species: Mink, long-tailed weasels, and striped skunks.

Notes: Although no single cranial feature will distinguish between western and eastern spotted skunks (*S. gracilis* and *S. putorius*), baculums reliably do so (Verts et al. 2001). Males are 7 percent larger in many cranial features (Van Gelder 1959).

Striped skunk, *Mephitis mephitis*

Greatest length: 67.9–88.0 mm ($2^7/_{10}$–$3^5/_{10}$ in.) (full table of measurements page 606, life-size image page 123, life-size jaw page 163)

Specimen illustrated: Adult male, LACM 8411

Dentition: i 3/3 c 1/1 p 3/3 m 1/2, total 34. Three premolars above, compared with two in *Conepatus* species.

Dorsal: Skunk skulls are somewhat like lithic arrowheads in outline, triangular from the zygomatic arches forward, with the broad mastoids and supraoccipital shield forming the squared base. The rostrum (1) is short, broad, and triangular; the nasal sutures (2) are visible only in immature specimens. The zygomatic arches (3) are wide-spreading and thin, strongly converging to the anterior. Postorbital processes (4) are reduced to just bumps; the orbits (5) are medium and less forward facing; the temporal fossa (6) is large. The interorbital breadth (7) is wider than the postorbital. The braincase (8) is large, rounded, and less than 50 percent of the greatest length of skull; temporal ridges (9) are well developed and converge to form sagittal crests (10) that extend the length of the braincases; occipital crests are well developed, and the supraoccipital shield (11) is broad. The mastoid processes (12) are large but not inflated.

Ventral: The broad, rectangular palate (13) terminates with the posterior edge of the last molar (14). Toothrows are relatively short. The incisive foramina (15) are small and forward of the canines. The pterygoid region (16) is broad. The mandibular fossa (17) is well developed. Auditory bullae (18) are small and flattened. The foramen magnum (19) is medium, and the occipital condyles (20) are strong. The toothrows are relatively short, and the posterior molar (21) is wide and flattened; a tiny premolar (22) sits just posterior to the canine, absent in *Conepatus* species.

Lateral: The apex of the skull (23) is above the orbit, especially apparent when the skull is resting on a flat surface. The anterior edges of the premaxillaries (24) extend

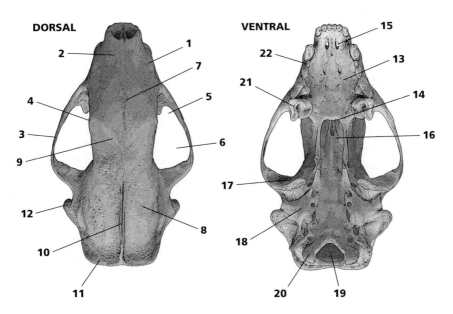

DORSAL

VENTRAL

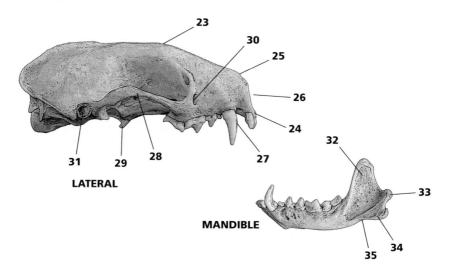

just beyond the nasals (25), and the nasal vacuity (26) is medium and relatively vertical; the anterior tips of the nasals align with the front edge of the canines (27). The zygomatics (28) are thin and less curved than in mustelids. The pterygoid processes (29) are short, and the infraorbital foramen (30) is a single, smaller hole just anterior to the zygomatic arch, divided by a wafer-thin bone often lost in specimens. The auditory meatus (31) is medium, and the foramen magnum is low.

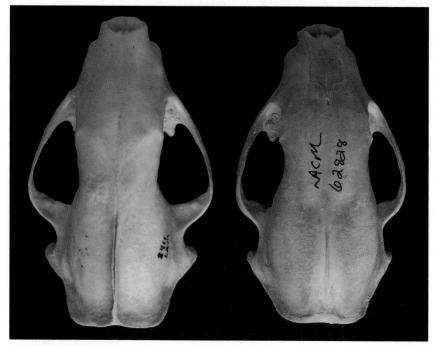

Larger male striped skunk on the left, and smaller female on the right. NATURAL HISTORY MUSEUM OF LOS ANGELES COUNTY 8411, 62828.

Mandible: The mandible is strong, and the body is slightly larger and curved. The coronoid process (32) is vertical, high, and rounded; overall, the coronoid is more triangular than in *Conepatus* species. The condyle (33) is stout and barrel-shaped, and it sits aligned with the toothrow. The angular process (34) is reduced and rounded, and the ventral outline at the posterior is very curved, creating a shallow step (35); it is straighter in spotted skunks. The dentition is jagged.

Similar species: Hooded and hog-nosed skunks, martens, and mink.

Notes: Difficult to distinguish from hooded skunks *(M. macroura)*, though hooded skunks often have larger, more inflated auditory bullae and wider postorbital breadths. Males are larger than females (see page 450).

White-backed hog-nosed skunk, *Conepatus leuconotus*

Greatest length: 65.0–84.5 mm (2⁶/₁₀–3³/₁₀ in.) (full table of measurements page 606, life-size image page 123, life-size jaw page 163)

Specimen illustrated: Adult female, LACM 59421

Dentition: i 3/3 c 1/1 p 2/3 m 1/2, total 32. Two premolars above, compared with three in *Mephitis* species.

Dorsal: Skunk skulls are somewhat like lithic arrowheads in outline, triangular from the zygomatic arches forward, with the broad mastoids and supraoccipital shield forming the squared base; the hog-nosed skunk skull is a more inflated, rounded version of the striped skunk's. The rostrum (1) is very short and broad. The nasal sutures (2) are visible only in immature specimens; the nasal vacuity (3) is large and broad. The zygomatic arches (4) are wide-spreading and thin, converging to the anterior. Postorbital processes (5) are essentially nonexistent; the orbits (6) are medium and less forward facing; the temporal fossa (7) is large. The interorbital breadth (8) is wider than the constricted postorbital breadth. The braincase (9) is larger, rounded, and slightly more than 50 percent of the greatest length of skull; temporal ridges (10)

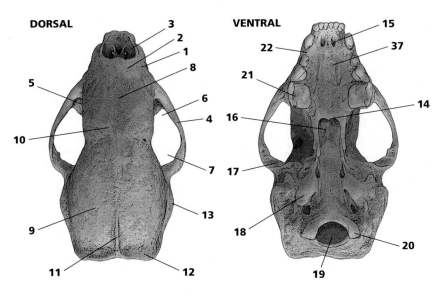

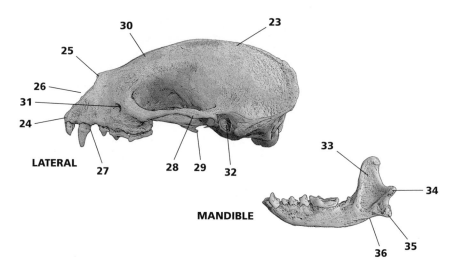

may be developed and converge to form sagittal crests (11) at the posterior of the skull. In some animals, crests are large and extend the length of the braincase; occipital crests are well developed, and the supraoccipital shield (12) is very broad. The mastoid processes (13) are not as pronounced as in *Mephitis* species.

Ventral: The broad, rectangular palate (37) terminates well beyond the last molars (14). The incisive foramina (15) are small, the posterior edges approximately in line with the posterior of the canines. The pterygoid region (16) is broad. The mandibular fossa (17) is well developed. Auditory bullae (18) are very small and flattened. The foramen magnum (19) is medium, and the occipital condyles (20) are strong. The

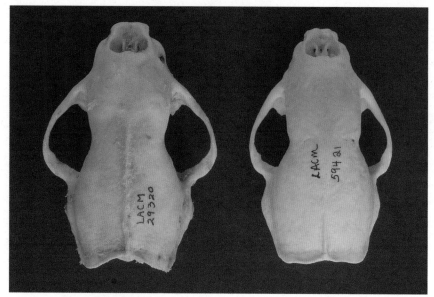

Adult male hog-nosed skunk on the left, and adult female on the right. NATURAL HISTORY MUSEUM OF LOS ANGELES COUNTY 29320, 59421.

toothrows are relatively short, and the posterior molar (21) is wide and flattened; the tiny premolar (22) that sits just posterior to the canine in *Mephitis* species, is absent.

Lateral: The dorsolateral outline is domed and rounded, and the frontals (30) are inflated; the apex of the skull (23) is posterior of the orbit above the braincase. The anterior edges of the premaxillaries (24) extend well beyond the nasals (25), and the nasal vacuity (26) is large and angled; the anterior tips of the nasals align with the posterior edge of the canines (27). The zygomatics (28) are thin and relatively straight. The pterygoid processes (29) are short, and the infraorbital foramen (31) is just anterior to the zygomatic arch and divided into two chambers by a sliver of bone. The auditory meatus (32) is medium, and the foramen magnum is low.

Mandible: The mandible is strong, and the body is slightly larger and curved. The coronoid process (33) is vertical, high, and rounded; overall, the coronoid is more slender than in *Mephitis* species. The condyle (34) is stout and barrel-shaped, and it sits just above the toothrow. The angular process (35) is reduced, rounded, and elevated; the ventral outline at the posterior is curved and forms a step (36) closer to the angular process than in *Mephitis* species. The dentition is jagged.

Similar species: Striped skunks, hooded skunks, mink, and martens.

Family Felidae: Cats

Cat skulls exhibit numerous characteristics of a predaceous and carnivorous lifestyle. The canines are long and slender, with increased nerve endings within; often the tips of the nerves are visible in teeth that are only slightly worn. These nerves increase sensitivity and help guide canines between vertebrae when making a kill. The carnassials also are

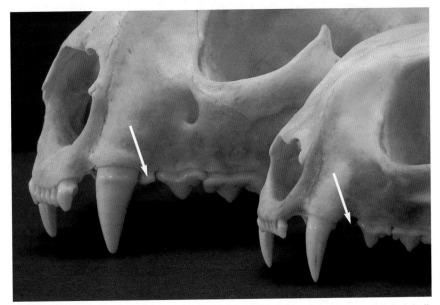

Note the tiny premolar just posterior to the canine in the larger cougar *(Puma concolor)* skull, and the lack thereof in the closer bobcat *(Lynx rufus)* skull. SANTA BARBARA MUSEUM OF NATURAL HISTORY 887, 891.

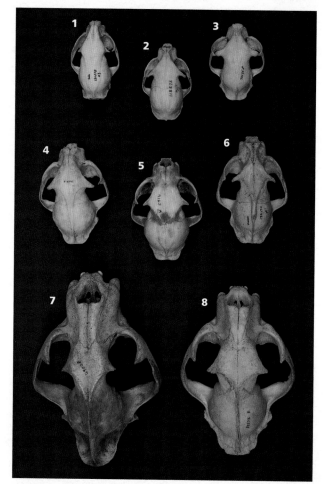

Members of Felidae. 1. Jaguarundi 184070 *(Herpailurus yaguarondi)*, 2. Margay 118878 *(Leopardus wiedii)*, 3. Feral cat, male 70135 *(F. catus)*, 4. Bobcat, male 7150 *(L. rufus)*, 5. Canada Lynx, male 4163 *(L. canadensis)*, 6. Ocelot, male 132174 *(Leopardus pardalis)*, 7. Jaguar, male 4900 *(Panthera onca)*, 8. Cougar, male 50278 *(Puma concolor)*. MUSEUM OF VERTEBRATE ZOOLOGY, UC BERKELEY.

long and bladelike. The incisors are horizontal. A single small molar sits on either side of the cranium. The articulation of the mandibles is very tight, focusing power into opening and closing the mouth rather than in lateral movements characteristic of crushing.

Cat skulls are characteristically rounded and squat, with shortened rostrums and wide-spreading and sturdy zygomatic arches. Large orbits are well forward, providing excellent binocular vision (see page 58), and large postorbital processes further support the temporalis muscles.

The number of premolars can sometimes be used in identifying felids. A tiny premolar grows just posterior to the canine in some species. It is present in cougars and ocelots, for example, but not bobcats; it may or may not be present in domestic cats. The dental formula will indicate the presence of this small tooth. In cats in which it is present, the formula for premolars is 3/2.

Differentiating between the skulls of bobcats *(Lynx rufus)* and Canada lynx *(L. canadensis)* can be difficult. Some loose generalizations can be made, but they do not

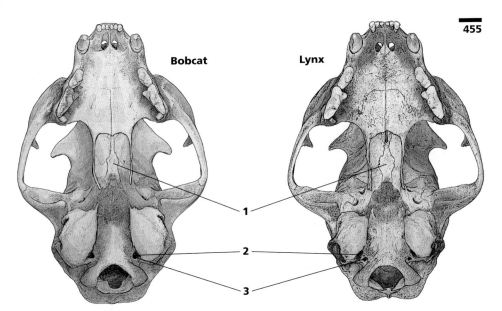

Bobcat **Lynx**

Differentiating between bobcat and lynx skulls. Compare the width and shape of the presphenoid bones (1). Compare the relative position and orientation of the hypoglossal canal (3) with the jugular foramen (2) in each species. Drawn after Jackson (1961).

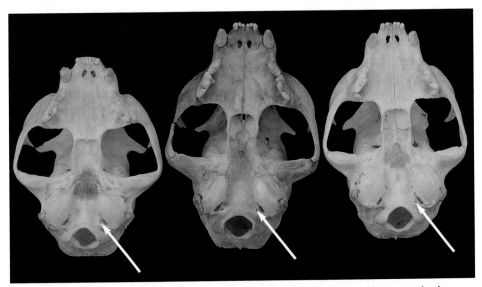

The position and orientation of the hypoglossal canal varies in bobcats, and in some animals will be orientated and positioned in a similar fashion to those found in lynx. From left to right compare the position of the hypoglossal canal in the typical bobcat, the typical lynx, and at the far right, a bobcat that shows characteristics similar to those in lynx. PRIVATE COLLECTION.

seem to hold across varied geographic populations or every skull from a single region. Lynx skulls frequently are larger, though there is tremendous variation in size. Often the postorbital processes from the frontal bones are smaller and more toward the anterior of the skull in lynx than in bobcats. Also, lynx in general exhibit broader interorbital regions than in bobcats. Roest (1991) suggests using an interorbital breadth of 30 millimeters as a cutoff between the two species. Yet neither the 30 millimeters cutoff for interorbital width nor any of the other characters mentioned above should be used alone to differentiate between bobcats and lynx. Rather, all should contribute to an interpretation that builds through the course of comparing numerous characters and the environmental context of the skull. If it is from central Alaska, for example, it will certainly be a lynx.

Anderson and Lovallo (2003) list several more reliable characters to distinguish between the two species, each found on the ventral surface of the cranium. In my own comparisons, the width of the presphenoid has been the most reliable in determining species. The authors suggest a cutoff of 4 millimeters wide, smaller than that being a bobcat, and larger being a lynx. This has been the case in the skulls I have compared, even when I found an unusual bobcat with a more swollen presphenoid; the larger presphenoids of lynx have most often been around 6 millimeters wide.

The location and orientation of the hypoglossal canal and jugular foramina are also useful, though variability creates certain complications. Refer to the illustrations and photographs on page 455 to gain a better understanding of these characters.

Domestic or feral cat, *Felis catus*

Greatest length: 77.5–101.0 mm (3¹/₁₀–4 in.) (full table of measurements page 608, life-size image page 126, life-size jaw page 164)

Specimen illustrated: Adult male, LACM 31041

Dentition: i 3/3 c 1/1 p 3/2 m 1/1, total 30. Grooved canines. Molars 1/1 distinct to cats.

Dorsal: Feline skulls are rounded, with wide-spreading zygomatics; short, broad rostrums; and large orbits. The rostrum (1) is very short, broad, and strong; the nasals (2) are broad at the anterior, quickly tapering to the posterior, where the tips converge and meet in a distinctive depression (3). The zygomatic arches (4) are long, heavy, and wide-spreading, converging slightly to the anterior; the zygomatic plates (5) are proportionately larger than in native counterparts. Postorbital processes from the frontals (6) are well developed, triangular, and long; postorbital processes are well developed on the zygomatics (7). The orbits (8) are very large, forward facing, and positioned completely forward of the midline of the skull. From this perspective, the temporal fossa (9) appears smaller than the orbits. The frontal region (10) and interorbital breadth are narrow and high; the interorbital breadth is narrower than the postorbital. The braincase (11) is large, rounded, and wider than the rostrum; temporal ridges are weak but converge in a V at the anterior of the braincase to form a small sagittal crest (12). Occipital crests are very well developed, and the supraoccipital shield (13) is prominent. Distinctive, thick bone extensions (14), sometimes two-tipped, run from the parietals over the frontals toward the temporal ridges, a reliable character for differentiating from bobcats. The mastoid processes (15) are medium for cats.

Ventral: The broad palate (16) is somewhat wedge-shaped, approximately as wide as the length of a toothrow, and then narrows considerably while extending well beyond the posterior molars. Toothrows are relatively short. The incisive foramina (17) are a bit larger and wider. The pterygoid region (18) is wide, and the pterygoid

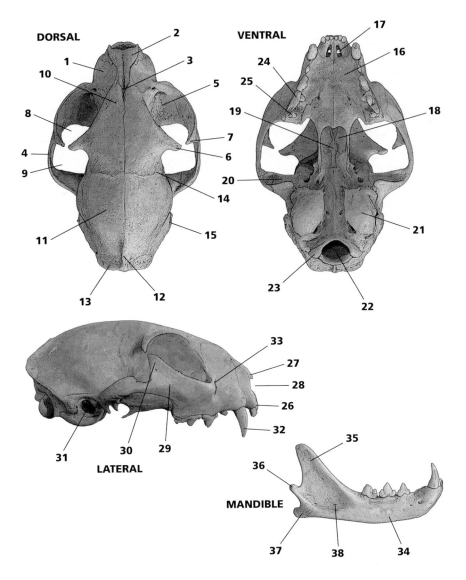

DORSAL

VENTRAL

LATERAL

MANDIBLE

processes are long. The presphenoid (19) is narrower than in margays. The mandibular fossa (20) is well developed. Auditory bullae (21) are large, oval, and inflated. The foramen magnum (22) is larger, and occipital condyles (23) are medium. The carnassial (24) is thin and strong, and the molar (25) is tiny.

Lateral: The dorsolateral outline is very curved, the line from the apex of the skull above the orbits sloping more gradually to the tips of the nasals. The premaxillaries (26) extend to just beyond the nasals (27), and the nasal vacuity (28) is relatively small and vertical. The zygomatics are stout; the jugals (29) are massive, with very large postorbital processes (30), which in older animals will make contact and fuse with the upper postorbital processes to form a complete postorbital bar. The audi-

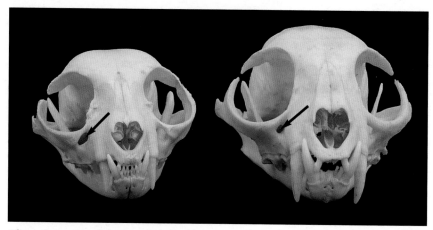

Often relative size of the overall skull and the comparative lengths of the canines are enough to differentiate between feral cat and bobcat skulls. Bone extensions of the parietal bones are also discussed in the text. Here compare the proportionately larger infraorbital foramen in the feral cat skull on the left with that of the bobcat on the right. This is a useful clue to skull fragments. PRIVATE COLLECTION.

tory meatus (31) is medium. Canines (32) are slender, conical, and grooved. The infraorbital foramina (33) are oblong and proportionately larger than in bobcats.

Mandible: The mandible is solid, the body (34) deep and curved to the anterior. The coronoid process (35) is more slender, rounded, and long. The condyle (36) is stout, barrel-shaped, and aligned with the toothrow. The angular process (37) is reduced and rounded. The masseteric fossa (38) is deep, and the dentition is jagged.

Similar species: Margays, jaguarundis, bobcats, and ocelots.

Notes: Domestic cats can often be distinguished from bobcats by size alone, especially after the relative age of an animal is determined. Some additional characters to consider are the relative size of the infraorbital canal, which is often larger in domestic cats; the temporal ridges, which are more V-shaped than U-shaped in bobcats; the zygomatic plates and jugals, which are proportionately larger in domestic cats; a depression at the posterior tips of the nasals, which often appears in domestic cats but is rare in bobcats; the presence of the small premolar (P1); and the tendency for thick bone extensions, sometimes two-tipped, to extend from the parietals over the frontals toward the temporal ridges in domestic cats.

Cougar or mountain lion, *Puma concolor*

Greatest length: 170.5–220.0 mm (6^{7}/$_{10}$–8^{7}/$_{10}$ in.) (full table of measurements page 608, life-size image page 139, life-size jaw page 171)

Specimen illustrated: Adult male, SBMNH 3037

Dentition: i 3/3 c 1/1 p 3/2 m 1/1, total 30. Grooved canines. Molars 1/1 distinct to cats.

Dorsal: Feline skulls are rounded, with wide-spreading zygomatics; short, broad rostrums; and large orbits. The rostrum (1) is very short, broad, and strong; the nasals (2) are broad, triangular, and shorter than in jaguars; the posterior tips converge and usually meet in a distinctive depression (3), though California populations lack this depression. The zygomatic arches (4) are long, heavy, and wide-spreading, converging to the anterior, and they are more than 50 percent of the greatest length of skull; postorbital processes from the frontals (5) are thick, triangular, and slightly longer than in canids and ursids; postorbital processes are well developed on the zygomatics (6). The orbits (7) are large, forward facing, and positioned completely forward of the midline of the skull; the temporal fossa (8) is very large. The frontal region (9) and interorbital breadth are narrow and high; the interorbital breadth is slightly larger than the postorbital. The braincase (10) is large, rounded, and approximately as wide as the rostrum; well-developed temporal ridges (11) converge in a V at the anterior of the braincase to form a large sagittal crest (12). Occipital

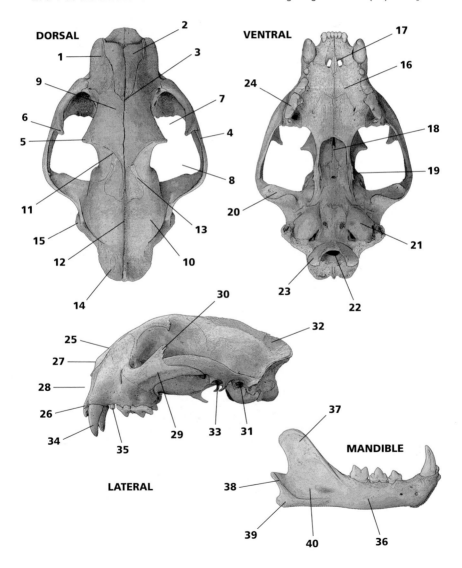

crests are very well developed, and the supraoccipital shield (14) is long. Distinctive, thin bone extensions (13) run from the parietals over the frontals toward the temporal ridges, a reliable character for identification. The mastoid processes (15) are large.

Ventral: The broad palate (16) is somewhat wedge-shaped, approximately as wide as the length of a toothrow, and extends well beyond the posterior molars. Toothrows are relatively short. The incisive foramina (17) are a bit larger and wider. The pterygoid region (18) is wide, and the pterygoid processes (19) are relatively long. The mandibular fossa (20) is well developed. Auditory bullae (21) are small, oval, and inflated. The foramen magnum (22) is smaller, and occipital condyles (23) are stout. The carnassial (24) is thin and strong.

Lateral: The dorsolateral outline is very rounded, the line from the apex of the skull above the orbits slopes steeply (25) to the tips of the premaxillaries. The premaxillaries (26) extend to just beyond the nasals (27), and the nasal vacuity (28) is very large and sloping. The jugals (29) are stout, with larger, narrow postorbital projections (30) far to the anterior. The auditory meatus (31) is small. From this perspective, also note the well-developed sagittal crest (32), mandibular fossa (33), and short toothrow. Canines (34) are large and conical. The extra premolar (35) situated behind the large canines is not present in bobcats or lynx.

Mandible: The mandible is heavy, the body (36) deep and curved to the anterior. The coronoid process (37) is large, stout, and rounded; the coronoid is more vertical than in jaguars. The condyle (38) is stout, barrel-shaped, and aligned with the

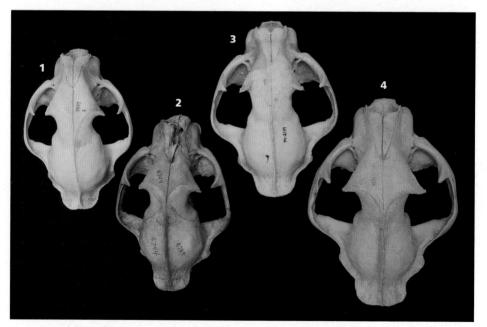

Sexual dimorphism is pronounced in cougars, and evident when comparing skulls. Skulls 1 and 2 are those of adult females, 3987 and 4744 respectively. Skull 3 is a subadult male, M-2159, and skull 4 that of an older, mature male, 3591. SANTA BARBARA MUSEUM OF NATURAL HISTORY.

toothrow. The angular process (39) is reduced and rounded. The masseteric fossa (40) is deep, and the dentition is jagged.

Similar species: Jaguars, ocelots, bobcats, lynx, and other large cats of the world, such as leopards.

Notes: Immature animals have large, rounded braincases. With age, the braincase becomes proportionately smaller as the frontal region extends forward, and crests develop to support larger muscles. In males, the sagittal crest is further developed and the zygomata are proportionately more widely spread than in females (see page 460). Hoffmeister (1986) distinguishes cougars from jaguars as follows: If the maxillary toothrow measures 69 millimeters or more in a male or 64 millimeters or more in a female, it's a jaguar. The length of the upper carnassial in male jaguars is 24 millimeters or more, and in females 23.5 millimeters or more.

Ocelot, *Leopardus pardalis*

Greatest length: 121.0–142.3 mm ($4^8/_{10}$–$5^6/_{10}$ in.) (full table of measurements page 608, life-size image page 136, life-size jaw page 167)

Specimen illustrated: Adult male, MVZ 132174

Dentition: i 3/3 c 1/1 p 3/2 m 1/1, total 30. Grooved canines. Molars 1/1 unique to cats.

Dorsal: Feline skulls are rounded, with wide-spreading zygomatics; short, broad rostrums; and large orbits. The rostrum (1) is very short, broad, and strong; the nasals (2) are broad at the anterior, tapering quickly, and their posterior tips converge and meet in a distinctive depression (3). The zygomatic arches (4) are long, heavy, and wide-spreading, converging to the anterior, and they are approximately 50 percent of the greatest length of skull; postorbital processes from the frontals (5) are thick, long, and triangular; postorbital processes are well developed on the zygomatics (6). The orbits (7) are large, forward facing, and positioned completely forward of the midline of the skull; the temporal fossa (8) is large. The frontal region (9) and interorbital breadth are narrow and high; the interorbital breadth is narrower than the postorbital. The braincase is large, rounded, and wider than the rostrum; temporal ridges (10) converge in a V at the anterior of the braincase to form a sagittal crest (11). Occipital crests are very well developed, and the supraoccipital shield (12) is very large. The mastoid processes (13) are large.

Ventral: The broad palate (14) is somewhat wedge-shaped, approximately as wide as the length of a toothrow, then narrows considerably as it extends well beyond the posterior molars. Toothrows are relatively short. The incisive foramina (15) are larger and wider. The pterygoid region (16) is wide, and the pterygoid processes (17) are long. The mandibular fossa (18) is well developed. Auditory bullae (19) are large, oval, and inflated. The foramen magnum (20) is large, and occipital condyles (21) are very wide apart. The carnassial (22) is thin and strong.

Lateral: The dorsolateral outline is very rounded, the line from the apex of the skull above the orbits sloping less steeply (23) to the tips of the premaxillaries. The premaxillaries (24) extend to just beyond the nasals (25), and the nasal vacuity (26)

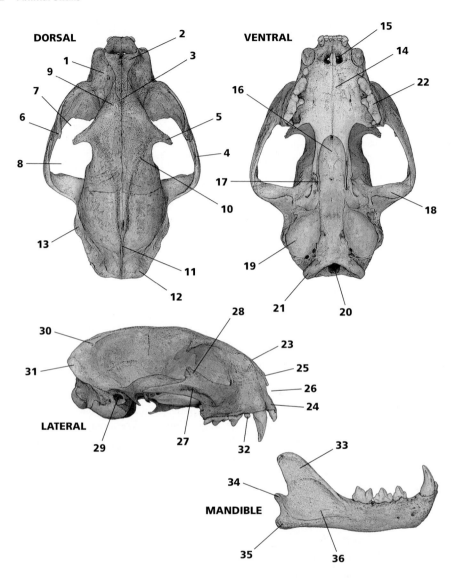

DORSAL

VENTRAL

LATERAL

MANDIBLE

is large and sloping. The zygomata are stout, especially the jugals (27), which have larger postorbital processes (28) to the anterior. The auditory meatus (29) is small. From this perspective, also note the well-developed sagittal (30) and occipital (31) crests. Canines are large and conical. The extra premolar (32) situated behind the large canines is not present in bobcats or lynx.

Mandible: The mandible is strong, the body deep and curved to the anterior. The coronoid process (33) is large, stout, and rounded. The condyle (34) is stout, barrel-shaped, and aligned with the toothrow. The angular process (35) is larger and rounded. The masseteric fossa (36) is deep, and the dentition is jagged.

Similar species: Bobcats, lynx, cougars, domestic cats, and jaguarundis.

Margay, *Leopardus wiedii*

Greatest length: 86.6–107.0 mm (3⁴/10–4²/10 in.) (full table of measurements page 608, life-size image page 125, life-size jaw page 164)

Specimen illustrated: Adult female, LACM 33944

Dentition: i 3/3 c 1/1 p 3/2 m 1/1, total 30. Grooved canines. Molars 1/1 unique to cats.

Dorsal: Feline skulls generally are rounded, with wide-spreading zygomata, short, broad rostrums, and large orbits, though the margay exhibits a more slender outline because of its very large and long braincase. The rostrum (1) is very short, broad, and strong; the nasals (2) are broad at the anterior and taper quickly to the posterior. The zygomatic arches (3) are long, heavy, and wide-spreading, slightly converging to the anterior; zygomatic plates (4) are proportionately larger than in other cats. Postorbital processes from the frontals (5) are slender and triangular, pointing to the posterior; postorbital processes are well developed on the zygomata (6). The orbits (7) are very large, forward facing, and positioned well forward of the midline of the skull, which is a useful character in identification. The temporal fossa (8) is large. The frontal region (9) is elevated and narrower; the interorbital breadth is much narrower than the postorbital. The braincase (10) is very large, oval, and approximately two-thirds the greatest length of skull; temporal ridges are weak, and sagittal crests are generally absent or very small. Occipital crests are less developed. The mastoid processes (11) are either just or not visible from this perspective.

Ventral: The broad palate (12) is somewhat wedge-shaped, approximately as wide as the length of a toothrow, then abruptly narrows and extends well beyond the posterior molars. Toothrows are relatively short. The incisive foramina (13) are larger and wider. The pterygoid region (14) is wide, and the pterygoid processes (15) are relatively long. The presphenoid (16) is wide. The mandibular fossa (17) is well

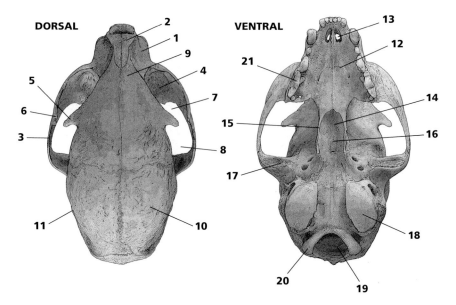

DORSAL

VENTRAL

developed. Auditory bullae (18) are large, oval, and inflated. The foramen magnum (19) is very large, and occipital condyles (20) are stout. The carnassial (21) is thin and strong.

Lateral: The dorsolateral outline is very rounded, the line from the point of the skull above the orbits slopes steeply (34) to the tips of the premaxillaries; the apex of the skull (22) is aligned with the posterior of the zygomatic arches, which is farther back than in domestic cats. The premaxillaries (23) extend to just beyond the nasals (24), and the nasal vacuity (25) is smaller and slightly angled. The jugals (26) are stout, with larger postorbital processes (27) far to the anterior. The auditory meatus (28) is smaller. Large, conical canines (29) are more slender and straighter.

Mandible: The mandible is strong, the body deep and very curved. The coronoid process (30) is large, slender, and rounded. The condyle (31) is stout and barrel-shaped, and it sits just above the toothrow. The angular process (32) is slightly larger and rounded. The masseteric fossa (33) is deep, and the dentition is jagged.

Similar species: Jaguarundis and domestic cats.

Jaguarundi, *Herpailurus yaguarondi*

Greatest length: 86.7–116.1 mm (3⁴/10–4⁶/10 in.) (full table of measurements page 608, life-size image page 125, life-size jaw page 165)

Specimen illustrated: Adult female, LACM 61144

Dentition: i 3/3 c 1/1 p 3/2 m 1/1, total 30. Grooved canines. Molars 1/1 unique to cats.

Dorsal: Feline skulls generally are rounded, with wide-spreading zygomatics, short broad rostrums, and large orbits, though the jaguarundi exhibits a more slender outline because of its very long braincase. The rostrum (1) is very short, laterally compressed, and angular; from this perspective, the lines (2) created by following the anterior edge of the postorbital processes forward to the midline of the nasals are very distinctive. The nasals (3) are broad at their anterior, then taper quickly, their posterior tips converging in a slight depression (4). The zygomatic arches (5) are very long, heavy, and wide-spreading, strongly converging to the anterior; the zygomatic plates (6) are very large. Postorbital processes from the frontals (7) are thick, triangular, and pointed; postorbital processes are well developed on the zygomata (8). The orbits (9) are very large, forward facing, and positioned well forward of the midline of the skull, which is a useful character in identification. The temporal fossa (10) is large. The frontal region (11) is well elevated, and the interorbital breadth is much narrower than the postorbital. The braincase is very large, oval, and well over 50 percent of the greatest length of skull. Temporal ridges are weak to absent, and a small sagittal crest may develop far to the posterior. Occipital crests are well developed, and the supraoccipital shield (12) is broad. The mastoid processes often are not visible from this perspective.

Ventral: The broad palate (13) is somewhat wedge-shaped, approximately as wide as the length of a toothrow, then abruptly tapers and extends well beyond the posterior molars; there is a concave outline (15) or notch in the posterior palate between the posterior molars and the pterygoid region. The posterior palate also has a small notch (14) along the midline, a smaller version of what is characteristic in jaguars. Toothrows are relatively short. The incisive foramina (16) are larger and wider. The pterygoid region (17) is very broad, and the pterygoid processes (18) are long. The mandibular fossa (19) is well developed. Auditory bullae (20) are very long, oval, and inflated. The foramen magnum (21) is large, and occipital condyles (22) are stout. The carnassial (23) is thin and strong.

Lateral: Perhaps the most distinctive feature of the jaguarundi is the dorsolateral outline, which is less rounded than other cats (24); the rostrum (25) is distinctively deep. The premaxillaries (26) extend to just beyond the nasals (27), and the nasal

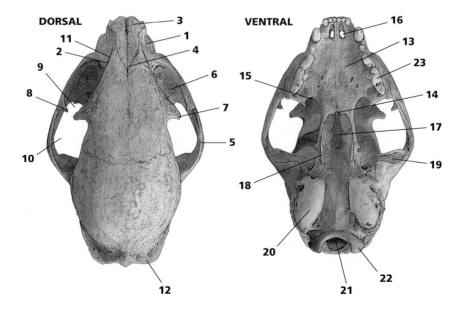

DORSAL

VENTRAL

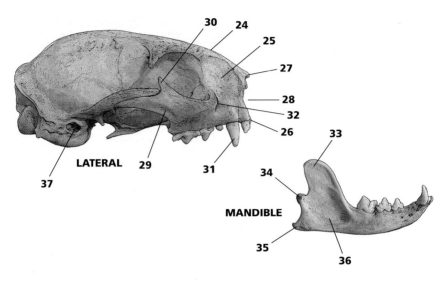

vacuity (28) is very large and vertical. The zygomata are stout, especially the jugals (29), which have slender postorbital processes (30) far to the anterior. The auditory meatus (37) is small. Canines (31) are smaller and conical, and the infraorbital foramen (32) is oval.

Mandible: The mandible is strong, the body deep and very curved. The coronoid process (33) is large, broad, and rounded. The condyle (34) is stout, barrel-shaped, and aligned with the toothrow. The angular process (35) is rounded and extends beyond the condyle. The masseteric fossa (36) is deep, and the dentition is jagged.

Similar species: Margays, domestic cats, ocelots, and bobcats.

Canada lynx, *Lynx canadensis*

Greatest length: 117.4–135.8 mm ($4^6/10$–$5^3/10$ in.) (full table of measurements page 608, life-size image page 136, life-size jaw page 167)

Specimen illustrated: Adult male, MVZ 4163

Dentition: i 3/3 c 1/1 p 2/2 m 1/1, total 28. Grooved canines. Molars 1/1 unique to cats.

Dorsal: Feline skulls are rounded, with wide-spreading zygomata; short, broad rostrums; and large orbits. The rostrum (1) is very short, broad, and strong; the nasals (2) are broad and triangular, tapering to the posterior, where the tips may converge in a slight depression (3) or may be flat. The zygomatic arches (4) are long, heavy, and wide-spreading, converging to the anterior. Postorbital processes from the frontals (5) are large and triangular, pointing well away from the midline of the skull; postorbital processes are well developed on the zygomata (6). The orbits (7) are very large, forward facing, and positioned completely forward of the midline of the skull; the temporal fossa (8) is large. The frontal region (9) and interorbital breadth are broad and elevated; the interorbital breadth is slightly narrower than the postorbital. The braincase (10) is large, rounded, and wider than the rostrum;

well-developed temporal ridges (11) converge in a ∪ at the posterior of the brain-case to form a small sagittal crest (12). Occipital crests are very well developed, and the supraoccipital shield (13) is long, especially in old animals. The mastoid processes often are not visible from this perspective.

Ventral: The broad palate (14) is somewhat wedge-shaped, approximately as wide as the length of a toothrow, and then narrows considerably before extending beyond the posterior molars. Toothrows are relatively short. The incisive foramina (15) are a bit larger and wider. The pterygoid region (16) is wide, and the pterygoid processes (17) are relatively long. The presphenoid (18) is wider than 4 mm, which is a more reliable character in differentiating from bobcats. The mandibular fossa (19) is well

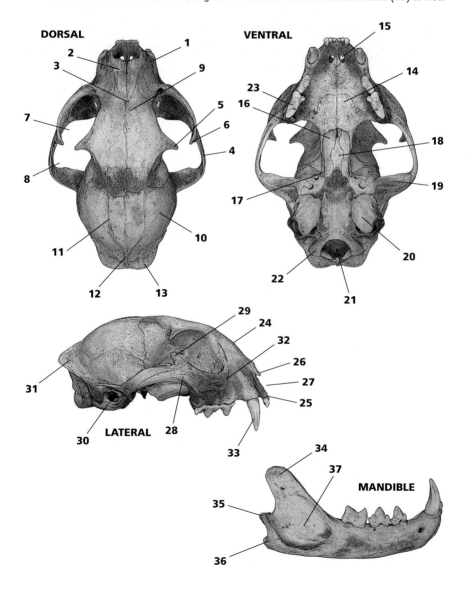

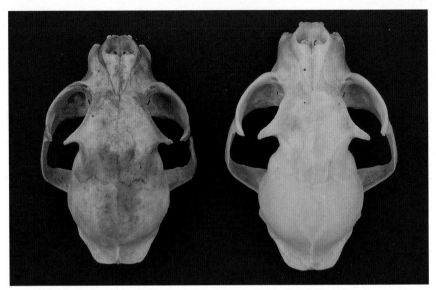

Compare the smaller, darker female lynx skull on the left with the lighter, larger adult male skull on the right. Both animals were trapped near Nome, Alaska. PRIVATE COLLECTION.

developed. Auditory bullae (20) are medium, oval, and less inflated. The foramen magnum (21) is medium, and occipital condyles (22) are stout. The carnassial (23) is thin and strong.

Lateral: The dorsolateral outline is very rounded, the line from the apex of the skull above the orbits slopes steeply (24) to the tips of the premaxillaries. The premaxillaries (25) extend to just beyond the nasals (26), and the nasal vacuity (27) is very large and sloping. The zygomatics are stout, especially the jugals (28), which have larger, narrow postorbital processes (29) to the anterior. The auditory meatus (30) is medium. From this perspective, also note the well-developed occipital shield (31) and oval infraorbital foramen (32). Canines (33) are long and conical.

Mandible: The mandible is strong, the body deep and curved to the anterior. The coronoid process (34) is large, stout, and rounded. The condyle (35) is stout, barrel-shaped, and aligned with the toothrow. The angular (36) process is reduced and rounded. The masseteric fossa (37) is deep, and the dentition is jagged.

Similar species: Difficult to distinguish from bobcats. Also, ocelots, domestic cats, and cougars.

Bobcat, *Lynx rufus*

Greatest length: 105.8–145.2 mm (4²/10–5⁷/10 in.) (full table of measurements page 610, life-size image page 134, life-size jaw page 166)

Specimen illustrated: Adult male, SBMNH 891

Dentition: i 3/3 c 1/1 p 2/2 m 1/1, total 28. Grooved canines. Molars 1/1 unique to cats.

Dorsal: Feline skulls are rounded, with wide-spreading zygomata; short, broad rostrums; and large orbits. The rostrum (1) is very short, broad, and strong; the nasals (2) are broad and triangular, tapering to the posterior, where the tips may converge in a slight depression (3) or may be flat. The zygomatic arches (4) are long, heavy, and wide-spreading, converging to the anterior. Postorbital processes from the frontals (5) are large and triangular, pointing well away from the midline of the skull; postorbital processes are well developed on the zygomata (6). The orbits (7) are very large, forward facing, and positioned completely forward of the midline of the skull; the temporal fossa (8) is large. The frontal region (9) and interorbital breadth are narrow and elevated; the interorbital breadth is slightly narrower than the postorbital. The braincase (10) is large, rounded, and wider than the rostrum; well-developed temporal ridges converge in a ∪ at the posterior of the braincase to form a small sagittal crest (11). Occipital crests are very well developed, and the supraoccipital shield (12) is long, especially in old animals. The mastoid processes (13) often are just visible from this perspective.

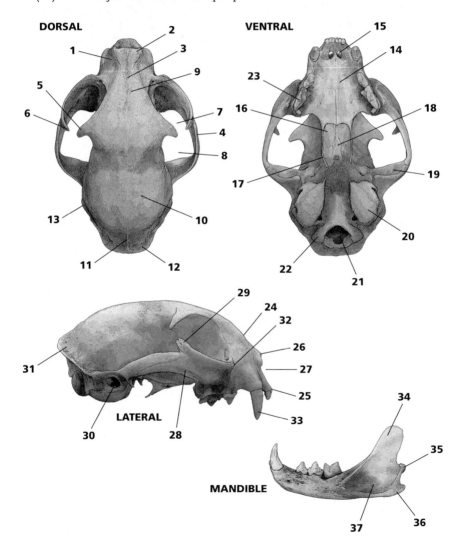

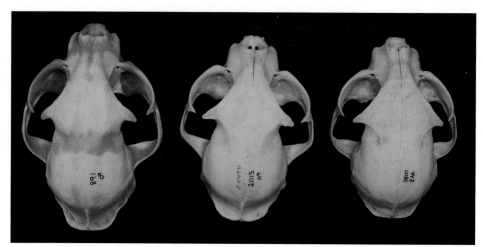

From left to right, two male bobcats and a female. SANTA BARBARA MUSEUM OF NATURAL HISTORY 891, 2015, 3807.

Ventral: The broad palate (14) is somewhat wedge-shaped, approximately as wide as the length of a toothrow, and then narrows considerably before extending beyond the posterior molars. Toothrows are relatively short. The incisive foramina (15) are a bit larger and wider. The pterygoid region (16) is wide, and the pterygoid processes (17) are relatively long. The presphenoid (18) is less than 4 mm wide, a more reliable character to differentiate from lynx. The mandibular fossa (19) is well developed. Auditory bullae (20) are medium, oval, and less inflated. The foramen magnum (21) is medium, and occipital condyles (22) are stout. The carnassial (23) is thin and strong.

Lateral: The dorsolateral outline is very rounded, the line from the apex of the skull above the orbits slopes steeply (24) to the tips of the premaxillaries. The premaxillaries (25) extend to just beyond the nasals (26), and the nasal vacuity (27) is very large and sloping. The zygomata are stout, especially the jugals (28), which have larger, narrow postorbital processes (29) to the anterior. The auditory meatus (30) is medium. From this perspective, also note the well-developed occipital shield (31) and infraorbital foramen (32), which is proportionately smaller than in domestic cats. Canines (33) are long and conical.

Mandible: The mandible is strong, the body deep and curved to the anterior. The coronoid process (34) is large, stout, and rounded. The condyle (35) is stout, barrel-shaped, and aligned with the toothrow. The angular process (36) is reduced and rounded. The masseteric fossa (37) is deep, and the dentition is jagged.

Similar species: Difficult to distinguish from Canada lynx. Also, ocelots, domestic cats, and cougars.

Notes: When specimens of similar age are compared, male skulls are longer, more sharply ridged, and more robust than female (see above). Yet sexual dimorphism is much less pronounced than in cougars, and an old female and a younger male could be confused. With age, the skull lengthens, ridges and crests develop, and postorbital processes lengthen; in old animals, they may touch and even fuse.

Jaguar, *Panthera onca*

Greatest length: 203.9–275.0 mm (8–10^{8}/$_{10}$ in.) (full table of measurements page 610, life-size image page 142, life-size jaw page 172)

Specimen illustrated: Adult male, MVZ 4900

Dentition: i 3/3 c 1/1 p 3/2 m 1/1, total 30. Grooved canines. Molars 1/1 unique to cats.

Dorsal: Feline skulls are rounded, with wide-spreading zygomata; short, broad rostrums; and large orbits. The rostrum (1) is slightly longer and broader than in cougars; the nasals (2) are broad and longer, the posterior tips converging and meeting in a depression (3). The zygomatic arches (4) are long, very heavy, and wide-spreading, strongly converging to the anterior; postorbital processes from the frontals (5) are thick, triangular, and longer than in canines and ursids; postorbital processes are well developed on the zygomata (6). The orbits (7) are large, forward facing, and positioned completely forward of the midline of the skull; the temporal fossa (8) is very large. The frontal region (9) and interorbital breadth are proportionately narrower than in cougars; the interorbital breadth is much larger than the postorbital. The braincase (10) is proportionately smaller and approximately as wide as the rostrum; well-developed temporal ridges (11) converge in a V at the anterior of the braincase to form a large sagittal crest (12). Occipital crests are very well developed, and the supraoccipital shield (13) is very long. The mastoid processes (14) blend in with the squamosal arm of the zygomatic arch (15).

Ventral: The broad palate (16) is somewhat wedge-shaped, approximately as wide as the length of a toothrow, and extends well beyond the posterior molars. There is a distinctive notch (17) in the palate at the posterior along the midline, a reliable character to differentiate from cougar. Toothrows are relatively short. The incisive foramina (18) are a bit larger and wider. The pterygoid region (19) is narrow, and

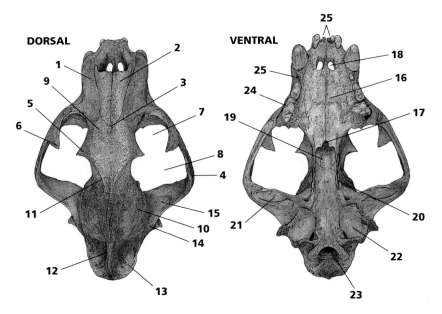

DORSAL

VENTRAL

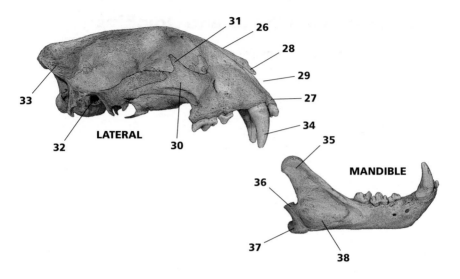

the pterygoid processes (20) are relatively long. The mandibular fossa (21) is well developed. Auditory bullae (22) are small, oval, and inflated. The foramen magnum (23) is proportionately smaller than in cougars. The carnassial (24) is thin and strong. Several teeth (25) are missing in this specimen.

Lateral: The dorsolateral outline is rounded, the line from the apex of the skull above the orbits sloping (26) to the tips of the premaxillaries (27), though to a lesser degree than in cougars. The premaxillaries extend well beyond the nasals (28), and the nasal vacuity (29) is large and sloping. The zygomata are very stout, with massive jugals (30) and narrow postorbital processes (31) far to the anterior. The auditory meatus (32) is small. From this perspective, also note the long occipital shield (33) and very large, conical canines (34).

Mandible: The mandible is heavy, the body deep and curved to the anterior. The coronoid process (35) is slightly longer and more slender than in cougars, and it points more to the posterior. The condyle (36) is stout, barrel-shaped, and aligned with the toothrow. The angular process (37) is reduced and rounded. The masseteric fossa (38) is deep, and the dentition is jagged.

Similar species: Cougars, other large cats, bears, and wolves.

Notes: The sagittal crest develops with age and is most pronounced in males. A biologist in Mexico told me, while working there inventorying carnivores, that the palatal notch is related to the jaguar's ability to roar; cougars, which lack the notch, are unable to do so. I've not found literature to substantiate this statement, but it has certainly burned the notch into my memory, which is a very useful character in identification.

Order Cetacea: Whales and Dolphins

Family Delphinidae: Dolphins

The vast diversity of porpoises, dolphins, and whales are divided into two large groups: the Mysticeti, the baleen whales; and the Odontoceti, the toothed whales, which include orcas, dolphins, porpoises, beaked whales, and sperm whales.

One can quickly surmise to which group an animal belongs from only its skull. The skulls of Mysticeti have long, arched rostrums, with concave ventral surfaces, creating ample space for baleen attachments (see page 474). The rostrums of the toothed whales are straight, and the presence of teeth is ample evidence.

Toothed whales also have concave, sloping foreheads, which create the necessary bony amphitheater to house the mass of fatty tissue used in echo location, and reflect and direct the sound waves used to project communication over vast distances; the

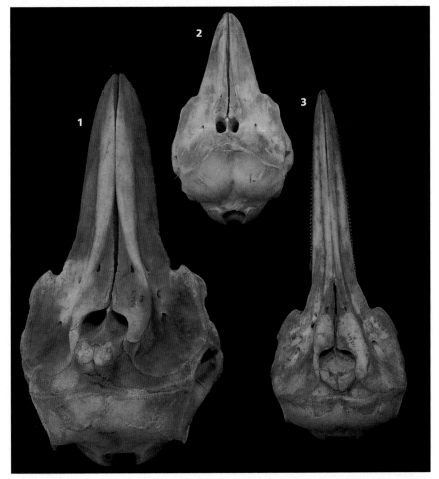

Three members of the order Cetacea: 1. Bottlenose dolphin 106609 *(Tursiops truncatus)*, 2. Harbor porpoise, female 208561 *(Phocoena phocoena)*, 3. Common dolphin, male 115339 *(Delphinus delphis)*. MUSEUM OF VERTEBRATE ZOOLOGY, UC BERKELEY.

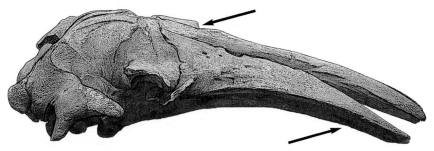

A gray whale *(Eschrichtius robustus)* and example of a baleen whale *(Mysticeti* species*)*. Note the concave ventral surface of the rostrum, where the baleen attaches, and the convex "forehead" region.

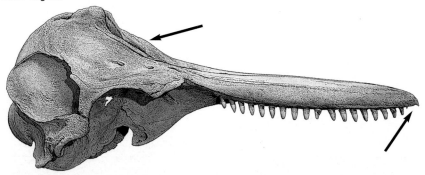

Bottlenose dolphin *(Tursiops truncatus)* an example of a toothed cetacean *(Odontoceti* species*)*. Note the straight ventral surface of the rostrum where the teeth are located and concave "forehead," which creates the bony amphitheater used to direct and launch sounds used in long distance communication.

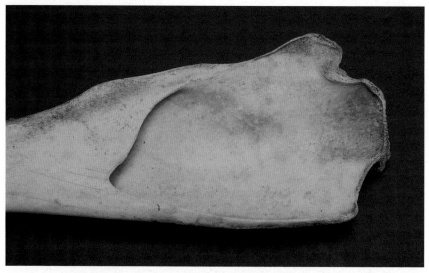

Here is pictured the inner surface of a bottlenose dolphin's mandible to show the bony structures characteristic of all members of Odontoceti, which funnel sound to the posterior of the mandible next to the free-floating ear bones. SANTA BARBARA MUSEUM OF NATURAL HISTORY 3669.

baleen whales are not able to do this. The sound receptacle is actually on the inside of each mandible, where sounds are funneled into a cavity at the posterior that sits just behind the free-floating ear bones.

The teeth of the Odontoceti are simple and peglike, ideal for gripping slippery prey. They are designed to prevent escape, as many toothed whales grip their prey, reposition it, and then gulp it whole.

Bottle-nosed dolphin, *Tursiops truncatus*

Greatest length: 425.0–517.5 mm (16⁷/10–20⁴/10 in.) (full table of measurements page 610, life-size image page 157, life-size jaw page 177)

Specimen illustrated: Adult, SBMNH 3669

Dentition: 20–26 above, 18–24 below, total up to 50.

Dorsal: Dolphin skulls are triangular, with long, slender rostrums and rounded posteriors. One peculiarity is that the nasal bones (1) are rounded projections toward the posterior at the apex of the skull. The two large vacuities (2) are the nares, which in many toothed whales are shifted to the left, and one is much larger than the other. The premaxillaries (3) extend forward down the center of the dorsal surface of the rostrum and are in contact with one another for 50 percent of their length. The maxillary bones (4) also extend the length of the rostrum. The occipital bone (5) is large and curved. This animal is not yet a full adult, as evidenced by the porous bone structures (6) in certain regions of the skull.

Ventral: Jugal bones (7) are very thin and are often lost in skulls found in the field; the jugal on the left-hand side is missing from this animal. The occipital condyles (8) are very large.

Lateral: The dorsolateral outline is dominated by the long, slender rostrum, and then rises sharply just posterior to the nares (9); the concave forehead (10) serves as the

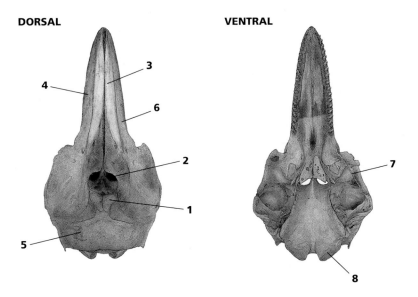

DORSAL   VENTRAL

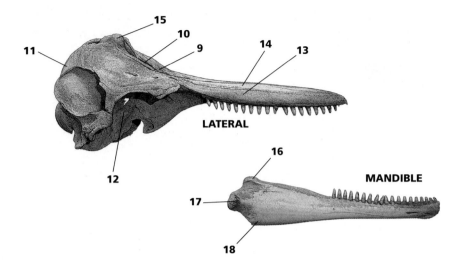

amphitheater. The posterior of the skull created by the large occipital bone (11) curves toward the anterior. The orbit (12) is large and low; the jugal bone is missing. The rostrum (13) is less deep than it is wide, and the premaxillaries (14) are flattened on their dorsal surfaces. Teeth are large, peglike, and smooth-crowned. Note the position of the nasals (15) at the apex of the skull.

Mandible: The mandible is long and triangular, tapering toward the anterior. The coronoid process (16) is reduced and rounded. The condyle (17) is large and stout, and the angular process (18) is small, creating a sharper corner along the ventral surface. The teeth are simple and peglike.

Similar species: Other dolphins, porpoises, and false killer whales.

Order Sirenia: Dugongs, manatees, and sea cows

Family Trichechidae: Manatees

The manatee is an entirely aquatic creature of heavy, dense bones. The jugals are heavy in fats and thought to be used in communication. The mandible is hollow and filled with lipid-rich adipose tissue that conducts sound energy (Hall 1981).

As in elephants, the molariform teeth are replaced from the posterior as anteriormost teeth become worn, useless, and drop out (Hall 1981). Look for the replacement teeth lined up in elevator fashion and emerging on the inside of the posterior mandible (see page 477).

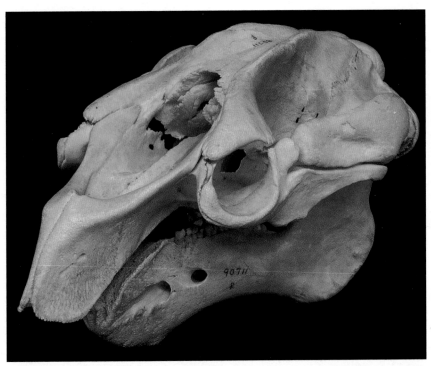

The North American member of this family is the West Indian manatee *(Trichechus manatus)*.
Female, MUSEUM OF VERTEBRATE ZOOLOGY, UC BERKELEY 90711.

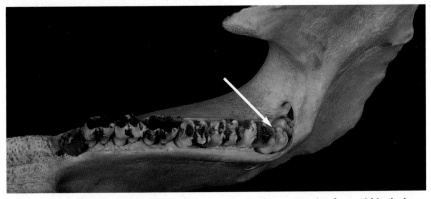

Look carefully to the posterior of the toothrow where teeth are emerging from within the bone as if on a conveyor belt. As teeth are worn and drop out to the anterior, new teeth shift forward from the posterior to replace them. Female, MUSEUM OF VERTEBRATE ZOOLOGY, UC BERKELEY 90711.

West Indian manatee, *Trichechus manatus*

Greatest length: 325.0–418.0 mm (12⁸/10–16⁵/10 in.) (full table of measurements page 610, life-size image page 152, life-size jaw page 176)

Specimen illustrated: Adult female, MVZ 90711

Dentition: Molariform teeth 11/11, but up to 6 showing at any given time. Incisors are very small and lost by adulthood.

Dorsal: Manatee skulls are large, heavy, and somewhat triangular in outline. The rostrum (1) is triangular and dominated by the massive nasal vacuity (2), which is enlarged due to the tiny, receded, and widely spaced nasal bones (3). The premaxillaries (1) are stout and have concave lateral surfaces (4) toward the anterior. Orbits (5) are small and well forward of the midline of the skull, protruding out and to the anterior. The zygomatic arches (6) are thick and heavy, converging toward the anterior. The postorbital breadth (7) is broad, flattened, and elevated. Temporal ridges (8) are well developed, as are the occipital crests (9), both of which obscure views of the smaller braincase (10).

Ventral: The palate (11) is long, very narrow, and notched (12) to the posterior. The pterygoid region (13) is narrow; mandibular fossae (14) are developed. The auditory bullae (15) are incomplete and ringlike, and the basioccipital region (16) is narrow. The foramen magnum (17) is large, and the occipital condyles (18) are large and stout. Molariform teeth are flat and squared; teeth are completely lacking to the anterior of the mouth.

Lateral: The dorsolateral outline is convex, with a step (19) midway along to the rostrum. The orbits (20) are oval and nearly completely surrounded by bone; the zygomatic arches (21) are massive.

Mandible: Manatee mandibles are massive and heavy, and they are very similar in form to those of elephants. The coronoid process (22) is very high, squared, and angled

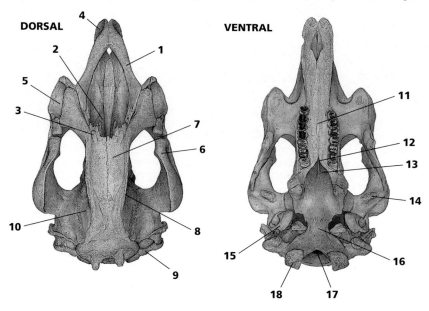

DORSAL VENTRAL

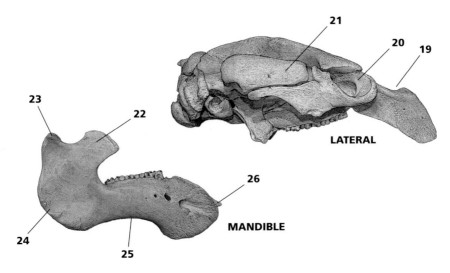

LATERAL

MANDIBLE

to the anterior; the anterior edge is concave. The condyle (23) is large, strong, high, and vertical, and it sits just below the apex of the coronoid. The angular process (24) is large and rounded, forming the posterior corner. The ventral surface of the mandible is concave (25), and high on the anterior edge is a small, pointed projection (26). The molariform teeth are replaced from the posterior as anteriormost teeth are worn and lost.

Similar species: Walrus, whales, and pygmy elephants.

Order Perissodactyla: Odd-Toed Ungulates

Family Equidae: Horses

Feral horses are an introduced species found in pockets throughout the West and in smaller numbers along the coast. The horse skull is distinctive due to its large incisors, which are ideal for cropping grass. The eyes are far to the back of the head, a characteristic of pure grazers. Additional bony structure on the lateral sides of the rostrum allows for the attachment of massive masseter muscles, responsible for grinding and milling. The articulation with the mandible allows ample lateral movement, and the body of the mandible is triangular, which moves the power to the posterior and away from the incisors when closing the mouth.

Feral horse or wild pony, *Equus caballus*

Greatest length: 567.0–628.0 mm ($22^3/_{10}$–$24^7/_{10}$ in.) (full table of measurements page 612, life-size image page 158, life-size jaw page 178)

Specimen illustrated: Adult, SBMNH

Dentition: i 3/3 c 0–1/0–1 p 3–4/3–4 m 3/3, total 36–44.

Dorsal: Horse skulls are massive and very slender, with large incisors to the anterior and orbits far to the posterior. The rostrum (1) is very long and triangular, with the premaxillary bones (2) projecting less to the anterior than in elk or moose; turbinate bones are not visible. Nasals (3) are very broad and long, tapering to points (4) at the anterior. Rostral fenestrae are absent. Orbits (5) are large and situated behind the midline of the skull; supraorbital foramina (6) are small. The braincase (7) is very small, oval, and smooth; temporal ridges are small but converge to form a small sagittal crest (8) at the posterior of the braincase. Zygomatic arches spread (9) less than the orbits protrude. Occipital crests are well developed, and the supraoccipital shield (10) is narrow.

Ventral: The palate (11) is long and narrow, extending to the posterior just beyond the anterior edge of the last molar (12); incisive foramina (13) are long, but very thin compared with those of cervids. Incisors (14) are large and distinctive, and a vestigial canine is evident. The pterygoid region (15) is narrow. The auditory bullae (16) are very small and not inflated; the basioccipital region (17) is very narrow. The foramen magnum (18) is medium, and the occipital condyles (19) are large and stout. Molariform teeth are large, flat, and squared.

Lateral: The dorsolateral outline is dominated by the deep rostrum (20). The premaxillaries (21) extend well beyond the anterior tips of the long nasals (22), and the nasal vacuity (23) is large and angled. The lacrimal bone (24) is large and in contact with the nasals (25); a lacrimal depression is absent. A significant ledge (26)

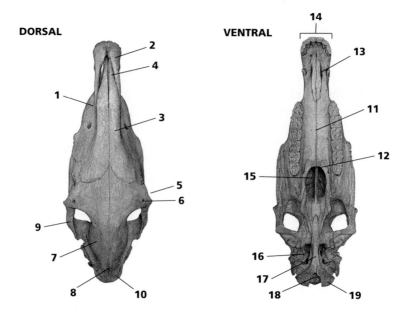

DORSAL VENTRAL

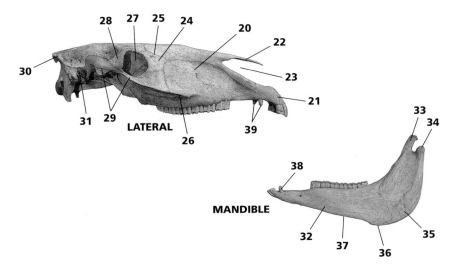

LATERAL

MANDIBLE

continues forward of the orbits along the maxillaries and provides additional bony attachments for the developed masseter muscles. The orbits (27) are oval in shape (the posterior edge is flattened in donkeys) and outlined to the posterior by a complete orbital bar (28); the zygomatic arches (29) are strong. The auditory meatus (31) is very small. The occipital crests (30) extend to the posterior over the occipital condyles. Note the small canine teeth (39).

Mandible: Horse mandibles are large and heavy. They are also long and slender, strongly tapering (32) toward the anterior, and have a posterior corner, which is the angular process. The coronoid process (33) is very high and slender, curving to the posterior. The condyle (34) is large and strong, and it sits well above the toothrows. The angular process (35) is large and rounded, forming the posterior corner. The ventral surface of the angular process (36) is below the ventral surface of the body (37) below the toothrows. The canine (38) is vestigial yet evident.

Similar species: Moose and elk.

Notes: Well-developed incisors for cropping grass. Canines may or may not be present, but when present, they are generally larger in males. Aging can be done quite reliably by examining tooth eruption and wear. A thorough description of the various characteristics used to age horses appears in Jenkins and Ashley (2003).

Order Artiodactyla: Even-Toed Ungulates

Family Suidae: Hogs and pigs

Feral hogs are difficult to classify and seem to be an interbred mix of wild hogs from Europe and domestic animals; they have since become feral and quite successful in North America. Morphologically, feral hogs provide a middle ground in many characters that differentiate the European wild hogs and domestic pigs.

Wild boar or feral hog, *Sus scrofa*

Greatest length: 258.0–322.0 mm (10²/₁₀–12⁷/₁₀ in.) (full table of measurements page 612, life-size image page 145, life-size jaw page 175)

Specimen illustrated: Adult male, SBMNH 1001

Dentition: i 3/3 c 1/1 p 4/4 m 3/3, total 44. Prominent canines are curved, 3 upper incisors rather than the 2 in peccaries, and 7 premolars rather than the 6 in peccaries.

Dorsal: Domestic and wild pig skulls are slender, with long rostrums, distinctive curving canines, and a large, triangular extension projecting from the posterior of the braincase. The rostrum (1) is very long and slender, with the maxillary bones (2) and curving canines projecting out to either side. Nasal sutures (3) are evident, and nasals (4) are long and slender, with pointed anterior tips; two smaller facial glands (5) are present between the orbits, but these should not be confused with the distinctive grooves of the peccary. The zygomatic arches (6) are heavy and thick; orbits (7) are relatively small, and postorbital processes (8) are well developed and triangular, pointing to the posterior. The braincase (9) is larger and angular, though obscured by large temporal ridges (10) that converge to the posterior but do not touch. The occipital crests are well developed, and the supraoccipital shield (11) is distinctly triangular but does not extend as far over the occipital condyles as in peccaries.

Ventral: The palate (12) is very long and narrow, extending to the posterior beyond the toothrows. The pterygoid region (13) is small. The auditory bullae (14) are small and inflated. The foramen magnum (15) is small, and occipital condyles (16) are stout. Six incisors (17) and large canines are obvious. Palatal pits (18) are present between the molars.

Lateral: The dorsolateral outline from the apex of the crests to the tip of the nasals is concave (19) and steeply slopes down the frontals. The tips of premaxillaries (20) and nasals (21) are aligned to the anterior, and the nasal vacuity (22) is smaller and notched. The zygomatic arches (23) are heavy, with large postorbital processes (24), but there is no complete postorbital bar. The infraorbital foramen (25) is medium and situated above the premolars. The auditory meatus is obscured. The very long paraoccipital processes (26) are a distinctive feature at the posterior. The canines (27) are curved out and up, and the molariform teeth are blunt.

Mandible: The mandible is long and heavy. The coronoid process (28) is reduced and pointed; the anterior edge (29) is convex. The condyle (30) is high and strong, and it sits well above the toothrows. The angular process (31) is large and rounded, forming the posterior corner. The ventral surface (32) of the mandible is relatively straight. The canine (33) is long and curves outward.

Similar species: Domestic pigs, peccaries, and horses.

Notes: Domestic pigs in general have larger, higher, and broader skulls, though some animals will be difficult to differentiate. Sweeney et al. (2003) describe a means of identifying the sex of a skull with a study of the canines: Males have enamel extending the length of the entire crown and roots of the teeth, while in females the roots

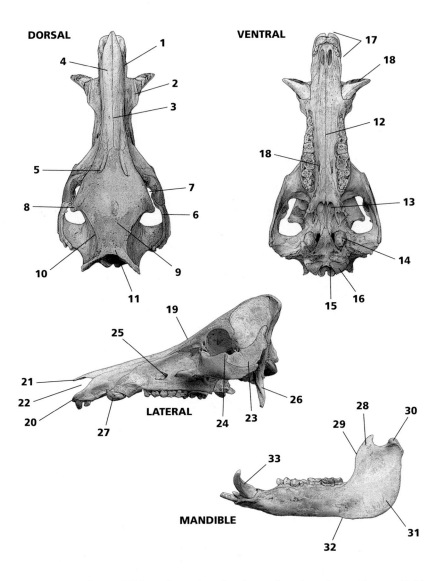

DORSAL

VENTRAL

LATERAL

MANDIBLE

are uncovered. In addition, the sockets for the canines in males are trapezoidal in cross section; in females, they are more triangular. A well-described and presented discussion on the aging of skulls from both tooth eruption and wear is included in Sweeney et al. (2003).

Family Tayassuidae: Peccaries

Peccaries are the native counterparts to Old World swine. Their skulls are distinctive in that the canines are enlarged and straight. The facial and palatal sutures fuse early in life. In 1974, Herring noted that the order in which sutures fuse in the peccary prioritizes those associated with the rostrum and palate, which is different from most other animals (Hellgren and Bissonette 2003). She hypothesized that this is due to an early strengthening of the snout, which is critical in rooting and food acquisition. Another peculiarity of the species is the interlocking molariform teeth (see page 485), which some researchers feel may stabilize the jaw when crushing tough mast crops.

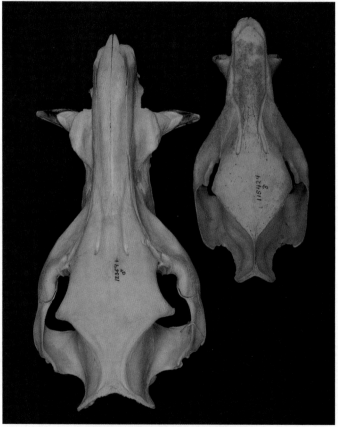

On the left is the skull of a feral pig *(Sus scrofa)*, and on the right the smaller collared peccary, male 115424 *(Pecari)*. MUSEUM OF VERTEBRATE ZOOLOGY, UC BERKELEY.

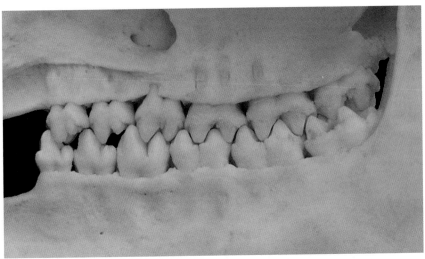

The interlocking teeth of a young collared peccary. With age, the sharp cusps and crowns wear down and thus interlocking components are less pronounced. PRIVATE COLLECTION.

Collared peccary or javelina, *Pecari tajacu*

Greatest length: 220.2–257.6 mm (8^{7}/$_{10}$–10^{1}/$_{10}$ in.) (full table of measurements page 612, life-size image page 141, life-size jaw page 172)

Specimen illustrated: Adult male, MVZ 115424

Dentition: i 2/3 c 1/1 p 3/3 m 3/3, total 38. Prominent, well-developed canines point straight up and down, 2 upper incisors rather than the 3 in wild hogs, and 6 premolars rather than the 7 in hogs.

Dorsal: Peccary skulls are robust, strong, and slender, with distinctive straight canines and a large, triangular extension projecting from the posterior of the braincase. The rostrum (1) is long, slender, and deep, with the maxillary bones (2) and canines projecting out to either side. Nasal sutures (3) fuse with adulthood and are obscured; two deep distinctive channels (4) start between the orbits and run the length of the rostrum. The zygomatic arches (5) are heavy and thick; orbits (6) are relatively small, and postorbital processes (7) are well developed and triangular. The braincase (8) is small and rounded, though obscured by elevated frontals (9) and large temporal ridges (10) that converge to form a large but short sagittal crest (11). The occipital crests are well developed, and the supraoccipital shield (12) is distinctly triangular and extends far to the posterior of the braincase.

Ventral: The palate (13) is very long and narrow, extending to the posterior beyond the toothrows; a pair of palatal ridges or grooves extends (14) between the canines and premolars. The pterygoid region (15) is small. The auditory bullae (16) are small, inflated, and they hang low. The foramen magnum (17) is small, and occipital condyles (18) are stout. Four incisors (19) and large canines (20) are obvious.

Lateral: The dorsolateral outline is one continuous slope (21) from the posterior crests to the tips of the nasals. The premaxillaries (22) extend well beyond the anterior

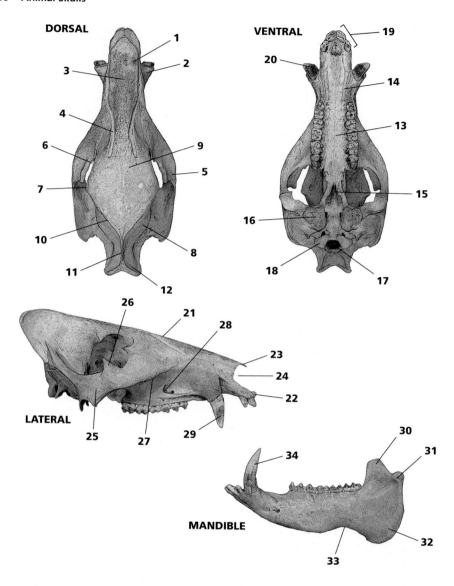

DORSAL

1
2
3
4
6
9
5
7
10
8
11
12

VENTRAL

19
20
14
13
15
16
18
17

LATERAL

26
21
28
23
24
22
25
27
29

MANDIBLE

30
31
34
32
33

tips of the nasals (23), and the nasal vacuity (24) is medium and angled. The zygomatic arches (25) are heavy, with large postorbital processes (26), but there is no complete orbital bar. A significant ledge (27) continues forward of the orbits along the maxillaries and provides additional bony attachments for the developed masseter muscles; the infraorbital foramen (28) is larger and situated above M1. The auditory meatus is obscured. The canines (29) are large and straight, and the molariform teeth are sharply cusped (except in very old animals) and interlock with the opposing teeth in the mandible.

Mandible: The mandible is long and heavy. The coronoid process (30) is low and squared. The condyle (31) is small and strong, and it sits above the toothrows. The angular process (32) is large and rounded, forming the posterior corner. There is a distinctive step (33) in the ventral surface of the angular process below the posterior molars. The canine (34) is long and vertical, curving slightly to the posterior.

Similar species: Other peccaries, feral hogs, and domestic pigs. The orbital notch is not present in the more southern white-lipped peccary *(Pecari pecari)*.

Notes: The large canines are thought to be used primarily as weapons and in competition between breeding males, though another hypothesis is that they stabilize the jaw while breaking tough tropical nuts (Hellgren and Bissonette 2003). Bissonette (1982) writes that adult dentition is reached in eighty-four weeks: Animals are born with four deciduous canines and the posterior pair of lower incisors. Between two and three months, the following teeth erupt in sequence: upper P3, lower p3, upper P2, lower p2, upper incisors I1, upper P4, lower p4, upper I2, lower i2. At about 5 months, M1 and lower m1 erupt. Then in sequence, canines are replaced, then i3 lower incisors, then upper molar M2 erupts, lower m2 erupts, and finally the remaining incisors are replaced and permanent premolars appear. This process is complete at about eighty-four weeks of age. Heffelfinger (1997) provides an excellent pictorial presentation of this process.

Family Cervidae: Deer

The skulls of cervids include numerous adaptations to support an herbivorous diet. The rostrum is long, allowing more anchorage for masseter muscles, and the mandibles are thin and long. Cervids lack incisors in the cranium altogether, and they feed by ripping vegetation caught between the lower incisors and the hard palate above. Their teeth are shorter than in Bovidae and have sharper cusps; this dentition grinds woody materials as well as herbaceous materials, and thus in general cervids are referred to as browsers and bovids as grazers.

A useful tool in identification of cervids is the length and form of the vomer bone. In deer and caribou, the vomer extends to the posterior to divide the nares into two chambers; in moose and elk, it does not. View the vomer ventrally, tilting it so that the rostrum is lower than the braincase. This thin and fragile bone is often damaged in skulls in the field, so infer as much as possible from jagged bone fragments. Refer to the photo on page 488.

Cervid males, and females in the caribou, grow and shed antlers every year. Bovids, such as bison and sheep, grow ever more impressive horns over a lifetime. Antlers grow directly from the skull, whereas horns are keratin and bone growths connected to the skull with cartilage.

There are only theories as to why horns and antlers began to grow on the heads of these animals long ago. Researchers believe that antlers were most likely developed for their contributions in scent communication during the mating season. The velvet, within which the antlers grow with astonishing speed, holds the highest concentration of oil- and scent-producing glands in the entire body, and very large glands occur on the skull above the orbits. Even when the velvet falls away and the antlers are "dead" bone, glands under the eyes are still rubbed on shrubs and trees, and then oils are transferred to the antlers during antler rubs. Some animals will, with some gymnastics, urinate on their own racks during the rut, when their urine is filled with tantalizing pheromones.

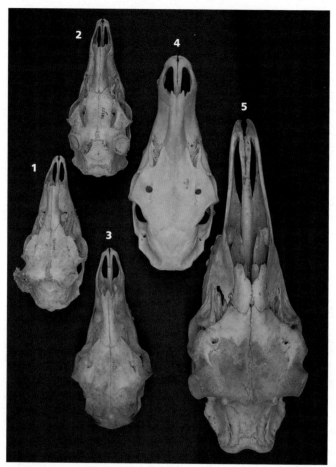

Members of Cervidae: 1. Mule deer, including black-tailed deer 104890 *(O. hemionus)*, 2. White-tailed deer 78255 *(O. virginianus)*, 3. Caribou 125629 *(Rangifer tarandus)*, 4. Elk or wapiti 133299 *(Cervus canadensis)*, 5. Moose 69929 *(Alces alces)*. MUSEUM OF VERTEBRATE ZOOLOGY, UC BERKELEY.

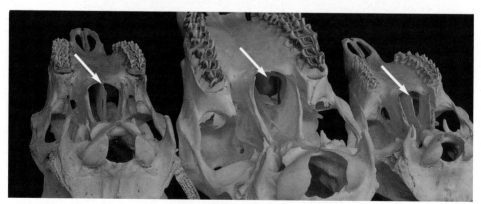

From left to right, white-tailed deer, elk or wapiti, and mule deer. Note the long vomer in the deer species, which divides the posterior of the nares into two chambers. MUSEUM OF VERTEBRATE ZOOLOGY, UC BERKELEY 78255, 133299,104890.

Antlers of North American cervids

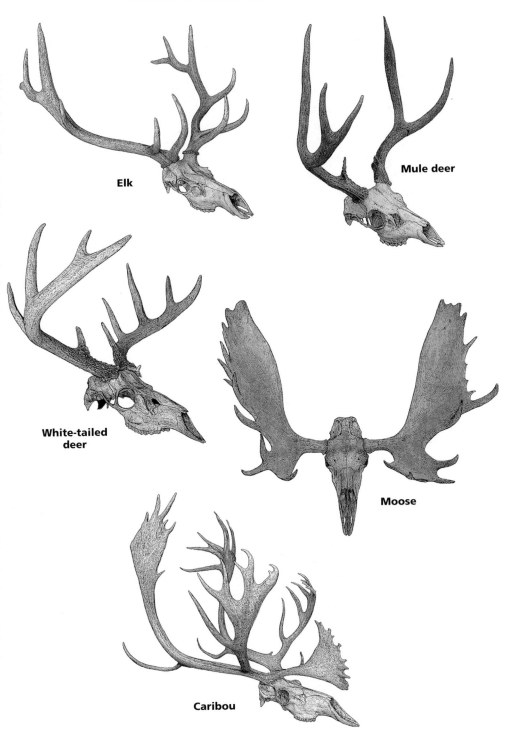

Elk

Mule deer

White-tailed deer

Moose

Caribou

The cells responsible for antler growth are the fastest-growing cells known—faster even than cancer. To give you a better sense of their amazing potential, Peterson (1991) reports that moose antlers grow from bump to fully exposed bone in 150 days. Antlers may weigh upward of 80 pounds, with the average about 50. Some simple math shows that 80-pound antlers would result from an average of just over half a pound of growth per day.

Antlers do offer some offensive and defensive benefits to the wearer. Yet they are designed to minimize the chance of injury during conflicts and were created for sparring, not spearing, competition. Antlers also visually display the health and vigor of males. A moose with a smaller rack would never challenge one with larger antlers. One researcher, Anthony Bubenik, put this to the test with Alaskan moose. After constructing incredibly large antlers for himself, he joined the courting arena. The males quickly backed off, and Bubenik was unexpectedly confronted with numerous receptive females (Peterson 1991).

The size of antlers varies from year to year, and the annual drop ensures that the current condition of a male is advertised to the females. Old and diseased animals grow less impressive racks and thus lose the opportunity to mate. Antler potential lies in a combination of age, health, nutrition (diets high in calcium, phosphorus, and protein), and genetics. The greatest antlers, a combination of good health and lineage, ensure that the strongest DNA packages will be passed on, thus contributing to the continuation of the species overall.

Mule deer

A third antler

As with other aspects of mammalian morphology, there are sometimes anomalies in antler growth, such as an extra tine, antlers that point down rather than up, or one side being much larger than the other. There are also cases of female moose growing small antlers (Bowyer et al. 2003).

Elk antlers generally have five or more tines, six being most common. Peek (2003) provides descriptions of the various elk antler forms: light and spreading with branches curved in Tule elk; light and spreading with branches straight in Rocky Mountain elk; and heavy and high with short branches in Roosevelt elk.

Mule deer antlers have a central beam that quickly forks into two, known as dichotomous branching, and each successive branch then forks to create a greater number of tines. White-tailed deer antlers exhibit single tines that grow from a single central beam.

Moose antlers are the largest of any cervid and are distinctly palmate. Small tines develop at the edges of very large dishes. Bowyer et al. (2001) report that males in their prime (between seven and eleven years of age in the Alaska population they studied) grow the largest and most symmetrical antlers; their research supports that both symmetry and size are variables in communicating health and vigor to prospective mates.

Caribou antlers are distinctively slender, with small palmate formations toward the tips; an additional lower growth to the anterior is called the shovel. The shovel often grows only on the left side and may or may not be present in females. Both female and male caribou grow antlers. Males cast their antlers at the end of the rut, which is end of fall, and then instantly lose their sex drive and return to foraging. Females lose their antlers the following spring, about the same time as calving (Miller 2003).

Elk, *Cervus canadensis*

Greatest length: 404.0–525.0 mm (15⁹/10–20⁷/10 in.) (full table of measurements page 612, life-size image page 153, life-size jaw page 177)

Specimen illustrated: Adult female, MVZ 133299

Dentition: i 0/3 c 1/1 p 3/3 m 3/3, total 34. Upper canines present in both sexes, and upper incisors absent.

Dorsal: Cervids have large, slender skulls, tapering to the anterior, and large orbits posterior to the midline of the skull. The rostrum (1) is long, slender, and triangular; the premaxillary bones (2) project far to the anterior, with large, distinctive incisive foramina (3). Nasals (4) are long and broadest near the posterior, tapering to the anterior. Rostral fenestrae (5) are large, and distinctive to the family. Orbits (6) are large and protrude to either side of the skull. Supraoccipital foramen (7) large and round. The braincase (8) is large, rounded, and smooth; temporal ridges (9) are weak and wide apart, and the occipital crests (10) are more developed. Zygomatic arches (11) spread less than the orbits protrude, and the squamosal arms of the zygomatic arches (12) join with the larger mastoid processes (13) to form a shelf.

Ventral: The palate (14) is long and broad, extending to the posterior to terminate within the posterior molar; deep palatal notches (15) are evident to either side. Small, rounded canines (16) are evident, but incisors are absent. The vomer (17) does not extend to the posterior to divide the nares into two chambers. The auditory bullae (18) are very small and less inflated. The foramen magnum (19) is medium, and occipital condyles (20) are stout. Dentition is sharply cusped.

Lateral: The dorsolateral outline is dominated by the rostrum (21); the braincase (22) is convex, and antlers are present in males. The premaxillaries (23) extend well beyond the anterior tips of the nasals (24), and the nasal vacuity (25) is large and angled; the premaxillaries are in contact with the nasals (26). The lacrimal bone (27) is large and does not make contact with the nasals; the lacrimal pit (28) or depression is relatively deep. The orbits are outlined to the posterior by a complete postorbital bar (29), and two lacrimal ducts (30) are prominent on the anterior rim; the zygomatic arches (31) are thinner but strong. The auditory meatus (32) is tiny and elevated. Paraoccipital processes (33) are long.

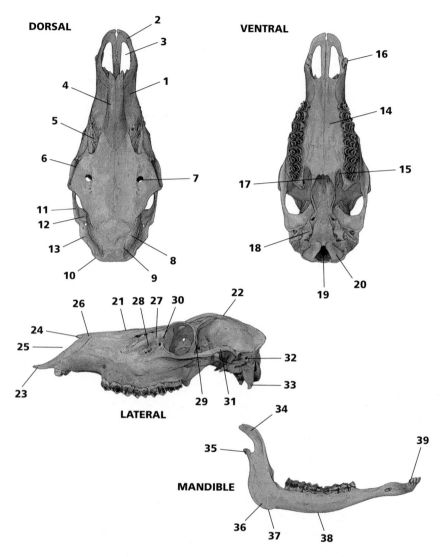

DORSAL

VENTRAL

LATERAL

MANDIBLE

Mandible: The mandible is long and slender, tapering toward the anterior, with a posterior corner that is the angular process. The coronoid process (34) is very high, slender, and very curved to the posterior. The condyle (35) is small and strong, and it sits well above the toothrows. The angular process (36) is large and rounded, forming the posterior corner. The ventral surface of the angular process (37) is below the ventral surface of the body (38) below the toothrows, which curve upward beneath the anterior molariform teeth. The canine (39) is incisoriform; the diastema is wide.

Similar species: Caribou, deer, and moose.

Notes: Males are larger than females. Peek (2003) describes the skull in various elk populations: short and broad in Tule elk; intermediate in Rocky Mountain elk; and long and slender in Roosevelt elk. Hoffmeister (1986) provides the following aging criteria by tooth eruptions in the cranium: M1 is just erupting at about seven months old; M2 is partially erupted and premolars show wear at about one year; M3 is partially erupted at about two years; M3 is equal in height to the other teeth and permanent premolars are in place at about three years. Heffelfinger (1997) provides a pictorial presentation of aging using molar eruption and wear in the mandibles.

Mule deer, including black-tailed deer, *Odocoileus hemionus*

Greatest length: 228.3–305.5 mm (9–12 in.) (full table of measurements page 612, life-size image page 144, life-size jaw page 173)
Specimen illustrated: Adult female, SBMNH 50
Dentition: i 0/3 c 0/1 p 3/3 m 3/3, total 32. No upper incisors.
Dorsal: Cervids have large, slender skulls, tapering to the anterior, and large orbits posterior to the midline of the skull. The rostrum (1) is long, slender, and triangular; the premaxillary bones (2) project far to the anterior, with large, distinctive incisive foramina (3); turbinate bones (4) are visible projecting out from the large nasal vacuity. Nasals (5) are broad, long, and rectangular. Rostral fenestrae (6) are large and distinctive to the family. Orbits are large (7) and protrude to either side of the skull. Supraoccipital foramina (8) are large and round. The braincase (9) is large, rounded, and smooth; temporal ridges are weak. Zygomatic arches (10) spread less than the orbits protrude.
Ventral: The palate (11) is long and broad, extending to the posterior beyond the toothrows. There are no teeth at the anterior of the mouth, no incisors or canines. The vomer (12) extends to the posterior to divide the nares into two chambers. The auditory bullae (13) are smaller and less inflated. The foramen magnum (14) is medium, and occipital condyles (15) are stout. Dentition is sharply cusped.

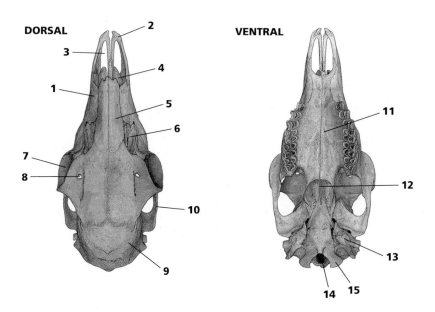

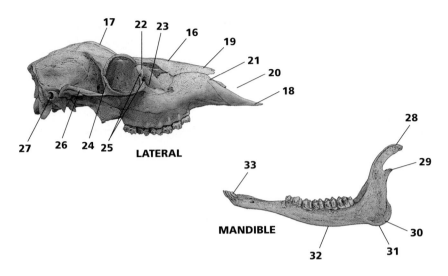

LATERAL

MANDIBLE

Lateral: The dorsolateral outline is dominated by the rostrum (16); the braincase (17) is convex, and antlers are present in males. The premaxillaries (18) extend well beyond the anterior tips of the nasals (19), and the nasal vacuity (20) is large and angled; the premaxillaries do not touch the nasals (21). The lacrimal bone (22) is large and does not make contact with the nasals; the lacrimal pit (23) or depression is deep, which is the primary means of differentiating from white-tailed deer. The orbits are outlined to the posterior by a complete postorbital bar (24), and two

Note the deep, long lacrimal pit in the mule deer in the foreground, and the much shallower, shorter lacrimal pit in the white-tailed deer in the background. SANTA BARBARA MUSEUM OF NATURAL HISTORY 62; private.

lacrimal ducts (25) are prominent on the anterior rim; the zygomatic arches (26) are strong. The auditory meatus (27) is small.

Mandible: The mandible is long and slender, tapering toward the anterior, with a posterior corner that is the angular process. The coronoid process (28) is very high, slender, and curved to the posterior. The condyle (29) is small and strong, and it sits well above the toothrows. The angular process (30) is large and rounded, forming the posterior corner. The ventral surface of the angular process (31) is aligned or nearly so with the ventral surface of the body (32) below the toothrows. The canine (33) is incisoriform; the diastema is wide.

Similar species: Elks, deer, and moose.

Notes: On occasion, small upper incisors have been recorded in animals. Cowan (1956) reports that skulls, dentition, and antlers do not reliably differentiate between all forms of white-tailed and mule deer (Anderson and Wallmo, 1984). Mackie et al. (1982) include research on aging using tooth eruption: Deciduous incisors and canines erupted by ten days of age. Premolars erupt within two to three months. M1 is just visible at two and a half to three months and fully erupted by twelve to fourteen months. M2 is just visible at eight months and fully erupted at twenty to twenty-three months. M3 emerges at fifteen months and is fully erupted at twenty-eight months, when adult dentition is complete. Heffelfinger (1997) provides an excellent pictorial guide to aging animals by tooth eruption in the mandible.

White-tailed deer, *Odocoileus virginianus*

Greatest length: 216.0–304.5 mm (8^5/$_{10}$–12 in.) (full table of measurements page 614, life-size image page 144, life-size jaw page 174)

Specimen illustrated: Adult male, MVZ 78255

Dentition: i 0/3 c 0/1 p 3/3 m 3/3, total 32. No upper incisors.

Dorsal: Cervids have large, slender skulls, tapering to the anterior, and large orbits posterior to the midline of the skull. The rostrum (1) is long, slender, and triangular; the premaxillary bones (2) project far to the anterior, with large, distinctive incisive foramina (3); turbinate bones (4) are visible projecting out from the large nasal vacuity. Nasals (5) are broad, long, and rectangular. Rostral fenestrae (6) are large and distinctive to the family. Orbits (7) are large and protrude to either side of the skull. Supraorbital foramina (8) are large and round. The braincase (9) is large, rounded, and smooth; temporal ridges are weak. Zygomatic arches (10) spread less than the orbits protrude.

Ventral: The palate (11) is long and broad, extending to the posterior beyond the toothrows; palatal notches (12) extend to the midpoint of the posterior molar. There are no teeth at the anterior of the mouth, no incisors or canines. The vomer (13) extends to the posterior to divide the nares into two chambers. The auditory bullae (14) are smaller and less inflated. The foramen magnum (15) is medium, and occipital condyles (16) are stout.

Lateral: The dorsolateral outline is dominated by the rostrum (17); the braincase (18) is convex, and antlers (19) are present in males. The premaxillaries (20) extend well

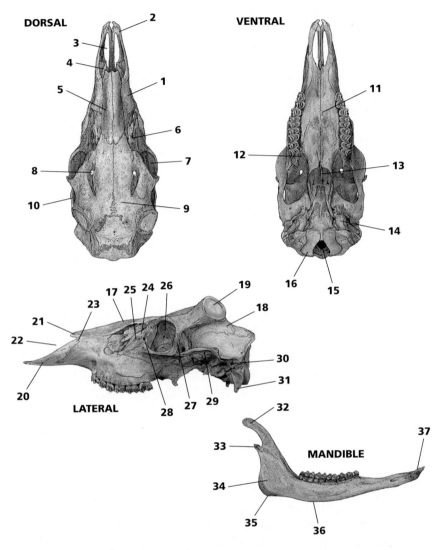

DORSAL

VENTRAL

LATERAL

MANDIBLE

beyond the anterior tips of the nasals (21), and the nasal vacuity (22) is large and angled; the premaxillaries do not touch the nasals (23). The lacrimal bone (24) is large and does not make contact with the nasals; the lacrimal pit (25) or depression is shallow, which is the characteristic most relied on to distinguish from mule deer. The orbits (26) are outlined to the posterior by a complete postorbital bar (27), and two lacrimal ducts (28) are prominent on the anterior rim; the zygomatic arches (29) are strong. The auditory meatus (30) is small. Paraoccipital processes (31) are long.

Mandible: The mandible is long and slender, tapering toward the anterior, with a posterior corner that is the angular process. The coronoid process (32) is very high, slender, and curved to the posterior. The condyle (33) is small and strong, and it sits well above the toothrows. The angular process (34) is large and rounded, forming the posterior corner. The ventral surface of the angular process (35) is aligned or nearly so with the ventral surface of the body (36) below the toothrows. The canine (37) is incisoriform; the diastema is wide.

Similar species: Elks, caribou, and moose.

Notes: Hesselton and Hesselton (1982) provide the following aging criteria using tooth eruption in the lower mandible: Full adult dentition is reached between sixteen and eighteen months. At four weeks, incisors and two premolars are partially to fully erupted. At ten weeks, the third premolar (P3) has erupted. At seven months, the first permanent molar (M1) has erupted. At thirteen months, the second molar (M2) has erupted. The third molar (M3) erupts soon after the second, but it isn't fully erupted until nineteen months of age. Cowan (1956) reports that skulls, dentition, and antlers do not reliably differentiate between all forms of white-tailed and mule deer (Anderson and Wallmo 1984). Miller et al. (2003) provides a wonderful visual presentation of tooth eruption and aging in white-tailed deer.

Moose, *Alces alces*

Greatest length: 540.0–633.0 mm (21$3/10$–24$9/10$ in.) (full table of measurements page 614, life-size image page 158, life-size jaw page 178)

Specimen illustrated: Adult male, MVZ 69929

Dentition: i 0/3 c 0/1 p 3/3 m 3/3, total 32. Upper incisors are absent.

Dorsal: Cervids have large, slender skulls, tapering to the anterior, and large orbits posterior to the midline of the skull. The rostrum (1) is very long, slender, and triangular; the premaxillary bones (2) project far to the anterior, with large, distinctive incisive foramina (3); turbinate bones (4) are well visible projecting out from the massive nasal vacuity. Nasals (5) are distinctly short and broad. Rostral fenestrae (6) are large and distinctive to the family. Orbits (7) are large and protrude to either side of the skull. Supraorbital foramina (8) are smaller and round, and between them is a significant depression (9) in the frontal bones. The braincase (10) is large, rounded, and smooth; temporal ridges are weak, though occipital crests are developed, and a supraoccipital shield (11) extends from the posterior of the braincase.

Ventral: The palate (12) is long and broad, terminating at the posterior edge of the last molar; palatal notches (13) are shallow. There are no teeth at the anterior of the mouth, no incisors or canines. The vomer (14) does not extend to the posterior to divide the nares into two chambers. Zygomatic arches (15) spread less than the orbits protrude. The auditory bullae (16) are very small and less inflated. The foramen magnum (17) is medium, and occipital condyles (18) are stout.

Lateral: The dorsolateral outline is dominated by the rostrum (19); the braincase (20) is convex, and antlers (21) are present in males. The premaxillaries (22) are enlarged and very long, extending well beyond the anterior tips of the nasals (23), and the nasal vacuity (24) is massive and angled; the premaxillaries do not touch the nasals (25). The lacrimal bone (26) is large and does not make contact with the nasals; the lacrimal pit or depression is shallow. The orbits (27) are outlined to the posterior

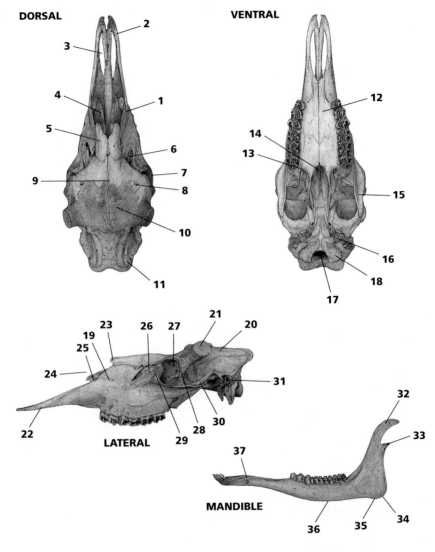

DORSAL

VENTRAL

LATERAL

MANDIBLE

by a complete postorbital bar (28), and two lacrimal ducts (29) are prominent on the anterior rim; the zygomatic arches (30) are slim but strong. The auditory meatus (31) is tiny.

Mandible: The mandible is long and slender, tapering toward the anterior, with a posterior corner that is the angular process. The coronoid process (32) is very high, slender, and curved to the posterior. The condyle (33) is small and strong and it sits well above the toothrows. The angular process (34) is large and rounded, forming the posterior corner. The ventral surface of the angular process (35) is aligned or nearly so with the ventral surface of the body (36) below the toothrows. The canine is incisoriform; the diastema (37) is wide.

Similar species: Elks, deer, caribou, and horses.

Caribou, *Rangifer tarandus*

Greatest length: 290.0–390.0 mm (11⁴/₁₀–15⁴/₁₀ in.) (full table of measurements page 614, life-size image page 151, life-size jaw page 176)

Specimen illustrated: Adult male, MVZ 125629

Dentition: i 0/3 c 1/1 p 3/3 m 3/3, total 34. Upper canines are vestigial, and upper incisors are absent.

Dorsal: Cervids have large, slender skulls, tapering to the anterior, and large orbits posterior to the midline of the skull. The rostrum (1) is long, slender, and triangular; the premaxillary bones (2) project far to the anterior, with large, distinctive incisive foramina (3); turbinate bones (4) are visible projecting out from the large nasal vacuity. Nasals (6) are broadest toward the posterior, constricted at their midpoints (5), and notched at their anterior tips; viewed together, the nasals are vase-shaped. Rostral fenestrae (7) are smaller and distinctive to the family. Orbits (8) are large and protrude to either side of the skull. Supraorbital foramina (9) are large and oval. The braincase (10) is large, rounded, and smooth; temporal ridges are weak. Zygomatic arches (11) spread less than the orbits protrude.

Ventral: The palate (12) is long and broad, extending to the posterior beyond the toothrows. Small canines (13) are present in the maxillary bone, but upper incisors are lacking. The vomer (14) extends to the posterior to divide the nares into two chambers. The auditory bullae (15) are very small and less inflated. The foramen magnum (16) is medium, and occipital condyles (17) are stout.

Lateral: The dorsolateral outline is dominated by the rostrum (18); the braincase (19) is convex, and antlers (35) are present in both sexes. The premaxillaries (20) extend well beyond the anterior tips of the nasals (21), and the nasal vacuity (22) is large and angled; the premaxillary bones touch the nasals (23). The lacrimal bone (24) is large and approaches (25) but does not make contact with the nasals; the lacrimal

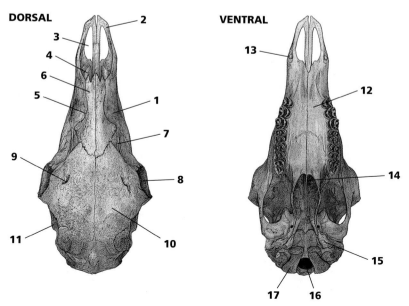

DORSAL

VENTRAL

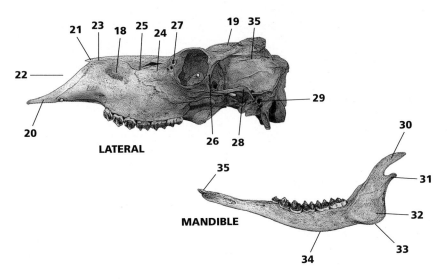

LATERAL

MANDIBLE

pit or depression is shallow. The orbits are outlined to the posterior by a complete postorbital bar (26), and two lacrimal ducts (27) are prominent on the anterior rim; the zygomatic arches are strong (28). The auditory meatus (29) is small.

Mandible: The mandible is long and slender, tapering toward the anterior, with a posterior corner that is the angular process. The coronoid process (30) is very high, slender, and very curved to the posterior. The condyle (31) is small and strong, and it sits well above the toothrows. The angular process (32) is large and rounded, forming the posterior corner. The ventral surface of the angular process (33) is above the ventral surface of the body (34) below the toothrows. The canine (35) is incisoriform, and the incisors are small; the diastema is wide.

Similar species: Elks, deer, and moose.

Notes: The sex of adult animals can be determined from the length of mandibles in a given population (Miller 1982). Miller also provides the following aging criteria using tooth eruption patterns: The first permanent molar M1 erupts between three and five months of age. Permanent incisors and M2 erupt at ten to fifteen months. Permanent premolars and M3 erupt at twenty-two to twenty-nine months. Tooth wear is slight until after three years old, and by ten years, molars are so worn they might lose some usefulness.

Family Antilocapridae: Pronghorn

The pronghorn has distinct horn cores that grow directly above the orbit. In a middle ground between cervids and bovids, horn cores are permanent and present in both sexes as in bovids, yet the horn sheaths are shed annually as in cervids. As opposed to the fingernail-like material which forms bovid horns, pronghorn horns are made of compressed hair.

Doe horns in general don't have prongs and tend to be less than 7 centimeters long. Males shed horn sheaths in early fall, while females, which are more variable in timing, tend to shed sheaths during the summer (Byers 2003).

An adult male pronghorn, the sole member of this family. MUSEUM OF VERTEBRATE ZOOLOGY, UC BERKELEY 44387.

Pronghorn, *Antilocapra americana*

Greatest length: 245.0–298.5 mm (9⁶/10–11⁸/10 in.) (full table of measurements page 614, life-size image page 143, life-size jaw page 174)

Specimen illustrated: Adult male, MVZ 44387

Dentition: i 0/3 c 0/1 p 3/3 m 3/3, total 32. Upper canines and incisors are absent.

Dorsal: Pronghorn have large, slender skulls, tapering to the anterior; large orbits posterior to the midline of the skull; and winglike projecting horn cores. The rostrum (1) is long, slender, and triangular; the premaxillary bones (2) project far to the anterior, with smaller distinctive incisive foramina (3); turbinate bones (4) are just visible projecting out from the large nasal vacuity. Nasals (5) are very long, slender, and slightly constricted at their midpoints (6). Rostral fenestrae (11) are deep and narrow. Orbits (7) are large and protrude to either side of the skull. Supraorbital foramina (8) are conspicuous and close to base of horn cores. The braincase (9) is large, rounded, and smooth; temporal ridges are weak. Occipital crests (10) are developed.

Ventral: The palate (34) is long and broad, terminating at the posterior edge of the last molar. There are no teeth at the anterior of the mouth, no incisors or canines.

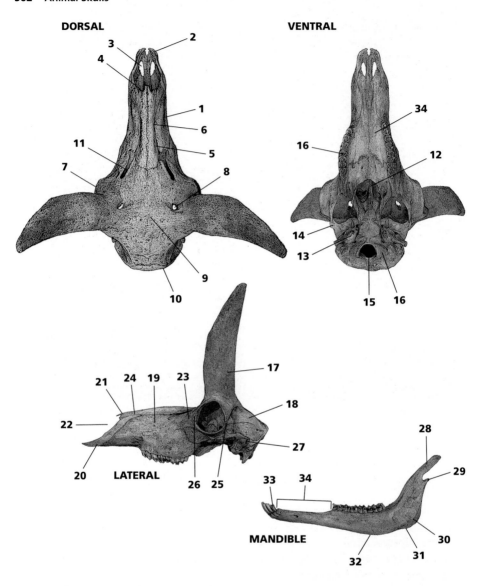

DORSAL

VENTRAL

LATERAL

MANDIBLE

The vomer (12) does not extend to the posterior to divide the nares into two chambers. The auditory bullae (13) are small and angular. The zygomatic arches (14) do not spread as wide as the orbits. The foramen magnum (15) is medium, and occipital condyles are stout. Dentition (16) is proportionately smaller than in deer.

Lateral: The dorsolateral outline is dominated by the rostrum (19), vertical horn cores (17), and convex braincase (18). The premaxillaries (20) extend well beyond the anterior tips of the nasals (21), and the nasal vacuity (22) is smaller and angled; premaxillaries touch the nasals (24). The lacrimal bone (23) is large and does not make contact with the nasals. The orbits are outlined to the posterior by a complete postorbital bar (25), and lacrimal ducts (26) are prominent on the anterior rim; the zygomatic arches are strong. The horn cores (17) rise vertically above the orbits, taper toward the tips, and are slender when viewed from the anterior. The auditory meatus (27) is small.

Mandible: The mandible is long and slender, tapering toward the anterior, with a posterior corner that is the angular process. The coronoid process (28) is very high, slender, straight, and angled to the posterior. The condyle (29) is small and strong, and it sits well above the toothrows. The angular process (30) is large and rounded, forming the posterior corner. The ventral surface of the angular process (31) is well above the ventral surface of the body (32) below the toothrows. The canine (33) is incisoriform and often separated from the remaining teeth; the diastema (34) is wide.

Similar species: Deer, elks, and caribou.

Notes: Hoffmeister (1986) reports a rather simple method to determine the sex of adult specimens: If the interorbital breadth is wider than the zygomatic breadth, it is a male; if the opposite is true, it is a female. Byers (2003) provides aging up to four years using tooth eruption sequences: At birth, only the first deciduous incisor is present. By day forty-four, all deciduous canines, incisors, and premolars are present, and M1 is partially erupted. At eighteen to twenty months, first permanent incisor and three molars are all erupted. During the third year, permanent incisors one and two, and premolars one to three are erupted. Between 3.4 and 4 years of age, the last deciduous tooth, the canine, is replaced. Heffelfinger (1997) provides an excellent pictorial guide to aging animals by tooth eruption in the mandible.

Family Bovidae: Cattle, antelope, sheep, and goats

Bovids are perhaps best recognized by their permanent and ever-growing horns and horn cores, which come in diverse sizes and forms. Often the frontal region or sinuses are enlarged and fortified to support heavy horn structures and protect the brain in head-butting contests. The dentition and skull structures of bovids support a grazing lifestyle. Their teeth are tall, flat, and high crowned, which provides more tooth to wear down over time. Their eyes are farther back on the skull, and orbits often protrude outward. Orbits farther to the posterior are thought to be characteristic of grazers, which feed when lowering the head; this eye placement allows a greater visual awareness of the environment.

The horns of bovids are ever-growing structures composed of two parts: a horny sheath of keratin and horn cores of bone that are permanently attached to the skull. Horns may have been an adaptation to help protect the skull, as many of the animals that they adorn are born with an instinctive need to butt heads. Corneal and frontal sinuses are both expanded to protect the brain.

As horns are ever-growing, they are a useful gauge in determining relative or definite age. Fuller (1959) has compiled several sources that describe the changes in buffalo horns with age. In calves, horns project laterally; they gradually turn upward in the first several years, and then turn inward in subadults and adults. Fuller also refers to the work of Mohr (1949), who writes that a feature of fully mature animals is the distinctive "stepped" horn tips; the tip of the new horn pierces the old sheath, leav-

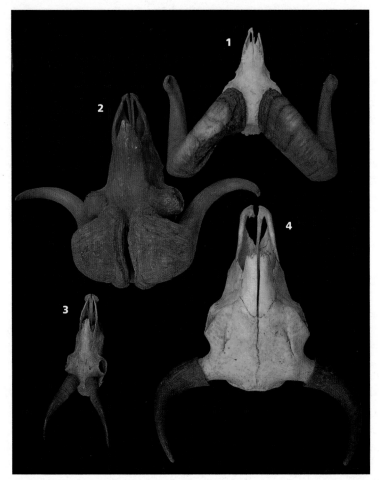

Select members of the family Bovidae: 1. Bighorn sheep, male 68739 *(Ovis canadensis)*, 2. Muskox *(Ovibus)*, 3. Mountain goat, male 4395 *(Oreamnos)*, 4. American bison, male 91037 *(Bos)*. MUSEUM OF VERTEBRATE ZOOLOGY, UC BERKELEY.

ing a ragged and blunted tip. In American bison, this occurs between seven and eight years of age and is carried into old adulthood. Refer to page 505.

Côté et al. (1998) use the circumference at the base of the right horn of mountain goats to determine a fairly accurate age class. The change with years for both males and females is depicted in the accompanying graph on page 506.

Bighorn sheep ewes exhibit much smaller horns than adult males, whose skulls and horns may account for more than 10 percent of their entire body mass. Yet in both sexes, annual horn rings can be a very useful tool in determining the age of the animal. Much of the horn growth in ewes occurs in early years; after six or seven years, it slows so much that differentiating new horn rings becomes very difficult, and thus a less useful means to determine age in old animals. In male bighorn sheep (see page 507), growth in the early years is great, and then it begins to slow after seven to eight years as well.

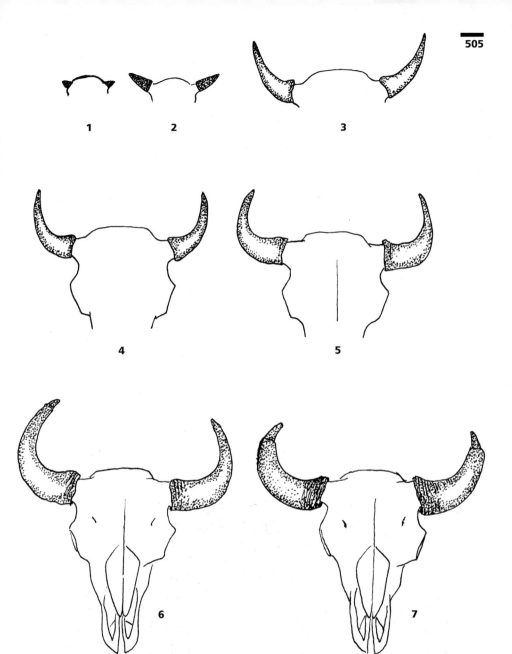

Horn growth in the buffalo bull: 1. Calf. 2. Yearling. 3. 2 years. 4. 3 years. 5. 4 years. 6. 8–9 years, when the tips first break through the horn layers. 7. Approximately 20 years old, stepped tips very apparent. Adapted from Hornaday (2002) and Garretson (1938).

Horn rings differ from the numerous other ridges and valleys on the surface in that they encircle the horns completely and can be detected on the back as well as the front. In older animals, it is considered the best strategy to identify the third-year growth rings, and then count from there. The first year or two can be lost to "brooming." Characteristic of the third year of growth is a series of widely spread horn rings

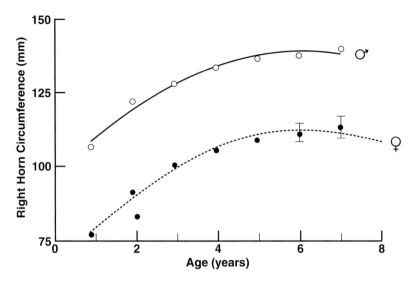

Côté et al. (1998) created this graph to illustrate the increase and then slight decrease in horn circumference in mountain goats as an animal ages. The horizontal axis is age in years. Used with permission of *J. Mamm.*

clumped together, as the horns start and stop growing several times during this year. Once you identify this cluster of rings, move toward the skull to locate the darker, thicker fourth ring. From there, count the darker complete rings, each of which represents a year of life. Because horn grown slows in mature animals, the distance between years may be considerably smaller. Look to Patricia Hansen's illustration on page 507 for a better understanding of horn rings and their characteristics.

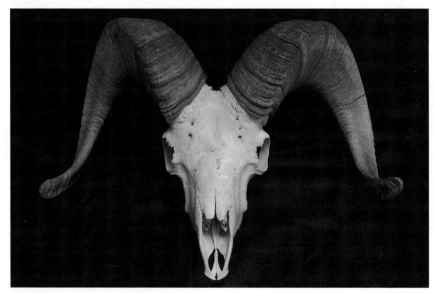

A male desert bighorn sheep *(Ovis canadensis).* SANTA BARBARA MUSEUM OF NATURAL HISTORY 2274.

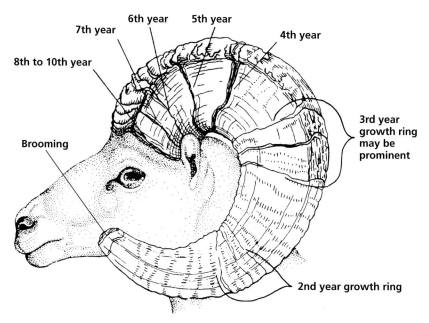

8th to 10th year

7th year

6th year

5th year

4th year

3rd year growth ring may be prominent

Brooming

2nd year growth ring

Bighorn sheep. Drawing by Patricia Hansen. Used with permission of the artist.

American bison, *Bos bison*

Greatest length: 279.0–604.0 mm (11–23⁸/₁₀ in.) (full table of measurements page 616, life-size image page 156, life-size jaw page 177)

Specimen illustrated: Adult male, MVZ 99970

Dentition: i 0/3 c 0/1 p 3/3 m 3/3, total 32.

Dorsal: Bison skulls are very broad and massive, with large, curving horns at the posterior. The rostrum (1) is long, broad, and triangular; the premaxillary bones (2) project far to the anterior, with large incisive foramina (3). Turbinate bones (4) are just visible projecting out from the large nasal vacuity. Nasals (5) are broad and triangular, tapering to points at the anterior. Orbits (6) are large and protrude to either side of the skull. Supraorbital foramina (7) are reduced. The braincase (8) is massive, flattened, and very broad; temporal ridges are weak, and horns (9) spread wide.

Ventral: The palate (10) is long and very broad, extending to the posterior beyond the toothrows; two palatal pits (11) are evident. There are no teeth at the anterior of the mouth, no incisors or canines. The pterygoid region (12) is narrow. The zygomatic arches (13) spread less than the orbits protrude. The auditory bullae (14) are small and less inflated. The foramen magnum (15) is smaller, and occipital condyles (16) are stout.

Lateral: The dorsolateral outline is dominated by the very deep rostrum (17), convex braincase, and curving horns. The premaxillaries (18) extend well beyond the anterior tips of the nasals (19), and the nasal vacuity (20) is very large and angled. The premaxillaries (21) do not touch or approach the nasals, as they do in domestic

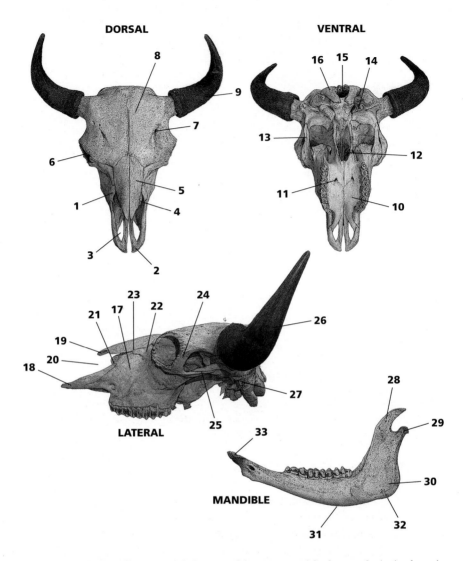

DORSAL

VENTRAL

LATERAL

MANDIBLE

cows. The lacrimal bone (22) is large and in contact with the nasals (23); there is no lacrimal depression. The orbits are outlined to the posterior by a complete post-orbital bar (24); the zygomatic arches (25) are strong. The horns (26) are circular at the base; curve out, up, and to the posterior; and taper to sharp points. The auditory meatus (27) is tiny.

Mandible: The mandible is long and slender, tapering toward the anterior, with a posterior corner that is the angular process. The coronoid process (28) is very high, slender, and curved to the posterior. The condyle (29) is tall and strong, and it sits well above the toothrows. The angular process (30) is large and rounded, forming the posterior corner. The ventral surface of the mandible (31) beneath the anterior molariform teeth curves steeply upward, and the ventral surface of the angular process (32) is above the ventral surface of the body. The canine (33) is incisoriform; the diastema is wide.

Similar species: Domestic cattle and musk oxen. Differentiating from domestic cattle is described on page 18.

Notes: Males are much larger and broader than females. Aging by tooth eruption is described in chapter 2. Aging by horn growth is illustrated on page 505 and described on page 503.

Mountain goat, *Oreamnos americanus*

Greatest length: 267.2–311.0 mm ($10^5/10$–$12^2/10$ in.) (full table of measurements page 616, life-size image page 147, life-size jaw page 174)

Specimen illustrated: Adult male, MVZ 4345

Dentition: i 0/3 c 0/1 p 3/3 m 3/3, total 32. Upper canines and upper incisors absent.

Dorsal: Mountain goat skulls are large and very slender, tapering to the anterior, with large, protruding orbits posterior to the midline and slender horns curved to the posterior. The rostrum (1) is long, slender, and triangular; the premaxillary bones (2) project far to the anterior, with large, narrow incisive foramina (3); the tips of the premaxillaries are flattened and broad (4). Turbinate bones (5) are visible projecting out from the large nasal vacuity. Nasals (6) are broad and long, tapering to the anterior to sharp points. Orbits (7) are large and protrude to either side of the skull. Supraorbital foramina (8) are reduced. The braincase (9) is large, oval, and smooth; temporal ridges are weak.

Ventral: The palate (10) is long and broad, extending to the posterior beyond the toothrows. There are no teeth at the anterior of the mouth, no incisors or canines. The pterygoid region (11) is narrow. The auditory bullae (12) are smaller and less inflated. The foramen magnum (13) is medium, and occipital condyles (14) are stout. The zygomatic arches (15) spread less than the orbits protrude.

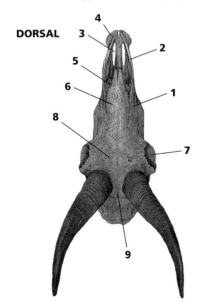

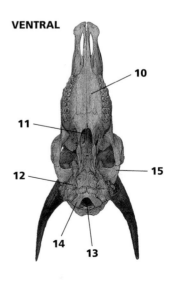

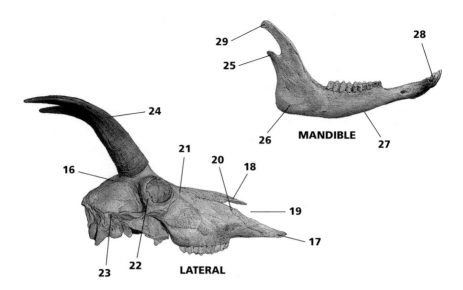

Lateral: The dorsolateral outline is dominated by the rostrum, convex braincase (16), and curving horns. The premaxillaries (17) extend well beyond the anterior tips of the nasals (18), and the nasal vacuity (19) is very large and angled. The premaxillaries do not touch or approach the nasals (20), as they do in many domestic goat breeds. The lacrimal bone (21) is large and in contact with the nasals; there is no lacrimal depression. The orbits are outlined to the posterior by a complete postorbital bar (22); the zygomatic arches are strong. The auditory meatus (23) is tiny. The horns (24) curve outward at the base and to the posterior, tapering to sharp points, with the tips converging inward; the horn cores are straight.

Mandible: The mandible is long and slender, tapering toward the anterior, with a posterior corner that is the angular process. The coronoid process (29) is very high, slender, and curved to the posterior. The condyle (25) is small and strong, and it sits well above the toothrows. The angular process (26) is large and squared, forming the posterior corner. The ventral surface of the mandible (27) beneath the anterior molariform teeth curves steeply upward. The canine (28) is incisoriform; the diastema is wide.

Similar species: Domestic goats, mountain and domestic sheep.

Notes: The nasal bones are slightly concave, which is a character useful in differentiating mountain goats from domestic goats. Côté and Festa-Bianchet (2003) describe aging by tooth eruption: Mountain goats are born with eighteen milk teeth. They replace i1 at fifteen to sixteen months, i2 at two years, i3 at three years, and incisiform canine between four and five years. Goats over eight years of age may have missing teeth and exhibit severe tooth wear.

Musk ox, *Ovibos moschatus*

Greatest length: 428.5–528.0 mm (16^9/$_{10}$–20^8/$_{10}$ in.) (full table of measurements page 616, life-size image page 155)

Specimen illustrated: Adult, MVZ

Dentition: i 0/3 c 0/1 p 3/3 m 3/3, total 32. Upper canines and upper incisors absent.

Dorsal: Musk ox skulls are massive and triangular, with distinctive broad, decurved, and tapering horns. The rostrum (1) is long, slender, and triangular; the premaxillary bones (2) project far to the anterior, with large, narrow incisive foramina (3). Turbinate bones are not visible projecting out from the large nasal vacuity. Nasals (4) are broad and long, tapering to sharp points at the anterior. Rostral fenestrae are absent. Orbits (5) are large and protrude far to either side of the skull, much farther than in bison. Supraorbital foramina (6) are reduced. The braincase (7) is large but hidden by the very broad and flattened bases of the horns (8).

Ventral: The palate (9) is long and broad, extending to the posterior just beyond the toothrows. There are no teeth at the anterior of the mouth, no incisors or canines. The pterygoid region (10) is narrow. The zygomatic arches (11) spread less than the orbits protrude. The auditory bullae (12) are smaller and less inflated. The foramen magnum (13) is medium, and occipital condyles (14) are very stout.

Lateral: The dorsolateral outline is dominated by the sloping rostrum (15) and massive horns. The premaxillaries (16) extend well beyond the anterior tips of the nasals (17), and the nasal vacuity (18) is very large and angled. The premaxillaries do not touch the nasals (19), as they do in domestic cows; the infraorbital foramina (21) are small and well forward on the side of the rostrum. The lacrimal bone (20) is large and in contact with the nasals; there is no lacrimal depression. The orbits are outlined to the posterior by a complete postorbital bar (22); the zygomatic arches are strong. Adult horns (23) and horn cores curve down, out, and then up again. The auditory meatus is hidden.

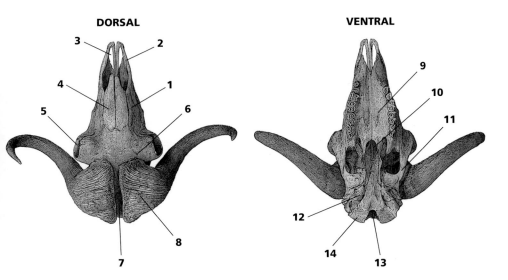

DORSAL   **VENTRAL**

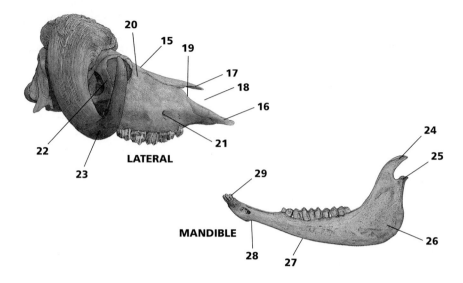

LATERAL

MANDIBLE

Mandible: The mandible is long and slender, strongly tapering toward the anterior, with a posterior corner that is the angular process. The coronoid process (24) is very high, slender, and curved to the posterior. The condyle (25) is small and strong, and it sits well above the toothrows. The angular process (26) is large and rounded, forming the posterior corner. The ventral surface of the mandible (27) beneath the anterior molariform teeth curves steeply upward and forms a distinctive step (28) just posterior to the incisors. To the posterior, the angular process is not separated by a step from the body of the mandible. The canine (29) is incisoriform; the diastema is wide.

Similar species: Domestic cattle, yaks, and buffalo.

Bighorn Sheep, *Ovis canadensis*

Greatest length: 237.5–324.0 mm ($9^4/10$–$12^8/10$ in.) (full table of measurements page 616, life-size image page 148, life-size jaw page 174)

Specimens illustrated: Adult male, SBMNH 2274; female, MVZ 78265

Dentition: i 0/3 c 0/1 p 3/3 m 3/3, total 32. Upper canines and upper incisors absent.

Dorsal: Mountain sheep skulls are triangular, with slender rostrums, protruding orbits posterior to the midline of the skull, and horns curved to the posterior, spiraling in males. The rostrum (1) is long, slender, and triangular, generally more slender than in domestic sheep; the premaxillary bones (2) project far to the anterior, with large, narrow incisive foramina (3); the tips of the premaxillaries are flattened and broad (4). Turbinate bones are not visible projecting out from the nasal vacuity. Nasals (5) are broad, with rounded anterior edges and sutures that fuse and become indistinct in adult animals; nasals are longer than in Dall's sheep. Orbits (6) are large and protrude to either side of the skull. Supraorbital foramina (7) are reduced. The braincase (8) is large, rounded, and smooth; temporal ridges are weak. The frontals (10) are expanded in males to support the massive horn cores (9); both frontals and horns are much smaller in females.

Ventral: The palate (11) is long and broad, extending to the posterior just beyond the anterior edge of the last molar. There are no teeth at the anterior of the mouth, no incisors or canines. The pterygoid region (12) is narrow. The zygomatic arches (13) spread less than the orbits protrude. The auditory bullae (14) are smaller and less inflated. The foramen magnum (15) is small, and occipital condyles (16) are stout. Toothrows are convex.

Lateral: The dorsolateral outline is dominated by the relatively level rostrum (17) and curving horns, massive in males. The premaxillaries (18) extend well beyond the

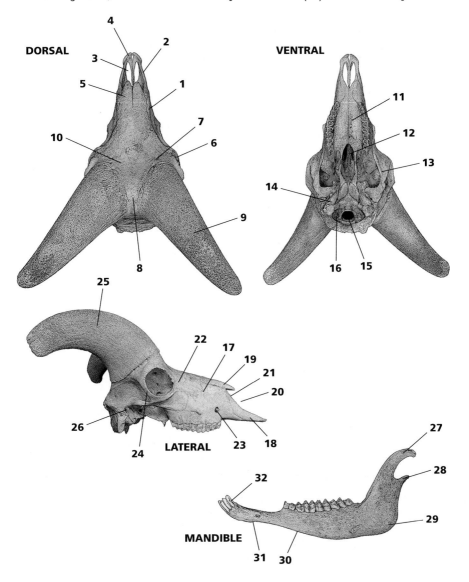

Female bighorn sheep

anterior tips of the nasals (19), and the nasal vacuity (20) is very large and angled. The premaxillaries do not touch the nasals (21). The lacrimal bone (22) is larger than in domestic sheep and in contact with the nasals; there is no lacrimal depression. The infraorbital foramen (23) is low on the side of the rostrum. The orbits are outlined to the posterior by a complete postorbital bar (24); the zygomatic arches are strong. The horns of males are distinctively spiraled, the horn cores (25) curve to the posterior and then down, and the ends are blunt. The auditory meatus (26) is tiny.

Mandible: The mandible is long and slender, tapering toward the anterior, with a posterior corner that is the angular process. The coronoid process (27) is very high, slender, and curved to the posterior. The condyle (28) is extended and strong, and it sits well above the toothrows. The angular process (29) is large and rounded, forming the posterior corner. The ventral surface of the mandible beneath the anterior molariform teeth curves steeply upward (30) and forms a distinctive step (31) just posterior to the incisors. The canine (32) is incisoriform; the diastema is wide.

Similar species: Dall's and domestic sheep, mountain and domestic goats.

Notes: Mountain sheep may interbreed with domestic sheep. Krausman and Bowyer (2003) write that desert bighorn sheep *(O. c. nelsoni)* have more diverging horns than their northern counterparts. They also provide a visual chart to determine age by tooth eruption in bighorn sheep, a method that is very accurate up to four years of age.

Dall's sheep, *Ovis dalli*

Greatest length: 275.0–282.0 mm ($10^8/_{10}$–$11^1/_{10}$ in.) (full table of measurements page 616)

Specimen illustrated: Adult male, MVZ 96105

Dentition: i 0/3 c 0/1 p 3/3 m 3/3, total 32. Upper canines and upper incisors absent.

Dorsal: Dall's sheep skulls are triangular, with slender rostrums, protruding orbits posterior to the midline of the skull, and horns curved to the posterior, spiraling in males. The rostrum (1) is long, slender, and triangular, generally more slender than in domestic sheep; the premaxillary bones (2) project far to the anterior, with large, narrow incisive foramina (3); the tips of the premaxillaries are flattened and broad (4). Turbinate bones are not visible projecting out from the nasal vacuity. Nasals (5) are broad, with rounded anterior edges and sutures that may fuse and become indistinct in adult animals; nasals are shorter than in bighorn sheep. Orbits (6) are large and protrude to either side of the skull. Supraorbital foramina (7) are reduced. The braincase (8) is large, rounded, and smooth; temporal ridges are weak. The frontals

(9) are expanded in males to support the massive horn cores; both frontals and horns are much smaller in females.

Ventral: The palate (10) is long and broad, extending to the posterior just beyond the anterior edge of the last molar. There are no teeth at the anterior of the mouth, no incisors or canines. The pterygoid region (11) is narrow. The zygomatic arches (12) spread less than the orbits protrude. The auditory bullae (13) are smaller and less inflated. The foramen magnum (14) is small, and occipital condyles (15) are stout. Toothrows are convex.

Lateral: The dorsolateral outline is dominated by the relatively level rostrum (16) and curving horns, massive in males. The premaxillaries (17) extend well beyond the

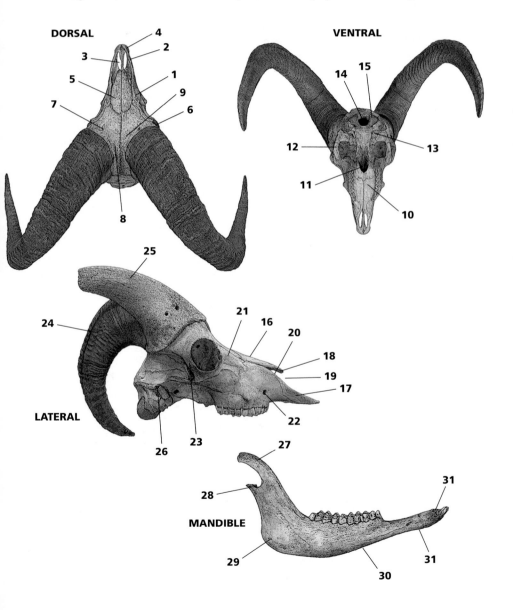

Dall's sheep

anterior tips of the nasals (18), and the nasal vacuity (19) is very large and angled. The premaxillaries do not touch the nasals (20). The lacrimal bone (21) is larger than in domestic sheep and in contact with the nasals; there is no lacrimal depression. The infraorbital foramen (22) is low on the side of the rostrum. The orbits are outlined to the poststerior by a complete postorbital bar (23); the zygomatic arches are strong. The horns (24) of males are distinctively spiraled, the horn cores (25) curve to the posterior and then down, and the ends are blunt. The auditory meatus (26) is tiny.

Mandible: The mandible is long and slender, tapering toward the anterior, with a posterior corner that is the angular process. The coronoid process (27) is very high, slender, and curved to the posterior. The condyle (28) is extended and strong, and it sits well above the toothrows. The angular process (29) is large and rounded, forming the posterior corner. The ventral surface of the mandible beneath the anterior molariform teeth curves steeply upward (30) and may form a distinctive step just posterior to the incisors. The canine is incisoriform, missing in this specimen; the diastema is wide.

Similar species: Bighorn and domestic sheep, mountain and domestic goats.

Notes: Horn cores are shorter and smaller than in bighorn sheep, and spiraling horns splay wider. Mountain sheep may interbreed with domestic sheep. Krausman and Bowyer (2003) provide a visual chart to determine age by tooth eruption in Dall's sheep, a method that is very accurate up to four years of age.

Mammal Species Accounts
Tables

Family Didelphidae

Table in millimeters. Mean and parameters on top. Total number
of specimens measured and specific number in cited sources below.

Species	Sex	Greatest length	Condylobasal length	Palatal length	Postpalatal length	Mastoidal breadth
Common opossum, *Didelphis marsupialis*	♀	98.84 (83.80–116.15)	96.81 (82.45–114.60)	60.14 (50.80–70.40)		
n=Total sample		n=112[5]	n=110[5]	n=111[5]		
	♂	108.25 (88.15–128.35)	104.85 (88.70–123.10)	63.33 (52.60–74.80)		
n=Total sample		n=118[5]	n=103[5]	n=111[5]		
Virginia opossum, *Didelphis virginiana*	♀	101.34 (77.85–128.0)	98.23 (77.10–116.10)	59.69 (45.65–70.06)	37.0 (32.0–48.3)	34.5 (30.42–39.08)
n=Total sample Sources		n=194 4[1],22[3],168[5]	n=157[5]	n=179 4[1],175[5]	n=22[3]	n=4[1]
	♂	111.37 (85.0–145.8)	106.59 (84.10–138.80)	63.81 (51.0–78.85)	41.6 (35.0–51.9)	40.08 (31.8–43.8)
n=Total sample Sources		n=221 4[1],22[3],194[5],1[6]	n=183 182[5],1[6]	n=210 5[1],205[5]	n=22[3]	n=6 5[1],1[6]
Mexican mouse opossum, *Marmosa mexicana*	♀♂	(29.9–40.8)	(30.1–33.2)	(16.70–21.4)		(11.18–12.68)
n=Total sample Sources		n=13 4[1],1[3],8[4]	n=8[4]	n=12 4[1],8[4]		n=4[1]

1=author, 2=Verts and Carraway (1998), 3=Lowery (1974), 4=Alonso-Mejía and Medellín (1992), 5=Gardner (1973), 6=Grinnell et al. (1937)

Family Soricidae

Table in millimeters. Mean and parameters on top. Total number
of specimens measured and specific number in cited sources below.

Species	Sex	Greatest length	Palatal length	Palatilar length	Postpalatal length
Marsh shrew, *Sorex bendirii*	♀	23.45 (22.45–24.23)			
n=Total sample		n=30[2]			
	♂	23.57 (22.29–24.22)			
n=Total sample		n=30[2]			

Braincase breadth	Zygomatic breadth	Interorbital breadth	Postorbital constriction	Maxillary toothrow	Mandible length
	48.28 (40.0–57.15)	18.56 (14.50–22.60)	11.63 (10.30–12.80)	41.98 (38.85–45.70)	79.88 (64.50–94.10)
	n=104[5]	n=110[5]	n=112[5]	n=84[5]	n=112[5]
	56.60 (44.60–68.70)	20.88 (16.40–29.96)	11.34 (10.25–12.45)	44.12 (39.70–48.40)	87.02 (70.40–103.25)
	n=114[5]	n=118[5]	n=120[5]	n=98[5]	n=117[5]
27.87 (20.95–34.76)	50.98 (38.2–67.92)	19.52 (13.6–28.7)	11.16 (9.5–13.05)	41.93 (34.05–48.50)	82.02 (62.35–104.75)
n=178 4[1],7[2],167[5]	n=192 4[1],7[2],22[3],159[5]	n=196 4[1],22[3],170[5]	n=175[5]	n=147 7[2],140[5]	n=187 4[1],7[2],176[5]
30.30 (21.6–42.97)	57.38 (40.6–83.37)	21.67 (15.75–30.15)	11.00 (9.4–12.70)	44.40 (35.59–51.80)	89.31 (68.85–116.90)
n=203 5[1],6[2],192[5]	n=217 5[1],6[2],22[3],185[5],1[6]	n=235 5[1],22[3],208[5]	n=208[5]	n=178 6[2],172[5]	n=215 5[1],6[2],204[5]
(11.43–14.3)	(16.3–21.8)	(4.88–6.04)	(5.48–7.3)	(11.0–13.0)	(22.05–29.5)
n=12 4[1],8[4]	n=12 3[1],1[3],8[4]	n=4[1]	n=12 4[1],8[4]	n=8[4]	n=12 4[1],8[4]

Braincase breadth	Maxillary breadth	Interorbital breadth	Maxillary toothrow	Mandibular toothrow	Mandible length
11.19 (10.55–11.78)	7.06 (6.50–7.58)	4.56 (4.22–5.14)	5.45 (5.18–5.6)	6.61 (6.05–7.09)	10.42 9.6–11.30)
n=30[2]	n=30[2]	n=30[2]	n=30[2]	n=30[2]	n=30[2]
11.31 (10.56–12.04)	7.03 (6.45–7.55)	4.59 (3.96–5.34)	5.45 (5.1–5.66)	6.57 (6.10–6.88)	10.56 (9.74–11.96)
n=30[2]	n=30[2]	n=30[2]	n=30[2]	n=30[2]	n=30[2]

Family Soricidae *continued*

Species	Sex	Greatest length	Palatal length	Palatilar length	Postpalatal length
Cinereus or masked shrew, *Sorex cinereus*	♀	16.55 (16.2–17.20)	6.64 (6.38–6.86)		
n=Total sample Sources		*n*=9 3[5],6[1]	*n*=6[1]		
	♂	16.33 (15.03–16.74)	6.79 (6.50–7.00)		
n=Total sample		*n*=6[1]	*n*=6[1]		
	♀♂	15.32* (14.6–17.2)	6.2 (5.7–6.6)		
n=Total sample Sources		*n*=32[14]+?[6]	*n*=151[13]		
Smoky shrew, *Sorex fumeus*	♀♂	(18.4–19.2)	7.7 (7.2–8.0)		
n=Total sample Sources		*n*=?[6]	*n*=24[9]		
Merriam's shrew, *Sorex merriami*	♀	16.62 (15.80–17.5)			
n=Total sample Sources		*n*=5 3[2],1[5],1[1]			
	♂	15.81 (15.33–16.6)			
n=Total sample Sources		*n*=10 9[2],1[5]			
	♀♂	15.69 (15.22–16.08)			
n=Total sample		*n*=11[3]			
Dwarf shrew, *Sorex nanus*	♀♂	14.38 (14.09–14.69)			
n=Total sample		*n*=15[3]			
American water shrew, *Sorex palustris*	♀	19.87 (18.86–21.52)	8.87 (8.46–9.16)		
n=Total sample Sources		*n*=27 21[2],1[5],5[1]	*n*=5[1]		
	♂	20.27 (19.27–20.96)	8.73 (8.24–9.26)		
n=Total sample Sources		*n*=28 17[2],4[5],7[1]	*n*=7[1]		
	♀♂	(21.2–22.4)	8.4 (8.1–8.8)		
n=Total sample Sources		*n*=?[6]	*n*=9[11]		

Braincase breadth	Maxillary breadth	Interorbital breadth	Maxillary toothrow	Mandibular toothrow	Mandible length
7.54 (7.1–7.9)	4.17 (4.1–4.2)	3.20 (2.88–3.96)	5.70 (5.5–5.8)		7.77 (7.44–8.05)
$n=9$ $3^5,6^{15}$	$n=3^5$	$n=6^1$	$n=3^5$		$n=6^1$
7.75 (7.56–7.96)		3.22 (2.82–3.52)			7.61 (6.50–8.30)
$n=6^1$		$n=6^1$			$n=6^1$
7.32 (6.4–8.2)	4.23 (3.8–4.55)	2.98 (2.6–3.2)	5.63 (5.2–6.1)		
$n=184+?^6$ $5^4,151^{13},28^{14}$	$n=198$ $5^4,151^{13},42^{14}$	$n=156$ $5^4,151^{13}$	$n=198$ $5^4,151^{13},42^{14}$		
8.97 (8.6–9.4)	5.24 (4.8–5.6)	3.70 (3.4–4.0)	6.70 (6.4–6.8)		
$n=16+?^6$ $4^4,12^9$	$n=29$ $6^4,23^9$	$n=31$ $6^4,25^9$	$n=31$ $5^4,26^9$		
8.36 (8.25–8.44)	5.21 (5.04–5.57)	3.74 (3.40–4.01)	5.93 (5.44–6.20)	4.71 (4.69–4.73)	7.49 (7.05–8.49)
$n=5$ $3^2,1^5,1^1$	$n=4$ $3^2,1^5$	$n=5$ $3^2,1^5,1^1$	$n=4$ $3^2,1^5$	$n=3^2$	$n=4$ $3^2,1^1$
8.15 (7.71–8.56)	4.98 (4.40–5.27)	3.70 (3.36–4.1)	5.80 (5.43–6.13)	4.62 (4.41–4.75)	7.06 (6.46–7.60)
$n=10$ $9^2,1^5$	$n=10$ $9^2,1^5$	$n=10$ $9^2,1^5$	$n=10$ $9^2,1^5$	$n=9^2$	$n=9^2$
8.32 (7.98–8.62)	5.24 (5.06–5.62)				
$n=11^3$	$n=11^3$				
7.28 (6.97–7.57)	4.12 (3.94–4.20)				
$n=15^3$	$n=15^3$				
9.81 (9.07–10.38)	5.79 (5.31–6.15)	3.84 (3.57–4.76)	7.09 (6.54–7.79)	5.67 (5.19–5.83)	9.05 (8.53–9.45)
$n=27$ $21^2,1^5,5^1$	$n=22$ $21^2,1^5$	$n=25$ $21^2,1^5,3^1$	$n=22$ $21^2,1^5$	$n=21^2$	$n=21^2$
10.01 (9.49–10.5)	5.93 (5.55–6.35)	4.05 (3.66–4.88)	7.17 (6.73–7.66)	5.48 (4.75–5.79)	9.14 (8.55–9.72)
$n=28$ $17^2,4^5,7^1$	$n=21$ $17^2,4^5$	$n=28$ $17^2,4^5,7^1$	$n=21$ $17^2,4^5$	$n=17^2$	$n=17^2$
9.72 (9.0–10.9)	5.92 (5.4–6.5)	3.81 (3.4–4.4)	7.70 (7.4–7.7)		
$n=90$ $2^4,88^{11}$	$n=73$ $3^4,70^{11}$	$n=98$ $3^4,95^{11}$	$n=12$ $3^4,9^{11}$		

Family Soricidae *continued*

Species	Sex	Greatest length	Palatal length	Palatilar length	Postpalatal length
Preble's shrew, *Sorex preblei*	♀	14.55 (14.31–14.74)			
n=Total sample		*n*=9[2]			
	♂	14.44 (13.17–14.86)			
n=Total sample		*n*=15[2]			
Trowbridge's shrew, *Sorex trowbridgii*	♀	17.22 (16.48–17.95)			
n=Total sample		*n*=30[2]			
	♂	17.39 (16.81–18.05)			
n=Total sample		*n*=30[2]			
Vagrant shrew, *Sorex vagrans*	♀	16.35 (14.93–19.50)			
n=Total sample Sources		*n*=401[12]			
	♂	16.46 (15.46–19.34)			
n=Total sample Sources		*n*=357[12]			
	♀♂	16.97 (16.38–17.94)			
n=Total sample		*n*=55[3]			
Northern short-tailed shrew, *Blarina brevicauda*	♀	22.60 (22.18–23.29)	9.80 (9.37–10.18)		
n=Total sample Sources		*n*=5[1]	*n*=5[1]		
	♂	22.87 (22.12–23.58)	9.96 (9.80–10.26)		
n=Total sample Sources		*n*=5[1]	*n*=5[1]		
	♀♂	21.49 (16.9–25.2)		7.6 (7.1–8.7)	8.2 (7.4–8.8)
n=Total sample Sources		*n*=184 75[7],109[14]		*n*=75[7]	*n*=75[7]
Least shrew, *Cryptotis parva*	♀	16.64 (16.14–17.98)	6.95 (6.76–7.04)		
n=Total sample Sources		*n*=6[1]	*n*=3[1]		

Braincase breadth	Maxillary breadth	Interorbital breadth	Maxillary toothrow	Mandibular toothrow	Mandible length
7.13 (7.01–7.4) n=9[2]	3.89 (3.7–4.04) n=9[2]	2.73 (2.49–2.89) n=9[2]	5.08 (4.84–5.35) n=9[2]	4.01 (3.89–4.16) n=9[2]	6.39 (6.05–6.64) n=9[2]
7.31 (6.98–8.3) n=15[2]	4.01 (3.79–4.21) n=15[2]	2.76 (2.54–3.03) n=15[2]	5.09 (4.72–5.43) n=15[2]	3.98 (3.77–4.13) n=15[2]	6.22 (5.65–6.75) n=15[2]
8.70 (8.1–9.09) n=30[2]	4.83 (4.63–5.18) n=30[2]	3.69 (3.54–3.89) n=30[2]	5.47 (4.19–6.79) n=30[2]	5.02 (4.8–5.60) n=30[2]	7.58 (6.6–8.02) n=30[2]
8.75 (8.13–9.02) n=30[2]	4.85 (4.45–5.02) n=30[2]	3.71 (3.45–3.96) n=30[2]	5.44 (4.21–6.47) n=30[2]	5.00 (4.76–5.23) n=30[2]	7.70 (7.2–8.15) n=30[2]
8.08 (7.36–9.69) n=415 401[12],14[5]	4.65 (3.97–5.99) n=415 401[12],14[5]	3.15 (2.67–4.3) n=415 401[12],14[5]	5.88 (5.12–6.6) n=74 60[2],14[5]	4.63 (4.22–5.21) n=60[2]	7.03 (6.29–8.81) n=401[12]
8.18 (7.55–9.41) n=369 357[12],12[5]	4.69 (4.15–5.81) n=370 357[12],13[5]	3.17 (2.8–4.2) n=370 357[12],13[5]	5.87 (5.29–6.6) n=74 61[2],13[5]	4.62 (4.27–4.95) n=61[2]	7.08 (6.43–8.43) n=357[12]
8.35 (7.99–8.65) n=55[3]	4.71 (4.42–5.20) n=55[3]				
11.65 (11.0–12.04) n=6 1[5],5[1]	7.5 n=1[5]	5.92 (5.4–7.31) n=6 1[5],5[1]	8.0 n=1[5]		11.40 (10.74–12.02) n=5[1]
12.02 (11.3–12.68) n=6 1[5],5[1]	7.6 n=1[5]	5.63 (5.4–5.85) n=6 1[5],5[1]	8.5 n=1[5]		11.39 (11.22–11.68) n=5[1]
11.43 (9.1–13.8) n=184 75[7],109[14]	7.92 (7.1–8.5) n=134 25[4],109[14]	5.53 (4.7–6.2) n=209 25[4],75[7],109[14]	8.28 (7.2–8.9) n=25[4]		
7.89 (7.41–8.12) n=7 1[5],6[1]	4.7 n=1[5]	3.90 (3.5–4.30) n=7 1[5],6[1]	4.8 n=1[5]		7.59 (7.30–8.12) n=6[1]

Family Soricidae *continued*

Species	Sex	Greatest length	Palatal length	Palatilar length	Postpalatal length
Least shrew, *Cryptotis parva*	♂	16.53 (15.96–16.85)	6.26, 6.83		
n=Total sample Sources		*n*=6[1]	*n*=2[1]		
	♀♂	15.32 (14.2–17.4)	6.5 (6.4–6.9)	6.00 (5.1–6.9)	7.24 (6.4–7.8)
n=Total sample Sources		*n*=213 148[7],65[14]	*n*=6[4]	*n*=148[7]	*n*=148[7]
Crawford's desert shrew, *Notiosorex crawfordi*	♀	16.69 (15.88–17.01)	7.26 (7.0–7.4)		
n=Total sample		*n*=7[1]	*n*=5[8]		
	♂	16.92 (16.03–17.62)	7.44 (7.1–7.7)		
n=Total sample		*n*=8[1]	*n*=7[8]		
	♀♂	15.83 (14.99–16.87)			
n=Total sample		*n*=19[3]			

1=author, 2=Verts and Carraway (1998), 3=Hoffmeister (1986), 4=Paradiso (1969), 5=Armstrong (1972), 6=Jackson (1961), 7=Lowery (1974), 8=Armstrong and Jones (1972), 9=Junge and Hoffman (1981) in Owen (1984), 10=Moncrief et al. (1982) in George et al. (1986), 11=Beneski and Stinson (1987), 12=Carraway (1990) in Gillihan and Foresman (2004), 13=French (1980) in Whitaker (2004), 14= Hoffmeister (1989)

*Mean created from specimens in Hoffmeister (1989) only

Family Talpidae

Table in millimeters. Mean and parameters on top. Total number of specimens measured and specific number in cited sources below.

Species	Sex	Greatest length	Palatal length	Palatilar length	Postpalatal length	Maxillary breadth
American shrew mole, *Neurotrichus gibbsii*	♀	21.99 (20.69–23.82)	10.90	9.43 (9.2–9.6)		5.89 (5.51–5.63)
n=Total sample Sources		*n*=37 30[2],7[5]	*n*=1[1]	*n*=7[5]		*n*=30[2]
	♂	22.22 (20.68–24.2)	9.10, 9.51	9.57 (9.1–10.0)		5.88 (5.24–7.12)
n=Total sample Sources		*n*=49 30[2],19[5]	*n*=2[1]	*n*=19[5]		*n*=30[2]
	♀♂	21.7 (21.1–22.3)				
n=Total sample		*n*=25[10]				

Braincase breadth	Maxillary breadth	Interorbital breadth	Maxillary toothrow	Mandibular toothrow	Mandible length
7.82 (7.7–8.10)	5.1	3.82 (3.56–4.16)	5.4		7.54 (6.99–7.98)
n=7 1[5],6[1]	n=1[5]	n=7 1[5],6[1]	n=1[5]		n=6[1]
7.60 (6.7–9.15)	5.15 (4.8–5.47)	3.62 (3.2–4.9)	5.82 (5.32–6.15)		
n=219 6[4],148[7],65[14]	n=71 6[4],65[14]	n=154 6[4],148[7]	n=71 6[4],65[14]		
8.20 (7.8–8.5)	5.20 (4.7–5.5)	3.81 (3.6–4.0)	6.16 (6.0–6.3)		7.76 (7.27–8.42)
n=5[8]	n=5[8]	n=5[8]	n=5[8]		n=7[1]
8.65 (8.4–8.8)	5.35 (5.3–5.4)	4.04 (4.0–4.1)	6.43 (6.0–6.7)		7.94 (7.46–8.83)
n=7[8]	n=7[8]	n=7[8]	n=7[8]		n=8[1]
8.36 (8.06–8.62)	5.00 (4.65–5.32)				
n=19[3]	n=19[3]				

Mastoidal breadth	Braincase breadth	Zygomatic breadth	Interorbital breadth	Maxillary toothrow	Mandible length
10.26 (9.6–10.6)	10.16 (9.51–10.75)	7.96	5.27 (4.93–5.85)	7.61 (6.9–8.25)	13.90 (12.82–15.98)
n=7[5]	n=31 30[2],1[1]	n=1[1]	n=39 30[2],2[1],7[5]	n=37 30[2],7[5]	n=32 30[2],2[1]
10.56 (10.1–11.1)	10.15 (9.56–10.62)	7.88	5.28 (4.72–5.7)	7.57 (6.9–8.35)	13.75 (12.63–14.52)
n=19[5]	n=32 30[2],2[1]	n=1[1]	n=50 30[2],1[1],19[5]	n=49 30[2],19[5]	n=32 30[2],2[1]
	9.9 (9.7–10.0)		5.1 (4.9–5.3)	9.7 (9.5–10.0)	
	n=25[10]		n=25[10]	n=25[10]	

Family Talpidae *continued*

Species	Sex	Greatest length	Palatal length	Palatilar length	Postpalatal length	Maxillary breadth
Broad-footed mole, *Scapanus latimanus*	♀	34.16 (31.0–36.6)	14.37 (13.72–14.91)	13.45 (12.2–14.5)		10.45 (10.19–11.06)
n=Total sample Sources		*n*=34 8[2],10[1],16[5]	*n*=10[1]	*n*=16[5]		*n*=8[2]
	♂	34.21 (30.46–38.13)	14.43 (13.12–15.34)	13.30 (12.1–14.7)		10.31 (9.73–10.9)
n=Total sample Sources		*n*=53 12[2],8[1],33[5]	*n*=8[1]	*n*=33[5]		*n*=12[2]
Townsend's mole, *Scapanus townsendii*	♀	41.43 (39.46–44.1)		17.67 (16.9–18.1)		11.62 (11.21–12.44)
n=Total sample Sources		*n*=34 17[2],17[5]		*n*=17[5]		*n*=17[2]
	♂	42.03 (39.66–44.6)		18.18 (17.4–18.8)		11.84 (11.11–12.73)
n=Total sample Sources		*n*=47 30[2],17[5]		*n*=17[5]		*n*=30[2]
Hairy-tailed mole, *Parascalops breweri*	♀	31.26 (30.27–32.39)	13.35 (12.96–13.64)	12.2		
n=Total sample Sources		*n*=6 5[1],1[5]	*n*=5[1]	*n*=1[5]		
	♂	(33.5–35.2)		12.6 (12.1–13.1)		
n=Total sample		*n*=10[5]		*n*=10[5]		
Eastern mole, *Scalopus aquaticus*	♀	33.50 (29.3–40.9)	15.45 (14.05–16.44)	13.43 (12.0–14.7)	14.21 (12.4–16.5)	
n=Total sample Sources		*n*=105 14[3],3[6],21[8], 7[1],33[5],27[11]	*n*=5[1]	*n*=68 14[3],21[8],33[5]	*n*=39 14[3],25[11]	
	♂	34.32 (30.0–40.8)	15.14 (14.05–16.38)	14.21 (12.4–17.0)	14.76 (13.3–16.3)	
n=Total sample Sources		*n*=161 23[3],5[6],21[8], 79[5],33[11]	*n*=5[1]	*n*=123 23[3],21[8],79[5]	*n*=56 23[3],33[11]	
Star-nosed mole, *Condylura cristata*	♀	34.11 (32.88–35.0)	14.14 (13.80–14.60)	13.3		
n=Total sample Sources		*n*=6 5[1],1[5]	*n*=5[1]	*n*=1[5]		

Mastoidal breadth	Braincase breadth	Zygomatic breadth	Interorbital breadth	Maxillary toothrow	Mandible length
16.36 (15.1–17.2)	16.52 (15.66–17.91)	13.07 (12.65–13.35)	7.63 (7.1–8.23)	11.02 (9.9–12.02)	22.00 (20.22–23.47)
n=16[5]	n=18 8[2],10[1]	n=8[1]	n=33 8[2],9[1],16[5]	n=24 8[2],16[5]	n=18 8[2],10[1]
16.32 (15.0–17.8)	16.56 (15.02–17.93)	13.36 (12.30–15.63)	7.53 (6.9–8.16)	10.91 (9.8–13.09)	21.53 (19.68–22.02)
n=33[5]	n=20 12[2],8[1]	n=7[1]	n=53 12[2],8[1],33[5]	n=45 12[2],33[5]	n=20 12[2],8[1]
19.91 (19.3–20.4)	19.66 (18.9–20.15)		8.61 (7.85–9.2)	13.99 (13.3–14.96)	27.43 (26.39–29.1)
n=17[5]	n=17[2]		n=34 17[2],17[5]	n=34 17[2],17[5]	n=17[2]
20.84 (20.0–21.8)	19.83 (19.05–20.55)		8.63 (7.63–9.5)	14.15 (13.5–15.21)	28.04 (27.11–29.68)
n=17[5]	n=30[2]		n=47 30[2],17[5]	n=47 30[2],17[5]	n=30[2]
14.3	14.37 (14.18–14.82)	11.60 (11.25–11.86)	7.12 (6.94–7.20)	9.6	20.22 (19.20–20.93)
n=1[5]	n=5[1]	n=5[1]	n=6 5[1],1[5]	n=1[5]	n=5[1]
14.5 (13.9–15.0)			7.3 (7.1–7.5)	9.9 (9.2–10.2)	21.04 (20.26–21.62)
n=10[5]			n=10[5]	n=10[5]	n=5[1]
17.54 (15.6–21.6)		14.25 (13.63–14.80)	7.48 (6.7–8.6)	11.75 (9.2–17.5)	20.43 (19.54–21.64)
n=105 14[3],3[6],21[8], 7[1],35[5],27[11]		n=5[1]	n=104 14[3],3[6],21[8], 7[1],33[5],26[11]	n=104 14[3],3[6],21[8], 7[1],33[5],26[11]	n=5[1]
18.14 (16.0–21.6)		14.54 (14.00–15.24)	7.61 (6.5–8.7)	12.07 (9.6–18.1)	20.77 (19.39–21.82)
n=161 23[3],5[6],21[8], 79[5],33[11]		n=5[1]	n=161 23[3],5[6],21[8], 79[5],33[11]	n=161 23[3],5[6],21[8], 79[5],33[11]	n=5[1]
13.4	13.32 (12.66–13.88)	9.84 (9.41–10.08)	6.48 (6.10–7.3)	11.5	21.33 (20.76–21.90)
n=1[5]	n=5[1]	n=4[1]	n=6 5[1],1[5]	n=1[5]	n=5[1]

Family Talpidae *continued*

Species	Sex	Greatest length	Palatal length	Palatilar length	Postpalatal length	Maxillary breadth
Star-nosed mole, *Condylura cristata*	♂	34.17 (33.1–35.2)	14.26 (13.86–14.66)	13.05 (12.7–13.6)		
n=Total sample Sources		n=20 5[1],15[5]	n=5[1]	n=15[5]		
	♀♂	33.05 (32.1–35.2)		13.7 (13.0–14.4)		
n=Total sample Sources		n=24+?[7] 2[4],22[9]		n=22[9]		

1=author, 2=Verts and Carraway (1998), 3=Lowery (1974), 4=Paradiso (1969), 5=Jackson (1915), 6=Armstrong (1972), 7=Jackson (1961), 8=Yates and Schmidley (1978), 9=Peterson and Yates (1980), 10=Dalquest and Burgner (1941) in Carraway and Verts (1991), 11=Hoffmeister(1989)

Families Mormoopidae, Phyllostomidae, and Molossidae

Table in millimeters. Mean and parameters on top. Total number of specimens measured and specific number in cited sources below.

Species	Sex	Greatest length	Condylobasal length	Palatal length	Rostrum breadth C–C
Ghost-faced bat, *Mormoops megalophylla*	♀	15.22 (14.84–15.63)		8.86 (8.58–9.12)	
n=Total sample Sources		n=9 1[4],8[1]		n=8[1]	
	♂	15.30 (15.02–15.67)		8.90 (8.32–9.22)	
n=Total sample Sources		n=7 1[4],6[1]		n=6[1]	
California leaf-nosed bat, *Macrotus californicus*	♀	22.88 (22.39–23.5)		10.11 (9.58–10.48)	3.42 (3.22–3.52)
n=Total sample Sources		n=18 10[2],8[1]		n=8[1]	n=10[2]
	♂	23.19 (22.60–23.85)		10.19 (9.58–10.47)	3.54 (3.45–3.6)
n=Total sample Sources		n=18 10[2],8[1]		n=8[1]	n=10[2]
Mexican long-tongued bat, *Choeronycteris mexicana*	♀	29.62 (28.55–30.6)		17.91 (17.46–18.50)	4.05 (3.95–4.15)
n=Total sample Sources		n=19 13[2],6[1]		n=6[1]	n=13[2]

Mastoidal breadth	Braincase breadth	Zygomatic breadth	Interorbital breadth	Maxillary toothrow	Mandible length
13.35 (12.6–14.0)	13.67 (13.44–14.02)	9.77 (9.35–10.52)	6.94 (6.04–7.4)	11.19 (10.6–11.5)	20.43 (19.54–21.64)
n=15[5]	n=5[1]	n=5[1]	n=20 5[1],15[5]	n=15[5]	n=5[1]
13.08 (12.7–14.2)			6.89 (6.6–7.2)	10.6 (10.0–11.0)	
n=24+?[7] 2[4],22[9]			n=24 2[4],22[9]	n=22[9]	

Mastoidal breadth	Braincase breadth	Zygomatic breadth	Interorbital breadth	Maxillary toothrow	Mandible length
8.51 (8.27–8.66)	8.72 (8.49–9.24)	9.57 (9.37–9.84)	5.48 (5.28–5.59)	8.9	12.69 (12.06–13.06) measured to angular process
n=8[1]	n=8[1]	n=9 1[4],8[1]	n=8[1]	n=1[4]	n=8[1]
8.66 (8.47–8.78)	8.83 (8.56–9.18)	9.62 (9.5–9.80)	5.48 (5.39–5.55)	9.0	12.93 (12.80–12.99) measured to angular process
n=6[1]	n=6[1]	n=7 1[4],6[1]	n=6[1]	n=1[4]	n=5[1]
9.83 (9.5–10.15)		11.06 (10.8–11.5)	3.40 (3.2–3.5)		14.73 (14.50–15.06)
n=10[2]		n=10[2]	n=10[2]		n=8[1]
10.03 (9.75–10.4)		11.52 (11.15–11.85)	3.42 (3.3–3.55)		14.72 (14.43–15.08)
n=10[2]		n=10[2]	n=10[2]		n=8[1]
9.37 (8.8–10.28)			3.85 (3.64–4.0)		21.51 (20.92–22.04)
n=19 13[2],6[1]			n=18 13[2],5[1]		n=6[1]

Families Mormoopidae, Phyllostomidae, and Molossidae *continued*

Species	Sex	Greatest length	Condylobasal length	Palatal length	Rostrum breadth C–C
Mexican long-tongued bat, *Choeronycteris mexicana*	♂	29.93 (29.34–31.02)		18.50 (17.78–19.24)	4.15 (3.9–4.3)
n=Total sample Sources		n=13 4[2],9[1]		n=9[1]	n=4[2]
	♀♂	(29.2–30.4)	(28.2–29.3)	(17.6–18.8)	
n=Total sample		n=13[3]	n=13[3]	n=13[3]	
Southern long-nosed bat, *Leptonycteris curasoae*	♀	26.77 (25.7–27.3)		14.72 (14.00–15.30)	4.39 (4.1–4.55)
n=Total sample		n=12[2]		n=11[1]	n=12[2]
	♂	26.68 (26.14–27.19)		14.83 (14.17–15.36)	
n=Total sample		n=10[1]		n=8[1]	
Hairy-legged vampire bat, *Diphylla ecaudata*	♀	22.37 (21.64–22.80)		6.45 (6.25–6.67)	
n=Total sample		n=8[1]		n=8[1]	
	♂	22.77 (22.22–23.30)		6.62 (6.20–7.24)	
n=Total sample		n=6[1]		n=6[1]	
Western bonneted bat, *Eumops perotis*	♀	30.80 (29.7–32.00)		12.80 (11.95–13.41)	
n=Total sample Sources		n=10 5[1],5[2]		n=5[1]	
	♂	31.61 (31.02–33.00)		13.15 (12.70–14.17)	
n=Total sample Sources		n=10 8[1],2[2]		n=8[1]	

1=author, 2=Hoffmeister (1986), 3=Baker (1956) in Arroyo-Cabrales et al. (1987), 4=Hall and Kelson (1959)

Family Vespertilionidae, genus *Myotis*

Table in millimeters. Mean and parameters on top. Total number of specimens measured and specific number in cited sources below.

Species	Sex	Greatest length	Condylobasal length	Postpalatal length	Zygomatic breadth	Mastoidal breadth
California myotis, *Myotis californicus*	♀	13.14 (12.90–13.64)	13.33 (12.51–14.14)		7.92 (6.93–8.6)	6.86 (6.42–7.18)
n=Total sample		n=10[1]	n=38[3]		n=38[3]	n=38[3]
	♂	13.24 (12.78–14.31)	13.14 (12.56–13.72)		7.85 (7.22–8.38)	6.85 (6.39–7.2)
n=Total sample		n=10[1]	n=39[3]		n=39[3]	n=39[3]

Mastoidal breadth	Braincase breadth	Zygomatic breadth	Interorbital breadth	Maxillary toothrow	Mandible length
10.01 (9.2–10.48)			3.98 (3.7–4.20)		21.85 (21.22–22.48)
n=13 4[2],9[1]			n=13 4[2],9[1]		n=9[1]
(9.9–10.5)	(9.4–10.1)		(3.6–4.1)	(8.6–9.3)	
n=13[3]	n=13[3]		n=13[3]	n=13[3]	
10.44 (10.0–10.8)		10.51 (10.25–10.9)	4.69 (4.4–4.9)		17.87 (17.36–18.64)
n=12[2]		n=12[2]	n=12[2]		n=12[1]
10.79 (10.38–11.22)		10.83 (10.46–11.28)	4.85 (4.48–5.14)		17.84 (16.80–18.58)
n=10[1]		n=10[1]	n=10[1]		n=10[1]
	11.97 (11.84–12.20)	12.52 (12.29–12.80)	6.84 (6.46–7.28)		13.50 (13.12–13.80)
	n=8[1]	n=8[1]	n=8[1]		n=8[1]
	12.20 (11.84–12.45)	12.75 (12.14–13.06)	6.90 (6.60–7.10)		13.83 (13.30–14.39)
	n=6[1]	n=6[1]	n=6[1]		n=6[1]
15.27 (15.04–15.50)		17.76 (17.34–18.32)	5.09 (4.85–5.32)	12.53 (12.2–12.85)	22.55 (21.95–23.28)
n=7 5[1],2[2]		n=10 5[1],5[2]	n=10 5[1],5[2]	n=5[2]	n=5[1]
15.43 (14.94–15.70)		18.03 (17.52–18.52)	5.12 (4.7–5.40)	12.45, 12.55	23.08 (22.20–23.96)
n=10 8[1],2[2]		n=10 8[1],2[2]	n=10 8[1],2[2]	n=2[2]	n=8[1]

Braincase breadth	Interorbital breadth	Rostrum width C–C	Maxillary toothrow	Skull depth	Mandible length
6.51 (6.11–6.84)	3.24 (3.01–3.49)				9.08 (8.55–9.86)
n=38[3]	n=38[3]				n=38[3]
6.47 (6.18–6.68)	3.29 (3.04–3.7)				8.99 (8.28–9.49)
n=39[3]	n=39[3]				n=39[3]

Family Vespertilionidae, genus *Myotis* continued

Species	Sex	Greatest length	Condylobasal length	Postpalatal length	Zygomatic breadth	Mastoidal breadth
California myotis, *Myotis californicus*	♀♂	13.36 (12.9–14.2)		6.96 (6.52–7.50)	8.06 (7.53–8.55)	6.83 (6.6–7.27)
n=Total sample		n=55[2]		n=55[2]	n=55[2]	n=55[2]
Western small-footed myotis, *Myotis ciliolabrum*	♀		13.47 (13.07–13.94)		8.12 (7.8–8.49)	6.83 (6.51–7.17)
n=Total sample			n=10[3]		n=10[3]	n=10[3]
	♂		13.49 (13.16–13.77)		8.17 (7.91–8.43)	6.8 (6.71–6.97)
n=Total sample			n=4[3]		n=4[3]	n=4[3]
Long-eared myotis, *Myotis evotis*	♀	15.2	15.46 (14.3–16.49)		9.01 (8.81–9.5)	7.63 (6.78–7.93)
n=Total sample Sources		n=1[6]	n=46 45[3],1[6]		n=46 45[3],1[6]	n=46 45[3],1[6]
	♂	15.58 (15.5–15.7)	15.43 (14.44–16.18)		9.03 (7.08–9.52)	7.62 (7.16–8.03)
n=Total sample Sources		n=4[6]	n=49 45[3],4[6]		n=47 45[3],2[6]	n=48 45[3],3[6]
	♀♂	16.67 (16.1–17.1)		8.25 (8.1–8.43)	9.76 (9.33–10.23)	8.10 (7.91–8.36)
n=Total sample		n=12[2]		n=12[2]	n=12[2]	n=12[2]
Eastern small-footed myotis, *Myotis leibii*	♀	14.1, 14.4	13.2, 13.6		8.2, 8.6	6.8, 7.2
n=Total sample		n=2[6]	n=2[6]		n=2[6]	n=2[6]
	♂	13.97 (13.5–14.2)	12.90 (12.4–13.3)		8.30 (8.0–8.5)	6.82 (6.7–7.0)
n=Total sample		n=4[6]	n=4[6]		n=4[6]	n=4[6]
	♀♂	14.44 (13.5–14.7)		7.4 (6.82–7.61)	8.89 (8.47–9.3)	7.32 (6.97–7.57)
n=Total sample		n=20[2]		n=20[2]	n=20[2]	n=20[2]
Little brown bat or myotis, *Myotis lucifugus*	♀	14.73 (13.8–15.6)	14.16 (13.2–15.1)		8.88 (8.01–10.3)	7.61 (6.95–8.6)
n=Total sample Sources		n=44 34[6],10[1]	n=108 74[3],34[6]		n=108 74[3],34[6]	n=108 74[3],34[6]
	♂	14.23 (13.74–14.71)	14.10 (13.43–14.75)		8.63 (7.99–9.12)	7.41 (6.95–7.83)
n=Total sample		n=10[1]	n=56[3]		n=56[3]	n=56[3]

Braincase breadth	Interorbital breadth	Rostrum width C–C	Maxillary toothrow	Skull depth	Mandible length
6.23 (5.96–6.67)	2.99 (2.74–3.3)	3.19 (3.0–3.37)	5.10 (4.8–5.43)	4.54 (4.12–4.91)	
n=55[2]	n=55[2]	n=55[2]	n=55[2]	n=55[2]	
6.53 (6.3–6.76)	3.15 (3.04–3.3)				9.29 (8.94–9.74)
n=10[3]	n=10[3]				n=10[3]
6.59 (6.42–6.8)	3.21 (3.15–3.27)				9.29 (9.18–9.48)
n=4[3]	n=4[3]				n=4[3]
7.35 (6.96–7.85)	3.77 (3.05–4.04)		5.9		10.75 (10.56–11.25)
n=45[3]	n=46 45[3],1[6]		n=1[6]		n=45[3]
7.28 (6.89–7.63)	3.78 (3.56–3.98)		5.98 (5.9–6.0)		10.71 (10.14–11.24)
n=45[3]	n=49 45[3],4[6]		n=4[6]		n=45[3]
7.42 (7.16–7.72)	3.80 (3.71–3.94)	3.93 (3.67–4.2)	6.58 (6.26–6.86)	5.39 (5.17–5.55)	
n=12[2]	n=12[2]	n=12[2]	n=12[2]	n=12[2]	
	3.2, 3.2		5.2, 5.6		
	n=2[6]		n=2[6]		
	3.20 (3.1–3.4)		5.35 (5.2–5.4)		
	n=4[6]		n=4[6]		
6.67 (6.41–7.05)	3.2 (3.04–3.45)	3.66 (3.49–3.82)	5.60 (5.43–5.81)	4.70 (4.35–4.91)	
n=20[2]	n=20[2]	n=20[2]	n=20[2]	n=20[2]	
7.09 (6.59–7.61)	3.92 (3.36–4.7)		5.66 (5.3–6.2)		9.82 (9.17–10.47)
n=74[3]	n=108 74[3],34[6]		n=34[6]		n=74[3]
7.07 (6.64–7.49)	3.83 (3.45–4.18)				9.71 (8.92–10.26)
n=56[3]	n=56[3]				n=56[3]

Family Vespertilionidae, genus *Myotis* continued

Species	Sex	Greatest length	Condylobasal length	Postpalatal length	Zygomatic breadth	Mastoidal breadth
Little brown bat or myotis, *Myotis lucifugus*	♀♂	14.52 (13.7–15.2)			8.99 (8.0–9.5)	7.9 (7.7–8.2)
n=Total sample Sources		*n*=27 +?[5] 7[4],20[8]			*n*=27 +?[5] 7[4],20[8]	*n*=20[8]
Fringed myotis, *Myotis thysanodes*	♀	15.5	15.54 (14.9–16.42)		9.50 (9.15–9.9)	7.91 (7.53–8.1)
n=Total sample Sources		*n*=1[6]	*n*=4 3[3],1[6]		*n*=4 3[3],1[6]	*n*=4 3[3],1[6]
	♂		16.06 (15.15–16.7)		9.59 (9.21–10.0)	7.84 (7.25–8.35)
n=Total sample			*n*=9[3]		*n*=9[3]	*n*=9[3]
	♀♂	16.83 (16.2–17.35)		8.41 (8.1–8.66)	10.40 (9.9–10.91)	8.32 (7.83–8.7)
n=Total sample		*n*=25[2]		*n*=25[2]	*n*=25[2]	*n*=25[2]
Cave myotis, *Myotis velifer*	♀♂	16.41 (15.8–17.0)		8.04 (7.76–8.32)	10.40 (10.04–10.83)	8.34 (7.98–8.70)
n=Total sample		*n*=24[2]		*n*=24[2]	*n*=24[2]	*n*=24[2]
Long-legged myotis, *Myotis volans*	♀	14.73 (14.6–15.0)	14.13 (13.66–14.63)		8.69 (7.98–9.1)	7.75 (7.22–8.1)
n=Total sample Sources		*n*=9[6]	*n*=47 38[3],9[6]		*n*=47 38[3],9[6]	*n*=47 38[3],9[6]
	♂	14.48 (14.3–14.7)	13.99 (13.54–14.49)		8.75 (8.0–9.1)	7.65 (7.2–7.98)
n=Total sample Sources		*n*=6[6]	*n*=44 38[3],6[6]		*n*=44 38[3],6[6]	*n*=44 38[3],6[6]
	♀♂	14.43 (13.95–14.85)		7.95 (7.57–8.4)	8.95 (8.4–9.45)	7.88 (7.57–8.32)
n=Total sample		*n*=23[2]		*n*=23[2]	*n*=23[2]	*n*=23[2]
Yuma myotis, *Myotis yumanensis*	♀	14.6, 14.6	13.90 (13.37–14.38)		8.34 (7.92–9.06)	7.24 (6.96–7.8)
n=Total sample Sources		*n*=2[6]	*n*=51 49[3],2[6]		*n*=51 49[3],2[6]	*n*=51 49[3],2[6]
	♂	14.6	13.85 (13.2–14.89)		8.31 (7.66–9.12)	7.23 (6.96–7.89)
n=Total sample Sources		*n*=1[6]	*n*=32 31[3],1[6]		*n*=32 31[3],1[6]	*n*=32 31[3],1[6]
	♀♂	14.01 (13.6–14.55)		7.19 (6.86–7.42)	8.32 (7.95–8.7)	7.21 (6.93–7.53)
n=Total sample		*n*=28[2]		*n*=28[2]	*n*=28[2]	*n*=28[2]

1=author, 2=Hoffmeister (1986), 3=Verts and Carraway (1998), 4=Paradiso (1969), 5=Lowery (1974), 6=Armstrong (1972), 7=Jackson (1961), 8=Hoffmeister (1989)

Braincase breadth	Interorbital breadth	Rostrum width C–C	Maxillary toothrow	Skull depth	Mandible length
7.5 (7.3–7.8)	4.07 (3.9–4.3)		5.1 (5.0–5.2)		
n=20[8]	n=27 7[4],20[8]		n=7[4]		
7.57 (7.29–7.71)	3.92 (3.83–4.07)		6.0		11.02 (10.62–11.31)
n=3[3]	n=4 3[3],1[6]		n=1[6]		n=3[3]
7.65 (7.18–8.08)	3.88 (3.64–4.03)				11.23 (10.71–11.60)
n=9[3]	n=9[3]				n=9[3]
7.99 (7.68–8.47)	4.07 (3.71–4.42)	4.27 (3.97–4.54)	6.55 (6.22–6.78)	5.68 (5.28–6.0)	
n=25[2]	n=25[2]	n=25[2]	n=25[2]	n=25[2]	
7.49 (7.2–7.72)	3.90 (3.64–4.09)	4.75 (4.46–4.95)	6.60 (6.41–6.86)	6.03 (5.7–6.33)	
n=24[2]	n=24[2]	n=24[2]	n=24[2]	n=24[2]	
7.22 (6.82–7.58)	3.97 (3.71–4.2)		5.41 (5.3–5.5)		9.90 (9.26–10.37)
n=38[3]	n=47 38[3],9[6]		n=9[6]		n=38[3]
7.18 (6.75–7.5)	3.98 (3.66–4.25)		5.40 (5.3–5.5)		9.83 (9.11–10.36)
n=8[3]	n=44 38[3],6[6]		n=6[6]		n=38[3]
7.40 (7.05–7.68)	4.00 (3.82–4.2)	3.83 (3.64–4.12)	5.47 (5.32–5.59)	5.49 (5.17–5.92)	
n=23[2]	n=23[2]	n=23[2]	n=23[2]	n=23[2]	
6.90 (6.57–7.31)	3.80 (3.59–4.4)		5.5, 5.6		9.55 (9.07–10.06)
n=49[3]	n=51 49[3],2[6]		n=2[6]		n=49[3]
6.89 (6.61–7.48)	3.81 (3.58–4.11)		5.6		9.49 (9.01–10.35)
n=31[3]	n=32 31[3],1[6]		n=1[6]		n=31[3]
7.03 (6.67–7.27)	3.67 (3.45–3.86)	3.57 (3.37–3.79)	5.36 (5.17–5.73)	5.23 (4.99–5.51)	
n=28[2]	n=28[2]	n=28[2]	n=28[2]	n=28[2]	

Family Vespertilionidae, genera *Lasiurus, Pipistrellus, Eptesicus,* and *Antrozous*

Table in millimeters. Mean and parameters on top. Total number of specimens measured and specific number in cited sources below.

Species	Sex	Greatest length	Condylobasal length	Postpalatal length	Mastoidal breadth
Eastern red bat, *Lasiurus borealis*	♀	13.04 (12.4–13.7)	12.95 (12.0–13.8)	5.3 (4.9–6.0)	7.92 (7.7–8.1)
n=Total sample Sources		n=7 4[2],3[6]	n=53 3[6], 50[5]	n=50[5]	n=4[2]
	♂	12.98 (12.3–13.9)	12.21 (11.9–13.9)	5.0 (4.7–5.4)	7.77 (7.7–7.9)
n=Total sample Sources		n=5 3[2],2[6]	n=31 2[6], 29[5]	n=29[5]	n=3[2]
Hoary bat, *Lasiurus cinereus*	♀	17.87 (16.90–19.0)	17.56 (17.82–17.88)		10.37 (9.96–10.76)
n=Total sample Sources		n=7 1[4],3[1],3[9]	n=3[3]		n=9 3[3],3[1],3[9]
	♂	17.32 (16.1–18.0)	16.58 (15.6–17.66)		10.07 (9.7–10.5)
n=Total sample Sources		n=38 9[2],1[4],28[6]	n=45 17[3],28[6]		n=54 9[2],17[3],28[6]
	♀♂	16.8 (13.1–17.7)		7.2 (6.9–7.8)	
n=Total sample		n=12[5],?[7]		n=12[5]	
Western pipistrelle, *Pipistrellus hesperus*	♀	11.52 (10.9–12.0)	11.88 (10.9–12.48)		6.35 (5.90–6.70)
n=Total sample Sources		n=31 29[2],2[6]	n=17 15[3],2[6]		n=46 29[2],15[3],2[6]
	♂	11.15 (10.35–11.8)	11.72 (11.0–12.25)		6.19 (5.45–6.44)
n=Total sample Sources		n=32 31[2],1[6]	n=13 12[3],1[6]		n=44 31[2],12[3],1[6]
Eastern pipistrelle, *Pipistrellus subflavus*	♀♂	12.72 (12.2–13.5)		4.4 (4.3–4.8)	
n=Total sample Sources		n=43 10[4],33[5]		n=33[5]	
Big brown bat, *Eptesicus fuscus*	♀	18.52 (18.0–19.7)	18.95 (17.3–20.34)		9.94 (9.15–10.86)
n=Total sample Sources		n=23 11[2],10[6],2[1]	n=36 26[3],10[6]		n=47 11[2],26[3],10[6]
	♂	18.31 (17.3–19.0)	18.74 (16.9–20.13)		9.70 (9.02–10.3)
n=Total sample Sources		n=19 11[2],3[6],5[1]	n=33 30[3],3[6]		n=41 11[2],30[3]

Braincase breadth	Zygomatic breadth	Interorbital breadth	Maxillary toothrow	Mandible length
7.72 (7.1–8.3)	9.79 (9.3–10.5)	4.33 (4.0–4.6)	4.47 (3.8–5.0)	
n=53 3[6], 50[5]	n=57 4[2],3[6], 50[5]	n=57 4[2],3[6], 50[5]	n=57 4[2],3[6], 50[5]	
7.44 (6.8–8.2)	9.07 (8.4–10.3)	4.22 (4.0–4.5)	4.20 (4.0–4.6)	
n=31 2[6], 29[5]	n=34 3[2],2[6], 29[5]	n=34 3[2],2[6], 29[5]	n=34 3[2],2[6], 29[5]	
9.46 (8.74–10.07)	12.52 (12.30–13.18)	5.19 (4.8–5.48)	6.2	13.24 (12.12–13.86)
n=9 3[3],3[1],3[9]	n=10 3[3],1[4],3[1],3[9]	n=10 3[3],1[4],3[1],3[9]	n=1[4]	n=6 3[3],3[1]
9.71 (9.00–10.08)	12.23 (11.4–12.70)	5.20 (4.80–5.5)	5.96 (5.7–6.3)	12.71 (12.15–13.16)
n=20 17[3],3[1]	n=55 9[2],17[3],1[4],28[6]	n=55 9[2],17[3],1[4],28[6]	n=38 9[2],1[4],28[6]	n=20 17[3],3[1]
9.6 (9.1–10.1)	12.1 (11.6–12.8)	5.2 (5.0–5.7)	5.7 (5.4–6.3)	
n=12[5]	n=12[5]	n=12[5]	n=12[5]	
6.23 (6.02–6.46)	7.55 (7.28–7.95)	3.13 (2.85–3.63)	4.05 (3.80–4.35)	8.04 (7.62–8.30)
n=15[3]	n=15[3]	n=46 29[2],15[3],2[6]	n=31 29[2],2[6]	n=15[3]
6.08 (5.84–6.33)	7.31 (6.82–7.57)	3.09 (2.80–3.41)	3.94 (3.65–4.2)	7.84 (7.39–8.15)
n=12[3]	n=13 12[3],1[6]	n=44 31[2],12[3],1[6]	n=32 31[2],1[6]	n=12[3]
6.8 (6.5–7.2)	7.90 (7.7–8.3)	3.58 (3.2–3.9)	4.15 (3.8–4.4)	
n=33[5]	n=43 10[4],33[5]	n=43 10[4],33[5]	n=43 10[4],33[5]	
9.51 (8.48–10.22)	12.70 (11.4–13.69)	4.28 (3.87–4.67)	6.96 (6.55–7.4)	14.16 (13.32–14.67)
n=28 26[3],2[1]	n=47 11[2],26[3],10[6]	n=47 11[2],26[3],10[6]	n=21 11[2],10[6]	n=28 26[3],2[1]
9.24 (8.26–9.82)	12.25 (10.7–13.18)	4.36 (3.8–5.0)	6.93 (6.6–7.15)	13.69 (12.82–14.91)
n=35 30[3],5[1]	n=47 11[2],30[3],6[6]	n=47 11[2],30[3],6[6]	n=14 11[2],3[6]	n=35 30[3],5[1]

Family Vespertilionidae, genera *Lasiurus, Pipistrellus, Eptesicus,* and *Antrozous continued*

Species	Sex	Greatest length	Condylobasal length	Postpalatal length	Mastoidal breadth
Big brown bat, *Eptesicus fuscus*	♀♂	18.46 (15.1–23.0)		6.5 (6.2–7.3)	
n=Total sample Sources		n=24+?[8]+?[7] 15[4],9[5]		n=9[5]	
Pallid bat, *Antrozous pallidus*	♀	20.66 (19.25–23.32)	21.43 (19.1–22.73)		10.14 (9.45–11.04)
n=Total sample Sources		n=16 11[2],5[1]	n=21 19[3],2[6]		n=37 11[2],19[3],2[6],5[1]
	♂	20.38 (18.7–23.16)	21.44 (20.16–22.72)		10.19 (9.2–10.9)
n=Total sample Sources		n=14 11[2],3[1]	n=30[3]		n=44 11[2],30[3],3[1]

1=author, 2=Hoffmeister (1986), 3=Verts and Carraway (1998), 4=Paradiso (1969), 5=Lowery (1974), 6=Armstrong (1972), 7=Jackson (1961), 8=Kurta and Baker (1990), 9=Hoffmeister (1989)

Order Primates

Table in millimeters. Mean and parameters on top. Total number of specimens measured and specific number in cited sources below.

Species	Sex	Greatest length
Mantled howler monkey, *Aloutta palliata*	♀	113.15 (108.69–119.12)
n=Total sample		n=3[1]
	♂	125.46 (118.18–132.46)
n=Total sample		n=3[1]

1=author

Family Dasypodidae

Table in millimeters. Mean and parameters on top. Total number of specimens measured and specific number in cited sources below.

Species	Sex	Greatest length	Palatal length	Palatilar length	Postpalatal length	Zygomatic breadth
Nine-banded armadillo, *Dasypus novemcinctus*	♀♂	98.54 (86.10–107.26)	63.16 (60.04–65.98)	62.5 (59.5–65.9)	15.1 (14.1–16.4)	39.97 (33.20–45.10)
n=Total sample Sources		n=60+?[3] 8[1],4[2],48[4]	n=4[1]	n=4[2]	n=4[2]	n=50 8[1],4[2],38[4]

1=author, 2=Lowery (1974), 3=Hall (1981), 4=Stangl et al. (1995)

Braincase breadth	Zygomatic breadth	Interorbital breadth	Maxillary toothrow	Mandible length
9.3 (8.8–10.6)	12.65 (11.1–14.2)	4.28 (3.9–4.8)	7.03 (6.5–9.8)	
$n=9^5$	$n=19+?^8$ $10^4,9^5$	$n=24$ $15^4,9^5$	$n=24+?^8$ $15^4,9^5$	
9.65 (9.11–10.56)	12.65 (11.6–14.06)	4.23 (3.55–4.77)	6.96 (6.4–7.5)	14.87 (13.75–16.60)
$n=24$ $19^3,5^1$	$n=36$ $11^2,19^3,2^6,4^1$	$n=37$ $11^2,19^3,2^6,5^1$	$n=13$ $11^2,2^6$	$n=24$ $19^3,5^1$
9.62 (9.03–10.42)	12.61 (11.61–13.72)	4.21 (3.7–4.80)	6.92 (6.5–7.3)	14.53 (13.66–16.30)
$n=33$ $30^3,3^1$	$n=44$ $11^2,30^3,3^1$	$n=44$ $11^2,30^3,3^1$	$n=11^2$	$n=33$ $30^3,3^1$

Zygomatic breadth	Interorbital breadth	Braincase breadth	Mandible length
72.63 (71.36–74.16)	10.85 (10.12–12.16)	50.54 (48.71–52.36)	83.23 (80.46–88.20)
$n=3^1$	$n=3^1$	$n=3^1$	$n=3^1$
82.50 (80.67–83.86)	12.11 (11.61–12.48)	52.35 (51.36–53.73)	97.03 (89.16–104.06)
$n=3^1$	$n=3^1$	$n=3^1$	$n=3^1$

Interorbital breadth	Braincase breadth	Mastoidal breadth	Maxillary toothrow	Mandibular toothrow	Mandible length
23.60 (21.30–26.10)	30.76 (29.4–32.02)	26.02 (24.52–28.30)	25.32 (20.80–28.28)	26.18 (22.34–29.18)	74.63 (71.58–79.24)
$n=72$ $8^1,4^2,60^4$	$n=4^1$	$n=4^1$	$n=52$ $8^1,44^4$	$n=63$ $8^1,55^4$	$n=8^1$

Families Ochotonidae and Leporidae

Table in millimeters. Mean and parameters on top. Total number of specimens measured and specific number in cited sources below.

Species	Sex	Greatest length	Basilar length	Palatal bridge length	Nasal length	Parietal breadth	Braincase breadth
American pika, *Ochotona princeps*	♀	43.43 (41.35–45.8)	38.32 (31.54–40.88)	2.21 (1.6–3.5)	13.98 (12.66–15.8)	7.97 (6.59–11.7)	19.13 (15.7–20.58)
n=Total sample Sources		n=14 11[6],3[1]	n=37[2]	n=10[6]	n=48 37[2],11[6]	n=37[2]	n=47 37[2],10[6]
	♂	43.81 (40.16–46.2)	38.52 (32.09–41.77)	2.24 (1.7–3.2)	14.10 (11.83–15.56)	8.33 (6.27–12.64)	19.14 (15.8–21.28)
n=Total sample Sources		n=24 18[6],6[1]	n=62[2]	n=18[6]	n=80 62[2],18[6]	n=62[2]	n=79 62[2],17[6]
	♀♂	43.6 (38.8–47.3)			13.5 (11.9–15.5)		17.3 (15.9–18.5)
n=Total sample		n=225[10]			n=225[10]		n=225[10]
Pygmy rabbit, *Brachylagus idahoensis*	♀	50.76 (47.58–51.87)	43.24 (37.5–50.24)	4.0 (3.5–4.6)	18.59 (16.18–21.14)	16.42 (15.21–18.02)	21.07 (18.58–23.59)
n=Total sample Sources		n=10[1]	n=31 22[2],9[11]	n=9[11]	n=31 22[2],9[11]	n=22[2]	n=30 22[2],8[11]
	♂	50.37 (46.34–52.24)	44.50 (36.9–48.79)	4.1 (3.3–4.6)	18.50 (15.41–20.11)	17.09 (15.49–18.84)	21.12 (19.05–23.4)
n=Total sample Sources		n=10[1]	n=36 30[2],6[11]	n=5[11]	n=36 30[2],6[11]	n=30[2]	n=35 30[2],5[11]
Swamp rabbit, *Sylvilagus aquaticus*	♀♂	87.5 (83.7–99.6)	68.1 (60.9–72.3)	17.0 (12.2–18.2)	37.4 (32.5–40.8)		27.64 (24.8–30.5)
n=Total sample Sources		n=34[5]	n=37[9]	n=37[9]	n=37[9]		n=61 24[5],37[9]
Desert cottontail, *Sylvilagus audubonii*	♀	68.42 (61.60–74.1)	52.85 (49.4–55.3)	5.64 (5.2–5.9)	29.80 (26.5–33.9)		22.63 (21.3–23.9)
n=Total sample Sources		n=22 12[6],10[1]	n=29[11]	n=45 12[6],33[11]	n=45 12[6],33[11]		n=27[11]
	♂	67.21 (61.07–72.92)	52.62 (48.1–55.67)	5.58 (4.5–6.4)	29.87 (26.7–31.8)		22.55 (21.0–23.6)
n=Total sample Sources		n=22 12[6],10[1]	n=33[11]	n=45 12[6],33[11]	n=45 12[6],33[11]		n=32[11]
	♀♂	66.88 (62.5–71.90)			28.53 (26.65–30.15)		25.59 (24.30–26.95)
n=Total sample		n=43[3]			n=43[3]		n=43[3]
Brush rabbit, *Sylvilagus bachmani*	♀	62.07 (58.20–65.20)	51.24 (44.5–61.37)	5.16 (3.7–6.6)	27.70 (23.4–32.1)	18.24 (15.54–21.38)	21.88 (19.6–25.09)
n=Total sample Sources		n=10[1]	n=93 30[2],63[11]	n=65[11]	n=96 30[2],66[11]	n=30[2]	n=93 30[2],63[11]

Zygomatic breadth	Interorbital breadth	Bulla length	Maxillary toothrow	Mandibular toothrow	Postorbital breath	Mandible length	Mandibular ramus depth
21.32 (20.14–22.74)	5.48 (4.9–6.2)	10.33 (9.28–12.29)	8.43 (7.67–9.42)	8.18 (7.06–9.44)		31.66 (27.03–34.21)	5.49 (4.94–6.19)
n=40 37[2],3[1]	n=11[6]	n=37[2]	n=37[2]	n=40 37[2],3[1]		n=40 37[2],3[1]	n=37[2]
21.31 (19.5–22.84)	5.38 (4.9–5.9)	10.36 (8.89–12.17)	8.44 (7.17–9.24)	8.19 (7.00–8.86)		31.43 (25.82–34.63)	5.56 (4.65–6.17)
n=68 62[2],6[1]	n=18[6]	n=62[2]	n=62[2]	n=68 62[2],6[1]		n=68 62[2],6[1]	n=62[2]
21.5 (19.6–23.1)	5.3 (4.2–6.5)	11.0 (8.0–12.5)	8.3 (7.4–9.0)				
n=225[10]	n=225[10]	n=225[10]	n=225[10]				
27.04 (24.8–28.95)		11.35 (9.37–12.85)	9.09 (7.94–9.72)	9.08 (7.93–9.82)	9.5 (8.9–10.5)	36.38 (31.48–40.39)	7.24 (6.04–8.15)
n=31 22[2],9[11]		n=22[2]	n=31 22[2],9[11]	n=22[2]	n=9[11]	n=22[2]	n=22[2]
27.28 (25.41–28.49)		11.51 (9.35–12.91)	9.18 (8.44–9.76)	9.01 (7.38–10.12)	9.2 (8.5–9.5)	36.89 (33.22–39.77)	7.14 (6.45–8.23)
n=36 30[2],6[11]		n=30[2]	n=36 30[2],6[11]	n=30[2]	n=6[11]	n=30[2]	n=30[2]
41.13 (37.1–49.8)	20.0 (17.5–29.7)		16.18 (12.2–18.2)			67.11 (64.72–69.85)	
n=64 27[5],37[9]	n=34[5]		n=76 39[5],37[9]			n=37[9]	
34.52 (31.8–36.7)	5.55 (5.30–5.84)		12.97 (11.8–14.3)		11.63 (8.9–11.8)	49.85 (47.20–52.50)	
n=44 12[6],32[11]	n=4[1]		n=45 12[6],33[11]		n=44 12[6],32[11]	n=10[1]	
34.23 (32.4–35.9)	9.36, 13.50		12.71 (11.7–13.6)		11.82 (10.4–13.4)	48.40 (43.24–52.36)	
n=43 12[6],31[11]	n=2[1]		n=45 12[6],33[11]		n=45 12[6],33[11]	n=10[1]	
33.23 (30.80–35.15)		12.83 (12.05–13.55)	12.61 (11.40–13.55)				10.61 (9.50–12.30)
n=43[3]		n=43[3]	n=43[3]				n=43[3]
31.65 (27.9–33.87)		10.10 (7.95–11.65)	12.63 (10.2–14.85)	13.23 (12.28–14.32)	10.51 (8.2–12.5)	51.08 (48.69–54.56)	9.89 (8.91–11.16)
n=92 30[2],62[11]		n=30[2]	n=97 30[2],67[11]	n=30[2]	n=67[11]	n=30[2]	n=30[2]

Families Ochotonidae and Leporidae *continued*

Species	Sex	Greatest length	Basilar length	Palatal bridge length	Nasal length	Parietal breadth	Braincase breadth
Brush rabbit, *Sylvilagus bachmani*	♂	61.14 (57.90–66.00)	52.63 (45.8–61.16)	5.31 (3.6–6.5)	27.80 (24.7–30.27)	18.99 (15.08–22.45)	22.08 (20.5–24.93)
n=Total sample Sources		n=10[1]	n=68 24[2],44[11]	n=46[11]	n=69 24[2],45[11]	n=24[2]	n=68 24[2],44[11]
Eastern cottontail, *Sylvilagus floridanus*	♀	74.29 (72.34–75.40)	63.55 (59.35–66.66)		31.76 (29.69–33.64)	20.80 (18.89–23.01)	24.35 (22.75–25.7)
n=Total sample Sources		n=5[1]	n=30[2]		n=30[2]	n=30[2]	n=30[2]
	♂	73.87 (71.39–76.14)	63.39 (60.29–66.95)		31.51 (29.37–33.52)	21.00 (19.38–23.11)	24.24 (23.35–25.82)
n=Total sample Sources		n=5[1]	n=30[2]		n=30[2]	n=30[2]	n=30[2]
	♀♂	71.20 (62.25–82.0)	57.0 (56.5–57.5)	6.5 (5.9–6.9)	31.49 (27.30–36.60)		26.38 (24.5–28.5)
n=Total sample Sources		n=74+?[8] 40[3],28[5],6[7]	n=3[4]	n=6[7]	n=40[3]		n=68 40[3],28[5]
Mountain cottontail, *Sylvilagus nuttallii*	♀	64.50 (56.60–72.4)	56.15 (48.1–61.41)	5.56 (4.5–6.1)	28.92 (26.71–32.2)	18.27 (15.15–21.25)	22.89 (21.47–24.46)
n=Total sample Sources		n=13 3[6],10[1]	n=41 30[2],11[11]	n=15 3[6],12[11]	n=45 30[2],3[6],12[11]	n=30[2]	n=41 30[2],11[11]
	♂	66.04 (61.06–72.6)	54.90 (48.2–61.51)	5.65 (5.1–6.8)	28.01 (24.7–31.1)	18.88 (15.74–21.1)	22.66 (20.9–24.26)
n=Total sample Sources		n=13 3[6],10[1]	n=47 30[2],17[11]	n=21 3[6],18[11]	n=51 30[2],3[6],18[11]	n=30[2]	n=48 30[2],18[11]
	♀♂	67.78 (65.30–70.60)			30.14 (27.25–31.50)		26.42 (24.35–27.35)
n=Total sample		n=22[3]			n=22[3]		n=22[3]
New England cottontail, *Sylvilagus transitionalis*	♀	72.23 (69.80–74.67)		6.57 (6.06–7.02)	29.47 (28.42–31.69)		26.47 (25.23–28.33)
n=Total sample		n=6[1]		n=6[1]	n=6[1]		n=6[1]
	♂	69.24 (65.50–75.04)		7.45 (6.80–7.76)	27.77 (25.10–31.18)		26.36 (25.40–27.20)
n=Total sample		n=6[1]		n=6[1]	n=6[1]		n=6[1]
	♀♂*		54.20 (52.69–55.71)	6.04 (5.60–6.48)	26.61 (24.08–29.14)	24.17 (23.34–25.00)	22.92 (22.35–23.49)
n=Total sample			n=14[12]	n=14[12]	n=12[12]	n=14[12]	n=14[12]
Antelope jackrabbit, *Lepus alleni*	♀♂	108.67 (97.0–115.1)			46.54 (38.2–50.9)		
n=Total sample		n=23[3]			n=23[3]		

Zygomatic breadth	Interorbital breadth	Bulla length	Maxillary toothrow	Mandibular toothrow	Postorbital breath	Mandible length	Mandibular ramus depth
31.90 (29.1–33.9)		10.33 (8.4–11.88)	12.56 (10.9–14.26)	12.93 (11.87–14.32)	10.38 (9.0–11.9)	50.44 (48.05–53.58)	9.74 (9.16–10.98)
n=67 24[2],43[11]		n=24[2]	n=70 24[2],46[11]	n=24[2]	n=45[11]	n=24[2]	n=24[2]
35.64 (33.55–37.49)		10.53 (9.49–11.49)	14.39 (13.42–15.32)	14.56 (12.92–15.48)		56.72 (53.55–59.16)	11.00 (9.87–11.72)
n=30[2]		n=30[2]	n=30[2]	n=30[2]		n=35 30[2],5[1]	n=30[2]
35.62 (34.04–38.55)		10.54 (9.25–11.95)	14.28 (13.2–15.22)	14.49 (13.33–15.43)		56.17 (53.20–60.10)	11.15 (10.07–12.43)
n=30[2]		n=30[2]	n=30[2]	n=30[2]		n=35 30[2],5[1]	n=30[2]
34.62 (32.1–37.15)	17.30 (15.4–20.0)	11.24 (10.10–12.45)	13.27 (11.80–16.00)				10.24 (9.10–11.60)
n=76 10[3],3[4],27[5],6[7]	n=40 3[4],37[5]	n=40[3]	n=83 40[3],3[4],34[5],6[7]				n=40[3]
32.90 (31.66–36.16)		9.73 (8.53–11.17)	13.03 (11.74–14.56)	13.15 (12.0–14.16)	11.30 (10.7–12.0)	50.85 (47.85–53.83)	9.81 (8.89–11.25)
n=45 30[2],3[6],12[11]		n=30[2]	n=45 30[2],3[6],12[11]	n=30[2]	n=15 3[6],12[11]	n=30[2]	n=30[2]
32.83 (30.7–34.9)		9.92 (8.47–11.71)	12.69 (11.75–14.26)	12.83 (11.86–14.14)	11.06 (10.3–11.8)	49.74 (45.59–53.83)	9.75 (9.02–10.86)
n=50 30[2],3[6],17[11]		n=30[2]	n=51 30[2],3[6],18[11]	n=30[2]	n=20 3[6],17[11]	n=30[2]	n=30[2]
34.83 (32.75–36.10)		11.09 (10.45–11.75)	12.38 (11.45–12.75)				9.50 (8.75–10.05)
n=22[3]		n=22[3]	n=22[3]				n=22[3]
35.59 (34.60–37.78)	15.15 (14.20–16.34)		14.41 (14.14–15.18)	13.95 (13.68–14.78)		53.80 (51.43–55.53)	
n=6[1]	n=6[1]		n=6[1]	n=6[1]		n=6[1]	
35.19 (33.74–36.72)	14.87 (13.46–17.00)		13.65 (12.48–15.54)	13.29 (12.52–14.64)		51.51 (49.06–54.69)	
n=6[1]	n=6[1]		n=6[1]	n=6[1]		n=6[1]	
36.29 (35.10–37.48)		10.12 (9.77–10.47)	13.63 (13.25–14.01)		14.32 (13.56–15.08)		
n=13[12]		n=14[12]	n=14[12]		n=14[12]		
47.66 (44.5–50.7)		15.13 (13.5–16.5)	19.01 (17.6–20.6)				
n=23[3]		n=22[3]	n=23[3]				

Families Ochotonidae and Leporidae *continued*

Species	Sex	Greatest length	Basilar length	Palatal bridge length	Nasal length	Parietal breadth	Braincase breadth
Snowshoe hare, *Lepus americanus*	♀	76.86 (72.9–84.10)	63.70 (54.0–71.08)	5.93 (4.4–6.8)	30.47 (27.1–37.35)	19.47 (17.37–21.67)	24.26 (21.79–29.36)
n=Total sample Sources		n=12 2[6],10[1]	n=33 25[2],8[11]	n=14 2[6],4[1],8[11]	n=39 25[2],2[6],8[11],4[1]	n=25[2]	n=35 25[2],4[1],6[11]
	♂	77.48 (73.94–80.06)	61.47 (52.9–68.97)	5.93 (4.9–6.6)	29.78 (25.96–33.26)	19.78 (17.67–21.46)	24.43 (22.07–30.34)
n=Total sample Sources		n=12 1[6],11[1]	n=30 19[2],11[11]	n=13 1[6],12[11]	n=37 19[2],1[6],6[1],11[11]	n=19[2]	n=35 19[2],6[1],10[11]
	♀♂	(73.5–85.5)					
n=Total sample		n=?[8]					
Black-tailed jackrabbit, *Lepus californicus*	♀	92.80 (87.04–99.80)	74.10 (68.2–85.02)	6.02 (5.1–6.9)	37.30 (31.59–44.86)	23.21 (20.71–26.07)	26.13 (22.02–29.5)
n=Total sample Sources		n=13 3[6],10[1]	n=69 25[2],44[11]	n=48 4[6],44[11]	n=73 25[2],4[6],44[11]	n=25[2]	n=68 25[2],43[11]
	♂	93.97 (85.42–99.0)	74.04 (66.4–81.99)	6.13 (5.0–7.7)	37.48 (30.63–44.9)	22.91 (20.59–25.7)	26.18 (23.24–29.1)
n=Total sample Sources		n=13 3[6],10[1]	n=71 25[2],46[11]	n=52 4[6],48[11]	n=75 25[2],2[6],48[11]	n=25[2]	n=70 25[2],45[11]
	♀♂	94.86 (87.0–101.9)			39.54 (35.5–45.6)		
n=Total sample		n=27[3]			n=27[3]		
White-tailed jackrabbit, *Lepus townsendii*	♀	92.91 (76.80–96.8)	71.98 (68.1–74.7)	5.95 (4.9–7.2)	39.28 (36.5–43.6)		28.99 (27.5–30.2)
n=Total sample Sources		n=23 14[6],9[1]	n=10[11]	n=24 14[6],10[11]	n=24 14[6],10[11]		n=10[11]
	♂	92.55 (77.48–96.41)	73.87 (67.6–82.63)	5.84 (4.4–7.1)	38.42 (34.3–41.8)	25.74 (23.71–27.48)	27.95 (25.72–30.6)
n=Total sample Sources		n=16 12[6],4[1]	n=19 7[2],12[11]	n=25 12[6],13[11]	n=30 7[2],12[6],11[11]	n=7[2]	n=19 7[2],12[11]
	♀♂	(88.8–102.5)					
n=Total sample		n=?[8]					

1=author, 2=Verts and Carraway (1998), 3= Hoffmeister (1986), 4=Paradiso (1969), 5=Lowery (1974), 6=Armstrong (1972), 7=Jones in Armstrong (1972), 8=Jackson (1961), 9=Lowe (1958) in Chapman and Feldhamer (1981), 10=Smith and Weston (1990), 11=Orr (1940), 12=Chapman and Morgan (1973)

*=Parameters incomplete, created from 1 Standard Deviation of means.

Zygomatic breadth	Interorbital breadth	Bulla length	Maxillary toothrow	Mandibular toothrow	Postorbital breath	Mandible length	Mandibular ramus depth
36.81	17.11	9.94	13.87	14.44	11.19	56.58	10.70
(34.3–41.71)	(15.88–18.78)	(8.61–11.14)	(12.2–15.72)	(13.25–16.22)	(10.0–12.3)	(52.24–64.18)	(9.78–11.49)
n=39	n=4[1]	n=25[2]	n=40	n=29	n=10	n=29	n=25[2]
25[2],2[6],4[1],8[11]			25[2],2[6],4[1],9[11]	25[2],4[1]	2[6],8[11]	25[2],4[1]	
36.64	15.70	9.78	13.65	14.46	10.96	56.02	10.50
(34.7–40.48)	(14.47–16.89)	(8.54–11.24)	(12.2–15.45)	(13.31–16.00)	(9.4–12.1)	(53.68–62.07)	(9.77–11.16)
n=38	n=6[1]	n=19[2]	n=38	n=25	n=13	n=25	n=19[2]
19[2],1[6],6[1],12[11]			19[2],1[6],6[1],12[11]	19[2],6[1]	1[6],12[11]	19[2],6[1]	
(36.5–42.0)							
n=?[8]							
41.40		12.52	15.70	16.45	12.52	66.19	13.39
(38.4–46.7)		(11.39–14.0)	(14.09–17.8)	(14.5–18.05)	(10.7–14.8)	(61.6–73.71)	(11.69–14.68)
n=73		n=25[2]	n=73	n=25[2]	n=48	n=25[2]	n=25[2]
25[2],4[6],44[11]			25[2],4[6],44[11]		4[6],44[11]		
41.37		12.63	15.77	16.43	12.32	65.31	13.37
(37.33–46.8)		(11.52–14.46)	(13.64–17.5)	(14.9–18.15)	(10.4–15.1)	(60.37–69.31)	(12.17–14.62)
n=77		n=25[2]	n=76	n=25[2]	n=52	n=25[2]	n=25[2]
25[2],4[6],48[11]			25[2],4[6],47[11]		4[6],48[11]		
42.48		14.21	16.59				
(40.8–45.5)		(13.1–15.2)	(15.1–18.1)				
n=27[3]		n=27[3]	n=27[3]				
44.89			16.78		13.63	68.82	
(42.1–46.7)			(15.8–17.5)		(11.1–16.0)	(58.38–72.85)	
n=24			n=24		n=24	n=9[1]	
14[6],10[11]			14[6],10[11]		14[6],10[11]		
43.92		11.78	16.53	16.86	13.58	67.50	13.26
(41.24–45.1)		(10.44–12.59)	(15.73–18.0)	(15.82–17.93)	(11.5–15.8)	(59.96–71.94)	(12.24–14.18)
n=31		n=7[2]	n=32	n=7[2]	n=25	n=11	n=7[2]
7[2],11[6],13[11]			7[2],12[6],13[11]		12[6],13[11]	7[2],4[1]	
(45.2–52.3)							
n=?[8]							

Family Sciuridae, genera *Neotamias* and *Tamias*

Table in millimeters. Mean and parameters on top. Total number of specimens
measured and specific number in cited sources below.

Species	Sex	Greatest length	Palatilar length	Postpalatal length	Nasal length	Braincase breadth
Yellow-pine chipmunk, *Neotamias amoenus*	♀	33.25 (31.66–34.62)				15.93 (14.94–16.83)
n=Total sample		*n*=60[2]				*n*=60[2]
	♂	32.93 (31.36–34.75)				16.01 (15.29–16.84)
n=Total sample		*n*=63[2]				*n*=63[2]
Cliff chipmunk, *Neotamias dorsalis*	♀	35.39 (34.8–36.1)			10.95 (10.5–11.7)	
n=Total sample		*n*=15[6]			*n*=15[6]	
	♂	35.28 (34.9–36.0)			10.77 (10.0–11.3)	
n=Total sample		*n*=9[6]			*n*=9[6]	
	♀♂ 38M+33F	35.85 (33.7–38.3)	14.52 (13.6–15.9)	13.03 (12.1–14.1)	10.95 (10.0–12.2)	16.40 (15.7–17.2)
n=Total sample		*n*=71[3]	*n*=71[3]	*n*=71[3]	*n*=71[3]	*n*=71[3]
Least chipmunk, *Neotamias minimus*	♀	30.72 (27.8–33.18)			9.44 (8.5–10.4)	14.87 (14.04–16.37)
n=Total sample Sources		*n*=94 30[2],54[6],10[7]			*n*=54[6]	*n*=40 30[2],10[7]
	♂	30.41 (27.45–32.4)			9.36 (8.6–10.3)	14.85 (13.82–15.68)
n=Total sample Sources		*n*=88 30[2],49[6],9[7]			*n*=43[6]	*n*=39 30[2],9[7]
	♀♂ 9M+20F	31.88 (30.9–33.0)	13.47 (12.5–14.4)	11.47 (11.1–11.9)	9.68 (9.0–10.3)	14.96 (14.5–15.3)
n=Total sample		*n*=29[3]	*n*=29[3]	*n*=29[3]	*n*=29[3]	*n*=29[3]
Colorado chipmunk, *Neotamias quadrivittatus*	♀	35.64 (34.4–36.9)			11.17 (10.3–12.1)	
n=Total sample		*n*=28[6]			*n*=28[6]	
	♂	35.48 (34.0–37.1)			11.03 (9.4–12.2)	
n=Total sample		*n*=35[6]			*n*=35[6]	
	♀♂ 34F+16M	35.23 (33.5–36.5)	14.76 (14.0–15.4)	12.41 (11.5–13.0)	10.63 (9.5–11.5)	16.15 (15.5–16.6)
n=Total sample		*n*=50[3]	*n*=50[3]	*n*=50[3]	*n*=50[3]	*n*=50[3]

Zygomatic breadth	Interorbital breadth	Postorbital constriction	Maxillary toothrow	Mandibular toothrow	Mandible length
18.49	8.18		5.50	5.27	17.70
(17.56–19.37)	(7.50–9.93)		(4.98–6.13)	(5.00–5.52)	(16.57–18.81)
n=60[2]	n=6[1]		n=60[2]	n=6[1]	n=60[2]
18.32	7.49		5.39	5.30	17.42
(17.55–19.47)	(6.64–8.05)		(4.05–6.06)	(4.96–5.62)	(16.49–18.52)
n=63[2]	n=8[1]		n=63[2]	n=8[1]	n=63[2]
19.75	7.80			5.47	18.76
(19.2–22.5)	(7.5–8.2)			(5.3–5.7)	(18.3–19.5)
n=15[6]	n=15[6]			n=15[6]	n=15[6]
19.36	7.80			5.44	18.50
(18.8–20.1)	(7.2–8.2)			(5.2–5.6)	(18.1–19.0)
n=9[6]	n=9[6]			n=9[6]	n=9[6]
19.56	7.93	11.36	5.66		
(18.7–20.7)	(7.3–8.8)	(10.5–12.2)	(5.1–6.2)		
n=71[3]	n=71[3]	n=71[3]	n=71[3]		
17.23	6.86		4.99	4.90	16.22
(15.5–19.24)	(6.2–7.8)		(4.49–5.46)	(4.4–5.5)	(14.66–18.49)
n=94	n=64		n=30[2]	n=64	n=84
30[2],54[6],10[7]	54[6],10[7]			54[6],10[7]	30[2],54[6]
16.97	6.74		4.93	4.81	16.01
(15.34–18.25)	(5.9–7.6)		(4.59–5.16)	(4.4–5.5)	(14.36–17.88)
n=88	n=58		n=30[2]	n=58	n=79
30[2],49[6],9[7]	49[6],9[7]			49[6],9[7]	30[2],49[6]
17.80	6.97	10.42	5.23		
(17.0–18.7)	(6.6–7.6)	(9.9–10.8)	(4.7–5.6)		
n=29[3]	n=29[3]	n=29[3]	n=29[3]		
19.64	7.78			5.84	18.90
(19.1–20.4)	(7.1–8.4)			(5.4–6.3)	(18.1–19.8)
n=28[6]	n=28[6]			n=28[6]	n=28[6]
19.38	7.74			5.90	18.75
(18.4–20.3)	(7.2–8.5)			(5.4–6.6)	(17.7–19.6)
n=35[6]	n=35[6]			n=35[6]	n=35[6]
19.60	7.90	11.14	5.81		
(18.0–20.3)	(7.1–8.7)	(10.1–11.9)	(5.3–6.2)		
n=50[3]	n=50[3]	n=50[3]	n=50[3]		

Family Sciuridae, genera *Neotamias* and *Tamias* *continued*

Species	Sex	Greatest length	Palatilar length	Postpalatal length	Nasal length	Braincase breadth
Townsend's chipmunk, *Neotamias townsendii*	♀	38.62 (36.42–41.43)				17.61 (16.78–22.14)
n=Total sample		n=60[2]				n=60[2]
	♂	38.18 (36.85–40.06)				17.46 (16.5–18.50)
n=Total sample		n=61[2]				n=61[2]
Uinta chipmunk, *Neotamias umbrinus*	♀	36.3, 36.5			11.1, 11.7	
n=Total sample		n=2[6]			n=2[6]	
	♂	35.67 (35.0–36.6)			11.03 (10.7–11.6)	
n=Total sample		n=14[6]			n=14[6]	
	♀♂ 8M+12F	35.29 (33.7–36.5)	14.74 (14.0–15.2)	12.64 (12.1–13.2)	10.88 (9.6–11.8)	15.83 (15.3–16.2)
n=Total sample		n=20[3]	n=20[3]	n=20[3]	n=20[3]	n=20[3]
Eastern chipmunk, *Tamias striatus*	♀	39.05 (36.38–41.32)				
n=Total sample		n=10[1]				
	♂	38.93 (36.35–40.49)				
n=Total sample		n=10[1]				
	♀♂	42.52 (38.9–49.6)	19.28 (17.5–24.1)	14.74 (13.6–15.9)	14.29 (12.5–16.1)	16.88 (15.7–20.8)
n=Total sample Sources		n=144 9[4],12[5],123[8]	n=135 12[5],123[8]	n=135 12[5],123[8]	n=148 13[4],12[5],123[8]	n=135 12[5],123[8]

1=author, 2=Verts and Carraway (1998), 3=Hoffmeister (1986), 4=Paradiso (1969), 5=Lowery (1974), 6=Armstrong (1972), 7=Johnson (1943) in Verts and Carraway (2001), 8=Hoffmeister (1989)

Zygomatic breadth	Interorbital breadth	Postorbital constriction	Maxillary toothrow	Mandibular toothrow	Mandible length
21.52 (20.22–22.47)			6.42 (5.65–7.0)		21.57 (19.26–22.8)
n=60[2]			n=60[2]		n=60[2]
21.18 (20.22–22.45)			6.35 (5.85–6.97)		20.70 (19.46–22.13)
n=61[2]			n=61[2]		n=61[2]
19.37 (19.2–19.5)	7.43 (7.2–7.6)			5.77 (5.7–5.8)	18.9 (18.6–19.2)
n=3[6]	n=3[6]			n=3[6]	n=3[6]
19.05 (18.6–19.3)	7.68 (7.3–8.4)			5.66 (5.5–5.9)	18.61 (18.0–19.2)
n=14[6]	n=14[6]			n=14[6]	n=14[6]
19.04 (18.4–19.6)	8.00 (7.1–8.9)	11.45 (10.5–12.2)	5.52 (5.1–6.0)		
n=20[3]	n=20[3]	n=20[3]	n=20[3]		
21.39 (19.93–22.87)				6.38 (6.08–6.94)	22.16 (20.69–23.62)
n=10[1]				n=10[1]	n=10[1]
21.27 (19.80–22.40)				6.26 (6.04–7.10)	22.34 (20.94–23.71)
n=10[1]				n=10[1]	n=10[1]
23.44 (19.9–26.4)	11.44 (10.1–12.8)	11.11 (10.5–12.2)	6.57 (5.9–8.6)		
n=148 13[4],12[5],123[8]	n=135 12[5],123[8]	n=13[4]	n=135 12[5],123[8]		

Family Sciuridae, genus *Marmota*

Table in millimeters. Mean and parameters on top. Total number of specimens measured and specific number in cited sources below.

Species	Sex	Greatest length	Condylobasal length	Palatal length	Postpalatal length	Nasal length
Hoary marmot, *Marmota caligata*	♀	96.69 (86.12–108.76)	96.44 (87.0–106.5)	55.10 (50.2–61.4)	36.63 (30.6–41.1)	39.42 (34.9–44.0)
n=Total sample Sources		n=10[1]	n=21 20[3],1[7]	n=21 20[3],1[7]	n=22 20[3],2[7]	n=22 20[3],2[7]
	♂	98.66 (82.76–107.83)	98.46 (85.4–107.4)	56.07 (49.6–62.7)	37.73 (32.3–41.7)	40.37 (34.9–45.3)
n=Total sample Sources		n=10[1]	n=23 22[3],1[7]	n=23 22[3],1[7]	n=23 22[3],1[7]	n=23 22[3],1[7]
Yellow-bellied marmot, *Marmota flaviventris*	♀	81.62 (73.8–88.82)	81.15 (71.3–94.1)	45.04 (39.4–50.3)	31.91 (27.0–36.9)	34.89 (29.4–41.5)
n=Total sample Sources		n=22 12[2],10[1]	n=57 43[3],14[6]	n=55 43[3],12[6]	n=43[3]	n=57 43[3],14[6]
	♂	85.13 (73.20–93.38)	89.27 (79.1–97.1)	48.76 (42.1–55.0)	35.38 (30.8–38.2)	38.12 (32.6–42.6)
n=Total sample Sources		n=18 8[2],10[1]	n=37 28[3],9[6]	n=36 28[3],8[6]	n=28[3]	n=37 28[3],9[6]
Woodchuck or groundhog *Marmota monax*	♀	89.33 (73.57–101.62)	84.79 (77.4–94.2)	49.79 (45.6–56.0)	31.11 (28.0–36.3)	35.42 (30.5–41.1)
n=Total sample Sources		n=17 10[1],7[8]	n=33 28[3],5[4]	n=33 28[3],5[4]	n=28[3]	n=35 28[3],7[8]
	♂	85.17 (77.30–89.68)	87.74 (75.0–102.6)	51.36 (43.7–59.5)	32.36 (27.5–37.7)	35.58 (29.9–41.8)
n=Total sample Sources		n=11[1]	n=40 37[3],3[4]	n=40 37[3],3[4]	n=37[3]	n=37[3]
	♀♂	(94.0–102.0)				
n=Total sample		n=?[5]				

1=author, 2=Verts and Carraway (1998), 3=Howell (1915), 4=Paradiso (1969), 5=Jackson (1961), 6=Armstrong (1972), 7=Bee and Hall (1956), 8=Hoffmeister(1989)

Braincase breadth	Zygomatic breadth	Interorbital breadth	Mastoidal breadth	Maxillary toothrow	Mandibular toothrow	Mandible length
	63.13 (55.8–68.4)	24.12 (20.9–27.2)	42.95 (37.9–49.4)	22.04 (20.2–24.4)	21.18 (19.26–22.04)	66.58 (61.14–74.74)
	n=22 20[3],2[7]	n=22 20[3],2[7]	n=22 20[3],2[7]	n=22 20[3],2[7]	n=10[1]	n=10[1]
	64.82 (56.2–69.8)	24.82 (21.5–29.0)	44.44 (38.0–49.2)	22.50 (21.1–24.1)	21.14 (19.87–22.40)	67.97 (57.52–73.56)
	n=23 22[3],1[7]	n=23 22[3],1[7]	n=23 22[3],1[7]	n=23 22[3],1[7]	n=10[1]	n=10[1]
30.65 (27.82–33.05)	54.88 (47.18–61.0)	18.72 (15.0–22.5)	39.80 (34.2–44.7)	19.57 (14.9–22.1)	18.78 (17.80–20.00)	55.02 (46.62–60.70)
n=12[2]	n=69 12[2],43[3],14[6]	n=57 43[3],14[6]	n=43[3]	n=69 12[2],43[3],14[6]	n=10[1]	n=22 12[2],10[1]
32.00 (29.77–33.66)	57.05 (42.1–63.7)	19.88 (16.1–23.2)	42.11 (37.5–46.2)	20.41 (19.0–22.2)	19.51 (18.44–20.58)	56.34 (48.21–62.66)
n=8[2]	n=45 8[2],28[3],9[6]	n=37 28[3],9[6]	n=28[3]	n=45 8[2],28[3],9[6]	n=10[1]	n=18 8[2],10[1]
33.9 (31.9–35.0)	59.14 (52.8–68.0)	23.45 (19.8–28.7)	40.75 (36.5–45.8)	20.26 (17.5–23.1)	19.57 (17.16–22.23)	61.11 (52.14–70.50)
n=7[8]	n=40 28[3],5[4],7[8]	n=40 28[3],5[4],7[8]	n=28[3]	n=40 28[3],5[4],7[8]	n=10[1]	n=10[1]
	60.05 (53.0–69.3)	23.85 (18.4–29.2)	42.11 (36.4–50.2)	20.06 (18.2–22.0)	19.39 (18.08–20.44)	60.50 (54.45–65.41)
	n=40 37[3],3[4]	n=40 37[3],3[4]	n=37[3]	n=40 37[3],3[4]	n=11[1]	n=11[1]

Family Sciuridae, genera *Ammospermophilus, Spermophilus,* and *Cynomys*

Table in millimeters. Mean and parameters on top. Total number of specimens measured and specific number in cited sources below.

Species	Sex	Greatest length	Condylobasal length	Palatilar length	Nasal length	Braincase breadth
Harris's antelope squirrel, *Ammospermophilus harrisii*	♀♂ 39M+36F +2?	39.69 (37.6–42.4)		17.79 (16.55–19.1)	11.87 (10.2–13.6)	19.06 (18.1–20.5)
n=Total sample		n=77[3]		n=77[3]	n=77[3]	n=77[3]
White-tailed antelope squirrel, *Ammospermophilus leucurus*	♀	39.17 (35.56–43.14)			12.26 (11.6–12.7)	18.78 (17.91–20.05)
n=Total sample Sources		n=25 15[2],10[6]			n=10[6]	n=15[2]
	♂	39.62 (37.01–41.9)			12.25 (11.2–13.0)	19.12 (18.36–20.03)
n=Total sample Sources		n=15 8[2],7[6]			n=7[6]	n=8[2]
	♀♂ 20M+38F	39.08 (36.7–41.5)		17.22 (16.05–18.05)	11.37 (10.0–12.4)	18.82 (17.7–20.1)
n=Total sample		n=58[3]		n=58[3]	n=58[3]	n=58[3]
California ground squirrel, *Spermophilus beecheyi*	♀	56.71 (51.6–63.64)		26.77 (23.5–30.0)	20.24 (17.5–22.4)	23.43 (22.0–25.2)
n=Total sample Sources		n=111 27[2],84[8]		n=84[8]	n=84[8]	n=111 27[2],84[8]
	♂	59.43 (53.9–65.35)		28.77 (25.0–31.0)	21.70 (19.0–24.0)	24.09 (22.2–25.9)
n=Total sample Sources		n=96 27[2],69[8]		n=69[8]	n=69[8]	n=96 27[2],69[8]
Columbian ground squirrel, *Spermophilus columbianus*	♀	52.40 (49.5–54.85)		25.13 (23.0–27.5)	18.92 (18.0–19.7)	21.28 (19.85–23.87)
n=Total sample Sources		n=31 20[2],11[8]		n=11[8]	n=11[8]	n=31 20[2],11[8]
	♂	53.22 (46.08–57.0)		24.41 (24.0–28.0)	18.55 (18.0–21.4)	21.49 (19.45–22.51)
n=Total sample Sources		n=49 31[2],18[8]		n=18[8]	n=18[8]	n=49 31[2],18[8]
Golden-mantled ground squirrel, *Spermophilus lateralis*	♀	42.28 (39.6–45.13)		19.46 (18.0–20.8)	14.87 (12.8–17.0)	19.43 (18.1–21.02)
n=Total sample Sources		n=129 51[2],9[6],69[8]		n=69[8]	n=78 9[6],69[8]	n=120 51[2],69[8]

Zygomatic breadth	Interorbital breadth	Postorbital breadth	Bulla length	Maxillary toothrow	Mastoidal breadth	Mandibular toothrow	Mandible length
22.93 (21.55–24.1)	9.44 (8.45–10.4)	13.79 (12.2–14.9)	10.50 (9.8–11.4)	7.20 (6.5–7.8)			
n=77[3]	n=77[3]	n=77[3]	n=77[3]	n=77[3]			
22.56 (20.94–25.72)		13.80 (12.7–14.8)		7.20 (6.1–8.88)		6.77 (6.42–7.18)	21.60 (20.32–22.9)
n=25 15[2],10[6]		n=10[6]		n=25 15[2],10[6]		n=10[1]	n=25 15[2],10[6]
22.80 (21.09–24.2)		13.83 (13.3–14.7)		7.11 (6.55–7.5)		6.63 (6.32–7.01)	21.91 (20.21–23.4)
n=15 8[2],7[6]		n=7[6]		n=15 8[2],7[6]		n=10[1]	n=15 8[2],7[6]
22.55 (20.8–23.8)	8.79 (7.7–9.9)	13.64 (12.6–15.1)	10.58 (9.75–11.6)	7.23 (6.5–8.5)			
n=58[3]	n=58[3]	n=58[3]	n=58[3]	n=58[3]			
35.14 (32.3–40.69)	13.54 (11.4–15.9)	15.75 (13.7–17.3)		11.49 (10.1–12.7)		11.11 (10.02–12.15)	35.20 (31.76–38.96)
n=111 27[2],84[8]	n=94 10[1],84[8]	n=84[8]		n=111 27[2],84[8]		n=10[1]	n=27[2]
37.30 (32.8–42.10)	14.14 (11.4–16.5)	15.66 (13.6–18.1)		11.75 (10.6–13.11)		11.26 (10.76–12.32)	36.40 (32.94–39.73)
n=96 27[2],69[8]	n=79 10[1],69[8]	n=69[8]		n=96 27[2],69[8]		n=10[1]	n=27[2]
32.59 (31.12–34.6)	11.67 (10.2–13.2)	12.04 (11.4–12.3)		11.54 (10.4–12.58)		10.84 (10.53–11.30)	32.04 (30.52–33.11)
n=31 20[2],11[8]	n=11[8]	n=11[8]		n=31 20[2],11[8]		n=10[1]	n=20[2]
33.11 (26.61–35.6)	10.80 (9.9–14.3)	10.96 (10.4–12.6)		11.64 (10.1–13.97)		10.80 (10.32–11.64)	32.02 (29.0–35.68)
n=49 31[2],18[8]	n=18[8]	n=18[8]		n=49 31[2],18[8]		n=10[1]	n=31[2]
26.02 (23.8–29.3)	9.90 (8.9–11.3)	12.71 (11.2–14.0)		8.34 (7.1–9.26)		8.23 (7.84–8.62)	24.72 (23.01–27.43)
n=129 51[2],9[6],69[8]	n=69[8]	n=78 9[6],69[8]		n=129 51[2],9[6],69[8]		n=10[1]	n=60 51[2],9[6]

Family Sciuridae, genera *Ammospermophilus,* *Spermophilus,* and *Cynomys* continued

Species	Sex	Greatest length	Condylobasal length	Palatilar length	Nasal length	Braincase breadth
Golden-mantled ground squirrel, *Spermophilus lateralis*	♂	42.96 (36.17–49.62)		19.91 (19.0–21.5)	15.16 (13.3–17.5)	19.64 (18.0–20.88)
n=Total sample Sources		n=122 51[2],5[6],66[8]		n=66[8]	n=71 5[6],66[8]	n=117 51[2],66[8]
	♀♂ 37M+64F	43.77 (41.7–45.8)		20.05 (18.6–21.2)	15.18 (14.0–17.0)	20.51 (19.5–21.9)
n=Total sample		n=101[3]		n=101[3]	n=101[3]	n=101[3]
Arctic ground squirrel, *Spermophilus parryii*	♀	56.45 (50.7–62.1)		28.43 (25.0–32.0)	20.89 (18.1–24.0)	22.81 (21.1–25.1)
n=Total sample Sources		n=72 11[5],61[8]		n=69 11[5],58[8]	n=65 11[5],54[8]	n=72 11[5],61[8]
	♂	58.98 (51.5–65.8)		29.89 (25.0–34.0)	21.86 (17.7–25.9)	23.73 (21.4–26.4)
n=Total sample Sources		n=80 14[5],66[8]		n=80 14[5],66[8]	n=80 14[5],66[8]	n=80 14[5],66[8]
Spotted ground squirrel, *Spermophilus spilosoma*	♀	40.18 (37.5–41.5)		18.2 (17.5–18.8)	14.1 (13.6–14.4)	18.7 (18.1–19.6)
n=Total sample		n=6[6]		n=10[8]	n=5[6]	n=10[8]
	♂	41.12 (37.2–43.0)		18.6 (18.0–19.5)	14.24 (12.8–15.3)	18.7 (18.1–19.6)
n=Total sample		n=5[6]		n=10[8]	n=5[6]	n=10[8]
	♀♂ 29M+36F	36.91 (34.8–39.6)		16.20 (14.9–17.8)	12.35 (11.35–13.7)	17.94 (16.6–19.4)
n=Total sample		n=65[3]		n=65[3]	n=65[3]	n=65[3]
Round-tailed ground squirrel, *Spermophilus tereticaudus*	♀♂	36.79 (34.7–39.8)		16.81 (15.6–18.6)	11.66 (9.9–13.7)	17.76 (16.6–19.3)
n=Total sample Sources		n=136 99[3],37[8]		n=115 99[3],16[8]	n=136 99[3],37[8]	n=136 99[3],37[8]
Thirteen-lined ground squirrel, *Spermophilus tridecemlineatus*	♀	37.67 (33.2–41.3)		17.09 (14.5–19.8)	13.01 (10.0–15.7)	16.53 (15.3–17.9)
n=Total sample Sources		n=56 2[3],20[6],5[1],29[8]		n=32 3[3],29[8]	n=52 3[3],20[6],29[8]	n=31 2[3],29[8]
	♂	38.74 (34.2–42.1)		17.61 (15.5–19.5)	13.56 (10.5–15.4)	16.95 (16.3–18.3)
n=Total sample Sources		n=52 1[3],23[6],5[1],23[8]		n=24 1[3],23[8]	n=48 2[3],23[6],23[8]	n=26 3[3],23[8]

Zygomatic breadth	Interorbital breadth	Postorbital breadth	Bulla length	Maxillary toothrow	Mastoidal breadth	Mandibular toothrow	Mandible length
26.49 (21.83–28.9)	10.20 (9.0–12.0)	12.83 (11.0–14.0)		8.35 (6.70–9.4)		8.27 (7.30–9.01)	24.92 (23.31–27.7)
n=122 51[2],5[6],66[8]	n=66[8]	n=71 5[6],66[8]		n=122 51[2],5[6],66[8]		n=10[1]	n=56 51[2],5[6]
27.19 (25.3–29.2)	9.86 (8.2–10.8)	12.67 (11.2–14.0)	9.24 (8.5–9.8)	8.77 (8.0–9.3)			
n=101[3]	n=101[3]	n=101[3]	n=101[3]	n=101[3]			
36.69 (32.0–42.0)	12.13 (10.0–14.6)	12.93 (11.0–14.4)		12.61 (10.3–15.0)			
n=72 11[5],61[8]	n=72 11[5],61[8]	n=61[8]		n=72 11[5],61[8]			
38.60 (33.5–44.3)	12.82 (10.2–15.6)	13.33 (11.4–15.5)		12.92 (11.2–15.0)			
n=80 14[5],66[8]	n=80 14[5],66[8]	n=66[8]		n=80 14[5],66[8]			
23.98 (23.1–24.8)		13.65 (12.7–14.8)		7.63 (6.9–8.2)			21.45 (18.3–22.8)
n=5[6]		n=6[6]		n=6[6]			n=6[6]
24.9, 25.5		13.54 (12.7–14.8)		7.68 (6.8–8.0)			22.26 (20.6–22.9)
n=2[6]		n=5[6]		n=5[6]			n=5[6]
22.10 (20.0–23.9)	7.71 (6.3–8.65)	12.96 (11.55–13.9)	9.58 (8.2–10.6)	6.79 (6.55–8.05)			
n=65[3]	n=65[3]	n=65[3]	n=65[3]	n=65[3]			
23.08 (21.3–25.4)	8.15 (6.9–10.3)	12.34 (10.7–13.6)	9.81 (8.8–10.7)	7.62 (6.7–8.5)			
n=136 99[3],37[8]	n=136 99[3],37[8]	n=136 99[3],37[8]	n=99[3]	n=136 99[3],37[8]			
22.02 (19.1–24.7)	7.36 (6.5–8.2)	11.17 (9.9–12.2)		6.80 (5.6–7.8)		6.63 (5.67–7.21)	21.10 (18.3–23.68)
n=48 1[3],20[6],27[8]	n=31 2[3],29[8]	n=43 2[3],20[6],21[8]		n=52 3[3],20[6],29[8]		n=10[1]	n=25 20[6],5[1]
22.78 (19.7–24.7)	7.72 (6.9–8.9)	11.51 (10.0–12.6)		6.94 (5.7–7.8)		6.73 (5.86–7.35)	21.80 (18.4–25.37)
n=47 1[3],23[6],23[8]	n=25 2[3],23[8]	n=49 3[3],23[6],23[8]		n=49 3[3],23[6],23[8]		n=10[1]	n=28 23[6],5[1]

Family Sciuridae, genera *Ammospermophilus, Spermophilus,* and *Cynomys* continued

Species	Sex	Greatest length	Condylobasal length	Palatilar length	Nasal length	Braincase breadth
Thirteen-lined ground squirrel, *Spermophilus tridecemlineatus*	♀ ♂	(40.8–45.8)				
n=Total sample		*n*=?[4]				
Rock squirrel, *Spermophilus variegatus*	♀	59.56 (54.8–65.7)		28.03 (25.9–32.5)	21.18 (18.8–23.7)	25.33 (23.5–26.7)
n=Total sample		*n*=50		*n*=44	*n*=52	*n*=44
Sources		19[3],8[6],23[8]		21[3],23[8]	21[3],8[6],23[8]	21[3],23[8]
	♂	61.77 (54.4–67.7)		29.50 (27.1–33.0)	22.32 (20.3–24.5)	25.77 (24.1–26.8)
n=Total sample		*n*=36		*n*=34	*n*=36	*n*=34
Sources		15[3],2[6],19[8]		15[3],19[8]	15[3],2[6],19[8]	15[3],19[8]
White-tailed prairie dog, *Cynomys leucurus*	♀	59.32 (53.17–63.15)			21.58 (20.8–22.5)	
n=Total sample		*n*=14			*n*=13[6]	
Sources		8[6],6[1]				
	♂	61.84 (58.88–64.1)			22.86 (22.5–23.2)	
n=Total sample		*n*=15			*n*=9[6]	
Sources		8[6],7[1]				
Black-tailed prairie dog, *Cynomys ludovicianus*	♀	63.09 (60.5–66.0)	59.98 (57.4–62.3)		23.58 (21.9–25.0)	
n=Total sample		*n*=17[6]	*n*=17[6]		*n*=17[6]	
	♂	64.02 (62.0–67.8)	61.40 (59.5–64.4)		22.91 (22.8–25.6)	
n=Total sample		*n*=17[6]	*n*=17[6]		*n*=17[6]	
	♀ ♂	62.89 (60.4–65.7)	59.9 (57.2–61.8)		23.4 (22.4–24.8)	24.5 (23.9–25.0)
n=Total sample		*n*=13[3]	*n*=212[7]		*n*=212[7]	*n*=212[7]

1=author, 2=Verts and Carraway (1998), 3=Hoffmeister (1986), 4=Jackson (1961), 5=Bee and Hall (1956), 6=Armstrong (1972), 7=Pizzimenti (1975) in Hoogland (1996), 8=Howell (1938)

Zygomatic breadth	Interorbital breadth	Postorbital breadth	Bulla length	Maxillary toothrow	Mastoidal breadth	Mandibular toothrow	Mandible length
36.42 (33.9–42.4)	14.04 (12.3–18.8)	17.26 (16.0–19.6)	11.97 (11.0–12.9)	12.05 (10.7–13.7)		11.75 (10.54–12.89)	35.53 (32.54–39.54)
n=52 21[3],8[6],23[8]	n=44 21[3],23[8]	n=52 21[3],8[6],23[8]	n=21[3]	n=52 21[3],8[6],23[8]		n=10[1]	n=18 8[6],10[1]
38.03 (34.8–41.8)	14.82 (13.1–18.1)	17.61 (16.3–19.1)	12.02 (11.4–12.7)	12.30 (11.3–14.0)		11.78 (11.15–12.46)	36.62 (33.35–40.33)
n=36 15[3],2[6],19[8]	n=34 15[3],19[8]	n=36 15[3],2[6],19[8]	n=15[3]	n=36 15[3],2[6],19[8]		n=10[1]	n=12 2[6],10[1]
43.69 (42.7–44.3)		13.30 (12.3–14.3)		15.65 (15.2–16.2)	28.43 (26.9–30.4)	13.96 (13.17–15.20)	39.63 (37.08–43.51)
n=13[6]		n=13[6]		n=13[6]	n=13[6]	n=6[1]	n=6[1]
45.14 (43.6–46.0)		13.37 (12.6–14.2)		16.06 (15.6–16.5)	29.77 (28.5–30.8)	13.69 (12.98–14.48)	41.29 (40.48–41.86)
n=9[6]		n=9[6]		n=9[6]	n=9[6]	n=7[1]	n=7[1]
44.71 (42.6–48.0)		13.42 (12.3–14.7)		16.54 (15.4–17.4)	28.24 (26.6–29.7)	14.82 (13.98–15.68)	42.77 (41.50–43.78)
n=17[6]		n=17[6]		n=17[6]	n=17[6]	n=10[1]	n=10[1]
45.20 (43.6–48.5)		13.29 (12.9–15.0)		16.12 (15.2–18.1)	29.73 (26.9–30.3)	14.86 (13.68–15.88)	42.88 (39.22–45.08)
n=17[6]		n=17[6]		n=17[6]	n=17[6]	n=10[1]	n=10[1]
30.7 (29.6–32.3)	12.9 (12.4–13.7)	13.6 (13.0–14.3)			27.63 (26.75–28.85)		
n=212[7]	n=212[7]	n=212[7]			n=10[3]		

Family Sciuridae, genera *Sciurus, Tamiasciurus,* and *Glaucomys*

Table in millimeters. Mean and parameters on top. Total number of specimens measured and specific number in cited sources below.

Species	Sex	Greatest length	Palatilar length	Nasal length	Braincase breadth
Abert's or tassel-eared squirrel, *Sciurus aberti*	♀♂	60.48 (58.1–62.9)		20.44 (18.75–22.25)	24.09 (22.9–24.9)
n=Total sample		n=94[3]		n=94[3]	n=94[3]
Arizona gray squirrel, *Sciurus arizonensis*	♀♂	62.73 (60.1–66.1)			
n=Total sample		n=174[3]			
Eastern gray squirrel, *Sciurus carolinensis*	♀	60.44 (55.78–62.82)			24.66 (24.16–25.02)
n=Total sample		n=8[1]			n=8[1]
	♂	61.73 (59.66–63.06)			24.75 (24.08–25.66)
n=Total sample Sources		n=11 3[4],8[1]			n=8[1]
	♀♂	59.35 (53.8–66.5)	25.4 (23.8–27.7)	19.77 (17.2–26.5)	23.76 (21.7–29.5)
n=Total sample Sources		n=207+?[7] 105[5],102[10]	n=105[5]	n=207 105[5],102[10]	n=210 105[5],105[10]
Western gray squirrel, *Sciurus griseus*	♀	66.69 (64.21–68.6)		23.79 (22.4–24.89)	26.95 (26.33–27.84)
n=Total sample		n=17[2]		n=17[2]	n=17[2]
	♂	67.12 (63.13–70.39)		24.21 (22.41–25.35)	27.18 (25.09–28.31)
n=Total sample		n=30[2]		n=30[2]	n=30[2]
Eastern fox squirrel, *Sciurus niger*	♀	63.15 (59.03–71.84)		21.11 (18.6–23.5)	25.05 (24.37–25.86)
n=Total sample Sources		n=33 7[2],16[6],10[1]		n=23 7[2],16[6]	n=7[2]
	♂	56.24 (47.06–71.12)		17.78 (14.53–22.2)	22.36 (20.49–26.23)
n=Total sample Sources		n=62 43[2],8[6],11[1]		n=51 43[2],8[6]	n=43[2]
	♀♂	63.62 (57.2–69.8)	27.96 (24.7–31.3)	21.54 (17.6–24.0)	25.54 (23.6–27.2)
n=Total sample Sources		n=133 8[4],90[5],35[10]	n=90[5]	n=125 90[5],35[10]	n=125 90[5],35[10]
Douglas's squirrel, *Tamiasciurus douglasii*	♀	47.59 (44.47–49.47)		14.46 (12.05–15.89)	20.54 (19.27–21.67)
n=Total sample		n=78[2]		n=78[2]	n=78[2]

Zygomatic breadth	Interorbital breadth	Postorbital breadth	Maxillary toothrow	Mandibular toothrow	Mandible length
35.44 (33.5–36.8)	19.14 (17.25–21.95)	18.54 (17.25–19.7)	11.63 (10.55–12.4)		
n=94[3]	n=94[3]	n=94[3]	n=94[3]		
36.25 (34.1–38.4)	20.85 (19.1–22.7)	20.64 (19.2–21.9)	11.64 (10.5–12.9)		
n=174[3]	n=174[3]	n=174[3]	n=174[3]		
33.87 (30.44–35.60)	18.22 (16.36–18.72)	19.43 (18.80–20.05)	10.87 (10.38–11.44)	10.58 (10.38–11.02)	34.27 (30.98–35.61)
n=8[1]	n=8[1]	n=8[1]	n=8[1]	n=8[1]	n=8[1]
33.62 (32.93–34.32)	18.29 (16.9–19.33)	19.20 (18.65–19.85)	11.00 (9.78–11.6)	10.93 (10.50–11.34)	35.06 (34.12–36.00)
n=11 3[4],8[1]	n=11 3[4],8[1]	n=8[1]	n=11 3[4],8[1]	n=8[1]	n=8[1]
32.91 (23.6–37.2)	17.0 (14.8–19.4)	19.15 (18.2–20.5)	10.69 (9.0–12.2)		
n=203+?[7] 105[5],98[10]	n=105[5]	n=106[10]	n=211 105[5],106[10]		
37.93 (35.87–40.15)	20.29 (18.78–21.66)		12.42 (11.51–13.11)	12.71 (11.87–13.40)	39.80 (37.95–41.19)
n=17[2]	n=10[1]		n=17[2]	n=10[1]	n=17[2]
37.94 (35.88–40.62)	20.78 (19.72–22.56)		12.49 (11.59–13.53)	12.66 (12.00–13.18)	39.94 (37.75–42.3)
n=30[2]	n=10[1]		n=30[2]	n=10[1]	n=30[2]
35.14 (33.12–37.2)		19.13 (17.5–20.7)	11.07 (10.3–12.1)	12.78 (11.68–13.54)	37.38 (33.07–42.28)
n=23 7[2],16[6]		n=16[6]	n=23 7[2],16[6]	n=10[1]	n=17 7[2],10[1]
31.01 (26.56–36.4)		19.22 (18.8–20.0)	9.70 (8.1–11.5)	12.14 (11.24–13.28)	31.74 (26.37–42.68)
n=51 43[2],8[6]		n=8[6]	n=51 43[2],8[6]	n=11[1]	n=54 43[2],11[1]
35.80 (32.4–39.8)	18.90 (16.7–22.3)	20.10 (19.2–21.2)	11.19 (9.2–12.3)		
n=133 8[4],90[5],35[10]	n=98 8[4],90[5]	n=35[10]	n=133 8[4],90[5],35[10]		
27.28 (24.04–29.21)			8.47 (7.35–9.5)		27.34 (25.34–28.78)
n=78[2]			n=78[2]		n=78[2]

Family Sciuridae, genera *Sciurus, Tamiasciurus,* and *Glaucomys* continued

Species	Sex	Greatest length	Palatilar length	Nasal length	Braincase breadth
Douglas's squirrel, *Tamiasciurus douglasii*	♂	47.90 (45.20–49.82)		14.66 (12.77–16.7)	20.65 (19.48–22.35)
n=Total sample		n=71[2]		n=71[2]	n=71[2]
Red squirrel, *Tamiasciurus hudsonicus*	♀	47.39 (42.35–51.34)		15.17 (13.78–16.37)	21.01 (20.15–21.99)
n=Total sample Sources		n=49 30[2],12[6],7[1]		n=42 30[2],12[6]	n=30[2]
	♂	46.16 (43.78–48.1)		15.29 (14.1–16.1)	
n=Total sample Sources		n=21 13[6],8[1]		n=13[6]	
	♀♂	47.69 (44.1–50.2)	21.64 (20.6–22.7)	13.64 (12.1–15.3)	20.21 (18.35–21.2)
n=Total sample Sources		n=83 54[3],29[10]	n=54[3]	n=29[10]	n=83 54[3],29[10]
Northern flying squirrel, *Glaucomys sabrinus*	♀	40.54 (38.27–44.19)		12.73 (10.91–14.06)	18.70 (17.61–19.76)
n=Total sample		n=65[2]		n=65[2]	n=65[2]
	♂	40.37 (36.0–44.2)		12.46 (10.0–14.0)	18.42 (17.11–19.46)
n=Total sample Sources		n=80 62[2],18[9]		n=80 62[2],18[9]	n=62[2]
Southern flying squirrel, *Glaucomys volans*	♀	34.76 (33.48–35.7)		9.7 (8.85–10.2)	
n=Total sample Sources		n=19 10[1],9[10]		n=9[10]	
	♂	34.35 (33.4–35.8)		9.5 (9.1–10.2)	
n=Total sample Sources		n=19 10[1],9[10]		n=9[10]	
	♀♂	34.17 (32.0–37.2)	15.14 (14.6–16.1)	9.76 (8.6–11.6)	
n=Total sample Sources		n=38+?[8] 8[4],30[5]	n=30[5]	n=30[5]	

1=author, 2=Verts and Carraway (1998), 3=Hoffmeister (1986), 4=Paradiso (1969), 5=Lowery (1974), 6=Armstrong (1972), 7=Jackson (1961), 8=Dolan and Carter (1977), 9=Howell (1918) in Wells-Gosling and Heaney (1984), 10=Hoffmeister (1989)

Zygomatic breadth	Interorbital breadth	Postorbital breadth	Maxillary toothrow	Mandibular toothrow	Mandible length
27.34 (24.28–29.8)			8.60 (7.98–9.35)		27.35 (24.86–29.28)
n=71[2]			n=71[2]		n=71[2]
27.59 (24.68–29.15)	14.67 (14.3–15.0)	14.82 (14.2–15.7)	8.64 (7.8–9.25)	7.21 (6.88–7.40)	27.59 (24.54–29.31)
n=37 30[2],7[1]	n=12[6]	n=12[6]	n=42 30[2],12[6]	n=7[1]	n=37 30[2],7[1]
25.71 (24.88–27.30)	14.94 (13.58–15.6)	14.80 (13.75–15.9)	7.96 (7.15–8.8)	7.41 (7.18–7.74)	26.74 (25.66–27.52)
n=8[1]	n=21 13[6],8[1]	n=21 13[6],8[1]	n=21 13[6],8[1]	n=8[1]	n=8[1]
27.47 (25.1–29.1)	14.75 (12.6–15.9)	14.70 (12.95–15.8)	8.16 (6.9–9.35)		
n=83 54[3],29[10]	n=83 54[3],29[10]	n=83 54[3],29[10]	n=83 54[3],29[10]		
23.92 (22.19–25.8)			8.63 (7.63–9.63)	7.92 (7.52–8.55)	23.18 (21.65–25.07)
n=65[2]			n=65[2]	n=12[1]	n=65[2]
23.49 (21.85–25.81)	7.44 (6.2–8.8)	9.04 (8.0–9.9)	8.26 (6.4–9.39)	7.72 (7.44–8.34)	23.16 (21.94–27.18)
n=80 62[2],18[9]	n=18[9]	n=18[9]	n=80 62[2],18[9]	n=13[1]	n=62[2]
21.11 (19.7–23.03)	6.98 (6.63–8.10)	8.4 (7.6–9.1)	6.46 (5.63–6.87)	6.06 (5.74–6.36)	19.14 (18.24–19.97)
n=19 10[1],9[10]	n=19 10[1],9[10]	n=9[10]	n=19 10[1],9[10]	n=10[1]	n=10[1]
20.67 (19.95–21.95)	6.96 (5.8–7.56)	8.6 (8.3–9.25)	6.36 (5.72–6.86)	6.01 (5.60–6.48)	18.84 (18.26–19.34)
n=19 10[1],9[10]	n=19 10[1],9[10]	n=9[10]	n=19 10[1],9[10]	n=10[1]	n=10[1]
20.48 (18.5–22.2)	6.99 (6.3–8.3)		6.19 (6.0–7.0)		
n=38+?[8] 8[4],30[5]	n=38 8[4],30[5]		n=38 8[4],30[5]		

Family Geomyidae

Table in millimeters. Mean and parameters on top. Total number of specimens measured and specific number in cited sources below.

Species	Sex	Greatest length	Basilar length	Palatal length	Nasal length	Rostrum length
Botta's pocket gopher, *Thomomys bottae*	♀	38.74 (34.82–43.78)	31.82 (26.3–35.9)*	23.41 (21.00–27.28)	12.80 (10.3–14.6)*	15.06 (11.4–17.1)*
n=Total sample Sources		n=10[1]	n=710 22[2],652[3],36[5]	n=8[1]	n=688 652[3],36[5]	n=650[3]
	♂	41.62 (34.02–46.42)	34.35 (28.2–40.1)*	24.46 (18.82–27.82)	13.93 (11.5–16.5)*	16.36 (13.7–17.8)*
n=Total sample Sources		n=10[1]	n=373 17[2],332[3],24[5]	n=8[1]	n=358 334[3],24[5]	n=332[3]
Northern pocket gopher, *Thomomys talpoides*	♀	37.10 (33.72–39.12)	30.73 (26.35–35.5)		13.92 (11.7–15.4)	16.23 (15.1–17.5)
n=Total sample		n=10[1]	n=191 74[2],20[3],97[5]		n=114 17[3],97[5]	n=17[3]
	♂	38.39 (35.54–40.83)	32.29 (27.28–37.1)		14.73 (12.5–15.8)	16.69 (15.7–17.3)
n=Total sample Sources		n=12[1]	n=147 72[2],17[3],58[5]		n=69 13[3],56[5]	n=13[3]
Plains pocket gopher, *Geomys bursarius*	♀	47.64 (40.60–55.3)	36.34 (34.2–38.5)	13.0 (11.4–15.3)	16.76 (12.8–20.2)	
n=Total sample Sources		n=28 10[1],18[7]	n=20[5]	n=18[7]	n=37 19[5],18[7]	
	♂	50.69 (40.51–59.98)	41.36 (31.5–45.1)	14.5 (11.6–17.0)	18.58 (15.5–23.0)	
n=Total sample Sources		n=28 10[1],18[7]	n=10[5]	n=18[7]	n=28 10[5],18[7]	
Yellow-faced pocket gopher, *Cratogeomys castanops*	♀	48.63 (41.48–53.00)	42.16 (40.3–43.5)	(33.2–35.5)	17.50** (16.8–18.6)	(20.9–23.2)
n=Total sample Sources		n=10[1]	n=13[5]	n=28[6]	n=41 13[5],28[6]	n=28[6]
	♂	52.26 (43.22–58.28)	47.52 (45.5–48.9)	(37.2–41.0)	20.64** (19.0–21.5)	(22.6–26.5)
n=Total sample Sources		n=10[1]	n=5[5]	n=15[6]	n=20 5[5],15[6]	n=15[6]

1=author, 2=Verts and Carraway (1998), 3=Hoffmeister (1986), 4=Jackson (1961), 5=Armstrong (1972), 6=Davidow-Henry et al. (1989), 7=Hoffmeister (1989)

*extremes created from a subset of the data
**means created only using Armstrong's data, ranges include Armstrong (1972) and Davidow-Henry et al. (1989)

Rostrum breadth	Mastoidal breadth	Braincase breadth	Zygomatic breadth	Interorbital breadth	Maxillary toothrow	Mandibular toothrow	Mandible length
7.66 (6.6–9.2)*	19.19 (16.0–21.2)*		22.82 (19.2–26.67)*	6.41 (5.8–7.1)*	7.98 (7.0–9.11)*	8.12 (7.07–9.26)	23.21 (20.25–29.04)
n=687 651[3],36[5]	n=710 22[2],652[3],36[5]		n=711 22[2],653[3],36[5]	n=711 22[2],653[3],36[5]	n=711 22[2],653[3],36[5]	n=30 22[2],8[1]	n=31 22[2],9[1]
8.27 (7.3–10.8)*	20.33 (17.7–23.9)*		24.76 (21.3–29.4)*	6.37 (5.7–7.6)*	8.18 (7.1–9.4)*	8.22 (7.34–9.58)	25.06 (21.48–30.10)
n=356 332[3],24[5]	n=373 17[2],332[3],24[5]		n=375 17[2],334[3],24[5]	n=375 17[2],334[3],24[5]	n=375 17[2],334[3],24[5]	n=25 17[2],8[1]	n=25 17[2],8[1]
7.47 (6.6–8.8)	17.89 (15.28–20.5)		20.83 (18.04–24.7)	6.24 (5.41–7.18)	7.37 (6.3–8.6)	7.21 (6.33–8.04)	20.20 (17.99–23.06)
n=114 17[3],97[5]	n=191 74[2],20[3],97[5]		n=189 74[2],20[3],95[5]	n=191 74[2],20[3],97[5]	n=191 74[2],20[3],97[5]	n=74[2]	n=74[2]
7.82 (6.9–9.2)	18.77 (15.11–21.6)		22.13 (18.73–26.1)	6.29 (5.2–7.66)	7.53 (6.14–8.71)	7.36 (6.39–8.25)	21.31 (18.77–24.3)
n=71 13[3],58[5]	n=143 72[2],13[3],58[5]		n=145 72[2],17[3],56[5]	n=143 72[2],13[3],58[5]	n=147 72[2],17[3],58[5]	n=72[2]	n=72[2]
10.38 (9.5–10.8)	25.89 (23.2–31.1)		28.21 (24.2–36.30)	6.63 (5.6–7.3)	8.79 (7.5–10.3)	8.45 (7.58–9.50)	29.82 (26.36–33.92)
n=20[5]	n=38 20[5],18[7]		n=36 20[5],16[7]	n=38 20[5],18[7]	n=38 20[5],18[7]	n=10[1]	n=10[1]
11.61 (10.2–12.7)	27.93 (23.8–32.0)		31.45 (26.4–37.25)	6.61 (5.7–7.3)	9.22 (8.2–10.5)	8.74 (8.20–10.10)	32.00 (25.84–39.45)
n=10[5]	n=28 10[5],18[7]		n=28 10[5],18[7]	n=28 10[5],18[7]	n=28 10[5],18[7]	n=10[1]	n=10[1]
10.29** (9.6–11.2)	27.58 (26.6–28.5)	(20.6–22.8)	31.18** (29.6–32.5)	6.78 (6.2–7.2)	9.80** (9.1–10.9)	8.53 (7.65–9.43)	32.46 (27.04–35.86)
n=41 13[5],28[6]	n=13[5]	n=28[6]	n=41 13[5],28[6]	n=13[5]	n=41 13[5],28[6]	n=10[1]	n=10[1]
12.60** (11.5–13.0)	30.78 (28.9–33.6)	(22.0–24.3)	36.73** (34.1–39.9)	6.92 (6.5–7.4)	10.42** (9.7–11.0)	8.82 (7.28–9.62)	34.48 (28.14–38.18)
n=20 5[5],15[6]	n=5[5]	n=15[6]	n=20 5[5],15[6]	n=5[5]	n=20 5[5],15[6]	n=10[1]	n=10[1]

Family Heteromyidae, genera *Perognathus, Chaetodipus,* and *Liomys*

Table in millimeters. Mean and parameters on top. Total number of specimens measured and specific number in cited sources below.

Species	Sex	Greatest length	Occipitonasal length	Nasal length	Bulla breadth
Silky pocket mouse, *Perognathus flavus*	♀	20.39 (19.54–21.36)	20.40 (19.3–21.3)	6.91 (5.50–7.5)	11.76 (11.23–12.2)
n=Total sample Sources		n=7 1[4],6[1]	n=14 5[4],9[5]	n=18 3[4],9[5],6[1]	n=19 5[4],9[5],5[1]
	♂	20.80 (20.29–22.0)	19.70 (18.8–20.9)	7.17 (6.40–8.1)	11.95 (11.44–12.4)
n=Total sample Sources		n=10 4[4],6[1]	n=9 1[4],8[5]	n=18 4[4],8[5],6[1]	n=18 5[4],8[5],5[1]
Little pocket mouse, *Perognathus longimembris*	♀	21.05 (20.24–22.05)	20.57 (19.95–21.35)	7.58 (6.9–8.0)	11.93 (11.4–12.3)
n=Total sample Sources		n=11 6[2],5[4]	n=10 6[2],4[4]	n=5[4]	n=6[4]
	♂	21.60 (20.60–22.61)	20.91 (20.37–21.46)	7.61 (7.3–8.05)	12.19 (11.4–13.2)
n=Total sample Sources		n=11 6[2],5[4]	n=8 6[2],2[4]	n=5[4]	n=5[4]
Great basin pocket mouse, *Perognathus parvus*	♀	24.90 (23.20–27.63)	24.86 (23.39–27.56)		
n=Total sample		n=40[2]	n=40[2]		
	♂	26.07 (23.77–28.98)	26.01 (23.74–29.02)	10.26 (9.1–11.25)	13.73 (12.95–14.45)
n=Total sample Sources		n=85 77[2],8[4]	n=82 77[2],5[4]	n=9[4]	n=9[4]
Bailey's pocket mouse, *Chaetodipus baileyi*	♀	28.67 (28.5–29.7)		10.73 (10.2–11.5)	14.3, 14.3
n=Total sample		n=3[4]		n=3[4]	n=2[4]
	♂	29.10 (28.5–29.7)	31.0	10.78 (10.0–11.25)	15.00 (14.3–15.6)
n=Total sample		n=3[4]	n=1[4]	n=3[4]	n=4[4]
Sonoran desert pocket mouse, *Chaetodipus penicillatus*	♀	24.60 (22.56–25.56)		9.38 (8.24–10.09)	12.86 (12.11–13.28)
n=Total sample Sources		n=6[1]		n=7 1[4],6[1]	n=7 1[4],6[1]
	♂	24.80 (23.0–27.10)	25.95 (22.7–27.55)	9.72 (7.7–11.10)	12.73 (11.9–13.7)
n=Total sample Sources		n=10 4[4],6[1]	n=3[4]	n=13 7[4],6[1]	n=13 7[4],6[1]

Maxillary arches breadth	Zygomatic breadth	Interorbital breadth	Maxillary toothrow	Mandibular toothrow	Mandible length
	10.32 (9.7–10.9)	4.50 (4.18–4.89)	3.07 (2.67–3.4)	2.71 (2.38–2.86)	9.07 (8.76–9.38)
	$n=17$ $2^4,9^5,6^1$	$n=21$ $6^4,9^5,6^1$	$n=21$ $6^4,9^5,6^1$	$n=6^1$	$n=6^1$
10.2, 10.3	10.73 (10.12–11.3)	4.46 (3.92–4.7)	3.04 (2.47–3.50)	2.57 (2.42–2.72)	9.11 (8.14–9.45)
$n=2^4$	$n=14$ $8^5,6^1$	$n=19$ $5^4,8^5,6^1$	$n=17$ $3^4,8^5,6^1$	$n=6^1$	$n=6^1$
	10.72 (9.8–11.24)	5.00 (4.8–5.3)	3.07 (2.78–3.4)	2.89 (2.69–3.21)	8.78 (8.56–9.10)
	$n=8$ $6^2,2^4$	$n=12$ $6^2,6^4$	$n=12$ $6^2,6^4$	$n=6^2$	$n=6^2$
	10.99 (9.8–11.97)	5.07 (4.6–5.51)	2.95 (2.6–3.11)	3.02 (2.93–3.13)	9.14 (8.72–9.72)
	$n=7$ $6^2,1^4$	$n=11$ $6^2,5^4$	$n=11$ $6^2,5^4$	$n=6^2$	$n=6^2$
	12.54 (11.17–13.32)	5.81 (5.31–6.39)	3.87 (3.33–4.30)	3.57 (3.14–4.16)	10.95 (9.67–12.00)
	$n=40^2$	$n=40^2$	$n=40^2$	$n=40^2$	$n=40^2$
11.8, 11.9	13.00 (12.11–14.22)	6.00 (5.00–6.81)	3.97 (3.34–4.81)	3.40 (3.17–4.40)	11.32 (10.22–12.85)
$n=2^4$	$n=77^2$	$n=86$ $77^2,9^4$	$n=81$ $77^2,4^4$	$n=77^2$	$n=77^2$
	15.17 (14.5–15.5)	6.4, 6.9	3.7, 4.5		
	$n=3^4$	$n=2^4$	$n=2^4$		
13.15	16.0	6.74 (6.5–7.0)	4.1 (4.0–4.2)		
$n=1^4$	$n=1^4$	$n=4^4$	$n=3^4$		
	12.57 (11.92–13.23)	6.18 (5.97–6.52)		3.18 (2.98–3.60)	11.02 (10.20–11.54)
	$n=6^1$	$n=7$ $1^4,6^1$		$n=6^1$	$n=6^1$
12.07 (11.25–12.9)	12.62 (11.5–14.2)	6.12 (5.5–6.6)	3.59 (3.20–4.0)	3.14 (2.82–3.34)	10.97 (10.34–11.32)
$n=3^4$	$n=8$ $2^4,6^1$	$n=13$ $7^4,6^1$	$n=9$ $3^4,6^1$	$n=6^1$	$n=6^1$

Family Heteromyidae, genera *Perognathus, Chaetodipus,* and *Liomys* continued

Species	Sex	Greatest length	Occipitonasal length	Nasal length	Bulla breadth
Mexican spiny pocket mouse, *Liomys irroratus*	♀	32.14 (30.26–35.44)		13.06 (11.6–15.44)	
n=Total sample Sources		n=9 4[4],5[1]		n=9 4[4],5[1]	
	♂	33.02 (29.76–37.84)		13.13 (11.6–15.40)	
n=Total sample Sources		n=6 1[4],5[1]		n=6 1[4],5[1]	

1=author, 2=Verts and Carraway (1998), 3=Hoffmeister (1986), 4=Williams et al. in Genoways and Brown (1993), 5=Armstrong (1972)

Family Heteromyidae, genera *Microdipodops* and *Dipodomys*

Table in millimeters. Mean and parameters on top. Total number of specimens measured and specific number in cited sources below.

Species	Sex	Greatest length	Occipitonasal length	Nasal length	Maxillary arches breadth
Dark kangaroo mouse, *Microdipodops megacephalus*	♀	27.77 (25.20–29.27)	25.17 (23.03–26.32)	9.96 (9.3–10.35)	11.52 (11.3–11.8)
n=Total sample Sources		n=33 30[2],3[4]	n=30[2]	n=4[4]	n=4[4]
	♂	27.93 (26.3–29.28)	25.49 (23.88–28.39)	9.53 (8.3–10.35)	11.61 (11.3–12.1)
n=Total sample Sources		n=37 30[2],7[4]	n=30[2]	n=7[4]	n=7[4]
California kangaroo rat, *Dipodomys californicus*	♀	39.52 (35.25–41.6)	37.96 (34.17–39.78)		
n=Total sample		n=19[2]	n=19[2]		
	♂	38.89 (34.01–42.13)	37.30 (32.91–40.28)		
n=Total sample		n=26[2]	n=26[2]		
Desert kangaroo rat, *Dipodomys deserti*	♀	44.19 (41.48–46.06)		16.18 (15.84–17.36)	22.84 (20.66–24.27)
n=Total sample Sources		n=9 1[4],8[1]		n=9 1[4],8[1]	n=9 1[4],8[1]
	♂	45.61 (43.88–46.70)		17.08 (16.2–18.52)	23.99 (22.20–24.82)
n=Total sample Sources		n=10 2[4],8[1]		n=10 2[4],8[1]	n=11 3[4],8[1]

Maxillary arches breadth	Zygomatic breadth	Interorbital breadth	Maxillary toothrow	Mandibular toothrow	Mandible length
15.02 (14.12–16.01)	15.13 (14.2–16.7)	8.24 (7.73–8.84)	5.21 (4.5–6.10)	5.14 (4.61–5.78)	15.32 (14.08–16.66)
n=5[1]	n=3[4]	n=9 4[4],5[1]	n=7 2[4],5[1]	n=5[1]	n=5[1]
16.01 (14.43–17.80)		8.36 (7.70–9.84)	5.36 (5.02–6.02)	5.14 (4.72–5.85)	16.19 (14.36–19.34)
n=5[1]		n=6 1[4],5[1]	n=6 1[4],5[1]	n=5[1]	n=5[1]

Bulla breadth	Interorbital breadth	Maxillary toothrow	Mandibular toothrow	Mandible length
18.82 (18.25–19.2)	6.70 (6.10–7.08)	3.40 (3.04–3.70)	3.15 (2.77–3.71)	10.16 (9.57–10.61)
n=4[4]	n=34 30[2],4[4]	n=33 30[2],3[4]	n=30[2]	n=30[2]
18.58 (17.7–19.05)	6.72 (6.2–7.52)	3.37 (2.66–3.84)	3.16 (2.79–3.96)	10.21 (9.34–10.85)
n=8[4]	n=38 30[2],8[4]	n=38 30[2],8[4]	n=30[2]	n=30[2]
	12.57 (11.55–13.16)	5.29 (4.99–5.83)	5.31 (4.78–6.55)	17.16 (14.72–19.23)
	n=19[2]	n=19[2]	n=19[2]	n=19[2]
	12.47 (11.39–13.65)	5.17 (4.68–6.10)	5.28 (4.65–6.15)	16.77 (14.92–18.27)
	n=26[2]	n=26[2]	n=26[2]	n=26[2]
29.52 (28.16–30.82)	14.01 (13.10–14.72)	5.66 (5.10–6.11)	5.71 (5.40–6.06)	19.16 (17.82–20.10)
n=9 1[4],8[1]	n=9 1[4],8[1]	n=9 1[4],8[1]	n=8[1]	n=8[1]
30.31 (28.83–31.5)	14.53 (13.12–15.40)	5.71 (5.00–6.10)	5.78 (5.44–5.99)	19.64 (19.12–20.49)
n=11 3[4],8[1]	n=10 2[4],8[1]	n=10 2[4],8[1]	n=8[1]	n=8[1]

Family Heteromyidae, genera *Microdipodops* and *Dipodomys* continued

Species	Sex	Greatest length	Occipitonasal length	Nasal length	Maxillary arches breadth
Giant kangaroo rat, *Dipodomys ingens*	♀	45.1 (43.6–46.0)		17.0 (16.2–17.4)	27.1 (26.5–27.5)
n=Total sample		n=7[5]		n=7[5]	n=7[5]
	♂	45.9 (44.0–47.5)		17.1 (16.3–18.0)	27.0 (26.2–28.3)
n=Total sample		n=15[5]		n=15[5]	n=15[5]
Merriam's kangaroo rat, *Dipodomys merriami*	♀	35.70 (33.52–37.9)	33.5	13.13 (12.7–14.1)	20.05 (18.65–21.3)
n=Total sample Sources		n=11 4[4],7[1]	n=1[4]	n=6[4]	n=5[4]
	♂	35.96 (34.6–37.6)	34.0, 34.3	13.21 (12.2–14.4)	20.12 (18.9–21.6)
n=Total sample Sources		n=15 9[4],6[1]	n=2[4]	n=10[4]	n=10[4]
Chisel-toothed kangaroo rat, *Dipodomys microps*	♀	35.78 (32.63–38.5)	34.07 (30.96–36.57)	12.18 (11.6–12.8)	19.34 (18.3–20.6)
n=Total sample Sources		n=25 19[2],6[4]	n=19[2]	n=5[4]	n=5[4]
	♂	36.37 (34.6–38.2)	34.33 (32.86–36.4)	12.68 (12.0–13.5)	19.94 (19.2–20.75)
n=Total sample Sources		n=21 15[2],6[4]	n=15[2]	n=6[4]	n=6[4]
Ord's kangaroo rat, *Dipodomys ordii*	♀	38.11 (34.92–41.9)	34.78 (30.3–36.88)	14.09 (12.7–15.7)	20.92 (18.7–22.8)
n=Total sample Sources		n=84 30[2],10[4],44[6]	n=33 30[2],3[4]	n=55 11[4],44[6]	n=54 10[4],44[6]
	♂	38.71 (35.6–42.4)	35.20 (28.4–39.0)	14.27 (12.3–16.0)	21.07 (19.1–22.8)
n=Total sample Sources		n=113 31[2],16[4],66[6]	n=39 31[2],8[4]	n=87 21[4],66[6]	n=86 20[4],66[6]

1=author, 2=Verts and Carraway (1998), 3=Hoffmeister (1986), 4=Williams et al. in Genoways and Brown (1993), 5=Grinnell (1932) in Williams and Kilburn (1991), 6=Armstrong (1972)

Bulla breadth	Interorbital breadth	Maxillary toothrow	Mandibular toothrow	Mandible length
29.0 (28.4–30.0)			5.91 (5.60–6.23)	20.27 (19.50–20.90)
n=7[5]			n=8[1]	n=8[1]
29.5 (28.1–30.4)			6.14 (5.60–6.49)	20.03 (18.49–21.10)
n=15[5]			n=7[1]	n=7[1]
22.64 (21.9–23.8)	12.83 (12.3–13.0)	4.43 (4.1–4.8)	4.57 (4.02–5.33)	14.46 (13.61–15.04)
n=6[4]	n=4[4]	n=3[4]	n=11[1]	n=11[1]
22.76 (21.7–23.45)	13.13 (12.4–13.7)	4.51 (4.1–4.8)	4.38 (3.97–4.98)	14.67 (13.99–15.12)
n=8[4]	n=4[4]	n=6[4]	n=11[1]	n=11[1]
23.66 (22.4–25.0)	11.85 (11.2–12.59)	4.56 (4.2–4.87)	4.81 (4.33–5.35)	16.01 (15.24–17.28)
n=6[4]	n=22 19[2],3[4]	n=23 19[2],4[4]	n=19[2]	n=19[2]
24.14 (23.55–25.3)	11.85 (11.14–12.75)	4.73 (4.4–5.1)	4.89 (4.53–5.22)	16.09 (15.35–17.36)
n=6[4]	n=21 15[2],6[4]	n=18 15[2],3[4]	n=15[2]	n=15[2]
24.26 (22.7–26.4)	12.39 (11.0–13.5)	4.96 (4.0–5.42)	4.53 (3.96–5.09)	15.08 (13.91–15.88)
n=53 9[4],44[6]	n=85 30[2],11[4],44[6]	n=76 30[2],2[4],44[6]	n=30[2]	n=30[2]
24.45 (22.5–27.5)	12.51 (11.27–13.7)	5.06 (4.2–6.0)	4.67 (3.99–5.10)	15.08 (13.99–15.94)
n=86 20[4],66[6]	n=115 31[2],18[4],66[6]	n=112 31[2],15[4],66[6]	n=31[2]	n=31[2]

Large Rodents: Families Aplodontiidae, Castoridae, Muridae, Erethizontidae, Dasyproctidae, Agoutidae, and Myocastoridae

Table in millimeters. Mean and parameters on top. Total number of specimens measured and specific number in cited sources below.

Species	Sex	Greatest length	Occipitonasal length	Condylobasal length	Basilar length	Palatal length
Mountain beaver or aplodontia, *Aplodontia rufa*	♀	69.14 (62.68–73.96)	70.36 (65.33–75.04)			44.26 (41.35–46.16
n=Total sample		n=11[1]	n=46[2]			n=11[1]
	♂	71.11 (64.23–77.10)	70.84 (65.71–77.96)			45.11 (40.92–49.58
n=Total sample		n=10[1]	n=58[2]			n=10[1]
	♀♂				59.13 (51.1–65.4)	
n=Total sample Sources					n=135 117[5],18[13]	
American beaver, *Castor canadensis*	♀	129.64 (100.84–140.16)	131.88 (117.02–146.15)	130.94 (121.9–136.4)	121.35 (111.7–130.5)	88.38
n=Total sample Sources		n=13 4[7],9[1]	n=21[2]	n=7 5[3],2[6]	n=10 5[3],5[4]	n=1[1]
	♂	137.41 (118.88–158.56)	135.63 (128.53–141.37)	126.32 (121.6–132.4)	123.38 (115.7–126.8)	80.31 (72.84–85.78
n=Total sample Sources		n=7[1]	n=16[2]	n=5 1[3],4[6]	n=6 1[3],5[4]	n=3[1]
Common muskrat, *Ondatra zibethicus*	♀	64.06 (60.40–71.32)	60.18 (55.88–67.14)	63.60 (60.4–66.0)	50.95 (48.1–54.2)	
n=Total sample Sources		n=16[1]	n=43[2]	n=4[6]	n=6[4]	
	♂	64.68 (58.20–69.16)	61.54 (56.41–68.05)	61.47 (60.0–63.4)	51.84 (46.4–55.2)	
n=Total sample Sources		n=16[1]	n=63[2]	n=3[6]	n=18[4]	
	♀♂	67.47 (58.8–72.3)		67.6 (63.9–72.2)		
n=Total sample Sources		n=357[9]		n=47 36[3],11[7]		
North American porcupine, *Erethizon dorsatum*	♀	102.88 (91.76–118.50)	94.49 (84.81–102.15)	102.30 (98.9–107.5)	91.05 (87.4–97.7)	48.6, 52.4
n=Total sample Sources		n=11[1]	n=30[2]	n=4 2[3],2[6]	n=4 2[3],2[6]	n=2[3]

Nasal length	Mastoidal breadth	Braincase breadth	Zygomatic breadth	Interorbital breadth	Maxillary toothrow	Mandibular toothrow	Mandible length
25.09 (2.58–28.84)		28.29 (24.04–36.24)	52.47 (47.91–58.46)	10.29 (9.16–11.36)	18.77 (17.48–20.22)		46.20 (41.96–50.42)
n=46[2]		n=46[2]	n=46[2]	n=11[1]	n=46[2]		n=46[2]
25.21 21.8–29.71)		30.26 (23.99–38.92)	53.41 (48.24–61.29)	10.84 (9.72–11.70)	18.55 (16.75–20.36)		46.15 (42.51–51.32)
n=58[2]		n=58[2]	n=58[2]	n=10[1]	n=58[2]		n=58[2]
25.86 (20.3–30.9)	52.21 (41.9–61.2)		55.16 (46.0–64.0)		18.98 (16.9–21.0)		47.41 (41.7–54.9)
n=109 91[5],18[13]	n=126[5]		n=142 124[5],18[13]		n=126[5]		n=125[5]
49.01 (40.7–57.3)	59.19 (44.1–69.7)	43.88 (39.33–47.56)	93.78 (82.37–111.6)	25.05 (21.8–28.6)	31.01 (27.7–34.2)	33.00 (28.94–37.46)	90.17 (73.28–100.54)
n=33 21[2],5[3],5[4],2[6]	n=14 5[3],5[4],4[7]	n=21[2]	n=46 21[2],5[3],5[4],2[6],4[7],9[1]	n=16 5[3],5[4],2[6],4[7]	n=37 21[2],5[3],5[4],2[6],4[7]	n=9[1]	n=30 21[2],9[1]
49.64 (41.9–57.7)	63.96 (47.45–70.1)	43.67 (41.44–46.57)	95.14 (86.34–109.88)	25.2 (23.6–29.6)	31.23 (27.2–34.6)	34.35 (30.35–37.78)	93.34 (82.80–107.90)
n=26 16[2],1[3],5[4],4[6]	n=6 1[3],5[4]	n=16[2]	n=33 16[2],1[3],5[4],4[6],7[1]	n=10 1[3],5[4],4[6]	n=26 16[2],1[3],5[4],4[6]	n=7[1]	n=23 16[2],7[1]
20.75 8.21–23.57)	24.03 (23.2–26.2)	19.81 (17.47–22.69)	37.75 (33.62–42.54)	5.86 (4.95–7.15)	15.33 (14.0–17.07)	16.30 (14.96–17.34)	42.55 (39.82–47.30)
n=43[2]	n=6[4]	n=43[2]	n=53 4[6],43[2],6[4]	n=53 4[6],43[2],6[4]	n=53 4[6],43[2],6[4]	n=16[1]	n=16[1]
21.32 9.15–24.44)	24.51 (21.6–26.9)	19.98 (16.70–23.98)	38.18 (31.4–43.04)	5.87 (4.49–7.16)	15.32 (13.8–17.28)	16.48 (15.66–17.44)	42.88 (38.78–45.76)
n=63[2]	n=18[4]	n=63[2]	n=82 3[6],63[2],16[4]	n=82 3[6],63[2],16[4]	n=82 3[6],63[2],16[4]	n=16[1]	n=16[1]
19.05 (17.8–20.1)		22.26 (19.7–24.8)	40.52 (33.8–45.3)	6.24 (4.2–7.9)	15.82 (13.5–17.7)		
n=36[3]		n=357[9]	n=395 36[3],11[7],348[9]	n=404 36[3],11[7],357[9]	n=404 36[3],11[7],357[9]		
36.88 28.64–40.63)		38.32 (34.93–40.96)	68.13 (62.27–87.6)	31.11 (29.9–32.5)	26.00 (23.74–28.33)	28.85 (26.16–33.04)	70.23 (62.84–81.75)
n=34 30[2],2[3],2[6]		n=32 30[2],2[3]	n=43 30[2],2[3],2[6],9[1]	n=4 2[3],2[6]	n=34 30[2],2[3],2[6]	n=11[1]	n=41 30[2],11[1]

Families Aplodontiidae, Castoridae, Muridae, Erethizontidae, Dasyproctidae, Agoutidae, and Myocastoridae *continued*

Species	Sex	Greatest length	Occipitonasal length	Condylobasal length	Basilar length	Palatal length
North American porcupine, *Erethizon dorsatum*	♂	105.66 (93.06–120.09)	96.95 (88.53–104.85)	104.98 (97.0–111.9)	93.85 (87.8–99.7)	51.93 (46.2–56.7)
n=Total sample Sources		n=8[1]	n=26[2]	n=9 6[3],3[6]	n=9 6[3],3[6]	n=6[3]
	♀♂	93–112[10]				
n=Total sample						
Nutria or coypu, *Myocastor coypus*	♀		118.43			
n=Total sample			n=1[2]			
	♀♂	116.3 (109.6–125.6)				
n=Total sample		n=11[7]				
Mexican black agouti, *Dasyprocta mexicana*	♀	106.74				
n=Total sample		n=1[1]				
Paca, *Agouti paca*	♀♂	150.67 (140.97–160.21)*				88.70 (81.36–97.5
n=Total sample		n=117[12]				n=132[12]

1=author, 2=Verts and Carraway (1998), 3=Hoffmeister (1986), 4=Grinnell et al. (1937), 5=Taylor (1918), 6=Armstrong(1972), 7=Lowery (1974), 8=Jackson (1961), 9=Gould and Kreeger (1948), 10=Woods (1973), 11=Gosling (1977) in Woods et al. (1992), 12=Nelson and Shump (1978), 13=Finley(1941)

*parameters created from partial data set

Nasal length	Mastoidal breadth	Braincase breadth	Zygomatic breadth	Interorbital breadth	Maxillary toothrow	Mandibular toothrow	Mandible length
38.22 (33.07–46.10)		38.76 (35.8–42.17)	70.05 (62.90–78.30)	31.50 (26.6–36.35)	26.24 (24.01–30.6)	28.77 (26.64–30.41)	72.95 (65.44–82.72)
n=35 26[2],6[3],3[6]		n=32 26[2],6[3]	n=41 26[2],6[3],2[6],7[1]	n=9 6[3],3[6]	n=35 26[2],6[3],3[6]	n=8[1]	n=34 26[2],8[1]
43.60		36.81	74.18		28.95		81.07
n=1[2]		n=1[2]	n=1[2]		n=1[2]		n=1[2]
43.4 (40.2–47.4)	50.1 (46.4–56.3)		71.9 (68.4–79.6)	31.4 (28.4–34.9)	29.1 (27.6–30.8)		
n=11[7]	n=11[7]		n=11[7]	n=11[7]	n=11[7]		
			50.26	30.16	19.02	20.63	60.81
			n=1[1]	n=1[1]	n=1[1]	n=1[1]	n=1[1]
		45.64 (42.46–48.02)*	98.32 (83.77–113.01)		31.44 (27.99–33.36)		76.08 (63.69–100.06)
		n=126[12]	n=124[12]		n=135[12]		n=4[1]

Family Muridae, genera *Reithrodontomys, Peromyscus, Podomys, Baiomys, Onychomys,* and *Mus*

Table in millimeters. Mean and parameters on top. Total number of specimens measured and specific number in cited sources below.

Species	Sex	Greatest length	Postpalatal length	Incisive foramen length	Nasal length	Bulla length
Fulvous harvest mouse, *Reithrodontomys fulvescens*	♀♂	21.44 (20.0–22.45)		4.43 (4.1–4.8)		
n=Total sample		n=49[3]		n=49[3]		
Western harvest mouse, *Reithrodontomys megalotis*	♀	20.90 (18.84–22.5)				
n=Total sample Sources		n=55 25[6],30[2]				
	♂	21.11 (19.4–22.5)				
n=Total sample Sources		n=60 30[6],30[2]				
	♀♂	20.67 (18.47–22.78)		4.43 (3.80–5.00)	7.78 (6.30–9.50)	
n=Total sample Sources		n=859 291[3],111[7],457[8]		n=748 291[3],457[8]	n=457[8]	
Salt marsh harvest mouse, *Reithrodontomys raviventris*	♀♂	20.84 (19.5–22.4)		4.07 (3.7–4.5)	7.51 (6.5–8.5)	
n=Total sample		n=414[9]		n=434[9]	n=457[9]	
White-footed mouse, *Peromyscus leucopus*	♀	26.91 (24.44–28.7)		5.03 (4.90–5.18)	10.72 (9.36–11.5)	
n=Total sample Sources		n=17 9[6],8[1]		n=3[1]	n=12 9[6],3[1]	
	♂	26.98 (24.94–28.3)		5.08 (4.84–5.24)	10.28 (9.50–11.0)	
n=Total sample Sources		n=17 9[6],8[1]		n=3[1]	n=12 9[6],3[1]	
	♀♂	26.60 (23.8–28.6)	9.44 (8.2–10.6)	9.0 (8.2–10.2)	9.98 (7.5–11.8)	
n=Total sample Sources		n=200 113[3],9[5],78[4]	n=191 113[3],78[4]	n=78[4]	n=191 113[3],78[4]	

Interorbital breadth	Zygomatic breadth	Braincase breadth	Skull depth	Maxillary toothrow	Mandibular toothrow	Mandible length
3.19 (3.0–3.5)	10.88 (10.45–11.25)	10.45 (9.9–10.9)	8.08 (7.65–8.4)	3.58 (3.25–3.8)		
n=49[3]	n=49[3]	n=49[3]	n=49[3]	n=49[3]		
3.24 (2.9–4.06)	10.64 (9.71–11.9)	10.09 (9.37–10.7)	7.77 (7.03–8.4)	3.21 (2.88–3.6)	3.02 (2.90–3.11)	10.67 (10.10–11.52)
n=55 25[6],30[2]	n=55 25[6],30[2]	n=55 25[6],30[2]	n=55 25[6],30[2]	n=55 25[6],30[2]	n=10[1]	n=10[1]
3.24 (2.92–3.5)	10.65 (9.88–11.3)	10.16 (9.57–10.9)	7.87 (7.19–8.5)	3.24 (2.97–3.6)	3.02 (2.92–3.20)	10.53 (9.42–11.18)
n=60 30[6],30[2]	n=58 28[6],30[2]	n=60 30[6],30[2]	n=59 29[6],30[2]	n=60 30[6],30[2]	n=10[1]	n=10[1]
3.14 (2.7–3.8)	10.53 (9.17–11.96)	10.13 (9.0–11.0)	7.75 (6.9–8.35)	3.27 (2.8–3.8)		
n=402 291[3],111[7]	n=774 291[3],26[7], 457[8]	n=859 291[3],111[7], 457[8]	n=291[3]	n=859 291[3],111[7], 457[8]		
		10.05 (9.3–10.7)				
		n=434[9]				
4.36 (4.00–4.5)	14.20 (12.97–15.0)	11.76 (11.63–11.94)	10.10 (10.0–10.4)	3.93 (3.58–4.2)	3.69 (3.44–3.94)	13.52 (12.72–14.03)
n=12 9[6],3[1]	n=12 9[6],3[1]	n=3[1]	n=9[6]	n=12 9[6],3[1]	n=9[1]	n=9[1]
4.35 (3.98–4.7)	14.06 (12.90–14.8)	11.87 (11.40–12.22)	10.44 (9.9–11.1)	4.01 (3.44–4.3)	3.76 (3.56–4.02)	13.61 (13.25–13.90)
n=12 9[6],3[1]	n=12 9[6],3[1]	n=3[1]	n=9[6]	n=12 9[6],3[1]	n=8[1]	n=8[1]
4.21 (3.5–4.7)	13.76 (11.8–15.25)	11.8 (11.2–13.0)		3.94 (3.4–4.5)		
n=200 113[3],9[5],78[4]	n=200 113[3],9[5],78[4]	n=78[4]		n=122 113[3],9[5]		

Family Muridae, genera *Reithrodontomys, Peromyscus, Podomys, Baiomys, Onychomys,* and *Mus* continued

Species	Sex	Greatest length	Postpalatal length	Incisive foramen length	Nasal length	Bulla length
Deer mouse, *Peromyscus maniculatus*	♀	25.46 (23.3–27.93)		5.12 (4.96–5.48)	10.27 (8.8–11.6)	
n=Total sample Sources		n=187 78[6],109[2]		n=10[1]	n=78[6]	
	♂	25.39 (23.35–27.3)		5.06 (4.63–5.74)	10.17 (8.8–11.3)	
n=Total sample Sources		n=215 97[6],118[2]		n=10[1]	n=97[6]	
	♀♂	25.59 (23.4–27.3)	9.00 (8.1–10.2)	5.51 (4.7–6.65)	10.44 (9.1–11.8)	3.48 (2.8–4.05)
n=Total sample Sources		n=237 226[3],11[5]	n=226[3]	n=226[3]	n=223[3]	n=224[3]
Florida mouse, *Podomys floridanus*	♀	30.84 (30.40–31.40)				
n=Total sample		n=4[1]				
Northern pygmy mouse, *Baiomys taylori*	♀♂	18.1 (17.1–19.35)	6.46 (6.05–7.05)		6.39 (6.0–6.7)	
n=Total sample		n=12[3]	n=12[3]		n=12[3]	
Northern grasshopper mouse, *Onychomys leucogaster*	♀	26.19 (25.05–27.87)				
n=Total sample Sources		n=19[2]				
	♂	26.59 (25.28–27.56)				
n=Total sample Sources		n=16[2]				
	♀♂	28.38 (27.0–29.9)	10.26 (9.3–11.1)	5.52 (4.9–6.12)	11.34 (10.2–13.0)	
n=Total sample		n=104[3]	n=104[3]	n=104[3]	n=104[3]	
Southern grasshopper mouse, *Onychomys torridus*	♀♂	25.43 (23.8–27.2)	9.51 (8.67–10.51)	4.89 (4.28–5.92)	9.90 (8.9–11.1)	
n=Total sample		n=72[3]	n=72[3]	n=72[3]	n=72[3]	

Interorbital breadth	Zygomatic breadth	Braincase breadth	Skull depth	Maxillary toothrow	Mandibular toothrow	Mandible length
3.98 (3.5–4.4)	12.99 (11.45–14.0)	11.68 (10.76–12.63)	8.98 (8.11–10.3)	3.73 (3.2–4.2)	3.62 (3.39–3.96)	13.08 (12.06–13.84)
n=187 78[6],109[2]	n=187 78[6],109[2]	n=109[2]	n=187 78[6],109[2]	n=187 78[6],109[2]	n=10[1]	n=10[1]
4.00 (3.20–4.61)	13.02 (11.58–14.53)	11.71 (10.80–13.19)	9.03 (8.19–16.2)	3.69 (3.27–4.3)	3.57 (3.39–3.77)	12.90 (11.97–13.71)
n=215 97[6],118[2]	n=215 97[6],118[2]	n=118[2]	n=215 97[6],118[2]	n=215 97[6],118[2]	n=10[1]	n=10[1]
3.94 (3.6–4.5)	12.79 (11.55–14.2)	11.54 (10.8–12.45)	9.16 (8.35–9.9)	3.49 (3.0–4.0)		
n=237 226[3],11[5]	n=228 217[3],11[5]	n=226[3]	n=226[3]	n=237 226[3],11[5]		
3.51 (3.3–3.7)	9.64 (9.3–10.1)	8.41 (8.15–8.75)		3.11 (2.9–3.3)		
n=12[3]	n=12[3]	n=12[3]		n=12[3]		
4.73 (4.4–5.1)	14.04 (12.71–15.3)	12.43 (11.64–12.93)	9.52 (9.17–10.01)	4.19 (3.45–4.8)	3.90 (3.26–4.47)	13.63 (12.52–15.08)
n=31 12[6],19[2]	n=31 12[6],19[2]	n=19[2]	n=19[2]	n=31 12[6],19[2]	n=10[1]	n=10[1]
4.78 (4.3–5.10)	14.27 (12.97–16.0)	12.62 (12.13–13.05)	9.61 (9.17–10.07)	4.16 (3.72–4.7)	4.29 (3.82–4.41)	14.39 (13.54–15.09)
n=24 8[6],16[2]	n=24 8[6],16[2]	n=16[2]	n=16[2]	n=24 8[6],16[2]	n=10[1]	n=10[1]
4.75 (4.2–5.1)	15.04 (13.9–16.0)	12.42 (11.7–13.2)		4.96 (4.3–5.3)		
n=104[3]	n=84[3]	n=104[3]		n=101[3]		
4.57 (4.2–4.85)	12.74 (11.6–14.0)	11.21 (10.5–12.0)		4.33 (3.88–4.69)	3.64 (3.42–3.96)	13.03 (12.26–14.03)
n=72[3]	n=59[3]	n=72[3]		n=72[3]	n=20[1]	n=20[1]

Family Muridae, genera *Reithrodontomys, Peromyscus, Podomys, Baiomys, Onychomys,* and *Mus* continued

Species	Sex	Greatest length	Postpalatal length	Incisive foramen length	Nasal length	Bulla length
House mouse, *Mus musculus*	♀	21.46 (20.2–23.5)		4.79 (4.26–5.10)	7.76 (7.0–9.0)	
n=Total sample Sources		n=20 11[3],9[2]		n=6[1]	n=11[3]	
	♂	21.47 (19.53–23.4)		4.71 (4.12–5.16)	7.92 (7.3–8.75)	
n=Total sample Sources		n=30 11[3],19[2]		n=5[1]	n=11[3]	
	♀♂	21.76 (19.8–22.9)	7.5 (6.1–9.6)		7.9 (7.1–9.0)	
n=Total sample Sources		n=32 25[4],7[5]	n=25[4]		n=25[4]	

1=author, 2=Verts and Carraway (1998), 3=Hoffmeister (1986), 4=Lowery (1974), 5=Paradiso (1969), 6=Armstrong (1972), 7=Whitaker and Mumford (1972), and Hooper (1952) in Webster and Jones (1982), 8=Collins and George (1990), 9=Fisler (1965)

Family Muridae, genera *Oryzomys, Sigmodon, Neotoma,* and *Rattus*

Table in millimeters. Mean and parameters on top. Total number of specimens measured and specific number in cited sources below.

Species	Sex	Greatest length	Postpalatal length	Incisive foramen length	Nasal length	Mastoid breadth
Marsh rice rat, *Oryzomys palustris*	♀	29.32 (28.52–31.18)		6.00 (5.04–6.80)		
n=Total sample		n=5[1]		n=5[1]		
	♂	33.53 (32.33–35.28)		7.14 (6.74–7.76)		
n=Total sample		n=5[1]		n=5[1]		
	♀♂	28.96 (26.2–32.8)	10.20 (8.8–11.8)	6.59 (5.4–7.35)	11.46 (9.5–13.7)	
n=Total sample Sources		n=98 1[5],89[4],8[8]	n=97 89[4],8[8]	n=8[8]	n=97 89[4],8[8]	
Hispid cotton rat, *Sigmodon hispidus*	♀	34.49 (30.54–36.7)			13.19 (10.7–15.3)	
n=Total sample Sources		n=16 6[6],10[1]			n=19 13[3],6[6]	
	♂	35.09 (30.53–39.30)			13.46 (12.2–14.6)	
n=Total sample Sources		n=12 2[6],10[1]			n=21 19[3],2[6]	

Interorbital breadth	Zygomatic breadth	Braincase breadth	Skull depth	Maxillary toothrow	Mandibular toothrow	Mandible length
3.58	11.01	9.78	7.67	3.61	2.93	11.38
(3.4–3.90)	(10.15–12.75)	(9.45–10.12)	(7.31–7.99)	(3.3–4.15)	(2.82–3.10)	(10.35–11.83)
n=20	n=20	n=9[2]	n=9[2]	n=20	n=6[1]	n=6[1]
11[3],9[2]	11[3],9[2]			11[3],9[2]		
3.59	10.91	9.64	7.58	3.56	2.96	11.09
(3.3–3.84)	(9.92–11.80)	(9.20–10.02)	(7.25–8.09	(3.20–4.06)	(2.78–3.14)	(10.51–11.96)
n=30	n=30	n=19[2]	n=19[2]	n=30	n=5[1]	n=5[1]
11[3],19[2]	11[3],19[2]			11[3],19[2]		
3.56	11.16	10.2		3.36		
(3.3–4.2)	(10.3–13.0)	(9.2–11.9)		(3.1–3.7)		
n=32	n=32	n=25[4]		n=32		
25[4],7[5]	25[4],7[5]			25[4],7[5]		

Interorbital breadth	Zygomatic breadth	Braincase breadth	Skull depth	Maxillary toothrow	Mandibular toothrow	Mandible length
4.88	15.28	12.92		4.55	4.61	15.63
(4.64–5.16)	(15.00–16.00)	(12.53–13.96)		(4.33–4.72)	(4.22–4.94)	(15.20–16.80)
n=5[1]	n=5[1]	n=5[1]		n=5[1]	n=5[1]	n=5[1]
5.52	17.46	13.59		4.98	5.10	17.62
(5.12–5.82)	(16.54–18.66)	(13.38–13.72)		(4.72–5.27)	(4.90–5.20)	(16.69–18.50)
n=5[1]	n=5[1]	n=5[1]		n=5[1]	n=5[1]	n=5[1]
4.90	14.92	12.78		4.68		
(4.4–5.5)	(13.5–16.7)	(11.8–13.5)		(4.4–5.1)		
n=98	n=90	n=97		n=7		
1[5],89[4],8[8]	1[5],89[4]	89[4],8[8]		1[5],6[8]		
4.66	19.53	14.55	11.45	6.44	6.66	19.31
(4.45–5.1)	(18.0–21.5)	(13.9–15.35)	(11.0–12.8)	(6.2–6.9)	(6.4–7.15)	(17.88–20.53)
n=19	n=19	n=12[3]	n=11[3]	n=19	n=13[3]	n=10[1]
13[3],6[6]	13[3],6[6]			13[3],6[6]		
4.73	19.97	14.84	11.77	6.43	6.69	20.29
(4.45–5.1)	(18.2–21.3)	(14.15–15.7)	(10.9–12.7)	(6.2–6.9)	(6.3–7.7)	(18.20–22.60)
n=21	n=21	n=19[3]	n=19[3]	n=21	n=19[3]	n=10[1]
19[3],2[6]	19[3],2[6]			19[3],2[6]		

Family Muridae, genera *Oryzomys, Sigmodon, Neotoma,* and *Rattus* continued

Species	Sex	Greatest length	Postpalatal length	Incisive foramen length	Nasal length	Mastoid breadth
Hispid cotton rat, *Sigmodon hispidus*	♀♂	37.65 (33.1–40.6)	12.1 (11.1–14.9)	9.9 (9.5–10.5)	14.88 (11.9–18.0)	
n=Total sample Sources		*n*=77 50[4],27[7]	*n*=50[4]	*n*=27[7]	*n*=77 50[4],27[7]	
White-throated woodrat, *Neotoma albigula*	♀	41.80 (39.82–43.79)			16.53 (15.5–17.4)	
n=Total sample		*n*=10[1]			*n*=17[6]	
	♂	41.71 (37.22–44.62)			17.13 (16.8–17.6)	
n=Total sample		*n*=10[1]			*n*=11[6]	
	♀♂	43.11 (39.05–46.3)		8.93 (7.45–10.1)	16.29 (14.3–18.3)	17.60 (16.5–19.0)
n=Total sample		*n*=67[3]		*n*=79[3]	*n*=77[3]	*n*=68[3]
Bushy-tailed woodrat, *Neotoma cinerea*	♀	48.72 (43.0–54.19)		10.57 (9.9–11.5)	18.67 (16.6–21.4)	
n=Total sample Sources		*n*=69 14[3],55[2]		*n*=14[3]	*n*=23 14[3],9[6]	
	♂	50.51 (45.4–55.62)		10.99 (10.2–12.0)	19.23 (17.3–21.4)	
n=Total sample Sources		*n*=67 11[3],56[2]		*n*=9[3]	*n*=20 11[3],9[6]	
Eastern woodrat, *Neotoma floridana*	♀	47.29 (44.64–49.36)			19.02 (18.7–19.4)	
n=Total sample		*n*=5[1]			*n*=4[6]	
	♂	47.43 (43.92–50.90)	20.28 (18.9–21.5)	10.36 (9.65–11.05)	20.02 (18.8–21.8)	19.10 (18.15–19.9)
n=Total sample Sources		*n*=10[1]	*n*=11[8]	*n*=11[8]	*n*=16 5[6],11[8]	*n*=11[8]
	♀♂	50.6 (47.9–55.6)	19.4 (18.0–21.7)		19.2 (18.6–22.5)	
n=Total sample		*n*=46[4]	*n*=46[4]		*n*=46[4]	
*Dusky-footed woodrat, *Neotoma fuscipes*	♀	49.68 (43.98–53.28)				
n=Total sample		*n*=30[2]				
	♂	51.37 (48.03–54.25)				
n=Total sample		*n*=30[2]				

Interorbital breadth	Zygomatic breadth	Braincase breadth	Skull depth	Maxillary toothrow	Mandibular toothrow	Mandible length
5.34 (4.6–6.2)	21.17 (18.4–25.4)	15.56 (14.4–17.6)		7.6 (7.1–8.2)		
n=77 50[4],27[7]	n=77 50[4],27[7]	n=77 50[4],27[7]		n=27[7]		
5.64 (5.2–5.9)	22.95 (20.9–25.0)			8.44 (7.9–9.1)	8.17 (7.95–8.44)	24.39 (22.29–26.08)
n=18[6]	n=18[6]			n=18[6]	n=10[1]	n=10[1]
5.80 (5.5–6.0)	23.30 (22.0–24.7)			8.53 (7.8–9.0)	8.26 (7.96–8.60)	23.88 (21.05–25.80)
n=11[6]	n=11[6]			n=11[6]	n=10[1]	n=10[1]
5.55 (5.0–6.1)	21.90 (19.55–24.1)			8.60 (7.8–9.15)		
n=79[3]	n=73[3]			n=80[3]		
5.84 (5.30–6.57)	25.22 (21.5–28.15)	18.17 (15.48–20.50)	15.58 (14.26–16.55)	9.94 (8.6–11.28)	9.76 (9.03–10.62)	28.92 (27.49–30.04)
n=78 14[3],9[6],55[2]	n=76 12[3],9[6],55[2]	n=55[2]	n=55[2]	n=78 14[3],9[6],55[2]	n=10[1]	n=10[1]
5.85 (5.25–6.92)	25.91 (23.42–29.29)	18.50 (16.65–20.39)	15.84 (14.76–17.00)	10.13 (9.1–11.66)	9.33 (8.68–9.98)	27.75 (25.95–30.16)
n=76 11[3],9[6],56[2]	n=74 9[3],9[6],56[2]	n=56[2]	n=56[2]	n=76 11[3],9[6],56[2]	n=8[1]	n=7[1]
6.70 (6.5–7.0)	25.55 (25.1–26.3)			9.60 (9.3–10.1)	8.65 (8.40–8.78)	27.19 (25.56–28.30)
n=4[6]	n=4[6]			n=4[6]	n=5[1]	n=5[1]
6.70 (6.25–7.6)	25.97 (23.3–27.8)	18.18 (17.55–18.85)	17.51 (16.2–18.2)	9.45 (8.8–10.3)	8.72 (8.17–9.14)	27.54 (25.12–29.32)
n=16 5[6],11[8]	n=16 5[6],11[8]	n=11[8]	n=11[8]	n=16 5[6],11[8]	n=10[1]	n=10[1]
6.6 (6.0–7.4)	26.2 (23.9–27.6)	19.2 (18.2–21.3)				
n=46[4]	n=46[4]	n=46[4]				
6.26 (5.45–6.96)	25.30 (22.87–27.02)	18.60 (16.90–20.14)	15.75 (14.89–16.44)	9.76 (9.21–10.37)	8.70 (8.33–9.16)	25.03 (23.51–27.31)
n=30[2]	n=30[2]	n=30[2]	n=30[2]	n=30[2]	n=10[1]	n=10[1]
6.29 (5.77–6.97)	25.99 (23.35–27.74)	18.92 (17.37–20.44)	15.99 (15.09–17.05)	9.87 (9.13–10.49)	8.71 (8.20–9.40)	25.72 (23.00–27.90)
n=30[2]	n=30[2]	n=30[2]	n=30[2]	n=30[2]	n=10[1]	n=10[1]

Family Muridae, genera *Oryzomys*, *Sigmodon*, *Neotoma*, and *Rattus* continued

Species	Sex	Greatest length	Postpalatal length	Incisive foramen length	Nasal length	Mastoid breadth
Desert woodrat, *Neotoma lepida*	♀	38.03 (35.0–41.2)		7.97 (7.25–8.9)	14.13 (7.25–8.9)	16.65 (15.4–18.0)
n=Total sample Sources		n=44 37[3],7[2]		n=37[3]	n=37[3]	n=37[3]
	♂	39.80 (33.33–46.04)		8.43 (7.55–9.2)	14.89 (13.85–16.1)	17.18 (16.0–18.5)
n=Total sample Sources		n=70 45[3],25[2]		n=45[3]	n=45[3]	n=45[3]
Norway rat, *Rattus norvegicus*	♀	46.82 (44.16–50.00)				
n=Total sample		n=7[2]				
	♂	46.83 (43.00–50.29)			15.95	
n=Total sample Sources		n=14[2]			n=1[3]	
	♀♂	49.3 (43.9–51.5)	16.5 (15.7–18.5)		17.7 (15.8–19.6)	
n=Total sample		n=20[4]	n=20[4]		n=20[4]	
Black rat, *Rattus rattus*	♀	40.66 (39.32–44.20)		7.46 (7.00–7.92)	14.42 (12.7–17.02)	
n=Total sample Sources		n=6 1[2],5[1]		n=5[1]	n=6 1[3],5[1]	
	♂	40.17 (35.68–42.84)		7.41 (6.86–8.03)	13.50 (11.27–15.34)	
n=Total sample Sources		n=5[1]		n=5[1]	n=7 2[3],5[1]	
	♀♂	42.20 (39.9–46.9)	14.6 (13.7–15.2)		15.2 (13.3–17.7)	
n=Total sample Sources		n=27 2[5],25[4]	n=25[4]		n=25[4]	

1=author, 2=Verts and Carraway (1998), 3=Hoffmeister (1986), 4=Lowery (1974), 5=Paradiso (1969), 6=Armstrong (1972), 7=Jimenez (1971) in Cameron and Spencer (1981), 8=Hoffmeister (1989)

*The Dusky-footed woodrat has recently been split into two distinct species: The Dusky-footed (*N. fuscipes*) north of San Francisco Bay, and the Big-eared woodrat (*N. macrotis*) south. The numbers presented here are from both species. All are *N. fuscipes* excepting the "Mandibular toothrow" and "Mandible length," which were created from *N. macrotis* specimens.

Interorbital breadth	Zygomatic breadth	Braincase breadth	Skull depth	Maxillary toothrow	Mandibular toothrow	Mandible length
4.97 (4.55–5.44)	19.71 (17.4–21.77)	15.89 (15.44–16.60)	13.64 (13.00–14.04)	8.04 (7.4–9.35)	7.86 (7.38–8.20)	23.13 (22.01–24.90)
n=44 37[3],7[2]	n=44 37[3],7[2]	n=7[2]	n=7[2]	n=44 37[3],7[2]	n=10[1]	n=10[1]
5.11 (4.65–5.90)	20.56 (18.89–23.76)	16.41 (15.37–17.48)	14.15 (13.32–15.67)	8.14 (7.55–8.65)	7.84 (7.54–8.13)	23.86 (22.03–26.20)
n=70 45[3],25[2]	n=70 45[3],25[2]	n=25[2]	n=25[2]	n=70 45[3],25[2]	n=10[1]	n=10[1]
6.66 (6.15–7.41)	22.93 (21.19–24.85)	16.91 (15.75–18.25)	14.31 (13.84–15.02)	7.78 (7.21–8.17)	7.14, 7.74	27.30, 27.51
n=7[2]	n=7[2]	n=7[2]	n=7[2]	n=7[2]	n=2[1]	n=2[1]
6.82 (6.0–7.48)	23.58 (20.0–25.96)	17.34 (16.39–18.31)	14.67 (13.56–15.69)	7.75 (7.15–8.36)	7.50 (7.32–7.66)	27.46 (25.81–29.00)
n=15 1[3],14[2]	n=15 1[3],14[2]	n=14[2]	n=14[2]	n=15 1[3],14[2]	n=3[1]	n=3[1]
6.5 (6.1–7.0)	23.0 (20.4–27.7)	18.4 (17.2–20.0)		6.6 (6.4–7.4)		
n=20[4]	n=20[4]	n=20[4]		n=20[4]		
5.96 (5.4–6.34)	19.39 (18.12–20.84)	16.86 (16.60–17.12)	13.58	6.89 (6.36–7.23)	6.63 (6.34–6.84)	22.72 (20.82–24.48)
n=7 1[3],1[2],5[1]	n=5 1[2],4[1]	n=6 1[2],5[1]	n=1[2]	n=7 1[3],1[2],5[1]	n=5[1]	n=5[1]
5.94 (5.45–6.62)	19.04 (16.95–20.92)	16.97 (15.32–19.20)		6.89 (6.2–7.65)	6.78 (6.36–7.42)	22.16 (18.54–24.66)
n=7 2[3],5[1]	n=7 2[3],5[1]	n=5[1]		n=7 2[3],5[1]	n=5[1]	n=5[1]
6.04 (5.4–6.9)	19.79 (18.3–22.3)	17.1 (16.1–18.9)		6.53 (5.5–7.0)		
n=27 2[5],25[4]	n=27 2[5],25[4]	n=25[4]		n=27 2[5],25[4]		

Family Muridae, genera *Clethrionomys,* *Microtus,* and *Lemmus*

Table in millimeters. Mean and parameters on top. Total number of specimens measured and specific number in cited sources below.

Species	Sex	Greatest length	Occipitonasal length	Condylobasal length	Nasal length	Incisive foramen length
Southern red-backed vole, *Clethrionomys gapperi*	♀	23.98 (21.54–26.42)	23.74 (22.41–25.64)	23.90 (23.0–25.2)	7.04 (6.33–8.28)	4.83 (4.37–5.24)
n=Total sample Sources		n=12[1]	n=31[2]	n=8[6]	n=31[2]	n=31[2]
	♂	24.06 (22.58–26.04)	23.89 (22.55–24.92)	23.61 (22.8–25.4)	7.09 (6.23–7.64)	4.83 (4.28–5.25)
n=Total sample Sources		n=12[1]	n=33[2]	n=15[6]	n=33[2]	n=36 33[2],3[1]
	♀♂		24.85 (23.9–25.7)	24.65 (23.1–25.8)	7.51 (6.8–7.95)	
n=Total sample Sources		n=?[7]	n=18[3]	n=28 18[3],10[5]	n=18[3]	
California vole, *Microtus californicus*	♀	28.11 (26.14–30.40)	28.13 (26.42–30.19)		9.14 (8.12–9.97)	5.61 (4.96–6.11)
n=Total sample		n=10[1]	n=21[2]		n=21[2]	n=21[2]
	♂	28.82 (26.86–31.38)	28.49 (26.18–30.72)		9.31 (8.11–10.40)	5.61 (4.89–6.65)
n=Total sample		n=12[1]	n=19[2]		n=19[2]	n=19[2]
Long-tailed vole, *Microtus longicaudus*	♀	27.91 (26.04–28.94)	26.95 (24.29–31.63)		7.86 (6.71–10.46)	5.11 (4.11–6.38)
n=Total sample		n=12[1]	n=61[2]		n=61[2]	n=61[2]
	♂	27.20 (25.88–28.34)	27.29 (24.50–33.85)	27.81 (26.8–29.2)	7.95 (6.42–9.88)	5.18 (4.20–6.77)
n=Total sample Sources		n=12[1]	n=72[2]	n=9[6]	n=72[2]	n=72[2]
	♀♂		27.52 (25.45–30.5)	27.13 (24.5–30.5)	8.45 (7.2–10.25)	
n=Total sample			n=141[3]	n=144[3]	n=145[3]	
Montane vole, *Microtus montanus*	♀	27.16 (25.40–29.36)	25.98 (24.32–27.23)	26.89 (26.2–27.8)	7.36 (6.42–8.54)	5.30 (4.70–6.04)
n=Total sample Sources		n=9[1]	n=54[2]	n=13[6]	n=54[2]	n=54[2]

Interorbital breadth	Zygomatic breadth	Braincase breadth	Skull depth	Maxillary toothrow	Mandibular toothrow	Mandible length
3.94	13.19	10.62	9.17	5.37	5.01	13.72
(3.5–4.2)	(12.36–13.81)	(9.67–11.42)	(8.86–9.71)	(4.82–5.80)	(4.84–5.50)	(12.68–15.74)
n=42	n=42	n=34	n=31[2]	n=42	n=12[1]	n=12[1]
8[6],31[2],3[1]	8[6],31[2],3[1]	31[2],3[1]		8[6],31[2],3[1]		
3.90	13.16	10.58	9.28	5.36	5.26	13.75
(3.4–4.5)	(11.95–14.40)	(9.90–11.58)	(8.69–9.77)	(4.88–7.18)	(4.93–5.98)	(13.00–15.32)
n=51	n=51	n=36	n=33[2]	n=51	n=12[1]	n=12[1]
15[6],33[2],3[1]	15[6],33[2],3[1]	33[2],3[1]		15[6],33[2],3[1]		
3.89	13.7			5.42		
(3.6–4.2)	(12.7–14.25)			(5.1–5.7)		
n=28	n=28			n=28		
18[3],10[5]	18[3],10[5]			18[3],10[5]		
3.66	16.54	11.32	10.31	7.24	6.58	17.17
(3.35–4.11)	(15.24–18.28)	(10.04–12.09)	(9.77–11.02)	(6.47–7.62)	(6.16–7.00)	(16.06–18.20)
n=21[2]	n=21[2]	n=21[2]	n=21[2]	n=21[2]	n=10[1]	n=10[1]
3.72	16.78	11.38	10.58	7.24	6.59	17.21
(3.41–4.01)	(15.26–18.00)	(10.64–12.59)	(10.10–11.07)	(6.73–7.90)	(6.17–7.00)	(16.36–19.72)
n=19[2]	n=19[2]	n=19[2]	n=19[2]	n=19[2]	n=12[1]	n=12[1]
3.79	14.97	11.28	9.96	6.82	6.18	16.66
(3.44–4.19)	(13.56–17.91)	(10.21–12.77)	(9.28–11.15)	(6.02–8.58)	(5.63–6.67)	(15.41–17.74)
n=61[2]	n=61[2]	n=61[2]	n=61[2]	n=61[2]	n=12[1]	n=12[1]
3.83	15.13	11.31	10.12	6.84	6.19	15.92
(3.49–4.33)	(13.13–17.77)	(10.12–12.74)	(9.25–11.18)	(5.85–8.53)	(5.68–6.68)	(14.58–17.28)
n=81	n=81	n=72[2]	n=72[2]	n=81	n=12[1]	n=12[1]
9[6],72[2]	9[6],72[2]			9[6],72[2]		
3.71	15.36			6.70		
(3.3–4.15)	(13.3–17.6)			(5.9–7.7)		
n=146[3]	n=144[3]			n=146[3]		
3.52	15.19	10.68	9.93	6.63	6.56	16.62
(3.2–3.85)	(13.93–17.56)	(9.73–11.43)	(9.33–10.91)	(5.97–7.66)	(5.94–7.14)	(15.51–17.82)
n=67	n=67	n=54[2]	n=54[2]	n=67	n=9[1]	n=9[1]
13[6],54[2]	13[6],54[2]			13[6],54[2]		

Family Muridae, genera *Clethrionomys*, *Microtus*, and *Lemmus* continued

Species	Sex	Greatest length	Occipitonasal length	Condylobasal length	Nasal length	Incisive foramen length
Montane vole, *Microtus montanus*	♂	27.72 (26.14–30.17)	26.39 (23.68–28.31)	27.31 (26.1–28.1)	7.47 (5.67–8.53)	5.39 (4.42–6.12)
n=Total sample Sources		n=12[1]	n=62[2]	n=16[6]	n=62[2]	n=62[2]
	♀♂		26.99 (25.2–28.35)	27.36 (25.4–30.1)	7.99 (7.1–9.2)	
n=Total sample			n=12[3]	n=58[3]	n=58[3]	
Meadow vole or field mouse, *Microtus pennsylvanicus*	♀	28.69 (26.92–31.04)		29.10 (27.7–30.6)	7.92 (7.16–8.90)	
n=Total sample Sources		n=10[1]		n=14[6]	n=10[1]	
	♂	28.14 (25.97–30.86)		28.68 (27.0–31.6)	7.38 (6.46–8.61)	
n=Total sample Sources		n=10[1]		n=13[6]	n=10[1]	
	♀♂	25.83 (23.8–27.8)		28.5 (28.1–29.0)	7.28 (6.3–8.4)	5.48 (4.6–6.3)
n=Total sample Sources		n=64[9]+?[7]		n=11[5]	n=64[9]	n=64[9]
Water vole, *Microtus richardsoni*	♀	35.04 (30.78–37.62)	31.80 (29.23–32.57)		9.43 (7.68–11.14)	6.19 (4.69–7.04)
n=Total sample		n=8[1]	n=32[2]		n=32[2]	n=32[2]
	♂	35.29 (30.12–37.68)	32.51 (30.12–34.93)		9.72 (8.34–11.96)	6.27 (5.33–7.29)
n=Total sample		n=8[1]	n=29[2]		n=29[2]	n=29[2]
Brown lemming, *Lemmus trimucronatus*	♀	31.41 (27.58–33.24)	31.0 (29.4–33.2)	31.3 (29.2–33.5)	9.1 (8.3–10.5)	
n=Total sample		n=10[1]	n=80[8]	n=80[8]	n=80[8]	
	♂	32.19 (28.52–35.14)	32.1 (29.7–35.6)	32.2 (29.3–35.8)	9.4 (8.1–10.7)	
n=Total sample		n=10[1]	n=80[8]	n=80[8]	n=80[8]	

1=author, 2=Verts and Carraway (1998), 3=Hoffmeister (1986), 4=Lowery (1974), 5=Paradiso (1969), 6=Armstrong (1972), 7=Jackson (1961), 8=Bee and Hall (1956), 9=Hoffmeister(1989)

Interorbital breadth	Zygomatic breadth	Braincase breadth	Skull depth	Maxillary toothrow	Mandibular toothrow	Mandible length
3.64	15.46	10.75	10.04	6.68	6.44	16.64
(2.71–4.28)	(13.44–17.25)	(9.70–11.67)	(9.20–11.06)	(5.9–7.33)	(5.84–7.12)	(15.06–18.54)
n=78	n=78	n=62[2]	n=62[2]	n=78	n=12[1]	n=12[1]
16[6],62[2]	16[6],62[2]			16[6],62[2]		
3.47	15.77			6.58		
(3.2–3.7)	(14.3–17.8)			(6.0–7.1)		
n=58[3]	n=58[3]			n=58[3]		
3.69	16.08	12.01		7.23	6.93	17.67
(3.2–4.00)	(14.54–17.7)	(11.02–12.45)		(6.50–8.2)	(6.21–7.38)	(16.45–19.34)
n=24	n=24	n=10[1]		n=24	n=10[1]	n=10[1]
14[6],10[1]	14[6],10[1]			14[6],10[1]		
3.73	15.62	11.89		6.92	6.63	16.98
(3.3–4.04)	(14.20–16.71)	(11.20–12.25)		(6.32–7.8)	(6.16–6.94)	(15.62–18.46)
n=23	n=23	n=10[1]		n=23	n=10[1]	n=10[1]
13[6],10[1]	13[6],10[1]			13[6],10[1]		
3.76	14.33			6.43		
(3.4–4.15)	(12.5–15.9)			(5.9–7.3)		
n=75	n=75			n=75		
11[5],64[9]	11[5],64[9]			11[5],64[9]		
4.90	20.02	12.63		8.30		
(4.63–5.27)	(17.37–22.36)	(11.33–14.35)		(7.01–9.58)		
n=32[2]	n=32[2]	n=32[2]		n=32[2]		
5.02	20.40	12.91		8.38		
(4.75–5.39)	(18.21–23.34)	(11.82–14.37)		(7.29–9.31)		
n=29[2]	n=29[2]	n=29[2]		n=29[2]		
3.8	21.1			9.0	7.93	20.36
(3.0–4.3)	(18.8–23.1)			(8.4–9.8)	(7.48–8.38)	(17.88–22.05)
n=80[8]	n=80[8]			n=80[8]	n=10[1]	n=10[1]
3.8	21.5			8.9	7.98	23.88
(3.3–4.2)	(18.9–23.7)			(8.3–9.8)	(7.58–8.74)	(18.88–23.04)
n=80[8]	n=80[8]			n=80[8]	n=10[1]	n=10[1]

Family Zapodidae

*Table in millimeters. Mean and parameters on top. Total number
of specimens measured and specific number in cited sources below.*

Species	Sex	Greatest length	Occipitonasal length	Condylobasal length	Nasal length	Incisive foramen length
Meadow jumping mouse, *Zapus hudsonius*	♀	22.78 (21.34–23.44)		20.18 (19.2–21.5)		
n=Total sample Sources		n=5[1]		n=9[6]		
	♂	22.51 (21.22–23.48)		20.6 (20.1–21.6)		
n=Total sample Sources		n=5[1]		n=3[6]		
	♀♂	22.15 (20.75–23.75)		20.83 (19.3–23.1)	8.81 (8.0–10.0)	4.30 (4.0–4.65)
n=Total sample Sources		n=32+?[7] 3[5],29[4]		n=16[3]	n=39 10[3],29[4]	n=10[3]
Western jumping mouse, *Zapus princeps*	♀		25.54 (22.83–25.88)	22.70 (22.0–23.6)		
n=Total sample Sources			n=30[2]	n=10[6]		
	♂		24.57 (23.12–26.19)	22.34 (20.7–23.9)		
n=Total sample Sources			n=33[2]	n=22[6]		
Pacific jumping mouse, *Zapus trinotatus*	♀		24.24 (22.21–25.63)			
n=Total sample			n=42[2]			
	♂		24.26 (23.14–25.54)			
n=Total sample			n=60[2]			
Woodland jumping mouse, *Napaeozapus insignis*	♀	23.87 (23.56–24.54)			9.36 (8.88–9.72)	
n=Total sample		n=5[1]			n=5[1]	
	♂	23.80 (23.00–24.08)			9.39 (8.90–9.86)	
n=Total sample		n=5[1]			n=6[1]	
	♀♂	23.1 (22.2–23.7)				
n=Total sample		n=6[5]				

1=author, 2=Verts and Carraway (1998), 3=Hoffmeister (1986), 4=Hoffmeister (1989), 5=Paradiso (1969), 6=Armstrong (1972), 7=Jackson (1961)

Interorbital breadth	Zygomatic breadth	Braincase breadth	Skull depth	Maxillary toothrow	Mandibular toothrow	Mandible length
4.12 (3.9–4.39)	11.01 (10.38–11.4)	9.89 (9.24–10.36)		3.37 (3.35–4.1)	3.35 (3.22–3.52)	11.62 (11.12–11.98)
n=14 9[6],5[1]	n=14 9[6],5[1]	n=5[1]		n=14 9[6],5[1]	n=5[1]	n=5
4.22 (3.7–4.56)	10.67 (10.24–11.2)	9.85 (9.73–9.95)		3.71 (3.34–4.0)	3.43 (3.26–3.48)	11.02 (10.64–11.26)
n=8 3[6],5[1]	n=8 3[6],5[1]	n=5[1]		n=8 3[6],5[1]	n=5[1]	n=5[1]
4.25 (3.7–5.0)	10.92 (9.9–12.0)	10.31 (10.1–10.6)		3.72 (3.3–4.25)		
n=50 18[3],3[5],29[4]	n=50 18[3],3[5],29[4]	n=9[3]		n=50 18[3],3[5],29[4]		
4.58 (4.1–4.96)	12.63 (11.55–13.31)	11.24 (10.48–11.87)	8.92 (8.09–9.79)	4.33 (4.10–4.70)		
n=40 10[6],30[2]	n=40 10[6],30[2]	n=30[2]	n=30[2]	n=40 10[6],30[2]		
4.61 (4.1–5.24)	12.48 (11.7–13.38)	11.20 (10.69–11.79)	8.95 (8.39–9.55)	4.25 (3.8–4.80)		
n=55 22[6],33[2]	n=55 22[6],33[2]	n=33[2]	n=33[2]	n=55 22[6],33[2]		
4.50 (3.99–4.84)	12.53 (11.74–13.20)	11.03 (10.45–12.35)	8.95 (8.34–9.41)	4.06 (3.73–4.45)		
n=42[2]	n=42[2]	n=42[2]	n=42[2]	n=42[2]		
4.58 (4.18–5.27)	12.36 (11.62–13.04)	11.01 (10.48–11.62)	8.97 (8.43–9.78)	4.11 (3.71–4.54)		
n=60[2]	n=60[2]	n=60[2]	n=60[2]	n=60[2]		
4.99 (4.94–5.13)	12.37 (12.18–12.52)	10.86 (10.56–11.20)		3.78 (3.56–4.02)	4.05 (3.88–4.23)	12.22 (11.58–12.66)
n=5[1]	n=5[1]	n=5[1]		n=5[1]	n=5[1]	n=5[1]
4.92 (4.78–5.18)	12.09 (11.62–12.48)	10.58 (10.28–10.92)		3.77 (3.63–3.88)	4.05 (3.84–4.19)	12.13 (11.62–12.34)
n=6[1]	n=6[1]	n=6[1]		n=6[1]	n=6[1]	n=6[1]
4.5 (4.1–4.7)	12.1 (11.8–12.3)			3.6 (3.4–3.8)		
n=6[5]	n=6[5]			n=6[5]		

Family Canidae

Table in millimeters. Mean and parameters above. Total number of specimens measured, and specific number in cited sources below.

Species	Sex	Greatest length	Condylobasal length	Basilar length	Palatal length	Palatilar length
***Coyote (New England), *Canis latrans*	♀	192.45 (173.76–205.84)				89.45 (81.30–95.62)
n=Total sample		n=5[1]				n=5[1]
	♂	207.85 (189.90–220.32)				95.77 (83.08–104.66)
n=Total sample		n=6[1]				n=6[1]
Coyote, *Canis latrans*	♀	187.09 (172.35–204.0)	166.79 (143.0–189.9)	153.61 (129.0–175.6)		88.73 (81.9–94.9)
n=Total sample Sources		n=35 30[4],5[3]	n=83 43[2],30[4],5[3],5[6]	n=80 43[2],30[4],7[1]		n=37 30[4],7[14]
	♂	192.14 (170.0–213.0)	173.59 (147.0–203.0)	161.06 (133.0–188.2)		90.97 (76.2–100.1)
n=Total sample Sources		n=39 30[4],9[3]	n=87 40[2],30[4],9[3],8[6]	n=91 40[2],30[4],21[14]		n=51 30[4],21[14]
	♀♂	196.88 (171.0–222.0)	184.41 (162.0–207.0)			
n=Total sample		n=57[5]	n=57[5]			
Coyote-dog hybrids from Illinois	♀♂			173.32 (168.8–192.9)		94.77 (85.8–106.2)
n=Total sample				n=14[14]		n=14[14]
Gray wolf, *Canis lupus*	♀	242.38 (213.6–280.5)	228.54 (191.33–263.5)	193.65 (183.0–211.07)		
n=Total sample Sources		n=134 15[3],119[10]	n=299 10[2],15[3],6[6], 119[10],149[16]	n=10[2]		
	♂	259.00 (221.0–293.7)	241.05 (205.0–286.78)	210.16 (193.0–228.0)		
n=Total sample Sources		n=171 18[3],153[10]	n=361 17[2],18[3],4[6], 153[10],169[16]	n=17[2]		
Eastern timber wolf, *Canis lycaon*	♀	237.5 (213.6–267.0)	222.3 (203.3–248.8)			
n=Total sample		n=19[10]	n=16[10]			
	♂	247.7 (233.0–259.3)	231.5 (219.3–247.7)			
n=Total sample		n=23[10]	n=22[10]			

Zygomatic breadth	Interorbital breadth	Rostrum width	Braincase breadth	Mastoidal breadth	Maxillary toothrow	Mandible length
97.66 (89.70–101.82)	32.44 (29.18–35.80)	28.63 (25.12–30.76)	57.96 (56.40–60.84)	60.52 (56.66–62.57)		139.63 (129.82–148.94)
n=5[1]	n=5[1]	n=5[1]	n=5[1]	n=5[1]		n=5[1]
106.98 (100.32–112.04)	35.62 (32.88–37.38)	32.29 (29.55–34.52)	59.79 (57.37–61.68)	64.67 (61.22–68.20)		150.99 (136.80–159.60)
n=6[1]	n=6[1]	n=6[1]	n=6[1]	n=6[1]		n=6[1]
92.99 (84.2–105.6)	30.77 (26.0–36.7)	27.86 (24.3–33.8)	56.38 (51.77–59.21)	59.82 (54.1–65.3)	81.09 (75.3–86.22)	133.73 (123.84–143.06)
n= 90 43[2],30[4],5[3], 5[6],7[14]	n= 90 43[2],30[4],5[3], 5[6],7[14]	n=42 30[4],5[3],7[14]	n=43[2]	n=42 30[4],5[6],7[14]	n=53 43[2],5[3],5[6]	n=43[2]
97.13 (84.5–106.4)	32.32 (26.5–37.76)	29.07 (24.5–33.2)	57.59 (53.05–62.02)	60.51 (52.8–67.8)	83.94 (76.44–91.62)	140.20 (125.82–151.49)
n= 108 40[2],30[4],9[3], 8[6],21[14]	n= 108 40[2],30[4],9[3], 8[6],21[14]	n=60 30[4],9[3],21[14]	n=40[2]	n=59 30[4],8[6],21[14]	n=57 40[2],9[3],8[6]	n=40[2]
99.30 (86.0–110.0)						
n=57[5]						
101.48 (92.4–111.2)	34.85 (31.5–38.4)	32.48 (30.2–35.7)	60.77 (52.4–66.0)	64.34 (59.0–70.6)		
n=14[14]	n=14[14]	n=14[14]	n=14[14]	n=14[14]		
130.09 (115.67–144.8)	43.03 (35.3–50.5)	41.60 (34.4–47.4)	66.00 (63.44–68.75)		101.70 (88.8–118.5)	175.34 (155.0–201.3)
n=150 10[2],15[3],6[6], 119[10]	n=149 10[2],15[3],5[6], 119[10]	n=140 15[3],6[6],119[10]	n=10[2]		n=152 10[2],15[3],8[6], 119[10]	n=129 10[2],119[10]
139.79 (112.17–156.5)	47.05 (35.1–59.8)	45.39 (38.2–54.3)	69.60 (65.42–78.0)		107.40 (87.5–121.5)	187.40 (161.9–210.3)
n=191 17[2],17[3],4[6], 153[10]	n=191 17[2],18[3],3[6], 153[10]	n=175 18[3],4[6],153[10]	n=17[2]		n=192 17[2],18[3],4[6], 153[10]	n=170 17[2],153[10]
126.0 (116.3–142.0)	41.6 (35.5–48.9)	38.4 (34.4–42.5)			99.0 (91.0–110.0)	170.2 (155.0–190.8)
n=18[10]	n=18[10]	n=19[10]			n=19[10]	n=18[10]
133.8 (122.4–140.7)	45.2 (38.6–50.6)	40.8 (35.7–44.5)			103.7 (95.6–113.1)	177.3 (165.5–194.4)
n=23[10]	n=23[10]	n=23[10]			n=23[10]	n=23[10]

Family Canidae *continued*

Species	Sex	Greatest length	Condylobasal length	Basilar length	Palatal length	Palatilar length
Red wolf, *Canis rufus*	♀	217.23** (198.5–247.0)	205.89 (187.5–215.8)			
n=Total sample Sources		n=114 45[10],69[11]	n=45[10]			
	♂	229.25** (208.0–261.0)	213.65 (196.5–233.7)			
n=Total sample Sources		n=136 62[10],74[11]	n=62[10]			
Arctic fox, *Vulpes lagopus*	♀	125.40 (121.76–128.96)	117.60 (105.19–130.67)	111.5 (108.8–115.5)	61.79 (59.32–64.28)	
n=Total sample Sources		n=8[1]	n=143[16]	n=5[9]	n=6[1]	
	♂	131.24 (126.70–134.86)	122.28 (107.41–133.13)	114.5 (110.8–118.4)	64.84 (63.66–67.00)	
n=Total sample Sources		n=7[1]	n=191[16]	n=7[9]	n=6[1]	
Kit fox, *Vulpes macrotis*	♀	110.71 (104.8–118.75)	108.88 (98.9–118.03)	105.34 (99.4–111.53)	55.54 (49.7–59.14)	54.21 (50.8–57.2)
n=Total sample Sources		n=19 13[4],6[3]	n= 45 6[3],13[4],8[6],18[15]	n=31 13[4],18[15]	n=24 6[3],18[15]	n=13[4]
	♂	111.57 (101.0–120.25)	110.24 (99.3–118.25)	105.60 (99.7–113.47)	55.10 (48.7–59.62)	55.11 (51.7–59.3)
n=Total sample Sources		n=39 21[4],18[3]	n=64 21[4],17[3],12[6],14[15]	n=35 21[4],14[15]	n=32 18[3],14[15]	n=21[4]
	♀♂		108.84 (102.21–118.45)*		54.75 (50.28–60.19)*	
n=Total sample			n=104[8]		n=104[8]	
Swift fox, *Vulpes velox*	♀	111.38, 113.00	106.96 (99.80–123.70)	107.94 (100.68–115.19)	56.28, 56.64	
n=Total sample Sources		n=2[1]	n=13 2[2],1[6],10[16]	n=2[2]	n=2[1]	
	♂	114.88, 116.80	111.77 (103.54–119.59)		55.66, 59.82	
n=Total sample Sources		n=2[1]	n=13 3[6],10[16]		n=2[1]	
Red fox, *Vulpes vulpes*	♀	138.89 (124.5–150.8)	134.25 (121.0–144.6)	122.01 (112.55–141.0)	71.03 (65.2–75.8)	64.1 (57.5–68.8)
n=Total sample Sources		n=137 6[4],131[7]	n=42 5[2],6[4],2[6],24[13],5[14]	n= 14 5[2],6[4],3[9]	n=31 24[13],7[14]	n=6[4]
	♂	145.81 (132.5–157.2)	140.36 (127.6–155.5)	128.40 (118.5–140.0)	73.56 (67.3–79.8)	67.12 (61.8–72.1)
n=Total sample Sources		n=153 4[4],149[7]	n= 39 4[2],4[4],4[6], 21[13],6[14]	n= 10 4[2],4[4],2[9]	n=29 21[13],8[14]	n=4[4]

Zygomatic breadth	Interorbital breadth	Rostrum width	Braincase breadth	Mastoidal breadth	Maxillary toothrow	Mandible length
113.40 (100.3–125.5) n=45[10]	36.60 (32.1–44.9) n=45[10]	33.71 (28.6–38.1) n=45[10]			92.47 (82.4–100.3) n=45[10]	155.23 (141.6–168.2) n=45[10]
118.73 (103.2–137.7) n=62[10]	37.15 (32.3–47.9) n=62[10]	35.46 (30.0–41.6) n=62[10]			96.98 (90.0–103.9) n=62[10]	163.48 (148.1–180.0) n=62[10]
66.58 (63.69–69.8) n=11 5[9],6[1]	26.83 (25.10–28.10) n=7[1]		45.6 (43.5–47.0) n=5[9]	41.18 (38.6–44.40) n=11 5[9],6[1]	45.2 (44.0–46.4) n=5[9]	89.81 (86.00–92.50) n=8[1]
69.44 (68.0–71.36) n=13 7[9],6[1]	27.02 (24.18–28.28) n=6[1]		46.2 (45.0–47.4) n=7[9]	41.56 (36.3–45.02) n=13 7[9],6[1]	46.5 (43.7–47.8) n=7[9]	95.53 (93.70–98.92) n=7[1]
59.81 (54.1–64.18) n= 45 6[3],13[4],8[6],18[15]	21.26 (19.3–23.4) n= 27 6[3],13[4],8[6]	17.17 (15.2–19.27) n=37 13[4],6[3],18[15]	43.43 (41.60–45.22) n=24 6[3],18[15]	38.57 (36.26–40.49) n=31 13[4],18[15]	50.84 (47.6–54.75) n=32 6[3],8[6],18[15]	82.87 (75.56–89.53) n=28 10[1],18[15]
59.77 (54.4–66.2) n=64 21[4],17[3],12[6],14[15]	21.27 (19.3–25.2) n=50 21[4],18[3],11[6]	16.76 (14.0–19.67) n=52 21[4],17[3],14[15]	42.95 (40.1–44.76) n=32 18[3],14[15]	39.11 (36.5–40.5) n=47 21[4],12[6],14[15]	51.75 (47.3–56.03) n=44 18[3],12[6],14[15]	86.13 (81.26–92.04) n=24 10[1],14[15]
59.09 (54.7–64.33)* n=104[8]	21.50 (19.78–24.23)* n=104[8]					
62.80 (57.54–67.74) n=5 2[2],1[6],2[1]	23.12 (20.27–25.39) n=5 2[2],1[6],2[1]		44.68 (41.82–47.54) n=2[2]		54.61 (50.94–60.17) n=3 2[2],1[6]	85.33 (80.07–95.62) n=4 2[2],2[1]
64.32 (63.6–65.04) n=5 3[6],2[1]	23.84 (23.12–24.7) n=5 3[6],2[1]			39.78, 40.10 n=2[1]	52.5 (51.6–54.1) n=3[6]	85.43 (83.27–86.66) n=3[1]
72.55 (66.2–84.2) n= 178 5[2],6[4],2[6],131[7],3[9],24[13],7[14]	26.52 (23.8–31.8) n=44 5[2],6[4],2[6],24[13],7[14]	20.59 (17.9–23.0) n=137 6[4],131[7]	46.64 (45.23–51.3) n=8 5[2],3[9]	45.62 (40.6–48.9) n=140 6[4],131[7],3[9]	62.48 (50.1–69.2) n=40 5[2],2[6],3[9],23[13],7[14]	99.06 (92.88–104.20) n=20 5[2],15[1]
75.76 (67.16–90.8) n= 190 4[2],4[4],4[6],149[7],2[9],21[13],6[14]	27.77 (22.8–33.2) n= 39 4[2],4[4],4[6],21[13],6[14]	21.28 (18.7–24.5) n=153 4[4],149[7]	48.63 (46.09–51.9) n=6 4[2],2[9]	46.99 (43.7–49.8) n=155 4[4],149[7],2[9]	65.40 (56.8–71.7) n=40 4[2],4[6],3[9],21[13],8[14]	105.57 (100.33–111.36) n=18 4[2],14[1]

Family Canidae *continued*

Species	Sex	Greatest length	Condylobasal length	Basilar length	Palatal length	Palatilar length
Red fox, *Vulpes vulpes*	♀♂	140.0 (132.5–154.5)	125.8 (119.2–140.5)			68.6 (65.2–75.0)
n=Total sample		n=8[5]	n=8[5]			n=8[5]
Common gray fox, *Urocyon cinereoargenteus*	♀	117.7 (111.6–131.3)	112.96 (90.71–126.83)	104.18 (84.05–117.55)	53.72 (41.48–61.3)	55.44 (51.7–61.7)
n=Total sample Sources		n=34 25[4],9[3]	n= 530 9[2],25[4],9[3],1[6], 7[14],479[15]	n= 513 9[2],25[4],479[15]	n=495 9[3],7[14],479[15]	n=25[4]
	♂	122.68 (114.1–131.9)	116.92 (94.91–128.04)	107.88 (101.61–118.49)	55.58 (44.06–62.36)	56.93 (52.5–62.5)
n=Total sample Sources		n=53 46[4],7[3]	n= 634 11[2],46[4],8[3],3[6], 5[14],561[15]	n= 618 11[2],46[4], 561[15]	n=574 8[3],5[14],561[15]	n=46[4]
	♀♂	117.9 (111.7–124.6)				54.7 (51.0–58.0)
n=Total sample		n=16[5]				n=16[5]
Island fox, *Urocyon littoralis*	♀	100.53 (96.8–107.6)	95.92 (88.6–103.9)	89.32 (86.4–95.1)		46.63 (45.0–50.0)
n=Total sample		n=33[4]	n=203[12]	n=33[4]		n=33[4]
	♂	102.52 (96.9–110.3)	99.01 (92.2–106.4)	90.88 (85.1–97.4)		47.92 (44.5–56.8)
n=Total sample		n=34[4]	n=201[12]	n=34[4]		n=34[4]

1=author, 2=Verts and Carraway (1998). 3=Hoffmeister (1986), 4=Grinnell et al.(1937), 5=Lowery (1974), 6=Armstrong (1972), 7=Storm et al. (1976), 8=Waithman and Roest (1977), 9=Bee and Hall (1956), 10=Young and Goldman (1944), 11=Paradiso and Nowak (1972), 12=Collins (1982–1983) in Moore and Collins (1995), 13=Rausch (1953), 14=Hoffmeister (1989), 15=Collins(1982), 16=Meiri et al. (2004b)

*parameters from partial data set
**means created with only Young and Goldman data
***Larger specimens from New England have been separated out for comparison with their southern and western counterpar

Family Ursidae

Table in millimeters. Mean and parameters on top. Total number of specimens measured and specific number in cited sources below.

Species	Sex	Greatest length	Condylobasal length	Basilar length	Palatal length	Palatilar length
American black bear, *Ursus americanus*	♀	260.51 (235.0–290.0)	244.80 (209.0–292.94)	212.93 (183.0–256.0)	130.94 (127.5–134.5)	133.0, 143.0
n=Total sample Sources		n=34 30[4],2[7],2[1]	n=82 12[2],2[3],25[4], 43[10]	n=17 12[2],4[3],1[7]	n=4[3]	n=2[7]
	♂	296.95 (262.0–349.0)	275.98 (229.0–318.0)	245.74 (206.0–291.0)	148.22 (141.6–158.3)	145.4, 150.6
n=Total sample Sources		n=55 50[4],2[7],3[1]	n=121 18[2],8[3],33[4], 62[10]	n=34 18[2],8[3],2[7],6[8]	n=9[3]	n=2[7]

Zygomatic breadth	Interorbital breadth	Rostrum width	Braincase breadth	Mastoidal breadth	Maxillary toothrow	Mandible length
70.8 (66.2–75.5)	23.4 (19.5–24.8)	20.1 (19.0–21.0)	46.8 (45.7–47.8)		61.7 (58.6–64.5)	
n=8[5]	n=8[5]	n=8[5]	n=8[5]		n=8[5]	
62.95 (49.36–72.6)	23.44 (20.0–27.1)	18.87 (14.97–23.34)	44.10 (37.39–49.10)	43.01 (34.06–48.5)	48.07 (38.16–54.47)	85.02 (69.39–95.28)
n= 530 9[2],25[4],9[3],1[6], 7[14],479[15]	n= 51 9[2],25[4],9[3], 1[6],7[14]	n=513 25[4],9[3],479[15]	n=497 9[2],9[3],479[15]	n=505 25[4],1[6],479[15]	n=505 9[2],9[3],1[6], 7[14],479[15]	n=498 9[2],10[1],479[15]
64.96 (51.05–72.3)	24.42 (20.3–27.9)	19.47 (15.18–22.74)	44.78 (37.94–48.94)	44.28 (33.33–48.81)	49.69 (38.76–55.86)	88.22 (70.81–97.39)
n= 634 11[2],46[4],8[3],3[6], 5[14],561[15]	n= 73 11[2],46[4],8[3], 3[6],5[14]	n=615 46[4],8[3],561[15]	n=580 11[2],8[3],561[15]	n=610 46[4],3[6],561[15]	n=584 11[2],4[3],3[6], 5[14],561[15]	n=582 11[2],10[1], 561[15]
65.1 (61.8–68.8)	23.7 (21.7–25.1)		44.2 (42.8–45.2)			
n=16[5]	n=16[5]		n=16[5]			
55.28 (51.1–61.4)	30.28 (27.0–34.2)	16.34 (15.4–17.8)	39.78 (37.6–42.2)	38.26 (37.0–40.4)	41.88 (38.5–45.5)	70.78 (66.48–74.24)
n=203[12]	n=203[12]	n=33[4]	n=203[12]	n=33[4]	n=203[12]	n=13[1]
57.04 (53.6–62.1)	31.06 (27.5–35.0)	16.67 (15.4–18.3)	40.37 (37.6–42.6)	38.73 (36.0–41.8)	43.15 (40.3–46.3)	72.92 (68.18–75.30)
n=201[12]	n=201[12]	n=34[4]	n=201[12]	n=34[4]	n=201[12]	n=11[1]

Rostrum width	Zygomatic breadth	Interorbital breadth	Postorbital constriction	Braincase breadth	Mastoidal breadth	Maxillary toothrow	Mandible length
53.41 (49.0–59.0)	147.96 (124.0–173.9)	53.46 (46.0–62.8)		77.72 (70.0–82.8)	117.8, 127.8	83.73 (78.0–94.0)	156.54 (144.0–172.62)
n=32[4]	n=45 12[2],4[3],27[4],2[7]	n=18 12[2],4[3],2[7]		n=12[2]	n=2[7]	n=12[2]	n=14 12[2],2[1]
61.46 (55.0–71.0)	172.35 (129.0–210.0)	63.09 (50.0–77.8)		83.23 (77.0–95.7)	146.49 (122.9–152.0)	91.09 (85.0–102.0)	176.03 (158.0–215.82)
n=63 54[4],9[8]	n=78 18[2],9[3],40[4],2[7],9[8]	n=29 18[2],9[3],2[7]		n=18[2]	n=9 2[7],7[8]	n=18[2]	n=22 18[2],4[1]

Family Ursidae *continued*

Species	Sex	Greatest length	Condylobasal length	Basilar length	Palatal length	Palatilar length
Brown or grizzly bear, *Ursus arctos*	♀	313.54 (230.32–367.0)	293.02 (271.5–308.0)	266.33 (263.0–270.0)	139.0	
n=Total sample Sources		n=9[1]	n=6 2[2],3[6],1[9]	n=3 2[2],1[8]	n=1[9]	
	♂	378.8 (299.0–422.0)	337.86 (236.30–429.10)	324.39 (305.1–343.0)	175.64 (124.8–208.9)	
n=Total sample Sources		n=10[1]	n=21 8[3],4[6],9[9]	n=10 8[3],2[8]	n=18 9[3],9[9]	
Polar bear, *Ursus maritimus***	♀	345.0 (337.0–350.0)	336.77 (333.79–347.2)			
n=Total sample		n=3[1]	n=53[5]			
	♂	386.0 (318.0–410.0)	387.83 (382.4–411.47)			
n=Total sample		n=6[1]	n=90[5]			

1=author, 2=Verts and Carraway (1998), 3=Hoffmeister (1986), 4=Graham (1991), 5=Manning (1971), 6=Armstrong (1972), 7=Lowery (1974), 8=Grinnell et al. (1937), 9=Rausch (1953), 10=Meiri et al. (2004b)

**adults only, and subset of data used to create parameters

Families Otariidae, Odobenidae, and Phocidae

Table in millimeters. Mean and parameters on top. Total number of specimens measured and specific number in cited sources below.

Species	Sex	Greatest length	Condylobasal length	Basilar length	Palatal length
Northern fur seal, *Callorhinus ursinus*	♀		170.0 (160.0–190.0)	152.8 (141.46–173.0)	
n=Total sample			n=3[2]	n=3[2]	
	♂		247.0	224.0	
n=Total sample			n=1[2]	n=1[2]	
Steller's sea lion, *Eumetopias jubatus*	♀		306.8 (300.0–312.0)	276.8 (271.0–282.0)	
n=Total sample			n=5[2]	n=5[2]	
	♂		361.92 (345.0–374.0)	331.2 (301.0–353.0)	
n=Total sample			n=4[2]	n=4[2]	
California sea lion, *Zalophus californianus*	♀	237.55 (232.92–253.29)			
n=Total sample		n=8[1]			
	♂	279.83 (265.22–304.80)	277.2 (261.0–293.0)	249.4 (232.0–264.0)	
n=Total sample		n=11[1]	n=14[2]	n=14[2]	

Rostrum width	Zygomatic breadth	Interorbital breadth	Postorbital constriction	Braincase breadth	Mastoidal breadth	Maxillary toothrow	Mandible length
68.8	185.69 (151.0–215.54)	68.74 (59.6–83.14)		91.0, 94.0	139.07 (108.8–166.18)	116.01 (108.5–126.5)	224.83 (202.0–292.45)
n=1[8]	n=11 2[2],4[6],1[8],3[1],1[9]	n=10 2[2],4[6],3[1],1[9]		n=2[2]	n=4 1[8],2[1],1[9]	n=7 2[2],4[6],1[9]	n=11 2[2],9[1]
78.0, 83.0	227.18 (131.8–295.0)	81.39 (53.10–96.68)			167.34 (95.1–264.66)	129.93 (109.1–157.4)	252.75 (203.0–287.2)
n=2[8]	n=24 8[3],4[6],4[1],8[9]	n=26 9[3],4[6],4[1],9[9]			n=11 2[8],3[1],6[9]	n=13 4[6],9[9]	n=10[1]
79.17 75.94–82.18)	198.75 (195.64–203.95)	81.50 (79.58–87.26)	66.29 (64.65–70.19)		145.67 (142.03–151.92)		233.11 (228.90–238.96)
n=3[1]	n=52[5]	n=53[5]	n=52[5]		n=45[5]		n=3[1]
95.93 87.06–100.62)	245.81 (242.03–260.39)	99.97 (97.99–109.04)	71.42 (70.43–73.67)		180.75 (178.92–185.41)		256.50 (213.84–278.68)
n=3[1]	n=85[5]	n=89[5]	n=82[5]		n=82[5]		n=5[1]

Zygomatic breadth	Interorbital breadth	Braincase breadth	Mastoidal breadth	Maxillary toothrow	Mandible length
98.31 (92.0–107.0)	21.29 (18.34–23.54)	89.95 (83.0–95.0)		45.43 (45.0–45.85)	106.19 (96.0–120.0)
n=3[2]	n=3[2]	n=3[2]		n=3[2]	n=3[2]
146.0	45.0	98.0		71.0	173.0
n=1[2]	n=1[2]	n=1[2]		n=1[2]	n=1[2]
169.82 (165.0–175.0)	62.39 (61.0–64.0)	123.52 (121.0–126.0)		108.56 (106.0–116.0)	222.64 (214.18–229.0)
n=5[2]	n=5[2]	n=5[2]		n=5[2]	n=4[2]
217.98 (203.0–234.0)	89.82 (83.0–96.0)	133.54 (125.0–139.0)		129.39 (126.0–134.56)	278.06 (266.0–291.24)
n=5[2]	n=5[2]	n=5[2]		n=4[2]	n=5[2]
123.27 (119.66–126.76)	34.86 (28.52–37.34)	100.39 (97.21–102.98)			154.78 (139.72–170.61)
n=8[1]	n=8[1]	n=8[1]			n=8[1]
158.71 (144.0–175.0)	49.14 (44.0–54.0)	105.86 (101.0–114.0)		81.86 (72.0–95.0)	200.79 (185.0–217.0)
n=14[2]	n=14[2]	n=14[2]		n=14[2]	n=14[2]

Families Otariidae, Odobenidae, and Phocidae *continued*

Species	Sex	Greatest length	Condylobasal length	Basilar length	Palatal length
Walrus, *Odobenus rosmarus*	♀ ♂	361.0 (319.0–396.0)	250.0–430.0		
n=Total sample		n=5[1]	n=?[4]		
Harbor seal, *Phoca vitulina*	♀	202.57 (182.66–221.04)	196.9 (180.0–210.0)	178.1 (161.0–190.0)	85.98 (77.86–93.68)
n=Total sample Sources		n=8[1]	n=5[2]	n=5[2]	n=8[1]
	♂	201.87 (174.86–216.72)	211.5 (210.0–213.0)	185.50 (185.0–186.0)	85.04 (71.7–95.73)
n=Total sample Sources		n=5[1]	n=2[2]	n=2[2]	n=5[1]
Northern elephant seal, *Mirounga angustirostris*	♀	263.29 (232.60–311.0)			
n=Total sample		n=3[1]			
	♂	512.33 (499.0–525.0)			
n=Total sample		n=3[1]			

1=author, 2=Verts and Carraway (1998), 3=Lowery (1974), 4=Heptner et al. (1976) in Fay (1985)

Family Procyonidae

Table in millimeters. Mean and parameters on top. Total number of specimens measured and specific number in cited sources below.

Species	Sex	Greatest length	Condylobasal length	Basilar length	Palatal length	Palatilar length
Ringtail, *Bassariscus astutus*	♀	76.40 (70.40–84.84)	74.01 (69.8–83.12)	68.19 (66.0–71.0)		32.86 (31.5–35.2)
n=Total sample Sources		n=23 8[3],4[5],11[1]	n=53 3[2],8[3],6[6],6[7],30[9]	n=12 6[3],6[7]		n=10 4[5],6[7]
	♂	79.49 (74.17–83.42)	76.76 (73.47–80.8)	70.51 (68.14–72.4)		34.51 (33.5–36.1)
n=Total sample Sources		n=19 6[3],3[5],10[1]	n=47 3[2],5[3],11[6],7[7],21[9]	n=14 3[2],4[3],7[7]		n=10 3[5],7[7]
Northern raccoon, *Procyon lotor*	♀	111.69 (93.6–126.5)	108.84 (89.4–120.5)	100.76 (92.61–111.0)		63.08 (56.8–71.6)
n=Total sample Sources		n=79 28[5],12[7],7[1],32[8]	n=81 29[2],6[4],2[6], 12[7],32[8]	n=42 30[2],12[7]		n=40 28[5],12[7]
	♂	115.35 (93.6–135.5)	113.68 (101.8–126.0)	105.65 (96.93–116.3)		64.72 (57.7–74.8)
n=Total sample Sources		n=119 13[3],45[5],13[7], 10[1],38[8]	n=103 30[2],13[3],7[4], 2[6],13[7],38[8]	n=43 30[2],13[7]		n=58 45[5],13[7]

Zygomatic breadth	Interorbital breadth	Braincase breadth	Mastoidal breadth	Maxillary toothrow	Mandible length
242.59 (203.54–274.60)	82.17 (71.89–90.14)		285.32 (226.46–322.0)		262.64 (229.27–290.39)
n=5[1]	n=5[1]		n=5[1]		n=5[1]
121.72 (106.74–144.01)	12.25 (9.65–17.08)	93.93 (87.8–101.26)		46.62 (37.25–57.21)	130.40 (116.07–151.42)
n=13 5[2],8[1]	n=13 5[2],8[1]	n=13 5[2],8[1]		n=5[2]	n=13 5[2],8[1]
126.96 (104.20–147.88)	14.50 (12.74–16.86)	94.76 (89.48–99.0)		57.0, 62.0	134.22 (109.90–144.66)
n=7 2[2],5[1]	n=7 2[2],5[1]	n=7 2[2],5[1]		n=2[2]	n=7 2[2],5[1]
176.42 (156.88–207.74)	34.91 (29.76–44.48)	143.73 (138.12–154.92)			177.01 (148.30–221.40)
n=3[1]	n=3[1]	n=3[1]			n=3[1]
302.67 (292.0–311.0)	62.37 (59.38–65.27)		271.65 (262.26–278.96)		357.67 (353.0–360.0)
n=3[1]	n=3[1]		n=3[1]		n=3[1]

Zygomatic breadth	Interorbital breadth	Braincase breadth	Mastoidal breadth	Maxillary toothrow	Mandible length
46.41 (40.8–50.7)	15.42 (14.0–17.2)	34.27 (33.53–35.2)	33.64 (31.9–36.0)	29.75 (29.2–31.16)	51.41 (46.54–58.72)
n=27 3[2],8[3],4[5],6[6],6[7]	n=27 3[2],8[3],4[5],6[6],6[7]	n=7 3[2],4[5]	n=18 6[3],6[6],6[7]	n=9 3[2],6[6]	n=14 3[2],11[1]
49.01 (45.97–55.4)	15.57 (14.3–17.7)	35.19 (33.18–37.3)	34.88 (33.3–37.9)	30.42 (28.5–31.8)	53.89 (47.73–56.88)
n=28 3[2],5[3],3[5],11[6],6[7]	n=29 3[2],6[3],3[5],11[6],6[7]	n=6 3[2],3[5]	n=22 4[3],11[6],7[7]	n=14 3[2],11[6]	n=13 3[2],10[1]
71.31 (48.03–82.7)	23.51 (15.57–28.87)	49.84 (33.42–56.53)	64.39 (59.3–68.5)	38.81 (31.29–44.3)	81.25 (72.47–86.17)
n=110 30[2],6[4],28[5],2[6], 12[7],32[8]	n=104 30[2],28[5],2[6], 12[7],32[8]	n=58 30[2],28[5]	n=14 2[6],12[7]	n=70 30[2],6[4],2[6],32[8]	n=38 30[2],8[1]
74.70 (57.8–90.66)	23.86 (19.3–28.8)	51.31 (43.9–58.85)	68.3 (64.2–72.7)	39.75 (34.85–46.9)	85.92 (74.65–91.33)
n=147 30[2],12[3],7[4], 45[5], 2[6],13[7],38[8]	n=141 30[2],13[3], 45[5], 2[6],13[7],38[8]	n=88 30[2],13[3],45[5]	n=15 2[6],13[7]	n=73 30[2],3[4],2[6],38[8]	n=40 30[2],10[1]

Family Procyonidae *continued*

Species	Sex	Greatest length	Condylobasal length	Basilar length	Palatal length	Palatilar length
White-nosed coati, *Nasua narica*	♀	123.10 (119.44–126.75)	116.55 (96.18–127.00)		76.28 (72.6–83.94)	
n=Total sample Sources		n=13 7[3],6[1]	n=15 7[3],8[9]		n=13 7[3],6[1]	
	♂	129.70 (123.27–138.00)	125.46 (121.08–130.25)		79.92 (76.2–85.78)	
n=Total sample Sources		n=11 4[3],7[1]	n=7 4[3],3[9]		n=11 4[3],7[1]	

1=author, 2=Verts and Carraway (1998), 3=Hoffmeister (1986), 4=Paradiso (1969), 5=Lowery (1974), 6=Armstrong (1972), 7=Grinnell et al. (1937), 8=Goldman (1950), 9=Meiri et al. (2004b)

Family Mustelidae

Table in millimeters. Mean and parameters on top. Total number of specimens measured and specific number in cited sources below.

Species	Sex	Greatest length	Condylobasal length	Basilar length	Palatal length	Palatilar length
American marten, *Martes americana*	♀	72.78 (67.68–78.88)	73.75 (66.51–86.25)	64.13 (59.8–69.03)	36.25 (32.48–39.8)	32.98 (30.8–34.7)
n=Total sample Sources		n=34 20[7],14[1]	n=361 27[2],2[6],20[7],5[11],307[13]	n=47 27[2],20[7]	n=11 5[1],6[11]	n=20[7]
	♂	79.99 (69.20–87.92)	80.26 (67.30–88.84)	70.93 (64.59–74.28)	40.13 (33.08–43.7)	37.77 (35.0–39.9)
n=Total sample Sources		n=36 24[7],12[1]	n=571 42[2],1[6],24[7], 11[11],493[13]	n=66 42[2],24[7]	n=16 5[1],11[11]	n=24[7]
Fisher, *Martes pennanti*	♀	101.71 (98.70–105.3)	100.56 (95.0–120.09)	91.80 (87.2–104.11)		50.09 (48.0–52.2)
n=Total sample Sources		n=23 10[7],13[1]	n=68 3[2],10[7],55[13]	n=13 3[2],10[7]		n=10[7]
	♂	122.06 (112.8–135.02)	113.69 (98.79–120.15)	104.9 (101.5–107.4)		58.7 (56.5–60.0)
n=Total sample Sources		n=22 10[7],12[1]	n=61 10[7],51[13]	n=10[7]		n=10[7]
Ermine or short-tailed weasel (northern), Mustela erminea	♀	37.99 (37.28–38.32)		33.95 (31.5–37.0)	15.44 (14.78–15.92)	
n=Total sample Sources		n=4[1]		n=31 1[8],30[9]	n=4[1]	
	♂	44.28 (43.20–46.03)		38.79 (35.6–45.2)	18.67 (17.41–19.42)	
n=Total sample Sources		n=5[1]		n=90 2[8],88[9]	n=5[1]	

Zygomatic breadth	Interorbital breadth	Braincase breadth	Mastoidal breadth	Maxillary toothrow	Mandible length
64.11 (57.30–66.85)	27.96 (25.66–30.2)	46.09 (45.55–46.8)	43.73 (42.44–46.10)	47.36 (46.0–48.5)	87.33 (83.76–91.66)
n=13 7[3],6[1]	n=13 7[3],6[1]	n=7[3]	n=6[1]	n=7[3]	n=6[1]
71.00 (59.20–82.78)	28.90 (25.50–32.48)	47.38 (46.7–48.0)	47.39 (44.41–49.19)	48.21 (46.6–50.8)	92.12 (87.98–98.65)
n=10 3[3],7[1]	n=11 4[3],7[1]	n=4[3]	n=7[1]	n=4[3]	n=7[1]

Zygomatic breadth	Interorbital breadth	Braincase breadth	Mastoidal breadth	Maxillary toothrow	Mandible length
40.54 (35.00–47.0)	16.26 (14.62–18.5)	33.34 (30.76–35.88)	32.38 (28.80–36.8)	27.38 (24.83–29.79)	45.16 (41.22–50.89)
n=60 27[2],2[6],20[7],5[1],6[11]	n=60 27[2],2[6],20[7],5[1],6[11]	n=32 27[2],5[1]	n=33 6[6],20[7],5[1],6[11]	n=35 27[2],2[6],6[11]	n=41 27[2],14[1]
46.17 (37.78–53.1)	18.15 (15.06–20.05)	34.98 (30.78–38.19)	35.67 (30.10–39.0)	29.89 (27.27–32.0)	50.94 (42.08–57.42)
n=83 42[2],1[6],24[7],5[1],11[11]	n=82 42[2],1[6],24[7],5[1],10[11]	n=47 42[2],5[1]	n=40 1[6],24[7],5[1],10[11]	n=53 42[2],1[6],10[11]	n=54 42[2],12[1]
57.35 (51.12–67.14)	22.62 (19.8–27.0)	42.34 (41.14–45.00)	45.20 (43.13–47.0)	40.51 (38.09–43.86)	67.17 (64.06–80.46)
n=20 3[2],10[7],7[1]	n=20 3[2],10[7],7[1]	n=10 3[2],7[1]	n=17 10[7],7[1]	n=3[2]	n=15 3[2],12[1]
71.03 (60.60–83.64)	25.99 (23.60–27.34)	45.77 (44.16–47.50)	53.44 (49.87–57.22)		81.56 (76.70–87.20)
n=19 10[7],9[1]	n=18 10[7],8[1]	n=8[1]	n=19 10[7],9[1]		n=11[1]
19.49 (17.1–23.0)	8.26 (7.2–10.3)		17.46 (15.4–19.4)	11.96 (10.8–13.4)	19.41 (18.68–21.08)
n=31 1[8],30[9]	n=30[9]		n=31 1[8],30[9]	n=31 1[8],30[9]	n=4[1]
23.43 (20.4–28.8)	10.6 (8.4–13.3)		20.33 (18.0–23.5)	13.81 (12.3–16.6)	23.74 (22.28–24.88)
n=90 2[8],88[9]	n=88[9]		n=90 2[8],88[9]	n=90 2[8],88[9]	n=5[1]

Family Mustelidae *continued*

Species	Sex	Greatest length	Condylobasal length	Basilar length	Palatal length	Palatilar length
Ermine or short-tailed weasel (southern), *Mustela erminea*	♀	35.51 (33.92–36.52)	32.01 (30.92–33.69)	30.00 (26.7–35.1)	13.87 (13.18–14.50)	
n=Total sample Sources		*n*=11[1]	*n*=28 26[2],2[6]	*n*=75 26[2],49[9]	*n*=11[1]	
	♂	40.82 (38.71–44.32)	35.54 (33.6–37.42)	34.44 (29.8–40.7)	16.24 (15.20–17.70)	
n=Total sample Sources		*n*=12[1]	*n*=28 26[2],2[6]	*n*=125 26[2],99[9]	*n*=12[1]	
Long-tailed weasel, *Mustela frenata*	♀	43.25 (38.40–46.62)	42.66 (34.79–49.5)	38.45 (33.55–47.3)	17.56 (16.1–20.0)	
n=Total sample Sources		*n*=14[1]	*n*=259 25[2],5[3], 12[6],217[13]	*n*=138 25[2],5[3], 3[4],105[9]	*n*=10 5[3],5[1]	
	♂	49.88 (45.60–53.6)	47.87 (39.49–54.52)	44.38 (37.32–51.3)	20.43 (17.8–22.62)	20.3 (18.4–22.0)
n=Total sample Sources		*n*=29 7[5],22[1]	*n*=522 57[2],4[3], 4[6],457[13]	*n*=282 57[2],4[3], 10[4],211[9]	*n*=10 4[3],6[1]	*n*=7[5]
Black-footed ferret, *Mustela nigripes*	♀		64.64 (60.1–68.4)	61.8	30.2	
n=Total sample Sources			*n*=13 1[3],6[6],6[13]	*n*=1[3]	*n*=1[3]	
	♂	67.62 (62.50–69.96)	67.63 (61.71–73.13)		32.40 (30.07–34.04)	
n=Total sample Sources		*n*=7[1]	*n*=33 3[6],30[13]		*n*=7[1]	
Least weasel, *Mustela nivalis*	♀	30.33 (29.04–32.96)	30.21 (26.88–37.31)	27.41 (24.7–28.8)	11.93 (10.90–13.24)	
n=Total sample Sources		*n*=10[1]	*n*=72 3[12],69[13]	*n*=14[9]	*n*=3[1]	
	♂	32.76 (30.28–35.46)	32.97 (29.41–43.99)	29.47 (27.6–30.7)	11.10	
n=Total sample Sources		*n*=10[1]	*n*=103 9[12],94[13]	*n*=16[9]	*n*=1[1]	
American mink, *Mustela vison*	♀	56.64 (53.28–60.1)	61.25 (54.8–73.02)	56.36 (51.73–65.69)	24.74 (23.40–26.38)	25.31 (23.4–27.5)
n=Total sample Sources		*n*=16 6[5],10[1]	*n*=47 19[2],6[6],10[7],12[12]	*n*=29 19[2],10[7]	*n*=10[1]	*n*=16 6[5],10[7]
	♂	64.53 (58.32–70.6)	67.39 (61.6–76.41)	61.27 (55.54–69.94)	27.09 (24.50–28.47)	28.24 (25.0–31.4)
n=Total sample Sources		*n*=28 19[5],9[1]	*n*=88 31[2],12[6],30[7],15[12]	*n*=61 31[2],30[7]	*n*=8[1]	*n*=49 19[5],30[7]

Zygomatic breadth	Interorbital breadth	Braincase breadth	Mastoidal breadth	Maxillary toothrow	Mandible length
16.54 (14.4–18.9)	7.31 (6.3–8.4)	14.88 (13.85–16.66)	15.37 (13.1–18.7)	9.93 (8.36–12.7)	16.45 (15.22–17.70)
n=72 26[2],2[6],44[9]	n=77 26[2],2[6],49[9]	n=26[2]	n=49[9]	n=77 26[2],2[6],49[9]	n=37 26[2],11[1]
19.66 (17.0–24.3)	8.66 (7.0–10.6)	16.35 (15.13–17.61)	17.87 (15.0–20.6)	11.83 (9.0–15.0)	19.11 (17.24–22.36)
n=121 26[2],2[6],93[9]	n=127 26[2],2[6],99[9]	n=26[2]	n=99[9]	n=127 26[2],2[6],99[9]	n=38 26[2],12[1]
22.76 (19.3–27.4)	9.10 (7.66–10.8)	19.76 (18.37–22.14)	20.31 (17.2–24.5)	13.96 (10.09–16.9)	23.42 (19.68–30.10)
n=149 25[2],5[3],2[4], 12[6],105[9]	n=150 25[2],5[3],3[4], 12[6],105[9]	n=25[2]	n=124 5[3],3[4],11[6], 105[9]	n=147 25[2],5[3], 12[6],105[9]	n=39 25[2],14[1]
27.66 (22.03–33.2)	10.78 (8.55–13.00)	21.69 (19.28–25.18)	24.04 (21.4–27.7)	16.36 (12.71–18.9)	27.46 (22.83–31.85)
n=292 57[2],4[3],10[4],7[5], 3[6],211[9]	n=293 57[2],4[3],10[4], 7[5],4[6],211[9]	n=64 57[2],7[5]	n=229 4[3],10[4], 4[6],211[9]	n=276 57[2],4[3], 4[6],211[9]	n=78 57[2],21[1]
38.71 (36.3–40.8)	16.26 (15.3–17.3)		34.83 (32.5–37.1)	20.33 (18.8–24.5)	
n=7 1[3],6[6]	n=7 1[3],6[6]		n=7 1[3],6[6]	n=7 1[3],6[6]	
41.72 (38.05–46.17)	17.23 (15.78–19.02)	29.11 (26.86–30.42)	36.01 (32.60–38.17)	20.03 (19.3–20.6)	42.28 (39.01–44.25)
n=9 2[6],7[1]	n=11 1[3],3[6],7[1]	n=7[1]	n=10 3[6],7[1]	n=3[6]	n=7[1]
15.11 (13.7–16.5)	6.22 (5.2–7.2)		13.92 (12.3–15.2)	9.31 (8.5–9.8)	15.20 (13.67–16.78)
n=15 12[9],3[12]	n=16 13[9],3[12]		n=16 13[9],3[12]	n=16 13[9],3[12]	n=3[1]
17.05 (15.2–18.0)	7.00 (6.3–7.8)		15.44 (14.0–16.3)	10.15 (9.6–15.0)	14.85, 15.92
n=22 17[9],5[12]	n=23 16[9],7[12]		n=24 17[9],7[12]	n=24 17[9],7[12]	n=2[1]
35.18 (30.3–43.87)	13.97 (11.8–17.52)	27.94 (25.00–31.37)	29.50 (26.9–31.7)	20.19 (16.15–23.63)	36.42 (30.58–45.96)
n=53 19[2],6[5],6[6],10[7],12[12]	n=47 19[2],6[5],10[7],12[12]	n=25 19[2],6[5]	n=27 6[6],9[7],12[12]	n=25 19[2],6[6]	n=29 19[2],10[1]
39.00 (33.5–45.99)	15.43 (12.5–18.7)	28.93 (26.45–32.81)	33.95 (31.0–37.1)	21.74 (19.0–25.31)	40.67 (33.47–47.30)
n=106 31[2],19[5],12[6], 29[7],15[12]	n=95 31[2],19[5], 30[7],15[12]	n=50 31[2],19[5]	n=57 12[6],30[7],15[12]	n=43 31[2],12[6]	n=40 31[2],9[1]

Family Mustelidae *continued*

Species	Sex	Greatest length	Condylobasal length	Basilar length	Palatal length	Palatilar length
Wolverine, *Gulo gulo*	♀	144.50 (135.77–150.5)	133.96 (121.52–147.40)	120.13 (117.5–123.7)	69.4 (65.6–72.5)	67.25 (65.3–68.3)
n=Total sample Sources		n=12 6[7],6[1]	n=71 6[7],10[11],55[13]	n=6[7]	n=9[11]	n=6[7]
	♂	162.02 (153.18–173.42)	144.96 (128.65–156.12)	132.7, 133.2	75.37 (69.1–78.8)	74.6, 75.0
n=Total sample Sources		n=17 2[7],15[1]	n=121 1[7],3[8],24[11],93[13]	n=2[7]	n=23 3[8],20[11]	n=2[7]
American badger, *Taxidea taxus*	♀	116.47 (107.98–122.16)	123.66 (113.86–136.66)	111.46 (104.6–122.24)		59.38 (57.3–61.4)
n=Total sample Sources		n=10[1]	n=52 30[2],9[6],5[7],8[12]	n=35 30[2],5[7]		n=5[7]
	♂	121.40 (112.1–131.58)	126.03 (115.87–138.60)	114.43 (104.0–124.42)	61.94 (58.6–66.3)	61.65 (56.5–64.4)
n=Total sample Sources		n=21 11[3],10[1]	n=59 30[2],19[6],8[7],2[12]	n=38 30[2],8[7]	n=13[3]	n=8[7]
Northern river otter, *Lontra canadensis*	♀	106.74 (101.52–118.5)	111.94 (100.43–126.82)	97.36 (87.5–106.1)	48.01 (46.31–49.14)	48.55 (45.8–51.9)
n=Total sample Sources		n=21 3[5],7[7],11[1]	n=130 3[2],1[3],6[7],120[13]	n=13 3[2],1[3],2[4],7[7]	n=5[1]	n=11 1[3],3[5],7[7]
	♂	111.21 (106.06–129.9)	115.10 (102.16–128.45)	100.97 (95.8–117.4)	50.89 (49.10–52.16)	50.94 (48.1–57.4)
n=Total sample Sources		n=20 4[5],8[7],8[1]	n=138 2[2],8[7],128[13]	n=12 2[2],2[4],8[7]	n=5[1]	n=12 4[5],8[7]
Sea otter, *Enhydra lutris*	♀	130.02 (125.14–133.53)	127.70 (115.0–136.0)		58.16 (55.20–59.38)	
n=Total sample		n=8[1]	n=149[10]		n=8[1]	
	♂	141.62 (137.90–148.60)	134.97 (124.0–144.0)		61.84 (59.52–64.64)	
n=Total sample		n=8[1]	n=123[10]		n=8[1]	

1=author, 2=Verts and Carraway (1998), 3=Hoffmeister (1986), 4=Paradiso (1969), 5=Lowery (1974), 6=Armstrong (1972), 7=Grinnel et al. (1937), 8=Bee and Hall (1956), 9=Hall (1951), 10=Roest (1973), 11=Rausch (1953), 12=Hoffmeister (1989), 13=Meiri et al. (2004b)

Family Mephitidae

Table in millimeters. Mean and parameters on top. Total number of specimens measured and specific number in cited sources below.

Species	Sex	Greatest length	Condylobasal length	Basilar length	Palatal length	Palatilar length
Western spotted skunk, *Spilogale gracilis*	♀	53.95 (49.44–58.66)	51.92 (45.2–59.03)	45.66 (40.1–51.53)		18.81 (16.3–20.7)
n=Total sample Sources		n=28 18[8],10[1]	n=73 35[2],14[3],6[6],18[8]	n=67 35[2],14[3],18[8]		n=32 14[3],18[8]

Zygomatic breadth	Interorbital breadth	Braincase breadth	Mastoidal breadth	Maxillary toothrow	Mandible length
94.84 (89.8–99.6)	38.05 (36.0–39.4)		78.52 (77.4–79.5)	49.97` (46.6–53.0)	93.61 (90.12–97.92)
n=16 6[7],10[11]	n=15 6[7],9[11]		n=6[7]	n=9[11]	n=6[1]
104.74 (95.0–111.8)	41.21 (38.6–46.7)		87.0, 90.7	53.1 (42.9–55.6)	103.49 (98.45–109.35)
n=31 2[7],3[8],26[11]	n=31 2[7],3[8],26[11]		n=2[7]	n=28 3[8],25[11]	n=14[1]
77.60 (72.8–86.56)	27.74 (24.27–32.01)	57.12 (53.92–61.04)	74.57 (70.8–79.0)	41.18 (38.6–44.31)	83.75 (75.66–93.91)
n=52 30[2],9[6],5[7],8[12]	n=43 30[2],5[7],8[12]	n=30[2]	n=22 9[6],5[7],8[12]	n=39 30[2],9[6]	n=40 30[2],10[1]
81.46 (68.9–91.8)	28.69 (24.3–33.92)	58.41 (55.93–61.67)	78.37 (69.6–86.9)	41.69 (37.4–45.41)	88.07 (81.99–96.16)
n=71 30[2],12[3],19[6],8[7],2[12]	n=52 30[2],12[3],8[7],2[12]	n=30[2]	n=29 19[6],8[7],2[12]	n=62 30[2],13[3],19[6]	n=40 30[2],10[1]
69.53 (61.67–75.1)	23.75 (22.08–26.3)	55.38 (53.36–58.21)	63.92 (56.7–71.9)	35.85 (32.9–38.7)	65.98 (59.83–72.55)
n=20 3[2],1[3],1[4],3[5],7[7],5[1]	n=19 3[2],1[3],3[5],7[7],5[1]	n=8 3[2],5[1]	n=18 1[3],2[4],3[5],7[7],5[1]	n=9 3[2],1[3],2[4],3[5]	n=14 3[2],11[1]
73.18 (65.3–82.3)	24.56 (21.92–29.9)	56.81 (54.80–58.18)	67.28 (62.38–75.5)	37.93 (35.2–40.0)	68.56 (65.97–72.06)
n=20 2[2],1[4],4[5],8[7],5[1]	n=19 2[2],4[5],8[7],5[1]	n=7 2[2],5[1]	n=19 2[4],4[5],8[7],5[1]	n=8 2[2],2[4],4[5]	n=10 2[2],8[1]
95.63 (92.52–98.90)	36.61 (35.26–38.83)		91.74 (88.66–94.42)		79.99 (77.34–85.24)
n=8[1]	n=8[1]		n=8[1]		n=8[1]
103.78 (100.90–108.18)	41.29 (37.89–44.10)		99.71 (96.84–102.56)		87.45 (81.37–95.78)
n=8[1]	n=8[1]		n=8[1]		n=8[1]

*The northern data for Ermine included specimens from Alaska, Canada, Minnesota, and North Dakota. The southern included the remainder of the lower 48 states.
**Only northern specimens, which are larger than southern animals, included for "Greatest length."

Zygomatic breadth	Interorbital breadth	Braincase breadth	Mastoidal breadth	Maxillary toothrow	Mandible length
32.95 (28.8–38.45)	14.60 (12.5–16.63)	25.10 (22.31–28.98)	28.59 (24.6–32.1)	16.86 (14.88–18.78)	33.55 (29.67–39.26)
n=73 35[2],14[3],6[6],18[8]	n=73 35[2],14[3],6[6],18[8]	n=35[2]	n=38 14[3],6[6],18[8]	n=55 35[2],14[3],6[6]	n=44 34[2],10[1]

Family Mephitidae *continued*

Species	Sex	Greatest length	Condylobasal length	Basilar length	Palatal length	Palatilar length
Western spotted skunk, *Spilogale gracilis*	♂	58.96 (52.18–63.6)	55.96 (47.5–62.62)	49.27 (44.5–55.71)		20.26 (17.8–22.7)
n=Total sample Sources		*n*=49 39[8],10[1]	*n*=118 35[2],37[3],7[6],39[8]	*n*=111 35[2],37[3],39[8]		*n*=76 37[3],39[8]
Eastern spotted skunk, *Spilogale putorius*	♀		52.77 (45.3–58.8)	46.78 (40.1–52.4)		19.06 (16.0–21.2)
n=Total sample			*n*=99[5]	*n*=98[5]		*n*=119[5]
	♂		55.52 (46.7–61.9)	49.28 (41.4–54.5)		19.87 (16.5–22.7)
n=Total sample			*n*=168[5]	*n*=164[5]		*n*=188[5]
Striped skunk, *Mephitis mephitis*	♀	73.22 (69.02–81.5)	71.54 (61.0–77.72)	60.70 (54.0–67.95)	27.81 (25.92–29.21)	25.57 (22.2–28.8)
n=Total sample Sources		*n*=83 53[7],24[8],6[1]	*n*=120 12[2],11[3],20[6], 53[7],24[8]	*n*=47 12[2],11[3],24[8]	*n*=53[7]	*n*=35 11[3],24[8]
	♂	78.73 (67.94–87.97)	74.98 (63.7–83.41)	65.07 (54.9–73.03)	29.71 (26.81–32.70)	27.14 (23.9–32.0)
n=Total sample Sources		*n*=89 60[7],21[8],8[1]	*n*=146 22[2],12[3],31[6], 60[7],21[8]	*n*=55 22[2],12[3],21[8]	*n*=60[7]	*n*=33 12[3],21[8]
	♀♂		60.8 (58.9–69.7)	56.4 (52.5–60.6)		24.2 (22.7–26.9)
n=Total sample			*n*=17[4]	*n*=17[4]		*n*=17[4]
Hooded skunk, *Mephitis macroura*	♀	63.59 (51.84–67.94)	61.94 (60.9–63.8)	54.26 (53.45–55.25)		22.76 (21.7–24.2)
n=Total sample		*n*=11[1]	*n*=8[3]	*n*=8[3]		*n*=8[3]
	♂	68.23 (64.76–72.40)	65.52 (62.9–72.4)	57.67 (55.2–63.7)		24.01 (22.7–26.65)
n=Total sample		*n*=5[1]	*n*=9[3]	*n*=9[3]		*n*=9[3]
White-backed hog-nosed skunk, *Conepatus leuconotus*	♀	70.05 (65.02–75.18)	66.77 (62.2–73.5)	58.05 (54.9–64.8)		26.66 (24.4–30.1)
n=Total sample Sources		*n*=10[1]	*n*=54 10[3],44[9]	*n*=53 10[3],43[9]		*n*=61 10[3],51[9]
	♂	80.05 (76.14–84.50)	71.59 (66.4–76.3)	62.34 (57.7–66.1)		28.77 (25.8–30.9)
n=Total sample Sources	–	*n*=10[1]	*n*=46 13[3],1[6],32[9]	*n*=44 13[3],31[9]		*n*=47 13[3],34[9]

1= author, 2=Verts and Carraway (1998), 3=Hoffmeister (1986), 4=Lowery (1974), 5=Van Gelder (1959), 6=Armstrong (1972), 7=Verts (1967), 8=Grinnell et al. (1937), 9=Van Gelder (1968)

Zygomatic breadth	Interorbital breadth	Braincase breadth	Mastoidal breadth	Maxillary toothrow	Mandible length
36.04	15.48	26.17	31.68	18.05	36.46
(31.9–41.78)	(13.1–19.57)	(23.17–28.91)	(28.1–35.2)	(15.5–20.61)	(32.46–40.48)
n=117	n=118	n=35[2]	n=83	n=79	n=45
35[2],37[3],6[6],39[8]	35[2],37[3],7[6],39[8]		37[3],7[6],39[8]	35[2],37[3],7[6]	35[2],10[1]
31.95	14.37		27.84	17.67	
(28.0–35.9)	(13.2–15.9)		(25.4–31.4)	(15.2–19.0)	
n=88[5]	n=114[5]		n=100[5]	n=127[5]	
34.05	15.06		29.29	18.31	
(28.4–37.8)	(13.3–16.9)		(25.4–34.2)	(15.6–20.5)	
n=166[5]	n=185[5]		n=167[5]	n=208[5]	
45.76	20.60	28.84	38.62	26.01	47.51
(38.6–49.3)	(18.3–23.98)	(27.54–29.8)	(32.5–40.6)	(20.3–29.46)	(42.02–51.14)
n=120	n=47	n=12[2]	n=108	n=85	n=18
12[2],11[3],20[6],53[7],24[8]	12[2],11[3],24[8]		11[3],20[6],53[7],24[8]	12[2],11[3],9[6],53[7]	12[2],6[1]
48.33	21.96	29.46	40.72	26.46	49.43
(39.8–55.0)	(18.9–25.4)	(26.97–32.35)	(32.7–47.1)	(20.8–32.16)	(45.18–56.23)
n=145	n=55	n=22[2]	n=124	n=109	n=30
22[2],12[3],30[6],60[7],21[8]	22[2],12[3],21[8]		12[3],31[6],60[7],21[8]	22[2],12[3],15[6],60[7]	22[2],8[1]
40.2	19.1		34.2	21.3	
(31.3–45.7)	(17.5–21.0)		(32.0–38.3)	(19.7–22.7)	
n=17[4]	n=17[4]		n=17[4]	n=17[4]	
40.01	19.07		33.18	21.73	40.88
(37.5–41.25)	(18.4–19.5)		(30.9–34.9)	(21.2–22.3)	(35.91–42.10)
n=8[3]	n=8[3]		n=8[3]	n=8[3]	n=11[1]
42.58	20.46		35.51	22.22	43.80
(38.4–46.6)	(18.1–22.0)		(33.4–39.9)	(20.6–23.9)	(42.67–45.57)
n=9[3]	n=9[3]		n=9[3]	n=9[3]	n=5[1]
43.10	21.70		36.66	21.51	43.79
(38.7–47.5)	(19.5–24.6)		(33.0–39.5)	(18.1–23.5)	(40.74–47.18)
n=51	n=58		n=55	n=62	n=10[1]
10[3],1[6],40[9]	10[3],1[6],47[9]		10[3],45[9]	10[3],1[6],51[9]	
46.14	22.70		38.98	22.65	49.27
(40.6–54.0)	(20.1–26.0)		(34.8–45.3)	(20.8–24.2)	(46.88–52.56)
n=43	n=48		n=47	n=48	n=10[1]
13[3],1[6],29[9]	13[3],1[6],34[9]		13[3],1[6],33[9]	13[3],1[6],34[9]	

Family Felidae

*Table in millimeters. Mean and parameters on top. Total number
of specimens measured and specific number in cited sources below.*

Species	Sex	Greatest length	Condylobasal length	Basilar length	Palatilar length	Zygomatic breadth
Domestic or feral cat, *Felis catus*	♀	89.35 (77.50–99.28)				62.86 (54.82–68.40)
n=Total sample		*n*=5[1]				*n*=5[1]
	♂	95.38 (89.32–101.00)				66.99 (64.20–69.84)
n=Total sample		*n*=8[1]				*n*=8[1]
Cougar or mountain lion, *Puma concolor*	♀	181.29 (170.5–194.2)	166.46 (138.0–197.20)	137.14 (120.0–168.0)	71.15 (68.5–73.8)	125.45 (114.87–149.95)
n=Total sample Sources		*n*=19 4[4],13[5],2[1]	*n*=85 22[2],4[4],13[5],2[7],44[14]	*n*=26 22[2],4[4]	*n*=4[4]	*n*=41 22[2],4[4],13[5],2[7]
	♂	210.63 (199.00–220.02)	184.52 (155.0–204.17)	159.07 (136.0–182.6)	80.21 (77.8–85.0)	144.92 (131.81–160.0)
n=Total sample Sources		*n*=29 10[4],2[3],6[5], 2[8],9[1]	*n*=88 28[2],10[4],2[3],6[5], 3[7], 2[8],37[14]	*n*=37 28[2],9[4]	*n*=12 10[4],2[8]	*n*=51 28[2],10[4],2[3], 6[5],3[7],2[8]
Ocelot, *Leopardus pardalis*	♀	127.1				81.6
n=Total sample		*n*=1[8]				*n*=1[8]
	♂	130.80 (121.0–142.3)	114.8 (114.0–115.6)			86.94 (82.0–94.76)
n=Total sample Sources		*n*=7 3[6],4[8]	*n*=3[6]			*n*=7 3[6],4[8]
	♀	(117.0–140.7)	(118.0–132.0)	(103.0–118.0)		(86.0–96.4)
n=Total sample		*n*=?[10]	*n*=?[10]	*n*=?[10]		*n*=?[10]
	♂	(129.0–158.0)	(130.0–139.0)	(105.0–139.0)		(90.0–108.0)
n=Total sample		*n*=?[10]	*n*=?[10]	*n*=?[10]		*n*=?[10]
Margay, *Leopardus wiedii*	♀♂	92.1* (86.6–107.0)	83.9 (81.1–94.0)			61.9* (55.9–72.2)
n=Total sample		*n*=33[12],?[13]	*n*=33[12]			*n*=33[12],?[13]
Jaguarundi, *Herpailurus yaguarondi*	♀♂	95.0 (86.7–116.1)	94.5 (81.2–109.2)		37.4 (33.4–41.6)	61.5 (55.6–72.7)
n=Total sample		*n*=23[11]	*n*=23[11]		*n*=23[11]	*n*=23[11]
Canada lynx, *Lynx canadensis*	♀	124.09 (117.60–129.30)	112.86 (98.99–126.24)	102.61 (99.49–105.66)	45.20 (42.68–47.66)	87.51 (82.18–91.40)
n=Total sample Sources		*n*=9[1]	*n*=135 4[2],131[14]	*n*=4[2]	*n*=9[1]	*n*=13 4[2],9[1]

Interorbital breadth	Rostrum width	Braincase breadth	Mastoidal breadth	Maxillary toothrow	Mandible length
17.30 (14.48–19.00) n=5[1]			39.76 (36.10–42.64) n=5[1]		59.02 (50.80–64.00) n=5[1]
18.03 (15.86–19.90) n=8[1]			42.71 (41.12–44.59) n=8[1]		62.18 (56.74–65.86) n=8[1]
37.15 (33.74–44.06) n=41 22[2],4[4],13[5],2[7]	50.9 (49.1–51.7) n=4[4]	68.73 (57.34–79.0) n=22[2]	68.36 (55.0–79.3) n=5 3[4],2[7]	57.03 (52.9–63.04) n=37 22[2],13[5],2[7]	123.93 (113.98–144.51) n=28 22[2],4[4],2[1]
43.56 (38.51–48.0) n=51 28[2],10[4],2[3], 6[5],3[7],2[8]	58.38 (55.3–60.6) n=10[4]	71.93 (66.63–77.06) n=28[2]	83.81 (59.9–96.4) n=15 10[4],3[7],2[8]	63.11 (57.5–66.81) n=41 28[2],2[3],6[5], 3[7],2[8]	141.69 (128.58–150.75) n=47 28[2],10[4],9[1]
21.8 n=1[8]				40.1 n=1[8]	80.04 (74.74–83.80) n=7[1]
23.69 (21.8–25.2) n=7 3[6],4[8]				39.44 (35.5–43.5) n=7 3[6],4[8]	87.81 (77.80–96.38) n=6[1]
(19.0–29.8) n=?[10]					
(24.0–32.0) n=?[10]					
16.6 (14.9–19.1) n=33[12]		44.5 (41.0–46.6) n=33[12]		27.9* (24.7–30.7) n=33[12],?[13]	58.25 (52.50–61.68) n=15[1]
17.0 (13.3–20.8) n=23[11]		44.4 (40.3–48.5) n=23[11]		29.8 (26.2–33.2) n=23[11]	61.94 (54.90–67.76) n=15[1]
27.83 (25.83–30.18) n=13 4[2],9[1]		56.93 (54.24–58.78) n=13 4[2],9[1]	53.10 (51.07–55.38) n=9[1]	40.46 (39.19–42.9) n=4[2]	81.95 (78.50–87.14) n=13 4[2],9[1]

Family Felidae *continued*

Species	Sex	Greatest length	Condylobasal length	Basilar length	Palatilar length	Zygomatic breadth
Canada lynx, *Lynx canadensis*	♂	130.28 (117.41–135.82)	118.02 (104.04–126.48)	106.62	47.56 (41.94–49.54)	91.84 (83.02–96.50)
n=Total sample Sources		n=9[1]	n=125 1[2],1[7],123[14]	n=1[2]	n=9[1]	n=11 1[2],1[7],9[1]
Bobcat, *Lynx rufus*	♀	116.16 (105.8–136.68)	109.65 (99.06–131.28)	97.53 (90.84–117.07)	42.56 (39.2–45.7)	83.79 (76.0–100.11)
n=Total sample Sources		n=27 12[4],6[3],5[8],4[1]	n=98 47[2],6[3],9[7],36[14]	n=58 47[2],11[4]	n=17 12[4],5[8]	n=78 47[2],12[4],6[3],9[7],4[8]
	♂	123.80 (114.5–145.20)	116.35 (94.28–134.15)	102.96 (94.8–118.96)	46.46 (42.4–53.67)	89.11 (79.4–104.33)
n=Total sample Sources		n=45 28[4],8[3],5[8],4[1]	n=111 39[2],8[3],8[7],56[14]	n=67 39[2],28[4]	n=34 28[4],6[8]	n=91 39[2],28[4],8[3],8[7],6[8],2[1]
Jaguar, *Panthera onca*	♀	221.68 (203.88–247.50)	193.1		87.52 (83.76–97.90)	154.47 (153.86–155.4)
n=Total sample Sources		n=4 1[3],3[1]	n=1[3]		n=3[1]	n=3 1[3],2[1]
	♂	256.04 (235.62–275.0)	232.40 (224.2–240.5)		99.05 (93.12–106.73)	173.54 (165.52–188.0)
n=Total sample Sources		n=8 4[3],4[1]	n=4[3]		n=4[1]	n=8 4[3],4[1]
	♀♂		218.2 (177.0–276.0)			165.2 (129.0–212.0)
n=Total sample			n=112[9]			n=112[9]

1=author, 2=Verts and Carraway (1998), 3=Hoffmeister (1986), 4=Grinnell et al. (1937), 5=Goldman(1946) in Hoffmeister (1986), 6=Goldman (1943) in Hoffmeister (1986), 7=Armstrong (1972), 8=Lowery (1974), 9=Seymour (1989), 10=Murray and Gardner (1997), 11=Oliveira (1998a), 12=Oliveira (1998b), 13=Hall (1981), 14=Meiri et al. (2004b)

*mean calculated without Hall (1981)

Families Delphinidae, Trichechidae, Equidae, Suidae, and Tayassuidae

Table in millimeters. Mean and parameters on top. Total number of specimens measured and specific number in cited sources below.

Species	Sex	Greatest length	Basal length	Palatal length	Nasal length	Braincase breadth
Bottle-nosed dolphin, *Tursiops truncatus*	♀♂	476.63 (425.0–517.5)				
n=Total sample		n=4[1]				
West Indian manatee, *Trichechus manatus*	♀♂	370.29 (325.0–418.0)				
n=Total sample Sources		n=7 6[1],1[4]				

Interorbital breadth	Rostrum width	Braincase breadth	Mastoidal breadth	Maxillary toothrow	Mandible length
29.40 (26.54–32.40)		57.92 (55.48–60.30)	55.21 (49.52–59.04)	39.1, 40.27	84.90 (76.58–88.24)
n=11 1[2],1[7],9[1]		n=10 1[2],9[1]	n=10 1[7],9[1]	n=2 1[2],1[7]	n=10 1[2],9[1]
23.90 (19.0–29.92)	30.92 (27.2–33.6)	53.43 (49.9–57.3)	51.77 (48.9–55.1)	36.67 (32.1–42.66)	78.55 (72.22–94.92)
n=78 47[2],12[4],6[3],9[7],4[8]	n=12[4]	n=47[2]	n=26 12[4],9[7],5[8]	n=67 47[2],6[3],9[7],5[8]	n=51 47[2],4[1]
25.57 (21.55–29.73)	32.80 (29.7–36.5)	54.78 (50.83–58.4)	55.34 (48.9–62.00)	38.68 (34.5–42.92)	83.90 (74.93–94.92)
n=90 39[2],28[4],8[3],8[7],7[8]	n=28[4]	n=39[2]	n=42 28[4],8[7],4[8],2[1]	n=62 39[2],8[3],8[7],7[8]	n=43 39[2],4[1]
44.3			92.57 (86.46–98.66)	69.1	148.35 (139.04–158.02)
n=1[3]			n=3[1]	n=1[3]	n=3[1]
50.43 (48.7–52.0)			103.70 (97.86–110.02)	79.8 (76.2–82.7)	156.76, 173.60
n=4[3]			n=4[1]	n=4[3]	n=2[1]
46.1 (33.8–68.1)	67.8 (55.4–89.8)				
n=112[9]	n=112[9]				

Zygomatic breadth	Greatest width	Interorbital breadth	Maxillary toothrow	Mandibular toothrow	Mandible length
248.98 (215.73–272.90)		183.49 (168.08–193.45)			405.0 (360.0–439.0)
n=4[1]		n=4[1]			n=4[1]
231.23 (199.18–255.20)					257.62 (227.64–294.76)
n=6[1]					n=6[1]

Families Delphinidae, Trichechidae, Equidae, Suidae, and Tayassuidae *continued*

Species	Sex	Greatest length	Basal length	Palatal length	Nasal length	Braincase breadth
Feral horse or wild pony, *Equus caballus*	♀ ♂	596.0 (567.0–628.0)	482.0 (471.0–489.0)		255.7 (253.0–259.0)	
n=Total sample		*n*=5[1]	*n*=4[2]		*n*=4[2]	
Wild boar or feral hog (California), *Sus scrofa*	♀	276.00 (258.0–304.0)			148.69 (132.00–162.66)	
n=Total sample		*n*=5[1]			*n*=5[1]	
	♂	291.90 (263.0–322.0)			159.27 (141.47–177.62)	
n=Total sample		*n*=5[1]			*n*=5[1]	
Collared peccary or javelina, *Pecari tajacu*	♀	228.64 (220.22–239.84)				
n=Total sample		*n*=5[1]				
	♂	241.98 (227.92–257.56)				
n=Total sample		*n*=6[1]				
	♀ ♂		191.8 (183.5–200.0)	132.9 (127.0–139.5)		54.5 (52.2–57.1)
n=Total sample			*n*=5[3]	*n*=5[3]		*n*=5[3]

1=author, 2=Bennett and Hoffman (1999), 3=Hoffmeister (1986), 4=Lowery (1974)

Family Cervidae

Table in millimeters. Mean and parameters on top. Total number of specimens measured and specific number in cited sources below.

Species	Sex	Greatest length	Condylobasal length	Basilar length	Nasal length
Elk or wapiti, *Cervus canadensis*	♀	424.00** (405.0–453.0)			146.42 (143.14–154.06)
n=Total sample Sources		*n*=5+? 4[1],1[2],?[6]			*n*= 4[1]
	♂	443.75** (404.0–525.0)			168.27 (152.79–185.42)
n=Total sample Sources		*n*=? 4[1],?[6]			*n*= 4[1]
Mule deer, including black-tailed deer, *Odocoileus hemionus*	♀	253.97 (228.34–276.63)		241.48 (230.0–259.0)	74.97 (62.5–85.98)
n=Total sample Sources		*n*=8 4[2],4[1]		*n*=16[3]	*n*=20 16[3],4[1]

Zygomatic breadth	Greatest width	Interorbital breadth	Maxillary toothrow	Mandibular toothrow	Mandible length
	132.7 (132.0–134.0)	87.5 (86.0–90.0)			428.8 (420.0–440.0)
	n=4[2]	n=4[2]			n=4[2]
146.54 (139.93–161.50)		74.57 (70.28–77.52)	104.50 (92.65–114.23)		247.30 (236.18–271.26)
n=5[1]		n=5[1]	n=5[1]		n=5[1]
143.34 (132.10–153.58)		75.00 (69.80–80.90)	103.64 (92.84–114.76)		250.25 (241.38–272.42)
n=5[1]		n=5[1]	n=5[1]		n=4[1]
95.96 (91.10–101.70)		50.99 (46.32–53.47)	64.05 (61.06–66.00)		153.49 (144.25–164.28)
n=5[1]		n=5[1]	n=5[1]		n=5[1]
109.38 (102.00–115.68)		54.09 (49.54–57.52)	66.04 (62.84–68.61)		163.30 (155.10–170.38)
n=5[1]		n=6[1]	n=6[1]		n=6[1]
103.5 (97.5–107.0)		52.32 (50.8–54.5)	61.0 (57.6–63.0)	68.55 (66.8–70.7)	
n=4[3]		n=5[3]	n=5[3]	n=4[3]	

Braincase breadth	Zygomatic breadth	Interorbital breadth	Maxillary toothrow	Mandibular toothrow	Mandible length
	167.33 (156.32–190.0)	127.73 (122.56–134.41)	136.0	143.0	345.50 (333.0–381.0)
	n=? 4[1],1[2],?[6]	n=4[1]	n=1[2]	n=1[2]	n=4[1]
	170.97** (150.84–218.0)	142.70 (123.74–162.38)			360.25 (329.0–387.0)
	n=? 4[1],?[6]	n=4[1]			n=4[1]
	107.69 (95.72–117.0)	68.13 (60.06–78.30)	77.15 (62.0–85.5)	86.68 (72.0–97.4)	201.19 (184.32–220.90)
	n=24 4[2],16[3],4[1]	n=4[1]	n=20 4[2],16[3]	n=13 4[2],9[3]	n=4[1]

Family Cervidae *continued*

Species	Sex	Greatest length	Condylobasal length	Basilar length	Nasal length
Mule deer, including black-tailed deer, *Odocoileus hemionus*	♂	284.53 (236.82–305.50)		266.68 (252.0–285.0)	87.07 (66.57–97.70)
n=Total sample Sources		*n*=9 5[2],4[1]		*n*=13[3]	*n*=15 11[3],4[1]
White-tailed deer, *Odocoileus virginianus*	♀	240.06 (216.0–274.54)	238.0 (230.0–252.0)	200.0, 200.0	59.0 (56.4–61.0)
n=Total sample Sources		*n*=37 33[2],4[1]	*n*=5[5]	*n*=2[3]	*n*=3[3]
	♂	263.44 (237.0–304.5)	261.09 (244.0–280.0)	223.48 (220.0–225.0)	66.21 (59.8–72.9)
n=Total sample Sources		*n*=27 24[2],3[1]	*n*=9 1[4],8[5]	*n*=4[3]	*n*=15[3]
Moose, *Alces alces*	♀	569.25** (540.0–610.0)			94.34 (85.08–103.16)
n=Total sample Sources		*n*=? 4[1],?[6]			*n*=4[1]
	♂	606.67** (560.0–633.0)			112.78 (99.40–129.60)
n=Total sample Sources		*n*=? 1[7],5[1],?[6]			*n*=5[1]
Caribou, *Rangifer tarandus*	♀		300.66 (274.0–336.0)		93.30 (76.0–111.0)
n=Total sample			*n*=40[8]		*n*=34[8]
	♂	359.50 (290.0–390.0)	333.44 (295.0–397.0)		104.77 (81.0–149.0)
n=Total sample		*n*=9[1]	*n*=72[8]		*n*=68[8]
Pronghorn, *Antilocapra americana*	♀	262.63 (245.0–279.0)		235.28 (218.9–250.3)	94.50 (78.0–104.6)
n=Total sample Sources		*n*=11 10[2],1[1]		*n*=4[3]	*n*=5[3]
	♂	270.67 (255.0–298.50)		244.8 (233.3–255.3)	104.08 (93.4–114.1)
n=Total sample Sources		*n*=9 7[2],2[1]		*n*=7[3]	*n*=9[3]

1=author, 2=Verts and Carraway (1998), 3=Hoffmeister (1986), 4=Paradiso (1969), 5=Lowery (1974), 6=Jackson (1961), 7=Bee and Hall (1956), 8=Manning (1960)

**=means calculated without Jackson's data

Braincase breadth	Zygomatic breadth	Interorbital breadth	Maxillary toothrow	Mandibular toothrow	Mandible length
	121.32 (97.92–139.0)	80.78 (62.23–88.58)	80.31 (72.9–89.1)	90.23 (81.3–97.6)	218.47 (187.72–238.12)
	n=21 5[2],12[3],4[1]	n=4[1]	n=17 5[2],12[3]	n=18 5[2],13[3]	n=4[1]
72.2 (69.7–76.5)	95.44 (85.0–105.7)	58.31 (50.1–65.82)	65.41 (52.0–78.6)	72.9 (67.0–86.2)	206.00 (183.28–219.96)
n=5[5]	n=42 33[2],4[3],5[5]	n=9 5[5],4[1]	n=42 33[2],4[3],5[5]	n=35 33[2],2[3]	n=7[1]
83.5 (78.3–97.0)	104.03 (95.0–122.0)	66.11 (52.4–78.05)	71.14 (62.0–88.0)	76.67 (68.0–95.0)	222.85 (188.70–239.15)
n=8[5]	n=45 24[2],13[3],8[5]	n=12 1[4],8[5],3[1]	n=49 24[2],15[3],2[4],8[5]	n=37 24[2],13[3]	n=6[1]
	197.90** (177.74–230.0)	146.38 (137.36–153.95)			477.50 (445.0–512.0)
	n=? 4[1],?[6]	n=4[1]			n=4[1]
	215.86** (209.26–240.0)	160.10 (155.22–167.28)			487.0 (481.0–495.0)
	n=? 1[7],5[1],?[6]	n=5[1]			n=4[1]
	119.74 (108.0–132.0)		87.50 (81.0–96.0)	95.64 (87.0–107.0)	242.97 (215.0–274.0)
	n=32[8]		n=41[8]	n=38[8]	n=37[8]
	129.83 (120.0–146.0)		92.13 (84.0–106.0)	100.62 (92.0–115.0)	262.96 (236.0–312.0)
	n=60[8]		n=75[8]	n=87[8]	n=82[8]
	114.57 (93.4–137.0)	93.42 (81.2–98.6)	66.01 (60.5–72.0)	70.93 (64.0–77.6)	216.80 (209.04–224.16)
	n=15 10[2],5[3]	n=5[3]	n=15 10[2],5[3]	n=15 10[2],5[3]	n=3[1]
	115.4 (97.1–149.0)	109.77 (104.9–118.1)	67.19 (59.5–74.0)	72.34 (63.5–79.1)	234.81 (225.00–245.18)
	n=17 7[2],10[3]	n=11[3]	n=18 7[2],11[3]	n=17 7[2],10[3]	n=10[1]

Family Bovidae

Table in millimeters. Mean and parameters on top. Total number of specimens measured and specific number in cited sources below.

Species	Sex	Greatest length	Basilar length	Palatal length	Nasal length
American bison, *Bos bison*	♀	472.46 (455.0–510.0)			180.57, 189.60
n=Total sample Sources		*n*=12+?[5] 2[1],10[2]			*n*=2[1]
	♂	481.29 (279.0–604.0)			177.36, 195.12
n=Total sample Sources		*n*=7+?[5]+?[6] 2[1],5[2]			*n*=2[1]
Mountain goat, *Oreamnos americanus*	♀	276.57 (267.22–292.10)			93.71 (91.96–96.92)
n=Total sample		*n*=3[1]			*n*=3[1]
	♂	310.0, 311.0			110.45 (103.41–115.18)
n=Total sample		*n*=2[1]			*n*=3[1]
Muskox, *Ovibos moschatus*	♂	487.15 (428.5–528.0)		263.41 (232.0–291.0)	152.86 (136.5–173.0)
n=Total sample		*n*=144[4]		*n*=59[4]	*n*=63[4]
Bighorn sheep, *Ovis canadensis*	♀	278.47 (237.5–296.0)	241.11 (226.0–256.0)		99.64 (86.0–113.0)
n=Total sample		*n*=9[1]	*n*=19[3]		*n*=25[3]
	♂	300.73 (262.24–324.0)	263.61 (247.0–280.0)		115.77 (99.0–134.0)
n=Total sample		*n*=12[1]	*n*=28[3]		*n*=30[3]
Dall sheep, *Ovis dalli*	♀		222.50 (215.0–238.0)		76.50 (72.0–84.0)
n=Total sample			*n*=8[3]		*n*=6[3]
	♂	278.57 (275.0–282.82)	252.73 (235.0–274.0)		92.39 (82.0–110.0)
n=Total sample		*n*=3[1]	*n*=33[3]		*n*=23[3]

1=author, 2=Verts and Carraway (1998), 3=Cowan (1940), 4= Tener (1965), 5=Jackson (1961), 6=MacDonald (1981) in Meagher (1986)

Zygomatic breadth	Interorbital breadth	Maxillary toothrow	Mandibular toothrow	Mandible length
245.31 (212.10–270.0)	196.22, 196.58	129.5 (120.0–162.0)	139.5 (137.0–142.0)	395.50 (388.0–407.0)
$n=12$ $10^2, 2^1$	$n=2^1$	$n=10^2$	$n=10^2$	$n=4^1$
271.64 (161.0–370.0)	222.12, 226.00	123.1 (92.32–135.0)	133.1 (92.3–163.0)	427.83 (409.5–439.5)
$n=7$ $5^2, 2^1$	$n=2^1$	$n=5^2$	$n=5^2$	$n=3^1$
98.97 (91.82–107.26)	75.62 (72.76–80.20)			220.84 (210.61–234.14)
$n=3^1$	$n=3^1$			$n=3^1$
112.03 (109.30–113.68)	88.68 (87.16–89.82)			244.87 (231.15–252.49)
$n=?^7$	$n=3^1$			$n=3^1$
168.04 (148.0–189.0)	190.53 (148.5–222.5)	149.05 (118.5–157.0)		
$n=101^4$	$n=84^4$	$n=381^4$		
115.92 (107.0–123.0)	104.76 (95.0–113.0)	85.63 (77.0–96.0)		189.28
$n=25^3$	$n=25^3$	$n=24^3$		$n=1^1$
129.41 (117.0–135.0)	120.16 (109.0–129.0)	87.45 (80.0–95.0)		231.13 (227.90–235.52)
$n=34^3$	$n=38^3$	$n=33^3$		$n=3^1$
113.29 (107.0–117.0)	98.50 (93.0–103.0)	70.50 (68.0–74.0)		
$n=7^3$	$n=8^3$	$n=8^3$		
123.30 (114.0–134.0)	115.59 (108.0–127.0)	76.51 (68.0–88.0)		
$n=30^3$	$n=29^3$	$n=37^3$		

Though far less comprehensive than the mammals accounts, it is hoped that enough diversity is presented to inspire you to look at bird skulls more carefully and with greater appreciation. Certainly the following accounts will help you narrow specimens to orders or families, and with any luck using such clues as geographic range and time of year, a species identification. The subject matter certainly deserves its own devoted publication.

There is much to compare when looking at bird skulls. Particularly useful are the varied palatine bones and associated structures on the ventral surface, as well as the fragile bone structures and fenestra viewed from the lateral between the orbits. These in combination with bill and nasal aperture characters should provide much material to weigh when attempting to identify bird skulls.

Additional resources for identifying bird skulls are relatively scarce, as avian systematics in the twentieth century has emphasized external morphology rather than comparative anatomy (Zusi 1993). Two noteworthy publications easily obtained are *Tracks and Signs of the Birds of Britain and Europe* (Brown et al., 2003) and *Guide to Raptor Remains: A Photographic Guide for Identifying the Remains of Selected Species of California Raptors* (Hurmence and Harness 2004), both listed in the bibliography. A reference for postcranial bones exists in *Avian Osteology* (Gilbert et al., 1986).

In the species accounts, three measurements are provided for each species: the greatest length of the skull, a linear measurement of the bill, and the greatest width

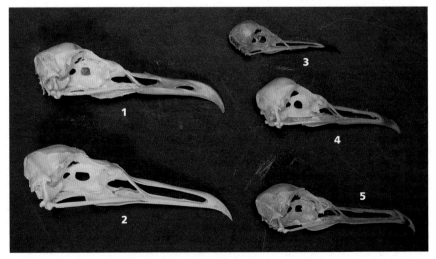

Gulls compared: 1. Herring gull *(Larus argentatus)* 1293, 2. Greater black-backed gull *(Larus marinus)*, 3. Bonaparte's gull *(Larus philadelphia)* 2543, 4. Ring-billed gull *(Larus delawarensis)* 1298, 5. California gull *(Larus californicus)* 3690. SANTA BARBARA MUSEUM OF NATURAL HISTORY.

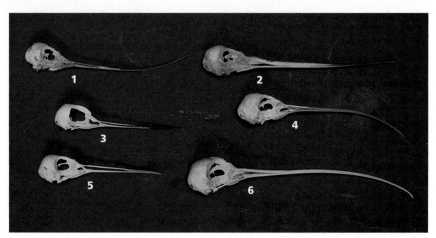

Shorebirds compared: 1. American avocet *(Recurvirostra americana)* 1644, 2. Marbled godwit *(Limosa fedoa)* 1858, 3. Black-necked stilt *(Himantopus mexicanus)* 1734, 4. Whimbrel *(Numenius phaeopus)* 1250, 5. Willet *(Tringa semipalmata)* 1755, 6. Long-billed curlew *(Numenius americanus)* 501. SANTA BARBARA MUSEUM OF NATURAL HISTORY.

of the skull, regardless of where that might fall. Brown et al. (2003) propose that the ratio of bill length over greatest length is a useful clue in identification. Following their lead, simple percentages representing this ratio have also been calculated using the means of the greatest length and bill length. Males and females are presented separately when resources provided the opportunity, and in certain species sexual dimorphism is pronounced.

Please note that the presence of the bill sheath significantly alters the length of the skull, and that in some accounts, both skulls with and without bill sheaths were measured. In general the bill sheath mimics the shape of the bones of the bill it covers, but not always. Consider the red crossbill *(Loxia curvirosta)* on page 690, which has a straight bony bill, yet a curved bill sheath. The curved bill sheaths provide the necessary tools for crossbills to extract seeds from cones which have yet to open, and before they are available to other bird species. Or compare the illustrations of the American kestrel *(Falco sparverius)* and Peregrine falcon *(Falco peregrinus)* on pages 640 and 641. In the kestrel the notched bill is emphasized by the presence of the bill sheath, but easily overlooked in the peregrine, where the sheath is absent. When present, bill sheaths are wondrous aids in identification, for the bills will better match those in field guides to birds, yet they may also block other useful characters, such as the shape and size of the nasal aperture.

A note on the sources for the measurements: Two others worked with me to compile the numbers. Neal Wight joined me as an intern from Prescott College and measured skulls in the Santa Barbara Museum of Natural History and the Museum of Vertebrate Zoology in Berkeley. Max Allen volunteered his time between his jobs with State Parks in Vermont and as an educator for the Vermont Wilderness School to measure skulls at the University of Massachusetts and the Museum of Comparative Zoology at Harvard.

Family Anatidae: Ducks, geese, and swans

Canada goose, *Branta canadensis*

Specimen illustrated: Adult, SBMNH 429. Life-size image page 185.

Features: (1) Interorbital region narrow; frontals thin to create shelflike orbital rims (11). (2) Palatines thin and curved; (4) posterior edges concave. (3) Narrow vomer pronounced. (5) Postorbital processes large and blunt. (6) Interorbital fenestra absent. (7) Bill lamellate (sieved), laterally compressed at base and narrower at tip; anterior flattened. (8) Nasal aperture large and oval. (9) Elevated foramen apparent through the occipital complex. (10) Craniofacial hinge very wide.

	Greatest length of skull	Length of bill	Bill/overall skull percentage	Greatest width of skull
♂	111.19 (105.70–125.37)	53.75 (51.88–62.90)	48%	38.14 (32.20–41.87)
Sample	N=5	N=5		N=5
♀	97.30 (83.13–118.51)	45.59 (37.78–57.83)	47%	32.58 (28.26–36.82)
Sample	N=6	N=6		N=6

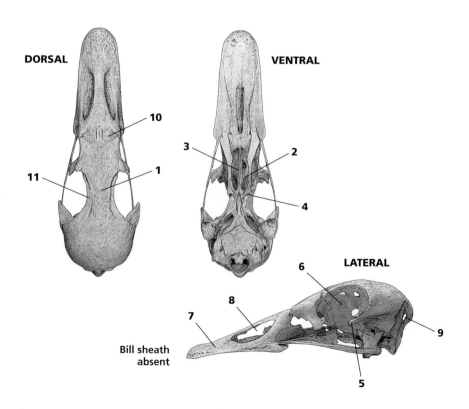

DORSAL

VENTRAL

LATERAL

Bill sheath absent

Mallard, *Anas platyrhynchos*

Specimen illustrated: Adult female, SBMNH 670. Life-size image page 185.

Features: (1) Interorbital region narrow and to posterior of skull; braincase (12) short and broad. (2) Palatines very slender and with concave posterior edges (4). (3) Narrow vomer well pronounced. (5) Postorbital processes long, large, and elevated. (6) Interorbital fenestra absent. (7) Bill lamellate (sieved), laterally compressed at base, and narrower at tip; anterior flattened; the nasal aperture (8) small and oval. (9) Elevated foramen apparent through occipital complex. (13) Craniofacial hinge very wide. (10) Lacrimal enlarged to further enclose orbit; orbit (11) smaller and more elevated than in Canada goose.

	Greatest length of skull	Length of bill	Bill/overall skull percentage	Greatest width of skull
♂	111.84 (106.86–116.73)	56.51 (55.22–61.96)	51%	30.15 (28.20–33.68)
Sample	N=7	N=7		N=7
♀	102.52 (95.83–107.44)	50.40 (45.92–52.46)	49%	28.28 (27.50–29.28)
Sample	N=6	N=6		N=6

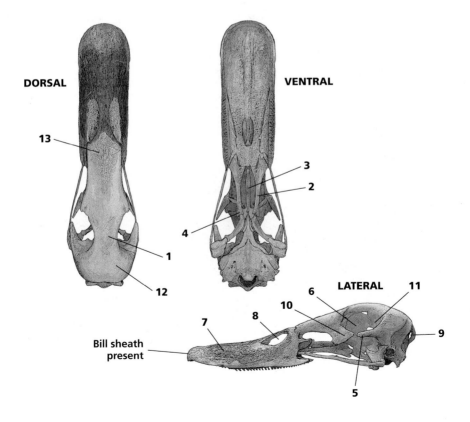

DORSAL

VENTRAL

LATERAL

Bill sheath present

Northern shoveler, *Anas clypeata*

Specimen illustrated: Adult male, SBMNH 4331. Life-size image page 185.
Features: (1) Interorbital region narrow. (2) Palatines slender, and posterior edges (3) notched. (4) Postorbital processes large and blunt. (5) Interorbital fenestra absent. (6) Lacrimal enlarged and rounded. (7) Large foramen apparent through elevated occipital complex. (8) Bill very broad, flattened, and spatulate; nasal aperture (9) oval.

	Greatest length of skull	Length of bill	Bill/overall skull percentage	Greatest width of skull
♂	114.87 (109.98–122.28)	62.39 (57.80–68.32)	54%	24.06 (22.10–26.40)
Sample	N=8	N=8		N=8
♀	105.77 (96.16–111.63)	56.34 (49.43–61.17)	53%	23.69 (22.34–25.07)
Sample	N=6	N=6		N=6

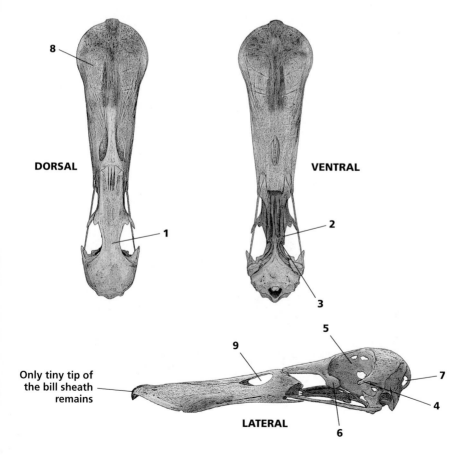

DORSAL

VENTRAL

Only tiny tip of the bill sheath remains

LATERAL

Green-winged teal, *Anas crecca*

	Greatest length of skull	Length of bill	Bill/overall skull percentage	Greatest width of skull
♂	80.11 (79.21–81.47)	36.56 (35.21–37.72)	46%	22.22 (21.68–23.00)
Sample	N=7	N=7		N=7
♀	78.14 (74.14–80.50)	36.80 (33.50–42.15)	47%	21.66 (21.12–22.17)
Sample	N=8	N=8		N=7

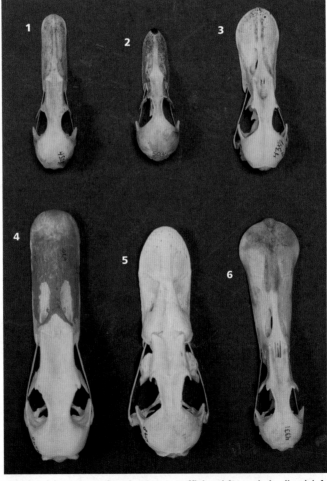

1. Green-winged teal *(Anas crecca)*, male 4528, 2. Bufflehead *(Bucephala albeola)*, female 5034, 3. Ruddy duck *(Oxyura jamaicensis)*, male 4357, 4. Mallard *(Anas platyrhynchos)*, female 670, 5. White-winged scoter *(Melanitta fusca)*, male 647, 6. Northern shoveler *(Anas clypeata)*, male 4331. SANTA BARBARA MUSEUM OF NATURAL HISTORY.

White-winged scoter, *Melanitta fusca*

Specimen illustrated: Adult male, SBMNH 647. Life-size image page 186.
Features: (1) Interorbital region very narrow. (2) Bill broad, gibbous (5) (referring to hump), and flattened to anterior (6). (3) Postorbital process long, blunt, and elevated. (4) Interorbital fenestra absent. (7) Nasal aperture tall and oval. (8) Premaxillaries broad. (9) Palatines slender with concave lateral edges (10).

	Greatest length of skull	Length of bill	Bill/overall skull percentage	Greatest width of skull
♂	112.32 (111.03–114.04)	53.72 (51.44–56.05)	48%	35.51 (33.28–41.21)
Sample	N=5	N=5		N=5
♀	108.05 (101.15–114.22)	51.86 (48.14–56.42)	48%	36.21 (33.83–36.26)
Sample	N=5	N=5		N=5

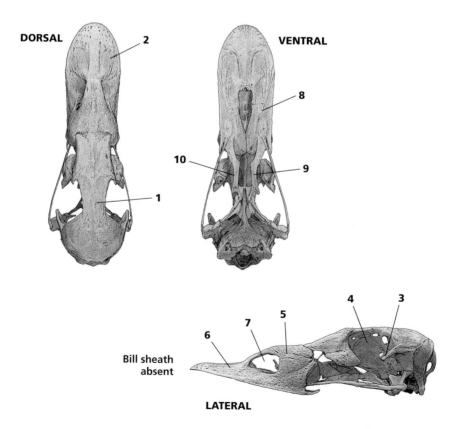

DORSAL · 2

VENTRAL · 8

10 · 9

1

4 · 3

5

7

6

Bill sheath absent

LATERAL

Bufflehead, *Bucephala albeola*

Specimen illustrated: Adult female, SBMNH 5034. Life-size image page 182.

Features: (1) Interorbital region very narrow. (2) Braincase longer, rounded, and smooth. (3) Palatines slender, curved, and with concave lateral edges (4). (5) Postorbital process long, slender, and less elevated than in mallard. (6) Interorbital fenestra oval. (7) Bill flattened and lamellate; (8) nasal aperture large and triangular. (9) Lacrimal long and relatively slender.

	Greatest length of skull	Length of bill	Bill/overall skull percentage	Greatest width of skull
♂	73.80 72.20	30.26 28.22	40%	27.44 25.08
Sample	N=2	N=2		N=2
♀	67.74 (65.18–73.64)	27.93 (25.66–30.32)	41%	23.31 (20.48–28.08)
Sample	N=6	N=6		N=6

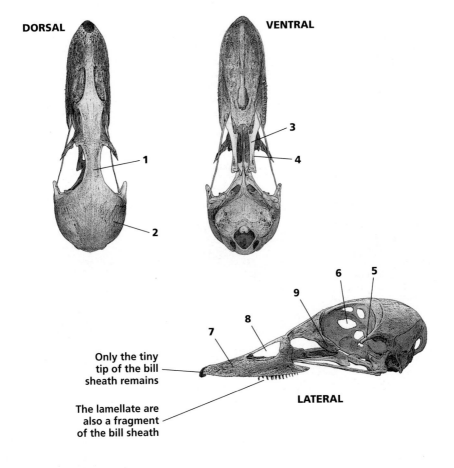

DORSAL

VENTRAL

1

2

3

4

6 5

9

8

7

Only the tiny tip of the bill sheath remains

The lamellate are also a fragment of the bill sheath

LATERAL

Common merganser, *Mergus merganser*

Specimen illustrated: Adult female, SBMNH 1835. Life-size image page 186.

Features: (1) Craniofacial hinge pronounced. (2) Interorbital region narrow. (3) Occipital crests well developed at posterior of skull. (4) Palatines thin and curved, with small bulbous processes (5) at posterior. (6) Thin vomer separates palatines except at posterior. (7) Postorbital process long and more vertical than in dabbling ducks. (8) Lacrimal process long and very slender. (10) Bill slender, long, terete, and serrate; nasal aperture (9) long and oval.

	Greatest length of skull	Length of bill	Bill/overall skull percentage	Greatest width of skull
♂	114.52 (109.62–116.88)	67.75 (65.32–71.72)	59%	32.96 (29.10–35.43)
Sample	N=9	N=9		N=9
♀	104.48 (100.11–107.04)	61.21 (55.92–64.71)	59%	31.08 (29.89–31.96)
Sample	N=10	N=10		N=10

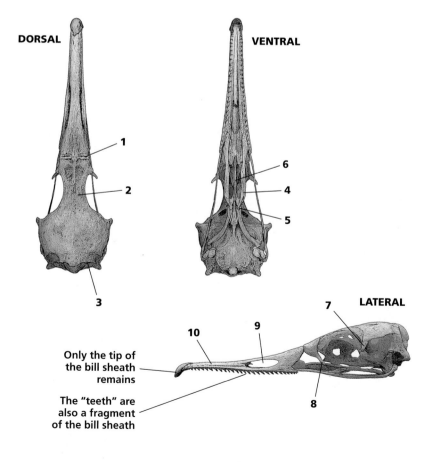

DORSAL

VENTRAL

LATERAL

Only the tip of the bill sheath remains

The "teeth" are also a fragment of the bill sheath

Family Phasianidae: Partridges, grouse, and turkeys

Ruffed grouse, *Bonasa umbellus*

Specimen illustrated: Adult male, MCZ 347936. Life-size image page 181.

Features: (1) Interorbital region narrrow. (2) Braincase rectangular and broader than wide. (3) Occipital crests less developed. (4) Palatines long, thin, and converging toward posterior. (5) Bill shorter than cranium, stout, and slightly decurved at tip. (6) Nasal aperture large, long, and oval. (7) Postorbital process long and thin. (8) Interorbital fenestra absent.

	Greatest length of skull	Length of bill	Bill/overall skull percentage	Greatest width of skull
♂	55.35 (52.30–58.64)	23.20 (21.59–27.64)	42%	27.66 (26.39–28.39)
Sample	N=8	N=8		N=8
♀	53.23 (50.63–57.31)	22.45 (19.92–25.84)	42%	26.21 (25.12–28.13)
Sample	N=8	N=8		N=8

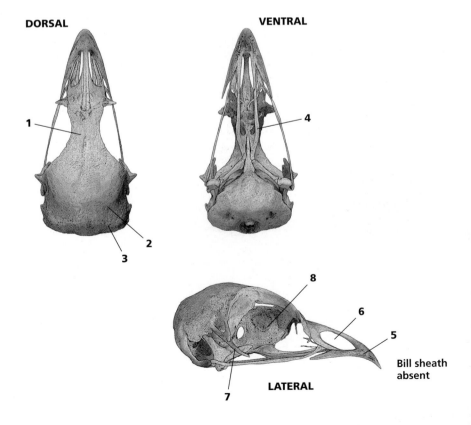

DORSAL

VENTRAL

1

4

2

3

8

6

5

Bill sheath absent

7

LATERAL

Wild turkey, *Meleagris gallopavo*

Specimen illustrated: Adult, MCZ 340819. Life-size image page 186.

Features: (1) Short, triangular lacrimals, or superciliary shields. (2) Long, squared braincase. (3) Occipital crests well developed. (4) Palatines long, thin, and converging toward posterior. (5) Bill shorter than cranium, stout, and slightly decurved at tip. (6) Nasal aperture large, long, and oval. (7) Postorbital process thick and blunt. (8) Interorbital fenestra absent.

	Greatest length of skull	Length of bill	Bill/overall skull percentage	Greatest width of skull
♂	103.15 (82.67–110.79)	55.33 (42.82–68.23)	54%	44.47 (35.53–50.72)
Sample	N=4	N=4		N=4
♀	89.23 (74.88–100.46)	47.74 (43.16–51.63)	54%	35.73 (31.33–39.56)
Sample	N=4	N=4		N=4

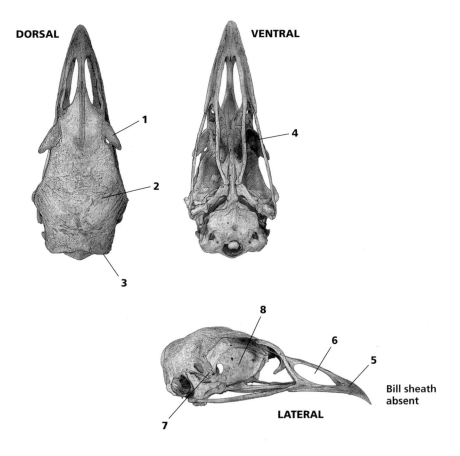

DORSAL

VENTRAL

LATERAL

Bill sheath absent

Family Odontophoridae: New World quail

Northern bobwhite, *Colinus virginianus*

Specimen illustrated: Adult male, SBMNH 1523. Life-size image page 179.
Features: (1) Short, triangular lacrimals, or superciliary shields. (2) Braincase rounded and smooth. (3) Interorbital region narrow. (4) Palatines long, thin, and converging toward posterior. (5) Bill short, stout, and slightly decurved at tip. (6) Nasal aperture large, tall, and oval. (7) Postorbital process triangular, tapering to a slender point. (8) Interorbital fenestra absent.

	Greatest length of skull	Length of bill	Bill/overall skull percentage	Greatest width of skull
♂	35.73	12.36	35%	18.36
Sample	N=1	N=1		N=1
♀	36.16 (32.78–36.76)	12.09 (10.60–13.26)	34%	18.20 (17.18–19.22)
Sample	N=4	N=4		N=4

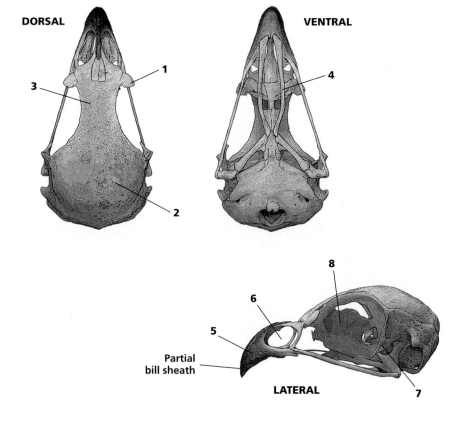

DORSAL

VENTRAL

Partial bill sheath

LATERAL

Family Procellariidae: Shearwaters and petrels

Sooty shearwater, *Puffinus griseus*

Specimen illustrated: Adult, SBMNH 1561. Life-size image page 184.

Features: (1) Bill long and straight, then hooked at the tip; (2) nasal aperture lacking. (3) Interorbital septum deep, and interorbital fenestra somewhat squared. (4) Postorbital process reduced. (5) Foramen through the occipital complex. (6) Frontals thin to create shelflike orbital rims and may be concave in shape. (7) Squamosals concave, forming broad grooves that constrict the braincase to the posterior. (8) Occipital crests well developed. (9) Palatines large and in contact with one another for their entire length. (10) Occipital condyle broad.

	Greatest length of skull	Length of bill	Bill/overall skull percentage	Greatest width of skull
♂	94.14 (90.90–97.50)	50.86 (48.34–54.65)	54%	30.29 (28.21–32.10)
Sample	N=10	N=10		N=8
♀	94.15 (92.11–97.18)	50.36 (48.12–52.55)	53%	31.97 (31.15–33.47)
Sample	N=7	N=7		N=7

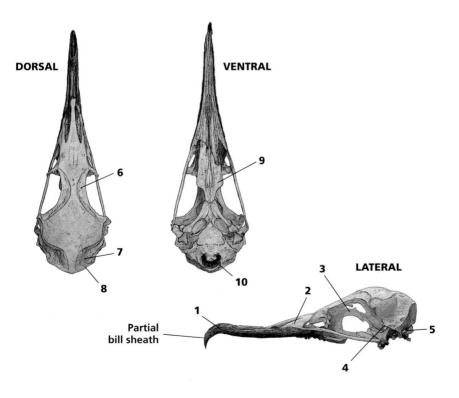

DORSAL

VENTRAL

6

9

7

8

10

3   LATERAL

2

1

5

Partial
bill sheath

4

Family Pelecanidae: Pelicans

Brown pelican, *Pelecanus occidentalis*

Specimen illustrated: Adult, SBMNH 1450. Life-size image page 188.

Features: (1) Bill very long and straight, with small hook at anterior tip; bill (7) broad and spatulate to anterior. Nasal aperture (2) lacking. (3) Occipital crests well developed and contributing to the squared posterior. (4) Palatines long, narrow, and in contact with one another for their entire length. (6) Small optic foramen to posterior of orbit; interorbital fenestra (5) absent. (7) The craniofacial hinge is wide and pronounced.

	Greatest length of skull	Length of bill	Bill/overall skull percentage	Greatest width of skull
♂	429.60 (412.00–438.00)	341.40 (327.00–348.00)	79%	75.36 (71.65–80.82)
Sample	N=5	N=5		N=5
♀	381.86 (343.31–399.00)	302.94 (275.71–318.00)	79%	67.87 (59.23–74.16)
Sample	N=5	N=5		N=5

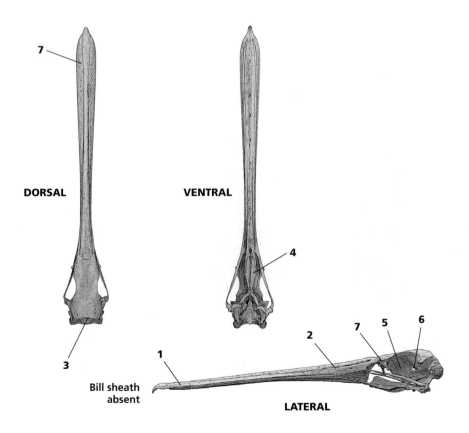

DORSAL

VENTRAL

7

4

3

1

2

7

5

6

Bill sheath absent

LATERAL

Family Phalacrocoracidae: Cormorants

Double-crested cormorant, *Phalacrocorax auritus*

Specimen illustrated: Adult, SBMNH 2449. Life-size image page 188.

Features: (1) Craniofacial hinge wide and pronounced. (2) Sagittal crest apparent at posterior of the braincase. (3) Occipital crests well developed. (4) Occipital complex extends to posterior and squared. (5) Palatines rectangular and in contact with one another for much of their length. (6) Bill long and straight, with a hooked anterior tip; nasal aperture (9) lacking. (7) Postorbital processes distinctive and elevated. (8) Interorbital fenestra and all foramina joined to form large, vacuous orbital region.

	Greatest length of skull	Length of bill	Bill/overall skull percentage	Greatest width of skull
♂	129.87 (121.51–138.15)	68.54 (64.07–71.77)	53%	35.71 (31.59–38.00)
Sample	N=8	N=8		N=8
♀	124.70 (118.65–135.49)	66.18 (61.82–72.31)	53%	34.40 (31.24–38.84)
Sample	N=8	N=8		N=8

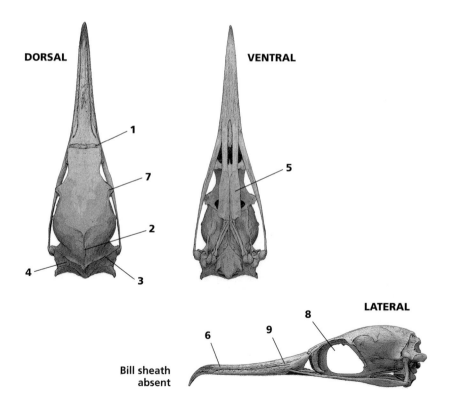

DORSAL

VENTRAL

LATERAL

Bill sheath absent

Family Ardeidae: Herons and bitterns

Great blue heron, *Ardea herodias*

Specimen illustrated: Adult male, SBMNH 2454. Life-size image page 188.

Features: (1) Sagittal crest well formed at posterior of braincase. (2) Occipital crests well developed, and occipital complex squared and extending well beyond braincase. (3) Palatines long, slender, in contact only at posterior and with convex lateral edges; premaxillaries (9) broad. (4) Slender vomer separates palatines. (5) Bill long, stout, and straight; nasal aperture (6) relatively small. (7) Interorbital fenestra large, and extension of interorbital septum (8) long and elevated.

	Greatest length of skull	Length of bill	Bill/overall skull percentage	Greatest width of skull
♂	208.91 (198.98–219.35)	136.84 (127.74–144.43)	66%	35.89 (34.28–36.81)
Sample	N=7	N=7		N=7
♀	202.98 (193.22–222.15)	134.28 (123.88–152.78)	66%	35.58 (33.89–37.40)
Sample	N=10	N=10		N=10

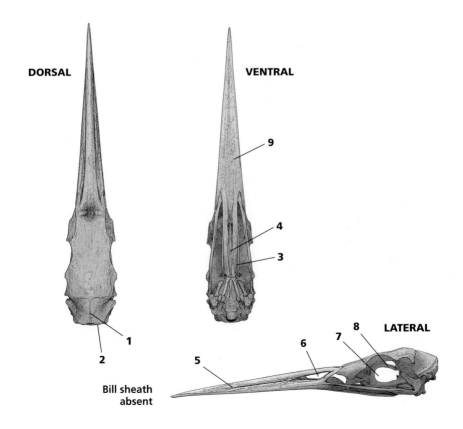

DORSAL

VENTRAL

LATERAL

Bill sheath absent

Family Threskiornithidae: Ibises and spoonbills

White-faced ibis, *Plegadis chihi*

Specimen illustrated: Adult female, MVZ 73320. Life-size image page 188.
Features: (1) Cranium smooth and rounded; interorbital breadth (9) broad. (2) Palatines long with rounded posterior corners. (3) Vomer thin, separating palatines except at far posterior. (4) Interorbital fenestra smaller. (5) Optic foramen larger, but still smaller than the interorbital fenestra. (6) Interorbital septum deep and angled. (7) Bill long and decurved, slender and cylindrical; nasal aperture (8) short and linear.

	Greatest length of skull	Length of bill	Bill/overall skull percentage	Greatest width of skull
♂	178.03 (165.76–184.38)	142.91 (132.44–148.84)	80%	24.49 (23.72–25.04)
Sample	N=3	N=3		N=3
♀	145.25 (138.28–155.53)	110.89 (104.55–122.08)	76%	21.95 (21.17–22.98)
Sample	N=4	N=4		N=4

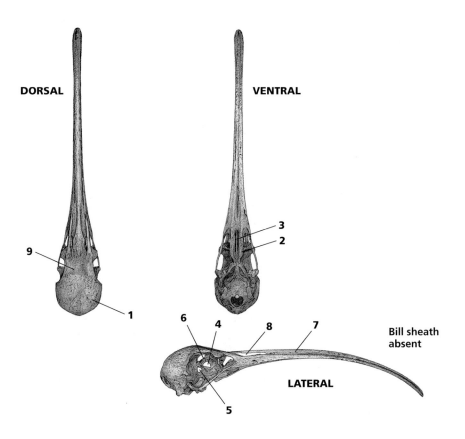

DORSAL

VENTRAL

9

3
2

1

6   4   8   7

Bill sheath absent

5

LATERAL

Family Cathartidae: New World vultures

Turkey vulture, *Cathartes aura*

Specimen illustrated: Adult, SBMNH 1352. Life-size image page 184.
Features: (1) Relatively broad interorbital region. (2) Rounded cranium. (3) Edge of orbit often rough and perforated. (4) Palatines long, broad, and rounded to posterior. (5) Postorbital process triangular and long. (6) Lacrimal bone stout, vertical, and squared. (7) Nasal aperture large and oval. (8) Bill hooked and cere, long and elevated to posterior; little rise (9) from bill to frontals. (10) Interorbital fenestra absent.

	Greatest length of skull	Length of bill	Bill/overall skull percentage	Greatest width of skull
♂♀	91.39 (83.28–98.26)	43.30 (37.93–47.10)	47%	37.29 (34.55–39.30)
Sample	N=11	N=11		N=11

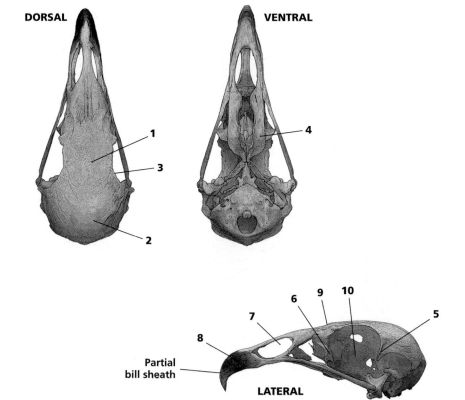

DORSAL

VENTRAL

Partial bill sheath

LATERAL

Family Accipitridae: Hawks, kites, and eagles

Bald eagle, *Haliaeetus leucocephalus*

Specimen illustrated: Adult, SBMNH 652. Life-size image page 187.

Features: (1) Supraocular bones (missing in this specimen) prominent and attach to lacrimal bones. (2) Broad interorbital region with rough and sometime perforated orbital edges. (3) Palatines broad with concave ventral surfaces (5) to the posterior. (4) Foramen magnum small and tubular. (7) Bill long, deep, and stout (much longer than in golden eagle), hooked and cere, with a smooth cutting edge; nasal aperture (6) oval, tapering to posterior and without bony tubercule. (8) Postorbital process stout with squared tip.

	Greatest length of skull	Length of bill	Bill/overall skull percentage	Greatest width of skull
Sex unknown	125.07 (110.33–140.00)	58.87 (49.79–69.13)	47%	64.55 (57.22–72.54)
Sample	N=14	N=14		N=14
♀	117.07 (110.33–124.62)	55.13 (49.79–58.54)	47%	60.37 (57.86–63.98)
Sample	N=3	N=3		N=3

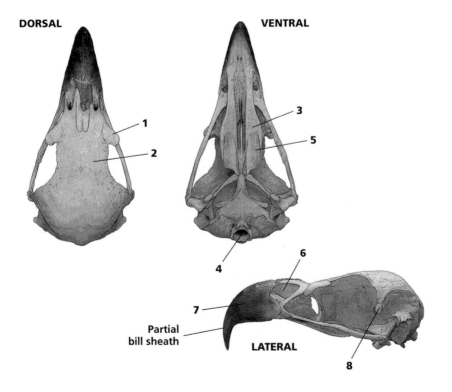

DORSAL

VENTRAL

Partial bill sheath

LATERAL

Cooper's hawk, *Accipiter cooperii*

Specimen illustrated: Adult male, SBMNH 5040. Life-size image page 181.

Features: (1) Supraocular bones prominent and attached to the lacrimal bones, but both bones often lost in the field or fall off during preparation. (2) Interorbital narrow. (3) Broad, rounded braincase. (4) Palatines broad to posterior, in contact for about one-third of length, with angular corners. (5) Bill tall at base, short and stout, hooked and cere; cutting edge rough but not toothed. (6) Nasal aperture oval and tallest at posterior. (7) Interorbital fenestra large and oval. (8) Interorbital septum elevated and angled. (9) Postorbital process well developed and with squared tip. (10) Posterior of braincase sloping steeply to posterior.

	Greatest length of skull	Length of bill	Bill/overall skull percentage	Greatest width of skull
♂	56.65 (53.88–61.47)	18.09 (14.54–20.98)	32%	32.83 (30.98–36.97)
Sample	N=8	N=8		N=8
♀	60.32 (58.1–63.27)	20.40 (18.76–21.98)	34%	34.35 (33.39–35.57)
Sample	N=10	N=10		N=10

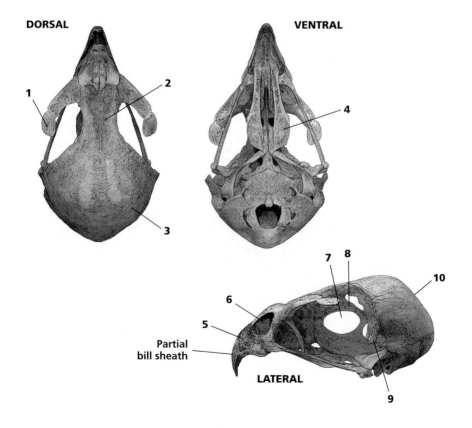

DORSAL

VENTRAL

1

2

4

3

7 8

10

6

5

Partial
bill sheath

9

LATERAL

Red-tailed hawk, *Buteo jamaicensis*

Specimens illustrated: Adult female without supraoculars, SBMNH 650; adult female without supraoculars and lacrimals, 2118M. Life-size image page 183.

Features: Supraocular bones (missing in this skull) pronounced and attached to lacrimal bones (1). (2) Interorbital relatively broad. (3) Large, broad, rounded braincase. (4) Palatines long and slender, broadest to posterior, with angular lateral and posterior edges. (5) Bill of median length and very hooked. (6) Nostrils oval and tapering to posterior. (7) Postorbital process slender and very long. (8) Interorbital fenestra small and oval.

	Greatest length of skull	Length of bill	Bill/overall skull percentage	Greatest width of skull
♂	82.13 (76.50–86.21)	27.92 (25.31–30.35)	34%	48.78 (47.05–50.09)
Sample	N=14	N=14		N=14
♀	85.74 (81.23–88.50)	30.36 (23.66–35.00)	35%	50.02 (46.62–51.96)
Sample	N=15	N=15		N=15

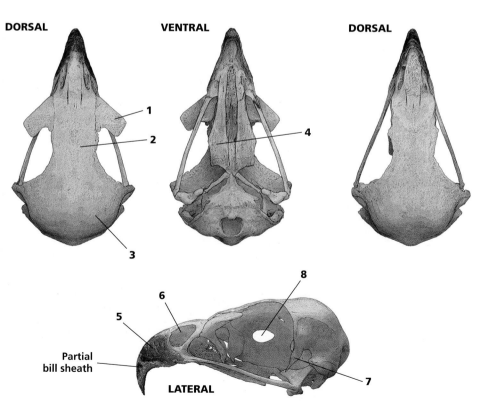

DORSAL

VENTRAL

DORSAL

Partial bill sheath

LATERAL

Family Falconidae: Falcons

American kestrel, *Falco sparverius*

Specimen illustrated: Adult male, SBMNH 5055. Life-size image page 180.

Features: (1) Supraocular bones and lacrimals one long, slender, straplike piece pointing to posterior. (2) Interorbital narrow. (3) Large, broad, rounded braincase. (4) Palatines squat and broad to posterior, in contact for 50 percent of length, tapering to posterior, with converging tips. (5) Foramen magnum relatively large. (6) Bill short, very hooked; bill sheath notched (10) and cere. (7) Nostrils round with bony tubercle at center. (8) Postorbital process slender. (9) Interorbital fenestra large and oval.

	Greatest length of skull	Length of bill	Bill/overall skull percentage	Greatest width of skull
♂	41.01 (40.00–42.48)	12.56 (9.64–14.88)	31%	24.96 (23.47–26.14)
Sample	N=16	N=16		N=16
♀	42.10 (40.63–44.46)	13.00 (9.26–15.63)	31%	25.80 (24.12–27.60)
Sample	N=15	N=15		N=15

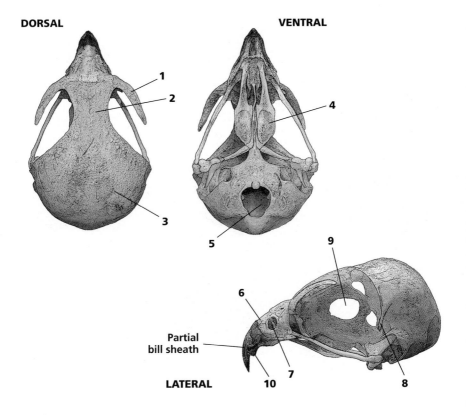

DORSAL

VENTRAL

Partial bill sheath

LATERAL

Peregrine falcon, *Falco peregrinus*

Specimen illustrated: Adult, MVZ 124693. Life-size image page 182.

Features: (1) Supraocular bones and lacrimals one long, slender straplike piece, pointing to posterior. (2) Interorbital broader. (3) Large, broad, rounded braincase. (4) Palatines squat and broad to posterior; posterior lateral edges (5) rounded. (6) Foramen magnum wider than tall. (7) Bill medium, very hooked; Bill sheath notched (absent in this specimen) and cere. Notch can be inferred from bony process (10). (8) Nostrils round with bony tubercle at center. (9) Interorbital fenestra very small and oval.

	Greatest length of skull	Length of bill	Bill/overall skull percentage	Greatest width of skull
♂	65.14	23.85	37%	38.70
Sample	N=1	N=1		N=1
♂♀	67.42 (62.77–73.14)	24.73 (21.42–27.10)	37%	39.77 (37.22–41.32)
Sample	N=8	N=8		N=8

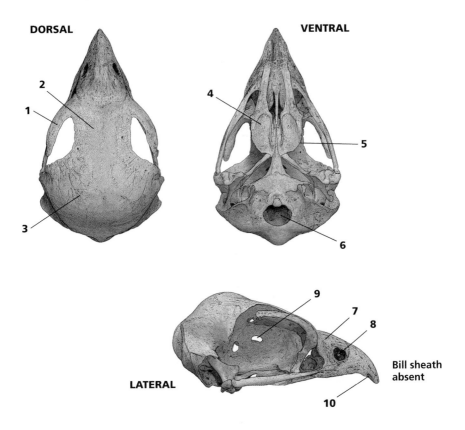

DORSAL

VENTRAL

LATERAL

Bill sheath absent

Family Rallidae: Rails, gallinules, and coots

American coot, *Fulica americana*

Specimen illustrated: Adult male, SBMNH 827. Life-size image page 182.

Features: Long, slender, and laterally compressed skull, with relatively broad bill. (1) Craniofacial hinge pronounced. (2) Interorbital breadth narrow. (3) Braincase smooth and rounded. (4) Palatines long and thin, broadest at posterior, where they are in contact; corners angular (5) and converging to sharp points at posterior edge. (6) Maxillopalatines larger and circular. (7) Postorbital processes reduced and elevated. (8) Interorbital septum narrow and high; interorbital fenestra large. (9) Line of commissure slightly angulate. (10) Nasal aperture large and linear, yet oval to posterior (12). (11) Bill slightly longer than cranium, and relatively deep and stout.

	Greatest length of skull	Length of bill	Bill/overall skull percentage	Greatest width of skull
♂	65.95 (63.45–68.12)	32.87 (31.44–34.49)	50%	21.17 (20.51–22.19)
Sample	N=10	N=10		N=10
♀	62.70 (59.69–67.17)	30.19 (24.25–33.83)	48%	20.90 (19.65–22.02)
Sample	N=10	N=10		N=10

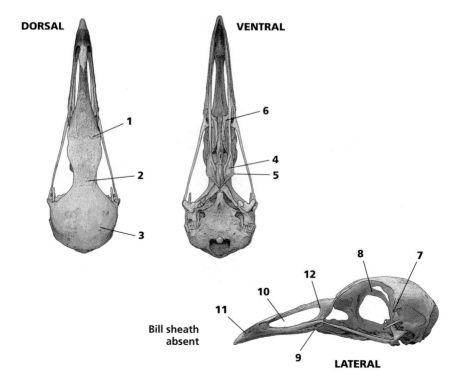

DORSAL

VENTRAL

Bill sheath absent

LATERAL

Family Charadriidae: Lapwings and plovers

Killdeer, *Charadrius vociferus*

Specimen illustrated: Adult male, SBMNH 4938. Life-size image page 180.

Features: (1) Braincase rounded and smooth. (2) Lacrimal bones project outward and upward above the level of the cranium. (3) Maxillopalatines to posterior of bill and circular. (4) Palatines long and thin, then broad at posterior, where contact (5) is minimal. Bill approximately equal in length to cranium, slender, and straight, with a slightly swollen, decurved tip (10). (6) Nasal aperture long and linear. (7) Orbit very large. (8) Interorbital septum long, narrow, and just above midline of orbit; interorbital fenestra only slightly larger than foramen above. (9) Low foramen apparent through occipital complex.

	Greatest length of skull	Length of bill	Bill/overall skull percentage	Greatest width of skull
♂	47.82 (46.18–50.44)	25.49 (22.63–27.50)	53%	16.86 (16.06–17.46)
Sample	N=8	N=8		N=8
♀	48.63 (47.47–50.35)	26.31 (23.96–29.01)	54%	16.99 (16.51–17.82)
Sample	N=6	N=6		N=6

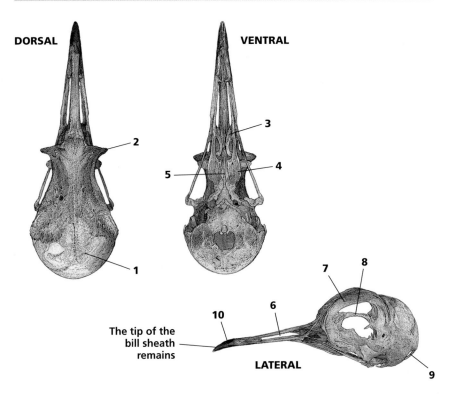

DORSAL

VENTRAL

The tip of the
bill sheath
remains

LATERAL

Family Recurvirostridae: Stilts and avocets

American avocet, *Recurvirostra americana*

Specimen illustrated: Adult female, SBMNH 1644. Life-size image page 187.

Features: (1) Cranium smooth and rounded. (2) Interorbital narrow. (3) Lacrimal bones project outward. (4) Maxillopalatines converge and make contact. (5) Palatines long and broad, with tapering posterior processes (6) at corners. (7) Bill very long, slender, and recurved. (8) Nasal aperture long and linear. (9) Postorbital process long and thin. (10) Interorbital septum long, narrow, and just above midpoint of orbit; interorbital fenestra (11) just larger than foramen (12) above.

	Greatest length of skull	Length of bill	Bill/overall skull percentage	Greatest width of skull
♂	128.05 (113.50–141.02)	97.88 (81.68–111.97)	77%	20.26 (19.55–21.18)
Sample	N=6	N=6		N=6
♀	117.08 (107.86–127.48)	88.39 (81.31–100.79)	75%	19.86 (18.90–20.40)
Sample	N=10	N=10		N=10

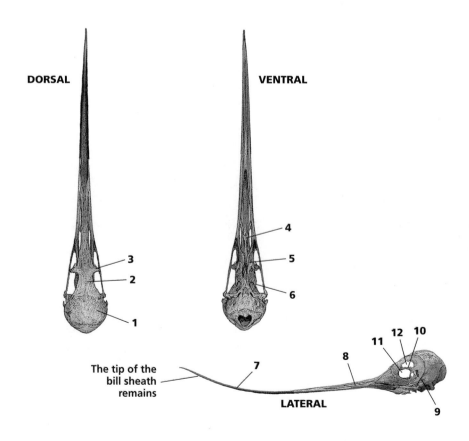

DORSAL

VENTRAL

The tip of the bill sheath remains

LATERAL

Family Scolopacidae: Sandpipers

Spotted sandpiper, *Actitis macularia*

Specimen illustrated: Adult, MVZ 63080. Life-size image page 180.

Features: (1) Cranium rounded and smooth. (2) Interorbital very narrow; palatine bones (3) visible below. (4) Posterior corners of palatines rounded. (5) Bill long, slender, and straight. (6) Nasal aperture long and linear. (7) Interorbital septum very long, narrow, and elevated; interorbital fenestra (8) approximately twice the size of foramen above. (9) Maxillopalatines circular. (10) Foramen through occipital complex.

	Greatest length of skull	Length of bill	Bill/overall skull percentage	Greatest width of skull
♂	46.49 (41.74–53.75)	27.78 (24.44–33.22)	60%	12.88 (12.44–14.06)
Sample	N=5	N=5		N=5
♀	47.35 (44.34–49.35)	28.12 (25.54–30.62)	59%	12.87 (12.54–13.52)
Sample	N=6	N=6		N=6

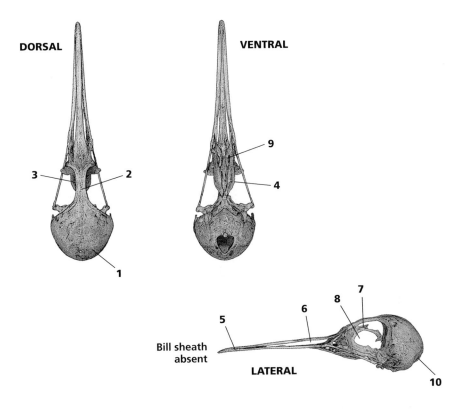

DORSAL

VENTRAL

LATERAL

Bill sheath absent

Long-billed curlew, *Numenius americanus*

Specimen illustrated: Adult, SBMNH 501. Life-size image page 188.

Features: (1) Cranium rounded and smooth. (2) Distinctive interorbital notch. (3) Lacrimal bones projecting slightly to anterior. (4) Posterior corners of palatines rounded. (5) Bill very long, slender, and decurved. (6) Nasal aperture linear but short in comparison with length of bill. (7) Interorbital septum long and deep, just above midline of orbit; interorbital fenestra (9) much larger than foramen above. (8) Foramen through occipital complex.

	Greatest length of skull	Length of bill	Bill/overall skull percentage	Greatest width of skull
♂	173.51 (159.42–193.07)	138.16 (122.84–158.48)	80%	24.46 (22.98–25.20)
Sample	N=5	N=5		N=5
♀	199.40 (169.22–222.54)	164.20 (131.10–187.52)	82%	25.58 (23.90–26.72)
Sample	N=8	N=8		N=8

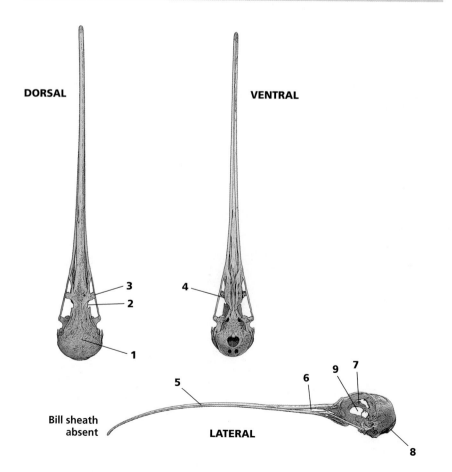

DORSAL

VENTRAL

3
2
1

4

5
6
9 7

Bill sheath absent

LATERAL

8

Marbled godwit, *Limosa fedoa*

Specimen illustrated: Adult female, SBMNH 1858. Life-size image page 188.
Features: (1) Braincase short, rounded, and smooth. (2) Lacrimal bones small. (3) Bill stout and broad for its length. (4) Palatines in contact for much of length and with rounded posterior corners (5). (6) Bill very long, slightly recurved, and with a swollen tip. (7) Nasal aperture short and linear, much broader to posterior. (8) Interorbital septum narrow and orbit slightly smaller. (9) Interorbital fenestra only slightly larger than foramen above.

	Greatest length of skull	Length of bill	Bill/overall skull percentage	Greatest width of skull
♂	144.70 (132.99–167.71)	115.21 (103.98–138.33)	80%	20.66 (19.86–21.25)
Sample	N=5	N=5		N=5
♀	157.19 (150.54–163.00)	125.89 (119.76–132.02)	80%	21.37 (21.13–21.92)
Sample	N=5	N=5		N=5

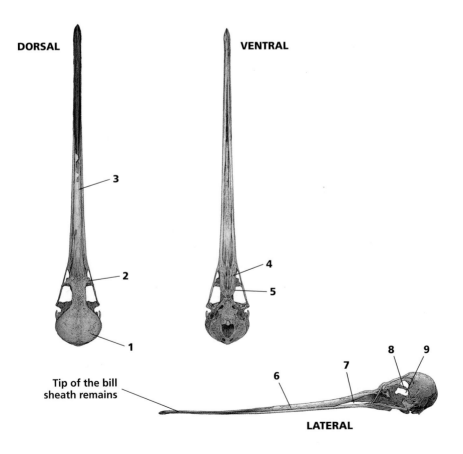

DORSAL

VENTRAL

3

2

1

4

5

Tip of the bill sheath remains

6

7

8 9

LATERAL

Wilson's snipe, *Gallinago delicata*

Specimen illustrated: Adult female, MVZ 68695. Life-size image page 184.

Features: (1) Braincase very short, rounded, and smooth. (2) Interorbital narrow, allowing views of inside of orbits (4); distinctive edge (3) to orbits. (6) Occipital complex shifted ventrally; foramen magnum (5) on ventral surface rather than posterior. (7) Craniofacial hinge large; second hinge (8) at anterior of bill. (9) Nasal aperture very long, linear, and broadest at anterior and posterior. (10) Orbit large, oval, and elevated; interorbital septum short, deep, and angled. (11) Foramen through occipital complex. (12) Foramen magnum, a second perspective.

	Greatest length of skull	Length of bill	Bill/overall skull percentage	Greatest width of skull
♂	91.43 (88.00–99.78)	69.29 (66.85–77.12)	76%	16.91 (16.39–17.95)
Sample	N=8	N=8		N=8
♀	94.41 (85.42–98.05)	73.15 (65.16–76.53)	77%	17.05 (16.66–17.84)
Sample	N=8	N=8		N=8

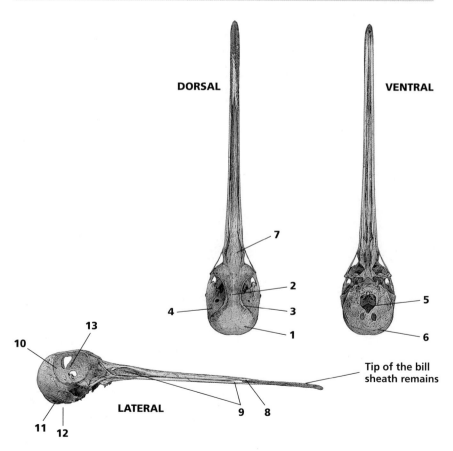

DORSAL

VENTRAL

Tip of the bill sheath remains

LATERAL

Family Laridae: Skuas, gulls, terns, and skimmers

Herring gull, *Larus argentatus*

Specimen illustrated: Adult female, SBMNH 1293. Life-size image page 187.

Features: (1) Frontals thin to create shelflike orbital rims, which may be concave in shape and perforate (2) to posterior; a median ridge (3) develops along the midline between the orbits. (4) Lacrimal bones stout and blunt. (6) Braincase high, angular, and reduced; squamosal (5) concave, creating deep grooves to posterior that constrict braincase. (7) Vomer sits between circular maxillopalatines (8). (9) Posterior corners of palatines rounded. (10) Foramen magnum small. (11) Postorbital process stout and elevated. (12) Interorbital septum deep; interorbital fenestra (13) reduced. (15) Bill straight, long, and hooked at tip; nasal aperture (14) linear, extending length of bill (partially covered here by bill sheath).

	Greatest length of skull	Length of bill	Bill/overall skull percentage	Greatest width of skull
♂	121.62 (115.61–127.02)	67.81 (65.55–69.79)	56%	41.98 (39.38–44.96)
Sample	N=8	N=8		N=8
♀	116.86 (112.96–122.04)	65.07 (61.64–69.06)	56%	40.22 (37.78–42.48)
Sample	N=8	N=8		N=8

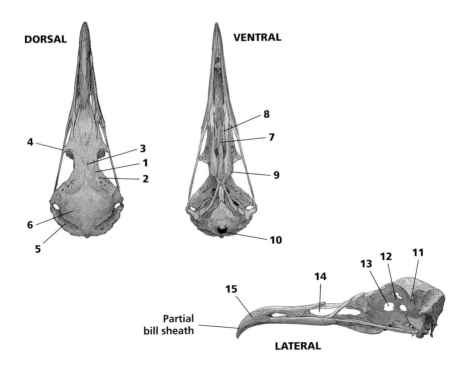

DORSAL

VENTRAL

Partial bill sheath

LATERAL

Common tern, *Sterna hirundo*

Specimen illustrated: Adult, MCZ 340442. Life-size image page 182.

Features: (1) Frontals thin to form shelflike orbital rims, which may be concave in shape. (2) Interorbital breadth very narrow, allowing views of palatines (6) below; medium ridge follows midline of skull between orbits. (3) Lacrimal bones larger than in gulls, broader and rounded. (4) Braincase rounded and smooth, except at posterior, where concave squamosals (5) create deep grooves to constrict braincase. (7) Maxillopalatines straighter. (8) Bill approximately the length of cranium, straight and acute; nasal aperture (9) linear, approximately half the length of bill. (10) Interorbital septum long and slender, at midline of skull; interorbital fenestra large, approximately equal to foramen above.

	Greatest length of skull	Length of bill	Bill/overall skull percentage	Greatest width of skull
♂	72.90 (70.13–75.88)	37.85 (34.57–39.39)	52%	22.06 (21.23–22.89)
Sample	N=5	N=5		N=5
♀	70.66 (63.68–77.89)	37.65 (33.78–42.91)	53%	21.42 (20.64–22.27)
Sample	N=9	N=9		N=9

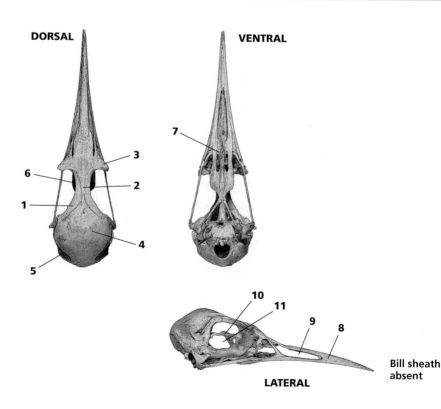

DORSAL

VENTRAL

LATERAL

Bill sheath absent

Black skimmer, *Rynchops niger*

Specimen illustrated: Adult male, MCZ 345002. Life-size image page 187.

Features: (1) Bill laterally compressed. (2) Craniofacial hinge pronounced. (4) Frontals thin at orbital edges to create narrow, shelflike orbital rims. (5) Braincase angular and reduced. (6) Squamosal broad and concave, creating distinctively large grooves at posterior of braincase; occipital ridges (3) well developed and give posterior of skull a squared appearance. (7) Palatines large, broad, and with concave surfaces (8) to posterior. (9) Postorbital process slender and elevated. (10) Interorbital septum large and fills orbit, the bridgelike extension between upper foramen and small interorbital fenestra short. (12) Bill deep, long, and straight; nasal aperture (11) smaller, linear, with rounded anterior edges.

	Greatest length of skull	Length of bill	Bill/overall skull percentage	Greatest width of skull
♂	124.65 (102.19–138.33)	76.39 (61.01–88.64)	61%	37.87 (31.36–40.14)
Sample	N=6	N=6		N=6
♀	114.68 (101.56–131.38)	69.36 (59.89–81.34)	60%	36.77 (32.00–42.64)
Sample	N=5	N=5		N=5

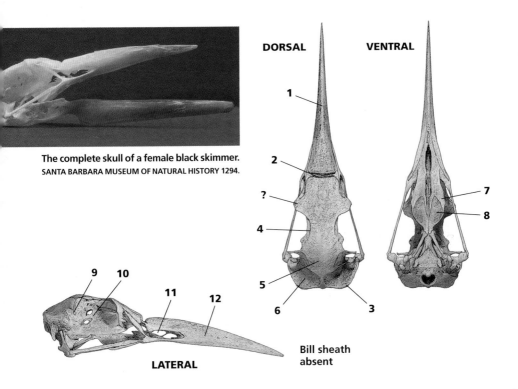

The complete skull of a female black skimmer.
SANTA BARBARA MUSEUM OF NATURAL HISTORY 1294.

DORSAL

VENTRAL

LATERAL

Bill sheath absent

Family Alcidae: Auks, murres, and puffins

Atlantic puffin, *Fractercula arctica*

	Greatest length of skull	Length of bill	Bill/overall skull percentage	Greatest width of skull
♂	75.32	36.93	49%	31.17
Sample	N=1	N=1		N=1
♀	72.05	36.07	50%	31.91
Sample	N=1	N=1		N=1

LATERAL

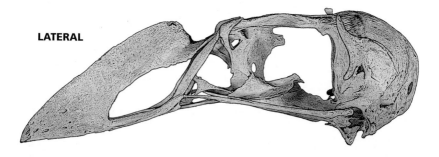

Bill sheath
absent

Horned puffin, *Fratercula corniculata*

Specimen illustrated: Adult male, MVZ 160699. Life-size image page 183.

Features: (1) Interorbital breadth very narrow and long, allowing views of palatine bones (3). (2) Frontal bones thin toward edges, creating shelflike orbital rims. (4) Maxillopalatine bones circular; palatine bones (5) broad to posterior, with more angular corners. (6) Bill large, distinctive, laterally compressed, and very deep; nasal aperture (7) very large and linear, with rounded anterior edges. (8) Interorbital septum long and curving; infraorbital fenestra (11) large and nearly round. (9) Postorbital processes large and distinctive, with both dorsal and ventral projections.

	Greatest length of skull	Length of bill	Bill/overall skull percentage	Greatest width of skull
♂	83.24 (82.04–85.31)	45.38 (42.81–47.97)	55%	33.49 (32.76–34.29)
Sample	N=4	N=4		N=4
♀	80.38 (77.77–82.31)	41.66 (36.69–44.83)	52%	32.44 (31.03–33.92)
Sample	N=5	N=5		N=5

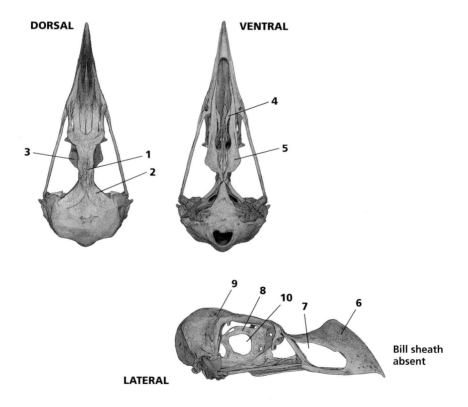

DORSAL

VENTRAL

LATERAL

Bill sheath absent

Family Columbidae: Pigeons and doves

Mourning dove, *Zenaida macroura*

Specimen illustrated: Adult female, SBMNH 4773. Life-size image page 180.
Features: (1) Braincase large, rounded, and smooth. (3) Occipital complex shifted ventrally; foramen magnum (2) on ventral surface of skull. (4) Palatines slender and long; maxillopalatines (5) rounded or circular. (7) Orbits very large; postorbital processes (11) very low. (8) Interorbital septum elevated, narrow, and curving, with hooklike projection (12) on ventral surface. (9) Bill short and slender, with slightly decurved tip; nasal aperture (10) long and linear, nearly 2/3 of the bill length.

	Greatest length of skull	Length of bill	Bill/overall skull percentage	Greatest width of skull
♂	41.67 36.68–44.39	16.99 14.59–18.32	41%	16.55 15.03–17.31
Sample	N=9	N=9		N=9
♀	41.54 (40.80–42.33)	16.00 (13.74–17.42)	39%	16.49 (16.18–16.96)
Sample	N=7	N=7		N=7

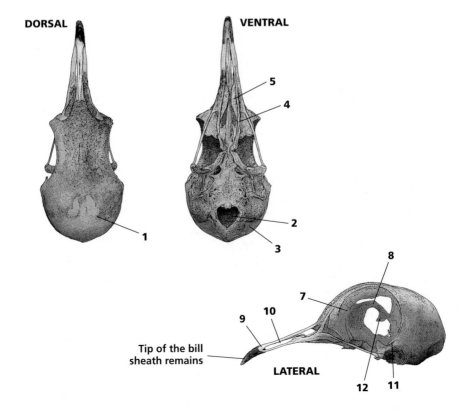

DORSAL

VENTRAL

5
4

1

2

3

8

7

10

9

Tip of the bill
sheath remains

LATERAL

12   11

Family Cuculidae: Cuckoos, roadrunners, and anis

Greater roadrunner, *Geococcyx californianus*

Specimen illustrated: Adult female, SBMNH 3285. Life-size image page 183.

Features: Skull long and slender (1) Lacrimal, or superciliary shield small, rounded, and angled to posterior. (2) Interorbital breadth wide; orbital rims sometimes perforate (3). (4) Posterior of short braincase squared. (5) Premaxillaries broad. (6) Palatines broad to anterior, with rounded corners to posterior (7). (8) Bill long, stout, and decurved at tip; nasal aperture (9) small, oval, and does not go through the bill all the way. (10) Interorbital septum short and deep; (11) interorbital fenestra somewhat square. (12) Postorbital process well elevated.

	Greatest length of skull	Length of bill	Bill/overall skull percentage	Greatest width of skull
♂	80.60 (72.53–89.97)	46.94 (39.90–54.88)	58%	28.58 (27.15–31.87)
Sample	N=4	N=4		N=4
♀	91.92 (84.00–99.61)	56.37 (50.62–60.35)	61%	28.96 (27.05–31.97)
Sample	N=8	N=8		N=8

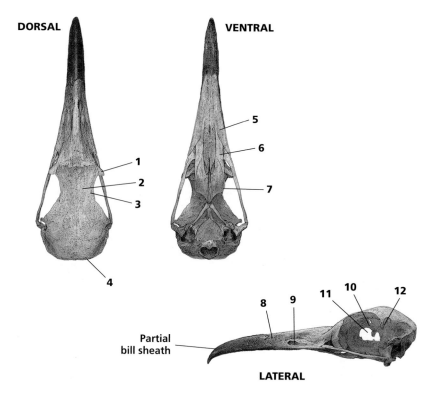

DORSAL

VENTRAL

1
2
3
4

5
6
7

8 9 11 10 12

Partial bill sheath

LATERAL

Family Tytonidae: Barn owls

Barn owl, *Tyto alba*

Specimens illustrated: Adult female, MCZ 334741; adult male with eye ring, MVZ 179980. Life-size image page 183.

Features: Skull longer and thinner than in other owls. (1) Interorbital region inflated and laterally compressed. (2) Braincase broad to posterior and tapering to anterior; posterior edge rounded and with prominent processes (11) to either side. (3) Concave surface to sharp edge of frontals. (4) Palatines broad for much of length and lacking posterior corners. (5) Dorsolateral outline distinctive; apex of skull above very elevated and swollen braincase, then sloping steeply down frontals; frontals (6) also rise steeply from plane of bill. (7) Postorbital process very long, curving, and low. (8) Bill long and straight for an owl, then hooked at anterior; nasal aperture (9) large and oval but only partially perforate through the skull. (10) Sclerotic ring may persist in skulls found in field and are longer than most birds, but small for an owl.

	Greatest length of skull	Length of bill	Bill/overall skull percentage	Greatest width of skull
♂	74.63 (71.78–77.40)	33.04 (31.62–34.47)	44%	41.72 (38.98–44.40)
Sample	N=7	N=7		N=7
♀	74.46 (72.02–77.00)	33.35 (32.28–34.51)	45%	43.06 (41.80–44.16)
Sample	N=7	N=7		N=7

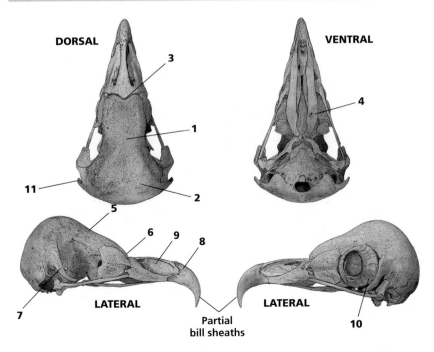

DORSAL

3

1

11

5

2

VENTRAL

4

6   9   8

LATERAL

7

LATERAL

Partial
bill sheaths

10

Family Strigidae: Owls

Western screech-owl, *Otus kennicottii*

Specimen illustrated: Adult male, SBMNH 5056

Features: Please refer to the eastern screech owl *(O. asio)* for a full description. The two species are very similar, but our measurements indicate that the bill may be proportionately larger in western screech owls that in eastern. This can be seen when comparing the bill/greatest length of skull ratio: 34% in western screech owls and 31% in eastern.

	Greatest length of skull	Length of bill	Bill/overall skull percentage	Greatest width of skull
♂	51.52 (49.22–53.39)	17.36 (16.01–18.85)	34%	38.37 (36.57–40.40)
Sample	N=6	N=6		N=6
♀	52.45 (50.73–53.69)	18.09 (16.80–19.96)	34%	38.72 (37.07–39.79)
Sample	N=10	N=10		N=10

LATERAL

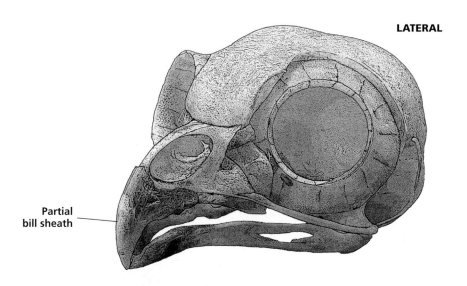

Partial bill sheath

Eastern screech-owl, *Otus asio*

Specimen illustrated: Adult, MCZ 341465. Life-size image page 181.

Features: (1) Skull short and squat, with very broad, short braincase; braincase rounded to posterior and with prominent processes (8) at corners. (2) Palatines long, slender, and curving; do not make contact (3). (4) Very large sclerotic rings; postorbital process (9) prominent. (5) Abrupt, steep rise of frontal bones from plane of the bill. (6) Bill short, deep, and hooked; nasal aperture (7) oval, tapering to posterior, and does not perforate the rostrum.

	Greatest length of skull	Length of bill	Bill/overall skull percentage	Greatest width of skull
♂♀	54.86 (53.39–57.04)	17.15 (15.34–18.77)	31%	39.67 (37.93–41.83)
Sample	N=8	N=8		N=8

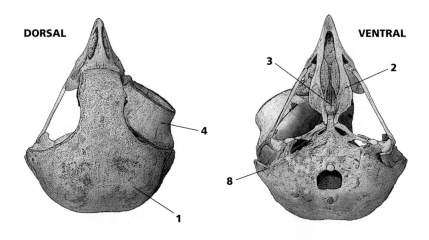

DORSAL

VENTRAL

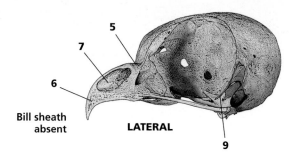

Bill sheath absent

LATERAL

Great horned owl, *Bubo virginianus*

Specimen illustrated: Adult male, MVZ 180469. Life-size image page 184.

Features: (1) Skull short and squat, with very broad, short braincase; braincase rounded to posterior and with prominent processes (8) at corners. (2) Palatines long, slender, and curving; they do not make contact (3). (4) Very large sclerotic rings, a distinctive feature of owl skulls; more often retained in owl skulls found in field than in other species. Postorbital process (9) prominent. (5) Abrupt, steep rise of frontal bones from plane of bill characteristic of owls. (6) Bill short, deep, and hooked (partially covered here by bill sheath); nasal aperture (7) oval, tapering to posterior.

	Greatest length of skull	Length of bill	Bill/overall skull percentage	Greatest width of skull
♂	87.22 (80.12–92.34)	34.82 (31.28–38.11)	40%	64.28 (61.65–67.98)
Sample	N=12	N=12		N=12
♀	90.34 (83.85–98.88)	35.85 (31.00–44.82)	40%	64.87 (57.01–67.92)
Sample	N=14	N=14		N=14

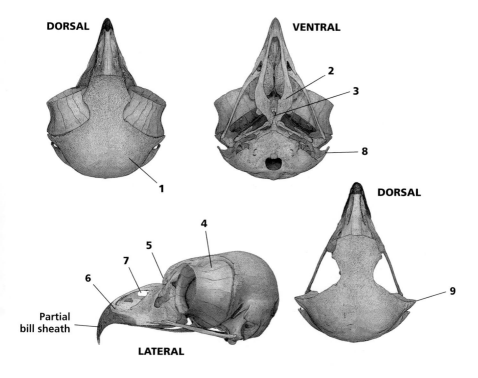

DORSAL

VENTRAL

2

3

8

1

DORSAL

4

5

7

6

9

Partial bill sheath

LATERAL

Family Caprimulgidae: Nighthawks and nightjars

Common nighthawk, *Chordeiles minor*

Specimens illustrated: Adult, MCZ 341480; adult male, ventral view, MVZ 69315. Life-size image page 179.

Features: (1) Braincase short, wide, and somewhat trapezoidal. (2) Bill very broad and triangular. (3) Interorbital breadth very wide, yet palatines (9) visible below. (4) Palatines massive and, viewed together, butterfly-shaped. (5) Orbit very large; interorbital fenestra (6) absent. (7) Bill short and flattened; nostrils (8) tubular.

	Greatest length of skull	Length of bill	Bill/overall skull percentage	Greatest width of skull
♂	36.11 (34.41–37.46)	14.23 (13.43–14.82)	39%	22.87 (22.24–23.23)
Sample	N=10	N=10		N=10
♀	35.10 (33.25–36.94)	13.49 (10.98–14.60)	38%	22.12 (20.86–22.86)
Sample	N=10	N=10		N=10

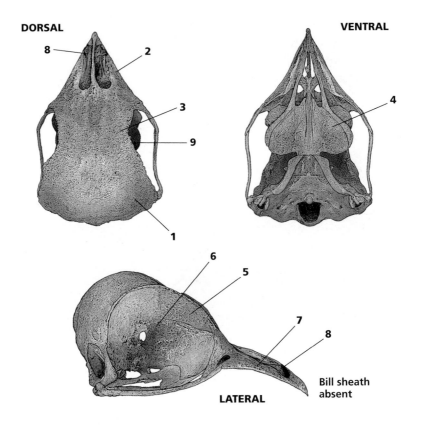

DORSAL

VENTRAL

LATERAL

Bill sheath absent

Family Trochilidae: Hummingbirds

Anna's hummingbird, *Calypte anna*

Specimen illustrated: Adult male, MVZ 180483. Life-size image page 179.
Features: (1) Braincase inflated, round, and smooth with a depressed midline (8). (2) Lacrimal bones large and curving. (3) Palatines long and slender, with long posterior extensions. (4) Foramen magnum on the ventral surface, as occipital complex has been shifted ventrally. (5) Orbits large. (6) Bill very long, slender, and terete; tip slightly decurved. (7) Nasal aperture long and linear, extending more than $1/2$ the length of the skull.

	Greatest length of skull	Length of bill	Bill/overall skull percentage	Greatest width of skull
♂	32.93 (30.92–34.48)	23.12 (20.96–25.04)	70%	9.28 (8.90–9.50)
Sample	N=10	N=10		N=10
♀	33.26 (31.93–34.04)	23.37 (21.18–24.08)	70%	9.06 (8.76–9.28)
Sample	N=10	N=10		N=10

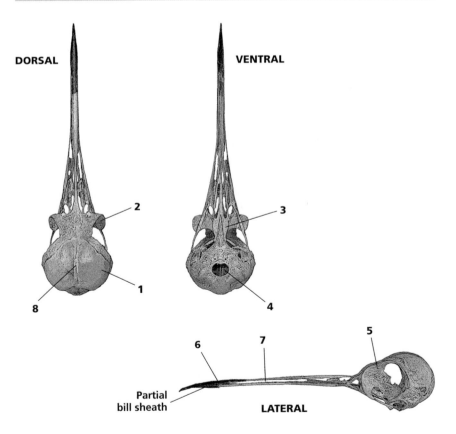

DORSAL

VENTRAL

Partial bill sheath

LATERAL

Family Alcedinidae: Kingfishers

Belted kingfisher, *Ceryle alcyon*

Specimen illustrated: Adult female, SBMNH 3157. Life-size image page 185.

Features: (1) Squamosals concave, creating large grooves at posterior of braincase; occipital crests (3) well developed. (2) Craniofacial hinge pronounced. (4) Palatines wide to posterior and distinctive; triangular shelves (5) at posterior edge, with small bone projections at their outside edges (6). (7) Interorbital fenestra absent. (8) Postorbital process small and elevated. (9) Bill long, straight, and slightly laterally compressed; nasal aperture (10) linear, and does not perforate the rostrum.

	Greatest length of skull	Length of bill	Bill/overall skull percentage	Greatest width of skull
♂	90.18 (79.50–99.48)	55.89 (47.03–63.06)	62%	27.37 (26.06–28.47)
Sample	N=8	N=8		N=8
♀	89.61 (79.81–99.34)	55.06 (50.78–63.16)	61%	27.79 (26.16–29.25)
Sample	N=7	N=7		N=7

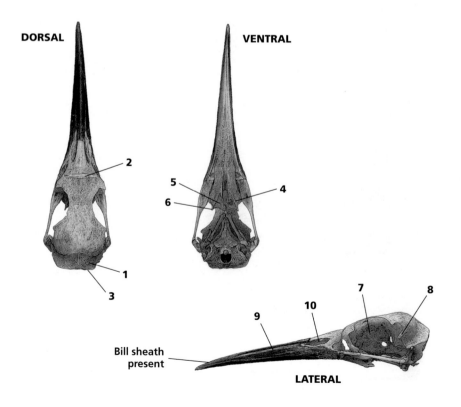

DORSAL

VENTRAL

Bill sheath present

LATERAL

Family Picidae: Woodpeckers

Nothern flicker, *Colaptes auratus*

Specimen illustrated: Adult female, SBMNH 2424. Life-size image page 182.

Features: (1) Braincase round and smooth. (2) Palatines long, tapering to points as tips converge to posterior. (3) Interorbital fenestra absent. (4) Bill long, flattened, and relatively straight; nasal aperture (5) oval.

	Greatest length of skull	Length of bill	Bill/overall skull percentage	Greatest width of skull
♂	62.36 (58.56–66.89)	32.80 (28.45–37.08)	53%	22.39 (21.50–23.29)
Sample	N=10	N=10		N=10
♀	65.66 (55.80–74.63)	35.54 (27.38–41.82)	54%	23.05 (21.92–24.42)
Sample	N=8	N=8		N=8

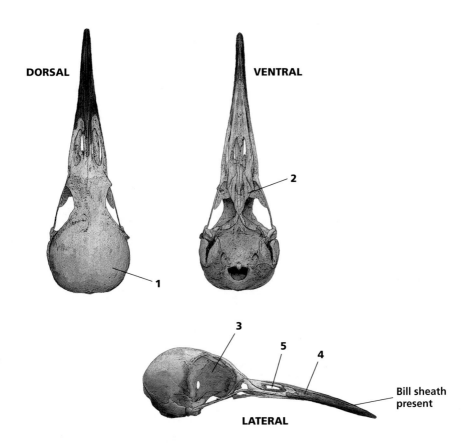

DORSAL

VENTRAL

2

1

3

5

4

Bill sheath present

LATERAL

Pileated woodpecker, *Dryocopus pileatus*

Specimen illustrated: Adult, MCZ 341129. Life-size image page 183.
Features: Woodpecker skulls are dense. (1) Braincase round and smooth. (2) Bill broad and triangular. (3) Orbital rims rugose. (4) Palatines with angular posterior corners, tapering to points as they converge to contact (8) at far posterior. (5) Interorbital septum short, deep, and sloping. (6) Bill long, flattened, and straight; nasal aperture (7) oval.

	Greatest length of skull	Length of bill	Bill/overall skull percentage	Greatest width of skull
♂♀	78.95 (74.33–83.77)	41.81 (36.29–43.97)	53%	28.35 (27.51–28.99)
Sample	N=7	N=7		N=7

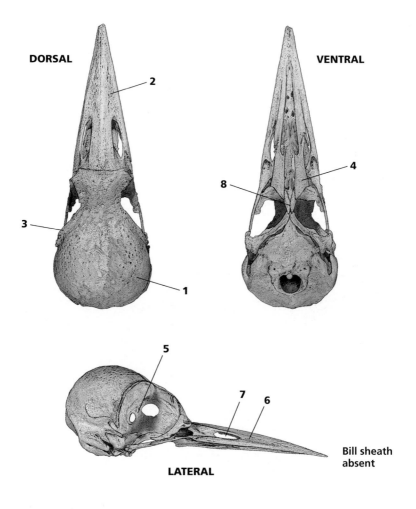

DORSAL

VENTRAL

LATERAL

Bill sheath absent

Family Tyrannidae: Tyrant and New World flycatchers

Eastern phoebe, *Sayornis phoebe*

Specimen illustrated: Adult male, MCZ 342566. Life-size image page 179.

Features: (1) Braincase rounded and smooth. (2) Interorbital breadth narrow. (3) Bill broad and triangular. (4) Premaxillaries large and broad. (5) Palatines long and very slender, with slender extensions at posterior corners (6). (7) Interorbital septum long and slender; interorbital fenestra (10) larger than foramen above. (8) Bill longer than cranium, flattened, and relatively straight (partial bill sheath creates angle in this specimen). (9) Nasal apertures long and relatively oval. (11) Craniofacial hinge straight.

	Greatest length of skull	Length of bill	Bill/overall skull percentage	Greatest width of skull
♂♀	34.23 (33.29–34.97)	16.43 (15.88–16.98)	48%	14.21 (13.92–14.52)
Sample	N=4	N=4		N=4

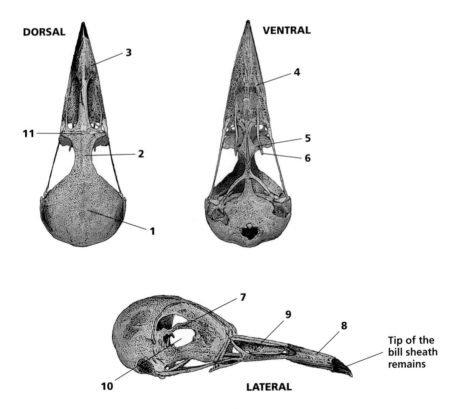

DORSAL

VENTRAL

Tip of the bill sheath remains

LATERAL

Eastern kingbird, *Tyrannus tyrannus*

Specimen illustrated: Adult, MCZ 34104. Life-size image page 180.

Features: (1) Braincase rounded and smooth. (2) Interorbital breadth narrow. (3) Bill broad and triangular; craniofacial hinge (11) slim and curved. (4) Premaxillaries large and broad. (5) Palatines long and slender, with broad, rounded processes at posterior corners (6). (7) Interorbital septum short and slender; interorbital fenestra (10) about equal to foramen above. (8) Bill longer than cranium, flattened, and relatively straight. (9) Nasal apertures oval.

	Greatest length of skull	Length of bill	Bill/overall skull percentage	Greatest width of skull
♂	38.44 (36.15–40.80)	18.61 (16.91–21.28)	48%	16.11 (15.31–16.67)
Sample	N=4	N=4		N=4
♀	39.39 (36.29–41.69)	19.40 (16.95–21.86)	49%	16.60 (14.97–17.98)
Sample	N=8	N=8		N=8

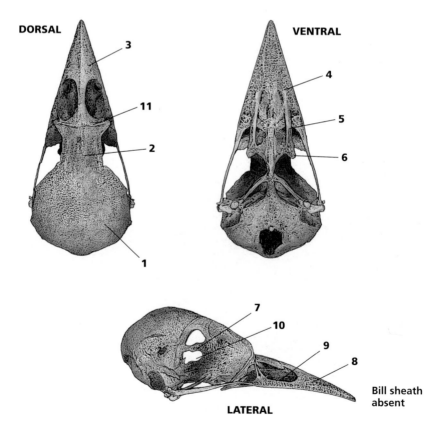

DORSAL

VENTRAL

LATERAL

Bill sheath absent

Family Laniidae: Shrikes

Loggerhead shrike, *Lanius ludovicianus*

Specimen illustrated: Adult male, MVZ 231. Life-size image page 180.
Features: (1) Cranium broader than long, rounded to posterior and smooth. (3) Interorbital breadth relatively narrow; palatines (2) visible below. (4) Palatines slender to anterior, but broad to posterior across angular corners; corners (5) sharp with long, slender processes pointing to posterior. (6) Interorbital septum elevated and long; interorbital fenestra round and smaller. (7) Bill shorter, stout, and hooked at tip; bill sheath (9) notched. (8) Nasal aperture small and round.

	Greatest length of skull	Length of bill	Bill/overall skull percentage	Greatest width of skull
♂	43.29 (40.56–45.28)	19.98 (17.98–22.05)	46%	21.18 (20.27–22.05)
Sample	N=8	N=8		N=8
♀	43.26 (41.40–45.02)	19.67 (18.81–21.32)	45%	21.17 (20.06–21.84)
Sample	N=7	N=7		N=7

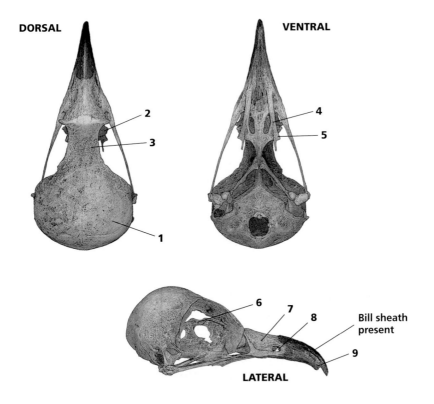

DORSAL

VENTRAL

LATERAL

Bill sheath present

Family Corvidae: Crows and jays

Blue jay, *Cyanocitta cristata*

Specimen illustrated: Adult, MCZ 1047. Life-size image page 181.

Features: (1) Braincase wider than long, rounded, and smooth. (2) Interorbital breadth medium; palatine bones visible below. (3) Bill relatively broad and triangular. (4) Palatine bones slender and parallel to anterior, and broad across angular posterior corners; additional processes at corners lacking. (5) Maxillopalatines damaged in this skull. (7) Interorbital septum deep and well fused with bones above; vertical and slender bone (6) separating interorbital fenestra (9) and optic canal (10) more apparent, as characteristic of corvids. (8) Bill approximately as long as cranium, stout, and slightly angulate; nasal aperture (11) large and oval.

	Greatest length of skull	Length of bill	Bill/overall skull percentage	Greatest width of skull
♂	58.59 (55.44–61.43)	28.81 (27.02–30.69)	49%	24.48 (22.67–24.44)
Sample	N=10	N=10		N=10
♀	55.89 (54.21–56.67)	26.91 (25.55–28.23)	48%	23.55 (23.23–25.52)
Sample	N=10	N=10		N=10

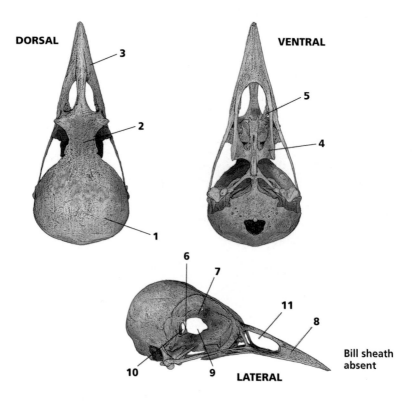

DORSAL

VENTRAL

LATERAL

Bill sheath absent

Black-billed magpie, *Pica hudsonia*

Specimen illustrated: Adult, MCZ 2097. Life-size image page 182.

Features: (1) Braincase wider than long, rounded, and smooth. (2) Interorbital breadth narrow; palatine bones visible below. (3) Bill relatively broad and triangular. (4) Palatine bones slender and parallel to anterior, and broad across angular posterior corners; posterior edges (7) notched. (5) Maxillopalatines damaged in this skull. (6) Vertical bone (6) separating interorbital fenestra (9) and optic canal (10) more apparent, as characteristic of corvids; interorbital septum large. (8) Bill approximately as long as cranium, stout, and slightly decurved; nasal aperture (11) is oval.

	Greatest length of skull	Length of bill	Bill/overall skull percentage	Greatest width of skull
♂	67.38 (65.54–69.31)	32.59 (30.12–34.92)	48%	29.21 (28.32–30.24)
Sample	N=8	N=8		N=8
♀	65.34 (61.96–71.98)	31.93 (27.88–39.96)	49%	28.68 (27.36–30.64)
Sample	N=8	N=8		N=8

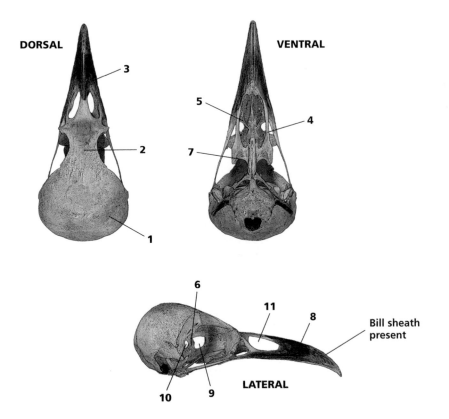

DORSAL
3
2
1

VENTRAL
5
4
7

6
11
8
Bill sheath present
10   9
LATERAL

American crow, *Corvus brachyrhynchos*

Specimen illustrated: Adult female, SBMNH 4356. Life-size image page 184.

Features: (1) Braincase wider than long, rounded, and smooth. (2) Interorbital breadth narrower than in raven, and palatine bones visible below. (3) Bill relatively broad and triangular. (4) Palatine bones slender and parallel to anterior, and broad across angular posterior corners; posterior edges (7) concave. (5) Maxillopalatines converge to posterior. Vertical bone (6) separating interorbital fenestra (9) and optic canal (10) more apparent; as characteristic of corvids; interorbital fenestra much larger than in ravens. Interorbital septum large. (8) Bill longer than cranium, stout, and slightly decurved; nasal aperture (11) oval.

	Greatest length of skull	Length of bill	Bill/overall skull percentage	Greatest width of skull
♂	85.43 (77.76–95.09)	46.62 (43.06–51.76)	53%	35.77 (32.96–39.37)
Sample	N=10	N=10		N=10
♀	85.14 (75.15–91.66)	46.20 (41.02–51.52)	54%	35.95 (33.53–38.75)
Sample	N=7	N=7		N=7

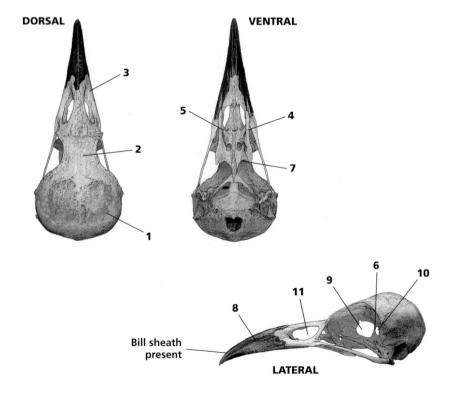

DORSAL

VENTRAL

LATERAL

Bill sheath present

Common raven, *Corvus corax*

Specimen illustrated: Adult, SBMNH 780. Life-size image page 186.

Features: (1) Braincase wider than long, rounded, and smooth. (2) Interorbital breadth wider than in crows and palatines are not visible below. (3) Bill relatively broad and triangular. (4) Palatine bones slender and parallel to anterior, and broad across angular posterior corners; posterior edges (7) concave. (5) Maxillopalatines converge to posterior. Vertical bone (6) separating interorbital fenestra (9) and optic canal (10) more apparent; as characteristic of corvids; interorbital fenestra much smaller than in crows. Interorbital septum large. (8) Bill longer than cranium, stout, and slightly decurved; nasal aperture (11) oval.

	Greatest length of skull	Length of bill	Bill/overall skull percentage	Greatest width of skull
♂	112.83 (107.05–116.46)	67.56 (63.18–69.63)	60%	45.90 (45.04–47.58)
Sample	N=4	N=4		N=4
♀	109.98 (107.13–114.75)	65.56 (63.08–70.45)	60%	45.77 (44.65–48.24)
Sample	N=4	N=4		N=4

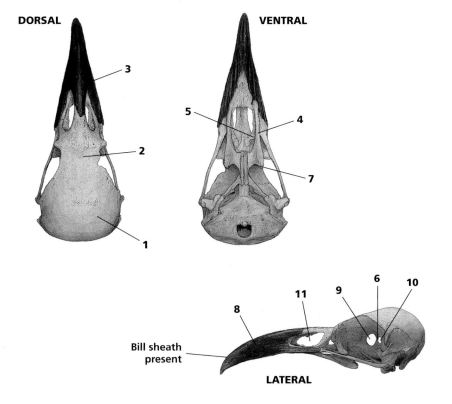

DORSAL

3

2

1

VENTRAL

5

4

7

6 10

11 9

8

Bill sheath present

LATERAL

Family Hirundinidae: Swallows

Cliff swallow, *Petrochelidon pyrrhonota*

Specimen illustrated: Adult male, MVZ 151930. Life-size image page 179.
Features: (1) Bill very broad, short, flattened (2), and slightly hooked at tip. (3) Interorbital breadth very narrow. (4) Braincase broader than long, rounded to posterior and smooth. (5) Slender jugal arches wide apart. (6) Palatines slender, taper to anterior, and broad across angular posterior corners; posterior edges (7) concave. (8) Interorbital septum horizontal, long, and slender. (9) Frontals rise abruptly from plane of bill. (10) Nasal apertures large and oval.

	Greatest length of skull	Length of bill	Bill/overall skull percentage	Greatest width of skull
♂	28.11 (27.77–29.00)	10.87 (9.88–11.56)	39%	15.00 (14.22–15.83)
Sample	N=10	N=10		N=10
♀	27.72 (26.67–28.67)	10.57 (9.96–11.33)	38%	15.11 (14.41–15.70)
Sample	N=10	N=10		N=10

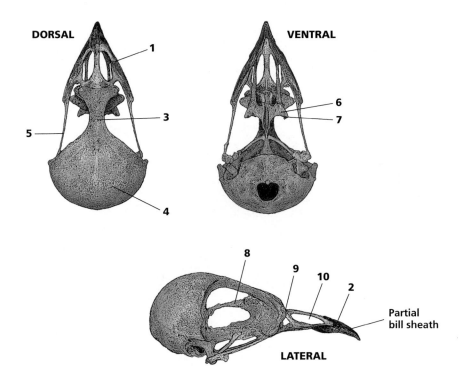

DORSAL

VENTRAL

LATERAL

Partial bill sheath

Family Paridae: Chickadees and titmice

Black-capped chickadee, *Poecile atricapillus*

Specimen illustrated: Adult, MCZ 7144. Life-size image page 179.

Features: (1) Braincase large, oval, and smooth. (2) Interorbital breadth very narrow. (3) Palatines proportionately shorter, with angular posterior corners; pointy processes (4) to posterior; posterior edges (5) concave. (6) Bill short, flattened, stout, and much shorter than the cranium; nasal aperture (7) oval. (8) Interorbital septum horizontal; ventral fenestra very small (9). (10) Foramen magnum on ventral surface. (11) Craniofacial hinge pronounced.

	Greatest length of skull	Length of bill	Bill/overall skull percentage	Greatest width of skull
♂	26.08 (24.44–27.65)	9.27 (7.43–10.24)	36%	14.26 (14.06–14.42)
Sample	N=9	N=9		N=9
♀	25.65 (23.69–27.24)	8.88 (7.10–9.71)	35%	13.99 (13.41–14.42)
Sample	N=6	N=6		N=6

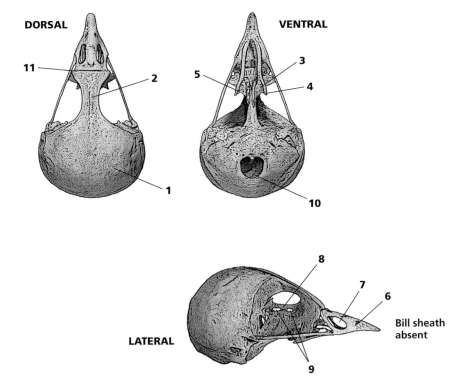

DORSAL

VENTRAL

LATERAL

Bill sheath absent

Family Troglodytidae: Wrens

House wren, *Troglodytes aedon*

Specimen illustrated: Adult male, SBMNH 4570. Life-size image page 179.
Features: (1) Braincase large, round, and smooth. (2) Interorbital very narrow. (3) Palatines slender and slightly convergent to anterior; angular posterior corners with concave posterior edges (4). (5) Interorbital septum slender and very long. (6) Post-orbital process slender and at about midline of skull. (7) Bill shorter than cranium, narrow, pointed, slightly decurved, and flattened; nasal aperture (8) long and oval. (9) Thin jugal arches with very narrow spread.

	Greatest length of skull	Length of bill	Bill/overall skull percentage	Greatest width of skull
♂	29.05 (27.46–32.65)	13.38 (11.98–15.46)	46%	13.16 (12.66–14.04)
Sample	N=9	N=9		N=9
♀	29.70 (28.68–30.56)	13.95 (12.42–15.32)	47%	13.28 (19.99–13.52)
Sample	N=5	N=5		N=5

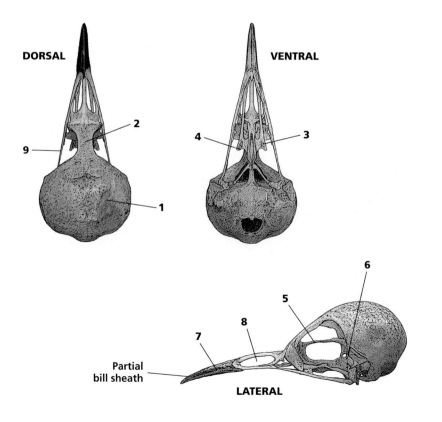

DORSAL

VENTRAL

Partial
bill sheath

LATERAL

Family Regulidae: Kinglets

Ruby-crowned kinglet, *Regulus calendula*

Specimen illustrated: Adult female, MVZ 150859. Life-size image page 179.

Features: (1) Braincase large, round, and smooth. (2) Interorbital very narrow. (3) Palatines slender and slightly bowed, with concave lateral edges to anterior; angular posterior corners with notched posterior edges (4). (5) Interorbital septum slender and very long. (6) Foramen magnum and occipital complex shifted ventrally. (7) Bill shorter than cranium, slightly decurved and flattened; nasal aperture (8) long and oval. (9) Thin jugal arches with very narrow spread.

	Greatest length of skull	Length of bill	Bill/overall skull percentage	Greatest width of skull
♂	25.30 (24.46–27.12)	11.21 (10.29–13.44)	44%	11.74 (11.28–12.32)
Sample	N=10	N=10		N=10
♀	24.64 (23.81–26.08)	10.54 (9.34–11.77)	43%	11.53 (10.46–12.04)
Sample	N=10	N=10		N=10

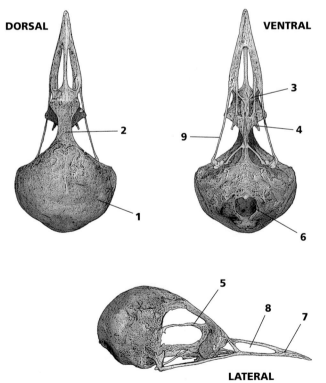

DORSAL

VENTRAL

2

9

3

4

1

6

5

8

7

LATERAL

Bill sheath absent

Family Turdidae: Thrushes

American robin, *Turdus migratorius*

Specimen illustrated: Adult female, SBMNH 7122. Life-size image page 180.

Features: (1) Braincase rounded and smooth. (2) Interorbital relatively narrow. (3) Maxillopalatines linear, converging to posterior on vomer. (4) Palatines slender and parallel to anterior, angular and notched (5) to posterior. (6) Interorbital septum long, slender, and just above midline of orbit; in this specimen, the vertical component (7) dividing interorbital fenestra and optic foramen broken. (8) Upper foramen long and slender. (10) Bill shorter than cranium and relatively slender, tip slightly decurved; nasal aperture (9) large and oval. (11) Thin jugal arches straight to outside edges of cranium.

	Greatest length of skull	Length of bill	Bill/overall skull percentage	Greatest width of skull
♂	47.71 (46.19–50.06)	22.15 (20.65–23.81)	46%	19.98 (19.49–20.55)
Sample	N=10	N=10		N=10
♀	47.52 (45.32–49.50)	22.20 (20.63–23.87)	47%	19.96 (19.23–20.70)
Sample	N=10	N=10		N=10

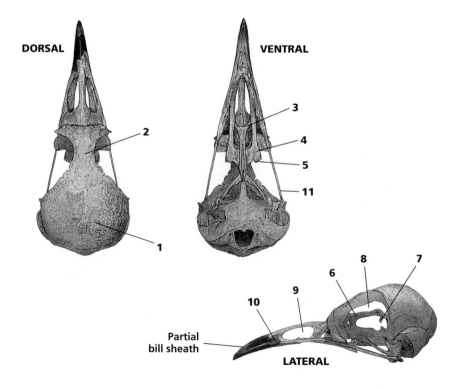

DORSAL

VENTRAL

LATERAL

Partial bill sheath

Family Mimidae: Mockingbirds and thrashers

Northern mockingbird, *Mimus polyglottos*

Specimen illustrated: Adult male, SBMNH 1801. Life-size image page 180.

Features: (1) Braincase round and smooth. (2) Interorbital narrow. (3) Maxillopalatines linear, converging to posterior. (4) Palatines slender and parallel to anterior, angular and notched (5) to posterior. (6) Interorbital septum long, slender, and just above midline of orbit; vertical component (7) dividing interorbital fenestra and optic foramen broken. (8) Upper foramen long and slender. (9) Bill shorter than cranium and slender, tip slightly decurved; nasal aperture (10) large and oval. (11) Craniofacial hinge prominent.

	Greatest length of skull	Length of bill	Bill/overall skull percentage	Greatest width of skull
♂	44.56 (40.57–46.20)	21.12 (18.77–23.32)	47%	18.24 (17.49–18.73)
Sample	N=10	N=10		N=10
♀	44.30 (41.84–46.50)	20.30 (17.19–22.52)	46%	17.88 (17.44–18.40)
Sample	N=7	N=7		N=7

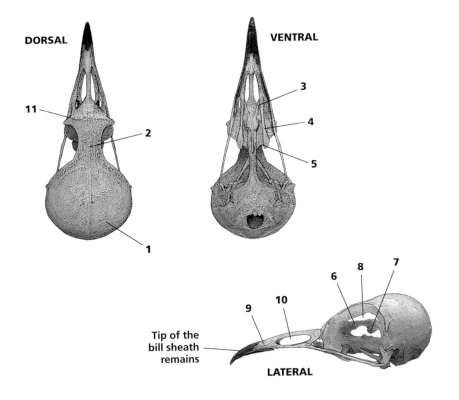

DORSAL

VENTRAL

11

2

3

4

5

1

6 8 7

9 10

Tip of the bill sheath remains

LATERAL

Brown thrasher, *Toxostoma rufum*

Specimen illustrated: Adult female, MCZ 343844. Life-size image page 181.

Features: (1) Braincase round and smooth. (2) Interorbital relatively narrow. (3) Palatines slender and, viewed together, narrower; also angular and notched (5) to posterior. (4) Foramen magnum and occipital complex shifted ventrally. (6) Interorbital septum long, slender, and just above midline of orbit; vertical component (7) dividing interorbital fenestra and optic foramen sloping. (8) Upper fenestra long and slender. (9) Bill shorter than cranium, slender, and slightly decurved; nasal aperture (10) large and oval. (11) Thin jugal arches with much narrower spread than in American robin.

	Greatest length of skull	Length of bill	Bill/overall skull percentage	Greatest width of skull
♂	53.05 (52.49–53.91)	25.63 (21.76–28.06)	48%	19.35 (18.74–19.75)
Sample	N=4	N=6		N=6
♀	55.50 49.04	25.67 (22.83–29.22)	49%	19.60 (19.39–19.79)
Sample	N=2	N=3		N=3

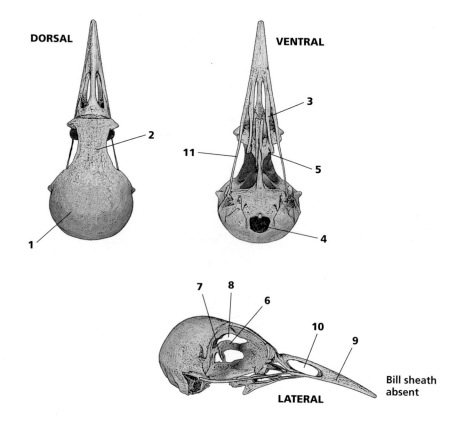

DORSAL

VENTRAL

LATERAL

Bill sheath absent

California thrasher, *Toxostoma redivivum*

Specimens illustrated: Adult male, SBMNH 1140; female with eye ring, 1839 (p. 31). Life-size image page 182.

Features: (1) Braincase rounded and smooth. (2) Interorbital narrow. (3) Maxillo-palatines linear, converging to posterior. (4) Palatines slender and parallel to anterior, angular and notched (5) to posterior. (6) Interorbital septum long, slender, and just above midline of orbit; vertical component (7) dividing interorbital fenestra and optic foramen broken. (8) Upper fenestra long and slender. (9) Bill long, slender, and decurved; nasal aperture (10) oval. (11) Thin jugal arches straight and attach at outside edges of cranium.

	Greatest length of skull	Length of bill	Bill/overall skull percentage	Greatest width of skull
♂	60.01 (56.97–66.25)	31.38 (28.14–39.31)	52%	21.27 (20.61–22.09)
Sample	N=10	N=10		N=10
♀	56.66 (54.52–58.51)	29.03 (26.54–33.04)	51%	21.10 (20.69–21.82)
Sample	N=6	N=6		N=6

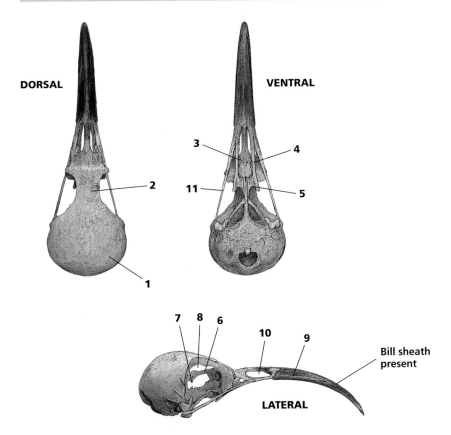

DORSAL

VENTRAL

LATERAL

Bill sheath present

Family Sturnidae: Starlings

European starling, *Sturnus vulgaris*

Specimen illustrated: Adult male, SBMNH 1979. Life-size image page 181.

Features: (1) Braincase very round and smooth. (2) Interorbital breadth narrow. (3) Palatines long, slender, and in contact for more than half of entire length; lateral edges (4) concave; posterior edges with rounded notches (9). (6) Interorbital septum of medium length; interorbital fenestra (5) rectangular. (7) Bill as long as cranium and straight; tomium slightly angulate. (8) Nasal aperture oval.

	Greatest length of skull	Length of bill	Bill/overall skull percentage	Greatest width of skull
♂	51.28 (48.20–59.04)	27.34 (25.45–34.09)	53%	19.30 (18.88–19.68)
Sample	N=7	N=7		N=7
♀	50.83	25.46	50%	19.11
Sample	N=1	N=1		N=1

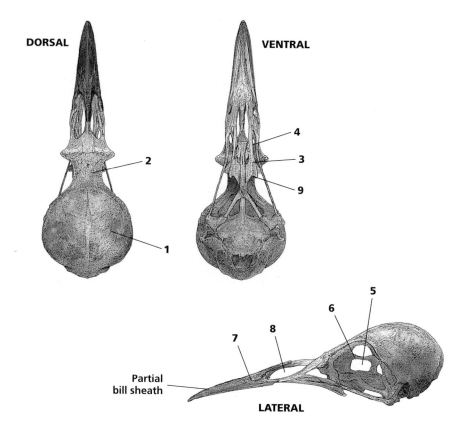

DORSAL

VENTRAL

2

4

3

9

1

5

6

8

7

Partial bill sheath

LATERAL

Family Parulidae: Wood warblers

Yellow warbler, *Dendroica petechia*

Specimen illustrated: Adult female, SBMNH 4619. Life-size image page 179.

Features: (1) Braincase very round and smooth. (2) Interorbital breadth relatively narrow. (3) Palatines very slender and angular; posterior corner (4) with two processes and posterior edges (5) notched. (6) Interorbital septum long, slender, horizontal, and at approximately two-thirds height of orbit. (7) Postorbital process long, slender, and low. (8) Bill short, straight, pointed, compressed, and slightly decurved; nasal aperture (9) oval.

	Greatest length of skull	Length of bill	Bill/overall skull percentage	Greatest width of skull
♂	28.45 (26.99–30.55)	12.56 (10.96–14.39)	44%	12.43 (11.80–13.44)
Sample	N=10	N=10		N=10
♀	28.79 (26.53–29.48)	12.95 (12.34–13.68)	45%	12.74 (12.16–13.52)
Sample	N=5	N=5		N=5

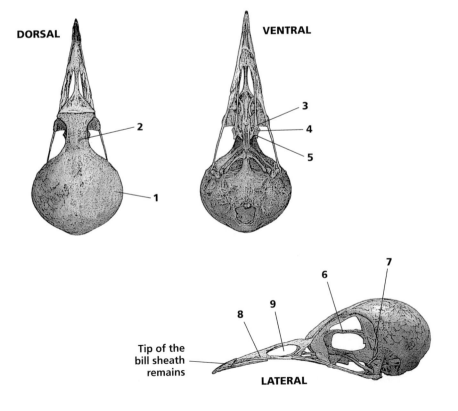

DORSAL

VENTRAL

Tip of the bill sheath remains

LATERAL

Family Emberizidae: Towhees, sparrows, longspurs, and buntings

Spotted towhee, *Pipilo maculatus*

Specimen illustrated: Adult male, MVZ 31378. Life-size image page 179.
Features: (1) Braincase relatively large, broad, and squared to posterior. (2) Bill relatively broad and triangular; tomium (3) angulate, and slope of culmen (4) steep. (5) Palatines converge to anterior and have long processes (6) projecting at posterior corners. (7) Interorbital septum long, slender, and horizontal; interorbital fenestra below and upper fenestra approximately equal in size. (8) Nasal aperture oval. (9) Slender jugal arches strongly converge to anterior and attach at outside edges of braincase.

	Greatest length of skull	Length of bill	Bill/overall skull percentage	Greatest width of skull
♂	34.25 (32.98–35.72)	12.02 (11.15–13.88)	35%	19.49 (18.94–20.20)
Sample	N=7	N=7		N=7
♀	33.56 (31.96–35.60)	12.49 (11.18–13.75)	37%	19.07 (18.14–20.01)
Sample	N=7	N=7		N=7

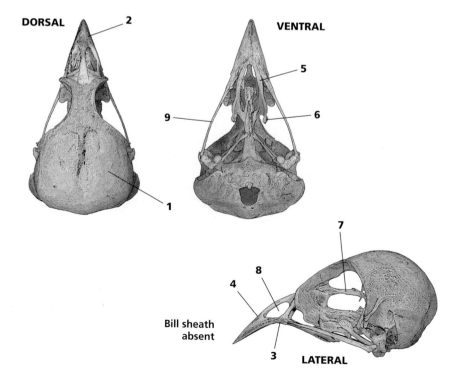

DORSAL

VENTRAL

Bill sheath absent

LATERAL

Song sparrow, *Melospiza melodia*

Specimen illustrated: Adult male, SBMNH 1392. Life-size image page 179.

Features: (1) Braincase relatively large, oval, and rounded to posterior. (2) Bill relatively broad and triangular; tomium (3) angulate, and slope of culmen (4) steep. (5) Palatines converge to anterior and have long, complex processes (6) projecting at posterior corners. (7) Interorbital septum long, slender, and horizontal; interorbital fenestra larger than upper fenestra. (8) Nasal aperture oval.

	Greatest length of skull	Length of bill	Bill/overall skull percentage	Greatest width of skull
♂	29.71 (28.64–30.96)	10.29 (9.63–11.28)	35%	15.67 (15.52–15.91)
Sample	N=5	N=5		N=5
♀	28.50 (26.80–29.98)	9.84 (8.00–10.93)	35%	15.24 (14.52–15.83)
Sample	N=6	N=6		N=6

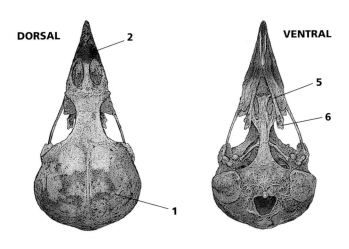

DORSAL 2

VENTRAL 5 6

1

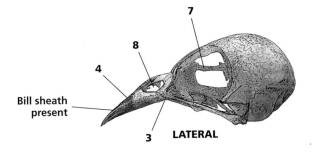

7

8

4

Bill sheath present

3 LATERAL

Dark-eyed junco, *Junco hyemalis*

Specimen illustrated: Adult female, SBMNH 4428. Life-size image page 179.
Features: (1) Braincase large, oval, and smooth. (2) Bill relatively broad and triangular; tomium (3) angulate, and slope of culmen (4) steep. (5) Palatines parallel to
anterior and have long, complex processes (6) projecting at posterior corners. (7)
Interorbital septum long, slender, and horizontal; interorbital fenestra larger than
upper fenestra. (8) Nasal aperture oval.

	Greatest length of skull	Length of bill	Bill/overall skull percentage	Greatest width of skull
♂	28.61 (26.66–29.97)	10.08 (8.90–11.18)	35%	15.28 (14.66–15.82)
Sample	N=10	N=10		N=10
♀	28.39 (26.98–29.64)	9.57 (8.14–10.85)	34%	15.72 (15.34–16.24)
Sample	N=7	N=7		N=7

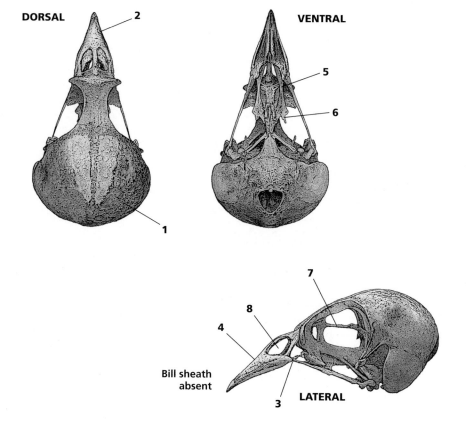

DORSAL

2

VENTRAL

5

6

1

7

8

4

Bill sheath
absent

3

LATERAL

Family Cardinalidae: Cardinal, grosbeaks, and buntings

Northern cardinal, *Cardinalis cardinalis*

Specimen illustrated: Adult female, MCZ 7974. Life-size image page 179.

Features: (1) Braincase rounded and smooth. (2) Bill broad and stout; tomium (3) very angulate, related culmen (4) sloping steeply. (5) Posterior processes of palatines very large and triangular. (6) Interorbital septum large, with extension far to posterior and short; much of interorbital region solid. (7) Nasal aperture oval.

	Greatest length of skull	Length of bill	Bill/overall skull percentage	Greatest width of skull
♂	35.28 (32.90–37.20)	12.72 (10.34–15.59)	36%	19.44 (18.29–20.23)
Sample	N=10	N=10		N=10
♀	34.64 (32.20–36.99)	12.44 (9.42–15.70)	36%	19.20 (17.66–20.19)
Sample	N=5	N=5		N=5

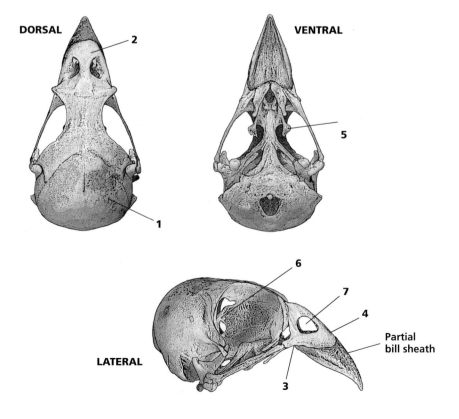

DORSAL

2

1

VENTRAL

5

6

7

4

Partial bill sheath

LATERAL

3

Family Icteridae: Blackbirds

Red-winged blackbird, *Agelaius phoeniceus*

Specimen illustrated: Adult male, SBMNH 3563. Life-size image page 180.

Features: (1) Braincase rounder, wider than long, and smooth. (2) Interorbital breadth narrow. (3) Palatines long, slender, curved, and widely separated (10); posterior corners with slender processes (4) that point to posterior. (5) Interorbital septum short; interorbital fenestra small, smaller than fenestra above. (6) Bill deep at base and tapering to tip; tomium (7) angled; culmen (8) first sloping up a short distance before sloping steeply to anterior. (9) Nasal aperture oval, with small hole through nasal septum.

	Greatest length of skull	Length of bill	Bill/overall skull percentage	Greatest width of skull
♂	42.11 (38.63–48.68)	18.61 (14.35–26.60)	44%	19.33 (18.87–19.80)
Sample	N=10	N=10		N=10
♀	35.28 (34.32–38.58)	16.09 (13.42–19.88)	46%	17.73 (15.32-18.54)
Sample	N=8	N=8		N=8

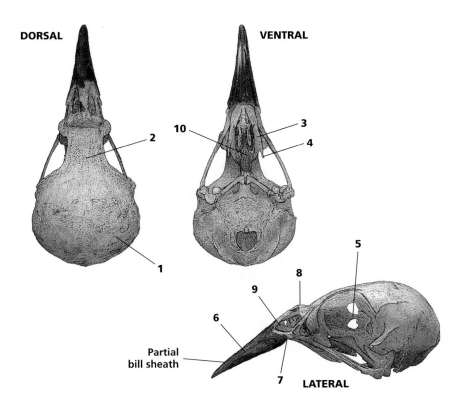

DORSAL

VENTRAL

2

10

3

4

1

5

8

9

6

7

Partial bill sheath

LATERAL

Western meadowlark, *Sturnella neglecta*

Specimen illustrated: Adult female, MVZ 54450. Life-size image page 181.

Features: (1) Braincase oval, wider than long, and smooth. (2) Interorbital breadth narrow. (3) Palatines long and slender, with concave lateral edges; posterior corners with slender, rounded processes (4) that point to posterior. (5) Interorbital septum long, slender, and sloping to posterior; interorbital fenestra much larger than fenestra above. (6) Bill deep at base and tapering to tip; tomium (7) angled; culmen (8) first sloping up a short distance before sloping steeply to anterior. (9) Nasal aperture oval.

	Greatest length of skull	Length of bill	Bill/overall skull percentage	Greatest width of skull
♂	54.91 (49.48–63.22)	27.92 (23.03–35.08)	51%	21.53 (20.78–22.12)
Sample	N=10	N=10		N=10
♀	52.13 (49.96–56.33)	26.45 (24.74–30.72)	51%	20.82 (20.11–21.61)
Sample	N=5	N=5		N=5

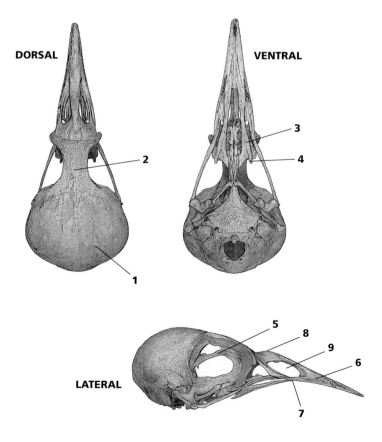

DORSAL

VENTRAL

LATERAL

Bill sheath absent

Common grackle, *Quiscalus quiscula*

Specimen illustrated: Adult male, MCZ 2486. Life-size image page 181.

Features: (1) Braincase oval, wider than long, and smooth. (2) Interorbital breadth narrow. (3) Palatines long and slender; posterior corners with slender, rounded processes (4) that point to posterior well forward of posterior edge (10). (5) Interorbital septum long and deep; interorbital fenestra slightly smaller than fenestra above. (6) Bill deep at base and tapering to tip; tomium (7) angled; culmen (8) first sloping up a short distance before sloping steeply to anterior. (9) Nasal aperture oval, with only a small opening through the nasal septum.

	Greatest length of skull	Length of bill	Bill/overall skull percentage	Greatest width of skull
♂	60.70 (56.14–64.10)	31.02 (26.70–32.51)	51%	22.30 (21.27–23.25)
Sample	N=10	N=10		N=10
♀	55.92 (53.76–57.96)	27.02 (24.06–28.47)	48%	21.13 (20.82–21.55)
Sample	N=7	N=7		N=7

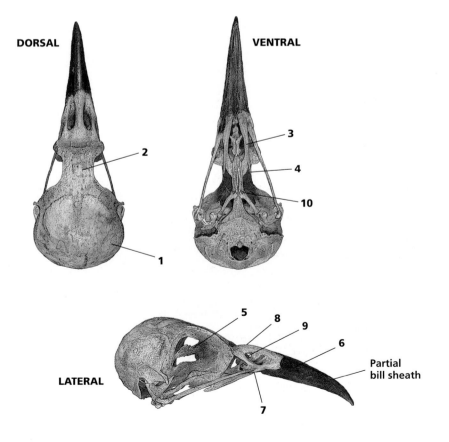

DORSAL

VENTRAL

LATERAL

Partial bill sheath

Baltimore oriole, *Icterus galbula*

Specimen illustrated: Adult female, MCZ 2584. Life-size image page 180.

Features: (1) Braincase oval and smooth. (2) Interorbital breadth narrow. (3) Palatines long and slender; posterior corners with slender processes (4) that point to the posterior. (5) Interorbital septum long, slender, and sloping to posterior; interorbital fenestra much larger than fenestra above. (6) Bill deep at base and tapering to pointed tip; tomium (7) angled; culmen (8) slopes to anterior. (9) Nasal aperture oval. (10) Maxillopalatines curved and converging to posterior.

	Greatest length of skull	Length of bill	Bill/overall skull percentage	Greatest width of skull
♂	38.79 (36.84–39.94)	18.06 (15.49–19.07)	47%	17.28 (16.78–17.67)
Sample	N=10	N=10		N=10
♀	37.51 (35.87–39.43)	16.84 (14.77–18.98)	45%	17.30 (17.11–17.52)
Sample	N=7	N=7		N=7

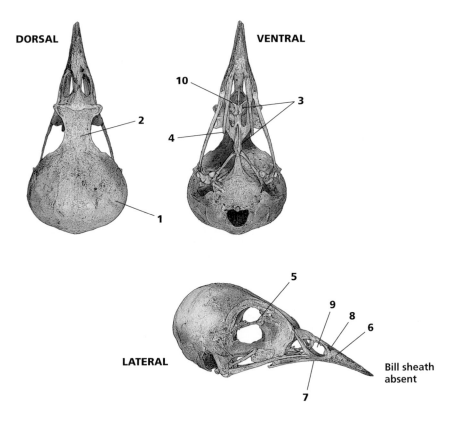

DORSAL

VENTRAL

LATERAL

Bill sheath absent

Family Fringillidae: Finches

Red crossbill, *Loxia curvirostra*

Specimens illustrated: Adult, MCZ 2426. Life-size image page 179.

Features: (1) Braincase oval, wider than long, and smooth. (2) Interorbital breadth relatively wide. (3) Bill sheath bent and curving right; actual bone of bill straight. The lower mandible bill sheath curves the opposite way, creating the crossed bill. (4) Palatines relatively short and broad; lateral edges (5) very curved and concave; posterior processes (4) large and rounded; posterior edges (6) deeply notched. (7) Interorbital septum large, with short, sloping extension at posterior edge of orbit; much of interorbital region solid. (8) Bill conical and stout; tomium (9) very angulate; culmen (10) steeply sloping to anterior. (11) Nasal aperture oval.

	Greatest length of skull	Length of bill	Bill/overall skull percentage	Greatest width of skull
♂	35.12 (30.94–38.04)	17.98 (13.90–19.56)	51%	19.27 (17.48–20.34)
Sample	N=8	N=8		N=7
♀	35.91 (33.83–37.78)	17.42 (15.16–18.33)	49%	19.32 (16.94–20.98)
Sample	N=7	N=7		N=7

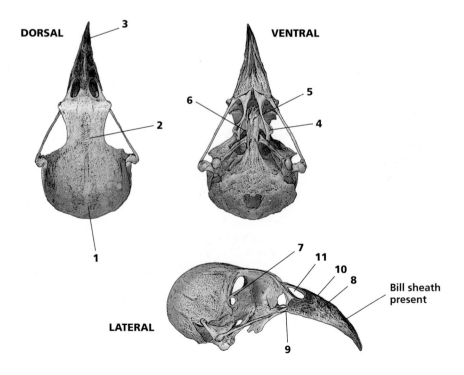

DORSAL

VENTRAL

LATERAL

Bill sheath present

American goldfinch, *Carduelis tristis*

Specimen illustrated: Adult male, SBMNH 4636. Life-size image page 179.

Features: (1) Braincase large and oval, wider than long, and smooth. (2) Interorbital breadth relatively broad. (3) Palatines short and wide apart (5); posterior processes (4) sharp and angular. (6) Postorbital processes long and slender. (7) Interorbital septum large, with short, sloping extension at posterior edge of orbit; much of interorbital region solid. (8) Bill conical and stout; tomium (9) very angulate; culmen (10) steeply sloping to anterior. (11) Nasal aperture oval.

	Greatest length of skull	Length of bill	Bill/overall skull percentage	Greatest width of skull
♂	23.73 (21.44–26.00)	9.66 (6.95–12.08)	41%	12.75 (12.19–13.43)
Sample	N=10	N=10		N=10
♀	23.44 (21.97–25.45)	9.78 (8.5–12.44)	42%	12.53 (12.24–12.90)
Sample	N=9	N=9		N=9

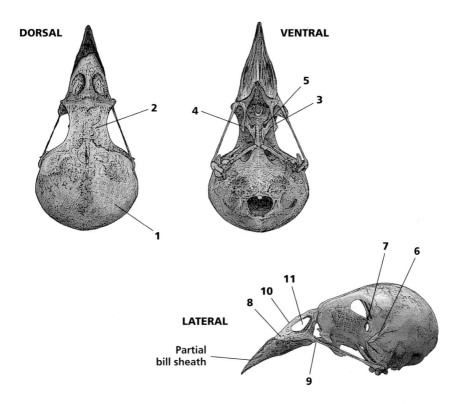

DORSAL

VENTRAL

LATERAL

Partial bill sheath

Evening grosbeak, *Coccothraustes vespertinus*

Specimen illustrated: Adult male, MCZ 7814. Life-size image page 180.

Features: (1) Braincase large and swollen, with ridges (4) developing in adults. (2) Interorbital breadth very wide. (3) Bill short, broad, and very stout; premaxillaries (5) very large and broad. (6) Palatines angled and converge to anterior; posterior processes (8) at corners large and notched; inner structures (7) slim and widely separated. (9) Postorbital processes stout. (10) Interorbital septum large, with short, sloping extension at posterior edge of orbit; much of interorbital region solid. (11) Bill conical, stout, and decurved; tomium (14) very angulate; culmen (12) steeply sloping to anterior. (13) Nasal aperture oval to round with only a very small perforation of the nasal septum. (15) Jugal arches are much taller than they are wide.

	Greatest length of skull	Length of bill	Bill/overall skull percentage	Greatest width of skull
♂	39.99 (36.26–41.73)	17.48 (14.90–18.45)	44%	20.35 (18.20–20.77)
Sample	N=10	N=10		N=10
♀	40.21 (38.60–41.08)	17.45 (15.79–18.35)	43%	20.39 (19.03–21.12)
Sample	N=10	N=10		N=10

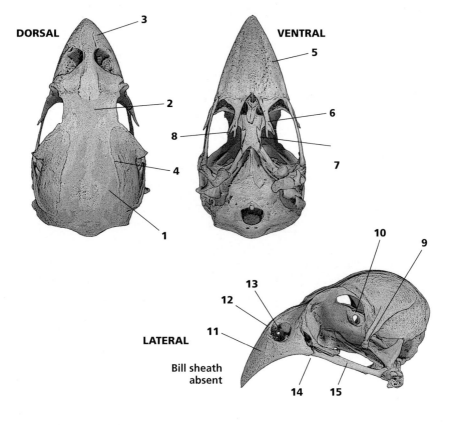

DORSAL

VENTRAL

LATERAL

Bill sheath absent

Here is a visual account of thirteen common and representative amphibians and reptiles from North America. Lizards often have a hole on the dorsal surface of the brain cavity, called the pineal foramen, which is a structure that senses light in the primitive nervous system. Also note the many simple teeth in most reptiles and amphibians. These are ideal for holding slick prey, maneuvering them, and then swallowing them whole. The pitted appearance of some species, such as the alligator, allows for an armorlike adherence of skin to bone. The following pages hint at the diversity in these vast and varied classes of creatures.

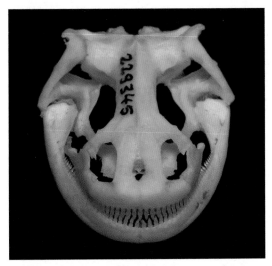

Pacific giant salamander *(Dicamptodon ensatus)*. MUSEUM OF VERTEBRATE ZOOLOGY, UC BERKELEY, 229345.

Gila monster

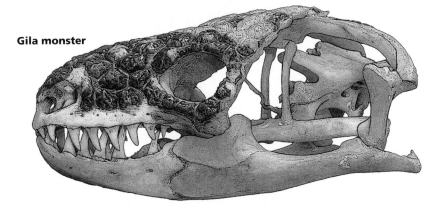

Order Anura: Frogs and toads

Western toad, *Bufo boreas*

Specimen illustrated: Adult, MVZ 142849
Greatest length of skull: 24.56 mm (1 in.), measured A–B
Life-size image page 189

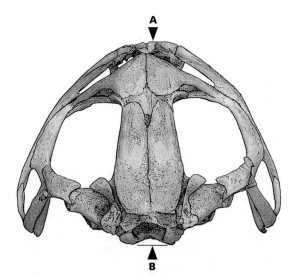

DORSAL

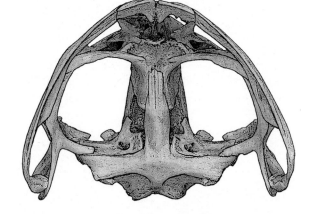

VENTRAL

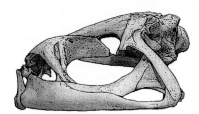

LATERAL

American bullfrog, *Rana catesbeiana*

Specimen illustrated: Adult, MVZ 175959
Greatest length of skull: 43.40 mm (1.7 in.), measured A–B
Life-size image page 189

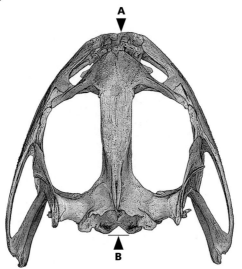

DORSAL

VENTRAL

LATERAL

Order Caudata: Salamanders

Pacific giant salamander, *Dicamptodon ensatus*

Specimen illustrated: Adult, MVZ 229345
Greatest length of skull: 24.49 mm (1 in.)
Life-size image page 189

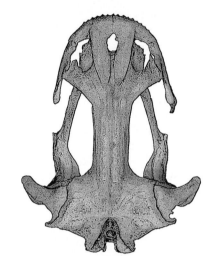

DORSAL

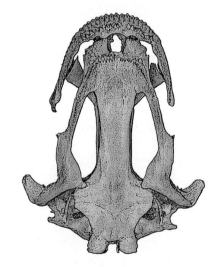

VENTRAL

LATERAL

Order Squamata: Lizards and snakes

Suborder Sauria: Lizards

Green anole, *Anolis carolinensis*

Specimen illustrated: Adult male, private collection
Greatest length of skull: 20.64 mm (⁸/10 in.)
Life-size image page 189

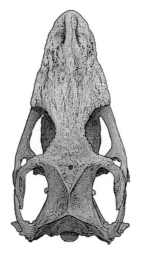

DORSAL

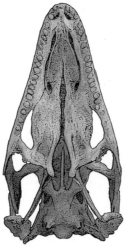

VENTRAL

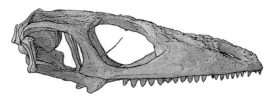

LATERAL

Gila monster, *Heloderma suspectum*

Specimen illustrated: Adult, MVZ 247626
Greatest length of skull: 57.52 mm (2³/₁₀ in.)
Life-size image page 189

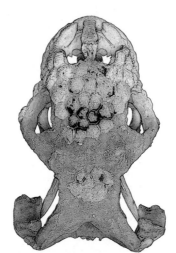

DORSAL

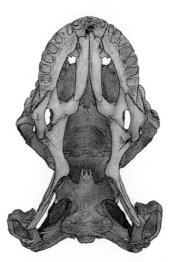

VENTRAL

LATERAL

Common chuckwalla, *Sauromalus ater*

Specimen illustrated: Adult, MVZ 52505
Greatest length of skull: 37.88 mm (1⁵/₁₀ in.)
Life-size image page 189

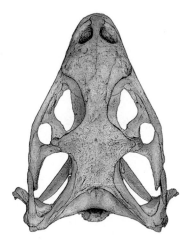

DORSAL

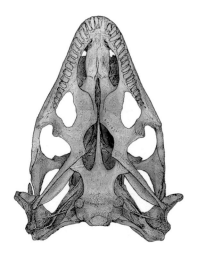

VENTRAL

LATERAL

Eastern fence lizard, *Sceloporus undulatus*

Specimen illustrated: Adult, MVZ 137647
Greatest length of skull: 12.08 mm (5/10 in.)
Life-size image page 189

DORSAL

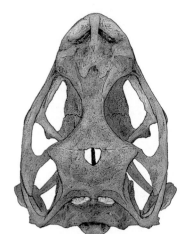

VENTRAL

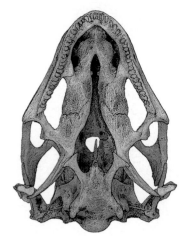

LATERAL

Suborder Serpentes: Snakes

Common garter snake, *Thamnophis sirtalis*

Specimen illustrated: Adult male, MVZ 93206
Greatest length of skull: 15.54 mm (⁶/10 in.), measured A–B
Life-size image page 189

DORSAL

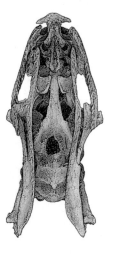

VENTRAL

LATERAL

Order Crocodilia: Crocodiles and relatives

Alligator, *Alligator mississippiensis*

Specimen illustrated: Subadult, MVZ 191313
Greatest length of skull: 271.22 mm (10⁷/10 in.)
Life-size image page 191

DORSAL

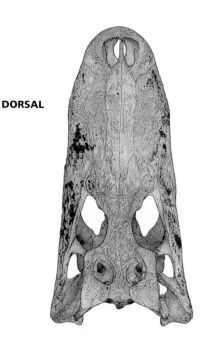

VENTRAL

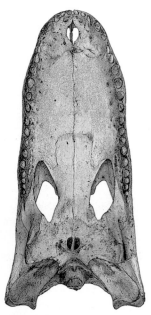

LATERAL

Order Testudines: Turtles and tortoises

Leatherback sea turtle, *Dermochelys coriacea*

Specimen illustrated: Subadult female, SBMNH 5085
Greatest length of skull: 272.04 mm (10⁷/10 in.)
Life-size image page 192

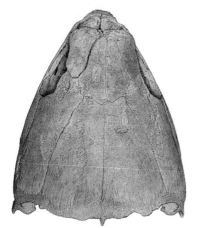

DORSAL

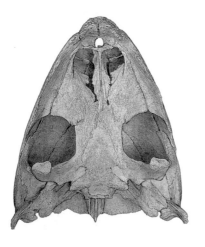

VENTRAL

LATERAL

Snapping turtle, *Chelydra serpentina*

Specimen illustrated: Adult male, SBMNH 3672
Greatest length of skull: 119.72 mm (4⁷/10 in.)
Life-size image page 190

DORSAL

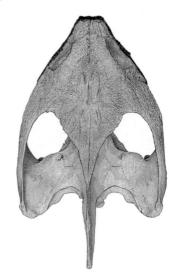

VENTRAL

LATERAL

Note presence
of bill sheath

Desert tortoise, *Gopherus agassizii*

Specimen illustrated: Adult female, SBMNH 2682
Greatest length of skull: 58.96 mm (2³/₁₀ in.)
Life-size image page 190

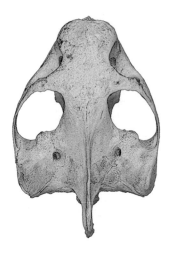

DORSAL

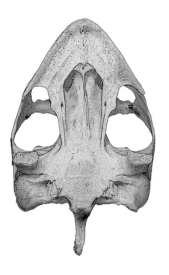

VENTRAL

LATERAL

Eastern box turtle, *Terrapene carolina*

Specimen illustrated: Adult, MVZ 38453
Greatest length of skull: 41.84 mm (1⁶/10 in.)
Life-size image page 189

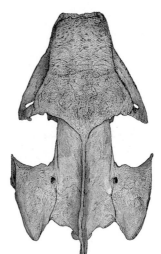

DORSAL

VENTRAL

LATERAL

Note presence
of bill sheath

BIBLIOGRAPHY

Allen, H. (1893) "A Monograph of the Bats of North America." *Bulletin of the United States National Museum* no. 43, 198. Washington, DC: Smithsonian Institution.

Alonso-Mejía, A., and Medellín, R. (1992) *"Marmosa mexicana."* *Mammalian Species* no. 421, 4. Lawrence, KS: American Society of Mammalogists.

Amorosi, T. (1989) "A Posteranial Guide to Domestic Neo-natal and Juvenile Mammals," *BAR International Series* (Oxford), 533.

Amstrup, S. (2003) "Polar Bear," in Feldhamer, G., Thompson, B., and Chapman, J., eds., *Wild Mammals of North America: Biology, Management, and Conservation,* 2nd ed. Baltimore: Johns Hopkins University Press, 587–610.

Anderson, A., and Wallmo, O. (1984) *"Odocoileus hemionus."* *Mammalian Species* no. 219, 9. Lawrence, KS: American Society of Mammalogists.

Anderson, E., and Lovallo, M. (2003) "Bobcat and Lynx," in Feldhamer, G., Thompson, B., and Chapman, J., eds., *Wild Mammals of North America: Biology, Management, and Conservation,* 2nd ed. Baltimore: Johns Hopkins University Press, 760.

Armstrong, D. (1972) "Distribution of mammals in Colorado." *Monograph of the Museum of Natural History* no. 3, 415. Lawrence: University of Kansas.

Armstrong, D., and Jones, J. K. (1972) *"Notiosorex crawfordi."* *Mammalian Species* no. 17, 5. Lawrence, KS: American Society of Mammalogists.

Arroyo-Cabrales, J., Hollander, R., and Jones, J. (1987) *"Choeronycteris mexicana."* *Mammalian Species* no. 291, 5. Lawrence, KS: American Society of Mammalogists.

Baker, B., and Hill, E. (2003) "Beaver," in Feldhamer, G., Thompson, B., and Chapman, J., eds. *Wild Mammals of North America: Biology, Management, and Conservation,* 2nd ed. Baltimore: Johns Hopkins University Press, 289.

Baker, R., Bradley, L., Bradley, R., Dragoo, J., Engstrom, M., Hoffman, R., Jones, C., Reid, F., Rice, D., and Jones, C. (2003) "Revised checklist of North American mammals north of Mexico, 2003." *Occasional Papers* no. 229, 23. Lubbock: Museum of Texas Tech University, Texas Tech University Press.

Bee, J., and Hall, E. R. (1956) "Mammals of northern Alaska." *Miscellaneous Publication* no. 8, 309. Lawrence: University of Kansas Museum of Natural History.

Bekoff, M. (1977) *"Canis latrans."* *Mammalian Species* no. 79, 9. Lawrence, KS: American Society of Mammalogists.

Beneski, J., and Stinson, D. (1987) *"Sorex palustris."* *Mammalian Species* no. 296, 6. Lawrence, KS: American Society of Mammalogists.

Bennett, D., and Hoffman, R. (1999) *"Equus caballus."* *Mammalian Species* no. 628, 14. Lawrence, KS: American Society of Mammalogists.

Birney, E., and Fleharty, E. (1966) "Age and sex comparisons of wild mink." *Transactions of the Kansas Academy of Science* 69(2): 139–145.

Bissonette, J. (1982) "Collared Peccary," in Chapman, J., and Feldhamer, G., eds. *Wild Mammals of North America: Biology, Management, and Economics.* Baltimore: Johns Hopkins University Press, 841–850.

Bond, C. (1956) "Correlations between reproductive condition and skull characteristics of beaver." *Journal of Mammalogy* 37: 506–512. Lawrence, KS: American Society of Mammologists.

Bowyer, R., Stewart, K., Kie, J., and Gasaway, W. (2001) "Fluctuating asymmetry in antlers of Alaskan moose: Size matters." *Journal of Mammalogy* 82(30): 814–824. Lawrence, KS: American Society of Mammologists.

Bowyer, R., Van Ballenberghe, V., and Kie, J. (2003) "Moose," in Feldhamer, G., Thompson, B., and Chapman, J., eds., *Wild Mammals of North America: Biology, Management, and Conservation,* 2nd ed. Baltimore: Johns Hopkins University Press, 933.

Brown, R., Ferguson, J., Lawrence, M., and Lees, D. (2003) *Tracks and Signs of the Birds of Britain and Europe,* 2nd ed. London: Christopher Helm Publishers, 272–318.

Byers, J. (2003) "Pronghorn," in Feldhamer, G., Thompson, B., and Chapman, J., eds., *Wild Mammals of North America: Biology, Management, and Conservation,* 2nd ed. Baltimore: Johns Hopkins University Press, 998–1008.

California Academy of Sciences. (2002) "Skulls in Culture." *www.calacademy.org/exhibits/skulls/skulls_in_culture.html*

Cameron, G., and Spencer, S. (1981) *"Sigmodon hispidus." Mammalian Species* no. 158, 9. Lawrence, KS: American Society of Mammalogists.

Campbell, J. (1988) *Historical Atlas of World Mythology.* Vol. 1. *The Way of the Animal Powers.* Part 1. *Mythologies of the Primitive Hunters and Gatherers.* New York: Harper and Row, 54–56, 118–125.

Carraway, L., and Verts, B. (1991) *"Neurotrichus gibbsii." Mammalian Species* no. 387, 7. Lawrence, KS: American Society of Mammalogists.

Chapman, J., and Feldhamer, G. (1981) *"Sylvilagus aquaticus." Mammalian Species* no. 151, 4. Lawrence, KS: American Society of Mammalogists.

Chapman, J., and Morgan, R. (1973) "Systematic status of the cottontail complex in western Maryland and nearby Virginia." *Wildlife Monograph* no. 36, 54. Bethesda, MD: Wildlife Society.

Childs, J. (1998) *Tracking the Felids of the Borderlands.* El Paso, TX: Printing Corner Press, 77.

Collins, P. (1982) Origin and differentiation of the island fox: A study of evolution in insular populations. Master's thesis, University of California at Santa Barbara, 228–272.

———. (1993) "Taxonomic and Biogeographic Relationships of the Island Fox and Gray Fox *(U. cinereoargenteus)* from Western North America," in Hochberg, F., ed., *Third California Islands Symposium: Recent Advances in Research on the California Islands.* Santa Barbara, CA: Santa Barbara Museum of Natural History, 351–390.

Collins, P., and George, S. (1990) "Systematics and taxonomy of island and mainland populations of western harvest mice *(Reithrodontomys megalotis)* in southern California." *Contributions in Science,* no. 420, 4–12. Los Angeles, CA: Natural History Museum of Los Angeles County.

Côté, S., and Festa-Bianchet, M. (2003) "Mountain Goat," in Feldhamer, G., Thompson, B., and Chapman, J., eds., *Wild Mammals of North America: Biology, Management, and Conservation,* 2nd ed. Baltimore: Johns Hopkins University Press, 1061–1075.

Côté, S., Festa-Bianchet, M., and Smith, K. (1998) "Horn growth in mountain goats *(Oreamnos americanus)." Journal of Mammalogy* 79(2): 406–414. Lawrence, KS: American Society of Mammalogists.

Cowan, I. (1940) "Distribution and variation in the native sheep of North America." *American Midland Naturalist* 24(3): 505–580.

Craighead, J., and Mitchell, J. (1982) "Grizzly Bear," in Chapman, J., and Feldhamer, G., eds., *Wild Mammals of North America: Biology, Management, and Economics.* Baltimore: Johns Hopkins University Press: 520.

Crothier, B., and the Society for the Study of Amphibians and Reptiles. (2000) "Scientific and standard English names of amphibians and reptiles of North America north of Mexico: With comments regarding confidence in our understanding," *Herpetological Circular* no. 29, 82. Society for the Study of Amphibians and Reptiles.

Davidow-Henry, B., and Jones, J. (1989) *"Cratogeomys castanops." Mammalian Species* no. 338, 6. Lawrence, KS: American Society of Mammalogists.

Dodge, W. (1982) "Porcupine," in Chapman, J., and Feldhamer, G., eds., *Wild Mammals of North America: Biology, Management, and Economics.* Baltimore: Johns Hopkins University Press, 355–366.

Dolan, P., and Carter, D. (1977) *"Glaucomys volans." Mammalian Species* no. 78, 6. Lawrence, KS: American Society of Mammalogists.

Duncan, N. (1976) "Theoretical aspects concerning transmission of the parasite *Skrjabingylus nasicola* (Leukart 1842) to stoats and weasels: With a review of the literature." *Mammal Review* 6(2): 63–74. London: Mammal Society.

Durrant, S. (1952) *Mammals of Utah: Taxonomy and Distribution.* Lawrence: University of Kansas, Museum of Natural History 6: 549.

Elbroch, M. (2003) *Mammal Tracks & Sign: A Guide to North American Species.* Mechanicsburg, PA: Stackpole Books, 779.

Elbroch, M., and Marks, E. (2001) *Bird Tracks & Sign: A Guide to North American Species.* Mechanicsburg, PA: Stackpole Books, 456.

Evans, H. and Heiser, J. (2004) "What's Inside: Anatomy and Physiology." *In Handbook of Bird Biology.* NY: Cornell Lab of Ornithology, Section 4–10.

Ewer, R. (1973) *The Carnivores.* Ithaca, NY: Comstock, Cornell University Press, 34–71.

Fay, F. (1985) *"Odobenus rosmarus." Mammalian Species* no. 238, 7. Lawrence, KS: American Society of Mammalogists.

Feldhamer, G., Thompson, B., and Chapman, J., eds. (2003) *Wild Mammals of North America: Biology, Management, and Conservation,* 2nd ed. Baltimore: Johns Hopkins University Press, 1216.

Fisler, G. (1965) "Adaptations and speciation in harvest mice of the marshes of the San Francisco Bay." *University of California Publications in Zoology* 77, 108.

Flyger, V., and Gates J. (1982) "Fox and Gray Squirrels" in Chapman, J., and Feldhamer, G., eds., *Wild Mammals of North America: Biology, Management, and Economics.* Baltimore: Johns Hopkins University Press, 209–229.

Fritzell, E., and Haroldson, K. (1982) *"Urocyon cinereoargenteus."* Mammalian Species no. 189, 8. Lawrence, KS: American Society of Mammalogists.

Fuller, W. (1959) "The horns and teeth as indicators of age in bison." *Journal of Wildlife Management* 23(3): 342–344. Bethesda, MD: Wildlife Society.

Gardner, A. (1973) "The systematics of the genus *Didelphis* (Marsupialia: Didelphidae) in North and Middle America." *Special Publications* no. 4, 81. Lubbock: Museum of Texas Tech University, Texas Tech University Press.

———. (1982) "Virginia Opossum," in Chapman, J., and Feldhamer, G., eds., *Wild Mammals of North America: Biology, Management, and Economics.* Baltimore: Johns Hopkins University Press, 3–36.

Gehrt, S. (2003) "Raccoon," in Feldhamer, G., Thompson, B., and Chapman, J., eds., *Wild Mammals of North America: Biology, Management, and Conservation,* 2nd ed. Baltimore: Johns Hopkins University Press, 611–634.

Genoways, H., and Brown, J., eds. (1993). "Biology of the Heteromyidae." *Special Publications* no. 10, 38–190. Lawrence, KS: American Society of Mammalogists.

George, S., Choate, J., and Genoways, H. (1986) *"Blarina brevicauda."* Mammalian Species no. 261, 9. Lawrence, KS: American Society of Mammalogists.

Gilbert, B. M. (1980) *Mammalian Osteology.* Columbia, MO: Missouri Archaeological Society, 428.

Gilbert, B. M., Martin, L., and Savage, H. (1986) *Avian Osteology.* Columbia, MO: Missouri Archaeological Society, 252.

Gillihan, S., and Foresman, K. (2004) *"Sorex vagrans."* Mammalian Species no. 744, 5. Lawrence, KS: American Society of Mammalogists.

Glass, B., and Thies, M. (1997) *A Key to the Skulls of North American Mammals,* 3rd ed. Self-published, 99.

Goheen, J., Swihart, R., and Robins, J. (2003) "The anatomy of a range expansion: Changes in cranial morphology and rates of energy extraction for North American red squirrels from different latitudes." *Oikos* 102: 33–44. Lund, Sweden: Nordic Ecological Society O: Kos.

Goldman, E. (1950) "Raccoons of North and Middle America." *North American Fauna* no. 60, 153. Washington, DC: U.S. Fish and Wildlife Service. U.S. Government Printing Office.

Gordon, K. (1977) "Molar measurements as a taxonomic tool." *Journal of Mammalogy* 58: 247–8. Lawrence, KS: American Society of Mammalogists.

Gould, H., and Kreeger, F. (1948) "The skull of the Louisiana muskrat *(Ondatra zibethica rivalicia).* 1. The skull in advanced age." *Journal of Mammalogy* 29(2): 138–149. Lawrence, KS: American Society of Mammalogists.

Graham, R. (1991) "Variability in the Size of North American Quaternary Black Bears *(Ursus americanus):* With the Description of a Fossil Black Bear from Bill Neff Cave, Virginia," in Purdue, J., Klippel, W., and Styles, B., eds., *Beamers, Bobwhites, and Blue-Points: Tributes to the Career of Paul W. Parmalee. Scientific Papers* 23: 242. Springfield: Illinois State Museum.

Grinnell, J., Dixon, J., and Linsdale, J. (1937) *Fur-bearing Mammals of California,* vols. 1 and 2. Berkeley: University of California Press, 777.

Hall, E. R. (1951) *American Weasels,* 4: 466. Museum of Natural History of University of Kansas. Lawrence: University of Kansas Publications.

————. (1981) *The Mammals of North America,* 2nd ed., vol. 2. New York: John Wiley and Sons, 601–1181.

————. (1995) *Mammals of Nevada.* Reno: University of Nevada Press, 710.

Hall, E. R., and Kelson, K. (1959) *The Mammals of North America,* vols. 1 and 2. New York: Ronald Press Company, 1083.

Hartman, G., and Yates, T. (2003) "Moles," in Feldhamer, G., Thompson, B., and Chapman, J. eds., *Wild Mammals of North America: Biology, Management, and Conservation,* 2nd ed. Baltimore: Johns Hopkins University Press, 30–55.

Heffelfinger, J. (1997) "Age criteria for Arizona game species." *Special Report* no. 19, 40. Phoenix: Arizona Game and Fish Commission.

Hellgren, E., and Bissonette, J. (2003) "Collared Peccary," in Feldhamer, G., Thompson, B., and Chapman, J., eds., *Wild Mammals of North America: Biology, Management, and Conservation,* 2nd ed. Baltimore: Johns Hopkins University Press, 867–876.

Hesselton, W., and Hesselton, R. (1982) "White-tailed Deer," in Chapman, J., and Feldhamer, G., eds., *Wild Mammals of North America: Biology, Management, and Economics.* Baltimore: Johns Hopkins University Press, 878–901.

Hildebrand, M., and Goslow, G. (2001) *Analysis of Vertebrate Structure,* 5th ed. New York: John Wiley and Sons, 635.

Hoffmeister, D. (1986) *Mammals of Arizona.* Tuscon: University of Arizona Press, 602.

————. (1989) *Mammals of Illinois.* Urbana: University of Illinois Press, 348.

Holdrege, C. (2003) *The Flexible Giant: Seeing the Elephant Whole.* Ghent, NY: Nature Institute, 72.

Hoogland, J. (1996) *"Cynomys ludovicianus." Mammalian Species* no. 535, 10. Lawrence, KS: American Society of Mammalogists.

Hornaday, W. (2002) *The Extermination of the American Bison.* Reprint, Washington, DC: Smithsonian Institution Press, 419.

Howard, W. (1949) "A means to distinguish skulls of coyotes and domestic dogs." *Journal of Mammalogy* 30(2): 169–171.

Howell, A. (1915) "Revision of the North American marmots." *North American Fauna* no. 37, 80. U.S. Department of Agriculture. Washington, DC: U.S. Government Printing Office.

————. (1938) "Revision of the North American ground squirrels." *North American Fauna* no. 56, 256. U.S. Department of Agriculture. Washington, DC: U.S. Government Printing Office.

Hurmence, J., and Harness, R. (2004) *Guide to Raptor Remains: A Photographic Guide for Identifying the Remains of Selected Species of California Raptors.* Fort Collins, CO: EDM International, 115.

Hwang, Y., and Lariviére, S. (2001) *"Mephitis macroura." Mammalian Species* Acct. No. 686. Lawrence, KS: The American Society of Mammalogy, 3.

Ingles, L. (1965) *Mammals of the Pacific States: California, Oregon, and Washington.* CA: Stanford University Press, 506.

Jackson, H. (1915) "A review of the American moles." *North American Fauna* no. 38, 100. U.S. Department of Agriculture. Washington, DC: U.S. Government Printing Office.

————. (1961) *Mammals of Wisconsin.* Madison: University of Wisconsin Press, 504.

Jenkins, S., and Ashley, M. (2003) "Wild Horse," in Feldhamer, G., Thompson, B., and Chapman, J., eds., *Wild Mammals of North America: Biology, Management, and Conservation,* 2nd ed. Baltimore: Johns Hopkins University Press, 1157–1158.

Jones, J. K., and Manning, R. (1992) *Illustrated Key to Skulls of Genera of North American Land Mammals.* Lubbock: Texas Tech University Press, 75.

Junge, J., and Hoffmann, R. (1981) "An annotated key to the long-tailed shrews (genus *Sorex*) of the United States and Canada: With notes of Middle American *Sorex.*" *Occasional Papers of the Museum of Natural History* no. 94, 48. Lawrence: University of Kansas.

Kastelein, R. (2002) "Walrus." Perrin, W., W.rsig, B., and Thewissen, J., eds., *Encyclopedia of Marine Mammals.* San Diego: Academic Press, 1294–1295.

Kochan, J. (1995) *Birds: Bills and Mouths.* Mechanicsburg, PA: Stackpole Books, 80.

———. (1995) *Birds: Heads and Eyes.* Mechanicsburg, PA: Stackpole Books, 85.

Krausman, P., and Bowyer, R. (2003) "Mountain Sheep," in Feldhamer, G., Thompson, B., and Chapman, J., eds., *Wild Mammals of North America: Biology, Management, and Conservation,* 2nd ed. Baltimore: Johns Hopkins University Press, 1095–1115.

Kurta, A., and Baker R. (1990) *"Eptesicus fuscus."* *Mammalian Species,* no. 356, 10. Lawrence, KS: American Society of Mammalogists.

Lariviere, S., and Messier, F. (1997) "Characteristics of waterfowl nest predation by the striped skunk *(Mephitis mephitis):* Can predators be identified from nest remains?" *American Midland Naturalist* 137(2): 393–397. South Bend, IN: University of Notre Dame.

Larsen, T. (1971) "Sexual dimorphum in the molar rows of the polar bear." *Journal of Wildlife Management* 35(2): 374–377. Bethesda, MD: Wildlife Society.

Lawson, B., and Johnson, R. (1982) "Mountainsheep," in Chapman, J., and Feldhamer, G., eds., *Wild Mammals of North America: Biology, Management, and Economics.* Baltimore: Johns Hopkins University Press, 1036–1055.

LeCount, A. (1986) *Black Bear Field Guide: A Manager's Manual.* Phoenix: Arizona Game and Fish Department, 62–66.

Liittschwager, D. (2002) *Skulls.* San Francisco: California Academy of Sciences, 112.

Lim, B. (1987) *"Lepus townsendii."* *Mammalian Species* no. 288, 6. Lawrence, KS: American Society of Mammalogists.

Lindzey, F. (2003) "Badger," in Feldhamer, G., Thompson, B., and Chapman, J., eds., *Wild Mammals of North America: Biology, Management, and Conservation,* 2nd ed. Baltimore: Johns Hopkins University Press, 683.

Linscombe, G., Kinler, N., and Aulerich, R. (1982) "Mink," in Chapman, J., and Feldhamer, G., eds., *Wild Mammals of North America: Biology, Management, and Economics.* Baltimore: Johns Hopkins University Press, 639.

Lowery, G. (1974) *The Mammals of Louisiana and Its Adjacent Waters.* Baton Rouge: Louisiana State University Press, 565.

Lynch, J., and Hayden, T. (1995) "Genetic influences on cranial form: Variation among ranch and feral American mink *Mustela vison* (Mammalia: Mustelidae)." *Biological Journal of the Linnean Society* 55: 293–307. London: Linnaean Society of London.

Lyver, P. (2000) "Identifying mammalian predators from bite marks: A tool for focusing wildlife protection." *Mammal Review* 30(1): 31–44. London: Mammal Society.

Mackie, R., Hamlin, K., and Pac, D. (1982) "Mule Deer," in Chapman, J., and Feldhamer, G., eds., *Wild Mammals of North America: Biology, Management, and Economics*. Baltimore: Johns Hopkins University Press, 862–877.

Manning, T. (1960) "The relationship of the Peary and barren Caribou." *Technical Paper* no. 4, 52. Montreal: Arctic Institute of America.

———. (1971) "Geographical variation in the polar bear" Ursus maritimus. *Canadian Wildlife Service Report Series* no. 13, 27. Ottawa, Ontario: Canadian Wildlife Service.

Martin, R., Pine, R., and DeBlase, A. (2001) *A Manual of Mammalogy*, 3rd ed. New York: McGraw-Hill, 333.

McManus, J. (1974) "Didelphis virginiana." *Mammalian Species* no. 40, 6. Lawrence, KS: American Society of Mammalogists.

Meagher, M. (1986) "Bison bison." *Mammalian Species* no. 266, 8. Lawrence, KS: American Society of Mammalogists.

Mech, D. (1974) *"Canis lupus."* *Mammalian Species* no. 37, 6. Lawrence, KS: American Society of Mammalogists.

Meiri, S., Dayan, T., and Simberloff, D. (2004a) "Carnivores, biases, and Bergmann's rule." *Biological Journal of the Linnean Society* 81: 579–588. London: Linnaean Society of London.

———. (2004b) Unpublished data.

Miller, F. (1982) "Caribou," in Chapman, J., and Feldhamer, G., eds., *Wild Mammals of North America: Biology, Management, and Economics*. Baltimore: Johns Hopkins University Press, 923–959.

———. (2003) "Caribou," in Feldhamer, G., Thompson, B., and Chapman, J., eds., *Wild Mammals of North America: Biology, Management, and Conservation*, 2nd ed. Baltimore: Johns Hopkins University Press, 969.

Miller, K., Muller, L., and Demarais, S. (2003) "White-tailed deer," in Feldhamer, G., Thompson, B., and Chapman, J., eds., *Wild Mammals of North America: Biology, Management, and Conservation*, 2nd ed. Baltimore: John Hopkins University Press, 906–930.

Moore, C., and Collins, P. (1995) *"Urocyon littoralis."* *Mammalian Species* no. 489, 7. Lawrence, KS: American Society of Mammalogists.

Morse, S. "Cougar conundrum." *Northern Woodlands*. (summer 2001): 19. Corinth, VT: Northern Woodlands.

Murmann, D., Brumit, P., and Schrader, B. (In Press) "A comparison of animal jaws and bite mark patterns. Colorado Springs, CO: *Journal of Forensic Sciences*. American Academy of Forensic Sciences. Also presented at the American Academy of Forensic Sciences Annual Meeting in 2005.

Murray, J., and Gardner, G. (1997) *"Leopardus pardalis."* *Mammalian Species* no. 548, 10. Lawrence, KS: American Society of Mammalogists.

National Geographic Society. (2002) *National Geographic Field Guide to the Birds of North America*, 4th ed. Washington, DC: National Geographic Society, 480.

Nelson, T., and Shump, K. (1978) "Cranial variation and size allometry in *Agouti paca* from Ecuador." *Journal of Mammalogy* 59(2): 387–394. Lawrence, KS: American Society of Mammalogists.

O'Connor, T. (2000) *The Archaeology of Animal Bones*. College Station: Texas A&M University Press, 206.

Oliveira, T. (1998a) *"Herpailurus yagouaroundi."* *Mammalian Species* no. 578, 6. Lawrence, KS: American Society of Mammalogists.

———. (1998b) *"Leopardus wiedii."* *Mammalian Species* no. 579, 6. Lawrence, KS: American Society of Mammalogists.

Orr, R. (1940) *The Rabbits of California. Occasional Papers of the California Academy of Sciences* no. 19, 227.

Owen, J. (1984) *"Sorex fumeus."* *Mammalian Species* no. 215, 8. Lawrence, KS: American Society of Mammalogists.

Paradiso, J. (1969) *Mammals of Maryland. North American Fauna* no. 66, 193. U.S. Department of Agriculture. Washington, DC: U.S. Government Printing Office.

Paradiso, J., and Nowak, R. (1972) *"Canis rufus."* *Mammalian Species* no. 22, 4. Lawrence, KS: American Society of Mammalogists.

Peek, J. (2003) "Wapiti," in Feldhamer, G., Thompson, B., and Chapman, J., eds., *Wild Mammals of North America: Biology, Management, and Conservation,* 2nd ed. Baltimore: Johns Hopkins University Press: 878.

Peterson, D. (1991) *Racks: The Natural History of Antlers and the Animals That Wear Them.* Santa Barbara, CA: Capra Press, 179.

Peterson, K., and Yates, T. (1980) *"Condylura cristata."* *Mammalian Species* no. 129, 4. Lawrence, KS: American Society of Mammalogists.

Pick, N. (2004) *The Rarest of the Rare: Stories behind the Treasures at the Harvard Museum of Natural History.* New York: HarperCollins Books, 178.

Podulka, S., Rohrbaugh, R., and Bonney, R. (2004) *Cornell Lab of Ornithology Handbook of Bird Biology.* Princeton, NJ: Princeton University Press, 1248.

Poole, K., Matson, G., Strickland, M., Magoun, A., Graf, R., and Dix, L. (1994) "Age and Sex Determination for American Martens and Fishers," in Buskirk, S., Harestad, A., Raphael, M., and Powell, K., eds., *Martens, Sables, and Fishers: Biology and Conservation.* Ithaca, NY: Cornell University Press, 204–223.

Powell, R., Buskirk, S., and Zielinski, W. (2003) "Fisher and Marten," in Feldhamer, G., Thompson, B., and Chapman, J., eds., *Wild Mammals of North America: Biology, Management, and Conservation,* 2nd ed. Baltimore: Johns Hopkins University Press, 635–649.

Proctor, N., and Lynch, P. (1993) *Manual of Ornithology: Avian Structure and Function.* New Haven, CT: Yale University Press, 120–129.

Rausch, R. (1953) "On the status of some arctic mammals." *Arctic* 6(2): 91–148. Calgary, Alberta, Canada: Arctic Institute of North America.

Reid, F. (1997) *A Field Guide to the Mammals of Central America and Southeast Mexico.* New York: Oxford University Press, 334.

Ritke, M., and Kennedy, M. (1993) "Geographic variation of sexual dimorphism in the raccoon, *Procyon lotor."* *American Midland Naturalist* 129: 257–265. South Bend, IN: University of Notre Dame.

Robertson, R., and Shadle, A. (1954) "Osteologic criteria of age in beavers." *Journal of Mammalogy* 35(2): 197–203.

Robinson, R. (1998) *Georgia O'Keeffe: A Life.* University Press of New England, 365.

Roest, A. (1973) "Subspecies of the sea otter, *Enhydra lutris."* *Contributions in Science* no. 252, 17. Los Angeles: Natural History Museum of Los Angeles County.

————. (1991) *A Key-Guide to Mammal Skulls and Lower Jaws.* Eureka, CA: Mad River Press, 39.

Roze, U., and Ilse, L. (2003) "Porcupine," in Feldhamer, G., Thompson, B., and Chapman, J., eds., *Wild Mammals of North America: Biology, Management, and Conservation,* 2nd ed. Baltimore: Johns Hopkins University Press: 372.

Samuel, D., and Nelson, B. (1982) "Foxes," in Chapman, J., and Feldhamer, G., eds., *Wild Mammals of North America: Biology, Management, and Economics.* Baltimore: Johns Hopkins University Press: 482.

Sauer, P. (1966) "Determining sex of black bears from the size of the lower canine tooth." *NY Fish and Game Journal* 13(2): 140–145.

Schartz, C., Miller, S., and Haroldson, M. (2003) "Grizzly Bear" in Feldhamer, G., Thompson, B., and Chapman, J., eds., *Wild Mammals of North America: Biology, Management, and Conservation,* 2nd ed. Baltimore: Johns Hopkins University Press: 561.

Searfoss, G. (1995) *Skulls and Bones: A Guide to the Skeletal Structures and Behavior of North American Mammals.* Mechanicsburg, PA: Stackpole Books, 277.

Seymour, K. (1989) *"Panthera onca."* *Mammalian Species* no. 340, 9. Lawrence, KS: American Society of Mammalogists.

Shaw, H. (1979) "Mountain lion field guide." *Special Report* no. 9, 47. Phoenix: Arizona Game and Fish Department.

Sheffield, S., and Thomas, H. (1997) *"Mustela frenata."* *Mammalian Species* no. 570, 9. Lawrence, KS: American Society of Mammalogists.

Smith, A., and Weston, M. (1990) *"Ochotona princeps."* *Mammalian Species* no. 352, 8. Lawrence, KS: American Society of Mammalogists.

Snyder, D. (1954) "Skull variation in the meadow vole *(Microtus p. pennsylvanicus)* in Pennsylvania." *Annals of the Carnegie Museum* 33(13): 201–234. Pittsburgh, PA: Carnegie Museum of Natural History.

Stangl, F., Beauchamp, S., and Konermann, N. (1995) "Cranial and dental variation in the nine-banded armadillo, *Dasypus novemcinctus,* from Texas and Oklahoma." *Texas Journal of Science* 47(2): 89–100. Kerrville: Texas Academy of Science.

Storm, G., Andrews, R., Phillips, R., Bishop, R., Siniff, D., and Tester, J. (1976) "Morphology, Reproduction, Dispersal, and Mortality of Midwestern Red Fox Populations." *Wildlife Monograph* no. 49, 74–77. Bethesda, MD: Wildlife Society.

Strickland, M., Douglas, C., Novak, M., and Hunziger, N. (1982) "Fisher and Marten," in Chapman, J., and Feldhamer, G., eds., *Wild Mammals of North America: Biology, Management, and Economics.* Baltimore: Johns Hopkins University Press: 594, 608.

Sweeney, J., Sweeney, J., and Sweeney, S. (2003) "Feral Hog," in Feldhamer, G., Thompson, B., and Chapman, J., eds., *Wild Mammals of North America: Biology, Management, and Conservation,* 2nd ed. Baltimore: Johns Hopkins University Press, 1173.

Taylor, W. (1918) "Revision of the rodent genus *Aplodontia." Publications in Zoology* 17(16): 435–504. Berkley: University of California.

Tener, J. (1965) *Muskoxen in Canada.* Ottawa, Ontario: Department of Northern Affairs and National Resources, Canadian Wildlife Service, 123–151.

University of Calgary. (2000) "Canada's First People." Joint project with Red Deer College. *www.ucalgary.ca/applied_history/tutor/firstnations/home.html*

Van Gelder, R. (1959) "A taxonomic revision of the spotted skunks." *Bulletin of the American Museum of Natural History* 117(5): 235–392. New York: American Museum of Natural History.

———. (1968) "The genus *Conepatus* (Mammalia, Mustelidae): Variation within a population." *American Museum Novitates* no. 2322, 37. New York: American Museum of Natural History.

Van Nostrand, F., and Stephenson, A. (1964) "Age determination for beavers by tooth development." *Journal of Wildlife Management* 28: 430–434.

Van Tyne, J., and Berger, A. (1971) *Fundamentals of Ornithology*. New York: Dover Publications, 40–45.

Verts, B. (1967) *The Biology of the Striped Skunk*. Chicago: University of Illinois Press: 9.

Verts, B., and Carraway, L. (1998) *Land Mammals of Oregon*. Berkeley: University of California Press, 669.

———. (2001) *"Tamias minimus."* *Mammalian Species* no. 653, 10. Lawrence, KS: American Society of Mammalogists.

Verts, B., Carraway, L., and Kinlaw, A. (2001) *"Spilogale gracilis."* *Mammalian Species* no. 674, 10. Lawrence, KS: American Society of Mammalogists.

Waithman, J., and Roest, A. (1977) "A taxonomic study of the kit fox, *Vulpes macrotis."* *Journal of Mammalogy* 58: 157–164. Lawrence, KS: American Society of Mammalogists.

Walker, P. (1987) "Archaeological evidence for the recent extinction of three terrestrial mammals on San Miguel Island," in Power, D., ed. *The California Islands: Proceedings of a Multi-disciplinary Symposium*. 703–717. Santa Barbara, CA: Santa Barbara Museum of Natural History.

Webster, W., and Jones, J. (1982) *"Reithrodontomys megalotis."* *Mammalian Species* no. 167, 5. Lawrence, KS: American Society of Mammalogists.

Wells-Gosling, N., and Heaney, L. (1984) *"Glaucomys sabrinus."* *Mammalian Species* no. 229, 8. Lawrence, KS: American Society of Mammalogists.

Whitaker, J. (2004) *"Sorex cinereus."* *Mammalian Species* no. 743, 9. Lawrence, KS: American Society of Mammalogists.

Williams, D., and Kilburn, K. (1991) *"Dipodomys ingens."* *Mammalian Species* no. 377, 7. Lawrence, KS: American Society of Mammalogists.

Woods, C. (1973) *"Erethizon dorsatum."* *Mammalian Species* no. 29, 6. Lawrence, KS: American Society of Mammalogists.

Woods, C., Contreras, L., Willner-Chapman, G., and Whidden, H. (1992) *"Myocastor coypus."* *Mammalian Species* no. 398, 8. Lawrence, KS: American Society of Mammalogists.

Yates, T., and Schmidly, D. (1978) *"Scalopus aquaticus."* *Mammalian Species* no. 105, 4. Lawrence, KS: American Society of Mammalogists.

Young, S., and Goldman, E. (1944) *The Wolves of North America*, vol. 2. New York: Dover Publications, 389–636.

Zusi, R. (1993) "Patterns of Diversity in the Avian Skull," in Hanken, J., and Hall B., eds., *The Skull*, vol. 2. Chicago: University of Chicago Press, 391–437.

INDEX

ABOUT THE AUTHOR

Mark Elbroch has contributed to numerous research projects in North America, including studies of black bears, brown bears, cougars; varied small mammals species: fisher, marten, lynx; and diverse animals in relation to wildlife corridors. Mark co-runs Ichneumon Wildlife Services with Kurt Rinehart, a consulting company specializing in wildlife inventories, monitoring, and research. His book *Mammal Tracks & Sign* is a National Outdoor Book Award winner. He is also lead author of *Bird Tracks & Sign* and coauthor of the *Peterson's Field Guide to Animal Tracks,* 3rd ed. Mark also works with CyberTracker Conservation in Africa and North America to establish an evaluation system and international standard for wildlife tracking skills as a means of testing and improving observer reliability in wildlife research and monitoring efforts. Mark maintains the following website: http://wildlifetrackers.com/.